HUMAN RIGHTS LAW

Human Rights Law is the first book in which the interpretation and application of the Human Rights Act 1998 by the courts in England and Wales is comprehensively examined and analysed. Part I of the book concerns the Human Rights Act itself, including the background to the Act and key principles of interpretation. Also examined in this part are: the benefit and burden of Convention rights; the identification of activities to which the Act applies; the process of determining incompatibility, encompassing the principles of proportionality and judicial deference; and the defence of primary legislation. This part concludes with a discussion of the remedies available for a breach of Convention rights, including a detailed examination of the power to award damages under the Act.

In Part II of the book, the application and interpretation of the Convention rights themselves by the courts in England and Wales is examined. Included in this part are: the right to life; the right to freedom from torture and inhuman or degrading treatment or punishment; the right to liberty; the right to a fair trial; the rights to respect for private life, family life and home; the right to freedom of expression; the prohibition of discrimination in securing Convention rights; and the right to the peaceful enjoyment of possessions. Each right is considered separately with a particular focus on its interpretation and practical application in the domestic context.

Human Rights Law will be of particular interest to teachers and students of domestic human rights law, constitutional law and administrative law. It will also be of considerable relevance to practitioners working in the area.

Human Rights Law

MERRIS AMOS

·H A R T·
PUBLISHING

OXFORD AND PORTLAND, OREGON
2006

Published in North America (US and Canada) by

Hart Publishing

c/o International Specialized Book Services
920 NE 58th Avenue, Suite 300
Portland, OR 97213-3786
USA
Tel: +1 503 287 3093 or toll-free: (1) 800 944 6190
Fax: +1 503 280 8832
Email: orders@isbs.com
Website: www.isbs.com

Hart Publishing, Salter's Boatyard, Folly Bridge, Abingdon Rd, Oxford, OX1 4LB

Telephone: +44 (0)1865 245533 Fax: +44 (0) 1865 794882

Email: mail@hartpub.co.uk

Website: http//:www.hartpub.co.uk

British Library Cataloguing in Publication Data

Data Available

ISBN-13: 978-1-84113-232-7 (hardback)
ISBN-10: 1-84113-232-2 (hardback)

ISBN-13: 978-1-84113-324-9 (paperback)
ISBN-10: 1-84113-324-8 (paperback)

Typeset by Forewords, Oxford, in Times 10/12 pt

Printed and bound in Great Britain by
Biddles Ltd, Kings Lynn

To Adam, Joel and Daniel

Preface

On 2 October 2000 the Human Rights Act 1998 came fully into force and a few days later I started teaching a new undergraduate course entitled 'United Kingdom Human Rights Law'. Looking back, this was quite an ambitious undertaking given that, apart from the cases generated under the human rights provisions of the Scotland Act 1998, which had come into force the year before, at the time there was actually very little case law to base a course on. Nevertheless, we soldiered on, and as the years went by, soon the gaps began to be filled and European Court of Human Rights jurisprudence was replaced with judgments of the House of Lords.

As the case law began to take shape, it became clear that what my course needed was a textbook in which the procedural and substantive aspects of the Human Rights Act were examined in detail. In 2001 I was lucky enough to meet Richard Hart and this book got underway. In the course of writing over the past four years, it has become evident to me that, as was hoped for in the White Paper and Parliamentary debates preceding the Act, British judges have made their own distinctive contribution to human rights jurisprudence, and I believe it vital that this is recognised and built upon. Whilst the Act greatly enhances the strength of Strasbourg jurisprudence in the domestic legal system, it is important to remember that it remains not legally binding. Human rights law is now predominantly what our judges have made it, and are making it, under the Human Rights Act.

As anyone who has ever written a book will know, the journey is not an easy one. Writing about human rights law was made even more difficult by the newness of the subject matter, the volume of the case law and the pace at which developments occurred. I freely admit almost to weeping every time the House of Lords handed down a ground-breaking Article 6 judgment. The fact that I have finished at all is a testament to the help of a number of people: in particular, my husband Adam, who has been immensely supportive and tolerated, with good humour, the ups and the downs; my son Joel, who is always understanding, even when I have not been as attentive to Bob the Builder as I perhaps should have been; Donna Gladwin and Helen Morgan, who have cared for Joel with the utmost dedication, love and professionalism; my mother-in-law Jean, for helping out when it all got too much (yes, it is possible to have over 5,000 footnotes); my parents and my father-in-law Ian, for their encouragement and support; my dear friend Richard Cornes, who steadfastly believed I could finish this book when I didn't believe it myself; and my colleagues in the Human Rights Centre and Department of Law at the University of Essex.

The law is correct as at 30 September 2005.

Merris Amos
London, December 2005

Summary of Contents

Contents

Table of Cases

Table of Statutes

Table of International Legislation

PART I

THE HUMAN RIGHTS ACT

1

Background and Interpretation

1. The Protection of Human Rights Prior to the Human Rights Act

Interest in the promotion and protection of human rights in England and Wales did not just start on 2 October 2000 with the coming into force of the Human Rights Act 1998 (HRA). For many years, the common law, primary and secondary legislation, and European Community Law have provided legal protection for human rights whilst international human rights law, although not directly enforceable in domestic courts, has provided an important benchmark for the courts, executive and legislature. With the coming into force of the HRA, these other mechanisms of protection have not disappeared but operate alongside the HRA, in some instances filling the gaps[1] and in others providing equivalent[2] or even stronger legal protection for human rights.[3] This important fact is made clear in section 11 of the HRA itself, which provides that a person's reliance on a Convention right does not restrict 'any other right or freedom conferred on him by or under any law having effect in any part of the United Kingdom' or restrict 'his right to make any claim or bring any proceedings which he could make or bring apart from sections 7 to 9' of the HRA.[4]

---

[1] In some instances the HRA may not apply. For example, if the act occurred before 2 October 2000 or the claimant does not fall within the definition of victim in s 7 of the HRA.

[2] For example, in *R v Secretary of State for the Home Department, ex p Daly* [2001] UKHL 26, [2001] 2 AC 532 the House of Lords reached the conclusion that the Secretary of State's policy governing the searching of prisoners' cells was unlawful on an 'orthodox application of common law principles derived from the authorities and an orthodox domestic approach to judicial review even though the same result was achieved by reliance upon Art 8 of the Convention.

[3] For example, in *Fitzpatrick v Sterling Housing Association Ltd* [2001] 1 AC 27, in deciding that the meaning of family in the Rent Act 1977 encompassed a same sex partner, a majority of the House of Lords was not influenced by the fact that the European Court of Human Rights had not so far accepted claims by same sex partners to family rights.

[4] It is clear that legislation can be compatible with Convention rights if it actually provides greater protection. See the comments of Lord Woolf in *R v Broadcasting Standards Commission, ex p British Broadcasting Corporation* [2001] QB 885 at [17].

Over the years, much has been written about these other important mechanisms for the promotion and protection of human rights, so the essential features of this machinery will not be repeated here.[5] The focus of this book is the Human Rights Act, which, whilst not the only means for the legal protection of human rights domestically, is at present clearly the most effective.

---

2. Background to the Human Rights Act

2.1 The Incorporation Debate

Constitutional tradition, in particular the principle of the sovereignty of Parliament and the protection for human rights provided by common law and statute, meant that for a long time there was very little interest in adopting a modern form of a Bill of Rights. But by the late 1970s this had changed, with bodies such as the National Council for Civil Liberties (now Liberty) campaigning for just such a bill. Agitation for a Bill of Rights soon transformed into calls for 'incorporation' of the European Convention on Human Rights (ECHR) into domestic law as the first—or only—step in the process of improving the legal protection of human rights.[6] Many NGOs joined the campaign, including JUSTICE, the Runnymede Trust, the Constitutional Reform Centre, the Institute for Public Policy Research, the British Institute of Human Rights and Charter 88. The shared view was that the traditional freedom of the individual 'under an unwritten constitution to do himself that which is not prohibited by law' gave no protection from misuse of power by the state, nor any protection from acts or omissions of public bodies which harmed individuals in a way that was incompatible with their human rights.[7]

Around this time judicial interest in human rights was also stirred. For example, in their decisions judges began referring to the 'right to freedom of expression',

[5] See further C McCrudden and G Chambers (eds), *Individual Rights and the Law in Britain* (Oxford University Press, 1994), ch 1; F Klug, K Starmer and S Weir, 'The British Way of Doing Things: The United Kingdom and the International Covenant on Civil and Political Rights, 1976–94' [1995] *PL* 504; B. Dickson (ed.), *Human Rights and the European Convention* (London, Sweet & Maxwell, 1997); M. Hunt, *Using Human Rights Law in English Courts* (Oxford, Hart Publishing, 1998); L Betten and N Grief, *EU Law and Human Rights* (London, Longman, 1998); M Demetriou, 'Using Human Rights through European Community Law' [1999] *EHRLR* 484; D Feldman, *Civil Liberties and Human Rights in England and Wales* (Oxford University Press, 2nd edn, 2002), ch 2; D Fottrell, 'Reinforcing the Human Rights Act—the Role of the International Covenant on Civil and Political Rights' [2002] *PL* 485.

[6] Whilst the prospect of a United Kingdom Bill of Rights and Responsibilities was mentioned in the Labour Party consultation paper by Jack Straw MP and Paul Boateng MP, 'Bringing Rights Home: Labour's plans to incorporate the European Convention on Human Rights into UK Law' (London, Labour Party, 1996) at 14, there was no mention of such an instrument in the Home Office White Paper *Rights Brought Home: The Human Rights Bill* (Cm 3782) (London, TSO, 1997), published once Labour assumed office.

[7] HL Deb, vol 582, col 1228 (3 November 1997), Lord Chancellor. On the campaign for incorporation, see KD Ewing, 'The Futility of the Human Rights Act' [2004] *PL* 829.

sometimes the 'constitutional right to freedom of expression'.[8] In many cases, Article 10 of the ECHR was also mentioned.[9] It is likely that this development was in some part driven by the finding in 1979 of a violation of Article 10 by the European Court of Human Rights in *Sunday Times v UK*.[10] In many quarters, the finding had shattered the illusion that acceptance of the Convention would have 'few implications for the United Kingdom' and the assumption that the United Kingdom 'as a democracy would have nothing to be concerned about.'[11]

The judicial interest in human rights continued, and by the 1990s many judges, writing and speaking extra judicially, had entered the rights debate. For example, in the 1993 Denning Lecture, Lord Bingham, then the Master of the Rolls, stated that

> the ability of English judges to protect human rights in this country and reconcile conflicting rights in the manner indicated is inhibited by the failure of successive governments over many years to incorporate into United Kingdom law the European Convention on Human Rights.[12]

He saw the European Convention as an instrument which lay ready to hand which, if not providing an ideal solution, nonetheless offered a clear improvement on the present position.[13] In the 1994 F. A. Mann Lecture Lord Woolf considered that it was unacceptable

> that our citizens should be able to obtain a remedy which the Government will honour in the European Court of Human Rights, which they cannot obtain from the courts in this country.

In his view, a

> British Bill of Rights would avoid the difficulty which exists at present in protecting some of our basic rights. It would enable us to play our part in the development of human rights jurisprudence internationally.[14]

Various attempts were also made via private members' bills in Parliament to achieve some measure of statutory human rights protection.[15] However, all suffered

---

[8] See, eg *Cassell & Co v Broome* [1972] 2 WLR 645 per Lord Kilbrandon at 726; *Harman v Secretary of State for the Home Department* [1982] 2 WLR 338 per Lord Scarman at 351; *Secretary of State for Defence v Guardian Newspapers Ltd* [1984] 3 WLR 986 per Lord Fraser at 1001.

[9] See, eg *R v Lemon* [1979] 2 WLR 281 at 315 per Lord Scarman; *Associated Newspapers Group Ltd v Wade* [1979] 1 WLR 697 at 708–9 per Lord Denning; *A-G v BBC* [1980] 3 WLR 109 at 130 per Lord Scarman; *Schering Chemicals Ltd v Falkman Ltd* [1981] 2 WLR 848 at 862, 864 per Lord Denning.

[10] (1979) 2 EHRR 245. See the comments of Lord Scarman in *A-G v BBC* [1980] 3 WLR 109 at 130.

[11] E Wicks, 'The United Kingdom Government's Perceptions of the European Convention on Human Rights at the Time of Entry' [2000] *PL* 438 at 441. This was not the first finding of a violation on the part of the United Kingdom which had occurred in *Golder v UK* (1975) 1 EHRR 524.

[12] See TH Bingham, 'The European Convention on Human Rights: Time to Incoroporate' (1993) 109 *LQR* 390 at 390.

[13] *Ibid*, at 393.

[14] The Rt Hon Lord Woolf of Barnes, 'Droit Public-English Style' [1995] *PL* 57 at 70. See also Sir Nicolas Browne-Wilkinson, 'The Infiltration of a Bill of Rights' [1992] *PL* 405; The Hon Sir John Laws, 'Is the High Court the Guardian of Fundamental Constitutional Rights?' [1993] *PL* 59 and 'Law and Democracy' [1995] *PL* 72; The Hon Sir Stephen Sedley, 'Human Rights: a Twenty-first Century Agenda' [1995] *PL* 386.

[15] See, eg the Human Rights Bill 1994 presented and First Reading HL Deb, vol 559, col 150 (22 November 1994). See further M Zander, *A Bill of Rights?* (London, Sweet & Maxwell, 1985).

from the fact that although there was considerable interest and enthusiasm for such a measure elsewhere, there was very little interest in the Conservative government. In 1994, in its Fourth Periodic Report to the UN Human Rights Committee under the Covenant on Civil and Political Rights,[16] the government of the day maintained that the rights and freedoms recognised in international instruments and in the constitutions of those countries that had enacted a comprehensive Bill of Rights were inherent in the United Kingdom's legal system and were protected by it and by Parliament unless they were removed or restricted by statute.

> The Government does not consider that it is properly the role of the legislature to confer rights and freedoms which are naturally possessed by all members of society. It also believes that Parliament should retain the supreme responsibility for enacting or changing the law, including that affecting individual rights and freedoms, while it is properly the role of the judiciary to interpret specific legislation.[17]

Furthermore, it stated its belief that the incorporation of an international human rights instrument into domestic law was not necessary to ensure that the United Kingdom's obligations under such instruments was reflected in the deliberations of government and of the courts.

> The United Kingdom's human rights obligations are routinely considered by Ministers and their officials in the formulation and application of Government policy, while judgments of the House of Lords have made clear that such obligations are part of the legal context in which the judges consider themselves to operate.[18]

It was clear that only a change in government would make any chance of incorporation possible.[19]

2.2 The Human Rights Bill

In March 1993, 'incorporation' of the ECHR was adopted as Labour Party policy. In December 1996 the Labour Party published 'Bringing Rights Home',[20] outlining its plans to incorporate the European Convention on Human Rights into UK law and thereby enable British people

> to bring grievances against the state covered by the Convention to a British court whilst still retaining a right of ultimate recourse to the Strasbourg court.[21]

The Labour Party saw incorporation as a way to

---

[16] CCPR/C/95/Add.3, 19 December 1994.
[17] *Ibid*, at [4].
[18] *Ibid*, at [5].
[19] For a background to the Human Rights Act generally, see: F Klug, *Values for a Godless Age The Story of the UK's New Bill of Rights* (London, Penguin, 2000); and H Fenwick, *Civil Liberties and Human Rights* (London, Cavendish, 2002), 117–32.
[20] Straw and Boateng, 'Bringing Rights Home', above n 6.
[21] *Ibid*, at 4.

change the relationship between the state and the citizen, and to redress the dilution of individual rights by an over-centralising government.

It also saw incorporation as a way to encourage citizens to better fulfil their responsibilities and to improve awareness of human rights thus nurturing a culture of understanding of rights and responsibilities at all levels in our society.[22]

With 'incorporation' a key manifesto commitment, Labour won the General Election in May 1997 with a majority of 179 seats. Little time was lost and in October 1997 the Home Office published the White Paper *Rights Brought Home*,[23] which accompanied a draft Bill. The Bill was an important part of the new government's commitment to a comprehensive policy of constitutional reform, including the establishment of a Scottish Parliament and a Welsh Assembly, reform of the House of Lords, freedom of information, an elected Mayor for London and a referendum on the voting system for the House of Commons.[24] It was seen as a 'key component' of the government's

> drive to modernise our society and refresh our democracy. It is part of a blueprint for changing the relationship between the Government and people of the United Kingdom to bring about a better balance between rights and responsibilities, between the powers of the state and the freedom of the individual.[25]

In *Rights Brought Home* the case for change comprised a number of points. First, the rights and freedoms guaranteed under the Convention were ones with which the people of this country were plainly comfortable.[26] Secondly, the growing awareness that it was not sufficient to rely on the common law and that incorporation was necessary.[27] Thirdly, the fact that the rights were no longer seen as British rights, and enforcing them took too long and cost too much.[28] Fourthly, the approach which the UK adopted towards the Convention did not sufficiently reflect its importance and had not stood the test of time—the most obvious proof lying in the number of cases in which violations had been found by the Commission and the Court.[29] The key argument was put as follows:

> Bringing these rights home will mean that the British people will be able to argue for their rights in the British courts—without this inordinate delay and cost. It will also mean that the rights will be brought much more fully into the jurisprudence of the courts throughout the United Kingdom, and their interpretation will thus be far more subtly and powerfully woven into our law. And there will be another distinct benefit. British judges will be enabled to make a distinctly British contribution to the development of the jurisprudence of human rights in Europe.[30]

---

[22] *Ibid*, at 14. For a discussion of possible models for incorporation see B Emmerson, 'Opinion: This Year's Model—The Options for Incorporation' [1997] *EHRLR* 313.

[23] Above, n 6.

[24] *Ibid*, 1.

[25] HC Deb, vol 306, col 783 (16 February 1998), Secretary of State for the Home Department, Mr Jack Straw.

[26] Home Office, *Rights Brought Home*, at [1.3].

[27] *Ibid*, at [1.4].

[28] *Ibid*, at [1.14].

[29] *Ibid*, at [1.15]–[1.16].

[30] *Ibid*, at [1.14].

Following lengthy parliamentary debates,[31] the Human Rights Bill was passed by both Houses and received the Royal Assent on 9 November 1998. However, it was not brought fully into force until 2 October 2000.

3. Purpose of the Human Rights Act

The purpose of the HRA is not obvious from the Act itself. In the Long Title it is described as 'An Act to give further effect to rights and freedoms guaranteed under the European Convention on Human Rights'. The reason the word 'further' was used was that prior to the HRA the courts already applied the Convention in many different circumstances.[32] More information is contained in the White Paper *Rights Brought Home*,[33] where the purpose of the Act is stated succinctly as

> to make more directly accessible the rights which the British people already enjoy under the Convention . . . to bring those rights home.[34]

The longer version provides as follows:

> . . . the time has come to enable people to enforce their Convention rights against the State in the British courts, rather than having to incur the delays and expense which are involved in taking a case to the European Human Rights Commission and Court in Strasbourg and which may altogether deter some people from pursuing their rights. Enabling courts in the United Kingdom to rule on the application of the Convention will also help to influence the development of case law on the Convention by the European Court of Human Rights on the basis of familiarity with our laws and customs and of sensitivity to practices and procedures in the United Kingdom . . . Enabling the Convention rights to be judged by British courts will also lead to closer scrutiny of the human rights implications of new legislation and new policies.[35]

It is interesting to note that the further purposes of nurturing a culture of understanding of rights and responsibilities at all levels in society and assisting public discussion of what might be the character of any future UK 'Bill of Rights and Responsibilities', originally present in the consultation paper 'Bringing Rights Home',[36] were not included, although it was noted that the Act would 'enhance the awareness of human rights in our society' and stand alongside the decision to put the promotion of human rights at the forefront of foreign policy.[37] In the Parliamentary debates the Lord Chancellor also noted that our 'courts will develop human rights

---

[31] See generally F Klug, 'The Human Rights Act 1998, *Pepper v Hart* and All That' [1999] *PL* 246.
[32] HL Deb, vol 583, col 478 (18 November 1997).
[33] Home Office, *Rights Brought Home*, above n 6.
[34] *Ibid*, at [1.19].
[35] *Ibid*, at [1.18]; see also [2.4].
[36] Straw and Boateng, 'Bringing Rights Home', above n 6, at 14.
[37] Home Office, *Rights Brought Home*, above n 6, at 1.

throughout society. A culture of awareness of human rights will develop.'[38] Lord Williams expanded on this, stating that every public authority 'will know that its behaviour, its structures, its conclusions and its executive actions will be subject to this culture,'[39] and in the House of Commons the Home Secretary noted that, over time, 'the Bill will bring about the creation of a human rights culture in Britain.'[40] Furthermore, in evidence to the Parliamentary Joint Committee on Human Rights, the Home Secretary stated that the HRA was intended, over time, to help bring about the development of a culture of rights and responsibilities.[41]

What judicial comment there has been on the purpose of the HRA is also reflective of the observations in *Rights Brought Home*. For example, in *Lambert*[42] Lord Clyde stated that the HRA did not incorporate the rights set out in the Convention into the domestic laws of the United Kingdom.

> The purpose of the Act, as set out in its preamble, was 'to give further effect to rights and freedoms' guaranteed under that Convention. The Convention rights have not become part of the constitution so as to obtain any superiority over the powers of Parliament or the validity of primary legislation . . . One principle achievement of the Act is to enable the Convention rights to be directly invoked in the domestic courts. In that respect the Act is important as a procedural measure which has opened a further means of access to justice for the citizen, more immediate and more familiar than a recourse to the Court in Strasbourg.

Lord Rodger emphasised in *Attorney General's Reference No 2 of 2001*[43] that these rights were to have effect in a way that had not previously been possible in domestic law in that the national courts were to have power to grant victims remedies in terms of the Act for violations of their rights.[44]

4. Structure of the Human Rights Act

The structure of the HRA is often described as unique[45] in addressing each of the three aspects of government.

> The Act . . . follows a scheme which recognises that the role of the judiciary is to apply and enforce the 'Convention rights' municipally, treats the executive branch of government, in the form of any public authority, as being civilly liable for any breach of the 'Convention

---

[38] HL Deb, vol 582, col 1228 (3 November 1997).
[39] *Ibid*, at col 1308.
[40] HC Deb, vol 317, col 1358 (21 October 1998).
[41] Minutes of evidence taken on Wednesday 14 March (2000–01 HL 66 HC 332){STYLE?}.
[42] *R v Lambert* [2001] UKHL 37, [2002] 2 AC 545.
[43] [2003] UKHL 68, [2004] 2 AC 72.
[44] *Ibid*, at [173].
[45] See, eg the comments of Lord Hobhouse in *Wilson v First County Trust* [2003] UKHL 40, [2003] 3 WLR 568.

rights' on its part and makes their offending conduct unlawful, and recognises that laws passed by the Legislature may be incompatible with a 'Convention right'.[46]

Section 1 defines the Convention rights given further effect by the HRA. Section 2 provides that a court or tribunal determining a question which has arisen in connection with a Convention right must take into account, inter alia, any judgment, decision, declaration or advisory opinion of the European Court of Human Rights or opinion of the Commission. Section 6, a key provision, provides that it is unlawful for a public authority to act in a way which is incompatible with a Convention right. However, this section also provides a defence to a public authority if, as a result of primary legislation, it could not have acted differently. The HRA clearly preserves the sovereignty of Parliament and this part of section 6 is an important part of that objective. Where primary legislation is itself incompatible with a Convention right, the courts have only two alternatives. First, they must apply section 3 of the Act and read and give effect to the legislation in a way which is compatible with Convention rights, so far as it is possible to do so. If this is not possible, the court may make a declaration of incompatibility under section 4 of the Act. However, such a declaration does not affect the validity, continuing operation or enforcement of the provision. Once a declaration is made, section 10 of the Act applies, empowering a minister to make such amendments to the legislation as he considers necessary to remove the incompatibility. Schedule 2 of the Act makes further provision about such remedial orders. Section 7 provides that only the victims of the unlawful acts of public as defined in section 6 may bring proceedings under the HRA or rely on the Convention rights in any legal proceedings. Finally, section 8 sets out the remedies that may be granted for the acts of public authorities incompatible with Convention rights.

As Lord Rodger commented in *Wilson*,[47] the HRA applies across the board.

While most statutes apply to one particular topic or area of law, the 1998 Act works as a catalyst across the board, wherever a Convention right is engaged. It may affect matters of substance in such areas as the law of property, the law of marriage and the law of torts. Or else it may affect civil and criminal procedure, or the procedure of administrative tribunals.[48]

5. Convention Rights Given Further Effect

5.1 The Nature and Scope of the Convention Rights

The HRA gives further effect to the 'Convention rights', and in section 1 these are defined as Articles 2–12 and 14 of the ECHR, Articles 1–3 of Protocol No 1 to the

---

[46] *Ibid*, at [126].
[47] *Ibid*.
[48] *Ibid*, at [182].

ECHR and Articles 1–2 of Protocol No 6 to the ECHR. All must be read with Articles 16 to 18 of the ECHR and have effect subject to any designated derogation or reservation.

These rights are predominantly what are known as civil and political rights and, given that the ECHR was drafted in 1950 and Protocol No 1 in 1952, are obviously not the most modern list of rights that could be given effect in domestic law.[49] However, it is often observed that these are the most fundamental and important rights.

> Those who negotiated and first signed the convention were not seeking to provide a blueprint for the ideal society. They were formulating a statement of very basic rights and freedoms which, it was believed, were very largely observed by the contracting states and which it was desired to preserve and protect both in the light of recent experience and in view of developments in Eastern Europe. The convention was seen more as a statement of good existing practice than as an instrument setting targets or standards which contracting states were to strive to achieve . . . Thus the rights guaranteed by the convention were minimum rights.[50]

The comment has also been made that the rights and freedoms guaranteed under the Convention are ones with which the people of the United Kingdom are plainly comfortable.[51]

It has been held that by virtue of sections 1(1) and 21 of the HRA, in the context of sections 2, 3, 6 and 7, the Convention rights are rights of the same scope as those enforceable under the Convention. There is no basis for construing the Act as providing rights with an autonomous United Kingdom meaning of greater scope than those in Strasbourg.

> Such a construction achieves the purpose of the statute, namely to allow victims to enforce those rights to which the Act refers in the United Kingdom and not be compelled to vindicate them in Strasbourg.[52]

However, such an interpretation of the Convention rights has some perhaps unforeseen consequences. For example, in *Al-Jedda*[53] the claimant, who had been detained by British forces in Iraq, alleged that his detention was incompatible with Article 5. The defendant Secretary of State argued that the claimant's detention was authorised by United Nations Security Council Resolution 1546 and that the effect of the resolution was to displace the claimant's rights under Article 5. Having already concluded that the Convention rights under the HRA were of the same scope as those enforceable in Strasbourg,[54] the Divisional Court held that as the Security Council Resolution would have had the effect of displacing Article 5 before the Strasbourg

---

[49] Compare, eg the EU Charter of Fundamental Rights. See further G Van Bueren, 'Including the Excluded: the Case for an Economic, Social and Cultural Human Rights Act' [2002] *PL* 456.

[50] *Procurator Fiscal, Linlithgow v Watson* [2002] UKPC D1, [2004] 1 AC 379 at [48]–[49] per Lord Bingham. See also the comments of Lord Bingham in *Brown v Stott* [2003] 1 AC 681 and in *Harrow London Borough Council v Qazi* [2003] UKHL 43, [2004] 1 AC 983 at [8]. As to the background to the rights included in the EHCR, see generally D Nicol, 'Original Intent and the European Convention on Human Rights' [2005] *PL* 152.

[51] Home Office, *Rights Brought Home*, above n 6, at [1.3].

[52] *R (on the application of Al-Jedda) v Secretary of State for Defence* [2005] EWHC (Admin) 1809 at [74].

[53] *Ibid.*

[54] *Ibid*, at [74].

Court as a matter of international law, Article 5 was also displaced in a claim under the HRA.[55]

5.2 The Convention as a 'Living Instrument'

However, it must also be appreciated that the ECHR is regarded as a 'living instrument'. The language in which the Convention rights is written is open textured and permits adaptation to modern conditions.[56] It has been held that

> As an important constitutional instrument the convention is to be seen as a 'living tree capable of growth and expansion within its natural limits.'[57]

As will become apparent in Part II of this book, which concerns the Convention rights, what is written down in the Convention and Protocol No 1 is not necessarily what you get. For example, the right not to incriminate oneself, the right of access to a court and the right to equality of arms are all rights that have been implied into Article 6, the right to a fair trial. Furthermore, the concept of living instrument means that the scope of a Convention right may change over time. For example, in *Bellinger*[58] the House of Lords took account of the fact that although previously the Court considered that non-recognition of a change of gender by a post-operative transsexual person did not constitute a violation of either Article 8 or Article 12, it had recently changed this view in *Goodwin v UK*,[59] finding that non-recognition by the state of a sex change constituted a violation of Articles 8 and 12.[60]

However, under the HRA the higher courts have made clear that there are limits to the living instrument approach. In *Brown*[61] Lord Clyde stated that the Convention is dealing with the realities of life and it is not to be applied in ways which run counter to reason and common sense. In his Lordship's view, if the Convention rights were to be applied by the courts in ways which would seem absurd to ordinary people then the courts would be doing a disservice to the aims and purposes of the Convention, and the result would simply be to prejudice public respect for an international treaty which seeks to express the basic rights and freedoms of a democratic society. Similarly in *Matthews*[62] Lord Bingham observed that

> the exact limits of such rights are debatable and, although there is not much trace of economic rights in the 50-year-old Convention, I think it is well arguable that human rights include the right to a minimum standard of living, without which many of the other rights would be a mockery. But they certainly do not include the right to a fair distribution of

---

[55] *Ibid*, at [92]–[93].
[56] *R (on the application of Pretty) v Director of Public Prosecutions* [2001] UKHL 61, [2001] 3 WLR 1598 at [56] per Lord Steyn.
[57] *Brown v Stott* [2003] 1 AC 681. See also the comments of Lord Clyde and the observations of Lord Bingham in *Procurator Fiscal, Linlithgow v Watson* [2002] UKPC D1, [2004] 1 AC 379 at [48]–[49].
[58] *Bellinger v Bellinger* [2003] UKHL 21, [2003] 2 AC 467.
[59] (2002) 35 EHRR 18.
[60] See also *R v Secretary of State for the Home Department, ex p Anderson* [2002] UKHL 46, [2003] 1 AC 837.
[61] *Brown v Stott* [2003] 1 AC 681.
[62] *Matthews v Ministry of Defence* [2003] UKHL 4, [2003] 1 AC 1163.

resources or fair treatment in economic terms—in other words, distributive justice. Of course distributive justice is a good thing. But it is not a fundamental human right.[63]

5.3 The Non-absolute Nature of the Majority of the Convention Rights

As discussed in more detail in Part II of this book, very few of the Convention rights are expressed in absolute terms. The majority are subject to exceptions, and it is the determination of the limits of these exceptions which forms the bulk of judicial decision making under the HRA. In relation to absolute rights, such as in Article 3, it has been held that such rights should not be capable in any circumstances of being overridden by the majority, even if it is thought that the public interest so requires.[64] This belief was of considerable importance in the case of *Millar*,[65] where the absolute right to an independent and impartial tribunal was upheld notwithstanding the prediction that the Scottish legal system would be 'plunged into chaos' as a result.[66]

With respect to the non-absolute rights, as Lord Steyn noted in *Brown*,[67] the framers of the Convention realised that from time to time the fundamental right of one individual may conflict with the human right of another.

> They also realised only too well that a single-minded concentration on the pursuit of fundamental rights of individuals to the exclusion of the interests of the wider public might be subversive of the ideal of tolerant European liberal democracies. The fundamental rights of individuals are of supreme importance but those rights are not unlimited: we live in communities of individuals who also have rights.

Such an interpretation was of particular importance in *McCann*,[68] which concerned a challenge to the making of anti-social behaviour orders. Lord Steyn pointed out that in Parliament the view was taken that proceedings for an antisocial behaviour order would be civil and would not 'attract the rigour of the inflexible and sometimes absurdly technical hearsay rule which applies in criminal cases.' In his view, if this supposition was wrong 'it would inevitably follow that the procedure for obtaining anti-social behaviour orders is completely or virtually unworkable and useless.' His starting point was 'an initial scepticism of an outcome which would deprive communities of their fundamental rights.'[69] Similarly Lord Hope stated that 'respect for the rights of others is a price that we all must pay for the rights and freedoms that it guarantees.'[70] He noted that if the proceedings were classified as criminal

---

[63] *Ibid*, at [26]. See also the comments of Lord Scott in *Harrow London Borough Council v Qazi* [2003] UKHL 43, [2004] 1 AC 983 at [123].
[64] *R v Secretary of State for the Environment, Transport and the Regions, ex p Alconbury Developments Ltd* [2001] UKHL 23, [2001] 2 WLR 1389 per Lord Hoffmann.
[65] *Millar v Procurator Fiscal* [2002] 1 WLR 1615.
[66] See, eg J Oldham and A Jamieson, 'Law Lords Rule Against Sheriffs', *The Scotsman*, 26 July 2001, 2.
[67] *Brown v Stott* [2003] 1 AC 681.
[68] *R (McCann) v Crown Court at Manchester* [2002] UKHL 39, [2003] 1 AC 787.
[69] *Ibid*, at [18].
[70] *Ibid*, at [41].

much of the benefit which the legislation was designed to achieve would be lost . . . It would greatly disturb the balance which section 1 of the Crime and Disorder Act 1998 seeks to strike between the interests of the individual and those of society.[71]

5.4 Derogations and Reservations

Section 1(2) of the HRA provides that the Convention rights given further effect are subject to any designated derogation or reservation. Derogations may be made pursuant to Article 15 of the ECHR and reservations pursuant to Article 57.[72] Following the withdrawal of a derogation to Article 5 in April 2005,[73] the United Kingdom currently maintains no derogations and only one reservation to Article 2 of Protocol No 1 accepting the second principle of Article 2 'only so far as it is compatible with the provision of efficient instruction and training, and the avoidance of unreasonable public expenditure.'

Although the HRA refers to derogations and reservations in sections 14–17, neither Article 15 nor Article 57 of the ECHR is included in the Convention rights given further effect by the HRA. Whilst few rules attach to the making of a reservation under Article 57, there are a number of requirements specified in relation to derogations under Article 15. Article 15(1) provides that

> in time of war or other public emergency threatening the life of the nation any High Contracting Party may take measures derogating from its obligations under this Convention to the extent strictly required by the exigencies of the situation, provided that such measures are not inconsistent with its other obligations under international law.

Pursuant to Article 15(2), no derogation from Article 2, except in respect of deaths resulting from lawful acts of war, or from Articles 3, 4 (paragraph 1) and 7 is possible under this provision. As Article 15 is not given further effect by the HRA, it is not clear how challenges to derogation orders can be brought domestically. Even in *A v Secretary of State*,[74] where a derogation order was successfully challenged, it was not made clear exactly how this was possible.[75]

Despite the questions surrounding the power to quash the derogation order in this case, it is important to examine the reasoning of their Lordships. The Order subject to challenge provided for a derogation from Article 5(1)(f) to allow legislation to detain a person against whom no action was being taken with a view to deportation.[76] The first argument of the claimants was that there was no public emergency

---

[71] *Ibid*, at [43]. See also Lord Hutton at [85] and [113].
[72] On derogations see A Mokhtar, 'Human Rights Obligations v. Derogations: Art 15 of the European Convention on Human Rights' (2004) 8 *IJHR* 65.
[73] This followed the declaration of incompatibility by the House of Lords in *A v Secretary of State for the Home Department* [2004] UKHL 56, [2005] 2 AC 68, the repeal of the detention provisions in the Anti-Terrorism Crime and Security Act 2001 and their replacement with control orders under the Prevention of Terrorism Act 2005.
[74] *Ibid*.
[75] It is likely that it was possible due to provisions of the Anti-terrorism, Crime and Security Act 2001, notably s 30 and s 25(2)(b), which provide that the Special Immigration Appeals Commission must cancel a certificate (certifying an individual as a terrorist) if it considers 'for some other reason the certificate should not have been issued.' It appears that the Secretary of State conceded that if the derogation order was not compatible with Art 15, this would constitute 'some other reason' within the meaning of s 25(2)(b).
[76] Human Rights Act 1998 (Designated Derogation) Order 2001 (SI 2001/3644).

threatening the life of the nation within the meaning of Article 15. A majority of their Lordships rejected this claim. Lord Bingham held that it had not been shown that the Special Immigration Appeals Commission or the Court of Appeal had misdirected themselves on this issue. He also found support in the conclusion of the European Court of Human Rights in *Lawless v Ireland (No.3)*[77] and stated that great weight should be given to the judgment of the Home Secretary, his colleagues, and Parliament on this question, because they were called upon to exercise a 'pre-eminently political judgment.'[78]

However, Article 15 also requires that the derogating measures must not go beyond what is 'strictly required by the exigencies of the situation'. 'Thus the Convention imposes a test of strict necessity or, in Convention terminology, proportionality.'[79] A majority of their Lordships found that this test was not satisfied in the present case and that the Order was disproportionate. Lord Bingham noted that the courts were not effectively precluded by any doctrine of deference from scrutinising the issues raised.[80] His Lordship concluded that the choice of an immigration measure to address a security problem had the inevitable result of failing adequately to address that problem (by allowing non-UK suspected terrorists to leave the country with impunity and leaving British suspected terrorists at large) while imposing a severe penalty of indefinite detention on persons who, even if reasonably suspected of having links with Al-Qaeda, may harbour no hostile intentions towards the United Kingdom.[81] A quashing order was made in respect of the Derogation Order.[82]

---

6. Principles of Interpretation

As discussed in the paragraphs above, a number of principles of interpretation relate to the Convention rights themselves, including the view that the rights given further effect are the most important and fundamental; the concept of the Convention as a living instrument, within limits; and the non-absolute nature of the majority of Convention rights. Other principles of interpretation of Convention rights, such as the principles of legality and proportionality and the practice of judicial deference, are discussed later in Chapter 4, which concerns the process of determining incompatibility. There are also a few principles of interpretation relating to the HRA itself. It has

---

[77] (1979–80) 1 EHRR 15.
[78] *Ibid*, at [27]–[29]. See also Lord Hope at [116], Lord Scott at [154], Lord Rodger at [166], Lord Walker at [208], Baroness Hale at [226].
[79] *Ibid*, at [30] per Lord Bingham.
[80] *Ibid*, at [42].
[81] *Ibid*, at [43]. See also Lord Hope at [131]–[132], Lord Scott at [155]–[156], Lord Rodger at [189], Baroness Hale at [231].
[82] See further TR Hickman, 'Between Human Rights and the Rule of Law: Indefinite Detention and the Derogation Model of Constitutionalism' (2005) 68 *MLR* 655; S Tierney, 'Determining the State of Exception: What Role for Parliament and the Courts?' (2005) 68 *MLR* 668; A Tomkins, 'Readings of *A v Secretary of State for the Home Department*' [2005] *PL* 259.

been held that a generous and purposive construction is to be given to that part of a constitution which protects and entrenches fundamental rights and freedoms, and that such an approach should be applied to the HRA.[83] It has also been held that the HRA 'must be given its full import' and that 'long or well entrenched ideas may have to be put aside, sacred cows culled.'[84]

The utilisation of a strong purposive approach to the construction of the HRA does not yet appear widespread, as evidenced by the approach of the courts to the issue of retrospective effect. As discussed in the paragraphs above, it is clear that at least one purpose of the HRA is to allow claims of violations of Convention rights to be heard in domestic courts rather than in the European Court of Human Rights. However, in *Lambert*,[85] only Lord Steyn interpreted section 6 of the HRA in the 'broader framework of an Act which was undoubtedly intended "to bring home" the adjudication on fundamental rights'[86] and thereby found that it could apply to a trial which took place before the Act came into force.[87] A strong purposive approach was far more evident in the case of *B*,[88] where the Court of Appeal held that, in determining whether the HRA could be applied to acts of UK public authorities outside of the territory of the United Kingdom, the approach taken to the interpretation of the Convention in such circumstances by the European Court of Human Rights should be followed.[89]

It has also been held that, in accordance with section 3 of the HRA, the HRA itself must be read and given effect in a way that is compatible with Convention rights.[90] Whilst this has had some impact on the interpretation of section 12 of the HRA, which concerns freedom of expression,[91] as Article 13 of the ECHR, the right to an effective remedy, is not a Convention right given further effect by the HRA, the potential for radical reinterpretation of the key provisions of the HRA using section 3 is limited. Indeed, it is likely that one of the fears prompting the non-inclusion of Article 13 was the possibility that a court would declare the HRA itself incompatible with Article 13 in that it failed to provide an effective remedy to those who had been subject to a violation of Convention rights perpetrated by primary legislation.

One final principle of interpretation which has emerged from the case law concerns satellite litigation within the criminal justice system. From early on in HRA

---

[83] *R v Director of Public Prosecutions ex p Kebilene* [2000] 2 AC 326 per Lord Hope endorsing the observations of Lord Wilberforce in *Minister of Home Affairs v Fisher* [1980] AC 319 at 328 and Lord Diplock in *Attorney-General of The Gambia v Momodou Jobe* [1984] AC 689 at 700. See also the speeches of Lord Steyn in *McCartan Turkington Breen v Times Newspapers Ltd* [2001] 2 AC 277 and *Brown v Stott* [2003] 1 AC 681.

[84] *R v Lambert* [2001] UKHL 37, [2002] 2 AC 545 per Lord Slynn. See also *Poplar Housing and Regeneration Community Association Ltd v Donoghue* [2001] EWCA Civ 595, [2000] QB 48 at [58] per Lord Woolf CJ. See further RA Edwards, 'Generosity and the Human Rights Act: the Right Interpretation?' [1999] *PL* 400; D Pannick, 'Principles of Interpretation of Convention Rights under the Human Rights Act and the Discretionary Area of Judgment' [1998] *PL* 545.

[85] *Ibid.*

[86] *Ibid*, at [29]. See also the speech of Lord Clyde at [135].

[87] See also Lord Steyn's speech in *Kebilene*, above n 83.

[88] *R (on the application of B) v Secretary of State for the Foreign and Commonwealth Office* [2004] EWCA Civ 1344, [2005] QB 643.

[89] *Ibid*, at [75]–[79]. See also *R (on the application of Al-Skeini) v Secretary of State for Defence* [2004] EWHC (Admin) 2911, [2005] 2 WLR 1401; and *Al-Jedda*, above n 52.

[90] See the speeches of Lords Hope and Clyde in *R v Lambert* [2001] UKHL 37, [2002] 2 AC 545.

[91] See *Douglas v Hello! Ltd* [2001] QB 967.

jurisprudence it was clear that such litigation was not to be encouraged. For example, in *Kebilene*[92] prior to trial it was argued that the enactment of the HRA gave rise to an enforceable legitimate expectation that the Director of Public Prosecutions would exercise his prosecutorial discretion in accordance with the ECHR. Lord Steyn, with whom Lords Slynn and Cooke agreed, held that once the HRA was fully in force it would not be possible to apply for judicial review on the ground that a decision to prosecute was in breach of a Convention right and the only available remedies would be in the trial process or on appeal.

> If the Divisional Court's present ruling is correct, it will be possible in other cases, which do not involve reverse legal burden provisions, to challenge decisions to prosecute in judicial review proceedings. The potential for undermining the proper and fair management of our criminal justice system may be considerable.[93]

His Lordship continued:

> While the passing of the Human Rights Act 1998 marked a great advance for our criminal justice system it is in my view vitally important that, so far as the courts are concerned, its application in our law should take place in an orderly manner which recognises the desirability of all challenges taking place in the criminal trial or on appeal. The effect of the judgment of the Divisional Court was to open the door too widely to delay in the conduct of criminal proceedings. Such satellite litigation should rarely be permitted in our criminal justice system.[94]

7. The Relationship with Strasbourg Jurisprudence

7.1 Section 2 of the Human Rights Act

Section 2(1) of the HRA provides that a court or tribunal determining a question which has arisen in connection with a Convention right must take into account, inter alia, any judgment of the European Court of Human Rights or opinion of the Commission, whenever made or given, so far as, in the opinion of the court or tribunal, it

---

[92] Above n 83.
[93] Per Lord Steyn.
[94] Lord Hope commented that he could see no reason why, in a clear case where the facts of the case were of no importance, a decision that a provision was incompatible should not be capable of being taken at a very early stage. However, he agreed that, absent dishonesty, bad faith or some other exceptional circumstance, the DPP's decisions to consent or not to consent to a prosecution were not amenable to judicial review. In *Pretty*, above n 56, per Lord Steyn at [67] stood by this rule as did Lord Hobhouse at [119], [121] [123]. Lord Hope at [78] held that in these exceptional circumstances it was open to Mrs Pretty to raise the issue by judicial review. In *R v Hertfordshire CC ex p Green Environmental Industries Ltd* [2000] 2 AC 483 Lord Cooke stated that the comments in *Kebilene* concerning satellite litigation in the criminal justice system had nothing to say about the general ability by a citizen to challenge by appropriate civil proceedings the validity of a requisition issued against him or her by a public authority—here a request for information under the Environmental Protection Act 1990. Lord Hobhouse agreed. See further *Alconbury*, above n 64.

is relevant to the proceedings in which that question has arisen. In HRA jurisprudence it is clear that the judgments of the Court and opinions of the Commission are regularly taken into account and followed.[95] In some instances courts have felt obliged by section 2 to take into account and follow Strasbourg jurisprudence even when they would obviously prefer not to.[96]

Reference to more than 50 years of jurisprudence has obviously expanded somewhat the task of the judge adjudicating in HRA cases. Furthermore, there is the need to keep constantly up to date, as the Court does not consider itself bound by its own previous judgments. For example, in *Bellinger*[97] the House of Lords took account of the fact that although previously the Court considered that non-recognition of a change of gender by post-operative transsexual persons did not constitute a violation of either Article 8 or Article 12, it had recently changed this view in *Goodwin v UK*,[98] finding that non-recognition by the state of a sex change constituted a violation of Articles 8 and 12.[99]

7.2 The Obligation to Take into Account *and* Follow?

In the majority of cases, the obligation to take into account Strasbourg jurisprudence is construed as an obligation to follow it as well. It has been held that, in the absence of some special circumstance, the court should follow any clear and constant jurisprudence of the European Court of Human Rights as, if it does not do so,

> there is at least a possibility that the case will go to that court which is likely in the ordinary case to follow its own constant jurisprudence.[100]

However, the case law reveals that there is also the possibility for some deviation. This was also recognised during the parliamentary debates, the Lord Chancellor noting that there may be occasions when it would be right for the United Kingdom courts to depart from Strasbourg decisions.

> We must remember that the interpretation of the convention rights develops over the years. Circumstances may therefore arise in which a judgment given by the European Court of Human Rights decades ago contains pronouncements which it would not be appropriate to apply to the letter in the circumstances of today in a particular set of circumstances affecting this country.[101]

---

[95] See, eg *R v P* [2001] 2 WLR 463 and *R (on the application of Amin) v Secretary of State for the Home Department* [2003] UKHL 51, [2004] 1 AC 653. On s 2(1), see generally R Masterman, 'Section 2(1) of the Human Rights Act 1998: Binding Domestic Courts to Strasbourg?' [2004] *PL* 725; E Wicks, 'Taking Account of Strasbourg? The British Judiciary's Approach to Interpreting Convention Rights' (2005) 11 *EPL* 405.

[96] See, eg the speech of Lord Hoffmann in *Alconbury*, above n 64, particularly at [74].

[97] *Bellinger v Bellinger* [2003] UKHL 21, [2003] 2 AC 467.

[98] (2002) 35 EHRR 18.

[99] See also *Anderson*, above n 60.

[100] *Alconbury*, above n 64 at [26] per Lord Slynn. See also his Lordship's comments in *Amin*, above n 95, at [44] and the observations of Lord Bingham in *Anderson*, ibid, at [18] and in *R v Special Adjudicator, ex p Ullah* [2004] UKHL 26, [2004] 2 AC 323 at [20].

[101] HL Deb, vol 584, col 1271 (19 January 1998) Lord Chancellor.

Nevertheless, the deviation from Strasbourg case law has proceeded slightly differently. Although in *Alconbury*[102] Lord Hoffmann stated that the House was not bound by decisions of the European court if these compelled a conclusion 'fundamentally at odds with the distribution of powers under the British constitution,'[103] the means by which conflicting Strasbourg jurisprudence is usually avoided is by a finding that the reasoning of the Court (or Commission) was inadequate. For example, in *Brown*[104] the Privy Council concluded that the leading of evidence by the prosecution obtained under section 172(2)(a) of the Road Traffic Act 1988 was not in violation of Article 6 although there was a judgment of the European Court of Human Rights arguably pointing to the opposite conclusion.[105] Lords Steyn and Hope and the Rt Hon Ian Kirkwood described the reasoning of the Court in this case as 'unsatisfactory', 'unconvincing' and a 'more absolute standard than the other jurisprudence of the court indicates.'[106] Lord Hope in particular noted that

> the general approach which is revealed by the judgment appears to be out of keeping with the mainstream of the jurisprudence which the court itself has developed as to the nature and application of the rights which it has read into art 6(1).

A similar approach was taken in *Boyd*,[107] where their Lordships were confronted with the judgment of the European Court of Human Rights in *Morris*[108] that the appointment of junior officer members to courts martial and the role of the reviewing authority were incompatible with Article 6. Exactly the same issue had arisen in the domestic proceedings. It was clear that their Lordships did not wish to follow the conclusion of the European Court on these two issues. Lord Bingham stated as follows:

> It goes without saying that any judgment of the European Court commands great respect, and section 2(1) of the Human Rights Act 1998 requires the House to take any such judgment into account, as it routinely does. There were, however, a large number of points in issue in *Morris*, and it did not seem clear that on this particular aspect the European Court did not receive all the help which was needed to form a conclusion . . . In my opinion the rules governing the role of junior officers as members of courts-martial are in practice such as effectively to protect the accused against the risk that they might be subject to 'external army influence', as I feel sure the European Court would have appreciated had the position been more fully explained.[109]

---

[102] Above n 64.
[103] *Ibid*, at [76]. Nevertheless Lord Hoffmann did follow such authority in concluding that the decisions of the Secretary of State were a determination of civil rights and obligations within the meaning of Art 6, despite his own views to the contrary. See [74].
[104] *Brown v Stott* [2003] 1 AC 681.
[105] *Saunders v UK* (1997) 2 BHRC 358.
[106] It is important to note that this was a devolution case and, although s 126 of the Scotland Act 1998 provides that the term 'Convention rights' has the same meaning as in the HRA, the Act does not include an equivalent of s 2 of the HRA. It is therefore possible that courts determining devolution issues concerning incompatibility with Convention rights are not obliged to take existing Convention jurisprudence into account. Nevertheless, this has been the approach generally followed.
[107] *Boyd v The Army Prosecuting Authority* [2002] UKHL 31, [2003] 1 AC 734.
[108] *Morris v United Kingdom* (2002) 34 EHRR 1253.
[109] *Ibid*, at [12]. Lords Steyn, Hutton and Scott agreed.

The same approach was taken in relation to the role of the reviewing authority.[110] Lord Rodger noted that the European Court was given rather less information than the House of Lords about the safeguards relating to the officers serving on courts-martial.

> And, like the European Court, the House must have regard to all the relevant factual information presented to it when deciding whether the safeguards of the independence and impartiality of the members of the courts-martial were adequate.[111]

It is also important to note that, conversely, particularly cogent reasoning on the part of the European Court of Human Rights has been used to support reasons for following a particular judgment. For example, in *Anderson*[112] it was argued for the Home Secretary that the House should not follow the judgment of the European Court of Human Rights in *Stafford*.[113] Lord Bingham held that the House would not, without good reason,

> depart from the principles laid down in a carefully considered judgment of the court sitting as a Grand Chamber . . . Here, there is very strong reason to support the decision, since it rests on a clear and accurate understanding of the tariff-fixing process and the Home Secretary's role in it.[114]

Similarly Lord Steyn found the decision of the European Court to be a coherent and inescapable one.

> The ECHR carefully took account of criticisms of the reasoning in *Wynne* in the judgments in the Court of Appeal in *Anderson*. The conclusion that the reasoning in *Wynne* is no longer supportable was inevitable. Moreover, the effective elimination by legislation in Scotland and Northern Ireland of the role of the executive in mandatory life sentence cases was regarded as important. And the ECHR was rightly influenced by the evolution and strengthening of the principle of separation of powers between the executive and judiciary which underlies article 6(1).[115]

Despite the development of mechanisms to get around Strasbourg jurisprudence, the bottom line is that a court is not bound to follow it. It remains international law not directly enforceable in domestic courts.

> Under the Convention, the United Kingdom is bound to accept a judgment of the Strasbourg court as binding: Article 46(1). But a court adjudicating in litigation in the United Kingdom about a domestic 'Convention right' is not bound by a decision of the Strasbourg court. It must take it into account.[116]

---

[110] *Ibid*, at [13].
[111] *Ibid*, at [66]. Lords Steyn, Hutton and Scott agreed. See also the comments of Lord Hoffmann in *R v Lyons* [2002] UKHL 44, [2003] 1 AC 976 at [46], where he stated that, if an English court considers that the European Court of Human Rights has misunderstood or been misinformed about some aspect of English law, it may wish to give a judgment which invites the ECHR to reconsider the question, and cited as an example *Z v UK* (2001) 34 EHRR 97.
[112] Above n 60.
[113] *Stafford v UK,* 28 May 2002
[114] *Ibid*, at [18].
[115] *Ibid*, at [54]. The others agreed.
[116] *In re McKerr* [2004] UKHL 12, [2004] 1 WLR 807 at [66] per Lord Hoffmann.

Whilst such a drastic approach has yet to appear, where a particular judgment of the European Court cannot be given effect via the HRA, the courts have been quick to affirm that the position of such jurisprudence remains as it was prior to the HRA. For example in *Lyons*[117] the appellants appealed against the refusal of the Court of Appeal to quash convictions recorded against them because the prosecution case against them at trial depended in significant part on answers given by them to inspectors armed with statutory power to compel answers. The admission of evidence of these answers at trial had since been held by the European Court to be in violation of Article 6. As the trial took place prior to the HRA coming into force, there was no recourse under it. Their Lordships made clear that international treaties 'do not form part of English law and that English courts have no jurisdiction to interpret or apply them.'[118] Lord Millett summed up the situation, stating that

> the obligation placed upon the United Kingdom by article 46 of the Convention to abide by a judgment of the ECHR is an international obligation of the United Kingdom. It has not been incorporated into our domestic law so as to be directly enforceable by individuals . . . while a judgment of the ECHR is binding on the United Kingdom, it is not directly binding as a matter of our domestic law on the courts.[119]

However, in *Hurst*[120] the Court of Appeal concluded that domestic tribunals were bound to give full weight to the international obligations to be found in the ECHR and that duty should in particular guide the exercise of discretions.[121] It concluded that when a coroner came to exercise his discretion under section 16(3) of the Coroners Act 1988 to decide whether or not there was sufficient cause to re-open an inquest, he had to take those international obligations into account. Here it held that it was not open to the coroner in terms of rationality as a matter of English domestic law to conclude otherwise than that obligations under Article 2 (the right to life) required the resumption of the inquest.[122]

7.3 A More Generous Interpretation of Convention Rights

A question which has arisen in a number of cases is whether it is possible for a domestic court to give a more generous interpretation to a Convention right than that which has been arrived at by the European Court of Human Rights. It has been held that what the Act has done

> is to create domestic rights expressed in the same terms as those contained in the Convention. But they are domestic rights, not international rights. Their source is the statute, not the Convention. They are available against specific public authorities, not the United

---

[117] *R v Lyons* [2002] UKHL 44, [2003] 1 AC 976.
[118] *Ibid*, at [27] per Lord Hoffmann.
[119] *Ibid*, at [104]–[105]. It is interesting to note that in *McKerr*, above n 116, Lord Steyn commented that it was difficult to see what relevance the dualist theory had to international human rights treaties which create fundamental rights for individuals against the state and its agencies. He also commented that a critical re-examination of this branch of the law may become necessary in the future. See [52].
[120] *The Commissioner of Police for the Metropolis v Hurst* [2005] EWCA Civ 890.
[121] *Ibid*, at [29].
[122] *Ibid*.

Kingdom as a state. And their meaning and application is a matter for domestic courts, not the court in Strasbourg.[123]

Arguably this would indicate that a more generous interpretation is possible. This is supported by the observation of Lord Woolf that legislation may be compatible with Convention rights if it provides greater protection[124] and the observation of the Court of Appeal in *Clays Lane*[125] that if the UK courts required a more rigorous test of proportionality where there was an interference under Article 1 Protocol No 1 than that required by the European Court, then that is the test that would have to be applied.[126] Similarly in *M*[127] a majority of the Court of Appeal held that, given the European Court of Human Rights had concluded that the question of whether two persons involved in a loving permanent same-sex relationship were members of the same family for the purposes of Article 8 was within the margin of appreciation, it was open to the United Kingdom to decide whether such a relationship was, for the purpose of the United Kingdom, within the concept of family life. 'In other words, it is not open to this court to shelter behind the margin of appreciation.'[128] It concluded that a stable same-sex relationship between two persons living together should, at least in most contexts, be treated as a family relationship and therefore within the ambit of Article 8.

However, the contrary opinion was put forward by Lord Bingham in *Ullah*,[129] where he stated that the Convention was an international instrument, the correct interpretation of which can be authoritatively expounded only by the Strasbourg court. In his Lordship's view, it followed from this that it was open to member states to

provide for rights more generous than those guaranteed by the Convention, but such provision should not be the product of interpretation of the Convention by national courts, since the meaning of the Convention should be uniform throughout the states party to it. The duty of national courts is to keep pace with the Strasbourg jurisprudence as it evolves over time: no more, but certainly no less.[130]

Similarly in *N*,[131] also in the context of deportation, Lord Hope stated that an enlargement of the scope of the Convention in its application to one contracting state was an enlargement for them all.

The question must always be whether the enlargement is one which the contracting parties would have accepted and agreed to be bound by.[132]

---

[123] *McKerr*, above n 116, at [65] per Lord Hoffmann.
[124] *British Broadcasting Corporation*, above n 4, at [17].
[125] *R (on the application of Clays Lane Housing Co-operative Limited) v The Housing Corporation* [2004] EWCA Civ 1658, [2005] 1 WLR 2229.
[126] *Ibid*, at [18].
[127] *Secretary of State for Work and Pensions v M* [2004] EWCA Civ 1343, [2005] 2 WLR 740.
[128] *Ibid*, at [114], although it was pointed out at [117] that where one was within the margin of appreciation the courts should be careful not to put themselves in the place of the legislature or the executive and there was a requirement for an appropriate degree of judicial self-restraint.
[129] Above n 100.
[130] *Ibid*, at [20].
[131] *N v Secretary of State for the Home Department* [2005] UKHL 31, [2005] 2 AC 296.
[132] *Ibid*, at [21].

His Lordship also found that it was for the Strasbourg court to decide whether its case law was out of touch with modern conditions and to determine what further extensions were needed to the rights guaranteed by the Convention. 'We must take the case law as we find it, not as we would like it to be.'[133]

7.4 A Conflict between Domestic Authority and Subsequent Strasbourg Authority

Finally, consideration needs to be given to the prospect that a judgment of a domestic court under the HRA may be found to conflict with a judgment of the European Court of Human Rights given after the HRA judgment. For example, in *Price*[134] the Court of Appeal found that the judgment of the House of Lords in *Qazi*[135] was inconsistent with the later judgment of the European Court of Human Rights in *Connors v United Kingdom*.[136] The court described the issue as a stark one.

> If a decision of the House of Lords in relation to the Convention is followed by a decision of the Strasbourg court that is incompatible with it, which decision should an inferior court follow?[137]

It concluded that the only permissible course was to follow the decision of the House of Lords but to give permission, if sought and not successfully opposed, to appeal to the House of Lords, thereby and to that extent taking the decision in *Connors* into account.[138]

---

8. Other Aids to Interpretation

8.1 Judgments of the Privy Council in Devolution Cases

Whilst human rights judgments of the Privy Council in devolution cases are not binding on the House of Lords and judgments of the House of Lords in HRA cases are not binding on the Privy Council, these are routinely taken into account by both parties. For example, in *Rezvi*[139] the House of Lords considered the compatibility of confiscation orders under drugs legislation with Article 6 and Article 1 Protocol No 1. Lord Steyn, with whom the others agreed, noted that the point had recently been

---

[133] *Ibid*, at [25]. See also *R (S) v Chief Constable South Yorkshire* [2004] UKHL 39, [2004] 1 WLR 2196 at [27] per Lord Steyn; *Al-Jedda*, above n 52.
[134] *Price v Leeds City Council* [2005] EWCA Civ 289, [2005] 1 WLR 1825.
[135] *Harrow London Borough Council v Qazi* [2003] UKHL 43, [2004] 1 AC 983.
[136] 27 May 2004.
[137] *Ibid*, at [31].
[138] *Ibid*, at [33]. See also *The Commissioner of Police for the Metropolis v Hurst* [2005] EWCA Civ 890.
[139] *R v Rezvi; R v Benjafield* [2002] UKHL 1, [2003] 1 AC 1099.

considered by the Privy Council in relation to confiscation proceedings in drugs legislation in Scotland.[140]

> The issue was considered in depth in the context of the law of Scotland and European jurisprudence. In these circumstances it is unnecessary to cover all the same ground again.[141]

His Lordship adopted the Privy Council's categorisation of the confiscation order as a penalty imposed for the offence of which he had been convicted but involving no accusation of any other offence.[142] A number of Privy Council human rights judgments in devolution cases under the Scotland Act 1998 are referred to in this book.[143]

However, it is important to note that divergences between human rights law in Scotland and England and Wales are possible. In *Watson*[144] Lord Hope warned that there may be room for the view that there is a fundamental difference of approach between the Scotland Act and the HRA in relation to the reasonable time guarantee in Article 6. Referring to a recent article,[145] he noted that the HRA does not impose a vires control upon UK Ministers—section 57(2) of the Scotland Act provides that a member of the Scottish Executive has no power to do any act so far as it is incompatible with any of the Convention rights.[146]

His Lordship's prediction came to fruition in *HM Advocate v R*,[147] where a majority of the Privy Council held that as a result of section 57(2) of the Scotland Act 1998, once it has been established that a proposed or continuing act was incompatible with a person's article 6(1) Convention right, the Lord Advocate was prohibited from doing that act by the statute. In the context of the reasonable time guarantee, this means that if it would be incompatible with the Convention right for the Lord Advocate to prosecute an individual because to do so would violate his right to a hearing within a reasonable time, to comply with the Scotland Act 1998 the proceedings must be stayed as the Lord Advocate has no power to proceed with the prosecution.[148] Lord Hope was careful to explain that he was basing his decision on section 57(2) of the Scotland Act 1998.

> [T]he accused does not have to go to article 6(1) to obtain his remedy. The remedy which Parliament has given to him is the right to a finding under section 57(2) of the Scotland Act 1998 that the Lord Advocate has no power to do the act which is incompatible with his Convention right.[149]

---

140 *McIntosh v Lord Advocate* [2003] 1 AC 1078.
141 *Ibid*, at [10].
142 See also the judgment of the Privy Council in *Mills v HM Advocate (No 2)* [2002] UKPC D2, [2004] 1 AC 441, where much reference was made to judgments of the House of Lords.
143 On human rights law in Scotland, see generally R Reed and J Murdoch, *A Guide to Human Rights Law in Scotland* (Edinburgh, Butterworths, 2001).
144 *Procurator Fiscal, Linlithgow v Watson* [2002] UKPC D1, [2004] 1 AC 379.
145 I Jamieson, 'Relationship between the Scotland Act and the Human Rights Act' [2001] *SLT (News)* 43.
146 *Watson*, above n 144, at [111].
147 [2002] UKPC D3, [2004] 1 AC 462.
148 Lords Steyn and Walker dissented on this point.
149 *Watson*, above n 144, at [66]. See also Lord Rodger at [128]–[129] and [155].

The opposite position has been reached in England and Wales in *Attorney General's Reference No 2 of 2001*.[150] A majority of the House of Lords confirmed that to hold a trial after the lapse of a reasonable time would not in itself be a breach of a Convention right and therefore it would not in itself comprise unlawful conduct under section 6 of the HRA.[151] In his dissenting judgment Lord Hope noted that a

> divergence of view between the two jurisdictions about the meaning of the reasonable time guarantee, as there is at present, is unfortunate but it may have to be accepted as inevitable. The last words as to its meaning must, of course, lie with Strasbourg. The doors of that court remain open to those who believe that, as a result of the decision in this case, they have not been provided in this jurisdiction with an effective domestic remedy.[152]

8.2 Case Law and Instruments from Other Jurisdictions

In interpreting both the HRA and the Convention rights, case law from other jurisdictions is often referred to. For example, in *Brown*[153] Lord Bingham, in discussing the right not to incriminate oneself, referred to the Constitution of the United States, the Indian Constitution, the Canadian Charter of Rights and Freedoms, the New Zealand Bill of Rights Act 1990, the Constitution of South Africa, the International Covenant on Civil and Political Rights and the Universal Declaration of Human Rights.[154] In *Pretty*[155] his Lordship referred to section 7 of the Canadian Charter of Rights and Freedoms and associated judgments, but noted that the judgments were directed to a provision with no close analogy in the ECHR.[156]

However, it still appreciated that, given section 2 of the HRA, Strasbourg jurisprudence is to be preferred.[157] The dangers of transplanting other human rights jurisprudence without question have also been appreciated. For example, in *British American Tobacco*[158] it was pointed out that US First Amendment jurisprudence should be treated with care.

> While it is instructive, in general terms, to see how another respected jurisdiction has dealt with a related but confined problem, the balance between State legislation and federal legislation in the United States is a subject of renowned complexity. Decisions on such matters can have limited effect on our consideration of the balance to be struck in considering a

---

[150] [2003] UKHL 68, [2004] 2 AC 72.
[151] Lords Hope and Rodger dissented on this point. The majority held that *HM Advocate v R* was wrongly decided.
[152] Above n 150, at [108].
[153] *Brown v Stott* [2003] 1 AC 681.
[154] See also the speech of Lord Steyn in *R v Lambert* [2001] UKHL 37, [2002] 2 AC 545, where he referred to judgments of the Canadian Supreme Court and South African Constitutional Court; *Aston Cantlow and Wilmcote with Billesley Parochial Church Council v Wallbank* [2003] UKHL 37, [2004] 1 AC 546, where reference was made to German constitutional law; and *Campbell v MGN Ltd* [2004] UKHL 22, [2004] 2 AC 457, where reference was made to privacy cases from Australia and New Zealand.
[155] Above n 56.
[156] *Ibid*, at [23]. See generally C McCrudden, 'A Common Law of Human Rights?: Transnational Judicial Conversations on Constitutional Rights' (2000) 20 *OJLS* 499.
[157] See the comments of Lord Hope in *Procurator Fiscal, Linlithgow v Watson* [2002] UKPC D1, [2004] 1 AC 379.
[158] *R (on the application of British American Tobacco UK Ltd) v The Secretary of State for Health* [2004] EWHC (Admin) 2493.

restriction of a limited Convention right and the measure of a discretion to be afforded to Parliament and ministers under our own rather different constitutional system.[159]

Finally, increasing reference is being made to other international human rights instruments and bodies. For example, in *A v Secretary of State for the Home Department*,[160] considerable reference was made to the Universal Declaration of Human Rights, the International Covenant on Civil and Political Rights, General Comments of the UN Human Rights Committee, Opinions of the Council of Europe Commissioner for Human Rights, Resolutions of the Parliamentary Assembly of the Council of Europe, Recommendations of the European Commission against Racism and Intolerance, Resolutions of the Security Council of the United Nations and the Convention on the Elimination of Racial Discrimination.[161]

8.3 Reports of the Joint Committee on Human Rights

The establishment of the Joint Committee on Human Rights was suggested in *Rights Brought Home*, where it was stated that

> [t]he new committee might conduct enquiries on a range of human rights issues relating to the Convention, and produce reports so as to assist the Government and Parliament in deciding what action to take. It might also want to range more widely, and examine issues relating to the other international obligations of the United Kingdom such as proposals to accept new rights under other human rights treaties.[162]

The Committee was established during the 2000–1 Parliamentary Session to consider matters relating to human rights in the United Kingdom, and proposals for remedial orders, draft remedial orders and remedial orders made under section 10 of and laid under Schedule 2 to the Human Rights Act 1988. All government bills are examined by the Committee for human rights compliance and its reports on such Bills are often referred to in HRA judgments.[163] It has also enquired into a number of general human rights issues and published some detailed and useful reports.[164]

---

[159] *Ibid*, at [36].

[160] Above n 73.

[161] For a similar scale of reference see also *Jones v Ministry of the Interior* [2004] EWCA Civ 1394, [2005] QB 699. See generally R. Singh, 'The use of international law in the domestic courts of the United Kingdom' (2005) 56 *NILQ* 119.

[162] Home Office, Rights Brought Home: The Human Rights Bill (Cmnd 3782) (London, TSO, 1997) at [3.7].

[163] See, eg *A v SS for the Home Department*, above n 73; *R (on the application of R) v Durham Constabulary* [2005] UKHL 21, [2005] 1 WLR 1184. On the work of the Committee generally, see: A Lester, 'Parliamentary Scrutiny of Legislation under the Human Rights Act 1998' [2002] *EHRLR* 432; D Feldman, 'Parliamentary Scrutiny of Legislation and Human Rights' [2002] *PL* 323; D Feldman, 'Can and Should Parliament Protect Human Rights?' (2004) 10 *EPL* 635; JL Hiebert, 'Parliamentary Review of Terrorism Measures' (2005) 68 *MLR* 676; and the Joint Committee's own report, *The Work of the Committee in the 2001–2005 Parliament*, Nineteenth Report (2004–05 HL 112, HC 552).

[164] See, eg *The Making of Remedial Orders*, Seventh Report (2001–02 HL 58, HC 473); *The Case for a Human Rights Commission*, Sixth Report (2002–03 HL 67, HC 489); *Work of the Northern Ireland Human Rights Commission*, Fourteenth Report (2002–03 HL 132, HC 142); *The Meaning of Public Authority Under the Human Rights Act*, Sixth Report (2003–04 HL 39, HC 382); *The International Covenant on Economic, Social and Cultural Rights*, Twenty-first Report (2003–04 HL 183, HC 1188).

The Benefit and Burden of the Human Rights Act

1. Introduction

Not every person may bring a claim under the HRA and not every person is obliged by the HRA to act compatibly with the Convention rights. The HRA contains a number of provisions concerning who may bring a claim under the Act or rely on Convention rights in legal proceedings (the benefit of the HRA) and which bodies must act compatibly with Convention rights (the burden of the HRA). These provisions have been carefully designed to mirror those employed in the international system for enforcement of the ECHR. The objective was obviously to ensure that it would be possible to bring any claim that could be brought before the European Court of Human Rights under the HRA before the domestic courts.

> The purpose of the Bill is to give greater effect in our domestic law to the convention rights. It is in keeping with this approach that persons should be able to rely on the convention rights before our domestic courts in precisely the same circumstances as they can rely upon them before the Strasbourg institutions.[1]

However, the effect is also to ensure that claims which could not be brought in Strasbourg also cannot be brought under the HRA.

---

[1] HL Deb, Vol 583, col 831, Lord Chancellor.

2. The Benefit of Convention Rights: Victims

2.1 Section 7 Human Rights Act

Section 7(1) of the HRA provides that a person who claims that a public authority has acted (or proposes to act) in a way which is made unlawful by section 6(1) may: (a) bring proceedings against the authority under the HRA in the appropriate court or tribunal; or (b) rely on the Convention right or rights concerned in any legal proceedings, but only if he is (or would be) a victim of the unlawful act.

The definition of 'victim' is given by reference to Article 34 of the ECHR. Section 7(7) provides that, for the purposes of the section, a person is a victim of an unlawful act only if he would be a victim for the purposes of Article 34 of the ECHR if proceedings were brought in the European Court of Human Rights in respect of that act. Article 34 provides that the Court

> may receive applications from any person, non-governmental organisation or group of individuals claiming to be the victim of a violation be one of the High Contracting Parties of the rights set forth in the Convention or the protocols thereto.

It has been held that, skilfully drawn though these provisions are,

> they leave a great deal of open ground. There is room for doubt and for argument. It has been left to the courts to resolve these issues when they arise.[2]

However, a few matters are plain. The victim test is clearly narrower than the test of standing to bring an application for judicial review. This is reflected in section 7(3) of the HRA, which provides that if the proceedings

> are brought on an application for judicial review, the applicant is to be taken to have a sufficient interest in relation to the unlawful act only if he is, or would be, a victim of that act.

Interest groups are able to bring claims under the HRA only it they themselves are victims of an unlawful act, although it is still possible for them to provide support to victims who bring cases and provide amicus written briefs.[3]

Furthermore, although it has been held that section 7 must be given a generous interpretation as befits its human rights purpose,[4] this does not extend to affording remedies under the HRA where the authority has not acted or proposed to act unlawfully. For example, in *Re S*[5] the House of Lords considered the Court of Appeal's proposed starring system in relation to care orders. In brief, if a starred milestone had not been achieved within a reasonable time after the date set at trial, the local

---

[2] *Aston Cantlow and Wilmcote with Billesley Parochial Church Council v Wallbank* [2003] UKHL 37, [2004] 1 AC 546 at [36] per Lord Hope.
[3] HL Deb, vol 583, col 833, Lord Chancellor. See further, M Arshi and C O'Cinneide, 'Third-party Interventions: The Public Interest Reaffirmed' [2004] *PL* 69; S. Hannett, 'Third Party Intervention: In the Public Interest?' [2003] *PL* 128.
[4] *Re S* [2002] UKHL 10, [2002] 2 WLR 720 at [48] per Lord Nicholls.
[5] *Ibid.*

authority was obliged to reactivate the process that had contributed to the creation of the care plan, and the child's guardian or the local authority had the right to apply to the court for further directions. Their Lordships concluded that the starring system would impose obligations on local authorities in circumstances where there had been no finding that the authority had acted unlawfully or was proposing to do so.[6]

Whilst it was not made clear in *Burke*[7] that the essential problem in relation to the HRA claim was that Mr Burke was not actually a victim or potential victim of any violation of Convention rights, the Court of Appeal explained the dangers of adjudicating upon claims where these were divorced from a factual context that required their determination. It stated that the

> court should not be used as a general advice centre. The danger is that the court will enunciate propositions of principle without full appreciation of the implications that these will have in practice, throwing into confusion those who feel obliged to attempt to apply those principles in practice. This danger is particularly acute where the issues raised involve ethical questions that any court should be reluctant to address, unless driven to do so by the need to resolve a practical problem that requires the court's intervention.[8]

2.2 The Victim Test and Sections 3 and 4 of the Human Rights Act

It is possible that the victim test does not apply where a claimant seeks a declaration of incompatibility under section 4 or for primary legislation to be construed compatibly with a Convention right, so far as it is possible to do so, under section 3. The issue has arisen in both the House of Lords and the Court of Appeal. In *Rusbridger*[9] the House of Lords considered proceedings brought by *The Guardian* for, inter alia, a declaration that section 3 of the Treason Act 1848, when read in the light of the HRA, did not apply to persons who evinced in print or in writing an intent to depose the monarch or deprive her of her imperial status or to establish a republican form of government unless their intent was to achieve this by acts of force, constraint or other unlawful means.

The Guardian had published articles which advocated republicanism and the editor sent a copy to the Attorney-General. No prosecutions were brought. Because of this, at first glance it would seem that there was no unlawful act. However, a majority of their Lordships held that as a matter of jurisdiction, it was possible to grant the relief claimed.

> *The Guardian* do not have to demonstrate that they are 'victims' under s.7 of the Human Rights Act 1998. That much is conceded and, in any event, obvious on a proper view of the place of s.3 in the scheme of the Human Rights Act 1998.[10]

---

[6] *Ibid*, at [49] per Lord Nicholls.
[7] *R (on the application of Burke) v The General Medical Council* [2005] EWCA Civ 1003.
[8] *Ibid*, at [21]. On the victim test generally, see: J Miles, 'Standing under the Human Rights Act 1998: Theories of Rights Enforcement and the Nature of Public Adjudication' (2000) 59 *CLJ* 133; J Marriott and D Nicol, 'The Human Rights Act, Representative Standing and the Victim Culture' [1998] *EHRLR* 730.
[9] *R (on the application of Rusbridger) v Attorney General* [2003] UKHL 38, [2004] 1 AC 357.
[10] *Ibid*, at [21] per Lord Steyn, with whom Lords Scott and Walker agreed.

Attention was drawn to the broad approach which the European Court of Human Rights adopts to the concept of victim. The example given was *Norris v Ireland*,[11] where a homosexual man complained that the criminalisation of homosexual conduct in Ireland violated his Article 8 right to respect for his private life, although he accepted that the risk of being prosecuted was remote. The Court accepted that he was a victim. 'For present purposes it is sufficient that *The Guardian* has an interest and standing. That is the threshold requirement.'[12]

However, their Lordships also made reference to the general principle that, save in exceptional circumstances, it is not appropriate for a member of the public to bring proceedings against the Crown for a declaration that certain proposed conduct is lawful and name the Attorney-General as the formal defendant to the claim. Whilst the majority concluded that the case may fall within the exceptional category,[13] it held that the matter ought not to be heard again by the Administrative Court.

> The idea that s.3 could survive scrutiny under the Human Rights Act is unreal. The fears of the editor of The Guardian were more than a trifle alarmist. In my view the courts ought not to be troubled further with this unnecessary litigation.[14]

Furthermore it was noted that sections 3 and 4 of the HRA are

> intended to promote and protect human rights in a practical way, not to be an instrument by which the courts can chivvy Parliament into spring-cleaning the statute book, perhaps to the detriment of more important legislation. Such a spring-cleaning process might have some symbolic significance but I can see no other practical purpose which this litigation would achieve.[15]

However, the judgment of the Court of Appeal in *Taylor*[16] indicates that obtaining a declaration of incompatibility in a purely hypothetical case is not possible. Here the claimant could not demonstrate breach of any substantive Convention right but sought a declaration of incompatibility.

> [E]ven if he could suggest that the 1986 Act discriminates against him, there is no realistic possibility that if, in consequence, a declaration of incompatibility was granted, any remedial action which could be taken would benefit him in any way.[17]

In addition, the court pointed out that the grant of a declaration of incompatibility was discretionary. It found it

> doubtful in the extreme that a court would exercise its discretion in favour of Mr Taylor if he could not be affected by the breach of the Convention on which he was attempting to rely.[18]

---

[11] (1989) 13 EHRR 186.
[12] *Ibid*, at [21] per Lord Steyn.
[13] *Ibid*, at [25] per Lord Steyn.
[14] *Ibid*, at [28] per Lord Steyn; at [40] per Lord Scott.
[15] *Ibid*, at [61] per Lord Walker.
[16] *Lancashire County Council v Taylor* [2005] EWCA Civ 284, [2005] HRLR 17.
[17] *Ibid*, at [41].
[18] *Ibid*, at [42].

Referring to the conclusion of the House of Lords in *Rusbridger*, the court noted that this flexible approach to the grant of declarations could not appropriately be applied in the

> circumstances that exist here where Mr Taylor has not been and could not be personally adversely affected by the repealed legislation on which he seeks to rely. To allow him to do so would be to ignore section 7 of the HRA.[19]

It therefore appears that whilst the victim test may not strictly apply to sections 3 and 4 of the HRA, it is still not possible to seek recourse to these sections in a purely hypothetical case where the outcome can have absolutely no effect on the claimant.

2.3 Categories of Victim

Usually the question of whether or not a claimant is a victim within the meaning of the HRA does not arise in litigation. However, there are some particular claimants where status as a victim is not clear cut. These are examined in the following paragraphs.

2.3.1 Core Public Authorities

Core public authorities themselves do not enjoy Convention rights and cannot be victims under the HRA.[20] For example, in *Westminster City Council*[21] it was confirmed that a local authority could not bring a claim under the HRA as it was not a victim within the meaning of section 7. However, it is clear that hybrid public authorities, those which exercise both public and private functions, can be victims under the HRA.[22]

2.3.2 Potential Victims

The concept of victim under the HRA includes potential victims. Provision for this is made in section 7(1) of the HRA, which applies to 'would be' victims if a public authority was proposing to act in a way which is made unlawful by section 6(1). This has also been confirmed in the case law. For example, in *H*[23] it was assumed that the claimant was a potential victim of the alleged unlawful act, namely the maintenance in force of the refusal to issue condoms pursuant to the defendant's (a secure hospital) Patients Relationships Policy.

---

[19] *Ibid*, at [44]. However, in *R (on the application of Trailer & Marina (Leven) Ltd) v Secretary of State for the Environment, Food & Rural Affairs* [2004] EWCA Civ 1580, [2005] 1 WLR 1267 it was held that, whilst reliance on hypothetical facts was not possible where executive action was being challenged, the power under s 4 was not so limited; see [69].
[20] *Aston Cantlow*, above n 2. However, there has been criticism of this conclusion. See H Davis, 'Public Authorities as "Victims" under the Human Rights Act' (2005) 64 *CLJ* 315.
[21] *R (on the application of Westminster City Council) v Mayor of London* [2002] EWHC (Admin) 2440 at [96].
[22] *Aston Cantlow*, above n 2.
[23] *R (on the application of H) v Ashworth Hospital Authority* [2001] EWHC (Admin) 872, [2002] FCR 206.

[T]he claimant himself could become infected (or further infected) by engaging in sexual activities with another patient infected with, for example, Hepatitis B.[24]

In *Hirst*,[25] an application for permission to appeal, Laws LJ rejected the view that the applicant would only become a victim if the Discretionary Life Panel, having first fixed him with the burden of proof, then also found against him on the merits. It was enough for the Panel merely to construe setion 28(6)(b) of the Crime (Sentences) Act 1997 as imposing a burden of proof as this would increase the chance that the Panel might not order his release.[26]

In certain circumstances, it may be necessary for a potential victim to have been active in some way in order to be considered a victim within the meaning of the HRA. For example, in *Hooper*[27] widowers complained that there had been a discriminatory denial of survivor's benefits to them. Commenting on this issue *obiter*, a majority of their Lordships held that a man in such a position could only be a victim if he had done something which identified him as having wished to make a claim.[28] Oral or written claims 'were held to' suffice as

any act will count if the appropriate official could reasonably have inferred that the applicant would have made a formal claim if there had been a form on which to make it.[29]

Whilst claims made before the HRA came into force do not count, an act which amounts to an express or implied reaffirmation of an earlier claim is sufficient.

It would convey to the official that the applicant would make a claim then and there if he was able to do so.[30]

2.3.3 Relatives of a Victim

In certain circumstances, the relatives of a victim may also be considered to be victims under the HRA. For example, in *McKerr*[31] the House of Lords accepted that a son questioning why his father was killed by agents of the state was a victim.[32]

---

[24] *Ibid*, at [75].
[25] *Hirst v Parole Board*, Court of Appeal, 25 September 2002. See also *Tangney v The Governor of HMP Elmley* [2005] EWCA Civ 1009.
[26] It is questionable whether the concept of potential victim could be extended to so-called 'satellite litigation' in the area of criminal justice. For example, in *R v Director of Public Prosecutions, ex p Kebilene* [1999] 3 WLR 972 the defence sought a ruling from the judge at the close of the case for the prosecution that the primary legislation reversed the burden of proof and was therefore in breach of Article 6(2). Lord Hobhouse pointed out that it was necessary to examine whether or not the relevant provision would in fact result in an injustice to the complainant.
[27] *R (on the application of Hooper) v Secretary of State for Work and Pensions* [2005] UKHL 29, [2005] 1 WLR 1681.
[28] *Ibid*, at [56] per Lord Hoffmann.
[29] *Ibid*, at [57] per Lord Hoffmann.
[30] *Ibid*, at [58] per Lord Hoffmann.
[31] *In re McKerr* [2004] UKHL 12, [2004] 1 WLR 807.
[32] See the comments of Lord Steyn at [43]. See also *R (on the application of Al-Skeini) v Secretary of State for Defence* [2004] EWHC (Admin) 2911, [2005] 2 WLR 1401.

2.3.4 Those Who Have Brought Proceedings Before the European Court of Human Rights

An individual may remain a victim within the meaning of the HRA even if he or she has succeeded in proceedings before the European Court of Human Rights and received compensation. In *McKerr*[33] a son brought proceedings in the European Court of Human Rights in 1993 questioning why his father was killed by agents of the state. The Court made an award of compensation on the basis that, due to the violation of the procedural obligation, the son suffered feelings of frustration, distress and anxiety.[34] In 2002 he commenced proceedings under the HRA seeking an order to compel the Secretary of State for Northern Ireland to hold an effective investigation into the circumstances of his father's death. A majority of their Lordships rejected the government's argument that he lacked standing as a victim because he had already received 'just satisfaction' from the European Court of Human Rights. Lord Steyn noted that the procedural obligation remained unfulfilled as the state had never conducted a proper investigation.

> The compensation was plainly not intended by the ECtHR to be the price which, if paid, relieved the Government of its unfulfilled procedural obligation even in circumstances where such an obligation was still capable of being fulfilled.[35]

2.3.5 Non-nationals and Those Living Outside the United Kingdom

Non-UK nationals living in the United Kingdom can be victims,[36] as can non-nationals living outside the UK.[37] In *Farrkhan*[38] it was conceded by the Secretary of State that the fact that an individual was neither a citizen of a Member State nor within the territory of a Member State did not, of itself, preclude the application of the Convention. This was also accepted by the court without an examination of whether or not the concession was correctly made.[39] Similarly in *Singh*[40] the court proceeded on the assumption that the HRA applied even though the claimant was not a UK citizen and lived in India. The claimant had been refused entry clearance to join his adoptive parents in the United Kingdom. Chadwick LJ commented that the court had not been invited to consider the question of whether the Convention or the Act should be treated as having extra-territorial reach and 'should not be taken to have reached any conclusion on that question.'[41]

It is established in European Court of Human Rights jurisprudence that the exclusion of a person from a State where members of his family are living might raise an issue under Article 8.[42] In relation to other Convention rights, the Court of Appeal

---

[33] Above n 31.
[34] *McKerr v United Kingdom* (2002) 34 EHRR 20.
[35] *Ibid*, at [43]. See also the comments of Lord Nicholls at [27].
[36] *A v Secretary of State for the Home Department* [2004] UKHL 56, [2005] 2 AC 68.
[37] *R (on the application of Farrakhan) v Secretary of State for the Home Department* [2001] EWHC (Admin) 781, [2002] 3 WLR 481.
[38] *Ibid.*
[39] *Ibid*, at [34].
[40] *Singh v Entry Clearance Officer New Delhi* [2004] EWCA Civ 1975, [2005] QB 608.
[41] *Ibid*, at [94].
[42] *Abdulaziz v United Kingdom* (1985) 7 EHRR 471 as cited in *Farrakhan*, above n 37, at [35].

accepted in *Farrakhan* that Strasbourg jurisprudence established that where the authorities of a State refuse entry to or expel an alien from its territory solely for the purpose of preventing the alien from exercising a Convention right within the territory, or by way of sanction for the exercise of a Convention right, the Convention would be directly engaged.[43] The court went on to actually modify the Strasbourg test in this case, concluding that even though only one object of the exclusion of Mr Farrakhan was to prevent him exercising the right to freedom of expression, Article 10 was engaged.[44]

Outside of the immigration context, in *Al-Skeini*[45] the Divisional Court found it was no obstacle to a claim under the HRA that the son, who had died in a British military prison in Iraq, and his father, who had brought the claim, had no connection with the United Kingdom

> other than as residents of a province in a foreign country where the United Kingdom is an occupying power . . .and other than, in the case of the son, as a prisoner in a British military prison.[46]

The court continued:

> It is hard to say that the Act was designed to bring rights home in their case, for the United Kingdom is in no way their home: in their case, it is not their rights which are brought home, but the United Kingdom's responsibilities. Even so, we would be reluctant to distinguish their case from that of a British resident or national where Convention rights are interfered with in a narrow extra-territorial context interpreted by Strasbourg jurisprudence (itself founded in concepts of international law) to be within a state party's essentially territorial jurisdiction under Art.1.[47]

2.3.6 Representative Bodies

Trade unions or other representative bodies which have an interest on behalf of their members in general or are otherwise interested in the point at issue in the case but are not themselves directly affected are not 'victims' within the meaning of section 7 of the HRA.[48] For example, in *Director General of Fair Trading*[49] the Proprietary Association of Great Britain (PAGB) sought compensation for the costs they wasted when a trial was vacated as a result of an Article 6 independence and impartiality breach on the part of one member of a court and proceedings were begun again before a reconstituted court. The PAGB was an association of manufacturers, importers and suppliers of branded 'pharmacy only' and 'general sales list' medicines, vitamins and mineral supplements sold over the counter (without the need for a prescription) in the

---

[43] *Ibid*, at [55] in reliance upon *Agee v United Kingdom* (1976) 7 D&R 164; *Swami Omkarananda and the Divine Light Zentrum v Switzerland* (1997) 25 D&R 105; *Piermont v France* (1995) 20 EHRR 301; *Adams and Benn v United Kingdom* (1997) 88A D&R 137.
[44] *Ibid*, at [62].
[45] Above n 32.
[46] *Ibid*, at [302].
[47] *Ibid*, at [302].
[48] *Director General of Fair Trading v Proprietary Association of Great Britain* [2001] EWCA Civ 1217, [2002] 1 WLR 269 in reliance upon *Hodgson v UK* (1987) 10 EHRR 503; *Ahmed v UK* (1995) 20 EHRR CD 72; *Bowman v UK* (1996) 21 EHRR CD 79.
[49] *Ibid*.

United Kingdom. It was alleged that the majority of PAGB members established and maintained a system of resale price maintenance in relation to the sale of such branded goods in the United Kingdom.

The Court of Appeal noted that it was possible under the Rules of the Restrictive Practices Court for the court on application to order that some or all of the suppliers, retailers or trade associations who were before the Court be represented by such a representative respondent as the Court may direct.[50] It concluded that

> the rules provided a route by which the individual parties could have been formally repre-
> sented by PAGB, but they chose not to follow that route. In those circumstances PAGB
> cannot be properly regarded as a victim for the purposes of making a claim under s.7(1) of
> the 1998 Act.[51]

However, a different conclusion was reached in relation to the Proprietary Articles Trade Association as it adduced evidence which showed that the proceedings in the Restrictive Practices Court were indeed determinative of its own civil rights and obligations because the outcome sought by the Director General rendered illegal an activity which constituted one of its constitutional objects and its primary practical objective.[52]

---

3. The Burden of Convention Rights: Public Authorities

Similar to the benefit of Convention rights, the burden of Convention rights closely reflects the position in international law. Section 6(1) provides that it is unlawful for a 'public authority' to act in a way that is incompatible with a Convention right. No comprehensive definition of public authority is provided in the Act, although section 6(3) provides that 'public authority' includes: (a) a court or tribunal, and (b) any person certain of whose functions are functions of a public nature. It also provides that 'public authority' does not include either House of Parliament or a person exercising functions in connection with proceedings in Parliament although Parliament does not include the House of Lords in its judicial capacity.[53] Furthermore, in relation to those exercising public functions, section 6(5) makes clear that a person is not a public authority by virtue only of subsection (3)(b) if the nature of the act is private.[54]

Whilst it is by no means clear from section 6, the HRA has actually created three classes of body which are obliged to act compatibly with Convention rights in different ways. The first are what as known as 'core public authorities'. All of the functions exercised by such bodies are public functions and they are bound by section 6 to act

---

[50] *Ibid*, at [12].
[51] *Ibid*, at [19].
[52] *Ibid*, at [9].
[53] Section 6(4).
[54] See generally D. Oliver, 'The Frontiers of the State: Public Authorities and Functions under the Human Rights Act', [2000] *PL* 476.

compatibly with Convention rights in respect of all of their acts. The second are what have been labelled 'hybrid public authorities'. These exercise both public and private functions, but are only bound by section 6 to act compatibly with Convention rights in respect of their public functions. It has been held that the definition of public authority and what is a public function should be given a generous interpretation,[55] and the HRA has been employed most frequently against these two types of bodies, in particular the first. Finally, the third type of body is private bodies which are indirectly bound to act compatibly with Convention rights essentially via the obligation of the courts, as public authorities, under section 6. All three types of body are discussed in the following paragraphs in more detail.

4. Core Public Authorities

4.1 Definition

It is clear that a core public authority is required to act compatibly with Convention rights in everything it does regardless of whether it is an act of a private or public nature.[56] However, the expression 'public authority' is not defined in the HRA in any detail, nor is it an expression in English law with a specific recognised meaning.[57] In determining the meaning of the expression, it has been held that the broad purpose to be achieved by the HRA is key.

> The purpose is that those bodies for whose acts the state is answerable before the European Court of Human Rights shall in future be subject to a domestic law obligation not to act incompatibly with Convention rights. If they act in breach of this legal obligation victims may henceforth obtain redress from the courts of this country.[58]

In other words, a purposive construction of section 6 indicates that

> the essential characteristic of a public authority is that it carries out a function of government which would engage the responsibility of the United Kingdom before the Strasbourg organs.[59]

It has also been held that the reference to non-governmental organisations in Article 34 of the Convention provides an important guide as to the nature of those persons who, for the purposes of section 6(1) of the Act and the remedial scheme which flows from it, are to be taken to be public authorities.

---

[55] *Poplar Housing and Regeneration Community Association Ltd v Donoghue* [2001] EWCA Civ 595, [2002] QB 48.
[56] *Aston Cantlow*, above n 2 at [7] per Lord Nicholls and [85] per Lord Hobhouse.
[57] *Ibid* per Lord Nicholls at [6].
[58] *Ibid*. See also the comments of Lord Hope at [44].
[59] *Ibid*, at [160] per Lord Rodger.

Non-governmental organisations have the right of individual application to the European Court of Human Rights as victims if their Convention rights have been violated. If the scheme to give effect to Art.13 is to be followed through, they must be entitled to obtain a remedy for a violation of their Convention rights under s.7 in respect of acts made unlawful by s.6.[60]

To this end it has been held that a distinction should be drawn between those persona who, in Convention terms, are governmental organisations on the one hand and those who are non-governmental organisations on the other.

A person who would be regarded as a non-governmental organisation within the meaning of Art.34 ought not to be regarded as a 'core' public authority for the purposes of s.6. That would deprive it of the rights enjoyed by the victims of acts which are incompatible with Convention rights that are made unlawful by s.6(1).[61]

As the House of Lords pointed out in *Aston Cantlow*,[62] the Convention institutions have developed their own jurisprudence as to the meaning which is to be given to the expression 'non-governmental organisation' in Article 34.[63] Indeed, in the opinion of their Lordships, this jurisprudence was far more relevant than the decided cases on the amenability of bodies to judicial review. Such cases

have been made for purposes which have nothing to do with the liability of the state in international law. They cannot be regarded as determinative of a body's membership of the class of 'core' public authorities . . .[n]or can they be regarded as determinative of whether a body falls within the 'hybrid' class.[64]

Similar observations were made by Lord Hope in relation to the concept of 'emanation of the state' in Community law.[65] However, in some instances it is possible that the judicial review and Community law case law may provide some assistance in determining what does and does not constitute a function of a public nature as discussed in the paragraphs below. Indeed, in *Beer*,[66] which was decided after *Aston Cantlow*, the Court of Appeal held that the test for a functional public authority and for amenability to judicial review were, for practical purposes, the same.[67]

Beyond this, some criteria have been specified to assist in identification, such as: the possession of special powers; democratic accountability; public funding in whole

---

[60] *Ibid* at [46] per Lord Hope.
[61] *Ibid*, at [47] per Lord Hope.
[62] *Ibid*.
[63] See, eg *Rothenthurm Commune v Switzerland, Commission*, 14 December 1988; *Ayuntamiento de Mula v Spain*, Court, 1 February 2001; *Holy Monasteries v Greece* (1995) 20 EHRR 1; *Hautanemi v Sweden* (1996) 22 EHRR CD 156. All cited by Lord Hope in *Aston Cantlow*, above n 2.
[64] *Aston Cantlow*, above n 2 at [52] per Lord Hope, [87] per Lord Hobhouse. Lord Scott agreed with Lord Hope. Lords Nicholls and Rodger did not mention judicial review cases, indicating that they regarded these as irrelevant to resolving the question. See also *R (on the application of Heather) v Leonard Cheshire Foundation* [2002] EWCA Civ 366, [2002] ACD 271 at [36]. But cf. *Poplar Housing*, above n 55 at [65] and *Hampshire County Council v Beer* [2003] EWCA Civ 1056, [2004] 1 WLR 233 at [29].
[65] *Aston Cantlow*, above n 2 at [53]–[55] per Lord Hope, citing *Johnston v Chief Constable of the Royal Ulster Constabulary* [1986] ECR 1651. See also the comments of Lord Hobhouse at [86].
[66] *Hampshire County Council v Beer* [2003] EWCA Civ 1056, [2004] 1 WLR 233.
[67] *Ibid*, at [14].

or in part; an obligation to act only in the public interest; a statutory constitution[68]; association with the process of either central or local government; statutory powers exercisable against the general public or a class or group; and surrender or delegation of state powers to it.[69]

4.2 Courts and Tribunals

Section 6(3)(a) clearly includes courts and tribunals within the definition of public authority, reflecting the fact that if, in complying with and applying the municipal law, the judiciary

> do not provide an outcome which is compliant with the rights of victims under the Convention, for example, by failing to recognise a right or grant an adequate remedy, the State is in breach of its Convention obligations and should change its municipal law.[70]

In criminal trials, it has been confirmed that it is appropriate to treat the court made up of both judge and jury as the public authority for the purposes of Article 6, and it is not possible to treat the jury as a separate entity.[71]

Requiring courts and tribunals to act compatibly with Convention rights has had a number of perhaps unforeseen consequences, and has given courts and tribunals a role where previously they had none. For example, in *Porter*[72] the House of Lords concluded that in exercising its discretion and determining whether an injunction for breach of planning control should be granted under section 187B of the Town and Country Planning Act 1990, the court was bound by section 6 of the HRA to act compatibly with Convention rights.

> [W]hen asked to grant injunctive relief under s.187B the court must consider whether, on the facts of the case, such relief is proportionate in the Convention sense, and grant relief only if it judges it to be so.[73]

Their Lordships appreciated that the new landscape of the HRA required a different perspective.[74]

> [I]t is not for the court to act merely as a rubber stamp to endorse the decision of the local planning authority to stop the user by a particular defendant in breach of planning control. Moreover the court is as well placed as the local planning authority to decide whether the considerations relating to the human factor outweigh purely planning considerations; the weight to be attached to the personal circumstances of a defendant in deciding whether a

---

[68] The previous five criteria were cited by Lord Nicholls in *Aston Cantlow*, above n 2 at [7].
[69] the previous two criteria were cited by Lord Hope in *Aston Cantlow* ibid at [59] and [61]. See further P Cane, 'Church, State and Human Rights: Are Parish Councils Public Authorities?' (2004) 120 *LQR* 41.
[70] *Wilson v Secretary of State for Trade and Industry* [2003] UKHL 40, [2003] 3 WLR 568 at [131] per Lord Hobhouse.
[71] *R v Mushtaq* [2005] UKHL 25, [2005] 1 WLR 1513.
[72] *South Buckinghamshire District Council v Porter* [2003] UKHL 26, [2003] 2 AC 558.
[73] *Ibid*, at [37] per Lord Bingham.
[74] *Ibid*, at [58] per Lord Steyn.

coercive order should be made against him is a task which is constantly performed by the courts.[75]

4.3 Parliament

As outlined above, section 6(3) also makes clear that either House of Parliament or a person exercising functions in connection with proceedings in Parliament is not a public authority within the meaning of the HRA. It is therefore not possible to bring proceedings under the HRA for a failure to legislate or for a failure to introduce legislation. This is also made clear in section 6(6), which provides that whilst an 'act' includes a failure to act, it does not include a failure to introduce in or lay before Parliament a proposal for legislation, or a failure to make any primary legislation or remedial order. The question actually arose in *Re S*,[76] where the principle contention was that the incompatibility with Articles 8 and 6 lay in the absence from the Children Act 1989 of an adequate remedy if a local authority failed to discharge its parental responsibilities properly and, as a direct result, the rights of the child or his parents were violated.

The House of Lords concluded that the failure

> to provide a young child with an effective remedy in this situation does not mean that the Children Act is incompatible with Article 8: failure to provide a remedy for a breach of Article 8 is not itself a breach of Article 8.[77]

With respect to Article 6, their Lordships continued this line of reasoning, noting that the Convention violation consisted of a failure to provide access to a court.

> The absence of such provision means that English law may be incompatible with Article 6(1). The United Kingdom may be in breach of its treaty obligations regarding this article. But the absence of such provision from a particular statute does not, in itself, mean that the statute is incompatible with Article 6(1). Rather, this signifies at most the existence of a lacuna in the statute.[78]

4.4 Which Core Public Authority is Responsible?

One issue which has arisen in a number of cases where more than one public authority is involved is the question of which particular core public authority should take responsibility for the violation of Convention rights. For example, *Noorkoiv*[79] concerned an individual serving an automatic life sentence. Although his tariff period expired on 21 April 2001, it was not until 22 June 2001 that the Parole Board held a hearing. This was due to the Secretary of State's policy, and a shortage of judicially

---

[75] *Ibid*, at [86] per Lord Clyde.
[76] *Re S* [2002] UKHL 10, [2002] 2 WLR 720.
[77] *Ibid*, at [64] per Lord Nicholls.
[78] *Ibid*, at [85] per Lord Nicholls. It was noted that the matter may be different regarding the inability of parents and children to challenge in court care decisions made by a local authority while a care order was in force. See [87].
[79] *R (on the application of Noorkoiv) v Secretary of State for the Home Department* [2002] EWCA Civ 770, [2002] 1 WLR 3284.

qualified chairmen and psychiatrists. The Secretary of State argued that the Parole Board lacked resources in terms of judges and psychiatrists because they had not been made available to it by other government departments. The Court of Appeal pointed out that if this matter was proceeding in Strasbourg, this argument would not avail the Secretary of State.[80] It concluded that, being a complaint about detention, it should be directed at the organ of the state actually responsible for the detention.

> Mr Noorkoiv was detained by the Secretary of State, who was implementing arrangements made by the state, including the slowness of consideration by the Board forced on it by the limited resources made available to it by the state. The Secretary of State cannot therefore excuse any failing under art.5(4) by pointing to policies adopted by other departments.[81]

Similarly in *K*,[82] also an Article 5(4) case, the Administrative Court held that it was for the state to ensure speedy hearings of detained patients' applications.

> It is therefore irrelevant to question whether there has been an infringement of art 5.4 which government department or other public authority was at fault.[83]

However, the court did make clear the respective responsibilities of central government and the tribunals themselves, concluding that the responsibility for the delays was that of central government rather than of the regional chairmen or their staff.[84]

It may also be the case that one of the decision makers cannot be challenged on Convention grounds. For example, in *Shetty*[85] proceedings were brought against the responsible medical officer (RMO) at a clinic and the Secretary of State in order to prevent the claimant being returned to prison. The Administrative Court found that the RMO's function and responsibility was to notify the Secretary of State if his patient no longer required treatment for a mental disorder. The court concluded that his duty was to exercise a clinical judgment and come to a clinical opinion.

> And assuming he has done it fairly and rationally he cannot be challenged on the grounds that the recommendation, if implemented by the Secretary of State, will or may involve a violation of his patient's Convention rights.[86]

4.5 Application: Core Public Authorities

It is actually very rare for questions about whether or not a body is a core public authority to arise in HRA litigation as usually the answer is obvious, and it has been assumed that the meaning of core public authority includes bodies such as

---

[80] *Ibid*, at [28].
[81] *Ibid*, at [30]. See also *R (K) v Camden and Islington Health Authority* [2001] EWCA Civ 240, [2002] QB 198. In *RA v Secretary of State for the Home Department,* Administrative Court, 30 July 2002, a similar case, the court held that damages were not therefore payable by the Secretary of State.
[82] *R (on the application of K) v Mental Health Review Tribunal* [2002] EWHC (Admin) 639.
[83] *Ibid*, at [112].
[84] *Ibid*, at [113].
[85] *R (on the application of R) v Shetty (Responsible Medical Officer)* [2003] EWHC (Admin) 3022.
[86] *Ibid*, at [40]. Cf. *R (on the application of B) v Responsible Medical Officer, Broadmoor Hospital* [2005] EWHC (Admin) 1936.

government ministers, coroners, NHS trusts, police, prisons, local authorities, Legal Services Commission, General Medical Council, Police Complaints Authority, Parole Board, Commissioners of Customs and Excise, Securities and Futures Authority, Nursing and Midwifery Council, General Optical Council, General Dental Council, Child Support Agency and Broadcasting Standards Commission.

Nevertheless, there have been a few cases where classification as a core public authority is not so obvious. In *Aston Cantlow*[87] the House of Lords concluded unanimously that parochial church councils were not core public authorities. Although the Church of England was found to still have special links with central government, it was found to be essentially a religious organisation.[88]

> It has regulatory functions within its own sphere, but it cannot be said to be part of government. The state has not surrendered or delegated any of its functions or powers to the Church.[89]

Furthermore, the constitution and functions of parochial church councils lent no support to the view that they should be characterised as governmental.

> The essential role of a parochial church council is to provide a formal means, prescribed by the Church of England, whereby ex officio and elected members of the local church promote the mission of the Church and discharge financial responsibilities in respect of their own parish church, including responsibilities regarding the maintenance of the fabric of the building. This smacks of a church body engaged in self-governance and promotion of its affairs. This is far removed from the type of body whose acts engage the responsibility of the state under the European Convention.[90]

It has also been held that housing associations, as a class, are not core public authorities[91] and that arbitrators are not public authorities as their jurisdiction springs from a private agreement.[92] However, if arbitration is compulsory, the nature of the arbitrator is more likely to be that of a public authority.[93] Adjudicators under the Housing Grants Construction and Regeneration Act 1996 have been held not to be public authorities[94] despite the fact that any construction agreement that does not contain adequate provision for adjudication is subjected to compulsory contract terms imposed by statute. The court reached its conclusion as it did not regard an adjudicator as a person before whom legal proceedings may be brought, and noted that his or her decision was not enforceable.[95] Furthermore, the adjudicator did not look like a tribunal to the court as he might be appointed once only and never appointed again.[96] 'Proceedings before an adjudicator are not legal proceedings. They are a process designed to avoid the need for legal proceedings.'[97]

---

[87] Above n 2.
[88] *Ibid*, at [13] per Lord Nicholls.
[89] *Ibid*, at [61] per Lord Hope.
[90] *Ibid*, at [14] per Lord Nicholls. See also the comments of Lord Rodger at [152]–[157] and [166].
[91] *Poplar Housing*, above n 55.
[92] *Austin Hall Building Ltd v Buckland Securities Ltd* [2001] BLR 272 at [27].
[93] *Ibid*, at [28].
[94] *Ibid*, at [40].
[95] *Ibid*, at [35].
[96] *Ibid*, at [39].
[97] *Ibid*, at [40].

5. Hybrid Public Authorities

5.1 Definition

Section 6(3)(b) makes clear that the obligations imposed by the HRA also extend to any person certain of whose functions are 'functions of a public nature'.[98] However, the extension only applies in respect of *public* functions, not if the nature of the act is private. This reflects the fact that there are many bodies which exercise both public and private functions.

> In a modern developed state governmental functions extend far beyond maintenance of law and order and defence of the realm. Further, the manner in which wide ranging governmental functions are discharged varies considerably. In the interests of efficiency and economy, and for other reasons, functions of a governmental nature are frequently discharged by non-governmental bodies.[99]

During the parliamentary debates, the Lord Chancellor gave the following examples:

> Railtrack would fall into that category because it exercises public functions in its role as a safety regulator, but it is acting privately in its role as a property developer. A private security company would be exercising public functions in relation to the management or a contracted-out prison but would be acting privately when, for example, guarding commercial premises. Doctors in general practice would be public authorities in relation to their National Health Service functions, but not in relation to their private patients.[100]

In relation to such bodies, there must be a twofold assessment, first of the body's functions and secondly of the particular act in question.[101] As in relation to core public authorities, no further definition is given in the HRA as to the meaning of 'function of a public nature'. Again, it has been suggested that essentially the contrast being drawn is between functions of a governmental nature and functions, or acts, which are not of that nature.[102] And, furthermore, that giving a generously wide scope to the expression 'public function'

> will further the statutory aim of promoting the observance of human rights values without depriving the bodies in question of the ability themselves to rely on Convention rights when necessary.[103]

---

[98] See, generally: Joint Committee on Human Rights, Seventh Report 'The Meaning of Public Authority under the Human Rights Act' (2003–04 HL 39, HC 382); M Sunkin, 'Pushing Forward the Frontiers of Human Rights Protection: The Meaning of Public Authority under the Human Rights Act', [2004] *PL* 643; D Oliver, 'Functions of a Public Nature under the Human Rights Act' [2004] *PL* 329.
[99] *Aston Cantlow*, above n 2 at [9] per Lord Nicholls.
[100] HL Deb, vol 583, col 811 (24 November, 1997).
[101] *Aston Cantlow*, above n 2 at [85] per Lord Hobhouse.
[102] *Ibid*, at [10] per Lord Nicholls.
[103] *Ibid*, at [11] per Lord Nicholls.

Unlike a core public authority, hybrid public authorities are not absolutely disabled from having Convention rights.[104]

No clear demarcation line can be drawn between public and private bodies and functions.[105]

What can make an act, which would otherwise be private, public is a feature or combination of features which impose a public character or stamp on the act.[106]

Criteria suggested to assist in deciding whether or not a function is public have included the extent to which, in carrying out the relevant function, the body is publicly funded[107]; is exercising statutory powers[108]; is taking the place of central government or local authorities; or is providing a public service.[109] Other factors include statutory authority for what is done and the extent of control over the function exercised by another body which is a public authority. The more closely the acts that could be of a private nature are enmeshed in the activities of a public body, the more likely they are to be public. However, it has also been held that the fact that the acts are supervised by a public regulatory body does not necessarily indicate that they are of a public nature.[110]

After considering the most important factors, it is desirable to step back and look at the situation as a whole.[111] Taking one factor as determinative appears problematic. For example, in *Donoghue*[112] the Court of Appeal held that the fact that a body performs an activity which otherwise a public body would be under a duty to perform cannot mean that such performance is necessarily a public function.

A public body in order to perform its public duties can use the services of a private body. Section 6 should not be applied so that if a private body provides such services, the nature of the functions are inevitably public. If this were to be the position, then when a small hotel provides bed and breakfast accommodation as a temporary measure, at the request of a housing authority that is under a duty to provide that accommodation, the small hotel would be performing public functions and required to comply with the Human Rights Act 1998.[113]

In the view of the court, this was not what the HRA intended.

The purpose of section 6(3)(b) is to deal with hybrid bodies which have both public and private functions. It is not to make a body, which does not have responsibilities to the public, a public body merely because it performs acts on behalf of a public body which would constitute public functions were such acts to be performed by the public body itself. An act can

---

[104] *Ibid*, at [11] per Lord Nicholls.
[105] *Poplar Housing*, above n 55 at [66].
[106] *Ibid*, at [65].
[107] *Heather*, above n 64, at [35].
[108] *Ibid*.
[109] The latter four were suggested by Lord Nicholls in *Aston Cantlow*, above n 2 at [12].
[110] The latter two were suggested in *Poplar Housing*, above n 55 at [65].
[111] *Ibid*, at [66].
[112] *Ibid*.
[113] *Ibid*, at [58].

remain of a private nature even though it is performed because another body is under a public duty to ensure that that act is performed.[114]

Similarly in *Heather*[115] the Court of Appeal held that whilst the degree of public funding of the activities of an otherwise private body was certainly relevant as to the nature of the functions performed, by itself it was not determinative of whether the functions were public or private.[116]

It has also been held that the fact that a body is a charity or is conducted not for profit means that it is likely to be motivated in performing its activities by what it perceives to be in the public interest. However, this does not point to the body being a public authority. In addition, even if such a body performs functions that would be considered to be of a public nature if performed by a public body, nevertheless such acts may remain of a private nature.[117]

5.2 Ensuring HRA Protection when Contracting Out

The provision of accommodation in a care home pursuant to section 21 of the National Assistance Act 1948 by a local authority is a public function. Making arrangements for the accommodation to be provided by a private sector provider is also a public function of the local authority. However, if a body which is a charity provides accommodation to those to whom the authority owes a duty under section 21 in accordance with an arrangement under section 26 of the National Assistance Act 1948, it does not follow that the charity is performing a public function.[118] Nevertheless, the courts have been careful to ensure that this does not thereby leave potential victims of Convention rights breaches in a vacuum.

> If this were a situation where a local authority could divest itself of its art 8 obligations by contracting out to a voluntary sector provider its obligations under s.21 of the 1948 Act, then there would be a responsibility on the court to approach the interpretation of s.6(3)(b) in a way which ensures, so far as this is possible, that the rights under art 8 of persons in the position of the appellants are protected.[119]

So far as protection is concerned, the Court of Appeal pointed out in *Heather*[120] that the local authority contracting out its care obligations under section 21 of the National Assistance Act 1948 remained under an obligation under section 21 and retained an obligation under Article 8 to those being cared for. In addition, residents of the care home had contractual rights against the private sector provider.[121] It also

---

[114] *Ibid*, at [59].
[115] Above n 64.
[116] at [35]. See further P.Craig, 'Contracting Out, the Human Rights Act, and the Scope of Judicial Review' (2002) 118 *LQR* 551; M.McDermont, 'The Elusive Nature of the 'Public Function': Poplar Housing and Regeneration Community Association v. Donoghue' (2003) 66 *MLR* 113; J. Morgan, 'The Alchemists' Search for the Philosophers' Stone: The Status of Registered Social Landlords under the Human Rights Act' (2003) 66 *MLR* 700.
[117] *Poplar Housing*, above n 55 at [65].
[118] *Heather*, above n 64 at [15].
[119] *Ibid*, at [33].
[120] *Ibid*.
[121] *Ibid*, at [33].

pointed out that if the arrangements which the local authorities had made with the private sector provider had been made after the HRA came into force, then it would arguably be possible for a resident to require the local authority to enter into a contract with its provider which fully protected the residents' Article 8 rights, and if this was done it would provide additional protection.

> Local authorities who rely on s.26 to make new arrangements should bear this in mind in the contract which they make with the providers. Then not only could the local authority rely on the contract, but possibly the resident could do so as a person for whose benefit the contract was made.[122]

In *Haggerty*,[123] obviously following this advice, the claimant residents of a private nursing home sought to argue that the St Helen's Council's decision not to enter into a revised and more onerous arrangement with the company which operated the home led to the company deciding to close the home. The Administrative Court agreed that there were two ways which the Council's actions in relation to the contract with the company could be impugned on ECHR grounds. First, pursuant to section 3 of the HRA, to read and give effect to the Council's obligations under section 26 of the National Assistance Act 1948 so that the claimant's Convention rights were taken into account by the Council in performing its section 26 obligations.[124] Secondly, the Council was potentially liable under section 6 of the HRA, which made it unlawful for it to act incompatibly with a Convention right.[125] The court assumed, without deciding, that commercial dealings by a local authority with a provider of residential care were public in nature.[126] However, the court found no breach of Articles 2, 3 or 8 on the part of the Council and the application was dismissed.[127]

5.3 Application: Hybrid Public Authorities

The question of the meaning of 'function of a public nature' has arisen more often in HRA litigation than the meaning of core public authority. However, there are still very few cases. Those that have been decided are examined in the following paragraphs.

5.3.1 Enforcement of Chancel Repairs

Having determined in *Aston Cantlow*[128] that parochial church councils were not core public authorities, the House of Lords turned to the question of whether such bodies were hybrid public authorities within the meaning of the HRA. The impugned act was the enforcement by the council of Mr and Mrs Wallbank's liability, as lay rectors, for the repair of the chancel of the church of St John the Baptist at Aston Cantlow. A

---

[122] *Ibid*, at [34].
[123] *R (on the application of Haggerty) v St Helens Council* [2003] EWHC (Admin) 803, [2003] ACD 304.
[124] *Ibid*, at [23].
[125] *Ibid*, at [24].
[126] *Ibid*, at [25].
[127] See further P Craig, 'Contracting Out, the Human Rights Act and the Scope of Judicial Review' (2002) 118 *LQR* 551.
[128] Above n 2.

majority of their Lordships concluded that the nature of the impugned act was private.

> If a parochial church council enters into a contract with a builder for the repair of the chancel arch, that could hardly be described as a public act. Likewise when a parochial church council enforces, in accordance with the provisions of the Chancel Repairs Act 1932, a burdensome incident attached to the ownership of certain pieces of land: there is nothing particularly 'public' about this. This is no more a public act than is the enforcement of a restrictive covenant of which church land has the benefit.[129]

5.3.2 Seeking Possession of a Property

In *Donoghue*[130] the Court of Appeal considered whether Poplar Housing and Regeneration Community Association Ltd was exercising a public function in seeking possession on the expiry of an assured shorthold tenancy. The Association had been created as a housing association by the London Borough of Tower Hamlets in order to transfer to it a substantial proportion of the Council's housing stock. The court took into account a number of factors, as outlined in the paragraphs above. However, it was particularly influenced by the closeness of the relationship between Tower Hamlets and Poplar. Poplar was created by Tower Hamlets to take a transfer of local authority housing stock; five of its board members were also members of Tower Hamlets; Poplar was subject to the guidance of Tower Hamlets as to the manner in which it acted towards the tenant. Furthermore, the tenant at the time of the transfer was a sitting tenant of Poplar and it was intended that she would be treated no better and no worse than if she remained a tenant of Tower Hamlets.

> While she remained a tenant, Poplar therefore stood in relation to her in very much the position previously occupied by Tower Hamlets.[131]

The court concluded that while activities of housing associations need not involve the performance of public functions, in this case, in providing accommodation for the defendant and then seeking possession, the role of Poplar was so closely assimilated to that of Tower Hamlets that it was performing public and not private functions. Poplar was therefore a functional public authority although the court was careful to point out that this did not mean that all of its functions were public.[132]

5.3.3 Care Home Closures and Management

In *Heather*[133] the Court of Appeal considered whether the Leonard Cheshire Foundation was exercising a public function in providing accommodation at one its care

---

[129] *Ibid*, at [16] per Lord Nicholls. See also the comments of Lord Hobhouse at [90] and Lord Rodger at [171]. Lord Rodger did note that, when, in the course of his pastoral duties, a minister marries a couple in the parish church, he may be carrying out a governmental function in a broad sense and so may be regarded as a public authority for the purposes of the HRA. See [170].
[130] *Poplar Housing*, above n 55.
[131] *Ibid*, at [65].
[132] *Ibid*, at [66]. It stated that the act of providing accommodation for rent was not, without more, a public function, at [65].
[133] Above n 64.

homes. The Foundation was the United Kingdom's leading voluntary sector provider of care and support services for the disabled. The majority of the residents at the home had been placed there by the social services departments of their local authority or by their health authority. In making the placements and providing the funding which the placements required, the authorities were exercising statutory powers. The court held that if a body like the Foundation provided accommodation to those to whom the authority owed a duty under section 21 of the National Assistance Act 1948, in accordance with an arrangement under section 26, it did not necessarily follow that the charity was performing a public function. Concluding that it was clearly not performing any public function, it took into account the fact that the degree of public funding was not determinative; that it was not standing in the shoes of the local authorities; and that, whilst there was statutory authority for the actions of the local authorities, the Foundation was not provided with any powers and was not exercising statutory powers in performing functions for the appellants.[134]

A similar issue arose in the *Partnerships in Care* case,[135] which concerned the decision of the managers of a private psychiatric hospital to change the focus of one of its wards. The claimant alleged that as a result she was denied the care and treatment appropriate to her condition. The Administrative Court held that the starting point was the statutory framework. In the present case the claimant came to be cared for by the private hospital as a result of her health authority making a contractual arrangement with the hospital pursuant to the National Health Service Act 1977. The hospital was registered as a mental nursing home under the provisions of Part II of the Registered Homes Act 1984 and it was subject to the Nursing Homes and Mental Nursing Homes Regulations 1984. Admission to the hospital, and the detention and treatment there of patients suffering from mental disorders, was governed by the Mental Health Act 1983.

The court found that the relationship between the managers of the hospital and the health authorities who had arranged for the hospital to provide care and treatment to patients with mental disorders was different from the relationship between the housing association and local authority in *Donoghue*.

> Accordingly, it may be that the statutory obligations of the Health Authorities ended when they arranged for the Defendant to provide care and treatment to patients with mental disorders, and that those statutory obligations, i.e. those of the Health Authorities, were not assumed by the defendant.[136]

However, in the view of the court, the question remained whether there were any other obligations imposed on the managers of the hospital which made the decision complained of an act of a public nature.[137] It concluded that the decision to change the focus of the ward was an act of a public nature.

---

[134] *Ibid*, at [35].
[135] *R (on the application of A) v Partnerships in Care Limited* [2002] 1 WLR 2610.
[136] *Ibid*, at [23].
[137] *Ibid*.

But whether facilities can and should be provided, and adequate staff made available, to enable the treatment which the psychiatrists say should take place is another matter entirely. That is the subject of specific statutory underpinning directed at the hospital.[138]

And further,

the need for the hospital's patients to receive care and treatment which may result in their living in the community again is a matter of public concern and interest.[139]

5.3.4 Denying Application to Participate in a Farmers' Market

In *Beer*[140] the Court of Appeal considered whether Hampshire Farmers' Markets Ltd was exercising a public function when it rejected an application by Mr Beer to be allowed to participate in the 2002 Farmers' Markets Programme. The Court of Appeal took into account a number of factors, including the fact that the power was being exercised in order to control the right of access to a public market[141]; the markets were held on town centre sites all owned by other local authorities[142]; the company owed its existence to Hampshire County Council and was set up using the Council's statutory powers[143]; the company stepped into the shoes of the Council in relation to these markets[144]; and from the date of incorporation of the company until the time when the company started operating the markets, the Council assisted the company in a number of respects.[145] The court concluded that the combined effect of these three features was sufficient to justify the conclusion that the decision was an exercise of a public function.

HFML was not simply another private company that was established to run markets for profit. It was established by a local authority to take over on a non-profit basis the running of the markets that the authority had previously been running in the exercise of its statutory powers in what it considered to be the public interest.[146]

5.3.5 Regulation of Membership

RSPCA v Attorney General,[147] a very earlier HRA case, concerned the RSPCA, a well-known charity devoted to the prevention of cruelty to animals. The case arose when the governing body of the charity, its council, adopted a policy which would enable it to exclude from membership those who had joined or were seeking to join the Society with the ulterior purpose of changing its policy against hunting with dogs. The Society brought charity proceedings seeking guidance. Some who had

---

138 *Ibid*, at [24].
139 *Ibid*, at [25].
140 *Hampshire County Council v Beer* [2003] EWCA Civ 1056, [2004] 1 WLR 233.
141 *Ibid*, at [30].
142 *Ibid*, at [32].
143 *Ibid*, at [36].
144 *Ibid*, at [37].
145 *Ibid*, at [38].
146 *Ibid*, at [40]. See further B Hough, 'Public Law Regulation of Markets and Fairs' [2005] *PL* 586.
147 [2001] 3 All ER 530.

joined or were seeking to join for this ulterior purpose brought arguments under the HRA, in particular Article 11, freedom of association.

Lightman J in the Chancery Court concluded that the RSPCA was not a public authority and had no public functions within the meaning of section 6 of the HRA. Furthermore, it was noted that, in any event, the acts in question were private acts relating to its regulation of membership. Therefore, pursuant to section 6(5), even if it was possible to argue that the RSPCA was a functional public authority, these acts were private and therefore section 6(5) meant that the Society was not subject to the HRA in this instance.[148] Whilst Lightman J's conclusions are undoubtedly correct in this case, it should not be concluded that a charity can never be a public authority within the meaning of section 6 of the HRA. Many perform what can only be described as public functions, for example, the National Trust, and should be required to act compatibly with Convention rights when doing so.

5.3.6 Approving Minority Buy-outs

Finally, in West[149] the Court of Appeal concluded that decisions of the Business Conduct Committee of Lloyd's approving minority buy-outs in four syndicates in which the claimant was a member were not the exercise of a public function.

> The objectives of Lloyd's are wholly commercial. The nature of Lloyd's is not governmental, even in the broad sense of that expression. If any question arises as to the performance of any obligation on the part of the state to protect investors, it is the FSA which is the governmental organisation which will be answerable to the Strasbourg court, and not Lloyd's.[150]

It also referred to the observation of Lord Woolf in Donoghue that the fact that the acts were supervised by a public regulatory body did not necessarily indicate that they were of a public nature.[151]

---

6. Private Bodies

The HRA does not directly oblige private bodies to act compatibly with Convention rights. Section 6 of the HRA does not

> give the applicant any cause of action under the HRA against a respondent which is not a public authority. In that sense the HRA does not have the same full horizontal effect as between private individuals as it has between individuals and public authorities.[152]

---

[148] Ibid, at [37].
[149] R (on the application of West) v Lloyd's of London [2004] EWCA Civ 506, [2004] 3 All ER 251.
[150] Ibid, at [38].
[151] Ibid.
[152] X v Y [2004] EWCA Civ 662 at [58].

However, an obligation to act compatibly with Convention rights can arise indirectly via the courts. There are two main routes by which the rights of private parties may be affected: firstly, through the interpretation of primary legislation pursuant to section 3 of the HRA; and secondly, via the development of the common law.

It is also possible for the rights of private bodies to be affected by the activities of regulatory bodies which, whilst not considered to be courts or tribunals, are nevertheless public authorities within the meaning of the HRA. For example, in *Ford*[153] the claimant sought permission to quash a decision of the Press Complaints Commission. With no argument the Commission accepted that it was a public authority within the meaning of the HRA. In making its determinations it was therefore obliged to act compatibly with Articles 8 and 10.

> [T]he sensitive task of the Commission is to consider not only the right to privacy but also the freedom of expression of the newspapers and then seek to balance them before reaching its conclusion.[154]

6.1 Interpreting Primary Legislation in Accordance with Section 3 of the HRA

It is clear that the section 3 obligation to interpret primary legislation, so far as it is possible to do so, in a way which is compatible with Convention rights, applies in cases between private parties, thereby indirectly imposing an obligation to comply with Convention rights on private parties.

> [T]he interpretative duty imposed by s 3 applies to the same degree in legislation applying between private parties as it does in legislation which applies between public authorities and individuals. There is nothing in the HRA which, either expressly or by necessary implication, indicates a contrary intention. If the position were otherwise, the same statutory provision would require different interpretations depending on whether the defendant was a public authority or a private individual.[155]

Whilst the significance of extending the duty to act compatibly with Convention rights to private parties was not commented upon directly, the judgment of the House of Lords in *Ghaidan v Godin-Mendoza*[156] is a prime example of this development. Pursuant to paragraph 2 of Schedule 1 to the Rent Act 1977, on the death of a protected tenant of a dwelling-house, his or her surviving spouse, if then living in the house, became a statutory tenant by succession. Marriage was not essential for this

---

[153] *R (on the application of Ford) v The Press Complaints Commission* [2001] EWHC (Admin) 683, [2002] EMLR 5.
[154] *Ibid*, at [23]. On horizontal effect see generally: R Buxton, 'The Human Rights Act and Private Law' (2000) 116 *LQR* 48; HWR Wade, 'Horizons of Horizontality' (2000) 116 *LQR* 217; A Lester and D Pannick, 'The Impact of the Human Rights Act on Private Law: The Knight's Move' (2000) 116 *LQR* 380; N Bamforth, 'The True "Horizontal Effect" of the Human Rights Act 1998' (2001) 117 *LQR* 34; D Beyleveld and SD Pattinson, 'Horizontal Applicability and Horizontal Effect' (2002) 118 *LQR* 623; J Morgan, 'Questioning the "True Effect" of the Human Rights Act' (2002) 22 *LS* 259; I Hare, 'Verticality Challenged: Private Parties, Privacy and the Human Rights Act' [2001] *EHRLR* 526; M Hunt, 'The 'Horizontal Effect' of the Human Rights Act' [1998] *PL* 423.
[155] *X v Y* [2004] EWCA Civ 662.
[156] [2004] UKHL 30, [2004] 2 AC 557.

purpose,[157] but this provision did not include persons in a same-sex relationship.[158] In the present case, in 1983 Wallwyn-James was granted an oral residential tenancy of a flat where he lived until his death in 2001 in a stable and monogamous homosexual relationship with Godin-Mendoza. The landlord brought proceedings claiming possession of the flat and the question was whether, subject to the HRA, Godin-Mendoza could succeed to the tenancy of the flat as the surviving spouse of Wallwyn-James within the meaning of paragraph 2 of Schedule 1 to the Rent Act 1977. A majority of their Lordships concluded that paragraph 2 of Schedule 1, construed without reference to section 3 of the HRA, violated Godin-Mendoza's Convention rights under Article 14 taken together with Article 8. Utilising section 3, the majority concluded that paragraph 2 should be read and given effect to as though the survivor of such a homosexual couple were the surviving spouse of the original tenant.

By contrast, in $X v Y$[159] the fact that section 3 of the HRA was being utilised in a case between private parties was of considerable comment. The Court of Appeal held that in the case of private employers under section 3, an employment tribunal, so far as it is possible to do so, must read and give effect to section 98 and the other relevant provisions in Part X of the Employment Rights Act 1996 in a way which is compatible with Articles 14 and 8.[160]

> In many cases if would be difficult to draw, let alone justify, a distinction between public authority and private employers. In the case of such a basic employment right there would normally be no sensible grounds for treating public and private employees differently in respect of unfair dismissal, especially in these times of widespread contracting out by public authorities to private contractors.[161]

In the present case the Court of Appeal noted that it was not immediately obvious how section 98 of the Employment Rights Act could be incompatible with or applied so as to violate Articles 8 and 14 and so attract the application of section 3.

> Considerations of fairness, the reasonable response of a reasonable employer, equity and substantial merits ought, when taken together, to be sufficiently flexible, without even minimum interpretative modification under s3, to enable the employment tribunal to give effect to applicable Convention rights.[162]

It did, however, appreciate that there may be cases where the HRA point could make a difference to the reasoning of the tribunal and even to the final outcome of the claim for unfair dismissal.[163] Here there was no need to apply section 3 as the facts did not engage either Articles 8 or 14.[164]

---

[157] Rent Act 1977 Sch 1, para 2(2).
[158] *Fitzpatrick v Sterling Housing Association Ltd* [2001] 1 AC 27.
[159] *X v Y* [2004] EWCA Civ 662.
[160] *Ibid*, at [57].
[161] *Ibid*.
[162] *Ibid*, at [59].
[163] *Ibid*.
[164] *Ibid*.

6.2 The Development of the Common Law

Whilst the HRA does not create any new cause of action between private parties,

> if there is a relevant cause of action applicable, the court as a public authority must act compatibly with both parties' Convention rights.[165]

This is particularly the case with respect to the development of the common law, although it has been observed that the common law will only relatively rarely not be Convention-compliant.

> One would normally expect the established common law to be consistent with the spirit of the Convention, and, given that the common law is always developing, one would expect it to develop along the same general lines as the Convention in any event.[166]

There have been a number of examples of the courts using Convention rights to develop the common law in cases between private parties. Most occur in the area of respect for private life in particular with respect to the tort of breach of confidence. It has been held that the

> values embodied in Arts 8 and 10 are as much applicable in disputes between individuals or between an individual and a non-governmental body such as a newspaper as they are in disputes between individuals and a public authority.[167]

The impact of the respective Convention rights is clear.

> Instead of the cause of action being based upon the duty of good faith applicable to confidential personal information and trade secrets alike, it focuses upon the protection of human autonomy and dignity—the right to control the dissemination of information about one's private life and the right to the esteem and respect of other people.[168]

In *Campbell*[169] a majority of the House of Lords concluded that, in relation to the fact that the claimant was receiving treatment at Narcotics Anonymous, the details of the treatment and the visual portrayal (photograph) of her leaving a specific meeting, the modified tort of breach of confidence had been made out and she was entitled to damages.[170]

The impact of the HRA has also been felt on the inherent jurisdiction of the High Court to restrain publicity. In *Re S*[171] the House of Lords considered the application for an injunction restraining the publication by newspapers of the identity of a defendant in a murder trial which had been intended to protect the privacy of her son who

---

[165] *Campbell v MGN Ltd* [2004] UKHL 22, [2004] 2 AC 457 at [132] per Baroness Hale.
[166] *Humberclyde Finance Group Limited v Hicks,* Chancery Division, 14 November 2001, at [44].
[167] *Campbell v MGN Ltd* [2004] UKHL 22, [2004] 2 AC 457 at [17] per Lord Nicholls.
[168] *Ibid,* at [51] per Lord Hoffmann.
[169] *Ibid.*
[170] See also *Douglas v Hello! Ltd* [2001] QB 967; *Theakston v MGN Limited* [2002] EWHC (QB) 137; *B&C v A* [2002] EWCA Civ 337, [2002] 3 WLR 542; *Archer v Williams* [2003] EWHC (QB) 1670, [2003] EMLR 38. See further, A Young, 'Remedial and Substantive Horizontality: the Common Law and Douglas v Hello! Ltd' [2002] *PL* 232.
[171] *Re S (A Child) (Identification: Restrictions on Publication)* [2004] UKHL 47, [2005] 1 AC 593.

was not involved in the criminal proceedings. Their Lordships observed that the foundation of the jurisdiction to restrain publicity in such a case was now derived from Convention rights.[172] Balancing Articles 8 and 10, it concluded that the injunction should not be granted.[173]

---

[172] *Ibid*, at [23] per Lord Steyn.
[173] See also *Arscott v The Coal Authority* [2004] EWCA Civ 892, [2005] Env LR 6 concerning the impact of the HRA on the tort of nuisance. There is obviously much further scope for the common law to develop in the light of the HRA. See generally R English and P Havers (eds), *An Introduction to Human Rights and the Common Law* (Oxford, Hart Publishing, 2000).

3

The 'Acts' to which the Human Rights Act Applies

1. Introduction

It is clear from sections 6 and 7 that the HRA applies to the acts of public authorities[1] incompatible with Convention rights as well as their proposed acts[2] and failures to act.[3] However, even if it is possible to identify an act, proposed act or failure to act of a public authority which is incompatible with Convention rights, it may not be possible to bring a claim under the HRA. First, there is a limitation period. Section 7(1)(5) provides that proceedings must be brought within one year from the date on which the act complained of took place.[4] Secondly, section 6(2)(a) provides a defence for a public authority if, as the result of one or more provisions of primary legislation, it could not have acted differently. This section and section 6(2)(b) are considered in more detail in Chapter 5, which concerns primary legislation.

In addition to these constraints, others have developed from the case law, including the finding that the HRA generally does not apply to acts which took place prior to 2 October 2000 (retrospective effect); issues relating to acts which occur outside of the United Kingdom (extra-territorial effect); considerations specific to failures to act; and claims relating to acts which do not appear directly to violate Convention rights (satellite litigation). These constraints on the 'acts' of public authorities which may be the subject of proceedings under the HRA are the subject of this chapter.

---

[1] Section 6(1).
[2] Section 7(1).
[3] Section 6(6).
[4] Or such longer period as the court or tribunal considers equitable having regard to all the circumstances. However, this is subject to any rule imposing a stricter time limit in relation to the procedure in question. Therefore, if proceedings are brought by way of an application for judicial review, the time limit would be three months.

2. Retrospective Effect

The HRA was passed on 9 November 1998 but did not come fully into force until 2 October 2000. Only sections 18, 20, 21(5) and 22 came into force on the passing of the Act. The sole reference in the HRA to any possible retrospective effect it may have is contained in section 22(4), which provides that

> section 7(1)(b) applies to proceedings brought by or at the instigation of a public authority whenever the act in question took place; but otherwise that subsection does not apply to an act taking place before the coming into force of that section.

Section 7(1)(b) allows a person who has claimed that a public authority has acted incompatibly with Convention rights to rely on the Convention rights in any legal proceedings.

With little guidance in the HRA itself, it was for the courts to determine whether or not the Act could apply to acts incompatible with Convention rights which took place before 2 October 2000. Early on, this was an important issue in HRA litigation, particularly in criminal cases where an act allegedly incompatible with Convention rights had occurred at trial prior to the HRA coming into force. However, as the years pass, the issue is waning in importance. It has now been firmly established that, apart from the exception created by section 22(4) and limited exceptions in relation to sections 3 and 4, the HRA does not apply to the acts of courts, tribunals or public authorities which took place prior to 2 October 2000.[5] Nevertheless, the process by which this conclusion was reached is worthy of closer examination.

2.1 Criminal Proceedings

The House of Lords first fully confronted the issue of the retrospective effect of the HRA in the case of *Lambert*.[6] Lambert had been convicted of possession of a controlled drug with intent to supply contrary to the Misuse of Drugs Act 1971 in April 1999. The judge had directed the jury that in order to establish possession of a controlled drug, the prosecution merely had to prove that he had the bag in his possession and that the bag in fact contained a controlled drug. Thereafter, under section 28 of the Act, the burden was on the defendant to prove, on the balance of probabilities, that he did not know that the bag contained a controlled drug. This was a legal rather than an evidential burden of proof. Lambert appealed relying on Article 6(2) and the Court of Appeal heard his appeal as if the HRA was in force. On appeal to the House of Lords, one certified question was whether a defendant whose trial took place before the coming into force of the HRA could rely, in the course of

---

[5] *R v Lambert* [2001] UKHL 37, [2002] 2 AC 545.
[6] *Ibid.* The issue actually first arose before their Lordships in *R v Director of Public Prosecutions, ex p Kebilene* [1999] 3 WLR 972. The HRA was not in force at the time of the trial or when the appeal went to the House of Lords. However, only Lord Steyn commented *obiter* on the question of retrospective effect, noting that the trial and appeal should be treated as part of the same process and, even if at the time of the trial the Act was not in force, the applicants on appeal would be entitled to rely on the HRA. Lords Slynn and Cooke agreed with this view.

an appeal, on an alleged breach of his Convention rights by the trial court or an investigating or prosecuting authority.

Lords Slynn, Hope, Clyde and Hutton approached the question as one concerning the effect of section 22(4) of the HRA. By contrast, Lord Steyn based his dissenting speech on the effect of section 6 of the HRA, stating that the effect of section 22(4) was 'obscure'.[7] To come within the exception provided by section 22(4) the victim must show that the proceedings where he wishes to rely on the Convention right are 'proceedings brought by or at the instigation of a public authority.' Lords Slynn, Clyde and Hutton were clear in their conclusions that 'proceedings brought by or at the instigation of a public authority' did not include an appeal from the decision of a court by an unsuccessful defendant.[8] Therefore, Lambert was not able to rely on Convention rights in respect of a conviction before the HRA came into force.

By contrast, Lord Hope concluded that proceedings brought by or at the instigation of a public authority included appeals:

> The appeal is treated by the Act as if it were part of the same legal proceedings as those brought by or at the instance of the public authority, irrespective of the person at whose instance the appeal is brought.[9]

However, Lord Hope introduced a further stumbling block. In order for section 22(4) to apply, not only must the public authority have brought the proceedings, it must also have committed the act incompatible with Convention rights. Lord Hope therefore concluded that if the appellant's complaint had been that the prosecuting authority had breached the Convention, he would have been entitled to rely on the Convention right in his appeal. But the complaint here concerned not an act of the prosecuting authority but an act of the court, therefore the appellant was not so entitled.

Discerning the intention of Parliament in including section 22(4) in the HRA is somewhat difficult, given that no comment was made on the section during the parliamentary debates on the Bill and no mention was made of it in *Rights Brought Home*. In *Lambert*, Lord Hope put forward the suggestion that section 22(4) was included to prevent a public authority seeking to rely on acts of its own which were lawful under the domestic law at the time when they were done but were incompatible with the Convention right. His Lordship saw it as a deliberate choice by Parliament in order to provide a person whose Convention rights had been violated with an effective remedy. Lord Clyde perhaps came far closer to solving the mystery by pointing out the positions in New Zealand and Canada. It has been made very clear in both jurisdictions that it is not possible to appeal against a conviction occurring before the coming into force of the Bill of Rights or Charter on Bill of Rights[10] or Charter[11] grounds. Furthermore, it has also been established in Canada that no

---

[7] *Lambert*, above n 5, at [28].

[8] Their Lordships were bolstered in reaching this conclusion by the distinction made in s 7(6) between 'proceedings brought by or at the instigation of a public authority' and 'an appeal against the decision of a court or tribunal'.

[9] *Lambert*, above n 5, at [104]. See further the speech of Lord Steyn in *Kebilene*, above n 6, with whom Lord Slynn and Lord Cooke agreed.

[10] New Zealand Bill of Rights Act 1990. *Minto and Cuthbert v Police* (1990–92) NZBORR 208.

[11] Canadian Charter of Rights and Freedoms 1982. *R v Stevens* [1988] 1 SCR 1153.

remedy under the Charter can be sought at trial in relation to an action of an executive or administrative kind, such as search, seizure, arrest or detention, which was
taken before the date the Charter came into force.[12]

It is possible therefore that, taking into account the experience in other jurisdictions, in particular Canada, section 22(4) was inserted in order to clarify the position
in this jurisdiction at the start and avoid a plethora of litigation over the issue of retrospective effect. Section 22(4) addresses two issues. First, as the majority of the
House of Lords concluded in *Lambert*, it is not possible to use the HRA to challenge
on appeal a conviction or adverse judgment obtained before 2 October 2000. As the
majority pointed out, if it had been intended that section 22(4) did extend to an
appeal, this would have been made clear in section 2(4), given that the distinction is
made between proceedings brought by a public authority and an appeal in section
7(6). Secondly, in contrast to the position in Canada, under the HRA it *is* possible at
trial to rely on a violation of a Convention right whenever it took place but only if
the proceedings are brought by or at the instigation of a public authority. As the
prime beneficiaries of section 22(4), the drafters would have had in mind criminal
defendants facing trial after 2 October 2000 where it is sought to lead against them
evidence obtained in violation of the HRA but prior to 2 October 2000.

If these assumptions concerning the intentions surrounding section 22(4) are correct, the majority of the House of Lords in *Lambert* reached the correct decision. But
even though the decision may have been technically correct, there still remains the
question of whether it furthered the purpose for which the HRA was passed by
affording an effective remedy for a violation of a Convention right. The experiences
of New Zealand and Canada are a little different to that of the United Kingdom.
The HRA gives further effect to certain Convention rights contained in the European
Convention on Human Rights—an international instrument which has imposed obligations in international law on the United Kingdom since 1953. Furthermore, it has
been open to individuals in the United Kingdom to take their complaints concerning
breach of the Convention to the European Court of Human Rights since 1966.
Despite the House of Lords' conclusion that Mr Lambert could not have recourse to
the HRA in his appeal, it remained open to Mr Lambert to take his case to the European Court of Human Rights. All of those in a similar position to Mr Lambert have
this avenue for redress, and many who have been denied a remedy under the HRA
due to problems of retrospective effect have already taken it.[13]

Concerns about giving the HRA retrospective effect are somewhat misplaced when
it is considered that public authorities, including courts, in the United Kingdom have
been bound in international law since 1953 to ensure that Convention rights are not
breached. Similarly, concerns about 'great confusion and uncertainty'[14] or increasing
the workload of the Court of Appeal and Criminal Cases Review Commission[15] are
also misplaced when the HRA is perceived not as a change in the law but as an instrument which gives 'further effect' to the Convention rights which have been operative

---

[12] *R v James* [1988] 1 SCR 669. See further, Hogg, *Constitutional Law of Canada* (Toronto, Carswell, 1998)
at 663.
[13] See, eg *Kansal v United Kingdom*, 10 November 2004; *Massey v United Kingdom*, 16 November 2004;
Kolanis v United Kingdom, 21 June 2005; *PM v United Kingdom*, 19 July 2005.
[14] Per Lord Slynn, *Lambert*, above n 5, at [10].
[15] *R v Kansal* [2001] EWCA Crim 1260, [2001] 3 WLR 751.

in our legal system since 1953. In short, if international human rights law were afforded appropriate respect in our legal system prior to the HRA coming into force, none of these concerns should arise. From the perspective of a purposive construction, far preferable is the dissenting judgment of Lord Steyn, who considered the HRA in the broader framework of an Act which was undoubtedly intended 'to bring home' the adjudication of fundamental rights.[16] Finding the meaning of section 22(4) obscure, Lord Steyn based his decision on section 6 of the HRA, concluding simply that it is unlawful for an appellate court to uphold a conviction obtained in breach of a Convention right.[17]

The difficulties with the judgment of the majority in *Lambert* were highlighted when the House of Lords returned to the question almost five months later in *R v Kansal*.[18] Here the majority of their Lordships, including Lord Hope, held that it was wrongly decided but should nevertheless be followed and could not be distinguished by reason of the fact that *Lambert* concerned the act of the trial judge whilst *Kansal* concerned the act of the prosecuting authority. Lord Lloyd concluded that the language of section 7(6) was not sufficiently clear to exclude by implication appeals in proceedings brought by or at the instigation of a public authority from the retrospective operation of section 22(4).[19] Similarly Lord Steyn held that the word 'proceedings' in section 22(4) covers both trials and appeals.[20] He also noted that the rationale of section 22(4) was recognition of the United Kingdom's international obligations under the ECHR. Finally, Lord Hope concluded that a defendant whose trial took place before the date of the coming into force of section 7(1)(b) was entitled to rely in an appeal after that date on an alleged breach of his Convention rights at the trial by the prosecutor.[21] He based his conclusion on a number of factors, including the judgment in *Kebilene*[22]; Article 13 and 46 of the Convention, 'These obligations have been binding on the United Kingdom in international law since ratification in 1951'[23]; and the underlying policy that the state should no longer be able to take advantage in proceedings brought by or at the instigation of a public authority of its breach of its obligation not to act incompatibly with the Convention rights.[24]

But despite the doubts, *Lambert* has been followed, and in subsequent litigation its effects have been felt. For example, in *R v Allen*[25] the House of Lords held that as the trial and conviction took place before 2 October 2000, it was not possible to consider the argument under Article 6.[26] Nevertheless, as often occurs in such instances, given that the point was one of general importance, opinions were expressed on it. Similarly in *R v Benjafield*,[27] when determining the compatibility of confiscation orders

---

[16] *Lambert*, above n 5, at [29].
[17] *Lambert*, above n 5, at [28].
[18] *R v Kansal* [2001] UKHL 62, [2001] 3 WLR 1562.
[19] *Ibid*, at [15].
[20] *Ibid*, at [26].
[21] *Ibid*, at [75].
[22] *Ibid*, at [52].
[23] *Ibid*, at [55].
[24] *Ibid*, at [74]. See further D Beyleveld, R Kirkham and D Townend, 'Which Presumption? A Critique of the House of Lords' Reasoning on Retrospectivity and the Human Rights Act' (2002) 22 *LS* 185.
[25] *R v Allen* [2001] UKHL 45, [2001] 4 All ER 768.
[26] *Ibid*, at [23].
[27] *R v Benjafield* [2002] UKHL 2, [2003] 1 AC 1099.

made under the Criminal Justice Act 1988 and Drug Trafficking Act 1994, the House of Lords accepted that the HRA was not applicable as the trial had been held prior to 2 October 2000. Nevertheless, bearing in mind the importance of the points raised, consideration was given to the impact of the Convention.[28]

2.2 Civil Proceedings

It was suggested by Lord Hope in *Porter v Magill*[29] that the conclusion of the majority in *Lambert* did not apply to civil proceedings and he approached the respondent's Article 6 submissions on the assumption that they were entitled to rely on their Convention rights in the appeal irrespective of the fact that all the acts in question took place before 2 October 2000.[30] However, in *JA Pye (Oxford) Ltd*,[31] also a civil case, it was conceded that the HRA did not affect the appeal as the original decision was made before 2 October 2000. And in *Bellinger*,[32] another civil case, Lord Hope held that section 3 of the HRA was not retrospective and could not be applied to a marriage celebrated in 1981.[33]

Any remaining doubt that there was the prospect of retrospective effect in civil cases was put to rest by the House of Lords in *Macdonald*,[34] which concerned discriminatory treatment well before the HRA came into force. Lord Nicholls held in relation to section 22(4) that

> [s]ubsequent steps in the proceedings, including an appeal, are all part of the proceedings. In the ordinary course they are not themselves separate proceedings for the purpose of s.22(4). To treat them as separate proceedings would lead to irrational and capricious results. It would mean that the law falling to be applied to a single set of proceedings would vary depending on the adventitious circumstance of which party was the appellant.[35]

2.3 The Application of Sections 3 and 4 of the Human Rights Act

In both criminal and civil proceedings, as discussed in the paragraphs above, it has been established that the HRA has no application to the acts of courts, tribunals or public authorities which took place prior to 2 October 2000 unless section 22(4) applies. However, the argument has also been made that the rules as to retrospective effect do not apply where sections 3 or 4 of the HRA are being applied. In *Offen*,[36] a

---

[28] at [5] per Lord Steyn. In *R v Lyons* [2002] UKHL 44, [2003] 1 AC 976 it was held that it made no difference that the European Court of Human Rights had found that the use made at the trial before 2 October 2000 rendered the trial unfair and in breach of Article 6. The Crown was entitled to rely after 2 October 2000 on the evidence in order to support the safety of the conviction and the court was entitled to hold the conviction safe in reliance on such evidence.

[29] *Porter v Magill* [2001] UKHL 67, [2002] 2 WLR 37.

[30] Lords Bingham, Steyn, Hobhouse and Scott agreed with Lord Hope on issues of fairness but did not comment on the issue of retrospective effect.

[31] *JA Pye (Oxford) Ltd v Graham* [2002] UKHL 30, [2002] 3 WLR 221.

[32] *Bellinger v Bellinger* [2003] UKHL 21, [2003] 2 AC 467.

[33] at [65].

[34] *Macdonald v Advocate General for Scotland* [2003] UKHL 34, [2004] 1 All ER 339.

[35] *Ibid*, at [23]. See also *Wilson v Secretary of State for Trade and Industry* [2003] UKHL 40, [2003] 3 WLR 568.

[36] *R v Offen* [2001] 1 WLR 253.

very early HRA case, the question of retrospective effect did not even arise and the Court of Appeal concluded that section 3 of the HRA should be utilised to construe section 2 of the Crime (Sentences) Act 1997 in relation to sentences imposed well before 2 October 2000.

> s 2 will not contravene convention rights if courts apply the section so that it does not result in offenders being sentenced to life imprisonment when they do not constitute a significant risk to the public.[37]

However, a couple of years later in *Wilson*[38] the House of Lords held that, in general, the principle of interpretation in section 3 does not apply to causes of action accruing before the section came into force.

> The principle does not apply because to apply it in such cases, and thereby change the interpretation and effect of existing legislation, might well produce an unfair result for one party or the other. The Human Rights Act was not intended to have this effect.[39]

It is important to note that their Lordships held that section 3 does not apply 'in general'—meaning that in certain circumstances section 3 can apply to acts which took place prior to 2 October 2000. It was held by Lord Nicholls that the application of section 3 to pre-Act events depended upon the application of the principle identified by Staughton LJ in *Tunnicliffe*,[40] which is as follows:

> [T]he true principle is that Parliament is presumed not to have intended to alter the law applicable to past events and transactions in a manner which is unfair to those concerned in them, unless a contrary intention appears. It is not simply a question of classifying an enactment as retrospective or not retrospective. Rather it may well be a matter of degree—the greater the unfairness, the more it is to be expected that Parliament will make it clear if that is intended.

An example Lord Nicholls gave of where section 3 might apply was a post-Act criminal trial in respect of pre-Act happenings. 'The prosecution does not have an accrued or vested right in any relevant sense.'[41] Similarly Lord Hope held that accrued rights and the legal effects of past acts should not be altered by subsequent legislation.

> [T]here is an important distinction to be made between legislation which affects transactions that have created rights and obligations which the parties seek to enforce against each other and legislation which affects transactions that have resulted in the bringing of proceedings in the public interest by a public authority.'[42]

In the present case it was concluded that Parliament could not have intended that application of section 3 should have the effect of altering the parties' existing rights and obligations under the Consumer Credit Act.

---

[37] *Ibid*, at [97].
[38] Above n 35.
[39] *Ibid*, at [20] per Lord Nicholls.
[40] *Secretary of State for Social Security v Tunnicliffe* [1991] 2 All ER 712 at 724.
[41] *Ibid*, at [21] per Lord Nicholls
[42] *Ibid*, at [98]. See further D Mead, 'Rights, Relationships and Retrospectivity: the Impact of Convention Rights on Pre-existing Private Relationships Following *Wilson* and *Ghaidan*' [2005] *PL* 459.

The case may be regarded as a typical example of the situation where legislation in question affects transactions that have created rights and obligations which the parties to it seek to enforce against each other.[43]

Furthermore, for the same reasons, no declaration of incompatibility could be made.

[I]t is only when a court is called upon to interpret legislation in accordance with s.3(1) that the court may proceed, where appropriate, to make a declaration of incompatibility. The court can make a declaration of incompatibility only where s.3 is available as an interpretative tool. That is not this case.[44]

It was also made clear that it was not possible to get around this conclusion by regarding the court as a public authority obliged to act compatibly with Convention rights.

The court's decision in these proceedings gives effect to the mandatory provisions of the Consumer Credit Act. An order giving effect to these provisions of primary legislation is excluded from the scope of s.6(1) by s.6(2)(a). Thus, reference to s.6(1) takes the matter no further forward.[45]

Applying the observations of their Lordships in *Wilson*,[46] in *Milton Gate Investments Ltd*[47] the Chancery Division held that section 3 could be applied to sections 141 and 142 of the Law of Property Act 1925, even though the headleases and underleases had been entered into before 2 October 2000. This was because, in the view of the court, the earliest that any vested rights could be said to have arisen under clause 5(6) of the lease was the date of the service of the Notice. It was argued that the underleases were determined on 24 June 2002 as a result of the service of the Notice. The response was that clause 5(6) meant that unless the headlease came to an end as a result of the notice, the underleases continued.

Unless and until clause 5(6) was operated, the rights and obligations of any of the parties as a result of the exercise were merely contingent, and not vested . . . If one approaches the question by reference to fairness, it does not appear to me to be unfair that the 1998 Act should be capable of being invoked to produce a result which the parties clearly intended at

---

[43] *Tunnicliffe*, above n 40, at [101] per Lord Hope.
[44] *Ibid*, at [23] per Lord Nicholls.
[45] *Ibid*, at [25] per Lord Nicholls. See also the comments of Lord Hope at [88]–[102]; Lord Hobhouse at [126]–[135]; Lord Scott at [152]–[162]; Lord Rodger at [186]–[220]. In *Lloyds UDT Finance Ltd v Chartered Finance Trust Holdings plc* [2002] EWCA Civ 806, [2002] STC 956 the court concluded that s 3 of the HRA did not apply to the construction of s 35(2) of the Capital Allowances Act 1990 since the events took place in 1999; in *Laws v Society of Lloyd's* [2003] EWCA Civ 1887 the court concluded that s 3 had no application to s 14(3) of the Lloyd's Act, which would allow for a claim in damages for negligent misrepresentation, especially in litigation between the parties which had commenced before the HRA came into force; in *Holland (executor of Holland, deceased) v Inland Revenue Commissioners* [2003] STC (SCD) 43 it was held that s 3 did not apply to s 18 of the Inheritance Tax Act 1984 where the death occurred before 2 October 2000.
[46] Above n 35.
[47] *PW & Co v Milton Gate Investments Ltd* [2003] EWHC (Ch) 1994.

the time when they entered into their contracts, and was intended by the person who exercised the unilateral right which gives rise to the relevant issue.[48]

More controversially, in *Hurst*[49] the Court of Appeal, relying on the observations in *Wilson*,[50] held that section 3 could be applied to section 11(5)(b)(ii) of the Coroners Act 1988 even though the death triggering the procedural duty to investigate had occurred prior to 2 October 2000.[51] It held that to require the coroner to apply section 11 compatibly with Article 2, so that he also had to establish not only by what means but also in what circumstances the deceased met his death,[52] would not interfere with vested rights or interests, or operate unfairly.

> [T]he language and tests set out in *Wilson* are grounded in the law of private rights, and apply only in a limited way to the obligations of public bodies.[53]

It also noted that the obligations were contained in the ECHR, and that there were no good reasons for holding that 'in an appropriate case a question that now arises as to the application of those rights to the interpretation of English legislation should not be answered by the application of the principles of article 2, even though the article 2 obligation rested upon the public authorities before 2 October 2000.'[54]

2.4 Section 22(4) of the Human Rights Act

As discussed in the paragraphs above, section 22(4) is the only section in the HRA in which reference is made to acts which took place before the coming into force of the HRA. It provides that section 7(1)(b) applies to proceedings brought by or at the instigation of a public authority whenever the act in question took place.

> [I]t was appreciated that victims of a violation by the state of their Convention rights were already entitled to obtain a remedy in the European Court of Human Rights under Art.41 of the Convention. In that context it made sense for the provisions of s.6(1) to be made available for use defensively where proceedings are brought against the victim by or at the instigation of a public authority, whenever the violation took place.[55]

---

[48] *Ibid*, at [114]–[115].
[49] *The Commissioner of Police for the Metropolis v Hurst* [2005] EWCA Civ 890.
[50] Above n 35.
[51] It had been held by the House of Lords in *In re McKerr* [2004] UKHL 12, [2004] 1 WLR 807 that the duty to investigate unexplained deaths imposed by Article 2 only applied to deaths occurring after 2 October 2000.
[52] *R (Middleton) v West Somerset Coroner* [2004] UKHL 10, [2004] 2 AC 182.
[53] *Hurst*, above n 49, at [52]. *McKerr*, above n 51, was distinguished as it did not address a case in terms of s 3; the obligation being enforced here was an obligation in international law; and there was no sign of any view that the investigation of deaths occurring before 2 October 2000 was necessarily to be avoided: see [55]–[61].
[54] *Hurst*, above n 49, at [53]. In response to the argument that s 3 could only be used to interpret compatibly with Convention rights given further effect by the HRA, the court held that s 3 imposed on the courts an obligation to give effect to the United Kingdom's international obligations and not merely its domestic obligations as created by the HRA.
[55] *Wilson*, above n 35 at [90] per Lord Hope.

However, recourse to the section is rare and a number of limits have been placed on its use. It was established in *Lambert*[56] that the section did not apply to allow a claimant to raise on appeal a breach of a Convention right occurring at his trial prior to the date of the HRA coming into force. It has also been held that judicial review proceedings are not proceedings brought 'by or at the instigation of a public authority' within the meaning of the section.

> When the provisions of s 7(3) are considered, they make it quite plain that, where a claim is brought in judicial review proceedings, it is the applicant for judicial review who is considered to be bringing the claim under s 7(1)(a).[57]

In *Preiss*[58] the section was used to allow an appeal against the Professional Conduct Committee (PCC) of the General Dental Council to take place. On 28 September 2000, before the HRA came into force, the PCC suspended the appellant's registration as a dentist for 12 months in consequence of a finding by them that he had been guilty of serious professional misconduct. In response to the argument that the HRA had no application here, the Privy Council distinguished *Lambert* as here the appellant had the benefit of section 22(4).

> The General Dental Council is a public authority within the meaning of ss 6(1) and 7(1). It is the action of the council, in bringing disciplinary proceedings under a system allegedly not complying with Article 6.1, of which he complains. In Lambert there was no question of the prosecuting authority having acted unlawfully.[59]

It has also been held that proceedings for possession brought by a local authority qualify as proceedings brought by or at the instigation of a public authority, enabling the appellant in *O'Sullivan*[60] to rely on alleged Convention breaches by the local authority between 1983 and 1991.

2.5 Getting Around the Problem of Retrospective Effect

In many cases, although the HRA has not strictly applied to the facts as the act in question occurred before 2 October 2000, the court has given consideration to the impact of the Convention.[61] It is also possible for counsel to invite the court to deal with the matter as if the HRA were applicable.[62] Beyond these options, considered in the following paragraphs are a few other techniques used to get the Convention rights issue before the court.

[56] *R v Lambert* [2001] UKHL 37, [2002] 2 AC 545.
[57] *R (on the application of Abdelaziz) v London Borough of Haringey* [2001] EWCA Civ 803, [2001] 1 WLR 1485 at [31].
[58] *Preiss v General Dental Council* [2001] UKPC 36, [2001] 1 WLR 1926.
[59] Per Lord Cooke.
[60] *Royal Borough of Kensington and Chelsea v O'Sullivan* [2003] EWCA Civ 371.
[61] See, eg *Allen*, above n 25; and *Benjafield*, above n 27.
[62] See, eg *R (McCann) v Crown Court at Manchester* [2002] UKHL 39, [2003] 1 AC 787; *Aston Cantlow and Wilmcote with Billesley Parochial Church Council v Wallbank* [2003] UKHL 37, [2004] 1 AC 546.

2.5.1 Ongoing Violation of Convention Rights

If the violation of Convention rights first occurred before 2 October 2000 but continued after that date, it may be considered an 'ongoing' violation and therefore within the scope of the HRA. For example, in *Bellinger*[63] the couple actually married in 1981 but, pursuant to section 11(c) of the Matrimonial Causes Act 1973, the marriage was void as the parties were not respectively male and female at the time. The House of Lords accepted that it could deal with the claim for a declaration of incompatibility as the non-recognition of their ability to marry continued to have adverse practical effects—the statute continued to prevent them from marrying each other.[64] Similarly in *Hooper*,[65] which concerned the denial to widowers of benefits that would have been payable to widows, the House of Lords held that in respect of acts or omissions before 2 October 2000 they could make no complaint. However, the submission that, in denying them the benefits after that date, the Secretary of State had acted incompatibly with Convention rights was considered.[66]

It may also be the case in an immigration context that a decision to deport adhered to after the HRA came into force engages the operation of Act.[67] However, in *Mahmood*,[68] the court rejected the submission that the HRA applied as, although the decision to deport was made before 2 October 2000, his actual removal would be after 2 October 2000.

> the court is required to review the legality of an administrative decision already made it is generally no part of its duty to go further and review also (as a distinct exercise) the legality of the decision-maker's carrying the decision into effect at some future date . . . It cannot be for the court, faced with a judicial review only of the earlier decision, in some way to police the considerations which might or might not impel the decision-maker to give effect to his decision.[69]

There are limits, however, to the notion of ongoing violations. In *McKerr*[70] the son of a man fatally shot in Northern Ireland in 1982 sought an order compelling the Secretary of State for Northern Ireland to hold an effective investigation into the circumstances of his father's death. The House of Lords concluded that the obligation to hold an investigation was an obligation triggered by the occurrence of a violent death and was consequential upon the death.

> If the death itself is not within the reach of s.6, because it occurred before the Act came into force, it would be surprising if s.6 applied to an obligation consequential upon the death . . . The event giving rise to the Art.2 obligation to investigate must have occurred post-Act.[71]

---

[63] Above n 32.
[64] *Bellinger*, above n 32, at [50] per Lord Nicholls.
[65] *R (on the application of Hooper) v Secretary of State for Work and Pensions* [2005] UKHL 29, [2005] 1 WLR 1681.
[66] *Ibid*, at [10] per Lord Hoffmann.
[67] See, eg *X v Secretary of State for the Home Department* [2001] 1 WLR 740 at [9].
[68] *R v Secretary of State for the Home Department, ex p Mahmood* [2001] 1 WLR 840.
[69] *Ibid*, at [29] per Laws LJ, with whom May LJ agreed.
[70] Above n 51.
[71] *Ibid*, at [22] per Lord Bingham. However, in *Hurst*, above n 49 the Court of Appeal held that the duty to investigate under Article 2 could be triggered by a death prior to 2 October 2000 if what was at issue was not s 6 of the HRA but the application of s 3 to a provision of primary legislation.

2.5.2 The 'Act' is Not Yet Complete

In *Aston Cantlow*[72] Lord Hope suggested that the HRA may be applicable as the unlawful act was the enforcement by the PCC of the liability for the cost of the repairs to the chancel. He considered the service of the notice to repair to be just the first step in the taking of proceedings under the Chancel Repairs Act 1932 to enforce the liability to repair.

> The final step in the process is the giving by the court of judgment for the responsible authority for such sums as appears to it to represent the cost of putting the chancel in proper repair.[73]

In Lord Hope's view, the proceedings to give effect to the notice were still on foot and in this situation there was no issue of retrospectivity.

> Mr and Mrs Wallbank do not need to rely on s.22(4). It is sufficient for their purpose to say that they wish to rely on their Convention right in the proceedings which the PCC are still taking against them with a view to having the notice enforced. This is something they are entitled to do under s.7(1)(b).[74]

Lord Hope also considered that the appeal here related to a preliminary issue only—the court had yet to reach the stage in the proceedings when effect could be given to the notice which the PCC had served.

> Section 7(6)(a) states that the expression 'legal proceedings' in s.7(1)(b) includes 'proceedings brought by or at the instigation of a public authority.' The preliminary issue has been examined as part of these proceedings.[75]

2.5.3 Utilising the Pre-HRA Position

It has been suggested that even if the HRA does not apply, if a decision maker has indicated that he or she has taken the Convention into account, the correctness of the Convention conclusion can be examined by the court. For example, in *Montana*[76] the Court of Appeal held that as the Secretary of State had contended that his decision on registering a child as a British citizen complied with the Convention, it would be unrealistic for the court to determine the appeal on any other basis.[77]

> If the applicant is to have an effective remedy against the decision which is flawed because the decision maker has misdirected himself on the Convention which he himself says he took into account, it must surely be right to examine the substance of the argument.[78]

---

[72] *Aston Cantlow and Wilmcote with Billesley Parochial Church Council v Wallbank* [2003] UKHL 37, [2004] 1 AC 546.
[73] *Ibid*, at [31].
[74] *Ibid*, at [31].
[75] *Ibid*, at [32]. However, the eventual conclusion was that the PCC was not a public authority.
[76] *R (on the application of Montana) v Secretary of State for the Home Department* [2001] 1 WLR 552.
[77] *Ibid*, at [14].
[78] *R v Home Secretary ex p Launder* [1997] 1 WLR 839 at 867 per Lord Hope. However, doubt was cast on such an approach in *Hurst*, above n 49 at [33].

There is also the possibility that the court may adopt the pre-HRA position and use the Convention as an interpretative tool.

[W]ords in a domestic statute should be construed in a manner which is consistent with Parliament's assumed intention to give effect to the UK's obligations under an international treaty or convention . . . But that is subject to the qualification that the words must be reasonably capable of bearing the meaning which it is sought to put upon them.[79]

For example, in *Hurst*,[80] to get around the problem of retrospective effect the Court of Appeal held that when a coroner came to exercise his discretion under section 16(3) of the Coroners Act 1988 and decide whether there was sufficient cause to reopen an inquest, he had to take the international obligations under the ECHR into account.[81]

2.5.4 Modified Common Law

Finally, in *Al-Hasan*[82] the House of Lords applied the common law test for bias to prison disciplinary proceedings held in 1998 and 1999. What was not commented upon in the judgments given was that the test that was applied had been modified as a result of the HRA

The question is whether the fair-minded and informed observer, having considered the relevant facts, would concluded that there was a real possibility that the tribunal was biased.[83]

It appears that modifications to the common law have escaped the problem of retrospective effect. Similarly in *R v H*[84] the defendant faced trial in 2001 for an offence contrary to section 47 of the Offences Against the Person Act 1861. His defence was that he was exercising his right as a parent to chastise his son. The issue was whether the trial judge and jury could take into account the Convention when determining the limits of this defence. The Court of Appeal concluded that this was possible.

The common law is evolutionary, as was indicated in the case of *R v R*. The directions which it is proposed the judge should give to the jury . . . seem to us to be an appropriate and accurate reflection of the current state of the common law in the light of the Strasbourg jurisprudence to which the English courts, by virtue of the Human Rights Act 1998, must now have regard.[85]

2.6 Judgments of the European Court of Human Rights

Given that courts are obliged under section 2 of the HRA to take into account, inter alia, judgments of the European Court of Human Rights when determining

---

[79] *Malcolm v Mackenzie* [2004] EWCA Civ 1748, [2005] 1 WLR 1238 at [26].
[80] Above n 49.
[81] *Ibid*, at [29].
[82] *R v Secretary of State for the Home Department, ex p Al-Hasan* [2005] UKHL 13, [2005] 1 WLR 688.
[83] *Ibid*, at [30] per Lord Brown citing *Porter v Magill*, above n 29 and *Lawal v Northern Spirit Ltd* [2003] UKHL 35, [2004] 1 All ER 187.
[84] *R v H* [2001] EWCA Crim 1024, [2002] 1 Cr App R 7.
[85] *Ibid*, at [35].

Convention rights questions, there is the possibility that should Strasbourg jurisprudence change, it would render what was once lawful in accordance with this jurisprudence unlawful. Such a situation raises obvious problems of retrospectivity. Would it be possible to bring a claim under the HRA concerning an act which was lawful in terms of Strasbourg jurisprudence when it occurred in 2003 if in 2004 The European Court changed its mind and reversed its earlier ruling thereby making the act unlawful?

The Administrative Court considered almost this exact situation in *Richards*,[86] although it is important to note that the case concerned Article 5(5), and the possibility of extending the principles established to other Convention rights is doubtful. The claimant was serving a mandatory life sentence for murder. The Parole Board recommended him for release on 16 November 2001 but he was not released by the Secretary of State for the Home Department until 12 August 2002. He sought compensation under Article 5(5) for the detention between the Parole Board's recommended date of release and his actual release date on 12 August 2002. Article 5(5) provides that

> everyone who has been the victim of arrest or detention in contravention of the provisions of this Article shall have an enforceable right to compensation.

The problem was that it was not until the judgment of the European Court of Human Rights in *Stafford v UK*[87] on 28 May 2002, reversing its earlier ruling in *Wynne v UK*,[88] that it could be said that the detention was incompatible with Articles 5(4) and 6(1).[89] The court noted that the conventional approach of the Strasbourg Court is that its decisions have both prospective effect and retrospective effect.[90] It concluded that the judgment in *Stafford* governed periods of detention that occurred both before and after the date of the judgment.

> First, the Strasbourg Court in *Stafford* considered that its judgment should have retrospective effect in that case and it awarded damages to the claimant in respect of periods before it published its judgment during which the established case law indicated that the detention in question was lawful. Second, the Strasbourg Court in two subsequent cases of *Van Bulow* and *Wynne (No.2)* followed that approach. Third, in *Stafford* the Strasbourg Court, unlike its approach in *Marckx*, did not dispense the United Kingdom from reopening release decisions, which pre-dated the date of that judgment.[91]

In light of this conclusion, it assessed compensation for the period from November 2001 to August 2002.

---

[86] *R (on the application of Richards) v The Secretary of State for the Home Department* [2004] EWHC (Admin) 93, [2004] ACD 69.
[87] (2002) 35 EHRR 1121.
[88] (1994) 19 EHRR 333.
[89] And it was not until 25 November 2002 that the House of Lords ruled that s 29 of the Crime (Sentences) Act 1997 was incompatible with Article 6(1).
[90] *Wynne*, above n 88, at [69].
[91] *Ibid*, at [81].

3. Acts which Occur Outside of the United Kingdom: Extra-territorial Effect

The application of the HRA to acts which occur outside of the territory of the United Kingdom is still being determined. At present it is clear that there are two categories of acts which take place outside the UK to which the HRA could apply. First, acts incompatible with Convention rights perpetrated by non-UK actors. Secondly, acts incompatible with Convention rights perpetrated by UK public authorities. There are also a number of issues concerning British Overseas Territories.

3.1 Acts of non-UK Actors

The label 'foreign cases' has been attached to cases in which it is not claimed that the state complained of has violated or will violate the applicant's Convention rights within its own territory but in which it is claimed that the conduct of a state in removing a person from its territory to another territory will lead to a violation of the person's Convention rights in that other territory.[92] Such cases

> represent an exception to the general rule that a state is only responsible for what goes on within its own territory or control. The Strasbourg court clearly regards them as exceptional.[93]

It is a little misleading to place this category of acts under the heading of extra-territorial effect as in addition to the act taking outside of UK territory in breach of Convention rights, there is an act within UK territory consisting of the decision to deport or extradite an individual. Such a case involves 'an exercise of power by the state affecting a person physically present within its territory.'[94]

It has been clearly established in both HRA and Strasbourg jurisprudence that whenever substantial grounds have been shown for believing that an individual would face a real risk of being subjected to treatment contrary to Article 3 if removed to another state, the responsibility of the contracting state to safeguard him or her against such treatment is engaged in the event of expulsion.[95] In *Ullah*[96] the House of Lords held that, in such cases, reliance may be placed on any Article of the Convention but it must be shown that there would be a flagrant denial or gross violation of

---

[92] See the explanation of Lord Bingham in *R (on the application of Ullah) v Special Adjudicator* [2004] UKHL 26, [2004] 2 AC 323 at [9].

[93] *R (on the application of Razgar) v Secretary of State for the Home Department* [2004] UKHL 27, [2004] 2 AC 368 at [42] per Baroness Hale.

[94] *Ullah*, above n 92, at [9] per Lord Bingham. In *R (on the application of Al-Skeini) v Secretary of State for Defence* [2004] EWHC (Admin) 2911, [2005] 2 WLR 1401 the court noted that this exception to territorial limitation was not a true exception because the victim and act of the respondent state were located in the home territory; see [246].

[95] See, eg *Soering v United Kingdom* (1989) 11 EHRR 439; *N v Secretary of State for the Home Department* [2005] UKHL 31, [2005] 2 AC 296.

[96] Above n 92.

the right whereby the right would be completely denied or nullified in the destination country.[97]

This principle has not just been applied in cases of deportation and extradition. In *Barnette*[98] the House of Lords concluded that Article 6 was capable of being applied to the enforcement in a Convention state of a judgment obtained in another state, whether or not the latter was an adherent to the Convention. However, such a jurisdiction was exceptional and a flagrant breach of the applicant's rights was required to trigger it. In the present case it concluded that the fugitive disentitlement doctrine under which the US Court of Appeals dismissed the appeal on the ground that the applicant was a fugitive from justice was not an arbitrary deprivation of a party's right to a hearing but was intended to be a means of securing proper obedience to the orders of the court. It could not be described as a flagrant denial of the applicant's Article 6 rights or a fundamental breach of Article 6.[99]

If the victim of the violation of Convention rights by non-UK actors is not within the territory of the United Kingdom, it has been held that no duty under the HRA is owed to him or her, although it is possible that a duty may be owed under the HRA to close relatives of the victim who are resident in the United Kingdom.[100] In *Abbasi*[101] the Court of Appeal held that the jurisdiction referred to in Article 1 of the ECHR was normally territorial jurisdiction. In addition,

[w]here a State enjoys effective control of foreign territory, that territory will fall within its jurisdiction for the purposes of Article 1.

Further,

[w]here, under principles of international law, a state enjoys extra-territorial jurisdiction over an individual and acts in the exercise of that jurisdiction, that individual will be deemed to be within the jurisdiction of the state for the purposes of Article 1, insofar as the action in question is concerned.[102]

However, in the present case the court concluded that the HRA did not afford any support to the contention that the Foreign Secretary owed Mr Abbasi, who was being

---

[97] *Ibid*, at [24] per Lord Bingham. The real risk of denial of a fair trial contrary to Article 6 has been argued in a number of extradition cases. See, eg *R (on the application of Elliot) v Secretary of State for the Home Department* [2001] EWHC (Admin) 559; *R (on the application of Ramda) v Secretary of State for the Home Department* [2002] EWHC (Admin) 1278; *Orechovsky v Government of Slovakia*, Divisional Court, 5 November 2003; *Sadutto v The Governor of HMP Brixton* [2004] EWHC (Admin) 563; *Daniels v Governor of HMP Holloway* [2005] EWHC (Admin) 148; *Okendeji v Government of Australia* [2005] EWHC (Admin) 471; *Government of Albania v Bleta* [2005] EWHC (Admin) 475, [2005] 3 All ER 351.
[98] *Barnette v United States* [2004] UKHL 35, [2004] 1 WLR 2241.
[99] *Ibid*, at [29] per Lord Carswell. See further A Briggs, 'Foreign Judgments and Human Rights' (2005) 121 *LQR* 185. It is also possible that the HRA applies to the return of a child to a foreign jurisdiction although in *Jomah v Attar* [2004] EWCA Civ 417 (pre the House of Lords' judgment in *Ullah*) the court rejected the argument that it would be in breach of Articles 6, 8 and 14 of the mother to return the child to Saudi Arabia. In any event, the court concluded that it would be open to an English judge to refuse to return the child if the evidence was that his welfare was likely to be compromised. 'Welfare is paramount: the fact that a return may or may not breach the art 6, 8, 9 or 14 rights of the abducting parent is secondary' at [58].
[100] *R (on the application of Suresh) v Secretary of State for the Home Department* [2001] EWHC (Admin) 1028. See also *R (on the application of Abbasi) v Secretary of State for Foreign and Commonwealth Affairs* [2002] EWCA Civ 1598, [2003] UKHRR 76.
[101] *Abbasi, ibid*.
[102] *Ibid*, at [76] in reliance upon *Al-Adsani v United Kingdom* (2002) 34 EHRR 11; *Bankovic v Belgium* 11 BHRC 435.

held by United States forces in Guantanamo Bay, Cuba, a duty to exercise diplomacy on his behalf.[103]

Nevertheless, putting the HRA to one side, the court did conclude that judicial review may be available.

[T]he Foreign Office has discretion whether to exercise the right, which it undoubtedly has, to protect British citizens. It has indicated in the ways explained what a British citizen may expect of it. The expectations are limited and the discretion is a very wide one but there is no reason why its decision or inaction should not be reviewable if it can be shown that the same were irrational or contrary to legitimate expectation; but the court cannot enter the forbidden areas, including decisions affecting foreign policy.[104]

3.2 Acts of UK Public Authorities

3.2.1 Jurisdiction as Defined by the European Court of Human Rights

It has been held that the HRA requires public authorities of the United Kingdom to secure Convention rights within the jurisdiction of the United Kingdom as that jurisdiction has been identified by the Strasbourg Court.[105]

The Strasbourg Court, when considering whether a Convention right has been infringed, will consider whether the events in issue have fallen within the jurisdiction of the Contracting State, within the meaning of Art.1. It is not realistic to divorce the right from the circumstances in which the right is enjoyed. It seems to us that we are under a duty, if possible, to interpret the Human Rights Act in a way that is compatible with the Convention rights, as those rights have been identified by the Strasbourg Court. This duty precludes the application of any presumption that the Human Rights Act applies within the territorial jurisdiction of the United Kingdom, rather than the somewhat wider jurisdiction of the United Kingdom that the Strasbourg Court has held to govern the duties of the United Kingdom under the Convention.[106]

3.2.2 Exceptions to Territorial Jurisdiction

A survey of authorities from the Commission and Court[107] reveals that there are instances where obligations under Article 1[108] have been held to apply notwithstanding that the applicants were not within the territory over which the defendant state

---

[103] *Ibid*, at [79].
[104] *Ibid*, at [106].
[105] *R (on the application of B) v Secretary of State for the Foreign and Commonwealth Office* [2004] EWCA Civ 1344, [2005] QB 643 at [79]. This conclusion was reached bearing in mind that the object of the HRA was to give effect to the obligations of the United Kingdom under the Convention; see [75].
[106] *Ibid*, at [78]. See also *Al-Skein*, above n 94, at [291].
[107] The following cases were cited in *B, ibid*: *X v Federal Republic of Germany*, 25 September 1965; *East African Asians v United Kingdom* (1973) 3 EHRR 76; *Drozd & Janousek v France & Spain* (1992) 14 EHRR 745; *WM v Denmark*, 14 October 1992, Commission; *Loizidou v Turkey*, 23 March 1995 and 18 December 1996; *Cyprus v Turkey* (2002) 35 EHRR 30; *Xhavara v Italy and Albania* (2001) 12 HRCD; *Bankovic v Belgium*, 12 December 2001; *Öcalan v Turkey*, 12 March 2003.
[108] 'The High Contracting Parties shall secure to everyone within their jurisdiction the rights and freedoms defined in Section I of this Convention.' Article 1 is not one of the Convention rights given further effect by the HRA.

exercised jurisdiction under international law.[109] However, it is not easy to identify a universal principle from these cases. In B[110] the Court of Appeal suggested that the HRA may apply where a claimant is 'sufficiently within the authority' of a UK public authority.[111] In *Al-Skeini*[112] the Divisional Court gave far more detailed guidance, holding that whilst the essential and primary nature of Article 1 jurisdiction was territorial, there were exceptions to this.[113] Two exceptions were identified, the first, where a state party had effective control of an area, lawful or unlawful.[114] However, the court was careful to point out that this exception only applied in territories inside the regional sphere of the party states of the Convention itself.[115]

The second exception identified was that relating to the authority or control of state agents of party states, wherever those agents operate.[116] However, the court was again careful to point out that that this was not a broad, worldwide extra-territorial jurisdiction arising from the exercise of authority by states' agents anywhere in the world, but only an

> extra-territorial jurisdiction which is exceptional and limited and to be found in specific cases recognised in international law. Such instances can be identified piece-meal in the jurisprudence.[117]

The court suggested that the recognised instances were ones where, although the violation of Convention rights had taken place outside the home territory of the respondent state, it had occurred by reason of the exercise of state authority in or from a location which had a form of

> discrete quasi-territorial quality, or where the state agent's presence in a foreign state is consented to by that state and protected by international law: such as diplomatic or consular premises, or vessels or aircraft registered in the respondent state.[118]

---

[109] *B*, above n 105, at [52]. These rare instances include: where a state, through the effective control of the relevant territory and its inhabitants abroad as a consequence of military occupation or through the consent, invitation or acquiescence of the government of that territory, exercises all or some of the public powers normally to be exercised by that government; the activities of diplomatic and consular agents abroad and on board craft and vessels registered in or flying the flag of that state. See *Bankovic v Belgium*, 12 December 2001, at [71] and [73].

[110] Above n 105.

[111] *Ibid*, at [66], although it is important to note that the court was only content to assume that this was the case, and that the HRA applied. It did not reach a positive conclusion on the point.

[112] Above n 94.

[113] *Ibid*, at [245].

[114] *Ibid*, at [248], in reliance upon *Loizidou v Turkey* (1995) 20 EHRR 99; *Loizidou v Turkey* (1997) 23 EHRR 513; *Cyprus v Turkey* (1997) 23 EHRR 244; *Cyprus v Turkey* (2002) 35 EHRR 300; *Ilascu v Moldova*, 8 July 2004

[115] *Ibid*, at [274] in reliance upon *Bankovic v Belgium*, 12 December 2001. The court also noted the possibility that this exception may not come within the HRA 'On our interpretation of this exception, it only applies within the sphere of the territories of the state parties, and does so in order to prevent a vacuum within that sphere. That is a rationale that applies strongly in the context of Strasbourg, but not to the United Kingdom for the very reason that there would always be a remedy, and thus no vacuum, via the Convention in Strasbourg.' *Ibid*, at [304].

[116] *Ibid*, at [249], in reliance upon *X v Republic of Germany*, 25 September 1965; *Cyprus v Turkey* (1976) 4 EHRR 482; *Hess v United Kingdom* (1975) 2 DR 72; *X and Y v Switzerland*, 14 July 1977; *X v United Kingdom* 15 December 1977; *Chrysostomos v Turkey*, 4 March 1991; *WM v Denmark*, 14 October 1993; *Ramirez v France*, 24 June 1996.

[117] *Ibid*, at [269].

[118] *Ibid*, at [270].

To this list it later added courts and prisons.[119]

The issue has actually arisen very rarely in HRA litigation. Those cases where it has are examined in the following paragraphs.

3.2.3 Application: Entry Clearance

The application of the HRA to the entry clearance function abroad is not clear. In *European Roma Rights Centre*[120] Lord Bingham had the very greatest doubt that the functions performed by British immigration officers in Prague, even though they were formally treated as consular officials, could possibly be said to be an exercise of jurisdiction in any relevant sense over non-UK nationals.[121] However, in *Singh*[122] the Court of Appeal proceeded on the assumption that the HRA applied to a decision of a British entry clearance officer in New Delhi, although Chadwick LJ commented that the court was not invited to consider the question of whether the Convention or the Act should be treated as having extra-territorial reach in this case; 'and we have not done so. We should not be taken to have reached any conclusion on that question.'[123]

3.2.4 Application: Activities of British Embassies

By contrast, the activities of British embassies abroad has been given far more detailed consideration in the case of *B*,[124] which concerned two boys, claiming to be of Afghan origin, who, having escaped from an asylum seeker detention centre, sought asylum in the British Consulate in Melbourne, Australia. Having reviewed Strasbourg authority, the Court of Appeal found that the authority closest to the situation here was *WM v Denmark*,[125] although there was a distinction in that the embassy officials in WM appear to have conducted negotiations with the DDR authorities on behalf of the applicant and 'may be said to have assumed some responsibility (or exercised some authority) in respect of the applicant.'[126] Taking into consideration that the applicants were told that while they were in the Consulate they would be kept safe, and that they were given some protection by being brought from the reception area into the office area, the court was content to assume, without reaching a positive conclusion on the point, that while in the Consulate the applicants were sufficiently within the authority of the consular staff to be subject to the jurisdiction of the United Kingdom for the purpose of Article 1.[127]

---

[119] *Ibid*, see [284]. See also *R (on the application of Al-Jedda) v Secretary of State for Defence* [2005] EWHC (Admin) 1809. For a critique of the judgment in *Al-Skeini*, above n 94 see P.Leach, 'The British military in Iraq—the applicability of the *espace juridique* doctrine under the European Convention on Human Rights' [2005] PL 448.

[120] *R (on the application of European Roma Rights Centre) v Immigration Officer, Prague Airport* [2004] UKHL 55, [2005] 2 AC 1.

[121] *Ibid*, at [21].

[122] *Singh v Entry Clearance Officer New Delhi* [2004] EWCA Civ 1075, [2005] QB 608.

[123] *Ibid*, at [94].

[124] Above n 105.

[125] *WM v Denmark*, 14 October 1993.

[126] *Ibid*, at [66].

[127] *Ibid*.

Assuming the HRA applied, the court then turned to whether there had been a breach here. It held that the UK officials could not be required by the Convention and the HRA to decline to hand over the applicants unless this was clearly necessary in order to protect them from the immediate likelihood of experiencing serious injury.[128] It found that this was not the case.

> The applicants were not subject to the type and degree of threat that, under international law, would have justified granting them diplomatic asylum. To have given the applicants refuge from the demands of the Australian authorities for their return would have been an abuse of the privileged inviolability accorded to diplomatic premises. It would have infringed the obligations of the United Kingdom under public international law.[129]

3.2.5 Application: Activities of the British Armed Forces

In *Al-Skeini*[130] the claimant relatives of deceased Iraqi civilians who had been killed by or in the course of action taken by British soldiers in the period following completion of major combat operations in Iraq, and prior to the assumption of authority by the Iraqi Interim Government, brought proceedings under the HRA against the Secretary of State for Defence, alleging violations of Articles 2 and 3. In a very lengthy judgment, the Divisional Court concluded that the 'effective control of an area' exception to the principle of territoriality did not apply here as Iraq was not a party to the ECHR.

> [S]ince Iraq is not within the regional sphere of the Convention, the complaints before us do not fall within the Art.1 jurisdiction of the United Kingdom under the heading of the extra-territorial doctrine of the 'effective control of an area' exception.[131]

However, in relation to the second exception to the principle of territoriality resulting from the extra-territorial activity of state agents, the court reached a different conclusion. In relation to the first five claimants, it held that this exception did not apply because the deaths occurred as a result of military operations in the field. In the opinion of the court, this did not come

> within any possible variation of the examples of acts by state authorities in or from embassies, consulates, vessels, aircraft, (or we would suggest, courts or prisons) to which the authorities repeatedly refer.[132]

In relation to the sixth claimant, the court found that the circumstances were different. This claimant had been arrested by British forces and taken into custody in a British military base, where he met his death.

> It seems to us that it is not at all straining the examples of extra-territorial jurisdiction discussed in the jurisprudence considered above to hold that a British military prison, operating in Iraq with the consent of the Iraqi sovereign authorities, and containing

---

[128] *Ibid*, at [89].
[129] *Ibid*, at [96].
[130] Above n 94.
[131] *Ibid*, at [281].
[132] *Ibid*, at [284].

arrested suspects, falls within even a narrowly limited exception exemplified by embassies, consulates, vessels and aircraft, and in the case of Hess v. United Kingdom, a prison.[133]

Finding the HRA applicable to this case, it later concluded that the procedural obligations arising under Articles 2 and 3 in relation this claimant's death had not been satisfied.[134]

3.3 The Channel Islands and the Isle of Man

The Channel Islands and the Isle of Man are dependencies of the Crown. Pursuant to Article 1 of the European Convention on Human Rights the United Kingdom is obliged to ensure that these dependencies comply with the European Convention on Human Rights. However, pursuant to the wishes of the appropriate Island governments, the Human Rights Act has not been extended to them.[135]

3.4 British Overseas Territories

Unless the Convention and Protocol No 1 have been extended to the particular British Overseas Territory, it is not possible to found a claim under section 7 of the HRA. For example, in *Quark Fishing Ltd*[136] the Court of Appeal concluded that as the First Protocol had not been extended to South Georgia, there was no breach of Convention rights capable of founding an HRA claim.

> However complete the control exercised by the Convention state over the dependent territory, the Convention applies to the territory only if there has been a notification under article 56 and, in the case of the Protocol, only if there has been a notification under its article 4.[137]

However, it was also established in this case that it is possible for United Kingdom powers to be exercised in an overseas territory where Her Majesty is queen and where there are competent local authorities.[138]

> The fact that Her Majesty the Queen is Head of State in the United Kingdom does not stand in the way of governmental actions in other territories where Her Majesty is Head of State from being treated as actions of the entities concerned, whether the territories are independent, self-governing or dependencies.[139]

Here it concluded that the instruction was given by the Secretary of State in right of the United Kingdom government.[140] He had directed the Commissioner for South

---

[133] *Ibid*, at [287].
[134] *Ibid*, at [336]. See also *Al-Jedda*, above n 119.
[135] See further, HL Deb, Vol 584, cols 1303–11 (19 January, 1998).
[136] *R (Quark Fishing Ltd) v Secretary of State for Foreign and Commonwealth Affairs* [2004] EWCA Civ 527, [2005] QB 93.
[137] *Ibid*, at [56], in reliance upon *Bui van Thanh v United Kingdom*, 12 March 1990; *Yonghong v Portugal*, Reports of Judgments and Decisions 1999—XI, p 385; and *Gillow v United Kingdom* (1986) 11 EHRR 335.
[138] *Ibid*, at [44].
[139] *Ibid*, at [45].
[140] *Ibid*, at [50].

Georgia, who in turn directed the Director of Fisheries for that territory, not to grant the fishing licence sought. If the First Protocol had been extended, this would have been an act to which the HRA would apply.

4. Failure to Act: Positive Duties

It is made clear in section 6(6) that an 'act' incompatible with Convention rights includes a failure to act. However, it is also made clear in this section that a failure to act does not include a failure to (a) introduce in, or lay before, Parliament a proposal for legislation; or (b) make any primary legislation or remedial order.

Expressly including failures to act within the meaning of acts which may be incompatible with Convention rights reflects the principle of positive obligations which has been a long-standing principle of Strasbourg jurisprudence.[141] As will become clearer in Part II of this book concerning the Convention rights, almost every right either expressly or impliedly requires public authorities not only to refrain from infringing rights, but also to take action. For example, Article 2, the right to life, imposes not only a duty not to take life but, in some circumstances, to take steps to prevent life being taken and, as part of that duty, an obligation to investigate the circumstances surrounding the death, should it occur.[142] Article 6(1) obliges public authorities to ensure that in the determination of civil rights and obligations, or any criminal charge, everyone has a fair and public hearing within a reasonable time by an independent and impartial tribunal established by law. There is also an implied duty attached to the right to respect for private life protected by Article 8 obliging public authorities to take reasonable measures so as to avoid an interference with private life.[143]

As outlined in Part II of this book, proceedings under the HRA for a failure to act which is incompatible with Convention rights have the tendency to be more controversial than proceedings for an act. This is generally because requiring a public authority to take action requires the expenditure of more resources than would otherwise be the case. Resources arguments have been a particular issue in claims which have arisen under Articles 3 and 8 in the context of welfare support.[144] Nevertheless, generally the courts have not shrunk from determining incompatibility in such instances.

---

[141] See further, A Mowbray, *The Development of Positive Obligations under the European Convention on Human Rights by the European Court of Human Rights* (Oxford, Hart Publishing, 2004).
[142] *R (on the application of Amin (Imtiaz) v Secretary of State for the Home Department* [2003] UKHL 51, [2004] 1 AC 653 at [40] per Lord Slynn.
[143] For a discussion of the meaning of 'reasonableness' in this context, see TR Hickman, 'The Reasonableness Principle: Reassessing its Place in the Public Sphere', (2004) 63 *CLJ* 166.
[144] See, eg *Anufrijeva v Southwark LBC* [2003] EWCA Civ 1406, [2004] QB 1124.

5. Satellite Litigation

5.1 Criminal Proceedings

An issue which has arisen in some criminal cases is the inappropriateness of what has been labelled 'satellite' litigation within the criminal justice system. Whilst it has not yet occurred, it is possible that a court will decline to exercise its jurisdiction under the HRA if it feels that the matter could have been more appropriately raised in the trial or on appeal. For example, in *Kebilene*,[145] at the close of the prosecution case at trial, the three defendants sought a ruling from the trial judge that section 16A of the Prevention of Terrorism (Temporary Provisions) Act 1989 reversed the burden of proof and was therefore in breach of Article 6. The jury was later discharged and a new trial date set. Meanwhile, the defendants applied for judicial review, arguing that the continuing decision of the Director of Public Prosecutions to give his consent to the prosecution under section 16A was incompatible with Article 6.

A majority of their Lordships held that, once the HRA was fully in force, it would not be possible to make such an application as the remedy would be in the trial process or on appeal. They concluded in the present case that, absent dishonesty or mala fides or an exceptional circumstance, the decision of the Director of Public Prosecutions to consent to the prosecution was not amenable to judicial review. Lord Steyn commented that while the passing of the HRA

> marked a great advance for our criminal justice system it is in my view vitally important that, so far as the courts are concerned, its application in our law should take place in an orderly manner which recognises the desirability of all challenges taking place in the criminal trial or on appeal . . . Such satellite litigation should rarely be permitted in our criminal justice system.[146]

A similar dilemma arose in *R v A*.[147] At a preparatory hearing, counsel for the defendant applied for leave to cross-examine the complainant about the alleged previous sexual relationship between the complainant and the defendant and to lead evidence about it. Relying on section 41 of the Youth Justice and Criminal Evidence Act 1999, the judge ruled that the complainant could not be cross-examined, nor could evidence be led about her alleged sexual relationship with the defendant and that the prepared statement could not be put in evidence. The defendant appealed. Only three members of the House of Lords commented on the timing of the challenge, although the silence of Lords Slynn and Hutton on the matter could be taken to mean that they also considered it important to resolve the issue at this stage. Lord

---

[145] Above n 6.
[146] See also *R (on the application of Pretty) v Director of Public Prosecutions* [2001] UKHL 61, [2001] 3 WLR 1598, where it was sought to challenge the refusal of the DPP to give an undertaking that he would not, under s 2(4) of the Suicide Act 1961, consent to the prosecution of Mr Pretty under s 2(1) if he were to assist his wife to commit suicide. Lord Hobhouse, at [123], commented that 'the procedure of seeking to by-pass the ordinary operation of our system of criminal justice by raising questions of law and applying for the judicial review of "decisions" of the Director cannot be approved and should be firmly discouraged. It undermines the proper and fair management of our criminal justice system.'
[147] *R v A* [2001] UKHL 25, [2002] 1 AC 45.

Steyn noted that the same issue arose in 13 other criminal cases, and it was therefore a matter of some urgency.[148] Lord Clyde also found that there were strong practical reasons for determining a matter of compliance with the Convention in advance of the trial.

> But the course has this consequence that the issue can only be answered on a very preliminary basis at this stage.[149]

Only Lord Hope held that the question of whether or not section 41 was incompatible with Article 6 could not be finally determined at this stage.

> [I]t will only be in rare and isolated cases, that the question of fairness will be capable of being determined before the trial.[150]

5.2 Civil Proceedings

It is also possible, although less common, for satellite litigation to arise in civil matters. For example, in *Alconbury*[151] the claimants sought clarification as to whether or not the role of the Secretary of State in planning matters was compatible with Article 6. The matters were by no means concluded but were merely at the stage where the Secretary of State had exercised his powers to intervene by referring a planning application to himself and appointing inspectors to hold public inquiries. Lord Clyde commented that their Lordships had been asked to form a view at a preliminary stage.

> It is not yet known what the decisions will be. Far less is it known what grounds, if any, will emerge for dissatisfaction with the decision.

However, in his Lordship's view the practical advantages of testing the issue at the early stage were obvious.

> A very considerable expenditure of effort, time and money would have been spent in vain if the decision of the Divisional Court was correct.[152]

---

[148] *Ibid*, at [26].
[149] *Ibid*, at [120].
[150] *Ibid*, at [106] and [107]. Under the Scotland Act 1998, satellite human rights litigation has been common. See, eg *Montgomery v HM Advocate* [2003] 1 AC 641; *Brown v Stott* [2001] 1 AC 681; *McLean v Procurator Fiscal, Fort William* [2001] 1 WLR 2425; *Millar v Procurator Fiscal, Elgin* [2001] 1 WLR 1615; and *HM Advocate v R* [2002] UKPC D3, [2004] 1 AC 462.
[151] *R v Secretary of State for the Environment, Transport and the Regions, ex p Alconbury Developments Ltd* [2001] UKHL 23, [2001] 2 WLR 1389.
[152] *Ibid*, at [171].

4

Determining Incompatibility

1. Introduction

Once it has been established that the HRA applies, the next step is to determine whether or not the act is incompatible with a Convention right or rights. The majority of the Convention rights are discussed in detail in Part II of this book and it is clear that very few are absolute rights. For example, the right to freedom of expression, as expressed in Article 10,

> may be subject to such formalities, conditions, restrictions or penalties as are prescribed by law and are necessary in a democratic society, in the interests of national security, territorial integrity or public safety, for the prevention of disorder or crime, for the protection of health or morals, for the protection of the reputation or rights of others, for preventing the disclosure of information received in confidence, or for maintaining the authority and impartiality of the judiciary.

Articles 8 (private life, family life, home and correspondence), 9 (freedom of thought, conscience and religion) and 11 (freedom of assembly and association) are drafted in a similar manner. In addition, some rights which appear absolute from the text of the Convention are also subject to exceptions. For example, differences in treatment contrary to Article 14 (prohibition of discrimination) may be subject to an interference which has a legitimate aim and bears a reasonable relationship of proportionality to that aim.[1] Any interference with the right to peaceful enjoyment of possessions is lawful as long as a fair balance is struck between the demands of the general interest of the community and the requirement of the protection of the individual's fundamental rights. Again, there must be a reasonable relationship of proportionality between the means employed and the aim pursued.[2]

---

[1] *R (on the application of S) v Chief Constable of South Yorkshire* [2004] UKHL 39, [2001] 1 WLR 2196 at [42] per Lord Steyn.
[2] *R v Dimsey; R v Allen* [2001] UKHL 46, [2001] 3 WLR 843.

Although there are different considerations attached to the interpretation of each Convention right (as discussed more fully in Part II), from this brief overview it is clear that certain concepts are key to determining incompatibility whatever Convention right is in play. First, the concept of 'prescribed by law'; secondly, the concept of proportionality; and thirdly, within the concept of proportionality, the concept of judicial deference to the executive, legislature and primary decision maker. Indispensable to the process of determining incompatibility, and the subject of considerable HRA case law, these concepts are the subject of this chapter.

2. Prescribed by Law

In determining whether or not an interference with a Convention right is prescribed by law, a court must address three distinct questions.

> The first is whether there is a legal basis in domestic law for the restriction. The second is whether the law or rule in question is sufficiently accessible to the individual who is affected by the interference, and sufficiently precise to enable him to understand its scope and foresee the consequences of his actions so that he can regulate his conduct without breaking the law. The third is whether, assuming that these two requirements are satisfied, it is nevertheless open to the criticism on the convention ground that it was applied in a way that was arbitrary because, for example, it has been resorted to in bad faith or in a way that is not proportionate.[3]

The principle of prescribed by law is reflective of the principle of legality at common law which means that

> Parliament must squarely confront what it is doing and accept the political cost. Fundamental rights cannot be overridden by general or ambiguous words . . . In the absence of express language or necessary implication to the contrary, the courts therefore presume that even the most general words were intended to be subject to the basic rights of the individual.[4]

Applying this principle in the case of *Simms*,[5] the House of Lords concluded that paragraphs 37 and 37A of the Prison Service Standing Order 5A left untouched the fundamental and basic right of the prisoners to freedom of expression and were therefore not ultra vires.[6]

Although a fundamental part of human rights jurisprudence, the principle of prescribed by law has actually given rise to very little litigation under the HRA and it is

---

[3] *R (on the application of Rottman) v Commissioner of Police of the Metropolis* [2002] UKHL 20, [2002] 2 WLR 1315 per Lord Hope at [35] in reliance upon *Sunday Times v United Kingdom* (1979) 2 EHRR 245 at 271; *R v Shayler* [2002] UKHL 11, [2002] 2 WLR 754 at [56].
[4] *R v Secretary of State for the Home Department, ex p Simms* [2000] 2 AC 115 per Lord Hoffmann.
[5] *Ibid.*
[6] See also *McCartan Turkington Breen (A Firm) v Times Newspapers Ltd* [2000] 3 WLR 1670.

very rare for primary legislation to be found lacking in this respect. Nevertheless, a few issues have arisen concerning accessibility, the common law and codes and guidelines. These are examined in the following paragraphs.

2.1 Sufficiently Accessible and Precise

Of the three requirements in order to be prescribed by law, it is the second, relating to accessibility and precision, which has given rise to the most case law, although not all of it is completely satisfying. In *Nadarajah*[7] the Court of Appeal was required to consider whether or not the detention of an asylum seeker, who was to be deported, was lawful. The policy of the immigration service was not to detain those to be imminently removed where proceedings challenging the right to remove had been instituted. However, it was also the policy to disregard information from those acting for asylum seekers that proceedings were about to be initiated. The latter aspect of the policy was not known or accessible, and the Court of Appeal therefore concluded on his ground that the detention was not lawful.[8]

By contrast, in *Gillan*[9] the police had carried out their stop and search in reliance upon an authorisation made under section 44 of the Terrorism Act 2000 by the Assistant Commissioner of the Metropolitan Police and its subsequent confirmation by the Secretary of State. It was argued that what took place was not in accordance with a procedure prescribed by law because the law was not published. The Court of Appeal did not agree, holding that the law that was under criticism was the statute, not the authorisation.

> [W]hile the authorisations and their confirmation are not published because not unreasonably it is considered publication could damage the effectiveness of the stop and search powers and as the individual who is stopped has the right to a written statement under s 45(5), in this context the lack of publication does not mean that what occurred was not a procedure prescribed by law.[10]

Nevertheless, the court also found that the use of the powers to police a protest was not a lawful use. It did not comment any further on this finding but it was clear that a requirement of 'prescribed by law', as discussed in the paragraphs above, was not met as there was no basis in domestic law for the interference with Convention rights.[11]

With respect to the requirement of precision, it is often argued that interferences on the grounds of obscenity, taste or decency are not prescribed by law. For example, it was argued in *R v Perrin*[12] that there was a lack of definition in the statutory definition of obscenity under the Obscene Publications Act 1959. Relying on Strasbourg jurisprudence, the Court of Appeal concluded that the offence was prescribed by

---

[7] *Nadarajah v Secretary of State for the Home Department* [2003] EWCA Civ 1768.
[8] *Ibid*, at [66]–[67].
[9] *R (on the application of Gillan) v The Commissioner of Police for the Metropolis* [2004] EWCA Civ 1067, [2005] QB 388.
[10] *Ibid*, at [49].
[11] *Ibid*, at [56].
[12] [2002] EWCA Crim 747.

law.[13] It has also been argued that the phrase 'national security' lacks clarity. However, in *Baker*[14] the Information Tribunal did not agree, holding that where the Strasbourg organs had considered the phrase it had never been suggested that the concept was so vacuous as to fail the test of clarity.

> The phrase itself is found in the 1981 Convention, in the Directive, and in the statutes and codes of Member States. The fact that it is incapable of comprehensive definition does not mean that it lacks adequate definition.[15]

One example of where the principle of precision was not met is *Briffett v DPP*,[16] where the Divisional Court held that the order imposing reporting restrictions under section 39 of the Children and Young Persons Act 1933 was insufficiently clear and unambiguous. It was held that to be sufficiently clear and unambiguous, the order must leave no doubt, in the mind of a reasonable reader or recipient, as to precisely what it is that is prohibited.[17]

2.2 The Common Law

Questions have often arisen in HRA cases as to whether or not the common law meets the test of prescribed by law. For example, in *Rottman*[18] the House of Lords considered whether under common law a police officer executing a warrant of arrest issued pursuant to section 8 of the Extradition Act 1989 had power to search for and seize any goods or documents which he reasonably believed to be material evidence in relation to the extradition crime in respect of which the warrant was issued. A majority of their Lordships concluded that the police had power under the common law, after arresting a person in his house or in the grounds of his house pursuant to section 8(1)(b) of the 1989 Act, to search the house and seize articles which they reasonably believed to be material evidence in relation to the crime for which they had arrested that person.[19] It also concluded that the search and seizure was in accordance with law as required by Article 8.[20] However, Lord Hope dissented, holding that the common law powers which were available to a police officer when effecting an arrest did not extend to a search of the premises where the person was arrested for the purpose of obtaining evidence.[21] Here he concluded that the search was unlawful because it was undertaken without the respondent's consent and because the police had not obtained a search warrant. He found there was no settled basis in domestic law for the carrying out by the police of a search of the respondent's house for evidence of an extradition crime without his consent and without having first obtained a

---

[13] *Ibid*, at [46], in reliance upon *Muller v Switzerland* (1991) 13 EHRR 212; *Handyside v United Kingdom* (1979–80) 1 EHRR 737; *Wingrove v United Kingdom* (1997) 24 EHRR 1; *Hoare v United Kingdom* [1997] EHRLR 678.
[14] *Baker v Secretary of State for the Home Department*, Information Tribunal, 1 October 2001.
[15] *Ibid*, at [68].
[16] [2001] EWHC Admin 841, [2002] EMLR 12.
[17] *Ibid*, at [13].
[18] Above n 3.
[19] *Ibid*, at [63] per Lord Hutton.
[20] *Ibid*, at [80]. Lord Hutton noted that the law was clearly stated by Lloyd LJ in *R v Governor of Pentonville Prison, ex p Osman* [1989] 3 All ER 701 and clearly set out at p 175 of the well-known textbook on extradition, A Jones, *Jones on Extradition* (London, Sweet & Maxwell, 1995).
[21] *Ibid*, at [32].

search warrant. Even if there was an undoubted power of search at common law, his Lordships found that the second and third requirements relating to accessibility, precision and lack of arbitrariness were not satisfied.[22]

Given that the common law continues to develop, it is conceivable that this could give rise to problems with the principle of prescribed by law. For example, in *Venables*[23] the court concluded that the law of confidence could extend to cover the injunctions sought to protect identities in the case and therefore the restriction imposed on freedom of expression was in accordance with the law.

> The common law continues to evolve, as it has done for centuries, and it is being given considerable impetus to do so by the implementation of the convention into our domestic law.

In light of such rapid development, the argument was made in *Douglas v Hello! Ltd*[24] that when Hello! took the decision to publish the unauthorised photographs the relevant law was so uncertain that it was not possible to predict that publication would be held to be unlawful. The Court of Appeal concluded that, given the interlocutory proceedings, it was reasonably foreseeable to Hello! when they decided to proceed with the publication that this developing area of English law might result in their being held to have infringed the Douglases' rights of privacy or confidence.[25]

> If one postulates that, at the time of the publication by Hello! of the unauthorised photographs, English law was insufficiently clear to satisfy the requirements of providing protection to privacy in a manner 'prescribed by law', the court was on the horns of a dilemma. If it gave a decision which developed the law so as to provide a protection to respect for privacy 'prescribed by law', it risked infringing Hello!'s Article 10 rights. If, however, it ruled that the law was insufficiently clear to provide a remedy, it perpetuated the infringement of the Douglases' Article 8 rights. It seems to us that in this situation the proper course was for the court to attempt to bring English law into compliance with the Convention, even if this was at the cost of a restriction, in the instant case, of Hello!'s Article 10 rights by findings which, up to that moment, could not be said to have been 'prescribed by law'.[26]

2.3 Codes and Guidelines

Codes and guidelines can satisfy the requirement of prescribed by law although it appears that there must be some legislative underpinning. For example, in *Matthias Rath*[27] it was held that the British Codes of Advertising and Sales Promotion, which have an underpinning of subordinate legislation and which are readily accessible, were prescribed by law.[28] In *E*[29] the Administrative Court held that the restrictions

---

[22] *Ibid*, at [36].
[23] *Venables v News Group Newspapers Ltd* [2001] 2 WLR 1038 at [80].
[24] [2005] EWCA Civ 595.
[25] *Ibid*, at [147].
[26] *Ibid*, at [150].
[27] *R (on the application of Matthias Rath BV) v The Advertising Standards Authority Ltd* [2001] EMLR 22.
[28] *Ibid*, at [26].
[29] *R (on the application of E) v Ashworth Hospital Authority* [2001] EWHC (Admin) 1089, [2002] ACD 149.

placed on a patient in a secure mental hospital to dress as a woman had a basis in the Mental Health Act 1983 and that this was accessible.

> [T]he requirement of forseeability is also met. Although the statutory provision itself is in very general terms, greater precision has been given to it by the case law . . . The limits on the exercise of the power, which are subject to the supervision of the court by way of judicial review, are sufficiently defined to provide the requisite protection against arbitrary interference with a patient's right to dress as a woman.[30]

The court also noted that the degree of precision required depended on the particular subject matter and that the subject matter here was not particularly important. Furthermore, the claimant knew in practice precisely what he was and was not permitted to do since the arrangements had been set out in a written plan.[31]

A breach of guidelines can result in a finding that an interference is not prescribed by law. For example, in *R v Mason*[32] the police had covertly taped the conversations of a number of suspects detained in the custody suite of the police station. These tapes played a fundamental role in the case for the prosecution against the defendants. The Chief Constable thought that he was applying the Home Office Guidelines on the Use of Equipment in Police Surveillance (1984), but his decision was not in accordance with a strict interpretation of the Guidelines. The Court of Appeal concluded that the prosecution could not rely on Article 8(2) to justify what took place because the surveillance was not conducted according to law.

> [T]his is because of the lack of any legal structure to which the public have access authorising the infringement. If there had been such authorisation there would have been no breach.[33]

---

3. Necessary

Whilst the phrase 'necessary in a democratic society' is the phrase which appears in a number of Convention rights, the meaning of necessary has received very little attention in the courts, most attention being focused on the meaning of proportionality. It has been held that to be necessary, relevant and sufficient reasons must be given by the national authority to justify the restriction; the restriction on disclosure must correspond to a pressing social need; and the restriction must be proportionate to the legitimate aim pursued.[34] It has also been held that there is a process of analysis that must be carried through.

---

[30] *Herczegfalvy v Austria* (1992) 15 EHRR 437 followed.
[31] *Ibid*, at [43].
[32] [2002] EWCA Crim 385, [2002] 2 Cr App R 38.
[33] *Ibid*, at [65], in reliance upon PG and *JH v United Kingdom* Judgment of 25 September 2001.
[34] *Shayler*, above n 3 at [58] per Lord Hope. See also Lord Bingham at [23].

The starting point is that an authority which seeks to justify a restriction of a fundamental right on the ground of a pressing social need has a burden to discharge. There is a burden on the state to show that the legislative means adopted were no greater than necessary.[35]

4. Proportionality

4.1 Definition

As discussed in the section above, in determining whether an interference with a Convention rights is necessary, a key element is the question of whether or not the interference is proportionate to the legitimate aim pursued.[36] Until the HRA, the principle of proportionality was only known in UK law via the medium of EC law and it still does not constitute a ground for non-HRA judicial review. Given the relative lack of experience of domestic courts with the concept, when it was first applied under the HRA, slight divergences in approach were evident. For example, in *Kebilene*,[37] when determining whether an interference with the presumption of innocence protected by Article 6(2) was justified, Lord Hope referred to striking a fair balance between the general interest of the community and the fundamental rights of the individual. However, in *R v A*[38] Lord Steyn set out the essence of the test as whether the means used to impair a right or freedom were no more than was necessary to accomplish the objective,[39] a slightly more difficult test to meet; meanwhile, Lord Hope continued to refer to striking a fair balance between the general interest of the community and the protection of the individual.[40]

Shortly after, in *Daly*,[41] the House of Lords unanimously addressed the meaning of proportionality in an attempt to clarify confusion which had arisen from judgments of the Court of Appeal.[42] Lord Steyn, with whom the others agreed, held that there was

a material difference between the *Wednesbury* and *Smith* grounds of review and the approach of proportionality applicable in respect of review where Convention rights are at stake.[43]

---

[35] *Ibid*, at [59] per Lord Hope.
[36] On the 'legitimate aim' test, see R Gordon, 'Legitimate Aim: A Dimly Lit Road', [2002] *EHRLR* 421.
[37] *R v Director of Public Prosecutions, ex p Kebilene* [1999] 3 WLR 972.
[38] *R v A* [2001] UKHL 25, [2002] 1 AC 45.
[39] *Ibid*, at [38].
[40] *Ibid*, at [91]. See also *Brown v Stott (Procurator Fiscal, Dunfermline)* [2001] 1 AC 681 and *McIntosh v Lord Advocate* [2001] 1 AC 1078.
[41] *R v Secretary of State for the Home Department, ex p Daly* [2001] UKHL 26, [2001] 2 AC 532.
[42] The cases leading to the confusion were *R (Mahmood) v Secretary of State for the Home Department* [2001] 1 WLR 840; *R v Secretary of State for the Home Department, ex p Isiko* [2001] 1 FLR 930; and *R v Secretary of State for the Home Department, ex p Samaroo*, Administrative Court, 20 December 2000.
[43] *Ibid*, at [26].

Adopting a recent decision of the Privy Council concerning the Constitution of Antigua and Barbuda,[44] his Lordship set out the contours of the principle of proportionality. In determining whether a limitation (by act, rule or decision) is arbitrary or excessive, the court should ask itself whether:

> (i) the legislative objective is sufficiently important to justify limiting a fundamental right;
> (ii) the measures designed to meet the legislative objective are rationally connected to it; and
> (iii) the means used to impair the right or freedom are no more than is necessary to accomplish the objective.[45]

Although in a few cases following *Daly* reference was still made to the fair balance test,[46] the principles outlined by Lord Steyn soon took hold. For example, in *Shayler*[47] Lord Bingham held that the acid test was whether, in all the circumstances, the interference with the individual's Convention right prescribed by national law was greater than was required to meet the legitimate object which the state sought to achieve.[48] Lord Hope essentially adopted the test outlined in *Daly* with slight modifications:

> The first is whether the objective which is sought to be achieved—the pressing social need—is sufficiently important to justify limiting the fundamental right. The second is whether the means chosen to limit that right are rational, fair and not arbitrary. The third is whether the means used impair the right as minimally as is reasonably possible.[49]

4.2 The Shift from *Wednesbury*

Clearly the criteria outlined by Lord Steyn in *Daly*[50] are more precise and more sophisticated than the traditional grounds of judicial review, and in his speech his Lordship suggested three concrete differences:

> First, the doctrine of proportionality may require the reviewing court to assess the balance which the decision maker has struck, not merely whether it is within the range of rational or reasonable decisions. Secondly, the proportionality test may go further than the traditional grounds of review inasmuch as it may require attention to be directed to the relative weight accorded to interests and considerations. Thirdly, even the heightened scrutiny test developed in . . . *Smith* . . . is not necessarily appropriate to the protection of human rights.[51]

---

[44] *De Freitas v Permanent Secretary of Ministry of Agriculture, Fisheries, Lands and Housing* [1999] 1 AC 69.

[45] *Ibid*, at [27].

[46] See, eg *R v Lambert* [2001] UKHL 37, [2002] 2 AC 545.

[47] Above n 3.

[48] *Ibid*, at [26]. Lords Hobhouse and Scott agreed.

[49] *Ibid*, at [61] and [111] per Lord Hutton. See also Lord Hope's comments in Rottman, above n 3 at [37]. It is clear that questions of proportionality have to be answered by reference to the time the events took place. If primary legislation is involved, it is not correct to merely examine the situation at the time the Act in question was passed. See *Wilson v Secretary of State for Trade and Industry* [2003] UKHL 40, [2003] 3 WLR 568 at [144] per Lord Hobhouse.

[50] Above n 41. On the meaning of proportionality in Convention law, see generally P Sales and B Hooper, 'Proportionality and the Form of Law' (2003) 119 *LQR* 426; D Feldman, 'Proportionality and the Human Rights Act 1998' in E Ellis (ed), *The Principle of Proportionality in the Laws of Europe* (Oxford, Hart Publishing, 1999).

[51] *Daly*, above n 41, at [27].

It is clear that in any application for judicial review alleging a violation of a convention right the court will now conduct a much more rigorous and intrusive review than was once sought to be permissible.[52] It is no longer enough to assert that the decision that was taken was a reasonable one.

A close and penetrating examination of the factual justification for the restriction is needed if the fundamental rights enshrined in the Convention are to remain practical and effective for everyone who wishes to exercise them.[53]

Merits Review?

In *Daly*,[54] noting that the differences in approach between traditional grounds of review and the proportionality approach may yield different results, Lord Steyn held that it was important that cases involving Convention rights must be analysed in the correct way. However, he was careful to point out that this did not mean that there had been a shift to merits review:

[T]he respective roles of judges and administrators are fundamentally distinct and will remain so. To this extent the general tenor of the observations in *Mahmood* . . . are correct. And Laws LJ rightly emphasised in *Mahmood* . . . 'that the intensity of review in a public law case will depend on the subject matter in hand'. That is so even in cases involving Convention rights. In law, context is everything.[55]

Despite the conviction with which it was made, Lord Steyn's claim warrants closer scrutiny.

As discussed in the preceding paragraphs, the process of determining whether or not a public authority has acted incompatibly with Convention rights can undoubtedly involve a far more intense form of review than *Wednesbury* or 'anxious scrutiny'. The role of a primary decision maker is to discover the facts, apply the law to those facts and thereby make a decision taking into account any relevant policy considerations and exercising judgment and discretion. If the individual to whom the decision applies complains that the decision is incompatible with a Convention right, the role of the court is to determine whether or not the Convention right was correctly interpreted and applied, and arguably not to substitute its own judgment for that of the primary decision maker. However, often in order to determine whether or not an act is compatible with a Convention right, a court will have to examine all the facts and policy arguments before the primary decision maker, accord a weighting to each, then engage in a balancing exercise to determine whether or not the interference is necessary in a democratic society in pursuit of a specified aim. Where a Convention right

---

[52] *Shayler*, above n 3, at [33] per Lord Bingham and [75] per Lord Hope.
[53] *Ibid*, at [61], per Lord Hope. See also Lord Hutton's comments at [111] and Lord Hope's comments in Rottman, above n 3, at [37]. See further T Hickman, 'The Reasonableness Principle: Reassessing its Place in the Public Sphere' (2004) 63 *CLJ* 166; J Jowell, 'Beyond the Rule of Law: Towards Constitutional Judicial Review' [2000] *PL* 671; P Craig, 'The Courts, the Human Rights Act and Judicial Review' (2001) 117 *LQR* 589; M Elliott, 'The Human Rights Act 1998 and the Standard of Substantive Review' [2001] *CLJ* 301; A Le Sueur, 'The rise and ruin of unreasonableness', (2005) 10 *JR* 32.
[54] Above n 41.
[55] *Ibid*, at [28].

stands at the heart of a claimant's case, a court performing this role will look very much like it is substituting its judgment for that of the primary decision maker—in effect, engaging in merits review.

It is well known that when exercising their powers of judicial review, courts are extremely reluctant to be seen to be engaging in merits review.

> On judicial review the court does not operate as a court of appeal, analysing the evidence and reaching its own conclusion as to the correct decision.[56]

However, it is clear that when determining whether or not an act is incompatible with Convention rights, merits review is entirely possible, albeit under another name. As the vast majority of cases brought under the HRA have reached the courts via the judicial review route, judges have been faced with a dilemma. Are they exercising judicial review and therefore unable to essentially retake the decision? Or are they exercising a new power—the power to ensure that public authorities act compatibly with certain human rights—which entitles them to effectively substitute their own decision free from the shackles of judicial review?[57] It is possible that it was in order to avoid engaging in full merits review that the practice of deference to the legislature, executive and primary decision maker has arisen. This forms the subject of the following section.

---

5. Deference

5.1 Definition

Prior to the HRA coming into force there was much discussion about what role the margin of appreciation would play in the domestic context.[58] Most commentators accepted that the doctrine of the margin of appreciation does not apply when a national court is considering the HRA. However, it was generally recommended that a similar doctrine should be recognised by national courts.[59] This recommendation was soon reflected in the case law. In *Kebilene*[60] Lord Hope held that the doctrine of margin of appreciation, exercised by the European Court of Human Rights, was not available to the national courts when they were considering Convention issues. However, his Lordship also stated that in this area

---

[56] *Champion v Chief Constable of the Gwent Constabulary* [1990] 1 WLR 1.
[57] See further I Leigh, 'Taking Rights Proportionately: Judicial Review, the Human Rights Act and Strasbourg', [2002] *PL* 265.
[58] See, eg D Pannick, 'Principles of Interpretation of Convention Rights under the Human Rights Act and the Discretionary Area of Judgment', [1998] *PL* 545; R Singh, M Hunt and M Demetriou, 'Current Topic: Is there a Role for the "Margin of Appreciation" in National Law after the Human Rights Act?' [1999] *EHRLR* 15.
[59] Pannick, *ibid*, 545, 549.
[60] Above n 37.

difficult choices may have to be made by the executive or the legislature between the rights of the individual and the needs of society. In some circumstances it will be appropriate for the courts to recognise that there is an area of judgment within which the judiciary will defer, on democratic grounds, to the considered opinion of the elected body or the person whose act or decision is said to be incompatible with the Convention.

The courts rarely define what exactly is meant by deference—apart from indicating that it involves affording 'weight' to the decisions of the legislature or executive.[61] In practice, deference usually only arises in the context of a decision on proportionality,[62] and it is important not to confuse deference when making a proportionality judgment with determining the limits of what is 'possible' under section 3 of the HRA.[63] Applying the test as set out in *Daly*,[64] in many instances it will not be obvious that an act is disproportionate and incompatible with Convention rights. By deferring, a court is not abdicating its role under the HRA but recognising, for one reason or another, the special competence of the primary decision maker by giving its view additional weight when determining whether or not the means used to impair a right or freedom are no more than is necessary to accomplish the objective.

In enacting legislation and reaching decisions Parliament and ministers must give due weight to fundamental rights and freedoms. For their part, when carrying out their assigned task the courts will accord to Parliament and ministers, as the primary decision-makers, an appropriate degree of latitude. The latitude will vary according to the subject matter under consideration, the importance of the human right in question, and the extent of the encroachment upon that right. The courts will intervene only when it is apparent that, in balancing the various considerations involved, the primary-decision maker must have given insufficient weight to the human rights factor.[65]

However, as will become clear in the following paragraphs, the practice is fraught with anomalies and inconsistencies, and still awaits some form of clarification.

5.2 Reasons to Defer

Many answers have been given by the courts to the question of why deference should be afforded. However, most reduce to a simple belief in the appropriate allocation of decision making power between the courts, legislature and executive.

---

[61] See *Brown*, above n 40, per Lord Bingham and *R v A*, above n 38 at [37] per Lord Steyn.

[62] Although it can also arise when a court is determining the scope of a Convention right. For example, in *R v Secretary of State for the Environment, Transport and the Regions, ex p Alconbury Developments Ltd* [2001] UKHL 23, [2001] 2 WLR 1389 deference to the executive was apparent in their Lordships' conclusion that a breach by the executive of the guarantee of independence and impartiality in Art 6(1) could be overcome by the existence of a sufficient opportunity for appeal or review. See also *R v Director of Public Prosecutions, ex p Pretty* [2001] UKHL 61, [2001] 3 WLR 1598. See further S Atrill, 'Keeping the Executive in the Picture: a Reply to Professor Leigh' [2003] *PL* 41; Leigh, 'Taking Rights Proportionately', above n 57; Craig, above n 53.

[63] See further A Young, 'Ghaidan v Godin-Mendoza: Avoiding the Deference Trap' [2005] *PL* 23.

[64] Above n 41.

[65] *A v Secretary of State for the Home Department* [2004] UKHL 56, [2005] 2 AC 68 at [80] per Lord Nicholls. On deference, see generally Lord Steyn, 'Deference: a Tangled Story' [2005] *PL* 346.

The courts are the independent branch of government and the legislature and executive are, directly and indirectly respectively, the elected branches of government. Independence makes the courts more suited to deciding some kinds of questions and being elected makes the legislature or executive more suited to deciding others. The allocation of these decision-making responsibilities is based upon recognised principles. The principle that the independence of the courts is necessary for a proper decision of disputed legal rights or claims of violation of human rights is a legal principle. It is reflected in Art.6 of the Convention. On the other hand, the principle that majority approval is necessary for a proper decision on policy or allocation of resources is also a legal principle. Likewise, when a court decides that a decision is within the proper competence of the legislature or executive, it is not showing deference. It is deciding the law.[66]

The legislature in particular is seen as the body charged with the primary responsibility for deciding whether the means chosen to deal with a social problem are both necessary and appropriate.

Assessment of the advantages and disadvantages of the various legislative alternatives is primarily a matter for Parliament. The possible existence of alternative solutions does not in itself render the contested legislation unjustified . . . The court will reach a different conclusion from the legislature only when it is apparent that the legislature has attached insufficient importance to a person's Convention rights.[67]

Similarly it has been noted that judicial recognition and assertion of the human rights defined in the convention is not a substitute for the processes of democratic government but a complement to them.

While a national court does not accord the margin of appreciation recognised by the European Court as a supra-national court, it will give weight to the decisions of a representative legislature and a democratic government within the discretionary area of judgment accorded to those bodies.[68]

5.3 Reasons Not to Defer

Whilst the arguments in favour of deference appear to be frequently raised, it is important not to overlook the fact that judicial arguments have also been made against the practice and that such statements are becoming increasingly common, perhaps signalling a change in the judicial approach. For example, in *R v A*,[69] whilst noting that weight should be given to the decision of Parliament, Lord Steyn also stated that when the question arose whether in a criminal statute Parliament had adopted a legislative scheme which made an excessive inroad into the right to a fair

---

[66] *R (on the application of Prolife Alliance) v British Broadcasting Corporation* [2003] UKHL 23, [2004] 1 AC 185 at [76] per Lord Hoffmann. See also *Alconbury Developments*, above n 62, at [48]–[49], [60], [68]–[72], [139]–[144] and [159]; Mahmood, above n 42, at [33] per Laws LJ and [38] per Lord Phillips MR; Isiko, above n 42; *R (on the application of Samaroo) v Secretary of State for the Home Department* [2001] EWCA Civ 1139 at [35].
[67] *Wilson*, above n 49, at [70] per Lord Nicholls.
[68] *Brown*, above n 40, per Lord Bingham. See also the speech of Lord Steyn. See also *R v A*, above n 38, at [58] per Lord Hope; *Marcic v Thames Water Utilities Ltd* [2003] UKHL 66, [2004] 2 AC 42 at [71] per Lord Hoffmann.
[69] Above n 38.

trial 'the court is qualified to make its own judgment and must do so.'[70] Similarly, in *Wilson*[71] Lord Hope commented that it did not follow from recognition that there was an area of judgment within which the judiciary would defer to the elected body on democratic grounds that the court was absolutely disabled from forming its own view as to whether or not the legislation was compatible. 'That question is ultimately for the court not for Parliament, as Parliament itself has enacted.'[72]

The most strident assertion of the role of the judiciary under the HRA was contained in *A v Secretary of State for the Home Department*.[73] The appellants had been certified under section 21 of the Anti-terrorism Crime and Security Act 2001 and detained under section 23 of that Act. All were foreign nationals. None had been the subject of a criminal charge and in none of their cases was a criminal trial in prospect. It was for their Lordships to determine whether there was a public emergency threatening the life of the nation within the meaning of Article 15. And, if there was, whether the measures taken went beyond what was strictly required by the exigencies of the situation.

Answering the second question, Lord Bingham did not accept the distinction drawn by the Attorney General between democratic institutions and the courts.

> [T]he function of independent judges charged to interpret and apply the law is universally recognised as a cardinal feature of the modern democratic state, a cornerstone of the rule of law itself. The Attorney-General is fully entitled to insist on the proper limits of judicial authority, but he is wrong to stigmatise judicial decision-making as in some way undemocratic. It is particularly inappropriate in a case such as the present in which Parliament has expressly legislated in s.6 of the 1998 Act to render unlawful any act of a public authority, including a court, incompatible with a Convention right, has required courts (in s.2) to take account of relevant Strasbourg jurisprudence, has (in s.3) required courts, so far as possible, to give effect to Convention rights and has conferred a right of appeal on derogation issues. The effect is not, of course, to override the sovereign legislative authority of the Queen in Parliament, since if primary legislation is declared to be incompatible the validity of the legislation is unaffected (s.4(6)) and the remedy lies with the appropriate minister (s.10), who is answerable to Parliament. The 1998 Act gives the courts a very specific, wholly democratic, mandate.'[74]

5.4 When is Deference Required?

As the above paragraphs indicate, there are a number of conflicting judicial opinions on the subject of deference under the HRA. The question of whether or not deference should be afforded has been answered in a number of different ways. However,

---

[70] *Ibid*, at [37].
[71] Above n 49.
[72] *Ibid*, at [116].
[73] Above n 65.
[74] *Ibid*, at [42]. See also the comments of Lord Nicholls at [80], Lord Hope at [114], [116] and [131], Lord Rodger at [176], Lord Scott at [145] and [154], Lord Walker at [192 and [196], and Baroness Hale at [226]. See also *International Transport Roth GmbH v Secretary of State for the Home Department* [2002] EWCA Civ 158, [2002] 3 WLR 344 at [27], [29] and [54] per Simon Brown LJ and [139] per Jonathan Parker LJ. See further T Hickman, 'above n 53; A Tomkins, 'Readings of A v Secretary of State for the Home Department' [2005] *PL* 259; and M Arden, 'Human Rights in the Age of Terrorism' (2005) 121 *LQR* 604.

there are two main indicators: first, the nature of the Convention right or rights at issue; and secondly, the subject matter of the legislation or act.

> The latitude will vary according to the subject matter under consideration, the importance of the human right in question, and the extent of the encroachment upon that right. The courts will intervene only when it is apparent that, in balancing the various considerations involved, the primary decision-maker must have given insufficient weight to the human rights factor.[75]

With respect to the nature of the convention, it has been held that deference should be afforded where a Convention right is qualified rather than absolute, and not of such high constitutional importance that the court is especially well placed to assess the need for protection.[76] For example, in *R v A*[77] Lord Steyn held that when a question arose whether, in the criminal statute in question, Parliament adopted a leg-islative scheme which made an excessive inroad into the right to a fair trial, the court was qualified to make its own judgment and must do so.[78] Given the fundamental nature of the right to life and the importance with which it is regarded, deference is rarely shown by the courts to primary decision makers in Article 2 cases. In *Re A*[79] Ward LJ commented that deciding matters of disputed life and death was 'surely and pre-eminently a matter for a court of law to judge. That is what courts are here for.'[80] Similarly, deference is rarely mentioned in the context of Article 5, reflecting the importance with which the right is regarded, its narrow construction and the fact that many of its protections are absolute.[81] However, deference is not uncommon when adjudicating on the right to respect for private life. Given the fact that the right is subject to exceptions, the subject matter raised by many private life claims and the fact that UK courts are not used to dealing with such a right at common law, this is not surprising.[82] The relative importance with which Convention rights are regarded by the courts is discussed more fully in Part II of this book.

In relation to the subject matter, it has been held that it is easier for deference to be recognised where the issues involve questions of social or economic policy,[83] or in fact, any question of policy.

---

[75] *A v Secretary of State*, above n 65, at [80] per Lord Nicholls. See also the observations of Laws LJ in *International Transport Roth*, ibid, at [83]–[87].

[76] *Kebilene*, above n 37 per Lord Hope.

[77] Above n 38.

[78] *Ibid*, at [37].

[79] *Re A (Children) (Conjoined Twins: Surgical Separation)* [2001] Fam 147.

[80] See also the comments of Dame Butler-Sloss in *NHS Trust A v Mrs M* [2001] 2 WLR 942 at [38] and *NHS Trust v P*, Family Division, 19 December 2000; *R (on the application of Wilkinson) v The Responsible Medical Officer Broadmoor Hospital* [2001] EWCA Civ 1545, [2002] 1 WLR 419; *R (on the application of H) v Ashworth Hospital Authority* [2001] EWHC (Admin) 872, [2002] 1 FCR 206. A similar approach has been taken to Art 3. See, eg *X v Secretary of State for the Home Department* [2001] 1 WLR 740 and *R (on the application of T) v Secretary of State for the Home Department* [2003] EWCA Civ 1285 at [19].

[81] See, eg *R v Secretary of State for the Home Department, ex p Noorkoiv* [2002] EWCA Civ 770, [2002] 1 WLR 3284 at [44].

[82] See, eg *Bellinger v Bellinger* [2003] UKHL 21, [2003] 2 AC 467 at [37] per Lord Nicholls and S, above n 1.

[83] *Kebilene*, above n 37 per Lord Hope; *Wilson*, above n 49, at [70] per Lord Nicholls; *Ghaidan v Godin-Mendoza* [2004] UKHL 30, [2004] 2 AC 557 at [19] per Lord Nicholls.

[T]he democratic powers in the State have a special responsibility. Policy making is their territory, and not that of the judges. Hence the margin of discretionary judgment accorded to the government policy-maker on democratic grounds. The courts are also likely to recognise that government is better equipped than the court to judge how needful the policy is to achieve the aim in view. So where policy is the subject-matter in hand, principle and practicality alike militate in favour of an approach in which the court's role is closer to review than appeal: where a degree of deference does not more than respect the balance to be struck between the claims of democratic power and the claims of individual rights.[84]

Examples of policy-making have included the payment of welfare benefits,[85] housing matters[86] and the protection of consumers.[87]

It has also been held that political judgments call for some deference on the part of the court.

The more purely political (in a broad or narrow sense) a question is, the more appropriate it will be for political resolution and the less likely it is to be an appropriate matter for judicial decision— and therefore the smaller the potential role of the court. It is the function of political and not judicial bodies to resolve political questions. Conversely, the greater the legal content of any issue, the greater the potential role of the court, because under our constitution and subject to the sovereign power of Parliament it is the function of the courts and not of political bodies to resolve legal questions.[88]

An example of a political matter was the judgment of the Secretary of State in *A v Secretary of State*[89] that there was a public emergency threatening the life of the nation within the meaning of Article 15 of the ECHR.

5.5 Problems with Deference

Deferring too readily to executive or legislative judgment can lead to inconsistency in decision-making, the categorisation of some groups as less deserving of the protection of the HRA, violation of Article 13 of the ECHR[90] and the abdication of judicial responsibility under the HRA. As Lord Steyn has noted extra-judicially,

[i]f the judges of today teach a new generation of lawyers, and judges, that complaisance by the judiciary to the view of the legislature and the executive in policy areas is the best way forward, one of the pillars of our democracy will have been weakened.[91]

---

[84] *Huang v Secretary of State for the Home Department* [2005] EWCA Civ 105, [2005] 3 All ER 435 at [53] per Laws LJ.
[85] *R (Hooper) v Secretary of State for Work and Pensions* [2005] UKHL 29, [2005] 1 WLR 1681.
[86] *Poplar Housing and Regeneration Community Association v Donoghue* [2001] EWCA Civ 595, [2001] QB 48.
[87] *Wilson*, above n 49.
[88] *A v Secretary of State*, above n 65 at [29] per Lord Bingham.
[89] *Ibid.*
[90] See further Leigh, above n 57.
[91] 'Deference: a Tangled Story' [2005] *PL* 346. For further critique of the practice of deference see KD Ewing, 'The Futility of the Human Rights Act' [2004] *PL* 829; R Clayton, 'Judicial Deference and "Democratic Dialogue": the Legitimacy of Judicial Intervention under the Human Rights Act 1998' [2004] *PL* 33; J Jowell, 'Judicial Deference: Servility, Civility or Institutional Capacity?' [2003] *PL* 592; Leigh, above n 57; RA Edwards, 'Judicial Deference under the Human Rights Act' [2002] 65 *MLR* 859.

It is possible to point to some judgments under the HRA where the court has simply taken the executive's justification for an interference without any supporting proof. For example, in *Samaroo*[92] the Court of Appeal held that it was not incumbent on the Secretary of State to prove that the withholding of a deportation order in any particular case would seriously undermine his policy of deterring crime and disorder.

> That would be to ask the impossible. Proof is not required. The subject matter is such that proof is usually impossible. What is required is that the Secretary of State justify a derogation from a Convention right, and that the justification be 'convincingly established'.[93]

That is not to say that some deference is never appropriate, but too much deference could result in a return to the pre-HRA position where the only argument a claimant would have to challenge an interference with human rights is *Wednesbury* unreasonableness. As Lord Bingham pointed out in *A v Secretary of State*,[94] the Convention regime for the international protection of human rights requires national authorities, including national courts, to exercise their authority to afford effective protection,[95] and domestic courts must themselves form a judgment as to whether a Convention right has been breached.[96] Similarly Lord Hope observed that the margin of appreciation afforded by the European Court of Human Rights could not be equated to the role of the domestic courts.

> [T]he fact that the European Court will accord a large margin of appreciation to the contracting states on the question whether the measures taken to interfere with the right to liberty do not exceed those strictly required by the exigencies of the situation cannot be taken as the last word on the matter so far as the domestic courts are concerned. Final responsibility for determining whether they do exceed these limits must lie with the courts, if the test which Art.15(1) lays down is to be applied within the domestic system with all the rigour that its wording indicates.[97]

Problems resulting from the judiciary deferring too readily have already arisen in the House of Lords and the Court of Appeal. For example, the *Prolife*[98] appeal in the House of Lords concerned the rejection of the Prolife Alliance's party election broadcast by broadcasters on the ground that it offended good taste, decency and public feeling. At the outset it is important to note that a majority, Lords Nicholls, Hoffmann and Millett, did not apply Article 10(2) as it was held that there was no right to use a television channel and therefore Article 10(1) was not engaged. What had to be established was that access to public media had been denied on discriminatory, arbitrary or unreasonable grounds. However, deference also entered into the judgments on these grounds.

---

[92] Above n 66.
[93] *Ibid*, at [39]. See also *R (on the application of Farrakhan) v Secretary of State for the Home Department* [2002] EWCA Civ 606, [2002] QB 1391.
[94] Above n 65.
[95] *Ibid*, at [40].
[96] *Ibid.*
[97] *Ibid*, at [114]. See also [116] and [131], Lord Rodger at [176], Lord Scott at [145] and [154], Lord Walker at [192] and [196], and Baroness Hale at [226].
[98] Above n 66.

A majority, Lords Nicholls, Hoffmann, Millett and Walker, afforded considerable deference to Parliament as it had established the taste and decency requirement as part of the Broadcasting Act 1990. Lords Hoffmann and Walker also afforded deference to the broadcasters in their decision that the taste and decency requirements had not been met in this instance. But it was the deference to Parliament which was most worrying. Lord Nicholls held that Parliament had decided where the balance (between freedom of political speech and the protection of the public from being unduly distressed in their own homes) should be held.

> The latter interest prevails over the former to the extent that the offensive material ban applies without distinction to all television programmes, including party broadcasts. In the absence of a successful claim that the offensive material restriction is not compatible with the Convention rights of ProLife Alliance, it is not for the courts to find that broadcasters acted unlawfully when they did no more than give effect to the statutory and other obligations binding on them. Even in such a case the effect of s.6(2) of the Human Rights Act 1998 would have to be considered.[99]

Lord Nicholls's conclusion was despite the fact that considerable discretion was held by the broadcasters as to the application of the legislation in a particular case. This was appreciated by Lords Hoffmann and Walker, who afforded deference to Parliament and the broadcasters.[100] Lord Walker noted that the court's task was not to substitute its own view for that of the broadcasters, but to review their decision with an intensity appropriate to all the circumstances of the case.[101]

This line of reasoning was continued in *Qazi*,[102] although the facts were slightly different as it could be said that the legislation did not confer any discretion on the primary decision maker or the court. At the heart of the case was the question of whether, having regard to the provisions of Article 8(1), it was lawful for a public authority to recover possession from a former tenant by a procedure which led to possession being granted automatically, or whether the court must always be given an opportunity to consider whether the making of an order for possession would be proportionate.[103] Mr Qazi had stayed on in the house after his former wife, a joint tenant, had served a notice to quit on the landlord, thereby terminating the tenancy.

Lord Hope stated that the joint tenancy had been brought to an end by the service of a tenant's notice to quit and the position in domestic law was that, in these circumstances, the whole of the joint tenancy was terminated. Therefore, the county court had no discretion as to whether or not it should grant an order for possession, and the making of an order for possession followed automatically.[104] His Lordship's understanding of European jurisprudence led him to the conclusion that Article 8(2) was met where the law afforded an unqualified right to possession on proof that the tenancy had been terminated. He saw such interference with the right to respect for home which came from the application of the law which enabled the public authority

---

[99] *Ibid*, at [16].
[100] *Ibid*, Lord Hoffmann at [77] and [80]; Lord Walker at [137] and [139].
[101] *Ibid*, at [139]. For further comment on this case, see J Rowbottom, 'Article 10 and Election Broadcasts' (2003) 119 *LQR* 553; and E. Barendt, 'Free Speech and Abortion' [2003] *PL* 580.
[102] *Harrow LBC v Qazi* [2003] UKHL 43, [2004] AC 983.
[103] *Ibid*, at [36] per Lord Hope.
[104] *Ibid*, at [74].

landlord to exercise its unqualified right to recover possession, with a view to making the premises available for letting to others, as not violating the essence of the right to respect for the home.[105]

Similarly Lord Millett held that whilst Article 8(2) might call for a balance to be struck, no such balancing exercise need be conducted where the outcome was a forgone conclusion.[106] In his view, the fact that a person could not be evicted without a court order did not mean that the court, as a public authority, was bound in each case to consider whether an order for possession would be disproportionate.[107]

> In most cases the statutory scheme established by Parliament will provide the objective justification for the council's decision to seek possession, which need not be demonstrated on a case by case basis.[108]

Lord Scott, having concluded that there was no interference with Article 8(1), did not discuss Article 8(2) but agreed with Lords Hope and Millett that the case should not be remitted to the County Court. Both Lords Bingham and Steyn dissented on this point, holding that the domestic law procedures should be subjected to scrutiny for conformity with the Article 8(2) standards and the issue of justification remitted to the County Court. Therefore, whilst a majority determined that the appeal should be dismissed, there was no majority decision on this point.[109]

The conclusion of Lords Hope and Millett that there was no need to consider Article 8(2) on a case-by-case basis as the balance has already been struck by the legislature is problematic. Although Mr Qazi's application to the European Court of Human Rights was declared inadmissible, in *Price*[110] the Court of Appeal held that this did not implicitly endorse the reasoning of the House of Lords.[111] Furthermore, the Court of Appeal held that the conclusion in *Qazi* was incompatible with the judgment of the European Court of Human Rights in *Connors v United Kingdom*.[112]

> The decision in *Connors* is unquestionably incompatible with the proposition that the exercise by a public authority of an unqualified proprietary right under domestic law to repossess its land will never constitute an interference with the occupier's right to respect for his home, or will always be justified under Article 8(2). To that extent *Connors* is incompatible with *Qazi*.[113]

However, despite this conclusion the Court of Appeal held that it was bound to follow *Qazi*, although it also stated that it would give permission, if sought and not successfully opposed, to appeal to the House of Lords.[114]

---

[105] *Ibid*, at [83].
[106] *Ibid*, at [103].
[107] *Ibid*, at [108].
[108] *Ibid*, at [109]. See also the comments of Lord Bingham in *Porter v Magill* [2001] UKHL 67, [2002] 2 WLR 37 [37] and Lord Clyde at [90].
[109] For a critique of the judgment, see I Loveland, 'The Impact of the Human Rights Act on Security of Tenure in Public Housing' [2004] *PL* 594.
[110] *Price v Leeds City Council* [2005] EWCA Civ 289, [2005] 1 WLR 1825.
[111] *Ibid*, at [15].
[112] 27 May 2004.
[113] *Ibid*, at [26].
[114] *Ibid*, at [33]. But see *Kay v London Borough of Lambeth* [2004] EWCA Civ 926, [2005] QB 352, where the Court of Appeal held that *Qazi* was compatible with *Connors*.

Problems with deference have also arisen in the Court of Appeal. In *Edore*,[115] an appeal against deportation based on the right to respect for family life, the court held that the concept of deference meant that the Secretary of State could fairly reach one of two opposite conclusions, one in favour of a claimant the other in favour of his removal.

> Of neither could it be said that the balance had been struck unfairly. In such circumstances, the mere fact that an alternative but favourable decision could reasonably have been reached will not lead to the conclusion that the decision maker has acted in breach of the claimant's human rights. Such a breach will only occur where the decision is outwith the range of reasonable responses to the question as to where a fair balance lies between the conflicting interests. Once it is accepted that the balance could be struck fairly either way, the Secretary of State cannot be regarded as having infringed the claimant's art 8 rights by concluding that he should be removed.[116]

Although this judgment led to considerable confusion in the lower courts, it is important to note that it was corrected almost two years later. In *Huang*[117] the court set out the proper approach to be taken by an adjudicator in an appeal where he is called upon to determine whether the Secretary of State's decision to remove the appellant from the United Kingdom, or refuse him leave to enter, is disproportionate, and therefore unlawful, interference with the appellant's right to respect for family life. The Court concluded that, pursuant to section 65 and paragraph 21 of Schedule 4 to the Immigration and Asylum Act 1999, which gives a right of appeal where it is alleged that there is a breach of human rights, the adjudicator must decide in substance whether the action appealed against involves a violation of the appellant's Convention rights.

> Any other approach would in our judgment perpetrate an abdication of his duty and ours, as public authorities, to vindicate and uphold Convention rights.[118]

In finding as such, the court expressly disapproved of the approach arrived at in *Edore*.[119]

With respect to the margin of discretion or discretionary area of judgment to be applied by the adjudicator, the Court of Appeal held that this was not relevant as the adjudicator was not required to pass upon any aspect of government policy.

> The principle of law by which respect for the democracy requires a margin of discretion to be accorded to the democratic decision maker primarily applies where the subject of the decision is the formation of policy.[120]

---

[115] *Edore v Secretary of State for the Home Department* [2003] EWCA Civ 716, [2003] 1 WLR 2979.
[116] *Ibid*, at [14] quoting from *R (on the application of Ala) v Secretary of State for the Home Department* [2003] EWHC 521 at [44].
[117] Above n 84.
[118] *Ibid*, at [26] in reliance upon *R (Razgar) v Secretary of State for the Home Department* [2004] UKHL 27, [2004] 2 AC 368.
[119] *Ibid*, at [45].
[120] *Ibid*, at [52].

In the present case it held that the task of the adjudicator was to see whether an exceptional case had been made out such that the requirement of proportionality required a departure from the relevant Rule in the particular circumstances.[121]

> In such a case the adjudicator is not ignoring or overriding the Rules. On the contrary it is a signal feature of his task that he is bound to respect the balance between public interest and private right struck by the Rules with Parliament's approval. That is why he is only entitled on Article 8 grounds to favour an appellant outside the Rules where the case is truly exceptional . . . The adjudicator's decision of the question whether the case is truly exceptional is entirely his own. He does defer to the Rules; for this approach recognises that the balance struck by the Rules will generally dispose of proportionality issues arising under Article 8; but they are not exhaustive of all cases. There will be a residue of truly exceptional instances.[122]

6. Deference in Practice

As outlined above, it appears the willingness of a court to defer to the judgment of the primary decision maker, whether that be the legislature, executive or other public authority, is closely linked to the Convention right or rights at issue and the subject matter concerned. To gain further insight into the practice of deference, it is very useful to consider the case law divided by reference to subject matter, although it is important to note that it is the combination of the Convention right and the subject matter which results in the level of deference shown. This study forms the remainder of this chapter.

6.1 Criminal Justice

6.1.1 Prevention of Terrorism

In *Kebilene*[123] the House of Lords considered section 16A of the Prevention of Terrorism (Temporary Provisions) Act 1989, which reversed the legal burden of proof and was therefore alleged to be incompatible with Article 6(2). Although agreeing with the majority that the decision of the Director of Public Prosecutions to consent to the prosecution was not amenable to judicial review, Lord Hope alone went on to consider the compatibility of the provision with Article 6(2). His Lordship commented that it was necessary to bear in mind the jurisprudence of the European Court which recognised that due account should be taken of the special nature of terrorist crime and the threat which it posed to a democratic society.[124] In striking a fair balance between the demands of the general interest of the community and the

---

[121] *Ibid*, at [56].
[122] *Ibid*, at [60]. Samaroo, above n 66, was distinguished as a policy case—see [61].
[123] Above n 37.
[124] In reliance upon *Murray v United Kingdom* (1994) 19 EHRR 193.

protection of the fundamental rights of the individual, his Lordship also took into account

> the nature of the threat which terrorism poses to a free and democratic society. It seeks to achieve its ends by violence and intimidation. It is often indiscriminate in its effects, and sophisticated methods are used to avoid detection both before and after the event. Society has a strong interest in preventing acts of terrorism before they are perpetrated—to spare the lives of innocent people and to avoid the massive damage and dislocation to ordinary life which may follow from explosions which destroy or damage property. Section 16A is designed to achieve that end.

However, his Lordship reached no final conclusion, holding that the problem of compatibility would have to await a decision after trial.

6.1.2 Drug Trafficking

In *McIntosh*[125] the Privy Council considered the compatibility with Article 6(2) of section 3(2) of the Proceeds of Crime (Scotland) Act 1995, which enabled a court making a confiscation order to make assumptions that certain property was the proceeds of drug trafficking. Deference to the legislature did not form a large part of the judgment given, although Lord Bingham did note that the statutory scheme contained in the 1995 Act was one approved by a democratically elected Parliament and should not be readily rejected.[126] A completely different issue arose in *Quayle*[127] where, in response to a defence of medical necessity, the Court of Appeal did not feel justified to express a view on the compatibility with Article 8 of legislation governing the cultivation, production, importation and possession of cannabis.

> [I]n certain matters of social, medical and legislative policy, the elected government of the day and Parliament are entitled to form overall policy views about what is best not just for particular individuals, but for the country as a whole, in relation to which the courts should be cautious before disagreeing.[128]

6.1.3 Road Traffic Offences

In *Brown*[129] the Privy Council considered the compatibility of section 172(2)(a) of the Road Traffic Act 1988 with the right not to incriminate oneself, as protected by Articles 6(1) and 6(2). At this trial for driving a car after consuming excessive alcohol, the prosecutor sought to rely on the claimant's admission that she was driving the car which was obtained compulsorily under this section. Lord Bingham, having already commented that the judiciary would give weight to the decisions of a representative legislature, noted that the high incidence of death and injury on the roads caused by the misuse of motor vehicles was a very serious problem and the need to address it in an effective way, for the benefit of the public, could not be doubted. He

---

125 *McIntosh v Lord Advocate* [2001] 1 AC 1078.
126 *Ibid*, at [36].
127 *R v Quayle* [2005] EWCA Crim 1415.
128 *Ibid*, at [68].
129 *Brown*, above n 40.

concluded that the section was not incompatible with Article 6. Lord Steyn also found deference to be of some relevance in the present case.

> Here s.172(2) addresses a pressing social problem, namely the difficulty of law enforcement in the face of statistics revealing a high accident rate resulting in death and serious injuries. The legislature was entitled to regard the figures of serious accidents as unacceptably high. It would also have been entitled to take into account that it was necessary to protect other convention rights, viz the right to life of members of the public exposed to the danger of accidents . . . On this aspect the legislature was in as good a position as a court to assess the gravity of the problem and the public interest in addressing it.

6.1.4 Prevention and Detection of Serious Crime

In S^{130} the House of Lords concluded that the retention of fingerprints and samples in cases where the suspect was subsequently acquitted or the charge discontinued was compatible with Articles 8 and 14. Lord Steyn, with whom the others agreed on this issue, held that there was a need to approach with due deference the policy decision made by Parliament in enacting this legislation in the fight against serious crime.[131]

6.1.5 Rape Complainant's Prior Sexual History

In *R v A*[132] the House of Lords considered the compatibility with Article 6 of section 41 of the Youth Justice and Criminal Evidence Act 1999 following the trial judge's ruling that the complainant could not be cross-examined, nor could evidence be led, about her alleged sexual relationship with the defendant. Lord Steyn noted that weight must be given to the decision of Parliament, yet concluded that

> when the question arises whether in the criminal statute in question Parliament adopted a legislative scheme which makes an excessive inroad into the right to a fair trial the court is qualified to make its own judgment and must do so.[133]

He concluded that whilst the statute pursued desirable goals, the methods adopted amounted to legislative overkill.[134]

By contrast, Lord Hope held that there were areas of law which lay within the discretionary area of judgment which the court ought to accord to the legislature and that prima facie section 41 was in that category.[135]

> The area is one where Parliament was better equipped than the judges are to decide where the balance lay. The judges are well able to assess the extent to which the restrictions will inhibit questioning or the leading of evidence. But it seems to me that in this highly sensitive and carefully researched field an assessment of the prejudice to the wider interests of the community if the restrictions were not to take that form was more appropriate for

---

[130] Above n 1.
[131] *Ibid*, at [55].
[132] Above n 38.
[133] *Ibid*, at [36].
[134] *Ibid*, at [43].
[135] *Ibid*, at [58].

Parliament. An important factor for Parliament to consider was the extent to which restrictions were needed in order to restore and maintain public confidence.[136]

However, using section 3 of the HRA, their Lordships concluded that the test of admissibility was whether the evidence was nevertheless so relevant to the issue of consent that to exclude it would endanger the fairness of the trial under Article 6.

6.1.6 Sentencing

In *Lichniak*[137] the House of Lords considered the compatibility of the mandatory life sentence for murder, pursuant to section 1(1) of the Murder (Abolition of Death Penalty) Act 1965, with Articles 3 and 5. Their Lordships noted that section 1(1) represented the settled will of Parliament.

> Criticism of the subsection has been voiced in many expert and authoritative quarters over the years, and there have been numerous occasions on which Parliament could have amended it had it wished, but there has never been a majority of both Houses in favour of amendment. The fact that section 1(1) represents the settled will of a democratic assembly is not a conclusive reason for upholding it, but a degree of deference is due to the judgment of a democratic assembly on how a particular social problem is best tackled . . . It may be accepted that the mandatory life penalty for murder has a denunciatory value, expressing society's view of a crime which has long been regarded with peculiar abhorrence.[138]

6.1.7 Policing

The police are also sometimes afforded some deference. For example, in *X*[139] the Court of Appeal held that the issuing of an Enhanced Criminal Record Certificate under section 115 of the Police Act 1997 by the Secretary of State on the basis of information provided by the Chief Constable was a matter where deference should be shown to the opinion of the Chief Constable.

> The statute properly conferred the responsibility of forming an opinion on the chief constable and, having formed that opinion perfectly properly that certain information might be relevant, it is not for the courts to interfere.[140]

6.1.8 Prisons

In *Ponting*[141] the Court of Appeal considered the complaint of a prisoner that he had been denied access to justice due to conditions imposed by prison authorities on the use of a computer and printer. Schiemann LJ did not directly discuss the issue of deference but referred to relevant paragraphs in *Samaroo*.[142] Clarke LJ also referred to

---

[136] *Ibid*, at [99].
[137] *R v Lichniak* [2002] UKHL 47, [2003] 1 AC 903.
[138] *Ibid*, at [14] per Lord Bingham.
[139] *R (on the application of X) v Chief Constable of the West Midlands Police* [2004] EWCA Civ 1068, [2005] 1 All ER 610.
[140] *Ibid*, at [47].
[141] *R (on the application of Ponting) v Governor of HMP Whitemoor* [2002] EWCA Civ 224.
[142] Above n 66.

Samaroo and the question of whether the Governor had struck the right balance. 'In answering that question the court must recognise and allow the Governor a discretionary area of judgment.'[143] Arden LJ discussed a number of factors indicating that deference should be shown. The right under Article 6 was not absolute; some restrictions imposed affected the allocation of resources by the prison authorities; the court had no relevant expertise in prison security or discipline; the right of access to court was subject to regulation by the state, which may take into account the needs and resources of the state as well as those of the individual.[144] No violation of Article 6 was found by a majority of the court.

Unusually in a right to life case, deference was afforded in *Bloggs 61*.[145] The Court of Appeal had to determine whether or not it was in breach of the claimant's right to life for him to be removed from a protected witness unit to a mainstream prison regime. As it was the positive aspect of the right to life that was involved, the court had to determine whether or not there was a risk to life. In doing so, Auld LJ held that, despite the fundamental and unqualified nature of the right to life, it was still appropriate to show some deference to and/or to recognise the special competence of the Prison Service in making a decision concerning the safety of an inmate's life.[146]

> [T]he Prison Service, with its experience of prison conditions, options and the relative efficacy of different protective regimes and measures—and the Police, with their expert and close knowledge of the level of risk—are generally better placed than the Court to assess the risk to life in such a context.[147]

He concluded that there was no risk to life. Whilst Mummery LJ agreed, Keene LJ was not so sure, stating that

> it could be argued that it is for the court to make its own judgment as to whether there would be an interference with the right to life under Article 2.[148]

However, he also pointed out that even were it to be for the court to make that primary judgment, the reality was that the court would have to attach considerable weight to the assessment of risk by those with professional involvement in the areas with which the case was concerned.

> It may therefore in most cases make little difference whether one describes the court's approach as one of deference or simply as one of attaching weight to the judgment reached by such bodies: the end result would be the same.[149]

---

[143] *Ibid*, at [79].
[144] *Ibid*, at [112].
[145] *R (on the application of Bloggs 61) v Secretary of State for the Home Department* [2003] EWCA 686, [2003] 1 WLR 2724.
[146] *Ibid*, at [65].
[147] *Ibid*, at [66].
[148] *Ibid*, at [81].
[149] *Ibid*, at [82].

In *Szuluk*[150] the Court of Appeal, in determining whether restrictions placed by the Governor on the prisoner's correspondence with his NHS consultant were compatible with Article 8, held that the

> court will ordinarily accept from the executive the evaluation of risk of serious abuse of outside mail because the prison service knows far more about it than the court does, and because it involves no immediate issue of law. The court's task is to consider whether, in the light of it, a sufficiently pressing need is demonstrated to justify what, will otherwise be the denial of a fundamental right. Once the facts are established, to abstain from adjudicating on them is not deference but abdication.[151]

6.2 National Security

In *Shayler*[152] the appellant argued that his prosecution under the Official Secrets Act 1989 was incompatible with Article 10. Lord Bingham, with whom Lords Scott and Hobhouse agreed, in response to the submission that the courts were reluctant to intervene in matters concerning national security, held that the court's willingness to intervene would very much depend upon the nature of the material which it was sought to disclose.

> If the issue concerns the disclosure of documents bearing a high security classification and there is apparently credible unchallenged evidence that disclosure is liable to lead to the identification of agents or the compromise of informers, the court may very well be unwilling to intervene. If, at the other end of the spectrum, it appears that while disclosure of the material may cause embarrassment or arouse criticism, it will not damage any security or intelligence interest, the court's reaction is likely to be very different.[153]

In the present case it was concluded that the sections of the Act were compatible with Article 10, essentially because the safeguards built into the Act were sufficient to ensure that unlawfulness and irregularity could be reported to those with the power and duty to take effective action.[154] By contrast, Lord Hope simply held that a wide margin of discretion was to be accorded to the legislature in matters relating to national security especially where the Convention rights of others, such as the right to life, may be put in jeopardy.[155] However, he also concluded that the choice of a system which favoured official authorisation before disclosure subject to judicial review on grounds of proportionality was within this margin of discretion.[156]

The issue of national security arose again in *A v Secretary of State for the Home Department*.[157] As discussed in the paragraphs above, the appellants had been certified under section 21 of the Anti-terrorism Crime and Security Act 2001 and

---

[150] *R (on the application of Szuluk) v The Governor of HMP Full Sutton* [2004] EWCA Civ 1426.

[151] *Ibid*, at [26]. See also *R (on the application of R) v Shetty (Responsible Medical Officer)* [2003] EWHC (Admin) 3022 concerning deference to the decision of the Secretary of State to transfer a prisoner from a mental health clinic back to prison.

[152] Above n 3.

[153] *Ibid*, at [33].

[154] *Ibid*, at [36] per Lord Bingham.

[155] *Ibid*, at [80].

[156] *Ibid*, at [83].

[157] Above n 65.

detained under section 23 of that Act. All were foreign nationals. None had been the subject of a criminal charge and in none of their cases was a criminal trial in prospect. It was for their Lordships to determine whether there was a public emergency threatening the life of the nation within the meaning of Article 15. And, if there was, whether the measures taken went beyond what was strictly required by the exigencies of the situation.

A majority of their Lordships concluded that there was a public emergency threatening the life of the nation and that this was an issue where great weight should be given to the judgment of the Home Secretary, his colleagues and Parliament 'because they were called on to exercise a pre-eminently political judgment.'[158] However, on the second question not as much deference was shown, a majority of their Lordships concluding that the measures taken were not strictly required. Lord Nicholls observed that

> Parliament must be regarded as having attached insufficient weight to the human rights of non-nationals. The subject matter of the legislation is the needs of national security. This subject matter dictates that, in the ordinary course, substantial latitude should be accorded to the legislature. But the human right in question, the right to individual liberty, is one of the most fundamental of human rights.[159]

Lord Hope noted that whilst the executive and legislature were to be afforded a wide margin of discretion in matters relating to national security, the width of the margin depended on the context.

> We are not dealing here with matters of social or economic policy, where opinions may reasonably differ in a democratic society and where choices on behalf of the country as a whole are properly left to government and to the legislature. We are dealing with actions taken on behalf of society as a whole which affect the rights and freedoms of the individual. This is where the courts may legitimately intervene, to ensure that the actions taken are proportionate. It is an essential safeguard, if individual rights and freedoms are to be protected in a democratic society which respects the principle that minorities, however unpopular, have the same rights as the majority.[160]

6.3 Immigration and Asylum

Given the amount of discretion involved in the area of immigration and asylum, it is rare for an opportunity for deference to the legislature to arise in such a case. The point arose in *International Transport Roth*[161] because the challenged decision was not a decision to deport but the scheme of penalties imposed on those intentionally or negligently allowing clandestine entrants into the United Kingdom. The scheme was contained in Part II of the Immigration and Asylum Act 1999. The Court of Appeal was divided in the conclusion reached. Simon Brown and Jonathan Parker LJJ, whilst noting that considerable deference should be afforded in this area to the

---

[158] *Ibid*, at [29] per Lord Bingham.
[159] *Ibid*, at [81].
[160] *Ibid*, at [108]. See also Lord Rodger at [176]-[178].
[161] Above n 74.

legislature,[162] concluded that the scheme was incompatible with Article 6 and Article 1 of Protocol No 1. Laws LJ, in his dissenting judgment, held that he had no doubt that the social consequences which flow from the entry into the United Kingdom of clandestine illegal immigrants in significant numbers were far reaching and in some respects complex.

> While the evidence before us gives more than a flavour of the problems, the assessment of these matters (and therefore of the pressing nature of the need for effective controls) is in my judgment obviously far more within the competence of government than the courts.[163]

The majority of judgments concerning deference to the executive in the context of immigration and asylum have come from the Court of Appeal. In the very early case of *X v Secretary of State for the Home Department*[164] the Court of Appeal was prepared to assume in the appellant's favour that the court had the duty of coming to a decision itself on the material before it as to whether the proposed course of action by the executive would infringe the appellant's human rights.[165] However, this line of reasoning changed soon after in *Mahmood*,[166] which concerned the claimant's challenge to his removal on the ground of his Article 8 right to respect for family life. Laws LJ noted that the HRA does not authorise the judges to stand in the shoes of Parliament's delegates who are decision makers given their responsibilities by the democratic arm of the state.

> It follows that there must be a principled distance between the court's adjudication in a case such as this and the Secretary of State's decision, based on his perception of the case's merits.[167]

Lord Phillips MR also stated that the court does not substitute its own decision for that of the executive as it 'reviews the decision of the executive to see whether it was permitted by law' and there will 'often be an area of discretion permitted to the executive of a country before a response can be demonstrated to infringe the Convention.'[168] The court concluded here that it was not in violation of the right to respect to family life to deport the claimant.

Similarly in *Isiko*[169] the Court of Appeal held that in this area

> difficult choices may have to be made by the executive or the legislature between the rights of the individual and the needs of society. In cases involving immigration policies and the rights to family life, it will be appropriate for the courts to recognise that there is an area of judgment within which the judiciary will defer, on democratic grounds, to the considered opinion of the elected body or person whose decision is said to be incompatible.[170]

---

[162] *Ibid*, at [26] and [139].
[163] *Ibid*, at [87].
[164] *X v Secretary of State for the Home Department* [2001] 1 WLR 740.
[165] *Ibid*, at [10].
[166] Above n 42.
[167] *Ibid*, at [33].
[168] *Ibid*, at [38].
[169] Above n 42.
[170] *Ibid*, at [31].

It concluded that the decision to deport was one the Secretary of State was allowed in law to make.[171]

In *Edore*,[172] also a deportation/family life appeal, the Court of Appeal took deference even further. The court held that the concept of deference meant that a decision maker could fairly reach one of two opposite conclusions, one in favour of a claimant the other in favour of his removal.

> Of neither could it be said that the balance had been struck unfairly. In such circumstances, the mere fact that an alternative but favourable decision could reasonably have been reached will not lead to the conclusion that the decision maker has acted in breach of the claimant's human rights. Such a breach will only occur where the decision is outwith the range of reasonable responses to the question as to where a fair balance lies between the conflicting interests. Once it is accepted that the balance could be struck fairly either way, the Secretary of State cannot be regarded as having infringed the claimant's art 8 rights by concluding that he should be removed. [173]

Whilst this would not appear to leave much room to the court at all, in the present case it was concluded that the decision reached by the Secretary of State was outside the range of permissible responses open to him and that removing the claimant was a violation of Article 8.

However, the approach in *Edore* was expressly disapproved of in *Huang*.[174] Here the Court of Appeal held that it was for the adjudicator to decide in substance whether the action appealed against involved a violation of the appellant's Convention rights.[175] In the view of the Court of Appeal, no deference was due as the adjudicator was not called upon to judge government policy.

> On the contrary, their duty was to see to the protection of individual fundamental rights, which is the particular territory of the courts (here the adjudicator), while policy is the particular territory of the elected powers in the State.[176]

It concluded that the adjudicator's duty, when faced with an Article 8 case, was to see whether an exceptional case had been made out such that the requirement of proportionality required a departure from the Rules.[177]

> The adjudicator's decision of the question whether the case is truly exceptional is entirely his own. He does defer to the Rules; for this approach recognises that the balance struck by the Rules will generally dispose of proportionality issues arising under Article 8; but they are not exhaustive of all cases. There will be a residue of truly exceptional instances.[178]

---

[171] *Ibid*, at [38]. See also *Shala v Secretary of State for the Home Department* [2003] EWCA Civ 233, where it was held that, although deference was shown, the delay in determining the application was taken to be an exceptional circumstance meaning that deportation was a disproportionate interference with family life.
[172] Above n 115.
[173] *Ibid*, at [14], quoting from *Ala*, above n 116, at [44].
[174] Above n 84.
[175] *Ibid*, at [26].
[176] *Ibid*, at [55].
[177] *Ibid*, at [56] in reliance upon *Razgar*, above n 118.
[178] *Ibid*, at [60].

It appears that if an individual is to be deported because he has committed a criminal offence, such as drug trafficking, the degree of deference is even greater. In *Samaroo*,[179] where the claimant alleged his right to family life would be infringed, the court held that a significant margin of discretion was required.

> The Convention right engaged is not absolute. The right to respect for family life is not regarded as a right which requires a high degree of constitutional protection. It is true that the issues are not technical as economic and social issues often are. But the court does not have expertise in judging how effective a deterrent is a policy of deporting foreign nationals who have been convicted of serious drug trafficking offences once they have served their sentences.[180]

It concluded his deportation was compatible with Article 8.[181] This case was distinguished in *Huang* as a policy case.

> The court was in particular asked to make an assessment, in the context of the case's facts, of the importance attached by the Secretary of State to the desirability of the appellant's deportation in light of his criminal past. In those circumstances the principle of respect for the democratic powers was plainly engaged.[182]

An additional factor adding to deference normally afforded in immigration matters was also present in *Farrakhan*.[183] In determining whether the decision of the Secretary of State to refuse Mr Farrakhan admission to the United Kingdom was compatible with Article 10, the Court of Appeal afforded a wide margin of discretion. This was due to a number of factors. First, this was an immigration decision and the Secretary of State was motivated by concern for public order within the United Kingdom. Secondly, the decision was the personal decision of the Secretary of State involving detailed consideration and wide consultation. Thirdly, the Secretary of State was far better placed than the court to reach an informed decision as to the likely consequences of admitting him. And fourthly, the Secretary of State was democratically accountable for his decision.[184] What was particularly concerning about the judgment, however, was the fact that the Secretary of State did not disclose his sources of information or the purport of that information.

> We can see that he may have had good reason for not disclosing his sources but feel that it would have been better had he been less diffident about explaining the nature of the information and advice that he had received.[185]

Nevertheless the court concluded that the decision was proportionate.

---

179 Above n 66.
180 *Ibid*, at [36].
181 See also *R (on the application of Kenya) v Secretary of State for the Home Department* [2004] EWCA Civ 1094.
182 *Ibid*, at [61].
183 Above n 93.
184 *Ibid*, at [71]-[74].
185 *Ibid*, at [78].

6.4 Pensions and Welfare Benefits

In *Hooper*[186] the House of Lords made very clear its view that it regarded the payment of welfare benefits, such as widow's benefit, a matter of social and economic policy.

> In a domestic system which (unlike the Strasbourg court) is concerned with the separation of powers, such decisions are ordinarily recognised by the courts to be matters for the judgment of the elected representatives of the people. The fact that the complaint concerns discrimination on grounds of sex is not in itself a reason for a court to impose its own judgment. Once it is accepted that older widows were historically an economically disadvantaged class which merited special treatment but were gradually becoming less disadvantaged, the question of the precise moment at which such special treatment is no longer justified becomes a social and political question within the competence of Parliament.[187]

It was concluded that the preservation of widow's pension for those bereaved before 9 April 2001 was objectively justified and involved no breach of Convention rights.[188]

Shortly after, in *Carson*,[189] the House of Lords considered the compatibility with the Convention rights of the non-payment of the annual pension uprate to certain UK pensioners living abroad and the difference in rates of jobseekers allowance and income support based on age. Lord Hoffmann noted that whilst certain grounds of discrimination (race, caste, noble birth, membership of a political party, gender) required careful examination by the courts, other differences in treatment (such as grounds of ability, education, wealth, occupation and age) usually depended upon considerations of the general public interest and were very much a matter for the democratically elected branches of government.[190] With respect to the differences in pensions, he noted that this was very much a case in which Parliament was entitled to decide whether the differences justified a difference in treatment.

> [I]n deciding what expatriate pensioners should be paid, Parliament must be entitled to take into account competing claims on public funds . . . Once it is conceded . . . that people resident outside the UK are relevantly different and could be denied any pension at all, Parliament does not have to justify to the courts the reasons why they are paid one sum rather than another. Generosity does not have to have a logical explanation. It is enough for the Secretary of State to say that, all things considered, Parliament considered the present system of payments to be a fair allocation of available resources.[191]

Similarly in relation to the levels of income support and jobseekers allowance his Lordship held that

> once it is accepted that the necessary expenses of young people, as a class, are lower than those of older people, they can properly be treated differently for the purpose of social

---

[186] Above n 85.
[187] *Ibid*, at [32] per Lord Hoffmann.
[188] Cf. *Secretary of State for Work and Pensions v M* [2004] EWCA Civ 1343, [2005] 2 WLR 740.
[189] *R (on the application of Carson) v Secretary of State for Work and Pensions* [2005] UKHL 37, [2005] 2 WLR 1369.
[190] *Ibid*, at [16].
[191] *Ibid*, at [25]–[26].

security payments. No doubt there are different ways of given effect to the distinction, but that is a matter for Parliament to choose.[192]

A majority concluded that there was no breach of Convention in relation to the pension uprate and it was unanimously concluded that there was no breach in relation to jobseekers allowance and income support.

6.5 Housing

Whilst the judgment of the House of Lords in *Qazi*[193] may have given the impression that national housing policy was an area of social policy where the courts were willing to defer to the opinion of the legislature, the judgment of the majority of their Lordships in *Ghaidan*[194] made clear that this is not always necessarily the case.

> National housing policy is a field where the court will be less ready to intervene. Parliament has to hold a fair balance between the competing interests of tenants and landlords, taking into account broad issues of social and economic policy. But, even in such a field, where the alleged violation comprises differential treatment based on grounds such as race or sex or sexual orientation the court will scrutinise with intensity any reasons said to constitute justification. The reasons must be cogent if such differential treatment is to be justified.[195]

In the present case a majority of their Lordships concluded that section 3 of the HRA could be used to construe the relevant legislation so that the survivor of a homosexual couple could become a statutory tenant by succession.[196]

However, if discrimination is not present, a different approach may be taken. In *Poplar Housing*[197] the Court of Appeal noted that the court had to pay considerable attention to the fact that Parliament intended, when enacting section 21(4) of the Housing Act 1988, to give preference to the needs of those dependent on social housing as a whole over those in the position of the defendant.

> The economic and other implications of any policy in this area are extremely complex and far-reaching. This is an area where, in our judgment, the courts must treat the decisions of Parliament as to what is in the public interest with particular deference.[198]

6.6 Taste and Decency in Broadcasting

In *Prolife Alliance*[199] the House of Lords considered the compatibility with Article 10 of the rejection by broadcasters of the ProLife Alliance's proposed party election broadcast. In accordance with section 6(1)(a) of the Broadcasting Act 1990 and

---

[192] *Ibid*, at [40]. See also Lord Rodger at [45] and Lord Walker at [80] and [91]. Cf Lord Carswell at [99].
[193] *Harrow LBC v Qazi* [2003] UKHL 43, [2004] AC 983.
[194] Above n 83.
[195] *Ibid*, at [19] per Lord Nicholls.
[196] See also *Secretary of State for Work and Pensions v M*, above n 188.
[197] Above n 86.
[198] *Ibid*, at [69]. See also *R (on the application of Smith) v Barking and Dagenham London Borough Council* [2002] EWHC (Admin) 2400.
[199] Above n 66.

paragraph 5.1(d) of the BBC's agreement with the Secretary of State for National Heritage, the broadcasters declined to transmit the programme on the grounds that it offended good taste, decency and public feeling. The major part of the proposed programme was devoted to explaining the processes involved in different forms of abortion, including prolonged and graphic images of the product of suction abortion.

Four of their Lordships afforded considerable deference to Parliament, Lord Nicholls stating that, in the absence of a successful claim that the offensive material restriction was not compatible with the Convention rights of ProLife Alliance,

> it is not for the courts to find that broadcasters acted unlawfully when they did no more than give effect to the statutory and other obligations binding on them.[200]

Lord Hoffmann also noted that the decision to make all broadcasts subject to taste and decency requirements represented Parliament's view that public opinion could not be totally disregarded in the pursuit of liberty and that this was 'an entirely proper decision for Parliament as representative of the people to make.'[201] The majority concluded that declining to transmit the programme involved no violation of Article 10.

Lords Hoffmann and Walker also afforded deference to the broadcasters in their decision applying the law to the facts. Given the considerable discretion involved in such decisions, it is submitted that this was the correct approach under the HRA. Lord Hoffmann noted that generally accepted standards on these questions were not a matter of intuition on the part of elderly male judges.[202] Lord Walker commented that the decision-maker was

> undoubtedly a broadcaster of great experience and high reputation. There is no reason to think that she and the others involved failed to approach their task responsibly and with a predisposition towards free speech. No doubt is cast on the good faith of any of them.[203]

6.7 Conclusion

This overview of subject areas is by no means a definitive guide and there are many other examples—some of which are discussed in Part II of this book. Deference has also been shown to the legislature in respect of: the right of serving prisoners to vote in Parliamentary or local government elections[204]; the placement of young offenders in secure accommodation[205]; the ban on the advertising of tobacco products in the interests of the protection of health [206]; the protection of consumers [207]; and the

---

[200] *Ibid*, at [16].
[201] *Ibid*, at [77].
[202] *Ibid*, at [80].
[203] *Ibid*, at [139].
[204] *R (on the application of Pearson) v Secretary of State for the Home Department* [2001] EWHC (Admin) 239.
[205] *R (on the application of SR) v Nottingham Magistrates' Court* [2001] EWHC (Admin) 802.
[206] *R (on the application of British American Tobacco UK Ltd) v The Secretary of State for Health* [2004] EWHC (Admin) 2493.
[207] *Wilson*, above n 49.

regulation of sewerage undertakers.[208] Particular deference has been shown to the Secretary of State in planning matters which have been held to be 'a matter of the formation and application of policy.'[209] This overview is also not particularly helpful in drawing conclusions as to the circumstances in which deference is likely to be afforded. For example, whilst it appears common in some areas, such as national social housing policy, the importance of the Convention right allegedly infringed may mean that the scope for any deference which would have otherwise arisen is thereby significantly reduced.

It is likely that deference when adjudicating upon Convention rights will continue to be sought by respondents to HRA claims. However a court approaches the task before it, as Lord Bingham outlined in *A v Secretary of State*,[210] it must be careful not to abandon its role under the HRA. As Lord Bingham emphasised, the Convention regime for the international protection of human rights requires national authorities, including national courts, to exercise their authority to afford effective protection[211] and domestic courts must themselves form a judgment whether a Convention right has been breached.[212]

---

[208] *Marcic*, above n 68.
[209] *Alconbury Developments*, above n 62, at [139] per Lord Clyde.
[210] Above n 65.
[211] *Ibid*, at [40].
[212] *Ibid.*

5

The Defence of Primary Legislation

1. Introduction

The HRA has been carefully drafted to preserve the sovereignty of Parliament.

> Parliamentary sovereignty means that Parliament can, if it chooses, legislate contrary to fundamental principles of human rights. The Human Rights Act 1998 will not detract from this power. The constraints upon its exercise by Parliament are ultimately political, not legal.[1]

Although section 6(1) provides that it is unlawful for a public authority to act in a way which is incompatible with a Convention right, section 6(2) provides that section 6(1) does not apply to an act if: (a) as the result of one of more provisions of primary legislation,[2] the authority could not have acted differently; or (b) in the case of one or more provisions of, or made under, primary legislation which cannot be read or given effect in a way which is compatible with the Convention rights, the authority was acting so as to give effect to or enforce those provisions.

Whilst section 6(2) appears to provide a fairly robust defence for public authorities bound by or relying on primary legislation in their decision making, sections 3 and 4 of the HRA must also be considered. Section 3 provides that, so far as it is possible to do so, primary legislation and subordinate legislation must be read and given effect in a way which is compatible with the Convention rights. Therefore, if an act is justified by reference to primary legislation incompatible with Convention rights, following the guidance in section 3, it may be possible for the court to construe the legislation so that it is compatible. If it is not possible to apply section 3, section 4 allows a court to make a declaration of incompatibility. Although this does not affect the validity,

---

[1] *R v Secretary of Sate for the Home Department, ex p Simms* [2000] 2 AC 115 per Lord Hoffmann.
[2] 'Primary legislation' is defined in s 21(1), the definition including Orders in Council made pursuant to Her Majesty's Royal Prerogative. See further P Billings and B Pontin, 'Prerogative Powers and the Human Rights Act: Elevating the Status of Orders in Council' [2001] *PL* 21.

continuing operation or enforcement of the provision, it does set in process a mechanism by which the offending provision may be quickly amended by Parliament.[3]

> It is crystal clear that the carefully and subtly drafted Human Rights Act 1998 preserves the principle of Parliamentary sovereignty. In a case of incompatibility, which cannot be avoided by interpretation under section 3(1), the courts may not disapply the legislation. The court may merely issue a declaration of incompatibility which then gives rise to a power to take remedial action.[4]

The final section of the HRA relating to primary legislation is section 19, which provides that a minister in charge of a Bill in either House of Parliament must, before the Second Reading of the Bill, make a statement to the effect that in his view the provisions of the Bill are compatible with the Convention rights (a 'statement of compatibility'). If this is not possible, he must make a statement to the effect that, although he is unable to make a statement of compatibility, the government nevertheless wishes the House to proceed with the Bill. This section and the others relating to primary legislation are the subject of this chapter.

---

2. Section 6(2) Human Rights Act

2.1 Introduction

Both sections 6(2)(a) and 6(2)(b) provide a public authority with a defence based on primary legislation.

> Paragraphs (a) and (b) both qualify the basic principle in section 6(1) that it is unlawful for a public authority to act in a way that is incompatible with the Convention rights. The purpose of these paragraphs is to prevent section 6(1) being used to undermine another of the Act's basic principles. This is that in the final analysis, if primary legislation cannot be interpreted in way that is compatible with them, Parliamentary sovereignty takes precedence over the Convention rights.[5]

However, it is not always clear which section applies. Further confusion has been caused by the judgment of the House of Lords in *Hooper*,[6] where Lords Hoffmann and Hope held that the appropriate defence was section 6(2)(b), Lords Scott and Brown held that it was section 6(2)(a), and Lord Nicholls held that it was not necessary to decide as section 6(2) clearly applied and the point was better left for a

---

[3] See s 10 and Sch 2.

[4] *R v Director of Public Prosecutions, ex p Kebilene* [1999] 3 WLR 972 per Lord Steyn. On the relationship between the judiciary, legislature and executive under the HRA, see generally TR Hickman, 'Constitutional Dialogue, Constitutional Theories and the Human Rights Act 1998', [2005] *PL* 306; CA Gearty, *Principles of Human Rights Adjudication* (Oxford University Press, 2004).

[5] *R (on the application of Hooper) v Secretary of State for Work and Pensions* [2005] UKHL 29, [2005] 1 WLR 1681 at [70] per Lord Hope.

[6] *Ibid.*

decision on another occasion. The respective views of their Lordships are discussed in the following paragraphs.[7]

2.2 Section 6(2)(a) Human Rights Act

Section 6(2)(a) provides that section 6(1), which makes it unlawful for a public authority to act in a way which is incompatible with a Convention right, does not apply to an act if, as the result of one or more provisions of primary legislation, the authority could not have acted differently. In *Hooper*,[8] Lord Hope held that the situation to which the paragraph was addressed arose where the effect of the primary legislation was that the authority had no alternative but to do what the legislation told it to do.

> The language of the paragraph tells us that this may be the result of one provision taken by itself, or that it may be the result of two or more provisions taken together. Where more than one provision is involved, they may be part of one enactment or they may be found in several different enactments. The key to its application lies in the fact that the effect of the legislation, wherever it is found, is that a duty is imposed on the authority. If the legislation imposes a duty to act, the authority is obliged to act in the manner which the legislation lays down even if the legislation requires it to act in a way which is incompatible with a Convention right. The authority has no discretion to do otherwise. As it is a duty which has been imposed on the authority by or as a result of primary legislation, Parliamentary sovereignty prevails over the Convention right. The defence is provided to prevent the legislation from being rendered unenforceable.[9]

Assuming section 6 applied, Lord Nicholls held in *Wilson*[10] that the court's decision in the proceedings gave effect to the mandatory provisions of the Consumer Credit Act 1974. 'An order giving effect to these provisions of primary legislation is excluded from the scope of s.6(1) by s.6(2)(a).'[11] Section 6(2)(a) was also held to clearly apply in *Wilkinson*.[12] Here a widower alleged discrimination in that he was not entitled to a widow's bereavement allowance by way of deduction from his liability for income tax under section 262 of the Income and Corporation Taxes Act 1988. Whilst there was a discretion which enabled the commissioners to formulate policy in the interstices of the tax legislation, it was held to not justify construing the power so widely as to enable the commissioners to concede, by extra-statutory concession, an allowance which Parliament could have granted but did not grant.[13] Their Lordships concluded that as the legislation gave the commissioners no power to act otherwise than to disallow claims for allowances by widows, they were therefore protected by section 6(2)(a).[14] Lord Hoffmann, with whom Lords Nicholls and Hope agreed, also

---

[7] See further P Cane, 'Church, State and Human Rights: Are Parish Councils Public Authorities?' (2004) 120 *LQR* 41.

[8] Above n 5.

[9] *Ibid*, at [71] per Lord Hope.

[10] *Wilson v Secretary of State for Trade and Industry* [2003] UKHL 40, [2003] 3 WLR 568.

[11] *Ibid*, at [25].

[12] *R (on the application of Wilkinson) v Inland Revenue Commissioners* [2005] UKHL 30, [2005] 1 WLR 1718.

[13] *Ibid*, at [21] per Lord Hoffmann. See also [36] and [39]–[40] per Lord Scott.

[14] *Ibid*, at [22] per Lord Hoffmann.

noted that if the powers of the commissioners had been wider, they would have been protected by s.6(2)(b),[15] although Lord Brown expressly disagreed with this reasoning.[16]

In *Hooper*,[17] only Lords Scott and Brown concluded that section 6(2)(a) was the appropriate defence. It had been claimed by widowers that the non-payment of payments corresponding to widow's payment and widowed mother's allowance under sections 36 and 37 of the Social Security Contributions and Benefits Act 1992 violated their Convention rights under Article 14 read with Article 1 of Protocol No 1. The Secretary of State claimed a defence under section 6(2). Lord Nicholls explained the problem in choosing 6(2)(a) or 6(2)(b) lay in the view taken of the Secretary of State's common law powers. In Lord Nicholls's view, if the effect of the statutory provision was that he could not lawfully have made corresponding payments to widowers in exercise of the Crown's common law powers, the case would fall within section 6(2)(a).[18] However, if, in the exercise of his common law powers, he could have lawfully made the payments, in Lord Nicholls's view the case fell within section 6(2)(b).

> Clearly, in making payments to widows the Secretary of State was giving effect to sections 36 and 37 of the Social Security Contributions and Benefits Act 1992. Likewise in not making corresponding payments to widowers the Secretary of State was giving effect to those statutory provisions . . . The fact that the Secretary of State could lawfully have made corresponding payments to widowers does not detract from the crucial fact that in declining to pay widowers he was 'giving effect' to the statute.[19]

Either way, Lord Nicholls held that section 6(2) provided a defence.

Both Lord Scott and Lord Brown concluded that the Secretary of State could not lawfully have made corresponding payments to widowers in exercise of the Crown's common law powers, and therefore section 6(2)(a) was the appropriate defence. Lord Scott stated that the

> widowers, and the widows who do not satisfy the statutory conditions, are not entitled to the statutory benefits. So the Secretary of State cannot authorise the payment to them of the statutory benefits.[20]

Similarly, Lord Brown held that the Secretary of State could not be required to act in such a way as to subvert the intention of Parliament.[21]

> Given Parliament's unambiguous intention in the matter it would seem to me an obvious abuse of power for the Secretary of State to have introduced a scheme to make matching extra-statutory payments to widowers.[22]

---

[15] *Ibid*, at [23].
[16] *Ibid*, at [43].
[17] Above n 5.
[18] *Ibid*, at [4].
[19] *Ibid*, at [6].
[20] *Ibid*, at [93]. However, similarly to Lord Nicholls, although preferring the s 6(2)(a) route, he also noted that the difference between (a) and (b) when applied to a case such as the present was immaterial. See [95].
[21] *Ibid*, at [122].
[22] *Ibid*, at [123].

He concluded that section 6(2)(a) was appropriate on the basis that, as a result of sections 36 and 37, the Secretary of State could not have acted differently: he had to pay the widows and could not lawfully have made matching payments to widowers.[23]

2.3 Section 6(2)(b) Human Rights Act

Section 6(2)(b) provides that section 6(1), which makes it unlawful for a public authority to act in a way which is incompatible with a Convention right, does not apply if, in the case of one or more provisions of, or made under, primary legislation which cannot be read or given effect in a way which is compatible with the Convention rights, the authority was acting so as to give effect to or enforce those provisions. In *Hooper*[24] Lord Hope held that the situation to which paragraph (b) was addressed arose where the authority had a discretion

> which it has the power to exercise or not to exercise as it chooses, to give effect to or enforce provisions of or made under primary legislation which cannot be read or given effect to in a way which is compatible with the Convention rights. The source of that discretion may be in a single statutory provision which confers a power on the authority which it may or may not choose to exercise . . . the source of the discretion that is given to the authority may also be found in several statutory provisions which taken together have that effect. Or, as there is nothing in the language of the paragraph to indicate the contrary, it may be found in the common law.[25]

In Lord Hope's view, the source of the discretion did not matter. What mattered was that the provision conferring the discretion could not be read or given effect compatibly with the Convention rights and that the authority had decided to exercise or not to exercise its discretion so as to give effect to those provisions or to enforce them.

> If it does this, this paragraph affords it a defence to a claim under section 7(1) that by acting or failing to act in this way it has acted unlawfully. In this way it enables the primary legislation to remain effective in the way Parliament intended. If the defence was not there the authority would have no alternative but to exercise its discretion in a way that was compatible with the Convention rights. The power would be a duty to act compatibly with the Convention, even if to do so was plainly in conflict with the intention of Parliament.[26]

In *Aston Cantlow*[27] Lord Nicholls held that, even assuming section 6 was applicable and the Act was incompatible with Convention rights, the Parochial Church Council would not be acting unlawfully in enforcing liability. Here the Chancel Repairs Act 1932 provided that if the defendant would have been liable to be admonished to repair the chancel by the appropriate ecclesiastical court, the court shall give

---

[23] *Ibid*, at [124]. His Lordship also noted that, the wider the ambit given to s 6(2), the more often the United Kingdom will be acting incompatibly with Art 13 of the ECHR. See [120].
[24] Above n 5.
[25] *Ibid*, at [72] per Lord Hope.
[26] *Ibid*, at [73]. See also *Aston Cantlow and Wilmcote with Billesley Parochial Church Council v Wallbank* [2003] UKHL 37, [2004] 1 AC 546 at [93] per Lord Hobhouse and *Ghaidan v Godin-Mendoza* [2004] UKHL 30, [2004] 2 AC 557 at [108] per Lord Rodger.
[27] *Aston Cantlow, ibid*.

judgment for the cost of putting the chancel in repair. Lord Nicholls found that when a Council acted pursuant to that provision, it was acting within the scope of the exception set out in section 6(2)(b).[28]

In *Hooper*[29] only Lords Hoffmann and Hope held that section 6(2)(b) was the appropriate defence as they had concluded that, in the exercise of his common law powers, the Secretary of State could have lawfully made the payments to the widowers. Lord Hoffmann noted that section 6(2)(b) assumed that the public authority could have acted differently but nevertheless excluded liability if it was giving effect to a statutory provision which could not be read as Convention-compliant in accordance with section 3.

> It follows that section 6(1) does not apply if the Secretary of State was acting incompatibly with Convention rights because he was giving effect to sections 36 and 37 of the 1992 Act.[30]

Lord Hope concluded that the Secretary of State's act in not exercising his common law power by making payment to widowers was not unlawful pursuant to section 6(2)(b).

> A common law power to make payments for which the statutes do not provide is only a power. By declining to exercise it, the Secretary of State was simply doing what the 1992 and 1999 Acts told him to do. He was giving effect to their provisions, as they obliged him to make payments to widows only and not to both widows and widowers.[31]

His Lordship found that it made no difference that the power the Secretary of State was declining to exercise was a common law power as section 6(2)(b) said nothing about the origin of the act or failure to act which gave effect to or enforced the provisions of primary legislation which cannot be read or given effect in a way which was compatible with Convention rights. In his view the failure to act which was incompatible with Convention rights could consist of a refusal to exercise a power which had its origins elsewhere because to exercise it in a way that was compatible with the Convention would conflict with the intention of Parliament.[32]

> There is no indication in section 6(2)(b) or elsewhere that public authorities whose powers are not derived from statute or whose powers are derived in part from the common law are in a less favourable position for the purposes of the defence which it provides than those which are entirely the creatures of statute. The primacy that is given to the sovereignty of Parliament requires that they be treated in the same way, irrespective of the source of the power.[33]

---

[28] *Ibid.* See also Lord Hobhouse at [93], Lord Scott at [137] and Lord Rodger at [172].
[29] Above n 5.
[30] *Ibid*, at [49].
[31] *Ibid*, at [81].
[32] *Ibid*, at [82].
[33] *Ibid*, at [83].

3. Section 3 Human Rights Act

3.1 Introduction

Section 3(1) provides that

> so far as it is possible to do so, primary legislation and subordinate legislation must be read
> and given effect in a way which is compatible with the Convention rights.[34]

The section applies to primary and subordinate legislation whenever enacted.[35] However, it does not affect the validity, continuing operation or enforcement of any incompatible primary legislation; nor does it affect the validity, continuing operation or enforcement of any incompatible subordinate legislation if (disregarding any possibility of revocation) primary legislation prevents removal of the incompatibility.[36]

It is clear that section 3 requires the court to 'interpret legislation in a manner which it would not have done before.' When it applies,

> the courts have to adjust their traditional role in relation to interpretation so as to give
> effect to the direction contained in section 3. It is as though legislation which predates the
> Human Rights Act 1998 and conflicts with the Convention has to be treated as being subsequently amended to incorporate the language of section 3.[37]

The section is often described as a key section of the HRA and one of the primary means by which Convention rights have been brought into the law.[38] The section is undoubtedly

> crucial to the working of the 1998 Act. It is the means by which Parliament intends that
> people should be afforded the benefit of their Convention rights—'so far as it is possible',
> without the need for any further intervention by Parliament.[39]

It has been held that section 3 applies to the interpretation of the HRA itself. For example, in *Douglas*[40] it was held that section 3 had to be applied to the interpretation of section 12 of the HRA. Therefore, consistently with other Convention rights, it was not possible to give the right of freedom of expression presumptive priority over other rights.[41] It is also clear that the interpretative duty imposed by section 3 applies to the same degree in legislation applying between private parties as it does in

---

[34] In *The Commissioner of Police for the Metropolis v Hurst* [2005] EWCA Civ 890 the Court of Appeal held that the 'Convention rights' referred to in s 3 were the international obligations of the United Kingdom as opposed to the obligations created by the HRA. See [44] and [58].

[35] Section 3(2)(a). It thereby removes the doctrine of implied repeal in that the HRA does not impliedly repeal inconsistent legislation.

[36] Sections 3(2)(b) and s 3(2)(c).

[37] *Donoghue v Poplar Housing* [2001] EWCA Civ 595, [2000] QB 48 per Lord Woolf CJ. See further F Bennion, 'What Interpretation is "Possible" under Section 3(1) of the Human Rights Act 1998?' [2000] *PL* 77.

[38] *Ghaidan*, above n 26, per Lord Nicholls at [26].

[39] *Ibid*, at [106] per Lord Rodger. See also Lord Steyn at [39] and [46].

[40] *Douglas v Hello! Limited* [2001] QB 967.

[41] *Ibid*, at [137] per Sedley LJ and [149] per Keene LJ.

legislation which applies between public authorities and individuals.[42] Finally, in order to apply section 3 the first step is to determine, using ordinary principles of statutory construction (both literal and purposive), whether or not the primary legislation is incompatible with a Convention right. Only if there is an incompatibility is it necessary to consider the section.[43] Whilst there may be some judicial deference afforded at this stage, it is important that this is not confused with the determination of what is possible under section 3 if an incompatibility is found.[44]

3.2 The Nature of Section 3

Section 3 is often described as a 'strong interpretative obligation'[45] and as a 'powerful tool', not an 'optional cannon of construction.'[46] It has also been held that the section requires a broad approach 'concentrating, amongst other things, in a purposive way on the importance of the fundamental right involved.'[47] It has been held that full weight must be given to the will of Parliament as expressed in the HRA[48] and that if Parliament disagrees with an interpretation by the courts under section 3 it is free to override it by amending the legislation and expressly reinstating the incompatibility.[49] It is clear that section 3 is also regarded by the courts as the prime remedial remedy whilst resort to a declaration of incompatibility under section 4 is regarded as an exceptional course.[50] Comparisons have been drawn with EC law as to the lengths to which a court may go.[51]

However, it is also plain from the case law that there are limits.

> The difficulty lies in the word 'possible'. Section 3(1), read in conjunction with ss.3(2) and 4, makes one matter clear: Parliament expressly envisaged that not all legislation would be capable of being made Convention-compliant by application of s.3. Sometimes it would be possible, sometimes not. What is not clear is the test to be applied in separating the sheep from the goats.[52]

The limits beyond which a Convention-compliant interpretation is not possible are examined in the following paragraphs.

---

[42] *X v Y* [2004] EWCA Civ 662, [2004] ICR 1634 at [66].
[43] *R v A* [2001] UKHL 25, [2002] 1 AC 45 at [58] per Lord Hope. See also *R v Crown Court at Leeds, ex p Wardle* [2001] UKHL 12, [2001] 2 WLR 865; and R v Hasan [2005] UKHL 22, [2005] 2 WLR 709 at [62] per Lord Steyn.
[44] See further A Young, 'Ghaidan v Godin-Mendoza: Avoiding the Deference Trap' [2005] *PL* 23.
[45] See, eg *Kebilene*, above n 4, per Lord Steyn and Lord Cooke; *Attorney General's Reference No.4 of 2002* [2004] UKHL 43, [2005] 1 AC 264 at [28] per Lord Bingham.
[46] *Re S* [2002] UKHL 10, [2002] 2 WLR 720 at [37] per Lord Nicholls.
[47] *Ghaidan*, above n 26, at [41] per Lord Steyn.
[48] *Ibid*, at [40] per Lord Steyn.
[49] *Ibid*, at [43] per Lord Steyn.
[50] *Ibid*, at [50] per Lord Steyn.
[51] *Ibid*, at [45] per Lord Steyn, citing *Marleasing SA v La Commercial Internacional de Alimentación SA* Case C–106/890 [1990] ECR I-4135 at 4159. See also Lord Rodger at [118].
[52] *Ibid*, at [27] per Lord Nicholls.

3.3 What is Not Possible

When adjudicating on section 3, the courts have been careful to warn that the section does not entitle the judges to act as legislators.[53]

> Section 3 is concerned with interpretation . . . In applying section 3 courts must be ever mindful of this outer limit. The Human Rights Act reserves the amendment of primary legislation to Parliament. By this means the Act seeks to preserve parliamentary sovereignty. The Act maintains the constitutional boundary. Interpretation of statutes is a matter for the courts; the enactment of statutes and the amendment of statutes, are matters for Parliament.[54]

To this end it has been held that it is not possible to use section 3 if the legislation contains provisions which expressly contradict the meaning which the enactment would have to be given to make it compatible or provisions which do so by necessary implication.[55] Furthermore, it is not possible to do 'violence' to the language or to the objective of the provision[56] so as to make it unintelligible or unworkable,[57] or to commit 'judicial vandalism' by giving the provision an effect quite different from that which Parliament intended.[58]

In short, it has been held that it is not possible to use section 3 if it would involve adopting a meaning which was inconsistent with a fundamental feature of the legislation.[59] It does not allow courts to change the substance of a provision completely.[60]

> That would be to cross the constitutional boundary s.3 seeks to demarcate and preserve. Parliament has retained the right to enact legislation in terms which are not Convention-compliant. The meaning imported by application of s.3 must be compatible with the under-lying thrust of the legislation being construed. Words implied must . . . 'go with the grain of the legislation'.[61]

Lord Rodger in *Ghaidan*[62] stated that the key lay in a careful consideration of the essential principles and scope of the legislation being interpreted.

> If the insertion of one word contradicts those principles or goes beyond the scope of the legislation, it amounts to impermissible amendment. On the other hand, if the implication of a dozen words leaves the essential principles and scope of the legislation intact but allows it to be read in a way which is compatible with Convention rights, the implication is a legitimate exercise of the powers conferred by s.3(1).[63]

---

[53] *R v A*, above n 43, at [108] per Lord Hope.
[54] *Re S*, above n 46, at [39] per Lord Nicholls.
[55] *R v A*, above n 43, at [108] per Lord Hope; *R v Lambert* [2001] UKHL 37, [2002] 2 AC 545 at [79] per Lord Hope; *Re S*, above n 46, at [40] per Lord Nicholls; *R v Secretary of State for the Home Department, ex p Anderson* [2002] UKHL 46, [2003] 1 AC 837 at [59] per Lord Steyn; *R (on the application of Rusbridger) v Attorney General* [2003] UKHL 38, [2004] 1 AC 357 at [8] per Lord Steyn; *Ghaidan*, above n 26, at [117] per Lord Rodger.
[56] *Lambert, ibid*, at [17] per Lord Slynn.
[57] *Ibid*, at [80] per Lord Hope.
[58] *Anderson*, above n 55, at [70] per Lord Bingham.
[59] *Re S*, above n 46, at [40] per Lord Nicholls.
[60] *Ghaidan*, above n 26, at [110] per Lord Rodger.
[61] *Ibid*, at [33] per Lord Nicholls.
[62] *Ibid*.
[63] *Ibid*, at [122].

It has also been held that the courts should not use section 3 to make decisions for which they are not equipped.

> There may be several ways of making a provision Convention-compliant, and the choice may involve issues calling for legislative deliberation.[64]

Even if the proposed interpretation does not run counter to any underlying principle of the legislation, it may involve reading into the statute powers or duties with far-reaching practical repercussions of that kind.

> In effect these powers or duties, if sufficiently far-reaching, would be beyond the scope of the legislation enacted by Parliament. If that is right, the answer to such questions cannot be clear-cut and will involve matters of degree which cannot be determined in the abstract but only by considering the particular legislation in issue. In any given case, however, there may come a point where, standing back, the only proper conclusion is that the scale of what is proposed would go beyond any implication that could possibly be derived from reading the existing legislation in a way that was compatible with the Convention right in question.[65]

3.4 What is Possible

It has been held that it is important not to approach section 3 in a too literal and technical way with too much emphasis on linguistic features.[66] Nevertheless, staying within the provisos outlined above, certain guidelines have developed. Section 3 can be applied even if there is no ambiguity in the language in the sense of the language being capable of two different meanings.[67]

> Even if, construed according to the ordinary principles of interpretation, the meaning of the legislation admits of no doubt, s.3 may nonetheless require the legislation to be given a different meaning.[68]

An interpretation which linguistically may appear strained can be adopted.[69]
It is possible to read in words to the legislation and to read down words.[70] It may be possible to

> isolate a particular phrase which causes the difficulty and to read in words that modify it so as to remove the incompatibility. Or else the court may read in words that qualify the provision as a whole. At other times the appropriate solution may be to read down the provision so that it falls to be given effect in a way that is compatible with the Convention rights in question.[71]

---

[64] *Ibid*, at [33] per Lord Nicholls.
[65] *Ibid*, at [115] per Lord Rodger. See also *Re S*, above n 46, at [40] per Lord Nicholls.
[66] *Ibid*, at [49] per Lord Steyn.
[67] *R v A*, above n 43 at [44] per Lord Steyn; *Re S*, above n 46, at [37] per Lord Nicholls.
[68] *Ghaidan*, above n 26, at [29] per Lord Nicholls citing *R v A*, above n 43, as an example. See also [44] per Lord Steyn.
[69] *R v A*, above n 43 at [44] per Lord Steyn.
[70] *Ibid*, at [44] per Lord Steyn.
[71] *Ghaidan*, above n 26, at [124] per Lord Rodger.

It also may be enough for the court to simply state what the effect of the provision is without altering the ordinary meaning of the words used.[72] It may be necessary for the words used to be expressed in different language in order to explain how they are to be read in a way that is compatible.[73]

Using these techniques, it has been accepted that it is possible for a court to modify the meaning, and hence the effect, of primary and secondary legislation.[74] It is also clear that the court may be required to depart from the intention of the enacting Parliament.[75]

> Once the 1998 Act came into force, whenever, by virtue of s.3(1), a provision could be read in a way which was compatible with Convention rights, that was the meaning which Parliament intended that it should bear. For all purposes, that meaning, and no other, is the 'true' meaning of the provision in our law.[76]

However, that is not to say that the limit outlined in the paragraphs above may be overstepped. It remains not possible to use section 3 if doing so would involve adopting a meaning which is inconsistent with a fundamental feature of the legislation.[77]

Observations have also been made by the courts concerning the correct procedure to be followed when applying section 3. It has been held that it is important to identify precisely the word or phrase which, if given its ordinary meaning, would otherwise be incompatible.

> So far as possible judges should seek to achieve the same attention to detail in their use of language to express the effect of applying s 3(1) as the parliamentary draftsman would have done if he had been amending the statute. It ought to be possible for any words that need to be substituted to be fitted in to the statute as if they had been inserted there by amendment.[78]

3.5 The Application of Section 3 in Hypothetical Cases

Although to date it has only occurred on one occasion, it appears that it is possible for a court to apply section 3 in a hypothetical case. In *Rusbridger*[79] the House of Lords had to determine whether or not to grant a declaration as to the construction of section 3 of the Treason Act 1848 in light of section 3 of the HRA and Article 10 (the right to freedom of expression). This was an application not for a declaration of incompatibility pursuant to section 4 of the HRA but for a declaration that certain proposed conduct was lawful. The proceedings were brought by the editor and a well-known journalist of *The Guardian* newspaper, which had published articles urging the abolition of the monarchy.

---

[72] *Lambert*, above n 55, at [81] per Lord Hope; *Ghaidan*, above n 26, at [107] per Lord Rodger.
[73] *Ibid*, at [81] per Lord Hope; *Ghaidan*, above n 26, at [124] per Lord Rodger.
[74] *Ghaidan*, above n 26, at [32] per Lord Nicholls.
[75] *Ibid*, at [30] per Lord Nicholls.
[76] *Ibid*, at [106] per Lord Steyn.
[77] *Re S*, above n 46, at [40] per Lord Nicholls.
[78] *Lambert*, above n 55, at [80] per Lord Hope; *Re S, ibid*, at [41] per Lord Nicholls.
[79] Above n 55.

Their Lordships made clear that, save in exceptional circumstances, it was not appropriate for a member of the public to bring proceedings against the Crown for a declaration that certain proposed conduct was lawful and name the Attorney-General as the formal defendant to the claim. However, there was jurisdiction for a civil court to make such a declaration.[80] It had been conceded that it was not necessary for *The Guardian* to demonstrate that they were victims under section 7 of the HRA and Lord Steyn held that this was obvious on a proper view of the place of section 3 in the scheme of the HRA. 'For present purposes it is sufficient that The Guardian has an interest and standing. That is the threshold requirement.'[81] His Lordship, with whom Lords Scott and Walker agreed, considered that *The Guardian* may be entitled to seek certainty[82]; that the case was not fact-sensitive[83]; and that the issue may be a matter of constitutional importance.[84] He concluded that the case may fall within the exceptional category.[85] However, he also concluded that the case did not have to be heard again by the Administrative Court.

> The idea that s.3 could survive scrutiny under the Human Rights Act is unreal. The fears of the editor of *The Guardian* were more than a trifle alarmist. In my view the courts ought not to be troubled further with this unnecessary litigation.[86]

It therefore appears that it may be possible, in an exceptional case, to seek a declaration as to the correct interpretation of a section of primary legislation in the light of section 3 of the HRA and a Convention right. However, the meaning of exceptional is not exactly clear from the judgment of the majority. Lord Steyn referred to three factors: the need for a genuine dispute about the subject matter, although noting that this could not by itself conclude the matter or be a weighty criterion if there were otherwise good reasons to allow the claim for a declaration to go forward[87]; whether the case was fact-sensitive or not, 'it has always been recognised that a question of pure law may more readily be made the subject matter of a declaration'[88]; and finally the question of whether there was a cogent public or individual interest which could be advanced by the grant of a declaration noting that the jurisdiction was in no way limited to life and death issues.[89]

3.6 The Application of Section 3 in Practice

A far better understanding of what is actually possible for a court to achieve by using section 3 can be gained by an examination of the cases in which it has been applied.

---

[80] *Ibid*, at [16].
[81] *Ibid*, at [21].
[82] *Ibid*, at [22].
[83] *Ibid*, at [24].
[84] *Ibid*, at [24].
[85] *Ibid*, at [25].
[86] *Ibid*, at [28]. Lord Hutton did not agree that this was an exceptional case and held that it was not a function of the courts to decide hypothetical questions which did not impact on the parties before them or to keep the statute book up to date using ss 3 and 4 of the HRA; see [33]–[36]. Lord Rodger reached a similar conclusion, see [57]–[58].
[87] *Ibid*, at [22].
[88] *Ibid*, at [23].
[89] *Ibid*, at [24].

In accordance with the view that this is the primary remedial measure, section 4 being a measure of last resort, section 3 has actually been applied in numerous cases. Many of these examples are examined in the following paragraphs.

3.6.1 Criminal Justice

(a) Admission of Evidence

R v A[90] concerned a trial for rape. During the trial the defendant alleged that, approximately three weeks prior to the date of the alleged rape, he and the complainant had a sexual relationship. His defence was that sexual intercourse took place with the complainant's consent or, alternatively, that he believed she consented. At a preparatory hearing, counsel for the defendant applied for leave to cross-examine the complainant about the alleged previous sexual relationship and to lead evidence about it. Relying on section 41 of the Youth Justice and Criminal Evidence Act 1999, the trial judge ruled that the complainant could not be cross-examined, nor could evidence be led, about her alleged sexual relationship with the defendant.

On appeal, the Court of Appeal held that questioning and evidence in relation to the alleged prior sexual activity was admissible in relation to the defendant's belief in her consent but inadmissible on the issue of consent. The Crown appealed and the appeal in the House of Lords turned predominantly on the meaning of section 3. On ordinary principles of construction, a majority concluded that section 41 was prima facie capable of preventing an accused person from putting forward evidence critical to his defence and, thus construed, was incompatible with Article 6.[91] Remitting the case to the Crown Court, the majority held that, applying section 3, the test of admissibility should be whether the evidence was so relevant to the issue of consent that to exclude it would endanger the fairness of the trial.[92]

(b) Burden of Proof

In *R v Lambert*[93] the claimant had been convicted of possession of a controlled drug with intent to supply contrary to the Misuse of Drugs Act 1971. The judge had directed the jury that in order to establish possession of a controlled drug, the prosecution merely had to prove that he had the bag in his possession and that the bag in fact contained a controlled drug. Thereafter, under section 28 of the Act, the burden was on the defendant to prove, on the balance of probabilities, that he did not know that the bag contained a controlled drug. This was a legal rather than a merely evidential burden of proof. One of the questions for their Lordships was whether, using section 3, section 28 could be interpreted so as to impose a merely evidential burden.

Having determined that the HRA did not actually apply here as it did not have retrospective effect, their Lordships did not have to consider this question, although most did. Lord Slynn held that it was possible

---

[90] Above n 43.
[91] Although Lord Hope concluded it was not necessary or appropriate to resort to s 3, he agreed with the test set out by Lord Steyn for the trial judge which entailed reading s 41 of the Youth Justice and Criminal Evidence Act 1999 compatibly with Art 6.
[92] *Ibid*, at [46] per Lord Steyn. See further P. Mirfield, 'Human Wrongs?' (2002) 118 *LQR* 20.
[93] Above n 55.

without doing violence to the language or to the objective of that section, to read the words as imposing only the evidential burden of proof.[94]

Lords Steyn, Hope and Clyde also held that, applying section 3, section 28 could be read as creating an evidential burden only.[95]

3.6.2 Sentencing

In *Offen*[96] the Court of Appeal determined that it was clear that there were circumstances where section 2 of the Crime (Sentences) Act 1997, imposing the automatic life sentence, could violate Articles 3 and 5. However, there was no need to impose such a sentence under the section if there were exceptional circumstances. Using section 3, the court concluded that 'exceptional circumstances' should be interpreted in such a way that offenders would not be sentenced to life imprisonment where they did not constitute a significant risk to the public.[97] It was held that this would still give effect to the intention of Parliament but in a more just, less arbitrary and more proportionate manner.[98]

> The objective of the legislature . . . will be achieved, because it will be mandatory to impose a life sentence in situations where the offender constitutes a significant risk to the public. Section 2 of the 1997 Act therefore provides a good example of how the 1998 Act can have a beneficial effect on the administration of justice, without defeating the policy which Parliament was seeking to implement.[99]

3.6.3 Parole Board

Section 3 has also had an impact on the role of the Parole Board. In *Sim*[100] the Court of Appeal held that it was necessary to apply section 3 to section 44A(4) of the Criminal Justice Act 1991, which provided that the Board shall direct the prisoner's release if satisfied that it is no longer necessary for the protection of the public that he should be confined. It was held that this gave rise to a presumption that the prisoner would be detained unless the Board was satisfied to the contrary and that this was incompatible with Article 5. However, applying section 3, section 44A could be interpreted in a such a way that the Board was obliged to conclude that detention was no longer necessary for the protection of the public unless it was positively satisfied that detention was necessary in the public interest.[101]

---

94 *Ibid*, at [17].
95 *Ibid*, at [42] per Lord Steyn, at [94] per Lord Hope and at [157] per Lord Clyde. Lord Hutton found that s 28 as drafted was not actually incompatible with Art 6(2). See also *Attorney General's Reference No.4 of 2002*, above n 45; *R v Daniel* [2002] EWCA Crim 959, [2003] 1 Cr Ap R 6; *Attorney-General's Reference No.1 of 2004* [2004] EWCA Crim 1025, [2004] 1 WLR 2111.
96 *R v Offen* [2001] 1 WLR 253.
97 *Ibid*, at [97].
98 *Ibid*, at [99].
99 *Ibid*, at [100].
100 *R (on the application of Sim) v Parole Board* [2003] EWCA Civ 1845, [2004] QB 1288.
101 *Ibid*, at [51].

3.6.4 Coroner's Inquests

In *Middleton*[102] the House of Lords held that the regime for holding inquests established by the Coroners Act 1988 and the Coroners Rules 1984 (SI 1984/553) as
hitherto understood and followed in England and Wales did not meet the requirements of the Convention under Article 2. However, it was concluded that only one
change was needed using section 3. 'How' in section 11(5)(b)(ii) of the Act and rule
36(1)(b) of the Rules was to be interpreted in the broader sense to mean not simply
by what means someone died but to include also 'by what means and in what circumstances'.[103]

> This will not require a change of approach in some cases, where a traditional short form
> verdict will be quite satisfactory, but it will call for a change of approach in others . . . In the
> latter class of case it must be for the coroner, in the exercise of his discretion, to decide how
> best, in the particular case, to elicit the jury's conclusion on the central issue or issues.[104]

The same conclusion was reached by their Lordships in *Sacker*.[105]

3.6.5 Family Law

In *Re S*[106] the House of Lords commented in detail on what it considered to be an
inappropriate use of section 3 by the Court of Appeal. In short, the Court of Appeal,
using section 3 to interpret the Children Act 1989, propounded a new procedure by
which the essential milestones of a care plan would be identified at the trial and ele-
vated to a starred status. If a starred milestone was not achieved within a reasonable
time after the date set at trial, the local authority was obliged to reactivate the inter-
disciplinary process that contributed to the creation of the care plan. At the least, the
local authority must inform the child's guardian of the position. Either the guardian
or the local authority would then have the right to apply to the court for further
directions.

Their Lordships concluded unanimously that the starring system could not be justified as a legitimate exercise in interpretation of the Children Act in accordance with
section 3.[107] It was found that a cardinal principle of the Children Act was that the
courts were not empowered to intervene in the way local authorities discharge their
parental responsibilities under final care orders.

> Parliament entrusted to local authorities, not the courts, the responsibility for looking after
> children who are the subject of care orders. To my mind the new starring system would
> depart substantially from this principle . . . In short, under the starring system the court will
> exercise a newly-created supervisory function.[108]

---

[102] *R (on the application of Middleton) v HM Coroner for Western Somerset* [2004] UKHL 10, [2004] 2 AC
182.
[103] *Ibid*, at [35] per Lord Bingham.
[104] *Ibid*, at [36] per Lord Bingham.
[105] *R (on the application of Sacker) v HM Coroner for the County of West Yorkshire* [2004] UKHL 11,
[2004] 1 WLR 796. See also Hurst, above n 34.
[106] Above n 46.
[107] *Ibid*, at [36] per Lord Nicholls.
[108] *Ibid*, at [42] per Lord Nicholls.

Their Lordships considered that this judicial innovation passed well beyond the boundary of interpretation.

> It would constitute amendment of the Children Act, not its interpretation. It would have far-reaching practical ramifications for local authorities and their care of children.[109]

It concluded that these were matters for decision by Parliament, not the courts.

> It is impossible for a court to attempt to evaluate these ramifications or assess what would be the views of Parliament if changes are needed.[110]

3.6.6 Housing

In *Ghaidan*[111] the question was whether section 3 could be applied to paragraphs 2 and 3 of Schedule 1 to the Rent Act 1977 so that it embraced couples living together in a close and stable homosexual relationship as much as couples living together in a close and stable heterosexual relationship so that the surviving spouse of a homosexual couple could succeed to the statutory tenancy. A majority of their Lordships concluded that section 3 could be so applied, finding that the provisions construed without reference to section 3 violated Article 14 taken together with Article 8.

> [T]he social policy underlying the 1988 extension of security of tenure under para.2 to the survivor of couples living together as husband and wife is equally applicable to the survivor of homosexual couples living together in a close and stable relationship . . . I see no reason to doubt that application of s.3 to para.2 has the effect that para.2 should be read and given effect to as though the survivor of such a homosexual couple were the surviving spouse of the original tenant. Reading para.2 in this way would have the result that cohabiting homosexual couples and cohabiting heterosexual couples would be treated alike for the purposes of succession as a statutory tenant. This would eliminate the discriminatory effect of para.2 and would do so consistently with the social policy underlying para.2.[112]

Lord Rodger simply saw this result as a modest development of the extension of the concept of spouse which Parliament itself made in 1988 when it provided that the couple did not have to be married. Therefore, it did not contradict any cardinal principle of the Rent Act, nor did it entail far-reaching practical repercussions which the House was not in a position to evaluate.[113]

In *Poplar Housing*[114] it was argued that section 21(4) of the Housing Act 1988 should be interpreted so that an order for possession was only to be made by a court if it was reasonable to do so. The Court of Appeal concluded that the effect of this amendment would be very wide indeed and would significantly reduce the ability of landlords to recover possession and defeat Parliament's original objective of provid-

---

[109] *Ibid*, at [43] per Lord Nicholls.
[110] *Ibid*, at [44] per Lord Nicholls. See further J Herring, 'The Human Rights of Children in Care' (2002) 118 *LQR* 534.
[111] Above n 26.
[112] *Ibid*, at [35] per Lord Nicholls.
[113] *Ibid*, at [128].
[114] Above n 34.

ing certainty. Section 3 was not employed.[115] In *Adan*,[116] also a housing case, a majority of the Court of Appeal did not think it possible to interpret section 204(1) of the Housing Act 1996 in such a way as to allow the County Court to allocate to itself jurisdiction to entertain an appeal on issues of fact so as to comply with Article 6.

3.6.7 Civil Procedure

In *Cachia v Faluyi*[117] the Court of Appeal used section 3 to interpret the word 'action' in section 2(3) of the Fatal Accidents Act 1976 as meaning 'served process' in order to give effect to rights under Article 6 of the children whose mother had died.[118] The Act provided that no more than one action shall lie for and in respect of the same subject matter of complaint. The problem was that a writ had been issued but never served—it was argued that this precluded the bringing of a new action. Similarly, in *Goode v Martin*[119] the Court of Appeal had to construe CPR 17.4(1) and (2), which precluded the amendment of a statement of case unless the new claim arose out of the same facts or substantially the same facts as a claim in respect of which the party applying for permission had already claimed a remedy in the proceedings. Finding that Article 6 altered the position, the court held that there was no sound policy reason why the claimant should not add to her claim the alternative plea.

> No new facts are being introduced: she merely wants to say that if the defendant succeeds in establishing his version of the facts, she will still win because those facts, too, show that he was negligent and should pay her compensation.[120]

It concluded that the Rule should be interpreted as if it contained the additional words 'are already in issue on', therefore reading

> if the new claim arises out of the same facts or substantially the same facts as are already in issue on a claim in respect of which the party applying for permission has already claimed a remedy in the proceedings.[121]

3.6.8 Other

Section 3 has been used to ensure that section 10 of the Contempt of Court Act 1981 is read and applied, so far as possible, compatibly with the Convention rights.

> This must mean that, to be necessary within what is now the meaning of s.10, disclosure [of a journalist's source] must meet a pressing social need, must be the only practical way of doing so, must be accompanied by safeguards against abuse and must not be such as to destroy the essence of the primary right.[122]

---

[115] *Ibid*, at [77].
[116] *Adan v Newham London Borough Council* [2001] EWCA Civ 1916, [2002] 1 WLR 2120.
[117] *Cachia v Faluyi* [2001] EWCA Civ 998, [2001] 1 WLR 1966
[118] *Ibid*, at [20].
[119] *Goode v Martin* [2001] EWCA Civ 1899, [2002] 1 WLR 1828.
[120] *Ibid*, at [42].
[121] *Ibid*, at [46].
[122] *Financial Times Ltd v Interbrew SA* [2002] EWCA Civ 274, [2002] EMLR 24.

Sedley LJ pointed out in *Wooder*[123] that section 3 clearly operated on section 132 of the Mental Health Act 1983, requiring the patient to be informed of the reasons for treatment without consent in order to ensure compatibility with Article 8.[124]

Section 3 has also been applied to:

- the State Immunity Act 1978, supporting a conclusion that it was not appropriate to give a blanket effect to a foreign state's claim to state immunity ratione materiae in respect of a state official alleged to have committed acts of systemic torture[125];
- the Bail Act 1976, so that a court is not entitled to deny a defendant bail simply on the basis that he has been arrested under section 7(3) of the Act[126];
- the Data Protection Act 1998, resulting in the conclusion that it was not possible for the Security Service to benefit from a blanket exemption relieving it of any obligation to give a considered answer to individual requests[127];
- section 21 of the National Assistance Act 1948 and section 17 of the Children Act 1989, so as to enable a local authority to provide financial assistance compatibly with Article 8[128];
- section 141(1)(b) of the Customs and Excise Management Act 1979 to make it compatible with Article 1 Protocol No 1[129];
- sections 141 and 142 of the Law of Property Act 1925 to ensure compatibly with Article 1 Protocol No 1 and thereby enable a landlord, under a head tenancy which has been determined by a break notice, to enforce the lessee's covenants as contained in the subtenancy[130];
- section 335A of the Insolvency Act 1986 to ensure that the immediate sale of a property would not violate a family's rights under Article 8.[131]

However, in *Wilkinson*[132] the House of Lords held that it was not possible to use section 3 to understand the word 'widow' as referring to the more general concept of a surviving spouse as the contrary indications in the language of Part VII of the Income and Corporations Taxes Act 1988 were too strong.[133]

---

[123] *R (Wooder) v Feggetter* [2002] EWCA Civ 554, [2002] 3 WLR 591.

[124] *Ibid*, at [48]–[49].

[125] *Jones v Ministry of the Interior* [2004] EWCA Civ 1394, [2005] QB 699 at [91]–[92], [96].

[126] *R (on the application of the Director of Public Prosecutions) v Havering Magistrates' Court* [2001] 1 WLR 805.

[127] *Baker v Secretary of State for the Home Department* [2001] UKHRR 1275.

[128] *R (on the application of J) v Enfield London Borough Council* [2002] EWHC (Admin) 432, [2002] 2 FLR 1.

[129] *Fox v HM Customs and Excise* [2002] EWHC (Admin) 1244, [2003] 1 WLR 1331.

[130] *PW & Co v Milton Gate Investments Ltd* [2003] EWHC (Ch) 1994, [2004] 2 WLR 443 at [130].

[131] *Barca v Mears* [2004] EWHC (Ch) 2170, [2005] 2 FLR 1.

[132] *R (on the application of Wilkinson) v Inland Revenue Commissioners* [2005] UKHL 30, [2005] 1 WLR 1718.

[133] *Ibid*, at [19] per Lord Hoffmann. See also *Secretary of State for Work and Pensions v M* [2004] EWCA Civ 1343, [2005] 2 WLR 740, where a majority of the court held that discrimination against absent parents living in same-sex relationships could be remedied by deleting the definition of unmarried couple in Reg 1(2) of the Child Support (Maintenance Assessments and Special Cases) Regulations 1992 so as to leave the meaning of married couple intact at the same time as liberating the meanings of family and partner, where there was no marriage, from the requirement of heterosexuality.

4. Section 4 Human Rights Act

4.1 Interpretation

Section 4 gives a court the power to make a declaration of incompatibility where a provision of primary legislation is incompatible with a Convention right[134] and where a provision of subordinate legislation is incompatible with a Convention right but the primary legislation prevents removal of the incompatibility.[135] It is only open to certain courts to make a declaration of incompatibility[136]; such a declaration does not affect 'the validity, continuing operation or enforcement of the provision in respect of which it is given' and is not binding on the parties to the proceedings in which it is made.[137] Furthermore, where a court is considering whether to make a declaration of incompatibility, the Crown is entitled to notice in accordance with the rules of court.[138] In *Rights Brought Home*[139] it was stated that whilst a declaration would not of itself change the law, 'it will almost certainly prompt the Government and Parliament to change the law.'[140] It was decided not to give the courts the power to set aside primary legislation due to the importance attached to Parliamentary sovereignty.

> To make a provision in the Bill for the courts to set aside Acts of Parliament would confer on the judiciary a general power over the decisions of Parliament which under our present constitutional arrangements they do not possess, and would be likely on occasions to draw the judiciary into serious conflict with Parliament. There is no evidence to suggest that they desire this power, nor that the public wish them to have it. Certainly, this Government has no mandate for any such change.[141]

Once a provision of legislation has been declared to be incompatible, a minister, if he considers that there are compelling reasons, may by order make such amendments to the legislation as he considers necessary to remove the incompatibility.[142] Again this power is discretionary, and the decision whether to seek a remedial order is a matter for the government to decide on a case-by-case basis. It was thought that it would be wrong for a declaration to automatically lead to a remedial order as this would in effect 'be tantamount to giving the courts power to strike down Acts of

---

[134] Sections 4(1) and 4(2).

[135] Sections 4(3) and 4(4).

[136] Section 4(5) lists the House of Lords; Judicial Committee of the Privy Council; Courts-Martial Appeal Court; in Scotland, the High Court of Justiciary sitting otherwise than as a trial court or the Court of Session; in England and Wales or Northern Ireland, the High Court or the Court of Appeal. It is therefore not open to the Employment Appeal Tribunal to make a declaration, although occasionally the opportunity arises. See, eg Whittaker v P&D Watson [2002] ICR 1244.

[137] Section 4(6).

[138] Section 5(1).

[139] Home Office, *Rights Brought Home: The Human Rights Bill* (Cm 3782) (London, TSO, 1997).

[140] *Ibid*, at [2.11].

[141] *Ibid*, at [2.13].

[142] Section 10(2). This section also allows amendment where, having regard to a finding of the European Court of Human Rights in proceedings against the United Kingdom, a provision of legislation is incompatible with an obligation of the United Kingdom arising from the Convention. See s 10(1)(b).

Parliament.'[143] The procedure for making such a remedial order is set out in Schedule 2 to the HRA. In brief, the procedure which must be followed is the affirmative procedure, and a draft of the order must be approved by a resolution of each House of Parliament. However, in urgent cases it is possible to make the order without the draft being so approved.[144] It is important to note that the victim of the incompatible act resulting in the declaration may actually have no other enforceable remedy although it may be possible for a remedial order affecting the legislation to take effect from a date earlier than that on which the order was made or for ex gratia compensation to be sought.[145] To date only two remedial orders have been made under the provisions set out in the HRA.[146]

As to the circumstances where a declaration may be made, these encompass the instances where it is not possible to use section 3 as discussed in the paragraphs above. It may be that the legislation contains provisions which expressly contradict the meaning which the enactment would have to be given to make it compatible or provisions which do so by necessary implication.[147] It may also arise that the use of section 3 would involve adopting a meaning inconsistent with a fundamental feature of the legislation[148] or involve the court in making a decision for which it was not equipped.[149] In keeping with the view that a declaration of incompatibility is a measure of last resort[150] and an exceptional course to take,[151] very few declarations of incompatibility have actually been made by the courts. During the parliamentary debates, the Lord Chancellor commented that in 99% of the cases that will arise, there will be no need for judicial declarations of incompatibility.[152] Of those which have survived the appeals process, at the time of writing there have been nine declarations in total: three by the House of Lords, three by the Court of Appeal and three by the High Court.

4.2 A Reasonable Period within which to Amend Domestic Law

It has been accepted by the courts that there may be circumstances where maintaining an offending law in operation for a reasonable period pending enactment of corrective legislation is justifiable and that, during the transitional period, an

---

[143] HL Deb, Vol 583, col 1139 (27 November 1997), Lord Chancellor.

[144] See paras 2(b) and 4 Sch 2. See further Joint Committee on Human Rights, *Seventh Report* (2001–02 HL 58, HC 473).

[145] HL Deb, Vol 583, col 1108 (27 November 1997), Lord Chancellor.

[146] These are: Mental Health Act 1983 (Remedial) Order 2001 as a result of the declaration of incompatibility in *R (H) v Mental Health Tribunal*, Court of Appeal, 4 April 2001; and Naval Discipline Act 1957 (Remedial) Order 2004 as a result of the judgment of the European Court of Human Rights in *Grieves v United Kingdom*, 16 December 2003. However, it is important to note that some declarations of incompatibility have been addressed via primary legislation such as the Nationality, Immigration and Asylum Act 2002, Gender Recognition Bill and the Criminal Justice Bill.

[147] *R v A*, above n 43, at [108] per Lord Hope; *Lambert*, above n 55, at [79] per Lord Hope; *Re S*, above n 46, at [40] per Lord Nicholls; *Anderson*, above n 55, at [59] per Lord Steyn; *Rusbridger*, above n 55, at [8] per Lord Steyn; *Ghaidan*, above n 26, at [117] per Lord Rodger.

[148] *Re S*, above n 46, at [40] per Lord Nicholls.

[149] *Ghaidan*, above n 26, at [33] per Lord Nicholls.

[150] *R v A*, above n 43, at [44] per Lord Steyn.

[151] *Ghaidan*, above n 26, at [50] per Lord Steyn. See also *Attorney General's Reference No.4 of 2002*, above n 45, at [28] per Lord Bingham.

[152] HL Deb, Vol 585, col 840 (5 February 1998).

individual would not be able to claim that his or her rights had been violated.[153] Therefore, where a declaration of incompatibility is likely to be made, it is not uncommon for the defendant Secretary of State to resist such a declaration on the ground that the government should be entitled to a reasonable period in which to amend domestic law. For example, in *Bellinger*[154] the Secretary of State submitted that the House of Lords should not make a declaration of incompatibility as the European Court of Human Rights in *Goodwin v United Kingdom*[155] envisaged that the government should have a reasonable period in which to amend domestic law on a principled and coherent basis.

However, this was not accepted by their Lordships. Lord Nicholls held that this was not a situation where legal acts or situations which antedated the judgment in *Goodwin* were being reopened. Section 11(c) of the Matrimonial Causes Act 1973 remained a continuing obstacle to Mr and Mrs Bellinger marrying each other[156] and was clearly not compatible with Articles 8 and 12.

> The European Court of Human Rights so found in July 2002 in *Goodwin*, and the government has so accepted. What was held to be incompatible in July 2002 has not now, for the purposes of s.4, become compatible. The government's announcement of forthcoming legislation has not had that effect, nor could it. That would make no sense.[157]

4.3 A Declaration where the Government already Has Plans to Legislate

It has also been submitted by respondent Secretaries of State that there is no need to make a declaration where the government already has plans to legislate in the area. However, such arguments are generally not successful. For example, it was also submitted in *Bellinger*[158] that a declaration would serve no useful purpose as the government had already announced its intention to bring forward primary legislation on this subject. Lord Nicholls was not persuaded.

> [W]hen proceedings are already before the House, it is desirable that in a case of such sensitivity this House, as the court of final appeal in this country, should formally record that the present state of statute law is incompatible with the Convention.[159]

Similarly, in M[160] it was submitted that the Mental Health Bill would resolve the problem. The Administrative Court rejected this argument, holding that it would be

---

[153] *Bellinger v Bellinger* [2003] UKHL 21, [2003] 2 AC 467 at [53] per Lord Nicholls.
[154] *Ibid.*
[155] (2002) 35 EHRR 18.
[156] *Ibid*, at [52].
[157] *Ibid*, at [53]. It was also held in *Hooper*, above n 5, that if a form of discrimination which was historically justified but, with changes in society, has gradually lost its justification, a period of consultation, drafting and debate must be included in the time which the legislature may reasonable consider appropriate for making a change and up to the point at which that time is exceeded, there is no violation of a Convention right. However, this did not apply in the present case. See [62]–[63] per Lord Hoffmann in reliance upon *Walden v Liechtenstein*, Judgment of 16 March 2000.
[158] Above n 153.
[159] *Ibid*, at [55].
[160] *R (on the application of M) v Secretary of State for Health* [2003] EWHC (Admin) 1094, [2003] ACD 389.

wrong to make assumptions about the form in which a Bill may be enacted or about the timing of its coming into force.

> If I make a declaration, it is for the Government to decide what, if anything, to do about it. It is not for me to express or imply any view as to what it, through Parliament, ought to do about it. If I make a declaration, the door is opened to a remedial order under s 10, but it remains a matter for the Secretary of State as to whether he wishes to walk through that door.[161]

4.4 Failure to Legislate

It is not possible to issue a declaration of incompatibility in relation to a failure to legislate. The absence of a particular provision from a statute does not, in itself, mean that the statute is incompatible with a Convention right. '[T]his signifies at most the existence of a lacuna in the statute.'[162] It is also clearly stated in section 6(6) that an act includes a failure to act but does not include a failure to introduce in, or lay before, Parliament a proposal for legislation, or make any primary legislation or remedial order.

Nevertheless, there have been deviations from this rule. In *MH*[163] the Court of Appeal declared that there was lacking from the scheme of the Mental Health Act 1983 provisions that were necessary to make that scheme compliant with the Convention rights. Section 2 was declared incompatible with Article 5(4) in that it was not attended by adequate provision for the reference to a court of the case of a patient detained pursuant to section 2 in circumstances where a patient had a right to make application to a Mental Health Review Tribunal but the patient was incapable of exercising that right on his own initiative.[164]

Furthermore, in *Rose*[165] the Administrative Court made a distinction between regulations falling with the affirmative resolution procedure and regulations falling within the negative resolution procedure. The claimants sought access to non-identifying information and, where possible, identifying information in respect of an anonymous sperm donor. The Administrative Court confirmed that section 6(6)(a) prevented the claimants from complaining of any failure to enact primary legislation or of any failure to make regulations under section 31(4)(a) of the Human Fertilisation and Embryology Act 1990. 'Any regulations under this subsection require the positive approval of both Houses of Parliament.'[166] However, the court pointed out that the claimants were not debarred from claiming that the Secretary of State had acted unlawfully in failing to make regulations under section 8(d) of the 1990 Act because such regulations would fall within the negative resolution procedure.[167] In the opinion of the court, where the primary legislation provides that a statutory

---

[161] *Ibid*, at [17]. See also [14]–[22].
[162] *Re S*, above n 46, at [85].
[163] *R (on the application of MH) v Secretary of State for Health* [2004] EWCA Civ 1609, [2005] 1 WLR 1209.
[164] *Ibid*, at [29]. Section 29(4) was also declared incompatible.
[165] *R (on the application of Rose) v Secretary of State for Health* [2002] EWHC (Admin) 1593, [2002] 3 FCR 731.
[166] *Ibid*, at [50].
[167] *Ibid*.

instrument shall be subject to annulment by resolution of either House after being made, it would not be a proposal for legislation within the meaning of section 6(6)(a) of the HRA. It contrasted the position where the primary legislation provided that a statutory instrument may not be made unless authorised by affirmative resolution as there the instrument would be a proposal for legislation for the purposes of section 6(6)(a).[168]

4.5 The Use of Section 4 in Hypothetical Cases

It has been held that the requirement for a claimant to be a victim within the meaning of section 7 of the HRA does not apply where a declaration of incompatibility is sought.[169] However, given that the grant of a declaration is discretionary, it appears that it is unlikely to be granted where the claimant has not been and could not be personally adversely affected by the legislation.

In *Taylor*[170] the issue was whether a litigant could obtain a declaration of incompatibility on a ground from which he could not benefit. The Court of Appeal held that it was not the intention of the HRA or the Convention that members of the public should use these provisions if they were not adversely affected by them to change legislation because they considered that the legislation was incompatible with the Convention. In the view of the court, this was made clear by the language of section 7, and the claimant here was not a victim.[171] In addition, it pointed out that the grant of a declaration of incompatibility was discretionary.

> It is doubtful in the extreme that a court would exercise its discretion in favour of Mr Taylor if he could not be affected by the breach of the Convention on which he was attempting to rely.[172]

Taking into account the judgment of the House of Lords in *Rusbridger*,[173] the court pointed out that the desirably flexible approach to the grant of declarations could not be applied in the present circumstances where the claimant has not been and could not be personally adversely affected by the repealed legislation on which he seeks to rely. 'To allow him to do so would be to ignore section 7 of the HRA.'[174]

4.6 The Application of Section 4 in Practice

Given that there have been so few declarations of incompatibility to date, the majority of those that have been made are examined in the following paragraphs.

---

168 *Ibid*, at [51].
169 *R (on the application of Trailer & Marina (Leven) Ltd) v Secretary of State for the Environment, Food & Rural Affairs* [2004] EWCA Civ 1580, [2005] 1 WLR 1267.
170 *Lancashire County Council v Taylor* [2005] EWCA Civ 284, [2005] HRLR 17.
171 *Ibid*, at [38]–[41].
172 *Ibid*, at [42].
173 Above n 55.
174 *Ibid*, at [44]. See also *Tangney v The Governor of HMP Elmley* [2005] EWCA Civ 1009.

4.6.1 Sentencing

In *Anderson*[175] the House of Lords found unanimously that it was not possible to apply section 3 to section 29 of the the the Crime (Sentences) Act 1997.

> Since, therefore, the section leaves it to the Home Secretary to decide whether or when to refer a case to the [Parole] board, and he is free to ignore its recommendation if it is favourable to the prisoner, the decision on how long the convicted murderer should remain in prison for punitive purposes is his alone. It cannot be doubted that Parliament intended this result when enacting section 29 and its predecessor sections . . . To read section 29 as precluding participation by the Home Secretary, if it were possible to do so, would not be judicial interpretation but judicial vandalism: it would give the section an effect quite different from that which Parliament intended and would go well beyond any interpretative process sanctioned by section 3 of the 1998 Act.[176]

Their Lordships therefore issued their first declaration of incompatibility, declaring section 29 incompatible with the right under Article 6 to have a sentence imposed by an independent and impartial tribunal.

4.6.2 Gender Reassignment

In *Bellinger*[177] the House of Lords unanimously declared section 11(c) of the Matrimonial Causes Act 1973 incompatible with Articles 8 and 12 as it made no provision for the recognition of gender reassignment. This step was taken even though it had no effect on the validity or otherwise of the marriage ceremony celebrated in 1981. Lord Hope recognised that

> problems of great complexity would be involved if recognition were to be given to same sex marriages. They must be left to Parliament. I do not think that your Lordships can solve the problem judicially by means of the interpretative obligation in s.3(1) of the 1998 Act.[178]

Similarly, Lord Hobhouse found a declaration appropriate, as to use section 3 to read section 11(c) so as to include additional words such as 'two people of the same sex' would be a legislative exercise of amendment.[179]

4.6.3 Prevention of Terrorism

In *A v Secretary of State for the Home Department*[180] the question of using section 3 to interpret section 23 of the Anti-Terrorism Crime and Security Act 2001 was not even discussed, it having been found incompatible with Article 14 taken together with Article 5. A majority of their Lordships simply made a declaration of incompatibility, declaring that the section was incompatible with Articles 5 and 14 insofar as it

---

[175] Above n 55.
[176] *Ibid*, at [30] per Lord Bingham. See also Lord Steyn at [59] and Lord Hutton at [81].
[177] Above n 153.
[178] *Ibid*, at [69].
[179] *Ibid*, at [78]. See further D Nicol, 'Gender Reassignment and the Transformation of the Human Rights Act' (2004) 120 *LQR* 194.
[180] *A v Secretary of State for the Home Department* [2004] UKHL 56, [2005] 2 AC 68.

was disproportionate and permitted detention of suspected international terrorists in a way that discriminated on the ground of nationality or immigration status.[181]

4.6.4 Mental Health

In *H*[182] the Court of Appeal concluded that section 73 of the Mental Health Act 1983 was incompatible with Articles 5(1) and 5(4) of the Convention in that the burden of proof was placed on the patient. The patient had to prove that the criteria for admission were not satisfied, whereas, in the opinion of the court, he should be entitled to be discharged if it could not be demonstrated that the criteria were satisfied. Section 3 was not considered and a declaration of incompatibility was made under section 4. As discussed above, in *MH*[183] the Court of Appeal declared section 2 of the Mental Health Act 1983 incompatible with Article 5(4) in that it was not attended by adequate provision for the reference to a court of the case of a patient detained pursuant to section 2 in circumstances where a patient had a right to make application to a Mental Health Review Tribunal but the patient was incapable of exercising that right on his own initiative.[184]

A declaration of incompatibility was also made in *D*,[185] where the Administrative Court found that the fact that a discretionary life prisoner who had served the minimum period of his detention but who remained also compulsorily detained under the Mental Health Act 1983 had no statutory right to apply to the Parole Board or to require the Secretary of State to refer his case to the Board under section 34(5) of the Criminal Justice Act 1991 in order for it to review the lawfulness of his detention was incompatible with Article 5(4). Section 74 of the Mental Health Act 1983 was declared incompatible. Sections 26 and 29 of the Mental Health Act 1983 were declared incompatible with Article 8 in *M*,[186] the Administrative Court finding that the absence of any possibility to apply to the court to change the claimant's nearest relative was incompatible with Article 8.

4.6.5 Immigration

In *International Transport Roth*[187] a majority of the Court of Appeal found that a penalty scheme created pursuant to section 32 of the Immigration and Asylum Act 1999 making carriers liable to a fixed penalty for every clandestine entrant found concealed in a vehicle was inconsistent with Article 6 and Article 1 of Protocol No 1. It was held that it was impossible to recreate the scheme by any interpretative process as one compatible with Convention rights.

---

[181] *Ibid*, at [73] per Lord Bingham.
[182] *R (on the application of H) v Mental Health Review Tribunal, North & East London Region* [2001] EWCA Civ 415, [2002] QB 1.
[183] Above n 163.
[184] *Ibid*, at [29]. Section 29(4) was also declared incompatible.
[185] *D v Secretary of State for the Home Department* [2002] EHC (Admin) 2805, [2003] 1 WLR 1315.
[186] Above n 160.
[187] *International Transport Roth GmbH v Secretary of State for the Home Department* [2002] EWCA Civ 158, [2003] QB 728.

> We cannot create a wholly different scheme . . . so as to provide an acceptable alternative means of immigration control. That must be for Parliament itself.[188]

Section 32 was declared incompatible with the Convention rights.[189]

4.6.6 Housing

Finally, a declaration of incompatibility was made by the Administrative Court in *Morris*[190] following its finding that the council's refusal to treat the claimant as having a priority need for accommodation in circumstances where a parent with a dependent child who was not subject to immigration control would have been treated as having a priority need was incompatible with Article 14 taken together with Article 8. It concluded that to read section 185(4) of the Housing Act 1996 compatibly with Article 14 would amount to amendment, not interpretation.[191] The court rejected the submission that a declaration could be avoided if the local authority could exercise another power.

> It may be that the consequences of the incompatibility of s.185(4) with art 14 can be ameliorated by converting the power in s.192(3) into a duty. But that does not make s.185(4) any the less incompatible with art 14. Its incompatibility should be brought home by a formal declaration under s.4(2) of the 1998 Act.[192]

---

5. The Use of Hansard and Other Materials in Compatibility Cases

It has been widely appreciated by the courts that the HRA requires them to exercise a new role in respect of primary legislation.

> This new role is fundamentally different from interpreting and applying legislation. The courts are now required to evaluate the effect of primary legislation in terms of Convention rights and, where appropriate, make a formal declaration of incompatibility. In carrying out this evaluation the court has to compare the effect of the legislation with the Convention right. If the legislation impinges upon a Convention right the court must then compare the policy objective of the legislation with the policy objective which under the Convention may justify a prima facie infringement of the Convention right.[193]

---

[188] *Ibid*, at [66] per Simon Brown LJ.
[189] See also Jonathan Parker LJ, *ibid*, at [184], [186].
[190] *R (on the application of Morris) v Westminster City Council* [2004] EWHC (Admin) 2191, [2005] 1 WLR 865.
[191] *Ibid*, at [38].
[192] *Ibid*, at [39].
[193] *Wilson*, above n 10, at [61] per Lord Nicholls.

When making these comparisons, it has been held that the court will look primarily at the legislation.

> The first question is whether the policy justification for the distinction which is in issue is apparent from the legislation, whether read by itself or with its antecedents and the cases decided on the provisions. Only if the policy is not apparent from these materials should it become necessary to look wider.[194]

However, it is also possible for a court to look outside the statute in order to see the complete picture.[195]

> [S]ometimes the court may need additional background information tending to show, for instance, the likely practical impact of the statutory measure and why the course adopted by the legislature is not appropriate. Moreover, as when interpreting a statute, so when identifying the policy objective of a statutory provision or assessing the 'proportionality' of a statutory provision, the court may need enlightenment on the nature and extent of the social problem (the 'mishchief') at which the legislation is aimed. This may throw light on the rationale underlying the legislation.[196]

Such background information may include published documents, such as a White Paper, or explanatory notes prepared by the relevant government department and published with the Bill.[197] It may also include information gleaned from the parliamentary debates on the Bill.

> By having regard to such material the court would not be 'questioning' proceedings in Parliament or intruding improperly into the legislative process or ascribing to Parliament the views expressed by a minister. The court would merely be placing itself in a better position to understand the legislation.[198]

However, it has been noted that such occasions when resort to Hansard is necessary will seldom arise and, if it did, the court must be careful

> not to treat the ministerial or other statement as indicative of the objective intention of Parliament. Nor should the courts give a ministerial statement, whether made inside or outside Parliament, determinative weight. It should not be supposed that members necessarily agreed with the minister's reasoning or his conclusions.[199]

Furthermore, it is clear that Hansard may only be used as a source of background information.

> The proportionality of a statutory measure is not to be judged by the quality of the reasons advanced in support of it in the course of parliamentary debate, or by the subjective state of mind of individual ministers or other members . . . The court is called upon to evaluate

---

194 *Taylor*, above n 170.
195 *Wilson*, above n 10.
196 *Ibid*, at [63].
197 *Ibid*, at [64].
198 *Ibid*.
199 *Ibid*, at [66]. See also Taylor, above n 170, at [58].

the proportionality of the legislation, not the adequacy of the minister's exploration of the policy options or his explanations to Parliament.[200]

In addition to concerns about the use of Hansard, particular issues have arisen surrounding the submission of witness statements by government ministers in compatibility cases. For example, in *Evans*[201] the Secretary of State filed a 19-page witness statement containing evidence as to the legislative history of the provision, the policy justification for the regime of the Act and relevant legal practice in other Council of Europe states. A majority of the Court of Appeal was concerned about its admissibility, commenting that they were not persuaded that the speeches in *Wilson* would accommodate the full ambit of the witness statement.

> If it is open to a minister whose predecessor was administratively responsible for a Bill to give evidence for s.4 purposes of the departmental policy and intent behind the measure, it is not immediately obvious why a minister may not give evidence—potentially conclusive evidence—of what he or his predecessor intended in making a statutory instrument of which the meaning is being debated in court.[202]

However, the majority did no more than record its concerns.[203]

The issue returned in *Taylor*,[204] where the Secretary of State submitted a witness statement containing: a summary of the history of legislative reform; substantial extracts from the reports of the Parliamentary debates on what became the predecessor Acts; a cutting from *Farmers' Weekly*; extracts from the drafter's Notes on Clauses on the 1976 Bill; correspondence dating from 1951 between the National Farmer's Union and the Ministry of Agriculture; some extracts from the 1947 Act; a comment on and gloss on the Hansard extracts; and an account of current government policy. The court pointed out that, insofar as this represented argument, its proper source was counsel, not a witness. Insofar as it recounted history, it was relevant and helpful. However, the use of drafter's Notes on Clauses was found to be problematic as they were not available to members of either House.

> To the extent that ministers used them in debate, they will feature in Hansard. It is therefore to Hansard that one needs principally to turn.[205]

It also concluded that, had it been necessary to go beyond the text and the legislative and judicial history of the 1986 Act, it would have admitted little if any of the parliamentary materials admitted in the court below, including contributions of members to the debates and ministerial statements which said no more than could be readily seen from the legislation itself.[206]

---

[200] *Ibid*, at [67]. Lord Hope reached a similar conclusion at [110]–[118], as did Lord Hobhouse at [139]–[144]. Lord Scott agreed with Lord Nicholls, and Lord Rodger made no comment on the issue. See further A Kavanagh, 'Pepper v Hart and Matters of Constitutional Principle', (2005) 121 *LQR* 98.
[201] *Evans v Amicus Healthcare Ltd* [2004] EWCA Civ 727, [2004] 3 WLR 681.
[202] *Ibid*, at [53].
[203] *Ibid*, at [56].
[204] Above n 170.
[205] *Ibid*, at [55].
[206] *Ibid*, at [59].

6. Section 19 Human Rights Act: Statements of Compatibility

The final provision of the HRA concerning primary legislation is section 19 which provides that a Minister of the Crown in charge of a Bill in either House of Parliament must, before Second Reading of the Bill: (a) make a statement to the effect that in his view the provisions of the Bill are compatible with the Convention rights; or (b) make a statement to the effect that although he in unable to make a statement of compatibility the government nevertheless wishes the House to proceed with the Bill. The statement must be in writing and be published in such manner as the Minister making it considers appropriate.[207] It was suggested by the Lord Chancellor during the Parliamentary debates that this section was a very large gesture, as well as a point of substance

> in favour of the development of a culture of awareness of what the convention requires in relation to domestic legislation.[208]

The Home Office has stated that in considering whether to make a statement of compatibility the basic test applied is whether, on the balance of probabilities, the provisions of the Bill would be found compatible with the Convention rights if challenged in court or tribunal. However, it is appreciated that

> the Minister's view is reached only after very careful consideration but is not legally binding. Ultimately, only a court can determine the Convention rights and give a definitive view as to whether a particular provision complies with those rights or not.[209]

Whilst a useful addition to mechanisms for the protection and promotion of human rights in the legislative process, section 19 statements have had little impact in HRA jurisprudence and such statements carry very little weight. Lord Hope in *R v A*[210] pointed out that the Secretary of State did not seek to rely on the statement of compatibility attached to the Youth Justice and Criminal Evidence Act 1999 in the course of his argument.

> I consider that he was right not to do so. These statements may serve a useful purpose in Parliament. They may also be seen as part of the parliamentary history, indicating that it was not Parliament's intention to cut across a Convention right . . . No doubt they are based on the best advice that is available. But they are no more than expressions of opinion by the minister. They are not binding on the court, nor do they have any persuasive authority.[211]

---

[207] More specific information on the human rights aspect of a Bill is provided in the Explanatory Notes which accompany the Bill.
[208] HL Deb, Vol 583, col 1163 (27 November 1997).
[209] Memo by Home Office to the Joint Committee on Human Rights, minutes of evidence taken on Wednesday 14 March 2001 (2000–01 HL 66, HC 332) at [15].
[210] Above n 43.
[211] *Ibid*, at [69].

Remedies

1. Introduction

In relation to any act of a public authority which a court finds unlawful, section 8(1) of the HRA provides that the court may grant such relief or remedy, or make such order, within its powers as it considers just and appropriate. As with other key features of the HRA, the remedies available closely mirror those which would be available to a claimant before the European Court of Human Rights under Article 41 of the ECHR,[1] which enables the Court to award 'just satisfaction to the injured party' for Convention violations. The approach of the UK courts should be no less liberal than those applied at Strasbourg

> or one of the purposes of the HRA will be defeated and claimants will still be put to the expense of having to go to Strasbourg to obtain just satisfaction.[2]

It has been rightly observed that where an infringement of an individual's human rights has occurred, the concern will usually be to bring the infringement to an end and any question of compensation will be of secondary importance.[3] The remedies most frequently sought for an act incompatible with Convention rights are the

> orders which are the descendants of the historic prerogative orders or declaratory judgments. The orders enable the court to order a public body to refrain from or to take action, or to quash an offending administrative decision or a public body. Declaratory judgments usually resolve disputes as to what is the correct answer in law to a dispute.[4]

---

[1] 'If the Court finds that there has been a violation of the Convention or the protocols thereto, and if the internal law of the High Contracting Party concerned allows only partial reparation to be made, the Court shall, if necessary, afford just satisfaction to the injured party.'

[2] *Anufrijeva v Southwark LBC* [2003] EWCA Civ 1406, [2004] QB 1124 at [57]. On remedies under the HRA generally, see D Feldman, 'Remedies for Violations of Convention Rights under the Human Rights Act', [1998] *EHRLR* 691.

[3] *Anufrijeva, ibid*, at [53]. However, it is important to note that, whilst a number of observations concerning the award of remedies, specifically damages, were made in this case, these were *obiter* given that the court actually found no violation of a Convention right.

[4] *Ibid.*

However, whilst this is the case, the focus of section 8, and HRA jurisprudence in this area, is primarily on the award of damages.

---

2. Just and Appropriate

A court's discretionary power under section 8(1) to grant a remedy extends to such remedy as it considers 'just and appropriate'. There has been very little consideration of this phrase in HRA case law apart from the observation that just and appropriate in Convention terms really means 'effective, just and proportionate'.[5]

The notion of a remedy being a 'just' remedy implies that it must be fair to all who are affected by it, including persons other than the person whose right was violated.[6] For example, in *Anufrijeva*[7] the Court of Appeal held that in considering whether to award compensation, and, if so, how much, there was a balance to be drawn between the interests of the victim and those of the public as a whole.[8] On the other hand, appropriateness suggests that the remedy, from the standpoint of the person whose Convention right was violated, will effectively address the grievance brought about by the violation.[9] For example, in relation to the reasonable time guarantee in Article 6, it has been held that if the breach is established before the hearing, the appropriate remedy may be a public acknowledgement of the breach, action to expedite the hearing to the greatest extent practicable and perhaps, if the defendant is in custody, his release on bail.[10]

---

3. Effective

It has also been suggested that, whilst it is not expressly referred to in section 8(1), any remedy awarded for an act incompatible with Convention rights should also be effective.

---

[5] *Attorney General's Reference No.2 of 2001* [2003] UKHL 68, [2004] 2 AC 72 at [24] per Lord Bingham.
[6] *Saskatchewan Human Rights Commission v Kodellas* (1989) 60 DLR (4th) 143 at 162 per Bayda CJS. This interpretation was of the remedies clause in the Canadian Charter of Rights and Freedoms, which is in very similar terms to s 8(1) empowering the court to award appropriate and just remedies for the infringement of rights.
[7] Above n 2.
[8] *Ibid*, at [56]. See also *R (on the application of Bernard) v London Borough of Enfield* [2002] EWHC (Admin) 2282, [2003] HRLR 4 at [58]–[59].
[9] *Ibid*.
[10] *Attorney General's Reference No.2 of 2001*, above n 5, at [24] per Lord Bingham, with whom Lords Nicholls, Steyn, Hoffmann, Hobhouse and Scott all agreed.

Since the aim of the Act is that the domestic courts, rather than the Strasbourg court, should be able to remedy violations of the convention, it can readily be inferred that a remedy will be just and appropriate if it constitutes the kind of effective remedy required by art 13 of the convention.[11]

The obligation to ensure that remedies are effective, as well as just and appropriate, could have a significant impact. Arguably an effective remedy under the HRA would adequately compensate those who have suffered damage as a result of the act of a public authority incompatible with a Convention right and, secondly, emphasise the importance of the Convention rights and deter future violations by public authorities.

However, the difficulty with obliging courts to ensure that remedies are also effective is that, despite parliamentary pressure, the government deliberately omitted Article 13 of the Convention (the right to an effective remedy)[12] from the HRA, stating that it was not necessary to include it as section 8 already 'provides effective remedies before our courts.'[13] Nevertheless, although courts as 'public authorities' are not obliged to act in a way which is compatible with Article 13,[14] the Lord Chancellor during the parliamentary debates did state that the courts may have regard to Article 13 when considering the provisions of section 8.[15]

Despite this encouragement, there has been little evidence of the impact of Article 13 or the notion of an effective remedy in the case law. In the majority of instances where it has been referred to by the courts, it has been to lament its non-inclusion as a Convention right given further effect by the HRA. For example, in *Lambert*[16] Lord Hope suggested his conclusion that the HRA did not have retrospective effect in the circumstances of the case may have been different if Article 13 had been one of the Convention rights given further effect by the HRA.[17] In *Re S*[18] it had been argued that the absence from the Children Act 1989 of an adequate remedy if a local authority failed to discharge its parental responsibilities properly was a violation of Article 8. The House of Lords disagreed, holding that failure by the state to provide an effective remedy for a violation of Article 8 was not itself a violation of Article 8.[19]

Article 13 is not a Convention right as defined in section 1(1) of the Human Rights Act. So legislation which fails to provide an effective remedy for infringement of Article 8 is not, for that reason, incompatible with a Convention right within the meaning of the Human Rights Act.[20]

---

[11] *Ibid*, at [175].

[12] Article 13: 'Everyone whose rights and freedoms as set forth in this Convention are violated shall have an effective remedy before a national authority notwithstanding that the violation was committed by persons acting in an official capacity.'

[13] Lord Chancellor, HL Deb, Vol 583, col 475 (18 November 1997). See also the observations of the House of Lords in *Re S* [2002] UKHL 10, [2002] 2 WLR 720 at [61] per Lord Nicholls.

[14] Section 6, Human Rights Act 1998.

[15] HL Deb, Vol 583, col 477 (18 November 1997).

[16] *R v Lambert* [2001] UKHL 37, [2002] 2 AC 545.

[17] *Ibid*, at [111]. See also the comments of Lord Clyde at [142]. However, in *R v Kansal* [2001] UKHL 62, [2001] 3 WLR 1562 Lord Hope indicated that it was the influence of Art 13 which lead to his conclusion that the HRA did have retrospective effect.

[18] *Re S* [2002] UKHL 10, [2002] 2 WLR 720.

[19] *Ibid*, at [59].

[20] *Ibid*, at [60] per Lord Nicholls.

Similarly, in relation to Article 6 it was held that Article 13 was the guarantee of an effective remedy for breach of a Convention right, not Article 6(1).[21]

4. The Power to Award Damages

It is not specifically stated in section 8 that a court may award damages, although 'damages' is defined in subsection 8(5) as 'damages for the unlawful act of a public authority'[22] and the remaining subsections of section 8 concern limitations on any award of damages indicating that such an award is possible.[23] There is also considerable extra-statutory evidence that this is the case the Lord Chancellor commenting during the Parliamentary debates that

> [o]ur aim is that people should receive damages equivalent to what they would have obtained had they taken their case to Strasbourg.[24]

It is clear that there is no right to damages for the violation of a Convention right,[25] and a number of pre-conditions relate to such an award.[26] First, there must be a finding of unlawfulness or prospective unlawfulness based on breach or prospective breach by a public authority of a Convention right.[27] Secondly, the court must have the power to award damages, or to order the payment of compensation, in civil proceedings.[28] Thirdly, the court should consider an award of damages to be just and appropriate.[29] Fourthly, the court should be satisfied, taking account of all the circumstances of the particular case, that an award of damages is necessary to afford just satisfaction to the person in whose favour it is made.[30] Finally, in deciding whether to award damages, and if so how much, the court is not strictly bound by the principles applied by the European Court in awarding compensation under Article 41 of the Convention, but it must take those principles into account.[31] These various constraints on the award of damages are considered in the following paragraphs.[32]

---

[21] *Ibid*, at [70] per Lord Nicholls.
[22] 'Unlawful act' is defined in subs 8(5) as 'unlawful under section 6(1).'
[23] See also s 9 of the Act, which concerns damages that may be awarded in respect of judicial acts, also indicating that such an award is possible.
[24] Lord Chancellor, HL Deb, Vol 582, col 1232 (3 November 1997).
[25] *Anufrijeva*, above n 2, at [55].
[26] See generally *R v Secretary of State for the Home Department, ex p Greenfield* [2005] UKHL 14, [2005] 1 WLR 673.
[27] Section 8(1).
[28] Section 8(2).
[29] Section 8(1).
[30] Section 8(3).
[31] Section 8(4).
[32] On damages under the HRA, see generally: Law Commission, Report No 266, *Damages under the Human Rights Act 1998*, Cm 4853 (2000); ME Amos, 'Damages for Breach of the Human Rights Act 1998' [1999] *EHRLR* 178; D Fairgrieve, 'The Human Rights Act 1998, Damages and Tort Law' [2001] *PL* 695; R Clayton, 'Damage Limitation: the Courts and Human Rights Act Damages' [2005] *PL* 429; J Hartshorne, 'The Human Rights Act 1998 and Damages for Non-pecuniary Loss' [2004] *EHRLR* 660.

5. Court Must Have the Power to Award Damages

Section 8(2) of the HRA provides that damages may be awarded only by a court which has power to award damages, or to order the payment of compensation in civil proceedings. It is therefore not possible for a criminal court to award damages.[33] In making this limitation, it was thought

> appropriate for an individual who considers that his rights have been infringed in such a case to pursue any matter of damages through the civil courts where this type of issue is normally dealt with; in other words, to pursue the matter in the courts that are accustomed to determining whether it is necessary and appropriate to award damages and what the proper amount should be.[34]

However, damages may be awarded by the High Court on an application for judicial review. The Supreme Court Act 1981 provides that on an application for judicial review, the High Court may award damages to the applicant if (a) he has joined with his application a claim for damages arising from any matter to which the application relates; and (b) the court is satisfied that, if the claim had been made in an action begun by the applicant at the time of making his application, he would have been awarded damages.[35] Obviously, the claim for damages joined would be a claim for damages for breach of the Act by the public authority. It is therefore quite possible for an applicant to bring judicial review proceedings against a public authority purely on Convention grounds, seeking, for example, certiorari and damages for the unlawful act of the public authority.[36]

---

6. Just Satisfaction

Section 8(3) of the HRA provides that no award of damages is to be made unless, taking account of all the circumstances of the case, including (a) any other relief or remedy granted, or order made, in relation to the act in question (by that or any other court) and (b) the consequences of any decision (of that or any other court) in respect of that act, the court is satisfied that the award is necessary to afford just satisfaction to the person in whose favour it is made.

It has been observed that the language of 'just satisfaction' is distinct from the approach in common law, where a claimant is invariably entitled, so far as money can achieve this, to be restored to the position he would have been in had he not suffered

---

[33] See, eg *R v Galfetti* [2002] EWCA Crim 1916.
[34] Lord Chancellor, HL Deb, Vol 583, cols 854–55 (24 November 1997).
[35] Subsection 31(4). See also RSC O53 r 7. Contrast the position under the old Order 53.
[36] HL Deb Vol 582, col 1232 (3 November 1997).

the injury of which the complaint is made.[37] 'Just satisfaction' is obviously a Convention concept, reflecting the wording of Article 41, and relevant judgments of the Court will be key to its interpretation. Nevertheless, two important circumstances are already referred to in the section.

6.1 Any Other Relief or Remedy Granted

In deciding whether an award is necessary to afford just satisfaction, pursuant to sub-section 8(3)(a) the court must take into account 'any other relief or remedy granted, or order made, in relation to the act in question.' Only those remedies that have already been granted are relevant, not the prospect of future alternative remedies. It is likely that when a violation of a Convention right occurs, the victim will have a number of alternative remedies available to him or her in addition to damages for breach of the Act. For example, on an application for judicial review, such remedies will include those available under section 31 of the Supreme Court Act—certiorari, prohibition, mandamus, injunction, declaration and damages for a private law wrong[38] or breach of Community law. Section 8(3)(a) is designed to avoid double recovery. Clearly no further compensation would be required under the HRA if the victim had already received just satisfaction via an alternative route.

However, what is not clear from the case law is whether a victim would receive a higher or similar level of compensation under the HRA than he or she would from a claim in tort. In *Anufrijeva*[39] the Court of Appeal warned against drawing too close an analogy between a claim for damages under the HRA and a claim against a public authority in tort.[40] And in *Greenfield*[41] the House of Lords held that, in awarding damages under the HRA, courts should not follow the domestic scale but that of the European Court.

> They are not inflexibly bound by Strasbourg awards in what may be different cases. But they should not aim to be significantly more or less generous than the Court might be expected to be, in a case where it was willing to make an award at all.[42]

Given the relative low level of damages awarded by the Strasbourg court, it may therefore be advisable, if it is open to a claimant to pursue damages via a common-law route, to take that path rather than the HRA.

6.2 The Consequences of Any Decision

Section 8(3)(b) also obliges the court to take into account the consequences of any decision (of that or any other court) in respect of that act. It is unclear what is meant by 'consequences'. One possible interpretation is that when contemplating an award of damages, the court should take into account that it might be opening the

---

[37] *Anufrijeva*, above n 2, at [55].
[38] Eg negligence, false imprisonment, nuisance, misfeasance in public office and breach of contract.
[39] Above n 2.
[40] *Ibid*, at [49].
[41] Above n 26.
[42] *Ibid*, at [19] per Lord Bingham.

'floodgates'. The consequences of any decision in respect of that act may be that the same duty is

> imposed in a wide range of similar situations with the result that the burden of liability on the class of defendant may be considered to be disproportionate to the conduct involved.[43]

To make an award of damages in respect of that act may mean that hundreds, even thousands, of potential applicants will have a similar claim—representing a considerable strain on the public purse.[44] However, as in the law of tort, the floodgates argument should be approached with caution. As Lord Roskill warned in *Junior Books Ltd v Veitchi Ltd*,

> if it be just that the law should henceforth accord that remedy, that remedy should [not] be denied simply because it will, in consequence of this particular development, become available to many rather than to few.[45]

Another possible interpretation, also related to the public purse, is that the consequences include the impact on public authorities generally and society as a whole. For example, in *Bernard*[46] the Administrative Court observed that on

> a simplistic view of local authority accounting, the larger the award to the claimants under section 8 the less there will be for the London Borough of Enfield to spend on providing social service facilities for the many others in need of care within the borough.[47]

However, it was also noted that, to set against this public disbenefit, it was very much in the interests of society as a whole that public authorities should be encouraged to respect individual's rights under the Convention.

> A 'restrained' or 'moderate' approach to quantum will provide the necessary degree of encouragement whilst not unduly depleting the funds available to the defendant for the benefit of others in need of care.[48]

6.3 Other Circumstances

In addition to the circumstances expressly set out in paragraphs (a) and (b) as discussed in the paragraphs above, other circumstances may be relevant. One circumstance may be any action the respondent public authority has taken following the finding of a violation. For example, if a court has found that a public authority has conducted a hearing in breach of Article 6, the public authority may then re-hear

---

[43] *Clerk & Lindsell on Torts* (London, Sweet & Maxwell, 1995, 17th edn), 229–32.
[44] See *M (A Minor) v Newham London Borough Council* [1995] 2 AC 633, at 674–75 per Staughton LJ; *X v Bedfordshire County Council* [1995] 2 AC 633 at 749-751 per Lord Browne-Wilkinson; *Stovin v Wise* [1996] AC 923 at 958 per Lord Hoffman.
[45] [1983] 1 AC 520 at 539. See also *McLoughlin v O'Brian* [1983] 1 AC 410 and *Dulieu v White & Sons* [1901] 2 KB 669.
[46] Above n 8.
[47] *Ibid*, at [58].
[48] *Ibid*, at [59]. See also *Anufrijeva*, above n 2, at [75].

the matter in accordance with Article 6. Other examples may be where a minister rescinds a deportation order following a court decision that it is in violation of Article 3 or allows a public assembly to proceed following a court decision that banning it is in violation of Article 11. Satisfactory outcomes such as these suggest that the applicant should not be entitled to damages as he or she already has been afforded 'just satisfaction' and a just, appropriate and effective remedy. The matter has been re-heard, he or she has not been deported, the assembly has been allowed to proceed; in effect, the violations of the Convention have been corrected.[49] Also relevant may be the action of a public authority once the problem has been drawn to its attention. In *Bernard*[50] the Administrative Court held that it may reduce the level of damages awarded if the public authority acknowledged that something had gone wrong and provided an explanation, an apology and an assurance that steps had been taken to ensure that the same mistake would not happen again.[51]

Another relevant circumstance may be the question of fault. Should it make any difference to an award of damages if the unlawful act was intentional, negligent or innocent? For example, in *Wainwright*[52] the House of Lords observed that, although Article 8 guarantees a right of privacy, a remedy in damages for invasion of privacy is not guaranteed irrespective of whether the defendant acted intentionally, negligently or accidentally.

> Article 8 may justify a monetary remedy for an intentional invasion of privacy by a public authority, even if no damage is suffered other than distress for which damages are not ordinarily recoverable. It does not follow that a merely negligent act should, contrary to general principle, give rise to a claim in damages for distress because it affects privacy rather than some other interest like bodily safety.[53]

Judgments of the European Court of Human Rights offer little assistance in answering this question. However, the manner in which questions of fault are dealt with in Community law may hold some useful lessons for the award of damages under section 8 of the Act. There is a right to reparation in Community law where three conditions are met: the rule of law infringed must be intended to confer rights on individuals; the breach must be sufficiently serious; and there must be a direct causal link between the breach of the obligation resting on the state and the damage sustained by the injured parties.[54] Both the European Court of Justice and national courts have given guidance as to how sufficient seriousness is to be assessed. Factors taken into consideration include

---

[49] It was held in *Director General of Fair Trading v Proprietary Association of Great Britain* [2001] EWCA Civ 1217, [2002] 1 WLR 269 at [34], in reliance upon *Kingsley v UK* (2001) 33 EHRR 288 that if a court has remedied a situation so that no violation of Art 6 will occur, those involved are not entitled to recover wasted legal costs as compensation.
[50] Above n 8.
[51] *Ibid*, at [39]. See also *W v Westminster City Council* [2005] EWHC (QB) 102.
[52] *Wainwright v Home Office* [2003] UKHL 53, [2004] 2 AC 406.
[53] *Ibid*, at [51] per Lord Hoffmann.
[54] *Brasserie du Pecheur SA v Germany* and *R v Secretary of State for Transport ex parte Factortame* [1996] ECR I–1029 at para 51. See also *Francovich and Bonifaci v Italy* [1991] ECR I–5357.

the clarity and precision of the rule breached, the measure of discretion left by that rule to the national or Community authorities, whether the infringement and the damage caused was intentional or involuntary, whether any error of law was excusable or inexcusable.[55]

A breach can be 'manifest and grave so as to make it sufficiently serious without it being intentional or negligent.' The 'lack of the intention to commit the breach or negligence or fault' are relevant circumstances, but their presence is not 'a condition precedent to a breach being sufficiently grave or manifest.'[56] Damages are therefore available even if the breach was innocent.

---

7. The Principles Applied by the European Court of Human Rights

7.1 Introduction

The final constraint on the award of damages is contained in section 8(4), which provides that, in determining whether to award damages, or the amount of the award, the court must take into account the principles applied by the European Court of Human Rights in relation to the award of compensation under Article 41 of the Convention.[57]

There are clear differences in wording between section 2(1) and section 8(4).

> The former requires the Court to take into account any judgment, decision etc. of the European Court; the latter requires the court to take into account 'the principles applied' by the European Court.[58]

However, it has been observed that the significance of the difference is not obvious.

> The only possible significance . . . is that Parliament may have wanted the UK court to have somewhat greater freedom in relation to decisions of the European Court on the amount of damages awarded in particular cases, quantum normally being a matter for the forum.[59]

Whilst there is nothing in the HRA or the jurisprudence of the European Court to prevent courts adjudicating on claims under the HRA from imposing more severe

---

[55] paragraphs 55-57. See also *R v HM Treasury ex parte British Telecommunications plc* [1996] ECR I–1631; *Denkavit Internationaal v Bundesamt fur Finanzen* [1996] ECR I–5063; *Dillenkofer and others v Federal Republic of Germany* [1996] ECR I–4845.

[56] *R v Secretary of State for Transport ex parte Factortame (No.5)* (1998) The Times, 28 April. See also *R v Secretary of State for the Home Department ex parte Gallagher* [1996] 2 CMLR 951; *Bowden v Secretary of State for the Environment and Others*, Divisional Court, 17 December 1997; *R v Ministry of Agriculture Fisheries and Food ex parte Lay*, Divisional Court, 15 May 1998.

[57] For a discussion of the principles applied, see Law Commission, Report No 266, above n 32, Part III.

[58] *R (on the application of KB) v Mental Health Review Tribunal* [2003] EWHC (Admin) 193, [2004] QB 936 at [22].

[59] *Ibid.*

sanctions,[60] this has not been the path taken and in those cases where damages have been considered, relevant guidance from the European Court has been closely followed. However, that is not to say that this guidance has universally been regarded as useful and the observation is often made that the assistance to be derived from Strasbourg jurisprudence is limited.

> The remedy of damages generally plays a less prominent role in actions based on breaches of the articles of the ECtHR, than in actions based on breaches of private law obligations where, more often than not, the only remedy claimed is damages.[61]

Extracting the 'principles' applied by the European Court of Human Rights when awarding compensation under Article 41 is a difficult task.[62] The Court treats its power as purely discretionary and the amount of compensation awarded, or whether compensation is awarded at all, depends very much on the circumstances of the case. Certain principles are clear. 'Just satisfaction' can only take the form of compensation[63] and the Court will not award damages, such as nominal damages and exemplary damages, which are not based strictly on compensation. The Court's awards for compensation are generally divided into an award for pecuniary damage and an award for non-pecuniary damage, although the Court does sometimes grant an aggregate sum where it is difficult to make a distinction.[64] Where a violation of the Convention is found, the Court may make an award for both types of damage, only one or neither, depending on its judgment of what is 'necessary' and what is 'just satisfaction'. Different considerations apply to the assessment of both types of damage and these are examined below.

Finally, it is important to note that the European Court routinely finds that a finding of a violation is, in itself, just satisfaction for the violation found. The House of Lords in *Greenfield*[65] noted that this reflected the fact that the focus of the Convention was on the protection of human rights and not the award of compensation.

> It is noteworthy that, in exercising its former jurisdiction under the original Art.32, the Committee of Ministers did not, before 1987, award compensation at all, even where a violation was found.[66]

Similarly, in *Anufrijeva*[67] the Court of Appeal found that the concern will usually be to bring the infringement of an individual's human rights to an end and any question of compensation will be of secondary, if any, importance.[68]

---

[60] *HM Advocate v R* [2002] UKPC D3, [2004] 1 AC 462 at [58].
[61] *Anufrijeva*, above n 2, at [52].
[62] *Bernard*, above n 8.
[63] See, eg *Vacher v France* (1997) 24 EHRR 482. The Court may also award costs and expenses and interest.
[64] *Allenet de Ribemont v France* (1996) 22 EHRR 582.
[65] Above n 26.
[66] *Ibid*, at [9] per Lord Bingham.
[67] Above n 2.
[68] *Ibid*, at [53].

7.2 Pecuniary Damage

In assessing compensation for pecuniary damage, the Court endeavours to put the applicant as far as possible in a situation equivalent to the one in which he or she would have been if there had not been a breach of the Convention.[69] The principle of *restitutio in integrum* is also familiar to domestic lawyers as the measure of damages in tort.[70]

There must be a causal link between the violation complained of and the alleged pecuniary damage.[71] The need to show a causal link is demonstrated by many of the Article 6 (right to a fair trial) cases where the Court, in assessing compensation for pecuniary damage, has refused to speculate on what the outcome of the proceedings would have been if the proceedings had complied with Article 6.[72] For example, in *Saunders v UK*[73] the Court would not speculate on whether the outcome of the trial would have been different had the prosecution not used the transcripts. The Court found 'no causal connection . . . between the losses claimed by the applicant and the Court's finding of a violation.'[74]

It is important for claims of pecuniary damage to be supported by evidence[75] and the burden is on the claimant to prove his or her damage. However, if there is no evidence but it is clear that pecuniary loss has occurred, the court will make a speculative assessment, assessing it as a whole and on an equitable basis.[76] It appears that there is no limit on the amount that may be awarded for this type of damage as long as the causal link is established.[77] Awards have been made for reduction in the value of property[78] and loss of past and future earnings.[79] The Court will also award compensation for pecuniary damage suffered through loss of opportunities. In *Weeks v UK* the Court awarded Mr Weeks compensation for the loss of opportunities he suffered by reason of the absence of proceedings to challenge the lawfulness of his re-detention in violation of Article 5(4). The award was made even though 'in the

---

[69] *Papamichalopoulos v Greece* (1996) 21 EHRR 439 at [38]. See also *Anufrijeva*, above n 2, at [59].
[70] *Livingstone v Rawyards Coal Co* (1880) 5 App Cas 25 at 39 per Lord Blackburn.
[71] *Vacher*, above n 63; *Coyne v UK* Judgment of 24 September 1997. See also *R (on the application of Richards) v Secretary of State for the Home Department* [2004] EWHC (Admin) 93, [2004] ACD 69.
[72] *Vacher*, above n 63; *Findlay v UK* (1997) 24 EHRR 221; *Schmautzer v Austria* (1996) 21 EHRR 511 at [44].
[73] (1997) 23 EHRR 313.
[74] *Ibid*, at [86]. However, a sum may be awarded for pecuniary and non-pecuniary damage if it can be shown that detention resulted from the use of evidence that was incompatible with Art 6. See *Windisch v Austria* Judgment of 28 June 1993 at [35]. See also *Teixeira de Castro v Portugal* Judgment of 9 June 1998, where the applicant was compensated for loss of earnings when he was deprived of his liberty and of opportunities when he came out of prison and also non-pecuniary damage.
[75] *Incal v Turkey* Judgment of 9 June 1998; *Pressos Compania Naviera SA v Belgium* Judgment of 3 July 1997.
[76] *Selçuk and Asker v Turkey* Judgment of 24 April 1998; *Akdivar v Turkey* Judgment of 1 April 1998; *Probstmeier v Germany* Judgment of 1 July 1997.
[77] One of the Court's highest awards for pecuniary damage was made in *Stan Greek Refineries and Stratis Andreadis v Greece* Judgment of 9 December 1994, where the Court awarded 116 million drachmas plus $16 million plus 614 thousand French francs plus interest. In *Pine Valley Developments v Ireland* (1993) 16 EHRR 379 the Court awarded IR£1,200,000 for pecuniary damage caused by a violation of Art 14 in conjunction with Art 1 of Protocol 1.
[78] See, eg *Pine Valley Developments, ibid.*
[79] See, eg *Young, James and Webster v UK* (1982) 4 EHRR 38

light of the recurrence of his behavioural problems the prospect of his realising them fully was questionable.'[80]

However, it appears the domestic courts have taken a harsher line. In *KB*[81] the Administrative Court stated that the jurisprudence of the European Court was replete with refusals to award damages for loss of a chance to obtain a favourable court or tribunal decision. 'The Court refuses to speculate on the prospects of success.'[82] It concluded that it would be contrary to these principles to award damages for loss of a chance of a favourable tribunal decision or for loss of opportunity as such. However, a claimant who seeks damages on the basis of an allegation that he would have had a favourable decision at an earlier date if his Convention right had been respected must prove his allegation on the balance of probabilities.[83] Similarly, in *Greenfield*[84] the House of Lords held that the key is to find a sufficient causal connection.

> [T]he Court will award monetary compensation under Art.41 only where it is satisfied that the loss or damage complained of was actually caused by the violation it has found, and it has repeatedly stressed that it will not speculate on what the outcome of the proceedings would have been but for the violation, it has on occasion been willing in appropriate cases to make an award if of the opinion that the applicant has been deprived of a real chance of a better outcome.[85]

7.3 Non-pecuniary Damage

Whilst in many cases the Court has found that its judgment is sufficient reparation for non-pecuniary damage, on numerous occasions the Court has also found that the applicant has suffered non-pecuniary damage (also referred to as 'moral damage') as the result of a breach of the Convention, for which the mere finding of a violation does not constitute sufficient reparation. The Court may make an award of compensation for this type of damage even if it has not awarded compensation for pecuniary damage. Here it is also important for the applicant to show a causal link between the violation of the Convention and the non-pecuniary damage suffered. For example, in *Halford v UK* the Court concluded that there was

> no evidence to suggest that the stress Ms Halford suffered was directly attributable to the interception of her calls, rather than to her other conflicts with the Merseyside Police.[86]

---

[80] (1988) 10 EHRR 293 para 13. See also *Probstmeier v Germany* Judgment of 1 July 1997; *Martins Moreira v Portugal* Judgment of 26 October 1988 at [65]; *Silva Pontes v Portugal* (1994) Series A No 286-A, at [46].
[81] Above n 58.
[82] *Ibid*, at [62].
[83] *Ibid*, at [64].
[84] Above n 26.
[85] *Ibid*, at [14] per Lord Bingham.
[86] (1997) 24 EHRR 523 at [76]. The Court did award Ms Halford £10,000 for non-pecuniary damage. Compensation for non-pecuniary damage may be awarded to surviving relatives. In *Kaya v Turkey* Judgment of 19 February 1998 the deceased's widow and children received £10,000 for violation of Articles 2 and 13.

It has also been suggested under the HRA that the claimant must provide some evidence for this type of damage.[87]

The Court has granted compensation for many types of non-pecuniary damage, including distress and anxiety,[88] loss of reputation,[89] bouts of depression,[90] enduring psychological harm,[91] feelings of helplessness and frustration,[92] and feelings of injustice.[93] The fact that a claimant is particularly vulnerable may also be taken into account. For example, in *KB*[94] the Administrative Court took into account that the claimants had been detained on account of their mental health and were therefore in a vulnerable condition.

> Damages may be awarded to such persons under Article 5.5 although in analogous circumstances no award would be made to a healthy person, because they may suffer compensatable injury in circumstances where those of more robust health would not.[95]

Such damage may have been caused by Convention violations such as inordinately lengthy proceedings,[96] the deprivation of property for a long period of time,[97] failure to provide a fair hearing,[98] ill treatment whilst in custody[99] and deprivation of liberty.[100] The Court assesses compensation on what it calls an 'equitable basis' and tends to be conservative, with the average award ranging from £5,000 to £15,000. However, on occasion, the Court makes larger awards. For example, in *Pine Valley Developments v Ireland*[101] Mr Healy was awarded IR£50,000 for non-pecuniary damage sustained through violation of Article 14 in conjunction with Article 1 of Protocol No 1. In *Leterme v France*[102] a violation of Article 6(1) was found in relation to the length of compensation proceedings brought by a haemophiliac who had been infected with the AIDS virus following blood transfusions. He was awarded 200,000 French francs (approximately £20,000) for non-pecuniary damage. The applicant in *Aydin v Turkey*[103] was awarded £25,000 for the serious violation of Article 3 suffered while she was in custody and the enduring psychological harm she suffered on account of being raped.

In assessing the amount of compensation, the Court also appears to take into account notions such as mitigation and contributory fault. For example, in *Johnson v UK*[104] the Court decided to award £10,000 for non-pecuniary damage sustained by

---

87 *Richards*, above n 71, at [128].
88 *Incal v Turkey* Judgment of 9 June 1998; *Cazenave de la Roche v France* Judgment of 9 June 1998; *Doustaly v France* Judgment of 23 April 1998.
89 *Doustaly v France* Judgment of 23 April 1998.
90 *Estima Jorge v Portugal* Judgment of 21 April 1998.
91 *Aydin v Turkey* (1998) 25 EHRR 251.
92 *Papamichalopoulos*, above n 69.
93 *Keegan v Ireland* (1994) 18 EHRR 342.
94 Above n 58.
95 *Ibid*, at [72]. Cf. *Anufrijeva*, above n 2.
96 *Cazenave de la Roche v France* Judgment of 9 June 1998.
97 *Vasilescu v Romania* Judgment of 22 May 1998.
98 *Papageorgiou v Greece* Judgment of 22 October 1997 [1998] HRCD 24.
99 *Aydin*, above n 91.
100 *Tsirlis and Kouloumpas v Greece* (1998) 25 EHRR 198.
101 (1993) 16 EHRR 379.
102 Judgment of 29 April 1998; see also *Henra v France* Judgment of 29 April 1998.
103 (1998) 25 EHRR 251.
104 Judgment of 24 October 1997 [1998] HRCD 41.

Mr Johnson when, no longer suffering from mental illness, he was detained in breach of Article 5(1).

> [T]he delay in his release cannot be attributed entirely to the authorities. In the first place, some period of deferment of release was inevitable having regard to the need to locate a hostel suited to the applicant's situation . . . Secondly, the applicant's negative attitude towards his rehabilitation did not facilitate their task and after October 1990 he refused to co-operate further with the authorities in finding a suitable hostel.[105]

Under the HRA in *Richards*,[106] in its assessment of non-pecuniary damages the Administrative Court took into account the fact that the claimant was responsible for some of the periods of delay.[107]

7.4 Exemplary Damages

The Court has not awarded aggravated or punitive (exemplary) damages even for serious violations.[108] Exemplary damages are also not available under the HRA.[109] However, on occasion, the European Court does make an award for non-pecuniary damage 'bearing in mind the seriousness of the violations,'[110] suggesting that an element of aggravated damage has infiltrated the awards of the Court, although it is not labelled as such. For example, in *Aksoy v Turkey*[111] the Court held that

> in view of the extremely serious violations suffered by Mr Zeki Aksoy, and the anxiety and distress that these undoubtedly caused to his father, who has continued with the application after his son's death . . . the Court has decided to award the full amounts of compensation sought as regards pecuniary and non-pecuniary damage.[112]

The ability to award a form of aggravated damages has also been commented upon domestically. In *KB*[113] the Administrative Court stated that it was in general not the function of an award of damages to mark a court's disapproval of the conduct complained of or to reflect the importance of the right infringed, although the tendency of the European Court to award greater damages where it disapproved of the conduct of the state in question or where there had been repeated infringements was noted. Whilst this was not expressly reflected in any principle applied by the Court,

---

[105] *Ibid*, at [77]. See also *A v Denmark* (1996) 22 EHRR 458; *McCann v UK* (1996) 21 EHRR 97.
[106] Above n 71.
[107] *Ibid*, at [131].
[108] *Tekin v Turkey* Judgment of 9 June 1998, where, in violation of Art 3, the applicant had been held in a cold, dark cell, blindfolded and treated so as to leave wounds and bruises. See also *Selçuk and Asker v Turkey* Judgment of 24 April 1998.
[109] *Anufrijeva*, above n 2, at [55]; *KB*, above n 58, at [50].
[110] See, eg *Selçuk and Asker v Turkey* Judgment of 24 April 1998, where the Court found that the burning the applicants' property by the security forces involved violations of Arts 3, 8 and 13, and Art 1 of Protocol 1. They were awarded £10,000 each for non-pecuniary damage 'bearing in mind the seriousness of the violations.' See also *Aydin*, above n 91.
[111] (1997) 23 EHRR 553
[112] *Ibid*, at [113]. See also the comments in *Anufrijeva*, above n 2, at [67] and [68].
[113] Above n 58.

it may be that it can be accommodated by the latitude (or 'margin of discretion') available to the court in awarding damages for non-pecuniary loss, or even, in an exceptional case of deliberate or persistent infringement, by an award of aggravated damages, which in principle are compensatory rather than penal.[114]

8. The Level of Damages

The House of Lords has held that, when awarding damages under section 8, courts should not apply the domestic scale.[115] Three reasons were cited as to why this was not the approach to follow. First, in the view of their Lordships, the HRA was not a tort statute.

> Its objects are different and broader. Even in a case where a finding of violation is not judged to afford the applicant just satisfaction, such a finding will be an important part of his remedy and an important vindication of the right he has asserted. Damages need not ordinarily be awarded to encourage high standards of compliance by member states, since they are already bound in international law to perform their duties under the Convention in good faith, although it may be different if there is felt to be a need to encourage compliance by individual officials or classes of official.[116]

Secondly, their Lordships pointed out that the purpose of the HRA was not to give victims better remedies at home than they could recover in Strasbourg but to give them the same remedies without the delay and expense of resort to Strasbourg.[117] Finally, it was noted that section 8(4) requires a domestic court to take into account the principles applied by the European Court under Article 41.

> There could be no clearer indication that courts in this country should look to Strasbourg and not to domestic precedents.[118]

Furthermore, it was noted that the Court describes its awards as equitable, which was taken to mean that they are not precisely calculated but were judged by the Court to be fair in the individual case.

> Judges in England and Wales must also make a similar judgment in the case before them. They are not inflexibly bound by Strasbourg awards in what may be different cases. But they should not aim to be significantly more or less generous than the Court might be expected to be, in a case where it was willing to make an award at all.[119]

---

[114] *Ibid*, at [50].
[115] *Greenfield*, above n 26.
[116] *Ibid*, at [19] per Lord Bingham.
[117] *Ibid*.
[118] *Ibid*.
[119] *Ibid*. See also the comments of Lord Hoffmann in *R (on the application of Wilkinson) v Inland Revenue Commissioners* [2005] UKHL 30, [2005] 1 WLR 1718 at [25].

This conclusion of the House of Lords is slightly at odds with jurisprudence in the lower courts. For example, in *Anufrijeva*[120] the Court of Appeal held that the suggestion that damages under the HRA should be moderate and on the low side in comparison with those awarded for torts should in future be ignored.[121] In *Bernard*[122] the Administrative Court noted that there was no justification for the view that the quantum should be low by comparison with tortious awards.

> Bearing in mind the importance of securing compliance with the Convention, I see no justification for a further reduction, pushing damages under section 8 below the level of tortious awards.[123]

Also, in *KB*[124] the Administrative Court saw no justification for an award of damages being lower under the HRA than it would be for a comparable tort. It postulated that, if there was a breach of Article 5(1), there should be no difference between the measure of damages awarded for this and for the tort of false imprisonment.[125] This line of reasoning was continued in *Dennis*,[126] where substantial damages of £950,000 were awarded for the tort of nuisance. Also finding violations of Article 8 and Article 1 of Protocol No 1, the Divisional Court held that, had the common law of nuisance not provided a remedy in this case, compensation would have been awarded in the same sum under the HRA.[127] Nevertheless, the judgment of the House of Lords in *Greenfield*[128] is the latest and most authoritative word on this subject. Observations in *Anufrijeva*[129] that appropriate guidance could be obtained from the guidelines issued by the Judicial Studies Board, the levels of awards made by the Criminal Injuries Compensation Board, and by the Parliamentary Ombudsman and the Local Government Ombudsman[130] are now subject to doubt, the House of Lords having held that the only appropriate guidance was that emanating from the European Court of Human Rights.

As with other procedural features of the HRA, the best indication of the approach to section 8 is to study its application in practice. Cases where damages have been considered, and sometimes awarded, are considered in the following paragraphs.[131]

---

[120] Above n 2.
[121] *Ibid*, at [73].
[122] Above n 8.
[123] *Ibid*, at [59].
[124] Above n 58.
[125] *Ibid*, at [53].
[126] *Dennis v Ministry of Defence* [2003] EWHC (QB) 793, [2003] 19 EG 118 (CS).
[127] *Ibid*, at [92].
[128] Above n 26.
[129] Above n 2.
[130] *Ibid*, at [74]. In *Bernard*, above n 8, the Administrative Court held that assistance may be obtained from: damages for discomfort, inconvenience and injury to health arising out of breaches of repairing covenants in residential tenancies; recommendations by Local Commissioners for Administration (Local Government Ombudsman) that local authorities pay compensation when claimants have suffered as a result of maladministration; the JSB Guidelines for the Assessment of General Damages in Personal Injury Cases; W Norris et al, *Kemp and Kemp: Quantum of Damages* (London, Sweet & Maxwell, 1975); and the awards for pain and suffering in cases of minor personal injury.
[131] For an article-by-article analysis of the practice of the European Court of Human Rights, see Law Commission, Report No 266, above n 32, Part VI.

9. Application: Article 5

9.1 Section 9(3) Human Rights Act and Article 5(5)

The first fact to note about the award of damages for violations of Article 5 is section 9(3), which provides that damages may not be awarded in respect of a judicial act done in good faith otherwise than to compensate a person to the extent required by Article 5(5) of the Convention.[132]

As originally drafted, without reference to Article 5(5), it was intended that this subsection would preserve the current position under section 2(5) of the Crown Proceedings Act 1947, which absolves the Crown of liability for the conduct of any person 'while discharging or purporting to discharge any responsibilities of a judicial nature vested in him.' However, following objections that this exemption was in breach of Article 5(5)[133] of the Convention, the government amended the section. The Lord Chancellor explained that where

> a complaint is made that Article 5 has been breached as a result of a judicial act or omission it will be necessary first to establish whether the judicial act complained of was unlawful, then to rule on whether the aggrieved person is entitled to compensation under Article 5(5) and then to determine the amount of compensation.[134]

The importance of the change was evident in the case of *KB*,[135] where the Administrative Court held that the Mental Health Review Tribunal was a judicial body for these purposes and that none of the acts or omissions leading to violations of Article 5(4) were done other than in good faith. Article 5(5) was therefore central to the claims.[136]

Furthermore, in *Richards*[137] it was confirmed that Article 5(5) gives a right to a person wrongfully detained to claim compensation for wrongful detention even though such a claim for compensation could not be made under section 6 of the HRA. It is a Convention right within the meaning of the HRA.[138] However, the right is only triggered if there has been an express or implied declaration that Article 5 has been contravened.

> [T]he claimant can obtain either an assessment by the court of the appropriate level of compensation payable by the defendant and a mandatory order that he pays such sums or damages under Article 5(5) of the Convention, provided that he can show first that he has suffered some form of damage and second, that he can establish a breach of art 5.[139]

---

[132] *Ibid*, Appendix A.
[133] Article 5(5) of the Convention provides 'Everyone who has been the victim of arrest or detention in contravention of the provisions of this Article shall have an enforceable right to compensation.'
[134] HL Deb, Vol 585, col 289 (29 January 1998).
[135] Above n 58.
[136] *Ibid*, at [11].
[137] Above n 71.
[138] *Ibid*, at [45].
[139] *Ibid*, at [48].

9.2 Article 5(4): Delay

In *KB*[140] the sole issue to be determined before the Administrative Court was the damages to be awarded to a number of claimants for violations of Article 5(4) resulting from the delay in the hearings of their applications before the Mental Health Review Tribunal for the review of their respective detentions. None made a claim for pecuniary loss, the claims being for frustration and distress, deprivation of liberty, damage to mental health and loss of chance to be discharged. As noted above, given section 9(3) of the HRA, the claimants had to rely upon Article 5(5), which provides that

> everyone who has been the victim of arrest or detention in contravention of the provisions of this article shall have an enforceable right to compensation.

Article 5(5) applies to a claim for breach of Article 5(4) even though the delay in obtaining a decision of a court did not prolong the victim's detention.[141] However, Article 5(5) does not compel the award of damages in every case.[142]

Damages under Article 5(5) depend upon there being proof of damage. Damage may be pecuniary or non-pecuniary.[143] However, in *KB* the court discovered some confusion in the European Court authorities.

> There are two principles applied by the Court: that damages are not recoverable in the absence of a deprivation of liberty, and that damages are recoverable for distress which may be inferred from the facts of the case. It follows that this court must itself determine the principles it is to apply.[144]

It stated that the object of an award of damages under Article 5(5) was to provide compensation for injury.

> Parliament requires the court to make an award of damages under Article 5.5 where that is required by the Convention. It must be taken to have provided the resources to meet such awards.[145]

Although the court found no comparable tort or other wrong under purely English law, it held that the damages awarded should so far as possible reflect the English level of damages.[146] Considerable assistance was derived from the decision of the Court of Appeal on damages in *Evans*.[147] This judgment emphasised the need to determine the precise consequences of any false imprisonment.

---

[140] Above n 58.
[141] *Ibid*, at [13].
[142] *Ibid*, at [28].
[143] *Ibid*, at [33].
[144] *Ibid*, at [41].
[145] *Ibid*, at [50].
[146] This conclusion is now subject to doubt. See *Greenfield*, above n 26.
[147] *R v Governor of Brockhill Prison, ex p Evans (No.2)* [1999] QB 1043.

As well as involving consideration of any distress caused, it is necessary to compare the conditions in which the claimant was detained with what his or her circumstances would have been if he or she had not been so detained.[148]

With respect to loss of chance, the Administrative Court drew attention to the fact that the jurisprudence of the European Court was replete with refusals to award damages for the loss of a chance to obtain a favourable court or tribunal decision.'The Court refuses to speculate on the prospects of success.'[149] It concluded that it would be contrary to these principles to award damages for the loss of a chance of a favourable tribunal decision or for loss of opportunity as such. However, a claimant who seeks damages on the basis of an allegation that he would have had a favourable decision at an earlier date if his Convention right had been respected must prove his allegation on the balance of probabilities. The Administrative Court also noted that the court will bear in mind that in practice a relatively low proportion of applications to tribunals succeed, and that a finding that a tribunal would have directed the discharge of a patient involved a finding that the Responsible Medical Officer was wrong—and convincing evidence would be required to justify such findings.[150]

The Administrative Court found that the relevant period to which any award of damages related was that between the time when the tribunal should have determined a patient's application and the date when it was actually determined.[151] It found that not every disappointment or feeling of distress constituted compensable damage for present purposes.

> Distress and disappointment are part of everyday life, and do not necessarily lead to claims for damages . . . There is a risk of creating anomalies between damages recoverable for breach of Convention rights and those for other civil wrongs. The Court should be reluctant to do so.[152]

However, it was taken into account that the patients were detained because of the state of their mental health and were thus in a vulnerable mental condition.

> Damages may be awarded to such persons under Article 5.5 although in analogous circumstances no award would be made to a healthy person, because they may suffer compensatable injury in circumstances where those of more robust health would not.[153]

However, the frustration and distress must be significant and 'of such intensity that it would in itself justify an award of compensation for non-pecuniary damage.'[154] An important touchstone was found to be if hospital staff considered it to be sufficiently relevant to the mental state of the patient to warrant its mention in the clinical notes.[155] Awards ranging from just a finding of breach to £4,000 were made.[156]

---

[148] *Ibid*, at [56].
[149] *Ibid*, at [62].
[150] *Ibid*, at [64].
[151] *Ibid*, at [65].
[152] *Ibid*, at [71].
[153] *Ibid*, at [72]. Cf. *Anufrijeva*, above n 2.
[154] *Ibid*, at [73].
[155] *Ibid*, at [73].
[156] See also *R (on the application of P) v Secretary of State for the Home Department* [2003] EWHC (Admin) 2953.

9.3 Article 5(4): Independence and Impartiality

In *Richards*[157] the claimant sought compensation in respect of his detention between the date on which the Parole Board recommended his release and his actual release, as he maintained that the Secretary of State's role in delaying his release was incompatible with Article 5(4). Interestingly, the court found that the Strasbourg decision in *Stafford*,[158] which made the detention unlawful, governed periods of detention that occurred both before and after the date of the decision.[159] The court then turned to the assessment of damages, noting that the main issue was to determine what would have happened to the claimant between November 2001 and his release in August 2002 if the Parole Board's recommendation in November 2001 that he be released had taken effect.[160]

A number of factors were taken into account, including the claimant's disability, which made it difficult for him to find a hostel; his excessive use of alcohol; his wish to be released to a hostel where he could be visited by friends and family; and that any licence on which he would have been released would have been subject to a residence requirement. Taking these factors into account, the court noted that the appropriate starting period for assessing compensation was 5 January 2002. Also taken into account was the breach of licence on 3 January, resulting in his return to prison on 4 January following release on temporary licence. It concluded that the claimant would have been recalled to prison even if released and would have been detained until the end of May 2002. Furthermore, there were difficulties finding him a suitable hostel and he had indicated that he was prepared to wait in custody until a suitable location was found. The court concluded that there was no causal link between the interference with his Convention rights and his detention from 18 November 2001 until August 2002, and found that he would not have enjoyed greater freedom had the recommendation of the Parole Board taken effect as a direct order.

No award of compensation was needed to place the claimant in the same position as if his Convention rights had not been infringed.[161] Furthermore, no damages were awarded for frustration, anxiety and uncertainty because his prospects of release were low even if the Board's recommendation had taken effect as an order; he was responsible for some of the periods of delay; and there was no evidence or allegation of frustration, uncertainty or anxiety on his part.[162] It concluded as follows.

> [T]he claim fails because no loss can be established. I consider that even if the Parole Board recommendation had taken effect as an instruction to release him, the claimant would still have been detained from the time of the Parole Board recommendation in November 2001 until his actual release on 12 August 2002. This was because of the claimant's severe disabilities, the consequential difficulties of finding accommodation for him, his previous misbehaviour and his unwillingness to move out of the area during some of this period.[163]

---

[157] Above n 71.
[158] *Stafford v United Kingdom* (2002) 35 EHRR 1121.
[159] *Ibid*, at [81].
[160] *Ibid*, at [92].
[161] *Ibid*, at [128].
[162] *Ibid*, at [131].
[163] *Ibid*, at [139].

Whilst irrelevant in light of the conclusion above, the court also commented on the 'period of grace' issue, holding that the Secretary of State was entitled to a reasonable time to consider the implications of *Stafford*[164] and that this would not have expired prior to the time of his actual release.[165]

---

10. Application: Article 6

10.1 Article 6(1) Reasonable Time: Post Conviction

In *Mills*[166] the Privy Council considered the remedy for a breach of the reasonable time guarantee post-conviction. Lord Steyn noted that the remedies available could include

> an order for discontinuance of a prosecution, quashing of the conviction, reduction of the sentence, monetary compensation or a declaration. A finding of a violation of a guarantee may itself sometimes be a sufficient vindication of the right.[167]

Lord Hope held that the circumstances of the present case provided a clear example of a situation where the setting aside of the conviction would be regarded in domestic law as both unjustified and unnecessary.

> It would be regarded as unjustified because the appellant's appeal against his conviction was . . . wholly without merit. No grounds exist for regarding the conviction itself as unsound, nor is there any question of its having been affected in any way by the delay. And the setting aside of the conviction would be regarded as unnecessary, because the effects of the delay can be recognised perfectly well by a reduction in the appellant's sentence.[168]

It was concluded that a reduction in the sentence by nine months was a just disposal in the spirit of Article 6(1).[169]

10.2 Article 6(1) Reasonable Time: Pre Conviction

Under the HRA in England and Wales, a majority of the House of Lords held in *Attorney General's Reference No.2 of 2001*[170] that if, through the action or inaction of a public authority, a criminal charge was not determined at a hearing within a reasonable time, there must be afforded such remedy as may be just and appropriate.

---

[164] *Ibid*, at [135].
[165] *Ibid*, at [138].
[166] *Mills v HM Advocate* [2002] UKPC D2, [2004] 1 AC 441.
[167] *Ibid*, at [16].
[168] *Ibid*, at [53].
[169] *Ibid*, at [23] per Lord Steyn. See also *R v Galfetti* [2002] EWCA Crim 1916 concerning delay between conviction and eventual disposal by way of hospital order under s 37 of the Mental Health Act 1983.
[170] Above n 5.

The appropriate remedy will depend on the nature of the breach and all the circumstances, including particularly the stage of the proceedings at which the breach is established. If the breach is established before the hearing, the appropriate remedy may be a public acknowledgement of the breach, action to expedite the hearing to the greatest extent practicable and perhaps, if the defendant is in custody, his release on bail. It will not be appropriate to stay or dismiss the proceedings unless (a) there can no longer be a fair hearing or (b) it would otherwise be unfair to try the defendant. The public interest in the final determination of criminal charges requires that such a charge should not be stayed or dismissed if any lesser remedy will be just and proportionate in all the circumstances.[171]

The majority confirmed that to hold a trial after the lapse of a reasonable time would not in itself be a breach of a Convention right and therefore would not in itself comprise unlawful conduct under section 6 of the HRA.[172] Lord Bingham appreciated that it was a powerful argument that, if a public authority caused or permitted such delay to occur that a criminal charge could not be heard against a defendant within a reasonable time, so breaching his right under Article 6(1), any further prosecution or trial of the charge must be unlawful within the meaning of the Article. But he cited four reasons which compelled its rejection. First, it would be anomalous if breach of the reasonable time requirement had an effect more far-reaching than breach of the defendant's other Article 6 rights when the breach did not taint the basic fairness of the hearing at all, and even more anomalous that the right to a hearing should be vindicated by ordering that there be no trial at all.[173] Secondly, he pointed out that a rule of automatic termination of proceedings on breach of the reasonable time requirement could not sensibly be applied in civil proceedings.

[T]ermination of the proceedings would defeat the claimant's right to a hearing altogether and seeking to make good his loss in compensation from the state could well prove a very unsatisfactory alternative.[174]

Thirdly, a rule of automatic termination had been shown to have the effect in practice of emasculating the right which the guarantee was designed to protect.

There is, however, a very real risk that if proof of a breach is held to require automatic termination of the proceedings the judicial response will be to set the threshold unacceptably high.[175]

---

[171] *Ibid*, at [24] per Lord Bingham, with whom Lords Nicholls, Steyn, Hoffmann, Hobhouse and Scott agreed. Lord Bingham thought it unwise to attempt to describe the category of cases in which it may be unfair to try a defendant, but did cite as possible examples bad faith, unlawfulness, executive manipulation and extreme breach of prosecutor's professional duty. Lords Hope and Rodger agreed that the remedy must be that which was just and appropriate, but held that to hold the trial after a lapse of a reasonable time was itself a breach of Art 6. For application of this principle, see *R v Wheeler* [2004] EWCA Crim 572.
[172] *Attorney General's Reference No.2 of 2001*, above n 5, per Lord Nicholls at [38]–[39]. Lords Hope and Rodger dissented on this point. The majority pointed out that if the very holding of the trial by the court would be unlawful, the trial must be stayed. Lord Bingham could not accept that it could ever be proper for a court, whose purpose was to uphold, vindicate and apply the law, to act in a manner which a statute declared to be unlawful. *Ibid*, at [30].
[173] *Ibid*, at [20].
[174] *Ibid*, at [21].
[175] *Ibid*, at [22].

Fourthly, his Lordship found that the Strasbourg jurisprudence gave no support to the contention that there should be no hearing of a criminal charge once a reasonable time had passed.[176]

However, in Scotland, a majority of the Privy Council held in *HM Advocate v R*[177] that, as a result of section 57(2) of the Scotland Act 1998, once it had been established that a proposed or continuing act was incompatible with a person's Article 6(1) rights, the Lord Advocate was prohibited from doing that act. In the context of the reasonable time guarantee, this meant that it would be incompatible with Article 6 for the Lord Advocate to prosecute an individual because to do so would violate his right to a hearing within a reasonable time. Therefore, the proceedings had to be stayed as the Lord Advocate had no power to proceed with the prosecution.[178]

10.3 Article 6(1): Independence and Impartiality

The just and appropriate remedy for a breach of the guarantee of independence and impartiality was considered by the House of Lords in *Greenfield*,[179] where the appellant had also been denied legal representation in violation of Article 6(3)(c). Their Lordships pointed out that, whilst the rights contained in Article 6 were important rights, it did not follow from a finding that the trial process involved a breach of Article 6 that the outcome of the trial process was wrong or would have been otherwise had the breach not occurred.

> There is a risk of error if Strasbourg decisions given in relation to one article of the Convention are read across as applicable to another.[180]

It also pointed out that, in the great majority of cases in which the European Court had found a violation of Article 6, it had treated the finding of the violation as, in itself, just satisfaction under Article 41.[181]

> Where Art.6 is found to have been breached, the outcome will often be that a decision is quashed and a retrial ordered, which will vindicate the victim's Convention right.[182]

However, their Lordships did find that the Court has been willing to depart from the practice of finding a violation of Article 6 to be, in itself, just satisfaction under Article 41, where it found a causal connection between the violation found and the loss for which an applicant claimed to be compensated.

---

[176] *Ibid*, at [23], citing *X v Germany* (1980) 25 DR 142; *Eckle v Germany* (1982) 5 EHRR 1; *Neuback v Germany* (1983) 41 DR 13; *Bunkate v Netherlands* (1995) 19 EHRR 477; *Beck v Norway* Judgment of 26 June 2001.

[177] Above n 60.

[178] In *Attorney General's Reference No.2 of 2001*, above n 5, at [83] Lord Hope held that the Human Rights Act did not require such an approach as it enabled one to say that the proposed act of bringing the defendant to trial after an unreasonable time had elapsed was unlawful, and then to provide a just and appropriate remedy. Lord Rodger agreed at [167]. However, the majority held that *HM Advocate v R*, above n 60, had been wrongly decided.

[179] Above n 26.

[180] *Ibid*, at [7] per Lord Bingham.

[181] *Ibid*, at [8] per Lord Bingham.

[182] *Ibid*, at [9] per Lord Bingham.

Such claim may be for specific heads of loss, such as loss of earnings or profits, said to be attributable to the violation.

However, it also pointed out that the court has been slow to award such compensation.[183] With respect to non-pecuniary damage, their Lordships pointed out that a

claim under this head may be put on the straightforward basis that but for the Convention violation found the outcome of the proceedings would probably have been different and more favourable to the applicant, or on the more problematical basis that the violation deprived the applicant of an opportunity to achieve a different result which was not in all the circumstances of the case a valueless opportunity. While in the ordinary way the Court has not been easily persuaded on this last basis, it has in some cases accepted it.[184]

In the view of their Lordships, the key was to find a sufficient causal connection.

[T]he Court will award monetary compensation under Art.41 only where it is satisfied that the loss or damage complained of was actually caused by the violation it has found, and it has repeatedly stressed that it will not speculate on what the outcome of the proceedings would have been but for the violation, it has on occasion been willing in appropriate cases to make an award if of opinion that the appellant has been deprived of a real chance of a better outcome.[185]

Their Lordships also discussed a second head of general or non-pecuniary damage which has been variously described in terms such as 'physical and mental suffering', 'prolonged uncertainty' and 'a certain feeling of frustration and helplessness'. Their Lordships noted that, in considering claims under this head and with its general approach, the Court has consistently only been willing to award compensation for anxiety and frustration attributable to the Article 6 violation.

It has recognised that for very many people involvement in legal proceedings is bound to cause anxiety irrespective of any Art.6 breach, and no award is made in such cases. In some cases the Court has found on the facts that the applicant had suffered attributable anxiety and frustration . . . In other cases the Court has found that the applicant 'must have' suffered such feelings . . . or that it is reasonable to assume he did . . . To gain an award under this head it is not necessary for the applicant to show that but for the violation the outcome of the proceedings would, or would probably, or even might, have been different, and in cases of delay the outcome may not be significant at all. But the Court has been very sparing in making awards.[186]

Their Lordships concluded that whatever the practice in other classes of case, the ordinary practice was not to make an award in cases of structural bias.

Where, having found a violation of Art.6, the Court has made an award of monetary compensation under Art.41, under either of the heads of general damages considered in this

---

[183] *Ibid*, at [11] per Lord Bingham .
[184] *Ibid*, at [12] per Lord Bingham citing *Goddi v Italy* (1984) 6 EHRR 457; *Colozza v Italy* (1985) 7 EHRR 516; *Lechner and Hess v Austria* (1987) 9 EHRR 490; *Weeks v United Kingdom* (1988) 13 EHRR 435; *O v United Kingdom* (1988) 13 EHRR 578; *Delta v France* (1990) 16 EHRR 574.
[185] *Ibid*, at [14] per Lord Bingham.
[186] *Ibid*, at [16] per Lord Bingham.

opinion, whether for loss of procedural opportunity or anxiety and frustration, the sums awarded have been noteworthy for their modesty.[187]

In the present case, in the determination of a criminal charge there had been a denial of independence and impartiality and legal representation by the deputy controller of a private prison when determining whether the prisoner had committed drugs offence. Their Lordships concluded that this was pre-eminently a case in which the finding in the appellant's favour afforded just satisfaction and an award of damages was not necessary.[188] The claim for loss of opportunity to achieve a different result if he had been legally represented was also rejected their Lordships finding that the adjudication was conducted with exemplary conscientiousness, patience and regard for the appellant's interests.

> The issue for Mr Parry was whether he believed the appellant and his witness. Clearly he did not. A legal representative might have persuaded Mr Parry or another tribunal to take a different view or he might not. It is inappropriate to speculate.[189]

The claim for damages for anxiety and frustration was also rejected.

> At the time, however, adjudication by a governor or deputy governor (or their private prison counterparts, also Crown servants) was the norm. The appellant had no expectation of any other procedure, and was treated no differently from anyone else. The conduct of the adjudication itself, as already noted, appears to have been exemplary. There is no special feature of this case which warrants an award of damages.[190]

---

11. Application: Article 8

Whilst its comments were strictly obiter, in *Anufrijeva*[191] the Court of Appeal observed that courts dealing with claims for damages for maladministration resulting in a breach of Article 8 should adopt a broad-brush approach.

> Where there is no pecuniary loss involved, the question whether the other remedies that have been granted to a successful complainant are sufficient to vindicate the right that has been infringed, taking into account the complainant's own responsibility for what has occurred, should be decided without a close examination of the authorities or an extensive and prolonged examination of the facts. In many cases the seriousness of the

---

[187] *Ibid*, at [17] per Lord Bingham.
[188] *Ibid*, at [26] per Lord Bingham.
[189] *Ibid*, at [28] per Lord Bingham. Cf. *R (on the application of Nunn) v First Secretary of State* [2005] EWCA Civ 101, [2005] 2 All ER 987, where the Court of Appeal held that, where the claimant had been deprived of her Art 6 rights to have her objections to the grant of planning permission heard and adjudicated upon, her only remedy would be a claim in damages.
[190] *Ibid*, at [29] per Lord Bingham.
[191] Above n 2.

maladministration and whether there is a need for damages should be capable of being ascertained by an examination of the correspondence and the witness statements.[192]

It held that where a breach of Article 8 did arise from maladministration, the scale of such damages should be modest.

> The cost of supporting those in need falls on society as a whole. Resources are limited and payments of substantial damages will deplete the resources available for other needs of the public including primary care. If the impression is created that asylum seekers whether genuine or not are profiting from their status, this could bring the Human Rights Act into disrepute.[193]

It was also held that similar considerations applied to delay in processing asylum claims or the procedure for admitting the relatives of a refugee.[194]

Despite these observations, damages have been awarded under the HRA for violations of Article 8. For example, in *Bernard*[195] the Administrative Court found serious violations of the claimant's private and family lives.

> The Council's failure to act on the September 2000 assessments showed a singular lack of respect for the claimants' private and family life. It condemned the claimants to living conditions which made it virtually impossible for them to have any meaningful private or family life for the purposes of Article 8 . . . the defendant was not merely in breach of its statutory duty under the 1948 Act. Its failure to act on the September 2000 assessments over a period of 20 months was also incompatible with the claimants' rights under Article 8 of the Convention.[196]

Turning to the question of relief, the court was satisfied that an award of damages was necessary to give just satisfaction to the claimants.

> This was a serious breach of their rights under Article 8. The claimants and their family had to live in deplorable conditions, wholly inimical to any normal family life, and to the physical and psychological integrity of the second claimant for a considerable period of time.[197]

The fact that the defendant belatedly discharged its duties under the 1948 Act and Article 8 did not affect the decision to award damages, only quantum.[198] This was not a case where the defendant had taken all necessary steps, reasonably promptly, once the problem had been drawn to its attention.[199]

---

[192] *Ibid*, at [65].
[193] *Ibid*, at [75].
[194] *Ibid*, at [76]. The court also made a number of suggestions as to the procedure to be followed in future where damages were sought under the HRA for maladministration. This was in an effort to avoid the situation which it found arose in the present case where it would cost more to try the case than the amount of damages likely to be awarded. *Ibid* at [80]–[81].
[195] Above n 8.
[196] *Ibid*, at [34].
[197] *Ibid*, at [36].
[198] *Ibid*, at [38].
[199] *Ibid*, at [40].

[T]here has been no acknowledgment that the defendant was in error, no explanation, no apology and nothing to indicate that the defendant's procedures have been improved so that the same kind of mistake . . is less likely to occur in the future.[200]

The threat to evict the claimants, whilst withdrawn, was also taken into account.[201]

In determining the level of damages, the court found no comparable tort. There was no evidence of mental or physical injury caused by the conditions. The first claimant's back problems were aggravated but this cause him discomfort, distress and inconvenience rather than injury. The second claimant suffered discomfort, distress and frustration.[202] The court found that the Judicial Studies Board's *Guidelines for the Assessment of General Damages in Personal Injury Case* and the awards noted in Part K of Kemp and Kemp's *The Quantum of Damages*, dealing with minor injuries where there is a complete or almost complete recovery and where damages are principally for pain and suffering, might provide a useful comparison.[203] It also took into account the reports of the Local Government Ombudsman and the awards for pain and suffering in the case of minor personal injury.[204] It stated that the award should not be minimal as that would undermine the policy underlying the Act that Convention rights should be respected by all public authorities, but it also noted that the consequences of awards for public authorities and society as a whole should not be ignored.[205]

The court concluded that the Local Government Ombudsman awards were the best comparables, finding that the case was, in essence, an extreme example of maladministration which deprived the second claimant of much needed social services care for a lengthy period.[206] The court also took into account that the ordeal was now over and the claimants had a home.

That said, they had to endure deplorable conditions, wholly inimical to private and family life, for a long time. They have received no explanation or apology and do not have the comfort of knowing that their sufferings have not been in vain. There is no indication that this case has prompted the Council to introduce revised procedures. The claimants' problems have been compounded by the defendant's conduct.[207]

In total, £10,000 was awarded, comprising £2,000 to the first claimant and £8,000 to the second.

In W[208] the Divisional Court also considered an award of damages for a violation of the right to respect for private life resulting from a disclosure of information. Taken into account was the fact that the defendant took steps reasonably promptly once the problem was drawn to its attention.

---

[200] *Ibid*, at [41].
[201] *Ibid*.
[202] *Ibid*, at [46].
[203] *Ibid*, at [47].
[204] *Ibid*, at [49].
[205] *Ibid*, at [58]. Such an approach is now subject to doubt due to the conclusion of the House of Lords *Greenfield*, above n 26, that only the judgments of the European Court should be looked to in determining the level of damages.
[206] *Ibid*, at [60].
[207] *Ibid*, at [61].
[208] *W v Westminster City Council, Divisional Court* [2005] EWHC (QB) 102.

He did acknowledge that something had gone wrong, provide an apology and an assurance that steps, in the form of the draft Correction, would be taken to ensure (so far as possible in an imperfect world) that the same mistake will not happen again.[209]

It concluded therefore that nothing more was required by way of monetary compensation to afford just satisfaction.[210] If damages were to be awarded, the court assessed these at £1,000. The violation was found to be not particularly grave, the publication was limited and there was an immediate agreement to investigate. The claimant received an apology and retraction.

> This is not a case which had to be brought in order to change procedures and prevent such an incident ever happening again.[211]

Whilst the claimant suffered frustration and distress, this did not result in him needing medical advice or assistance, nor was he shunned by anyone.[212] Whilst he was a particularly susceptible individual, the defendants were not responsible for that lack of understanding on his part.[213]

12. Application: Article 14

In *Wilkinson*[214] their Lordships agreed that the general principle applied to affording just satisfaction was to put the applicant so far as possible in the position in which he would have been if the state had complied with its obligations under the HRA. However, this may not result in an award of damages in a discrimination case. As their Lordships pointed out, where

> the wrongful act is treating A better than B, this involves forming a view about whether the State should have complied by treating A worse or B better. Normally one would conclude that A's treatment represented the norm and that B should have been treated better. In some cases, however, it will be clear that A's treatment was an unjustifiable anomaly.[215]

An example given of such a case was *Van Raalte v Netherlands*,[216] where a breach of Article 14 with Article 1 of Protocol No 1 was found as the law exempted unmarried childless women over 45 from paying contributions under the General Child Benefits Act without exempting unmarried childless men. The European Court rejected a claim for repayment of the contributions from which the appellant would have been exempt if he had been a woman. In the view of their Lordships, the reason

---

[209] *Ibid*, at [247].
[210] *Ibid*.
[211] *Ibid*, at [251].
[212] *Ibid*, at [252].
[213] *Ibid*, at [252].
[214] Above n 119.
[215] *Ibid*, at [26] per Lord Hoffmann.
[216] (1997) 24 EHRR 503.

for the rejection of the claim was that if the state had complied with its Convention obligations, it would not in 1989 have exempted men or women.

It follows that the applicant would have been no better off. He would still have had to pay. In the circumstances, the judgment itself was treated as being sufficient just satisfaction.[217]

Their Lordships concluded that the same principle applied in the present case.

There was no justification whatever for extending the widows' allowance to men. If, therefore, Parliament had paid proper regard to article 14, it would have abolished the allowance for widows. Mr Wilkinson would not have received an allowance and no damages are therefore necessary to put him in the position in which he would have been if there had been compliance with his Convention rights.[218]

---

[217] *Ibid*, at [27] per Lord Hoffmann.
[218] *Ibid*, at [28] per Lord Hoffmann. See also the comments of Lord Brown at [44]–[53].

PART II

THE CONVENTION RIGHTS

Article 2: The Right to Life

1. Introduction

The right to life is often described as the most fundamental of all human rights[1] and the fact that no derogation from Article 2 is permitted under Article 15 reinforces the importance of this right.[2] Compliance must

> rank among the highest priorities of a modern democratic state governed by the rule of law. Any violation or potential violation must be treated with great seriousness.[3]

However, despite its fundamental nature, it is not expressed in the Convention in absolute terms. Article 2(1) preserves the death penalty whilst Article 2(2) permits the use of force, though no more than is absolutely necessary, in three instances.[4] But although the death penalty is expressly preserved in Article 2(1), the HRA has given further effect in UK law to Articles 1 and 2 of Protocol No 6 to the Convention. These Articles provide for the complete abolition of the death penalty except in respect of acts committed in time of war or of imminent threat of war.[5]

On its face, Article 2 provides that 'everyone's right to life shall be protected by law' and that no one 'shall be deprived of his life intentionally.' These words have

---

[1] See, eg *Re McKerr* [2004] UKHL 12, [2004] 1 WLR 807 at [18] per Lord Nicholls; *R (on the application of Bloggs 61) v Secretary of State for the Home Department* [2003] EWCA Civ 686, [2003] 1 WLR 2724 at [63] per Auld LJ; *R v Director of Public Prosecutions, ex p Manning* [2001] QB 330; *R (on the application of H) v Ashworth Hospital Authority* [2001] EWHC (Admin) 872, [2002] 1 FCR 206 at [77].
[2] *Venables v News Group Newspapers* [2001] 2 WLR 1038.
[3] *R (on the application of Middleton) v HM Coroner for Western Somerset* [2004] UKHL 10 [2004] 2 AC 182 at [5].
[4] In defence of any person from unlawful violence; in order to effect a lawful arrest or to prevent the escape of a person lawfully detained; and in action lawfully taken for the purpose of quelling a riot or insurrection.
[5] HC Deb, Vol 312, cols 987–1013 (20 May 1998).

been interpreted by the European Court of Human Rights and UK courts as including

> not only a duty not to take life, but in some circumstances to take steps to prevent life being taken and as part of that duty an obligation to investigate the circumstances surrounding the death.[6]

Underpinned by the principle of the sanctity of human life,[7] Article 2 does not extend beyond this and, in particular, does not confer a right to die or to enlist the aid of another in bringing about one's own death. In *Pretty*[8] the House of Lords confirmed that voluntary euthanasia, suicide, physician-assisted suicide and suicide assisted without the intervention of a physician do not derive protection from an article designed to protect the sanctity of life.[9]

Given the fundamental nature of the right to life and the importance with which it is regarded, deference is rarely shown by the courts to primary decision makers in Article 2 cases. In *Re A*[10] Ward LJ commented that deciding matters of disputed life and death was 'surely and pre-eminently a matter for a court of law to judge. That is what courts are here for.'[11] With respect to intentional deprivations of life and the procedural duty to investigate, there is in fact little room for the court to show any deference to the primary decision maker. Its essential role is to look at the facts and determine whether or not the allegation of breach of Article 2 is made out. Even when assessing whether or not there is a risk to life, the courts have given little margin to the primary decision maker. For example, *Wilkinson*[12] concerned a challenge to a decision to carry out medical treatment without consent. Article 2 was raised because of the risk of the claimant suffering a fatal heart attack if the treatment was administered. Articles 3 and 8 were also argued. Given the importance of the Convention rights involved, the Court of Appeal concluded that it was necessary for the court to reach its own view as to the relevant issues.

> [W]hat would be required on a substantive challenge here would be a full merits review of the propriety of the treatment proposed and, for that purpose, cross-examination of the specialists.[13]

Resources arguments have also been given short shrift in Article 2 jurisprudence. For example, in *Wright*[14] it was submitted by the Home Secretary that the costs and resources of setting up an inquiry should be taken into consideration. The Administrative Court held that, whilst it was conscious of the costs and resources which would be involved,

---

[6] *R (on the application of Amin (Imtiaz) v Secretary of State for the Home Department* [2003] UKHL 51, [2004] 1 AC 653 at [40] per Lord Slynn.
[7] *Ibid*, at [30] per Lord Bingham.
[8] *R v Director of Public Prosecutions, ex p Pretty* [2001] UKHL 61, [2001] 3 WLR 1598.
[9] *Ibid*, at [6] per Lord Bingham.
[10] *Re A (Children) (Conjoined Twins: Surgical Separation)* [2001] Fam 147.
[11] See also the comments of Dame Butler-Sloss in *NHS Trust A v Mrs M* [2001] 2 WLR 942 at [38] and *NHS Trust v P*, Family Division, 19 December 2000.
[12] *R (on the application of Wilkinson) v The Responsible Medical Officer Broadmoor Hospital* [2001] EWCA Civ 1545, [2002] 1 WLR 419.
[13] *Ibid*, at [36] per Simon Brown LJ. See also [83] per Hale LJ.
[14] *R v Home Office, ex p Wright* [2001] EWHC (Admin) 520, [2002] HRLR 1.

[i]f this unsatisfactory situation is to be avoided in the future, steps should be taken to ensure that, in every case where Article 2 of the Convention may be engaged, the coroner's inquest complies with the procedural obligations arising under that article.[15]

However, there is only so far that the courts will go. Whilst the Article 2 argument was only a small part of the case, in *Pretty*[16] the claimant argued that she had a right to her husband's assistance in committing suicide and that section 2 of the Suicide Act 1961, so far as it made this a criminal offence requiring the Director of Public Prosecutions (DPP) to prosecute, was incompatible with various Convention rights. Lord Bingham stated that the Judicial Committee of the House of Lords was not a legislative body, nor entitled or fitted to act as a moral or ethical arbiter.[17] Lord Steyn stated that any change in this area was a role for the legislature.[18]

[A]n interpretation requiring states to legalise euthanasia and assisted suicide would not only be enormously controversial but profoundly unacceptable to the people of many member states.[19]

2. Scope

Article 2 provides that 'everyone's' right to life shall be protected by law, but there has been little discussion in the judgments as to the meaning of 'everyone'. Either end of the spectrum is clear. Life begins, it was established in pre-HRA case law, if, after birth, the child exists as a live child,

that is to say, breathing and living by reason of its breathing through its own lungs alone, without deriving any of its living or power of living by or through any connection with its mother.[20]

Post-HRA, in *Evans*[21] the CA confirmed that a foetus, prior to the moment of birth, does not have independent rights or interests.[22] Life ends, it has also been established in pre-HRA case law, with brainstem death.[23]

---

[15] *Ibid*, at [68]. See also *Manning*, above n 1, at [33] and *R (Khan) v Secretary of State for Health* [2003] EWCA Civ 1129, [2004] 1 WLR 971. Cf. *R (Haggerty) v St Helens Council* [2003] EWHC Admin 808, [2003] ACD 304.
[16] Above n 8.
[17] *Ibid*, at [2].
[18] *Ibid*, at [57].
[19] *Ibid*, at [56].
[20] *Rance v Mid-Downs Health Authority* [1991] 1 QB 587 at 621 per Brooke J. See also *R v Poulton* (1832) 5 C&P 329 at 330 per Littledale J and *R v Handley* (1874) 13 Cox CC 79 at 81 per Brett J.
[21] *Evans v Amicus Healthcare Ltd* [2004] EWCA Civ 727, [2005] Fam 1.
[22] *Ibid*, at [19] per Thorpe and Sedley LJJ in reliance upon *Re F (in utero)* [1988] 2 All ER 193 and *Re MB (an adult: medical treatment)* [1997] 2 FCR 541. See also Arden LJ at [106]–[107].
[23] *Re A (A Minor)* [1992] 3 Med L Rev 303. See also *Airedale NHS Trust v Bland* [1993] AC 789.

Between the extremes of life and death, the courts have taken a broad approach. In *Pretty*[24] Lord Hope stated that the right to life is assumed to be inherent in the human condition which we all share.[25] It has been held that the terminally ill have a right to life,[26] as do patients diagnosed as in a permanent vegetative state within the guidelines of the Royal College of Physicians.[27] Seriously disabled babies and children with very short life expectancies[28] have a right to life. In *Re A*,[29] a case concerning the separation of conjoined twins, the Court of Appeal unanimously held that Mary was alive even though she was not capable of separate survival from her sister Jodie, to whom she was joined at the lower abdomen. She had her own brain, heart and lungs, other vital organs, and arms and legs. She was alive because of a common artery which enabled Jodie, who was stronger, to circulate oxygenated blood for both of them. Ward LJ commented that

> it would be contrary to common sense and to everyone's sensibilities to say that Mary is not alive or that there are not two separate persons.

3. Definition of 'Life'

Another question which arises from Article 2 is whether the 'life' everyone has a right to is merely a right to exist or whether it is a right to a life which meets certain qualitative benchmarks. Given the dangers inherent in making any assessment of someone's quality of life, understandably there has been little discussion of this question in the judgments given. In *Pretty*,[30] although the claimant suffered from motor neurone disease, a progressive degenerative illness from which she had no hope of recovery, had only a short time to live and faced the prospect of a humiliating and distressing death, the House of Lords resoundingly rejected the suggestion that it would be permissible under Article 2 for her husband to assist in her suicide and escape prosecution.[31]

Withholding or discontinuing treatment of the seriously disabled or those in a permanent vegetative state has been characterised as an omission rather than the intentional deprivation of the life of someone who has no quality of life. There is only a duty to treat a patient who does not have the capacity to accept or refuse

---

[24] Above n 8.
[25] *Ibid*, at [87].
[26] See, eg *Pretty*, above n 8.
[27] *NHS Trust A v Mrs M*, above n 11, at [17]. See also *Airedale NHS Trust v Bland* [1993] AC 789.
[28] See, eg *A National Health Service Trust v D* [2000] 2 FCR 577; *Re J (a minor) (wardship: medical treatment)* [1991] FCR 370.
[29] Above n 10.
[30] Above n 8.
[31] See the comments of Lord Steyn at [50] and [54].

treatment when treatment is in the patient's best interests.[32] However, if treatment is in a patient's best interests, any failure to treat will be in violation of Article 2:

> Article 2 therefore imposes a positive obligation to give life-sustaining treatment in circumstances where, according to responsible medical opinion, such treatment is in the best interests of the patient but does not impose an absolute obligation to treat if such treatment would be futile.[33]

Although kept from centre stage, it is clear that quality of life issues do play some part in the determination of what is in a patient's best interests. For example, in *NHS Trust A*,[34] a test case concerning the withdrawal of treatment from two patients in permanent vegetative states, Dame Butler-Sloss agreed that the quality of life may be relevant to the clinical assessment of whether it was in the patient's best interests for treatment to continue.[35] She later explained this decision as a conclusion to

> treat these patients with respect and to allow them to die with dignity and in peace by withdrawing that which keeps them artificially alive.[36]

In *D*[37] Cazalet J concluded that treatment of I which would include non-resuscitation in the event of a respiratory and/or cardiac failure and/or arrest with palliative care to ease his suffering and to permit his life to end peacefully with dignity was in I's best interests:

> Having regard to the minimal quality of life that I has in the short life span left to him through his irreversible and worsening lung condition, I weigh, from I's assumed standpoint, any possible very limited short-term extension to this that mechanical ventilation might give him against the increasing pain and suffering caused by the further mechanical ventilation . . . I consider that the thorough and careful analysis of the way ahead through full palliative treatment as advocated by the paediatricians in the declaration as sought is in the best interests of I.[38]

The issue presented itself slightly differently in *Re A*,[39] the case of the conjoined twins. Although the case was actually decided on common law principles, the Court of Appeal was unanimous in concluding that no different decision would have been made under Article 2. As discussed in the preceding paragraphs, Mary and Jodie were joined at the lower abdomen. If separated, Mary would die within minutes but Jodie would have some chance of a life 'which will be worthwhile.'[40] If they remained joined, doctors estimated they would both die within 3–6 months.

---

[32] *NHS Trust A v Mrs M*, above n 11, at [37]. See also the pre-HRA case in which the same conclusion was reached: *Airedale NHS Trust v Bland* [1993] AC 789 per Lord Goff at 867 and Lord Brown Wilkinson at 884–85.
[33] *NHS Trust A*, ibid, at [37].
[34] *Ibid.*
[35] *Ibid*, at [32].
[36] *Re G (adult incompetent: withdrawal of treatment)* [2002] 65 BMLR 6.
[37] *A National Health Service Trust v D* [2000] 2 FLR 677.
[38] see also the pre-HRA case of *Re J (a minor) (wardship: medical treatment)* [1991] FCR 370.
[39] Above n 10.
[40] Per Ward LJ.

Ward and Brooke LJJ did not characterise the operation to separate the twins as being in Mary's best interests.[41] Ward LJ, with whom Brooke LJ agreed on this point, held that the sanctity of life doctrine compelled him to accept that each life had an equal inherent value and that life was worthwhile in itself whatever the diminution in one's capacity to enjoy it and however gravely impaired some of one's vital functions of speech, deliberation and choice may be.[42] Therefore, in his view, Mary's life, 'desperate as it is,' still had its 'own ineliminable value and dignity.' Whilst this seemed to indicate that he would conclude the operation could not go ahead, instead he placed in the scales the question of whether the treatment was worthwhile and held that this was a different exercise from the proscribed consideration of the worth of one life compared with another:

> In summary, the operation will give Jodie the prospects of a normal expectation of relatively normal life. The operation will shorten Mary's life but she remains doomed for death. Mary has a full claim to the dignity of independence which is her human entitlement . . . Mary is 'designated for death' because her capacity to live her life is fatally compromised. The prospect of a full life for Jodie is counterbalanced by an acceleration of certain death for Mary. That balance is heavily in Jodie's favour . . . it is . . . impossible not to put in the scales of each child the manner in which they are individually able to exercise their right to life. Mary may have a right to life, but she has little right to be alive. She is alive because and only because, to put it bluntly, but none the less accurately, she sucks the lifeblood of Jodie and she sucks the lifeblood out of Jodie.

It is difficult to see how Ward LJ thought he was doing anything but balancing the worth of the one life compared with the other. As he himself concluded, what was proposed was an intentional deprivation of life, not a failure to treat, meaning that under existing law, questions as to whether or not treatment was in the patient's best interests did not arise. Once it was concluded that Mary was a life and had a right to life, a strict Article 2 interpretation would imply that under no circumstances could the operation go ahead unless it fell within one of the exceptions outlined in Article 2(2)—an unlikely prospect.[43] However, in the judgments given, whilst it was pointed out that no different conclusion would be reached under Article 2, it was not discussed in detail and all members of the Court of Appeal were careful to point out that their judgments were only authoritative in the particular unique circumstances which had given rise to the proceedings. In short, *Re A* is very unlikely to open the floodgates to 'quality of life'-based litigation.[44]

---

[41] Robert Walker LJ held that the operation would be in Mary and Jodie's best interests 'since for the twins to remain alive and conjoined in the way they are would be to deprive them of the bodily integrity and human dignity which is the right of each of them.'

[42] Ward LJ quoted extensively from J. Keown, 'Restoring Moral and Intellectual Shape to the Law after Bland' (1997) 113 *LQR* 481 at 485–87.

[43] As discussed in following paragraphs, Ward LJ suggested that Art 2 was subject to an implied limitation which justified balancing. Brooke LJ was reluctant to find that a right as fundamental as Art 2 could be subject to an implied limitation which destroyed its value.

[44] See generally S. Michalowski, 'Sanctity of Life—Are Some Lives More Sacred Than Others?' (2002) 22 *LS* 377; R Huxtable, 'Separation of Conjoined Twins: Where Next for English Law?' [2002] *CLR* 459.

4. Intentional Deprivation of Life

Proceedings concerning the intentional deprivation of someone's life by a public authority are rare. The bulk of litigation has concerned the positive duty to safeguard life and the procedural duty to investigate deaths. Those cases which have raised the question of intentional deprivation have all centred on one question: what actually constitutes an intentional deprivation of life? Although the case law is far from clear, brief definitions have been given. To fall within this limb of Article 2, it must be a deliberate act, as opposed to an omission, which results in death[45] and the purpose must be to cause death.[46] However, determining what is a deliberate act with the purpose of causing death is not as simple as it would first appear.

It is clear that assisted suicide and voluntary euthanasia fall within the category of intentional deprivation.[47] It has been held that if an NHS doctor were deliberately to bring about the death of a competent patient by withdrawing life-prolonging treatment contrary to that patient's wishes, Article 2 would be infringed.[48] In *Re A*,[49] the case of the conjoined twins discussed in preceding paragraphs, it was beyond doubt that separation would lead to the death of the weaker twin, Mary. In the Court of Appeal, Ward LJ and Brooke LJ held that the operation was not in Mary's best interests and would be an intentional deprivation of life. Ward LJ stated that it would be utterly fanciful to classify the invasive treatment as an omission in contradistinction to an act. Nor did he believe it could be classified as not continuing to provide treatment. Robert Walker LJ dissented on this point, holding that the word 'intentionally' in Article 2 must be given its natural and ordinary meaning and that it applied only to cases where the purpose of the prohibited action was to cause death. He concluded that Mary would die as a result of the operation 'not because she was intentionally killed, but because her own body cannot sustain her life.'

Difficult questions have also arisen concerning the treatment of seriously disabled children and those in a permanent vegetative state. To summarise, following on from the pre-HRA reasoning in the *Bland*[50] decisions on the part of NHS Trusts to withhold further treatment, or discontinue life support, have not been characterised by the courts as intentional deprivations of life under Article 2. The first so-called 'test case' was *NHS Trust A v Mrs M*,[51] which concerned two patients in a permanent vegetative state (PVS). In the Family Division of the High Court, Dame Butler-Sloss held that the first step was to confirm that the diagnosis of PVS fell within the guidelines of the Royal College of Physicians. Finding that this was so, she concluded that it would not be in the best interests of either patient to continue treatment. She then considered the question of whether or not an omission to provide a life-sustaining treatment constituted an intentional deprivation of life within the meaning of Article 2.

---

[45] *NHS Trust A v Mrs M*, above n 11.
[46] *Re A*, above n 10 per Robert Walker LJ.
[47] *Pretty*, above n 8.
[48] *R (on the application of Burke) v The General Medical Council* [2005] EWCA Civ 1003 at [39].
[49] Above n 10.
[50] *Airedale NHS Trust v Bland* [1993] AC 789.
[51] Above n 11.

Pointing out that the question of discontinuing artificial nutrition and hydration to a patient in a PVS state had not yet arisen in the European Court of Human Rights, she held that guidance could be gleaned from decisions of that court dealing with entirely different situations.[52] She also relied upon the judgment of Robert Walker LJ in *Re A*. She concluded that there were limits to the extent of the negative obligation under Article 2(1). Here the purpose of the action was not to cause death:

> Although the intention in withdrawing artificial nutrition and hydration in PVS cases is to hasten death, in my judgment the phrase 'deprivation of life' must import a deliberate act, as opposed to an omission, by someone acting on behalf of the state, which results in death. A responsible decision by a medical team not to provide treatment at the initial stage could not amount to intentional deprivation by the state. Such a decision based on clinical judgment is an omission to act. The death of the patient is the result of the illness or injury from which he suffered and that cannot be described as a deprivation.[53]

She also concluded that there was no difference between this situation and a decision to discontinue treatment which was no longer in the best interests of the patient. She found the analysis of the House of Lords in *Bland*[54] to be entirely in accordance with Article 2.

The conclusion of Dame Butler-Sloss could be described as the only viable solution in the circumstances. If discontinuing treatment was to be characterised as an intentional deprivation, this would place hospitals in a difficult position. PVS patients would have to be kept alive indefinitely, and seriously disabled children would have to be resuscitated despite their pain and suffering and poor quality of life.[55] As Dame Butler-Sloss commented,

> in view of the absolute nature of the prohibition on intentional killing . . . there would be a duty in every case to take steps to keep a terminally ill patient alive by all means possible, and to continue those steps indefinitely, until the patient's body could no longer sustain treatment, irrespective of the circumstances or the prognosis.[56]

In order to provide some way out in such circumstances, the courts may even have been tempted to embark down the dangerous road of defining who was to benefit from the right to life or whether life had to be of a certain quality. Classification as non-intentional has definitely resolved some problems, but, as discussed in the following paragraphs, it has also raised new ones given the positive obligation under Article 2 to take steps to safeguard life.

---

[52] *Widmer v Switzerland* Application 20527/92 (1993); *Association X v United Kingdom* (1978) 14 D&R 31 were cited.
[53] *Ibid*, at [30].
[54] *Airedale NHS Trust v Bland* [1993] AC 789.
[55] See, eg *A National Health Service Trust v D* [2000] 2 FCR 577.
[56] *Ibid*, at [29].

5. Positive Duty to Safeguard Life

5.1 Nature of the Duty

Although not apparent on its face, Article 2(1) also requires public authorities to take appropriate steps to safeguard the lives of those within its jurisdiction. The origin of this duty can be found in the judgment of the European Court of Human Rights in *Osman*[57]:

> The Court notes that the first sentence of Article 2(1) enjoins the State not only to refrain from the intentional and unlawful taking of life, but also to take appropriate steps to safeguard the lives of those within its jurisdiction . . . Article 2 of the Convention may also imply in certain well-defined circumstances a positive obligation on the authorities to take preventive operational measures to protect an individual whose life is at risk from the criminal acts of another individual . . . where there is an allegation that the authorities have violated their positive obligation to protect the right to life in the context of their above-mentioned duty to prevent and suppress offences against the person, it must be established to its satisfaction that the authorities knew or ought to have known at the time of the existence of a real and immediate risk to the life of an identified individual or individuals from the criminal acts of a third party and that they failed to take measures within the scope of their powers which, judged reasonably, might have been expected to avoid that risk.[58]

Initially the *Osman* test was adopted wholesale by UK courts.[59] However, in *R (A) v Lord Saville of Newdigate*[60] slight alterations began to appear. The case concerned a challenge to a procedural order of the tribunal conducting the Bloody Sunday Inquiry. The retired soldiers, due to give evidence in the Inquiry, challenged the decision that they must give evidence in the Guildhall in Londonderry rather than in London or some other venue. The primary ground of challenge was that the soldiers had reasonable grounds for fearing for their lives if they went to Londonderry to give evidence.

The Court of Appeal considered that the *Osman* duty was directly engaged; however, it found it very difficult to find a phrase 'which encapsulates a threshold of risk which engages article 2.'[61] It held that the degree of risk described as real and immediate in *Osman*, as used in that case, was very high, calling for positive action from the authorities to protect life. It was a real and immediate risk to the life of an identified individual or individuals from the criminal acts of a third party which was, or ought to have been, known to the authorities. It concluded:

---

[57] *Osman v United Kingdom* (1997) 29 EHRR 245.
[58] *Ibid*, at [115]–[116].
[59] See, eg *Venables*, above n 2; *H*, above n 1.
[60] *R(A) v Lord Saville of Newdigate* [2001] EWCA Civ 2048, [2002] 1 WLR 1249.
[61] *Ibid*, at [28] per Lord Phillips MR giving the judgment of the court.

Such a degree of risk is well above the threshold that will engage article 2 when the risk is attendant upon some action that an authority is contemplating putting into effect itself. It was not the appropriate test to invoke in the present context.[62]

Given that the facts of *Osman* were unique and it is far more likely for the risk to life to be posed by unidentified individuals, arguably in the majority of instances the Court of Appeal had lowered the threshold at which the positive duty arose, keeping in mind that it is entirely possible for UK courts to provide greater protection than that provided by the European Court.[63] This was the view reached by a differently constituted Court of Appeal in *Bloggs 61*,[64] which concerned the Prison Service's decision to move a prisoner from a protected witness unit to a mainstream prison regime. The Court of Appeal held that there is no single or all-purpose formulation of the test to be applied when considering what steps a person should take in order to protect a person from a threat to his life from a third party or parties. 'It all depends on the facts of the case.'[65]

If a risk to life is not 'real', it is not a risk to life. If a risk to life is not 'immediate' in the sense that it is not present at the time or during the period when it is claimed that a protective duty is owed by a public body, it is not a risk that can engage article 2. It is future risk that may, at some later date do so. To be a candidate for engaging article 2, all that is needed is 'a risk to life'. To engage it depends, in the circumstances of each case, on the degree of risk, which necessarily includes considerations of the nature of the threat, the protective means in being or proposed to counter it and the adequacy of those means.[66]

It concluded that the word 'risk' in the general context of risk to life engaging Article 2 was one of common-sense application to individual circumstances and can and should be used without a qualifying adjective.[67]

5.2 Assessing a Risk to Life

Given the judgments in *R(A)* and *Bloggs 61*, it is clear that the duty to take reasonable measures arises where there is a risk to life. The next step is to determine what actually qualifies as a risk to life sufficient to engage Article 2. In *R(A)*[68] the Court of Appeal held that the appropriate course was to consider first the nature of the subjective fears of the soldier witnesses, to consider the extent to which those fears were objectively justified and then to consider the extent to which those fears, and the grounds giving rise to them, would be alleviated if the soldiers gave their evidence

---

[62] *Ibid*, at [28].
[63] In *R (on the application of F) v Chief Constable of Norfolk Police* [2002] EWHC (Admin) 1738 the court, considering a prisoner's request to be placed in a protected witness unit, distinguished decisions of the Prison Service from the kind of actions contemplated in *R(A)*. It held that the question to be asked was whether there was a real and immediate risk to the life of the prisoner if he was not admitted to the unit. However, it is difficult to discern from the judgment the difference that would have been made if the test had simply been one of 'risk to life'.
[64] Above n 1.
[65] *Ibid*, at [55] per Auld LJ, with whom the others agreed.
[66] *Ibid*, at [61] per Auld LJ.
[67] *Ibid*, at [62] per Auld LJ.
[68] Above n 60.

somewhere else.[69] With respect to the objective test, the Court of Appeal held in *Officer A*[70] that there must be reasonable grounds which show that the fears of a witness are objectively justified.[71] Although it has been held that the evidence supporting the case must demonstrate convincingly the risk to life, often there are no concrete facts or statistics as to future probability.[72]

The role that deference to the primary decision maker should play in any risk assessment exercise by the court is not clear. In *Bloggs 61*[73] the Court of Appeal held that any potential interference with the right to life required the most anxious scrutiny by the court since it was the most fundamental of human rights, but also held that this stopped short of merits review.[74] Despite the fundamental and unqualified nature of the right to life, the court held that

> it is still appropriate to show some deference to and/or to recognise the special competence of the Prison Service in making a decision going to the safety of an inmate's life.

However, it did hold that the degree of deference would be less and the intensity of the court's review would be greater—perhaps greatest—in an Article 2 case than for those human rights where the Convention required a balance to be struck.[75]

It is questionable whether this aspect of the judgment of the Court of Appeal is correct. It is not an approach which has been taken in any other case where the positive duty under Article 2 has been raised.[76] For example, in *H*[77] the Administrative Court held that, given the fundamental nature of the right to life, the court had to examine the factual evidence for itself to determine whether or not there was a risk to life.[78] But despite the comments concerning deference in *Bloggs 61*, it is clear that the court did not simply accept the Prison Service's word as to the safety of the prisoner. A police risk assessment had been carried out and the concerns of the Assistant Chief Probation Officer were taken into account. Whilst deference was urged, it appears that the facts justifying the conclusion of the court were apparent, Auld LJ stating that he would have reached the same conclusion as the Prison Service based on the reasons it gave.[79] Keene LJ, who agreed, pointed out that, even were it for the court to make the primary judgment, the court would have to attach considerable weight to the assessment of risk made by those with professional involvement in the areas with which the case was concerned.

---

[69] *Ibid*, at [31].
[70] *R (on the application of Officer A) v HM Coroner for Inner South London* [2004] EWCA Civ 1439, [2005] UKHRR 44.
[71] *Ibid*, at [30] per Gale LJ, with whom the others agreed.
[72] See, eg *Venables*, above n 2.
[73] Above n 1.
[74] *Ibid*, at [63] per Auld LJ.
[75] *Ibid*, at [65] per Auld LJ in reliance upon *R v DPP ex p Kebilene* [2000] 2 AC 326 at [80] per Lord Hope and *R v BBC ex p Prolife Alliance* [2003] UKHL 23, [2004] 1 AC 185 at [139] per Lord Walker.
[76] *Bloggs 61* was not even referred to in *Officer A*, a later Court of Appeal judgment.
[77] Above n 1.
[78] *Ibid*, at [86]. See also *Wilkinson*, above n 12.
[79] *Ibid*, at [70].

It may therefore in most cases make little difference whether one describes the court's approach as one of deference or simply as one of attaching weight to the judgment reached by such bodies: the end result would be the same.[80]

It appears that the court was not really affording deference but merely appreciating the expertise of those providing the evidence. Given the importance of the right to life, the appropriateness of deference in the true sense of the term at the stage of risk assessment is open to serious question.

5.3 Reasonable Measures

If a risk to life has been found, the next stage is to determine what should be done to avoid it. In *Osman*[81] such measures were described as 'reasonable measures', the European Court also holding that the obligation must be interpreted in a way which did not impose an impossible or disproportionate burden on the authorities.[82] It is clear that the term 'reasonable' imports an element of balancing and may require the assessment of different alternatives. For example, as mentioned above, in *R(A)*[83] the Court of Appeal considered the extent to which the fears of the soldiers, and the grounds giving rise to them, would be alleviated if the soldiers gave their evidence somewhere else. It then balanced this against the adverse consequences to the inquiry of the move of venue, applying commonsense and humanity.[84] Although no mention was made of the original *Osman* formulation of 'reasonable measures', the approach taken by the court was essentially along those lines.

Given the balancing involved, it has been held that at this stage some degree of deference to the primary decision maker is appropriate. In *H*[85] the Administrative Court held that there was a discretionary area of judgment to which a court should accord due weight to the views of the decision maker.[86] However, it is clear that the court only had a limited degree of deference in mind, stating that the court's task was to

subject the contested policy to anxious scrutiny on an objective basis to satisfy itself that there is no other step which might reasonably have been required of the defendant, giving proper weight to all the various factors, including the absolute nature of the right in issue.[87]

5.4 Application

5.4.1 Protection of Identity

Often the disclosure of a person's identity can rise to a risk to life. For example, *Officer A*[88] concerned a request for anonymity from two police officers due to give

---

[80] *Ibid*, at [82]. See also *F*, above n 63, where the AC held that the risk assessment carried out by the Prison Service in relation to a request for admission to a protected witness unit was flawed and a new decision was required.
[81] Above n 57.
[82] *Ibid*, at [116].
[83] Above n 60.
[84] *Ibid*, at [31].
[85] Above n 1.
[86] *Ibid*, at [111].
[87] *Ibid*, at [113]. See also *Haggerty*, above n 15.
[88] Above n 70.

evidence to a coroner's inquest into the death of a man who had been shot by Officer A accompanied by Officer B. The two officers feared for their own safety and for that of their families. Taking the evidence as a whole, the Court of Appeal concluded that there were clear grounds which objectively justified the fears of the officers and Article 2 was therefore engaged.[89] It then considered countervailing considerations and concluded that there were none of sufficient weight to tip the balance in favour of an order for anonymity being refused.

> It is relevant to note that the respondents still have to give evidence before a jury. Their evidence will be given by video-link and will be subject to cross examination. This is not a case where the court is concerned with the trial of a defendant. It is a fact-finding exercise conducted by the coroner and the jury. The appellant's interest in the proceedings, although very important and significant, is not in the same category as the interest of a defendant in a criminal trial.[90]

In *Venables*[91] protection of identity was also at issue. The claimants sought injunctions to restrain the publication of information relating to their identities and whereabouts. They had both been convicted of the murder of two-year-old James Bulger in 1993 when they were ten years old, a case which was widely publicised in the media. Although only three news groups were named as defendants, the injunction was sought *contra mundum*—against the world at large. The case pre-dated the judgment in *R(A)* and the Family Division of the High Court applied the *Osman* test. It took into account evidence from the Home Secretary, press reports, evidence of risk reported by the press, evidence from defendant newspapers and judicial observations. It concluded that there was a real possibility that someone would seek them out and, if they were found, the media would be likely to reveal that information.

> If their new identities were discovered, I am satisfied that neither of them would have any chance of a normal life and that there is a real and strong possibility that their lives would be at risk.[92]

Balancing Article 10 against Article 2, Dame Butler-Sloss concluded that the court had jurisdiction in exceptional cases to extend the protection of confidentiality of information

> where not to do so would be likely to lead to serious physical injury, or to the death, of the person seeking that confidentiality.[93]

Taking into account the high risk of serious physical harm and the possibility that a claimant might be killed if identified, the injunctions protecting identity were granted.

---

[89] *Ibid*, at [36].
[90] *Ibid*, at [37].
[91] Above n 2.
[92] *Ibid*, at [94]. See also *Secretary of State for Defence v Times Newspapers Limited*, Divisional Court, 28 March 2001.
[93] *Ibid*, at 933.

5.4.2 Witness Protection

Witness protection, particularly in relation to serving prisoners, has also given rise to Article 2 claims. In *Bloggs 61*[94] a serving prisoner challenged the Prison Service's decision to remove him from a protected witness unit to a mainstream prison regime. The Prison Service, relying on a police risk assessment containing a division of opinion, had determined that he be returned to mainstream prison conditions although there was a subsequent report revising his risk from high to medium. As discussed above, the Court of Appeal held that the Prison Service and police were better placed than the court to assess risk to life in such a context.[95] Subjective and objective tests were not explicitly applied, although the judgment in *R(A)* was referred to. Subjecting the decision of the Prison Service to the most anxious scrutiny, the court concluded that it was correct, stating that it was 'not just well within the bounds of what was reasonable,'[96] and therefore Article 2 was not engaged.[97]

Although identities may be protected, the actual location of proceedings may give rise to an additional risk to life. In *R(A)*[98] the Court of Appeal concluded that if soldier witnesses had to go to Londonderry to give evidence, many would be subjectively in fear for their lives.[99] Taking into consideration the evidence of the agencies concerned with security, the unique attractiveness of the soldiers as targets to some terrorists, and the scale of the security problem given that between 200 and 400 soldier witnesses were to be called to give evidence, this fear was found to be objectively justified.[100]

But, before concluding that a change of venue was required, the court weighed the risk at the alternative venue, the risk to the likelihood of the tribunal getting at the truth and the impact on the families. The court was also concerned that a public authority should not be required to desist from a lawful and peaceful activity because of a terrorist threat. The

> desirability of carrying on lawful activities in a democracy can constitute compelling justification for continuing to do so despite terrorist threats, leaving it to the security agencies to do their best to provide protection.[101]

However, it concluded that the risk posed in Londonderry to the soldier witnesses constituted a compelling reason why their evidence should be taken in a venue other than Londonderry.

> [W]e do not see why, should we direct a change of venue for these witnesses, this should threaten the credibility of the tribunal or confidence in their inquiry.[102]

---

[94] Above n 1.
[95] *Ibid*, at [66] per Auld LJ.
[96] *Ibid*, at [70] per Auld LJ.
[97] See also *F*, above n 63. Applying the rest of real and immediate risk to life, the court concluded that the Prison Service had not carried out a proper risk assessment and a new decision was required as to whether or not the claimant should be admitted to the protected witness unit.
[98] Above n 60.
[99] *Ibid*, at [33].
[100] *Ibid*, at [50]–[52].
[101] *Ibid*, at [17]. Reference was made to the judgment of the European Court of Human Rights in *Ergi v Turkey*, 28 July, 1998.
[102] *Ibid*, at [56].

5.4.3 Care Home Closures

In a number of cases it has been claimed that closure of a care home will result in a risk to the lives of the residents. For example, in *Haggerty*[103] it was argued that the Council's decision not to enter into a more onerous arrangement with the private provider led to the provider deciding to close the home. Putting to one side chain of causation issues, the Administrative Court spent considerable time assessing whether or not there was a risk to the claimant's lives by moving them. Not only measures proposed by the Council to facilitate the move but also reports from general practitioners and a consultant psychiatrist were taken into account. The court concluded that Article 2 was not engaged in the light of the precautions and steps to be taken by the Council.[104] Despite this conclusion, it did go on to consider reasonable measures and held that the courts accord a broad area of discretionary judgment to a public authority in deciding what is a fair balance between the interests of the individual and that of the community.[105] It concluded that the Council had done all that was reasonable to prevent lives being put at risk. For example, it had liaised with relatives, sought alternative placements, attempted to preserve friendship groups and agreed to liaise with a consultant in geriatric psychiatry on the best way of moving the claimants. The court also considered the council's statutory obligation to take expense into account.[106]

5.4.4 PVS Patients and Medical Treatment

Although one set of problems was avoided by characterising the withdrawal of treatment from PVS patients as an omission rather than an intentional deprivation of life, another was created by holding that the positive obligation under Article 2 was engaged in these instances.[107] Applying *Osman*, the court held that reasonable measures had to be taken. However, it concluded that in a case

> where a responsible clinical decision is made to withhold treatment, on the grounds that it is not in the patient's best interests, and that clinical decision is made in accordance with a respectable body of medical opinion, the positive obligation under Article 2 was discharged.[108]

It was also noted that assistance in determining the scope of the positive duty in such instances could be gained from the right to autonomy and self-determination as protected by Article 8.[109] The court summarised the position as follows:

---

[103] Above n 15.
[104] See also *R (on the application of Dudley) v East Sussex County Council* [2003] EWHC (Admin) 1093, [2003] ACD 353; *McKellar v Mayor & Burgess of the London Borough of Hounslow* [2003] EWHC (QB) 3145.
[105] *Ibid*, at [49].
[106] *Ibid*.
[107] *NHS Trust A v Mrs M*, above n 11, at [35].
[108] *Ibid*, at [35]. Reliance was placed on *Widmer* and *Association X*, above n 52.
[109] *Ibid*, at [41]. See also *A National Health Service Trust v D* [2000] 2 FCR 577, where the court referred to Art 3 as protecting the right to die with dignity.

Article 2 therefore imposes a positive obligation to give life-sustaining treatment in circumstances where, according to responsible medical opinion, such treatment is in the best interests of the patient but does not impose an absolute obligation to treat if such treatment would be futile.[110]

Where a competent patient makes it clear that he does not wish to receive treatment which is, objectively, in his medical best interests, it is unlawful for doctors to administer that treatment. Personal autonomy or the right of self-determination prevails.[111] Furthermore, Article 2 does not entitle anyone to continue with life-prolonging treatment where to do so would expose the patient to inhuman or degrading treatment breaching Article 3.[112]

5.4.5 No Condoms Policy

Article 2 has also been raised in relation to a hospital's no condoms policy. In H[113] the claimant, a patient detained at Ashworth Hospital who was also a carrier of hepatitis C and a practising homosexual, challenged the policy. The Administrative Court pointed out that this was not a case of protection from the criminal acts of a third party nor of self-harm. '[T]he means to protect himself lie in the first instance in his own abstention from such activities.'[114] Nevertheless, *Osman* was applied. Making its own assessment of the evidence, the court held that, given the no-sex policy of the hospital and the security and observation regimes in force, the risk of any relevant sexual activity taking place was low, although it could not be wholly eliminated.[115] Secondly, the risk of infection with hepatitis B or C was regarded as very low.[116] The court concluded that the no-condoms policy did not present a real and immediate threat to life within the meaning of Article 2, even assuming that in some circumstances hepatitis B or C could be life threatening illnesses 'as to which there is no evidence before the court.'[117]

Despite this conclusion, the question of reasonable measures was also considered. According due weight to the views of the decision maker,[118] the court took into account the kinds of patient with whom Ashworth deals, the therapeutic need to have a no-sex policy, the need to apply that policy consistently and the security issues. The Administrative Court concluded that the defendant had not acted unreasonably in adopting as part of its no-sex policy a no-condoms policy. Furthermore, balancing the needs of consistent treatment, safety and security against the very low risk of

---

[110] *Ibid*, at [37]. See also *NHS Trust v P*, above n 11; *NHS Trust A v H* [2001] 2 FLR 501.
[111] *Burke*, above n 48, at [30].
[112] *Ibid*, at [39]. See further SAM McLean, 'Death, Decision-making and the Law' (2004) 3 *JR* 265.
[113] Above n 1.
[114] *Ibid*, at [84].
[115] *Ibid*, at [99].
[116] *Ibid*, at [103].
[117] *Ibid*, at [104].
[118] *Ibid*, at [111].

infection, the defendant had not unreasonably failed to make exceptions to the policy.[119]

6. Duty to Investigate

6.1 Nature of the Duty

As with the positive duty to safeguard life, the duty to investigate has its origins in Strasbourg case law. In *McCann*[120] the European Court held as follows:

> The obligation to protect the right to life under [Article 2(1)], read in conjunction with the State's general duty under Article 1 of the Convention to 'secure to everyone within their jurisdiction the rights and freedoms defined in [the] Convention,' requires by implication that there should be some form of effective official investigation when individuals have been killed as a result of the use of force by, *inter alios*, agents of the State.[121]

The essential purpose of the investigation is to secure the effective implementation of the domestic laws which protect the right to life and, in those cases involving state agents or bodies, to ensure their accountability for deaths occurring under their responsibility.[122] Lord Bingham expanded on this in *Amin*[123]:

> The purposes of such an investigation are clear: to ensure so far as possible that the full facts are brought to light; that culpable and discreditable conduct is exposed and brought to public notice; that suspicion of deliberate wrongdoing (if unjustified) is allayed; that dangerous practices and procedures are rectified; and that those who have lost their relative may at least have the satisfaction of knowing that lessons learned from his death may save the lives of others.[124]

The duty to investigate is secondary to the duties not to take life unlawfully and to protect life in the sense that it only arises where a death has occurred or life-threatening injuries have occurred. But 'in any case where a death has occurred in custody it is not a minor or unimportant duty.'[125] The duty is partly one owed to the next of kin of the deceased as representing the deceased and partly to others who may in similar

---

[119] *Ibid*, at [116]. See also *T v Mental Health Review Tribunal* [2002] EWHC (Admin) 247, [2002] Lloyd's Rep Med 354, where the claimant argued that she should be given a copy of the tribunal's decision in relation to her former partner. The court held that the case fell a long way short of the threshold in *Osman*. In *R (on the application of T) v Secretary of State for Health*, Court of Appeal, 29 July 2002 the court held that Art 2 was engaged if an HIV-positive mother, in whose case the state had assumed responsibility for making financial provision, was provided with insufficient money to buy formula milk for her baby. However, the court was not satisfied that the claimant had insufficient funds to buy the formula.
[120] *McCann v United Kingdom* (1996) 21 EHRR 97. See also *Yasa v Turkey* (1998) 28 EHRR 408 at [98]; *Salman v Turkey* (2002) 34 EHRR 17 at [104]; and *Jordan v United Kingdom* (2003) 37 EHRR 2 at [105].
[121] *Ibid*, at [161] as quoted in *Amin*, above n 6, at [20] per Lord Bingham with whom the others agreed.
[122] *Jordan*, above n 120, at [105] as quoted in *Amin* ibid at [20] per Lord Bingham.
[123] *Ibid*.
[124] *Ibid*, at [31]. See also *Middleton*, above n 3, at [9]–[15].
[125] *Amin*, above n 6, at [31] per Lord Bingham.

circumstances be vulnerable and whose lives may need to be protected.[126] It is clear that it has had a major impact on the system for investigating deaths in England and Wales. For example, in *Clayton*[127] it was noted that a coroner's inquest has become a means by which the state fulfils its positive obligations under Article 2 to investigate effectively and publicly any death in the hands of the police or prison service.

> The time is past when coroners' courts could be regarded as an anachronism with practices and standards that would not be acceptable elsewhere in the system of justice.[128]

6.2 When Does the Duty Arise?

6.2.1 Death or Life-threatening Injuries

The duty to investigate only arises where a death or life-threatening injuries have occurred.[129] In *McKerr*[130] the House of Lords held that the duty was consequential on the death. Therefore, if the death itself was not within the reach of the HRA because it occurred before 2 October 2000, when the HRA came into force, there was no duty to investigate. 'The event giving rise to the Article 2 obligation to investigate must have occurred post-Act.'[131] It is not possible to characterise the failure to investigate as an ongoing failure to which the HRA would apply if the death had occurred prior to 2 October 2000. However, as the judgment of the Court of Appeal in *Hurst*[132] demonstrates, it is possible to get around this requirement if what is at issue is not section 6 of the HRA but the application of section 3 to a provision of primary legislation. Here the Court of Appeal held that section 11(5)(b)(ii) of the Coroners Act 1988 had to be interpreted compatibly with Article 2, thereby requiring an inquest to resume and determine in what circumstances the deceased met his death, even though the death had occurred prior to 2 October 2000.[133]

6.2.2 Intentional or Non-intentional Killing by an Agent of the State

It is beyond doubt that there should be some form of effective official investigation when individuals have been killed as a result of use of force by agents of the state.[134]

> Where agents of the state have used lethal force against an individual the facts relating to the killing and its motivation are likely to be largely, if not wholly, within the knowledge of

---

[126] *Ibid*, at [41] per Lord Slynn.
[127] *Clayton v HM Coroner for South Yorkshire (East District)* [2005] EWHC (Admin) 1196.
[128] *Ibid*, at [9].
[129] *Amin*, above n 6, at [31] per Lord Bingham in reliance upon *Menson v United Kingdom* (2003) 37 EHRR CD 220. Where life threatening injuries have occurred, it is possible that the duty to investigate may also arise under Art 3. In *R (on the application of Green) v Police Complaints Authority* [2004] UKHL 6, [2004] 1 WLR 725 only Lord Scott held that the allegation of the claimant that the police officer had driven the car at him deliberately in order to kill or seriously injury him engaged Art 2.
[130] Above n 1.
[131] *Ibid*, at [22] per Lord Nicholls. See further C Bell and J Keenan, 'Lost on the Way Home? The Right to Life in Northern Ireland' (2005) 32 *JLS* 68.
[132] *The Commissioner of Police for the Metropolis v Hurst* [2005] EWCA Civ 890.
[133] *Pearson v Inner London North Coroner* [2005] EWHC (Admin) 833, not followed.
[134] *McCann, Yasa, Salman* and *Jordan*, above n 120, as quoted in *Amin*, above n 6, at [20] per Lord Bingham.

the state, and it is essential both for the relatives and for public confidence in the administration of justice and in the state's adherence to the principles of the rule of law that a killing by the state be subject to some form of open and objective oversight.

It is clear that the duty is not limited to deliberate killing and also arises where there has been a negligent failure to protect life.

[W]hile any deliberate killing by state agents is bound to arouse very grave disquiet, such an event is likely to be rare and the state's main task is to establish the facts and prosecute the culprits; a systemic failure to protect the lives of persons detained may well call for even more anxious consideration and raise even more intractable problems.[135]

For example, the duty was found to arise in *Amin*,[136] where the deceased had been beaten to death by his cell-mate in Feltham Young Offender Institution. The possibility of systemic failure on the part of the Prison Service was clear. It also arose in *Middleton*,[137] where the deceased prisoner had hanged himself in his cell[138]; in *Khan*,[139] where a little girl had died in hospital and there were allegations of gross negligence and concern that there may have been a medically orchestrated cover up[140]; and in *Hurst*,[141] where the roles of the police and local authority were called into question following the manslaughter of the deceased outside his home by a man who lived on the same estate.

There is even more reason for an effective official investigation where an individual has died in custody.

Persons in custody are in a vulnerable position and the authorities are under a duty to protect them. Consequently, where an individual is taken into police custody in good health and is found to be injured on release, it is incumbent on the State to provide a plausible explanation of how those injuries were caused. The obligation on the authorities to account for the treatment of an individual in custody is particularly stringent where that individual dies.[142]

6.2.3 Intentional or Non-intentional Killing by a Non-state Agent

The obligation to ensure that there is some form of effective official investigation when individuals have been killed as a result of the use of force is not confined to cases where it is apparent that the killing was caused by an agent of the state.[143]

---

[135] *Amin, ibid*, at [21] per Lord Bingham in reliance upon *Edwards v United Kingdom* (2002) 35 EHRR 19. See also the comments of Lord Slynn at [41], Lord Steyn at [50] and Lord Hope at [62].
[136] *Ibid.*
[137] Above n 3.
[138] See also *R (on the application of Sacker) v HM Coroner for the County of West Yorkshire* [2004] UKHL 11, [2004] 1 WLR 796.
[139] *Khan*, above n 15.
[140] See also *R (on the application of Davies) v Birmingham Deputy Coroner* [2003] EWCA Civ 1739, [2004] HRLR 13.
[141] *Hurst*, above n 132.
[142] *Salman*, above n 120, at [99] as quoted in *Amin*, above n 6, at [20] per Lord Bingham and at [30]–[31]. See also *Middleton*, above n 3, at [5] and *R (on the application of Al-Skeini) v Secretary of State for Defence* [2004] EWHC (Admin) 2911, [2005] 2 WLR 1401 at [323]
[143] *Salman* ibid at [105] as quoted in *Amin*, above n 6, at [20] per Lord Bingham.

Although in *Challender*[144] the Administrative Court held that, as the death had occurred before 2 October 2000, it could not consider the application under Article 2, it did go on to consider whether the duty arose. The deceased was found dead in a friend's flat. His sister and partner applied for public funding to be legally represented at the inquest into his death. The Legal Services Commission argued that the Article 2 obligation did not arise as the state was not involved in the death. The Administrative Court disagreed and, relying on the admissibility decision in *Menson*,[145] held that there is an obligation to carry out an effective investigation where there is reason to believe an individual had died or sustained life-threatening injuries in suspicious circumstances.[146]

It is therefore clear that the duty may arise

> even where the state is not directly involved in the death (whether through the acts of agents of the state or because the deceased was in the care of the state). The involvement of the state in the death gives rise to additional reasons why an effective investigation is needed, but the state's obligation to ensure the effective implementation of domestic laws protecting the right to life can be a sufficient basis for the need to carry out an effective investigation even in cases with no state involvement in the death.[147]

Here the court concluded that, as there was some evidence to suggest the deceased's death occurred in circumstances that amounted to unlawful killing, the investigative obligation was engaged.[148]

6.2.4 Exculpating Factors

The argument has been made that in some cases the full investigative duty under Article 2 should not apply if the contextual situation causes particular difficulties for the state. In *Al-Skeini*[149] the Divisional Court noted that the European Court of Human Rights had consistently rejected the idea that there was any displacement of the investigative duty by reason of a security situation.[150] In the present case, it had been argued that the application of the Convention to an Iraqi held in British custody during the period of the occupation of Iraq would create a raft of intractable legal issues. This was rejected by the court, it holding that where a prisoner held in the custody of British forces had been tortured or killed, such difficulties shrank before the importance of state accountability.[151] However, in relation to the other deaths, where the deceased persons were shot at and killed by British troops—one in the course of an exchange of fire between British troops and Iraqi gunmen—assuming the HRA applied, the court held that the extremely difficult situation in which investigations had to be carried out were not to be discounted, and accepted that these must have

---

[144] *R (on the application of Challender) v Legal Services Commission* [2004] EWHC (Admin) 925, [2004] ACD 57.
[145] *Menson v United Kingdom*, Admissibility Decision, 6 May 2003.
[146] *Ibid*, at [48].
[147] *Ibid*, at [49].
[148] *Ibid*, at [50].
[149] Above n 142.
[150] *Ibid*, at [324] in reliance upon *Kaya v Turkey* (1998) 28 EHRR 1; *Guleç v Turkey* (1998) 28 EHRR 121; *Ergi v Turkey* (2001) 32 EHRR 18; *Özkan v Turkey*, Judgment of 6 April 2004.
[151] *Ibid*, at [335].

amounted to grave impediments for anyone concerned to conduct investigations. However, it still concluded that these investigations did not satisfy the Article 2 duty.[152]

6.3 Form of the Investigation

The form of investigation which will achieve the aims of securing the effective implementation of the domestic laws protecting the right to life and ensuring accountability will vary in different circumstances.[153] The European Court has not required that any particular procedure be adopted to examine the circumstances of a killing by state agents, nor is it necessary that there be a single unified procedure.

> But it is 'indispensable' that there be proper procedures for ensuring the accountability of agents of the state so as to maintain public confidence and allay the legitimate concerns that arise from the use of lethal force.[154]

The more serious the events that call for inquiry, the more intensive should be the process of public scrutiny.[155] Certain minimum requirements have been specified.

6.3.1 Authorities Must Act of their Own Motion

The authorities must act of their own motion once the matter has come to their attention. They cannot leave it to the initiative of the next of kin either to lodge a formal complaint or to take responsibility for the conduct of any investigative procedures.[156]

6.3.2 Investigation Must be Effective

The investigation must be effective in the sense that it is capable of leading to a determination of whether the force used was or was not justified in the circumstances, and to the identification and punishment of those responsible. 'This is not an obligation of result, but of means.'[157] The authorities must have taken the reasonable steps available to them to secure the evidence concerning the incident, and a requirement of promptness and reasonable expedition is implicit in this context.[158]

6.3.3 Independence

For the investigation to be effective, it is generally regarded as necessary for the persons responsible for and carrying out the investigation to be independent from those

---

[152] *Ibid*, at [340]. At [341] the court noted that this conclusion did not mean that in other circumstances, it would ignore the strategic difficulties of the situation. '[T]here may come a point when that state's responsibility can only be measured against what is possible, and not against entirely objective standards.'
[153] *Jordan*, above n 120, as quoted in *Amin*, above n 6, at [20] per Lord Bingham.
[154] *Amin*, *ibid*, at [20] per Lord Bingham in reliance on *Jordan*, *ibid*, at [143]–[144].
[155] *Khan*, above n 15, at [62] per Brooke LJ giving the judgment of the court.
[156] *Jordan*, above n 120, at [105] as quoted in *Amin*, above n 6, at [20] per Lord Bingham.
[157] *Jordan*, *ibid*, at [107] as quoted in *Amin*, *ibid*, at [20] per Lord Bingham.
[158] *Edwards*, above n 135, at [71]–[72] as quoted in *Amin*, *ibid*, at [22] per Lord Bingham.

implicated in the events. 'This means not only a lack of hierarchical or institutional connection but also a practical independence.'[159]

6.3.4 Public Scrutiny

While public scrutiny of police investigations cannot be regarded as an automatic requirement under Article 2, there must be a sufficient element of public scrutiny of the investigation or its results to secure accountability in practice as well as in theory. The degree of public scrutiny required may well vary from case to case.[160]

6.3.5 Involvement of Next of Kin

In all cases, the next of kin of the victim must be involved in the procedure to the extent necessary to safeguard his or her legitimate interests.[161] In certain circumstances financial support to family members to allow them to play a part may be required. For example, in *Khan*[162] the Court of Appeal held that the inquest would not be an effective one unless the family of the deceased could play a part in it—and they were in no fit state to play that part. Whilst making no final decision on the issue, it noted that it was seriously open to question whether a provision which required someone in the position of the father to fund the entire cost of his lawyer's appearance at the inquest into his daughter's death out of his own pocket in such a serious and complex case was compatible with Article 2.

> After all, the Convention imposes on states the obligation to conduct an effective investigation in a case like this, and without Mr Khan's participation the inquest cannot fulfil that role.[163]

The court was unimpressed by the suggestion that economic exigencies might be called in aid by a state to whittle down its obligations in a case as serious as this.[164]

A similar issue arose in *Challender*,[165] where the sister and partner of the deceased sought public funding to be legally represented at the coroner's inquest into the death. As the death occurred prior to 2 October 2000, the Administrative Court held that it could not consider the case. Nevertheless, it made observations on this point. It concluded that the Legal Services Commission's refusal of funding was correct as it had considered the question of whether, in the absence of legal representation, it would be possible for the family to have effective representation.[166] In the opinion of the court, the case was not of exceptional factual or legal complexity. It was within the competence of the coroner to carry out the necessary investigation without assistance from legal representatives for the family.

---

[159] *Jordan*, above n 120, at [106] as quoted in *Amin*, *ibid*, at [20] per Lord Bingham.
[160] *Jordan*, *ibid*, at [121] and [109] as quoted in *Amin*, *ibid*, at [20] per Lord Bingham.
[161] *Jordan*, *ibid*, at [109] as quoted in *Amin*, *ibid*, at [20] per Lord Bingham.
[162] *Khan*, above n 15.
[163] *Ibid*, at [98].
[164] *Ibid*, at [99].
[165] Above n 144.
[166] *Ibid*, at [67].

An important additional consideration is that the claimants will be able to obtain advice and assistance under the Legal Help scheme, which will cover the making of written submissions to the coroner, and will enable them to attend the inquest themselves. All that they will be denied through lack of funding will be legal representation in the form of advocacy at the inquest. It does not seem to me that the circumstances are such as to place this case into the exceptional category where legal representation is needed in order to ensure effective participation by the deceased's family and an effective investigation.[167]

6.3.6 Outcome of the Investigation

It is now clear that the procedural duty under Article 2 may also extend to the outcome of the investigation. In *Middleton*[168] the House of Lords held that if an official investigation was to meet the state's procedural obligation under Article 2, the prescribed procedure had to work in practice and fulfil the purpose for which the investigation was established.[169] It concluded that the procedural obligation was unlikely to be met if it was

plausibly alleged that agents of the state had used lethal force without justification, if an effectively unchallengeable decision has been taken not to prosecute and if the fact-finding body cannot express its conclusion on whether unjustifiable force has been used or not, so as to prompt reconsideration of the decision not to prosecute.

If an inquest was the instrument by which the state sought to discharge its investigative obligation, the House of Lords concluded that to comply with Article 2, an explicit statement, however, brief, of the jury's conclusion on the disputed factual issues at the heart of the case was required.[170] And in their Lordship's view, this applied in all categories of cases.[171]

In some instances the procedural obligation may be discharged by criminal proceedings. This is most likely where the defendant pleads not guilty and the trial involves a full exploration of the facts.[172] In other cases short inquest verdicts in the traditional form will enable the jury to express their conclusion on the central issue canvassed at the inquest, such as whether the deceased took his own life or was killed by another.[173] However, in order to ensure that the requirements of Article 2 are met using section 3 of the HRA, it is now necessary to read the Coroners Act 1988 and Rules 1984 as allowing the jury to express an opinion on by what means and in what circumstances the deceased came by his death.[174] It must be for the coroner

to decide how best, in the particular case, to elicit the jury's conclusion on the central issue or issues. This may be done by inviting a form of verdict expanded beyond those suggested in . . . the Rules. It may be done . . . by inviting a narrative form of verdict in which the

---

167 *Ibid*, at [68].
168 Above n 3.
169 *Ibid*, at [8].
170 *Ibid*, at [16] in reliance upon *McCann*, above n 120; *Jordan*, above n 120; *Keenan v United Kingdom* (2001) 33 EHRR 913; *Edwards*, above n 135; *Mastromatteo v Italy*, 24 October 2002.
171 *Ibid*, at [17].
172 *Middleton*, above n 3, at [30].
173 *Ibid*, at [31].
174 *Ibid*, at [35].

jury's factual conclusions are briefly summarised. It may be done by inviting the jury's answer to factual questions put by the coroner.[175]

Article 2 has also had a limited impact on the decision of whether or not to prosecute. In *Manning*[176] the sisters of a man who had died in Blakehurst Prison challenged the decision taken by the DPP not to prosecute anyone for manslaughter as a result of the manner in which the deceased met his death. They argued that no adequate reasons were given for the decision. The High Court held that neither domestic law nor Strasbourg law imposed an absolute and unqualified obligation to give reasons for a decision not to prosecute. Relying on *McCann*,[177] the court held that, where an inquest culminated in a verdict of unlawful killing implicating a person who, although not named in the verdict, was clearly identified, who was living and whose whereabouts were known, 'the ordinary expectation would naturally be that a prosecution would follow.' It concluded that, in the absence of compelling grounds for not giving reasons:

> . . . we would expect the Director to give reasons in such a case: to meet the reasonable expectation of interested parties that either a prosecution would follow or a reasonable explanation for not prosecuting be given, to vindicate the Director's decision by showing that solid grounds exist for what might otherwise appear to be a surprising or even inexplicable decision and to meet the European Court's expectation that if a prosecution is not to follow a plausible explanation will be given.[178]

It was appreciated that review of the DPP was a power to be exercised sparingly.[179] Nevertheless, it was also appreciated that the standard of review should not be set too high since judicial review was the only means by which the citizen could seek redress against a decision not to prosecute.[180]

6.4 Application

Alongside the positive duty to protect life, this aspect of Article 2 has given rise to the most litigation under the HRA. Whilst the practice of inquiries into deaths was well established in the United Kingdom prior to the passage of the HRA, flaws in the system have become apparent.

6.4.1 Deaths in Custody

Deaths in custody have given rise to a number of Article 2 claims and sadly, in the majority of cases, the investigations carried out have found to be lacking at a number of levels. In *Amin*[181] the deceased, a young Asian man, was beaten to death by his

---

[175] *Ibid*, at [36]. See also [37]–[38]. See also *Sacker*, above n 138; *Davies*, above n 140.
[176] Above n 1.
[177] Above n 120.
[178] *Ibid*, at [33]. See also *R v Weaver* [2001] EWCA Crim 2768 where the Court of Appeal held that Art 2 provides no basis upon which to approach sentencing for homicide in the English courts and English criminal law provides its own machinery to punish those who take life unlawfully.
[179] *Ibid*, at [23].
[180] *Ibid*.
[181] Above n 6.

cell-mate, Stewart, in Feltham Young Offenders Institution. Stewart was considered to be very dangerous, a threat to both staff and other inmates, and possibly violently racist. Stewart was convicted of the murder and the inquest into the death was adjourned, never to be resumed. A police investigation resulted in the advice of counsel that there was insufficient evidence to provide a realistic prospect of securing any convictions against Prison Service staff relating to the deceased. The Prison Service set up an internal inquiry but, whilst the family of the deceased were consulted about the terms of reference, they were not present at any stage of the investigation and did not avail themselves of the opportunity to meet the person conducting the inquiry. The report was made available to the family, police and Commission for Racial Equality (CRE), but was not published. The CRE conducted an investigation into racial discrimination in the Prison Service. The family were involved in the preparation of the terms of reference and expressed views on the procedures proposed, but the CRE declined their request to be allowed to participate in the inquiry and for its hearings to be in public.

The House of Lords concluded that the state's duty to investigate was undoubtedly engaged in this case and that, given that the death had occurred in custody, this duty was particularly important.[182] The House of Lords found a number of defects in the procedure that had been followed. There was no inquest. The police investigation had been conducted in private without any participation by the family. The murder trial was directed solely at establishing Stewart's mental responsibility and there was little exploration of wider issues concerning the death. The man conducting the internal inquiry did not enjoy institutional or hierarchical independence. His investigation was conducted in private, his report was not published and the family were not able to play any effective part in the investigation. The CRE inquiry was confined to race-related issues and was conducted almost wholly in private. Again, the family were not able to play any effective part.[183] The House of Lords restored the order of the lower court that an independent public investigation be held.

In *Middleton*[184] the deceased had taken his own life by hanging himself in his cell. At the inquest the jury found the cause of death to be hanging and returned a verdict that the deceased had taken his own life when the balance of his mind was disturbed. It also gave the coroner a note which communicated its opinion that the Prison Service had failed in its duty of care for the deceased. The family asked that the note should be appended to the inquisition, but the coroner declined to do so. The sole issue before the House of Lords was whether the requirements of Article 2 had thereby been met. It concluded that they had not. In the view of their Lordships, the crux of the argument was whether the deceased should have been recognised as a suicide risk and whether appropriate precautions should have been taken to prevent him taking his own life. It held that the jury's verdict did not express its conclusions on these crucial facts which might have been done by a short and simple verdict such as

the deceased took his own life, in part because the risk of his doing so was not recognised and appropriate precautions were not taken to prevent him doing so.[185]

---

[182] *Ibid*, at [31] per Lord Bingham.
[183] *Ibid*, at [33]–[37] per Lord Bingham.
[184] Above n 3.
[185] *Ibid*, at [45]. See also *Sacker*, above n 138; *Davies*, above n 140.

Although doubt was cast by the Court of Appeal on the Administrative Court's judgment in *Wright*,[186] it was expressly confirmed by the House of Lords in *Amin*.[187] This case also concerned a death in custody. Paul Wright died in prison as a result of a severe asthma attack. During the inquest the questions as to inadequate medical treatment were not addressed. Following a review of Strasbourg case law, Jackson J held that the inquest did not constitute an effective official investigation.[188] Mr Wright's cell mate on the evening he died was not called as a witness and the jury were directed to disregard his written statement. There was no consideration of the short-comings in the medical treatment, and his mother and aunt were not represented. Jackson J also held that the civil action did not constitute an effective official investigation because liability was admitted at an early stage.[189] There was never a hearing at which evidence concerning the circumstances of the deceased's death was adduced or tested. He concluded that the proper remedy was an order that the Home Secretary set up an independent investigation into the circumstances of Mr Wright's death.[190]

A death in a British military prison in Iraq has also been examined for conformity with the Article 2 procedural duty. In *Al-Skeini*[191] the Divisional Court found that the investigation had not been adequate.

> Even if an investigation solely in the hands of the SIB [Special Investigation Branch] might be said to be independent . . . it is difficult to say that the investigation which has occurred has been timely, open or effective.[192]

More than a year had elapsed since the death. Other than in the early stages of the autopsy, the family was not involved and the outcome of the SIB report was not known. There were no conclusions and there had been no public accountability. 'All this in a case where the burden of explanation lies heavily on the United Kingdom authorities.'[193]

6.4.2 Deaths in Hospital

Khan[194] concerned the death of a little girl in hospital. The police conducted an extensive inquiry but no criminal proceedings were taken. The NHS Trust made its own investigations. The family were not involved in either investigation. The Court of Appeal concluded that it was the coroner's inquest which furnished the natural occasion for the effective judicial inquiry into the cause of death.

> The police investigation, in which the family played no part, and which culminated in a decision not to prosecute, could not act as a substitute. Nor could the investigations carried

---

[186] Above n 14.
[187] Above n 6.
[188] *Ibid*, at [60].
[189] *Ibid*, at [61].
[190] *Ibid*, at [67].
[191] *Al Skeini*, above n 142.
[192] *Ibid*, at [331].
[193] *Ibid*, at [332].
[194] *Khan*, above n 15.

out privately by the Trust, in which again the family played no part, particularly as the Trust could not be regarded as having the requisite independence.[195]

It concluded that the inquest would not be effective unless the family could play a part in it, and they were in no fit state to play that part.[196] To discharge the obligation under Article 2 the Court of Appeal held that reasonable funding could be provided at the inquest to ensure the family was represented or to set up some other type of inquiry at which such funding would be possible.[197]

> With a wife and four other children to support it seems absurd, on the information at present available to the court, that he could reasonably be expected to fund the whole cost of his own representation himself in order to enable the state to perform the obligations that rest on it, and not on him.[198]

However, no final judgment on the point was given, the hearing being adjourned to allow the state to make further representations as to the route to be followed.

---

7. Exceptions

The exceptions expressly set out in Article 2(2) have not yet been the subject of litigation under the HRA. As discussed in preceding paragraphs, in *Re A*,[199] the case of the conjoined twins, as a majority of the Court of Appeal had characterised the operation as an intentional deprivation of life, it was appreciated that it would therefore be necessary for it to be justified under Article 2(2). However, the reasoning was far from satisfactory. Relying on the opinion of the Commission in *Paton*,[200] Ward LJ held that Article 2 was subject to an implied limitation 'which would justify the balancing act we have undertaken.' Brooke LJ did not agree, stating that he would be reluctant to hold that a right as fundamental as the right to life could be subject to an implied limitation which destroyed its value and reached no firm conclusion on the point. Again, as the judgments given were confined to the unique facts of the case, Ward LJ's comments are unlikely to lead to the development of an implied exceptions jurisprudence.

---

[195] *Ibid*, at [69].
[196] *Ibid*, at [74].
[197] *Ibid*, at [87].
[198] *Ibid*, at [98].
[199] Above n 10.
[200] *Paton v United Kingdom* (1980) 3 EHRR 408.

8

Article 3: Prohibition of Torture and Inhuman or Degrading Treatment or Punishment

1. Introduction

Article 3, which proscribes torture and inhuman or degrading treatment or punishment, is considered to be one of the most fundamental and important of all the Convention rights.[1] It is expressed in absolute terms, permitting of no qualification or excuse, and derogation under Article 15 is not possible in any circumstances.

The majority of Article 3 HRA claims have arisen in the context of proposed deportations by the Home Secretary. This is because under the HRA it is not lawful to expel an individual within this jurisdiction to a destination state where there are strong grounds for believing that the person, if returned, faces a real risk of being subjected to torture or to inhuman or degrading treatment or punishment.[2] Outside of this context, there are no cases concerning torture and very few concerning punishment. When referring to inhuman or degrading treatment, generally the courts do not delineate between the two types of treatment and refer instead to the 'proscribed treatment' encompassing both.[3]

The importance with which Article 3 is regarded is reflected in the fact that deference to the primary decision maker is rarely mentioned when it is at issue. Often the underlying factual material is considered so as to enable the court to conclude for

---

[1] See, eg the comments of Lord Bingham in *R (Pretty) v Director of Public Prosecutions* [2001] UKHL 61, [2001] 3 WLR 1598 at [10] and [13].
[2] *R v Special Adjudicator, ex p Ullah* [2004] UKHL 26, [2004] 2 AC 323 at [24] per Lord Bingham.
[3] See, eg *R v Drew* [2003] UKHL 25, [2003] 1 WLR 1213.

itself whether or not a violation of Article 3 is made out.[4] The courts have even gone so far as to admit fresh evidence during appeal proceedings where Article 3 is possibly engaged.[5] For example, prior to the coming into force of the HRA, the Court of Appeal held in *Turgut*[6] that the question of an illegal entrant being returned to Turkey to face treatment contrary to Article 3 was not an area in which the court would pay any especial deference to the Secretary of State's conclusion on the facts. Similarly, in *X*,[7] concerning a deportation allegedly in violation of Article 3, the court held that it had a duty to come to a decision itself on the material before it as to whether the proposed course of action by the executive would infringe the appellant's human rights.

Outside of the deportation context, this has also been the approach taken. For example, in *T*,[8] in considering whether the state's treatment of an asylum seeker was inhuman or degrading, the Court of Appeal commented that, once the facts were known, the question of whether they brought the applicant actually or imminently within the protection of Article 3 was one which could be answered by the court without deference to the initial decision maker.[9]

It appears the only scope for some deference to the primary decision maker would be at the stage of assessing what reasonable steps need to be taken in order for a public authority to meet its positive obligation under Article 3. This is the path that Article 2 jurisprudence has followed and there are already signs of this in the Article 3 case law. For example, in *Watts*[10] the Administrative Court recognised that the Health Authority was allocating finite funds between competing resources. In *Gezer*[11] Laws LJ employed his spectrum metaphor, first referred to in his judgment in *Limbuela*,[12] intended to demonstrate a sliding scale of instances in which Article 3 might be engaged from those where the state enjoyed no power of discretion to those 'where the State might enjoy a considerable margin of discretion as to the adoption and exercise of policy.'[13]

---

[4] See, eg *R v Secretary of State for the Home Department, ex p Turgut* [2001] 1 All ER 719; *R (on the application of Wilkinson) v The Responsible Medical Officer Broadmoor Hospital* [2001] EWCA Civ 1545, [2001] 1 WLR 419; *R (on the application of T) v Secretary of State for the Home Department* [2003] EWCA Civ 1285, [2003] UKHRR 1321; *R (on the application of B) v Responsible Medical Officer, Broadmoor Hospital* [2005] EWHC (Admin) 1936. But see *R (on the application of N) v M* [2002] EWCA Civ 1789, [2003] 1 WLR 562 and the comments of Carnwath LJ in *R (on the application of Limbuela) v Secretary of State for the Home Department* [2004] EWCA Civ 540, [2004] QB 1440 at [129]–[130].

[5] See, eg *A v Secretary of State for the Home Department* [2003] EWCA Civ 175 at [20]; *Khan v Secretary of State for the Home Department* [2003] EWCA Civ 530. Cf. *A v Secretary of State for the Home Department* [2004] EWCA Civ 255.

[6] Above n 4.

[7] *X v Secretary of State for the Home Department* [2001] 1 WLR 740.

[8] Above n 4.

[9] at [19].

[10] *R (Watts) v Beford Primary Care Trust* [2003] EWHC Admin 2401.

[11] *Gezer v Secretary of State for the Home Department* [2004] EWCA Civ 1730, [2005] HRLR 7.

[12] Above n 4.

[13] *Ibid*, at [33].

2. Severity of Ill-treatment

Whilst it is difficult to define all the human conditions that will engage Article 3,[14] it is clear that the standard of what constitutes inhuman or degrading treatment must be set at a high level. Only serious ill-treatment falls within the scope of the expression 'inhuman or degrading treatment or punishment.'[15] But although ill-treatment must obtain a minimum level of severity, assessment of the minimum is relative as it all depends on the circumstances of the case.[16] Relevant factors are the nature and context of the treatment, the manner of its execution, its duration, and its physical and mental effects, including, where relevant, its impact on the health of the person involved, both positive and negative.[17] In *Pretty v UK*[18] the European Court of Human Rights made some observations on the type of treatment which would fall within the scope of Article 3. Whilst not universally adopted by UK courts, some have found this to be a useful benchmark.[19] The Court held as follows:

> As regards the types of 'treatment' which fall within the scope of art 3 of the Convention, the court's case law refers to 'ill-treatment' that attains a minimum level of severity and involves actual bodily injury or intense physical or mental suffering. Where treatment humiliates or debases an individual showing lack of respect for, or diminishing, his or her human dignity or arouses feelings of fear, anguish or inferiority capable of breaking an individual's moral and physical resistance, it may be characterised as degrading and also fall within the prohibition of art 3. The suffering which flows from naturally occurring illness, physical or mental, may be covered by art 3, where it is, or risks being, exacerbated by treatment, whether flowing from conditions of detention, expulsion or other measures, for which the authorities can be held responsible.[20]

It has also been held that, with respect to degrading treatment, it is not enough for a victim to feel that he has suffered a loss of dignity.

> How he sees himself and how he is seen by others are matters which may be relevant, but they are not determinative.[21]

It is relevant, but not requisite, that the purpose of the treatment is to debase or humiliate. What matters more is effect. Emotional distress of itself is not enough, but

---

[14] *R (on the application of Q) v Secretary of State for the Home Department* [2003] EWCA Civ 364, [2004] QB 36 at [60].

[15] *Pretty*, above n 1, at [90] per Lord Hope; *Secretary of State for the Home Department v Z* [2002] EWCA Civ 952.

[16] *Ibid*, at [91] per Lord Hope. See also the comments of Carnwath LJ in *Limbuela*, above n 4, at [89]–[90].

[17] *B*, above n 4, at [52].

[18] Judgment of 29 April 2002.

[19] See, eg *Q*, above n 14, at [62]–[63]; *Watts*, above n 10, at [54]; *T*, above n 8.

[20] *Pretty v UK*, above n 18, at [52].

[21] *T*, above n 8, at [12] in reliance upon *East African Asians v UK* (1973) 3 EHRR 76; *Lorsé v Netherlands* (2003) 37 EHRR 3.

it is a factor.[22] Each case must be judged in relation to all the circumstances which are relevant to it.[23]

3. Negative and Positive Duties

3.1 Distinguishing Negative from Positive

It is clear that Article 3 imposes both negative and positive duties on public authorities encompassing both acts and failures to act or, in the context of the article, treatments and failures to treat. The negative duty imposed by Article 3 is an absolute duty: 'no one shall be subjected to torture or to inhuman or degrading treatment or punishment.' However, the positive Article 3 duty is generally not absolute. It is therefore particularly important, when Article 3 is raised, to determine whether or not the activities of a public authority constitute treatment or a failure to treat.

This is no simple task and caused considerable difficulty in Q,[24] which concerned the denial of support to asylum seekers who had not claimed asylum as soon as reasonably practicable on arrival. The court agreed that Article 3 did impose positive duties that required states to

> take measures designed to ensure that individuals within their jurisdiction are not subjected to torture or inhuman and degrading treatment or punishment, including such treatment administered by private individuals.[25]

However, it found that the regime imposed on asylum seekers who were denied support engaged the negative duty and constituted treatment within the meaning of Article 3.[26] It found that here the state had been more than passive. Asylum seekers could not lawfully be removed until their claims had been determined.

> The imposition by the legislature of a regime which prohibits asylum-seekers from working and further prohibits the grant to them, when they are destitute, of support amounts to positive action directed against asylum-seekers and not to mere inaction.[27]

As the court itself pointed out, the problem with characterising the issue as such was that some who apply for asylum may already be in a condition which verges on the degree of severity capable of engaging Article 3. With others, their fate will be

---

[22] *Ibid.*
[23] *Ibid*, at [16]. Closure of a care home does not engage Art 3 (*R (Haggerty) v St Helens Council* [2003] EWHC (Admin) 803, [2003] ACD 304); nor does the eviction of travellers from a site (*R (on the application of Fuller) v Chief Constable of Dorset Police* [2001] EWHC (Admin) 1057, [2003] QB 480); a striking off from the Solicitors Roll (*Re a Solicitor No.11 of 2001* [2001] EWCA Civ 153801); or the supply of heroin (*R (on the application of M) v Merseyside Police* [2003] EWHC (Admin) 1121).
[24] Above n 14.
[25] *Ibid*, at [51].
[26] *Ibid*, at [56].
[27] *Ibid*, at [57].

uncertain—charitable bodies or individuals may come to their assistance.[28] But the court did not believe it was unlawful for the Secretary of State to decline to provide support unless it was clear that charitable support had not been provided and the individual was incapable of fending for himself—the 'wait and see' approach. Such an approach risked clogging the courts with hundreds of asylum seekers claiming to have fallen into a condition sufficient to engage Article 3. It was also contrary to the rationale behind the European Court's development of the positive duty under Article 3 'to ensure that individuals within their jurisdiction are not subjected to torture or inhuman or degrading treatment or punishment.'[29] It could be said that it was like waiting until a preventable death had occurred before finding a violation of Article 2.

In *Limbuela*[30] the Court of Appeal did not agree that the court in *Q* had proposed a pure wait-and-see approach. The judgment was taken to mean that the individual had to show that he was 'verging on' the necessary degree of severity for Article 3 to be engaged—there was no need to show the actual onset of severe illness or suffering.[31] Whilst it was not made explicit in the judgments of the majority, the court in *Limbuela* could be said to have reverted to a positive duty test.

> Once it is accepted that Article 3 is potentially in play, it must follow in my view that the State has some responsibility in the matter.[32] . . . The obligation 'to take measures' seems to me to imply more than simply acting as a longstop in individual cases as they arise.

Carnwath LJ concluded that if the scale of the problem was such that the system was unable to cope, it was the responsibility of the state to take reasonable measures to ensure that it could cope.

> [T]here will be considerable room for executive judgment as to the steps necessary to achieve it, balanced against the policy objectives of the legislation.[33]

Jacob LJ agreed, stating that the 'verging on' test was 'abhorrent, illogical and very expensive.'[34] Both found that the circumstances of each appellant met the Article 3 threshold and effectively told the Home Secretary that the courts would do as such in each of the 600 plus cases waiting to be heard. Jacob LJ commented:

> although one may not be able to say of any particular individual that there is more than a very real risk that denial of food and shelter will take that individual across the threshold, one can say that collectively the current policy of the Secretary of State will have that effect in the case of a substantial number of people. It seems to me that it must follow that the current policy . . . is unlawful as violating Article 3.[35]

---

[28] *Ibid*, at [62].
[29] *A v United Kingdom* (1998) 3 FCR 597 at [22].
[30] Above n 4.
[31] *Ibid*, at [95] per Carnwath LJ.
[32] Per Carnwath LJ at [120]–[121] in reliance upon *Pretty v UK* (2002) 12 BHRC 149.
[33] *Ibid*, at [121].
[34] *Ibid*, at [142].
[35] *Ibid*, at [149].

A far simpler way to proceed would have been that suggested in the court below in *Q*—a risk test along the lines of that developed in Article 2 jurisprudence. There was obviously a risk that the majority denied support would fall into conditions which would engage Article 3. The state obviously knowing what was occurring, the next question would be what reasonable or proportionate measures should be taken to avoid the risk. As asylum seekers could not lawfully be returned until their claims had been determined and as they were prohibited from working, it would seem that the reasonable response of the state in such circumstances would be to supply some minimum support until their claims were determined and, if resources were the major concern, speed up the decision-making process. It would also be possible for the court to take into account the length of time before asylum was claimed and resources considerations. This would not open up the floodgates as asylum seekers are in a unique position.[36]

Given the difficulties in determining whether negative or positive duties are engaged, in *Gezer*,[37] Laws LJ, with whom the other members of the Court of Appeal agreed, stated that the utility of this distinction in the context of Article 3 was limited.[38] He reiterated his judgment in *Limbuela*,[39] where he proposed the metaphor of a spectrum between the worst class of case—state-sponsored violence—and a decision made in the exercise of lawful policy which may expose the individual to a marked degree of suffering:

> The figure of a spectrum seems to imply the existence of a point upon the spectrum which marks the dividing line, in terms of State acts or omissions, between what violates Article 3 and what does not. There is such a point, but it does not, I fear, provide a brightline rule by which the court may readily determine whether any particular set of facts falls on this or that side of the line. The point is at the place between cases where government action is justified notwithstanding the individual's suffering, and cases where it is not. Various factors will determine where this place is to be found. They will include the severity of the threatened suffering, its origin in violence or otherwise, and the nature of the government's reasons or purpose in acting as it does.[40]

Whilst encapsulating the difficulties thrown up by the gamut of Article 3 cases, it is clear that this approach also has the potential to unnecessarily complicate matters. Exactly the same factors could be taken into account if the far simpler approach employed by the courts in relation to the positive duty under Article 2 were to be utilised. And the eventual conclusion reached would most likely remain the same. Despite earlier confusion, it appears that this is the path now being taken, and the distinction between negative and positive duties has been maintained.

---

[36] For example, in *R (on the application of K) v Lambeth London BC* [2003] EWCA Civ 1150 it was held that the state owed no duty to support a foreign national a foreign who was in a position to return home.
[37] Above n 11.
[38] *Ibid*, at [28].
[39] Above n 4.
[40] *Ibid*, at [71].

3.2 Positive Duty

3.2.1 When Does the Duty Arise?

In Q[41] the Court of Appeal held that Article 3 imposes a positive duty on public authorities to take action to prevent the subjection of individuals to proscribed treatment.[42] What is not clear is when this positive obligation arises. With respect to Article 2, it has been established that the positive duty to take reasonable measures to safeguard life arises where the authorities know, or ought to know, of the existence of a risk to life. However, in Q the Court of Appeal expressly disapproved of the risk test Collins J applied in the lower court. Collins J considered that there would be a breach of Article 3 if the Secretary of State refused support to an asylum seeker where there was a real risk that, because he would receive no support from any alternative source, he would decline into the state described in *Pretty*. The Court of Appeal noted that the real risk test had been applied by Strasbourg in the case of removal to a country in circumstances where the removing state was no longer in a position to influence events. It did not believe it was an appropriate test in the present context.[43] That is not to say it would not be an appropriate test in a different context.

This conclusion of the Court of Appeal is rather odd, given that, in the removal cases, a UK public authority is not itself carrying out the torture or inhuman or degrading treatment or punishment. These cases therefore arguably fall within the category of positive obligation to protect. Given that the real risk test is well established in this branch of Article 3 jurisprudence, it is questionable why it has not carried over to non-deportation/extradition cases. The most likely explanation is that it has not been appreciated that what is being put into effect here is the positive duty of the state under Article 3.

The most straightforward explanation of the positive duty under Article 3 was given by the Court of Appeal in *Bagdanavicius*,[44] a judgment later upheld by the House of Lords,[45] although it is important to note that the central issue of the appeal was the meaning of a real risk of Article 3 ill-treatment when a person threatened with removal to another state alleged that if returned there he would be at risk from non-state actors. Nevertheless, there is no reason why the principles should not apply outside of this context. The Court of Appeal held that the starting point for consideration of Article 3 ill-treatment in non-state actor cases and of the response of the state to it was *Osman*.[46] It concluded that there was a duty to take positive protective action against ill-treatment by non-state actors. However, sufficiency of state protection was not a guarantee of protection from Article 3 ill-treatment.

> Where the risk falls to be judged by the sufficiency of state protection, that sufficiency is judged, not according to whether it would eradicate the real risk of the relevant harm, but according to whether it was a reasonable provision in the circumstances.

---

[41] Above n 14.
[42] *Ibid*, at [53] in reliance on *A v UK* [1998] 3 FCR 597; *Z v UK* [2001] 2 FCR 246; *Pretty v UK*, above n 32. See also *Watts*, above n 10, at [54] at [45].
[43] at [61].
[44] *R (on the application of Bagdanavicius) v Secretary of State for the Home Department* [2003] EWCA Civ 1605, [2004] 1 WLR 1207.
[45] [2005] UKHL 38, [2005] 2 WLR 1359.
[46] *Osman v UK* (1988) 29 EHRR 245 at [115]–[116]. Referred to at [18].

Notwithstanding such systemic sufficiency of state protection in the receiving state,

> a claimant may still be able to establish an Article 3 claim if he can show that the authorities there know or ought to know of particular circumstances likely to expose him to risk of Article 3 ill-treatment.[47]

In a differently constituted Court of Appeal in *Gezer*, despite agreeing with Laws LJ's judgment, Carnwath LJ and Elias J essentially followed the approach in *Bagdanavicius*. Carnwath LJ simply held that, where state action or inaction may lead to suffering sufficiently serious to engage Article 3, the relevant state agency had a duty to take reasonable steps to avoid it.[48] Elias J held that, where there is a real risk of ill-treatment at the hands of non-state agents, and the treatment would, absent any protection afforded by the state, involve a breach of Article 3, the state must provide reasonable protection in the circumstances.[49]

Whilst the picture remains far from clear, what seems to be emerging is an approach along the lines of that developed in relation to Article 2. The positive duty to take reasonable measures to avert a violation of Article 3 arises where the authorities know or ought to know of the existence of a risk of torture or of inhuman or degrading treatment or punishment. It is not clear whether what is required is a risk or a real risk and, in any event, what difference this would make. Given the predominance of 'real risk' in the deportation cases, it is likely that this is the appropriate standard. Borrowing again from this jurisprudence, the burden of proof is on the claimant and the standard of proof is that there must be substantial grounds for believing that he or she is at real risk of prohibited ill-treatment contrary to Article 3.[50] A claimant may be able to meet this test either by referring to evidence specific to his own circumstances or by evidence applicable to a class of which he or she is a member.[51]

3.2.2 Knew or Ought to Have Known

Whilst this aspect of the *Osman* test has not yet featured in Article 2 cases, it is important to remember that it was held in this case that it must also be shown that the authorities knew or ought to have known, at the time, of the existence of the risk.[52] Using this approach would have made the task of the Court of Appeal in *Gezer*[53] far simpler. Only Carnwath LJ agreed with the finding of the court below that the claimant had not established a particular and specific danger of ill-treatment within Article 3 directed against asylum seekers in the estate of which the public authority ought to have been aware.[54]

---

[47] *Ibid*, at [55]. See also *McPherson v Secretary of State for the Home Department* [2001] EWCA Civ 1955.
[48] *Gezer*, above n 11, at [46].
[49] *Ibid*, at [55].
[50] *McPherson*, above n 47.
[51] *Batayav v The Secretary of State for the Home Department* [2003] EWCA Civ 1489 at [7].
[52] *Osman v UK* (1998) 29 EHRR 245 at [116].
[53] Above n 11.
[54] *Ibid*, at [52].

3.2.3 Reasonable Measures

When it arises, in contrast to the negative duty, it has been held that the positive obligation is not absolute and unqualified. In *Pretty*[55] Lord Bingham referred to the observations of the European Court of Human Rights in *Osman*,[56] where it had been held that a positive obligation to protect life must be interpreted in a way which did not impose an impossible or disproportionate burden on the authorities. He also referred to *Rees*,[57] where the European Court held that, in determining whether or not a positive obligation existed, regard had to be had to the fair balance that has to be struck between the general interests of the community and the interests of the individual. Lord Hope agreed that issues of proportionality would arise where a positive obligation was implied.[58] Both Carnwath LJ and Elias J in *Gezer* referred to reasonable steps[59] and reasonable protection.[60]

However, this interpretation of the positive obligation may not be of universal application. In *Munjaz*[61] the Court of Appeal held that *Osman* and *Rees* had no relevance to cases where the state itself had deprived a vulnerable person of his liberty, and the state itself was responsible for how that person was treated. It held that in such cases

the state ought to know enough about its own prisoner or patient to provide effective protection from inhuman or degrading treatment by the state's own agents.[62]

Therefore, in relation to conditions of detention, it may be that any failure to act resulting in inhuman or degrading treatment or punishment will be measured by an absolute standard and questions of reasonableness and proportionality will not arise.

---

4. Illness and Medical Treatment

Article 3 requires respect for physical and human integrity[63] and in this respect, overlaps to some extent with the protection provided by Article 8 although there may be circumstances in which Article 8 can be regarded as affording a protection in relation to conditions which do not attain the level of severity required by Article 3.[64]

---

[55] Above n 1.
[56] Above n 52, at [115]–[116].
[57] *Rees v United Kingdom* (1986) 9 EHRR 56 at [37].
[58] *Ibid*, at [90] and [93] See also Lord Steyn at [60].
[59] *Gezer*, above n 11, at [46].
[60] *Ibid*, at [55]. See also the judgment of Carnwath LJ in *Limbuela*, above n 4.
[61] *R (on the application of Munjaz) v Mersey Care NHS Trust* [2003] EWCA Civ 1036, [2004] QB 395.
[62] *Ibid*, at [58].
[63] *Pretty*, above n 1, at [13] per Lord Bingham.
[64] *Watts*, above n 10.

4.1 Responsibility of a Public Authority

For Article 3 to be engaged, it is first necessary to show that the treatment, or failure to treat, by a public authority, is the cause of the suffering. Article 3 imposes positive obligations to take measures to ensure that the right is effectively protected[65] and such obligations may be imposed upon the authorities even where the underlying problem is the claimant's physical or mental illness.[66] It is rare for a public authority to be found to have subjected someone to inhuman or degrading treatment in this area. For example, in *Pretty*[67] the claimant suffered from motor neurone disease, a progressive degenerative illness from which she had no hope of recovery. She faced the prospect of a humiliating and distressing death and wished to bring her life to her end. As she could not take her own life without help, her husband was willing to assist if the Director of Public Prosecutions (DPP) undertook not to prosecute him. The DPP refused to give such an undertaking. Ms Pretty argued that, in denying her the opportunity to bring her life to an end, the DPP was subjecting her to inhuman and degrading treatment. The House of Lords did not agree, holding that it could not plausibly be suggested that the 'Director or any other agent of the United Kingdom is inflicting the proscribed treatment on Mrs Pretty, whose suffering derives from her cruel disease.'[68] However, it did go on to consider the positive duty imposed by Article 3 as discussed below.

4.2 The Right to Die and the Right to Die with Dignity

It is clear that Article 3 is not concerned with an individual's right to live or to choose not to live.[69] In *Pretty*,[70] although it concluded there was no 'treatment' by the DPP within the meaning of Article 3, the House of Lords went on to consider the positive obligation—did the DPP's failure to give his consent mean that the claimant would go on suffering in a manner which engaged Article 3? Their Lordships were clear that this was not an absolute duty.

> [W]hile states may be absolutely forbidden to inflict the proscribed treatment on individuals within their jurisdiction, the steps appropriate or necessary to discharge a positive obligation will be more judgmental, more prone to variation from state to state, more dependent on the opinions and beliefs of the people and less susceptible to any universal jurisdiction.[71]

The House of Lords concluded that there was no positive obligation to ensure that a competent terminally ill person who wished but was unable to take his or her own life should be entitled to seek the assistance of another without that other being exposed to the risk of prosecution.[72] Lord Hope held as follows:

[65] *Ibid*, at [45].
[66] *Ibid*, at [46] in reliance upon *D v United Kingdom* (1997) 24 EHRR 423; *Bensaid v United Kingdom* (2001) 33 EHRR 205; and *Price v United Kingdom* (2001) 34 EHRR 128.
[67] Above n 1.
[68] *Ibid*, at [13] per Lord Bingham. See also Lord Steyn at [60] and Lord Hope at [92]. The European Court of Human Rights also agreed with this conclusion. See *Pretty v UK*, above n 32, at [53].
[69] *Pretty*, *ibid*, at [13] per Lord Bingham and [60] Lord Steyn.
[70] *Ibid*.
[71] *Ibid*, at [15] per Lord Bingham.
[72] *Ibid*. See also [27]–[28].

the object which s 2(1) was designed to achieve struck the right balance between the interests of the individual and the public interest which seeks to protect the weak and vulnerable. . . although the effect of the Director's decision that he had no power to give the undertaking is likely to expose Mrs Pretty to acute distress as she succumbs to her illness, his act cannot be said to be unfair or arbitrary or to have impaired her Convention right more than is reasonably necessary.[73]

The European Court agreed, holding that Article 3 must be construed in harmony with Article 2, which is

first and foremost a prohibition on the use of lethal force or other conduct which might lead to the death of a human being and does not confer any claim on an individual to require a State to permit or facilitate his or her death.[74]

However, whilst it does not extend to a right to die, it has been held that Article 3 does protect the right to die with dignity.[75] Article 2 does not entitle anyone to continue with life-prolonging treatment where to do so would expose the patient to inhuman or degrading treatment.[76]

4.3 Medical Treatment

Forcible medical treatment inflicted upon an incapacitated patient which is not a medical necessity may be inhuman or degrading. The same applies to forcible measures inflicted upon a capacitated patient.[77] However, it has been held that, as a general rule, treatment administered to a detained patient will not amount to a violation of Article 3 if the therapeutic or medical necessity for it has been convincingly shown.[78] The court itself must determine whether such necessity has been shown to the appropriate standard.[79] The capacity of a patient is a relevant factor but is not determinative.[80] As the court has no particular medical expertise, it is proper for the court to place particular weight on the evidence of the Responsible Medical Officer and Second Opinion Appointed Doctor.[81]

With respect to PVS patients in *NHS Trust A v Mrs M*[82] it was held that the continuation of futile treatment or the withdrawal of such treatment did not engage Article 3, which

requires the victim to be aware of the inhuman and degrading treatment which he or she is experiencing or at least to be in a state of physical or mental suffering. An insensate patient

---

[73] *Ibid*, at [97]. See also Lord Steyn at [60] and the judgment of the European Court in *Pretty v UK*, above n 32, at [54]–[56].
[74] *Pretty v UK, ibid*, at [54].
[75] *A National Health Service Trust v D* [2000] 2 FLR 677.
[76] *R (on the application of Burke) v The General Medical Council* [2005] EWCA Civ 1003 at [39].
[77] *Wilkinson*, above n 4, at [79] per Hale LJ in reliance upon *Herczegfalvy v Austria* (1992) 15 EHRR 437. See also *R (on the application of B) v Haddock* [2005] EWHC (Admin) 921; and *R (Wooder) v Feggetter* [2002] EWCA Civ 554, [2002] 3 WLR 591 in relation to the duty to give reasons in such circumstances.
[78] *B*, above n 4, at [55] in reliance upon *Herczegfalvy v Austria* (1993) 15 EHRR 432.
[79] *Ibid*, at [67].
[80] *Ibid*, at [63].
[81] *Ibid*, at [68].
[82] *NHS Trust A v Mrs M* [2001] 2 WLR 942.

suffering from permanent vegetative state has no feelings and no comprehension of the treatment accorded to him or her.[83]

It is possible that hospital waiting times may give rise to an Article 3 claim. For example, in *Watts*[84] the claimant, who needed urgent hip replacements and was unwilling to wait, had the operation in France, then sought to recover her costs from her NHS Trust. The Administrative Court confirmed that Article 3 imposed positive obligations to take measures to ensure that the right was effectively protected[85] and that such obligations may be thrown upon the authorities even where the underlying problem was the claimant's physical or mental illness.[86] However, no breach of the article was found here. First, the court was not satisfied that the ill-treatment had attained a minimum level of severity and involved actual bodily injury or intense physical or mental suffering. Even making every allowance for the constant pain and suffering that she was having to endure, it was not so 'severe or so humiliating as to engage Article 3.'[87] Secondly, given that the positive duty was not absolute, the court held that Article 3 was not designed for the circumstances of this sort where the challenge was to a health authority's allocation of finite funds between competing demands.[88]

---

5. Conditions of Detention

The conditions of detention in prisons, secure hospitals and other places can undoubtedly engage Article 3, and it has been held that more might be required of the authorities where vulnerable people have been deprived of their liberty.[89] Distinctions can be made between types of vulnerable people such as prisoners and compulsory psychiatric patients. The imprisonment of criminal offenders is an end in itself.

> The necessary ingredients of imprisonment, provided that they meet the standards considered acceptable at the time, are unlikely to amount to inhuman or degrading treatment or punishment under Art 3.

However, the detention of psychiatric patients is a means to an end, the assessment and treatment of their mental disorder.

---

[83] *Ibid*, at [49].
[84] Above n 10.
[85] *Ibid*, at [45].
[86] *Ibid*, at [46] in reliance upon *D*, *Bensaid* and *Price*, above n 66.
[87] *Ibid*, at [54].
[88] *Ibid*, at [50]–[53] in reliance upon *R v North West Lancashire Health Authority, ex p A* [2000] 1 WLR 977 at 996A; *Matthews v Ministry of Defence* [2003] UKHL 4, [2003] 1 AC 1163 at [26] per Lord Hoffmann.
[89] *Munjaz*, above n 61, at [54] in reliance upon *Keenan v UK* (1998) 26 EHRR CD 64. See also *R (on the application of R) v Shetty (Responsible Medical Officer)* [2003] EWHC (Admin) 3022 at [23].

Conditions of detention which defeat rather than promote that end are much more likely to amount to inhuman or degrading treatment.[90]

The distinction between regular prison and detention where treatment for a mental disorder was received was made clear in *Shetty*.[91] Here the claimant argued that transfer back to prison from the psychiatric clinic where he was receiving treatment would violate Article 3. The Responsible Medical Officer of the clinic had concluded that the claimant no longer required treatment for mental disorder. The Administrative Court considered whether it was more likely than not that if the claimant was remitted to prison he would suffer treatment so damaging to him as to amount to inhuman and degrading treatment. It held that the claimant had to demonstrate that, following a transfer back to prison, he would relapse; that the treatment provided in response would be inadequate; and that as a consequence severe suffering would occur such that there would be a violation of Article 3.[92] The claimant failed to establish this to the satisfaction of the court, which held that it was open to the Home Secretary to conclude that remittal to prison would not violate Article 3.[93]

Where a detainee is particularly vulnerable, the assessment of severity under Article 3 is adjusted accordingly. For example, in *Spinks*[94] the claimant, serving a life sentence for murder, had been diagnosed as suffering from terminal cancer of the colon with no prospect of recovery and a short life expectancy. His Article 3 complaint concerned a number of difficulties, including attending appointments at the hospital; handcuffing during treatment; the availability of colostomy bags; and problems with day attendance at a hospice. The relief sought was the quashing of a decision of the Secretary of State that he should not be released from prison on compassionate grounds. The Court of Appeal concluded that a breach of Article 3 had not been made out. It found that, for the moment, the claimant was fit and mobile, that there had been no recommendation that he should be treated full-time in a specialist clinic or removed to hospital and that there was no evidence of significant psychological harm.[95] With respect to the handcuffing, it found that this also did not constitute a violation of Article 3, and there had been a risk assessment carried out indicating a continuing significant degree of risk although the observation was made that such rigorous security may not be necessary in hospital.[96]

Segregation from the prison community or other detained patients does not of itself constitute a form of inhuman or degrading treatment.[97] However, the use of seclusion, consisting of the supervised confinement of a patient alone in a room which may be locked for the protection of others from significant harm, is capable of violating Article 3.[98] Given the risk of violation, Article 3 imposes a positive duty on public authorities to take steps to prevent this from happening. In *Munjaz*[99] it was

---

[90] *Munjaz, ibid*, at [55] in reliance upon *Keenan, ibid*. See also *Drew*, above n 3.
[91] Above n 89.
[92] *Ibid*, at [87].
[93] *Ibid*, at [77].
[94] *R (on the application of Spinks) v Secretary of State for the Home Department* [2005] EWCA Civ 275.
[95] *Ibid*, at [42] in reliance upon *Mouisel v France* (2004) 38 EHRR 34.
[96] *Ibid*, at [47].
[97] *Munjaz*, above n 61, at [54] in reliance upon *Dhoest v Belgium* [1987] Application No 10448/83; *Koskinen v Finland* Application (1994) 18 EHRR CD 14.
[98] *Ibid* in reliance upon *A v United Kingdom* (1980) 3 EHRR 131.
[99] *Ibid*.

argued that the Code of Practice issued by the Secretary of State under section 118 of the Mental Health Act 1983 was one of those steps. The Court of Appeal agreed, holding that, in these circumstances, the positive duty under Article 3 was not modelled on that under Article 2 as discussed in *Osman*[100] and *Z*.[101]

> [T]hese remarks referred to the steps which the state should take to protect individuals from threats to their life or ill-treatment by other private individuals. In our view, they have no relevance to cases where the state itself has deprived a vulnerable person his liberty, and the state itself is responsible for how that person is treated. In such cases, the state ought to know enough about its own prisoner or patient to provide effective protection from inhuman or degrading treatment by the state's own agents.[102]

The court accepted that the Code should be afforded a status and weight consistent with the state's obligation to avoid ill-treatment of patients detained by or on the authority of the state,[103] and concluded that the Code should be followed unless there was good reason to depart from it.[104]

---

6. Violence

Violence and serious racial abuse engage Article 3.[105] It is beyond doubt that public authorities must not engage in either. In certain circumstances there may be a positive duty to protect individuals from such behaviour perpetrated by other private individuals. In *Gezer*, the claimant asylum seekers—Turkish nationals of Kurdish origin—had been provided with accommodation in the Toryglen council estate in Glasgow. Within days they were subjected to racial abuse and hostility, and their home was attacked by three men, one of whom tried to stab the youngest son. They were eventually returned to London.

Before the Court of Appeal there was no challenge to the finding in the court below that such behaviour undoubtedly engaged Article 3.[106] The question was whether or not the National Asylum Support Service (NASS), as the agency which conducted the dispersal, could be held responsible. Laws LJ employed his spectrum metaphor, first referred to in his judgment in *Limbuela*,[107] intended to demonstrate a sliding scale of instances in which Article 3 might be engaged, from those where the state enjoyed no power of discretion to those 'where the State might enjoy a

---

[100] Above n 52.
[101] *Z v UK* (2001) 34 EHRR 97.
[102] *Munjaz*, above n 61, at [58].
[103] *Ibid*, at [60].
[104] *Ibid*, at [74]. See also *R v Governor of HMP Frankland ex p Russell* [2000] 1 WLR 2027, where the decision of the governor to only provide one meal per day to the prisoners in segregation who refused to wear prison clothes may well breach Art 3. See further S Foster, 'Prison Conditions, Human Rights and Article 3 ECHR' [2005] *PL* 35.
[105] *Gezer*, above n 11.
[106] *Ibid*, at [26] per Laws LJ.
[107] Above n 4.

considerable margin of discretion as to the adoption and exercise of policy.'[108] He concluded that in the present case the key question was what duty of enquiry was owed by NASS to obtain information as to the conditions prevailing on the estate before offering accommodation there.[109] Finding that it was open to the claimants to refuse the accommodation, he located the case at the lower end of the spectrum and NASS was not required to make special enquiries to save the claimant from harm.[110]

Carnwath LJ and Elias J reached the same conclusion via a far simpler process of reasoning. Carnwath LJ, whilst agreeing with Laws LJ, found that NASS did not know, nor ought to have known, about the risk to the claimants.

> In the light of the knowledge which NASS had, and the advice which it was receiving from the responsible authorities in the Glasgow area, the steps taken were reasonable.[111]

Elias J also agreed, but applied a real risk test.[112] He stated that there must be an ability and willingness to provide an effective system of protection, having regard to the practical realities.[113] Given the information available to NASS, he concluded that it was fully entitled to take the view that the protection was adequate.[114] He also expressly disagreed with Laws LJ's finding that the Article 3 duty owed was affected by the fact that the claimants had a choice.

> It cannot in my opinion be justified in requiring the appellant to accept a higher risk of treatment whose severity would infringe Article 3 because he could choose to give up altogether the rights which Parliament has conferred on him.[115]

---

7. Sentencing

The question of inhuman or degrading punishment has arisen in relation to sentencing, specifically the automatic life sentence and the mandatory life sentence. For punishment to be inhuman or degrading, it has to attain a minimum level of severity.[116] However, punishment which is arbitrary or disproportionate can be regarded as inhuman.[117]

---

[108] *Ibid*, at [33].
[109] *Ibid*, at [34].
[110] *Ibid*, at [41].
[111] *Ibid*, at [52].
[112] *Ibid*, at [55].
[113] *Ibid*, at [55].
[114] *Ibid*, at [56].
[115] *Ibid*, at [57].
[116] *R v Lichniak* [2002] UKHL 47, [2003] 1 AC 903 at [25] per Lord Hutton in reliance upon *Costello-Roberts v United Kingdom* (1993) 19 EHRR 112.
[117] *Ibid*, at [25] per Lord Hutton in reliance upon *Weeks v United Kingdom* (1987) 10 EHRR 293. See generally D van Zyl Smit and A Ashworth, 'Disproportionate Sentences as Human Rights Violations' (2004) 67 *MLR* 541.

The automatic life sentence is imposed for a second serious offence where there are no exceptional circumstances.[118] In *Offen*[119] the Court of Appeal concluded that it was possible in some circumstances for the imposition of an automatic life sentence to be arbitrary and disproportionate. It gave the example of an unjustified push which

> can result in someone falling, hitting his head and suffering fatal injuries. The offence is manslaughter. The offender may have committed another serious offence when a young man. A life sentence in such circumstances may well be arbitrary and disproportionate and contravene art 5. It could also be a punishment which contravenes art 3.[120]

Using section 3 of the HRA, the court concluded that there would be no contravention if the section was applied so that it did not result in offenders being sentenced to life imprisonment when they did not constitute a significant risk to the public.[121]

In *Lichniak*[122] it was argued that imposition of the mandatory life sentence[123] was incompatible with Article 3 because it required the same life sentence to be passed on all convicted murderers, whatever the facts of the case or the circumstances of the offender, and irrespective of whether they were thought to present a danger to the public or not. Relying on the judgment of the European Court of Human Rights in *V v United Kingdom*,[124] the House of Lords held that an indeterminate sentence, in its operation in practice, did not constitute an arbitrary or disproportionate punishment. In particular, their Lordships held that it was not arbitrary to postpone to the end of the tariff period the decision whether a person who has committed a murder would be a danger to the public if released, rather than decide this at the time of the trial. Whilst it was appreciated that this would cause uncertainty, it was not considered that such uncertainty

> can constitute treatment of such severity as to come within the ambit of inhuman punishment forbidden by Article 3 or can make the sentence of life imprisonment an arbitrary one.[125]

It also concluded that the fact that the imposition of a life sentence made the prisoner released on licence liable to recall to prison for the remainder of his life did not fall foul of Article 3.[126]

---

[118] See s 109, Powers of Criminal Courts (Sentencing) Act 2000.
[119] *R v Offen* [2001] 1 WLR 253.
[120] *Ibid*, at [95].
[121] *Ibid*, at [97]. See also *R v Kelly* [2001] EWCA Crim 1030, [2002] 1 Cr Ap 11; *Drew*, above n 3.
[122] Above n 116.
[123] Section 1(1) Murder (Abolition of Death Penalty) Act 1965.
[124] (1999) 30 EHRR 121.
[125] *Ibid*, at [35] per Lord Hutton. Lord Bingham reached a similar conclusion but also held that, if it had been the case that on imposition of a mandatory life sentence the convicted murderer forfeited his liberty to the state for the rest of his days, to remain in custody until (if ever) the Home Secretary concluded that the public interest would be better served by his release than by his continued detention, this would violate Art 3. See [8].
[126] *Ibid*, at [37] per Lord Hutton in reliance upon *V v United Kingdom* (1999) 30 EHRR 121. See also *R v Parchment* [2003] EWCA Crim 2428.

8. Criminal Law

The positive duty under Article 3 for the state to take action to prevent the subjection of individuals to the proscribed treatment has ramifications for the criminal law. However, the only aspect of the criminal law to come under scrutiny has been the defence of reasonable chastisement available to parents in relation to children. In *R v H*[127] a father who beat his son with a leather belt pleaded not guilty to the offence of actual bodily harm, his defence being that he was exercising his right as a parent to chastise his son who was not obeying a request to write his own name. Although the offence occurred before the HRA came into force, the Court of Appeal held it was appropriate for the trial judge to balance the rights of the child under Article 3 with the rights of a defendant under Articles 6 and 7. It held that the jury should be directed in detailed terms as to the factors relevant to whether the chastisement was reasonable and moderate.

> [T]hey must consider the nature and context of the defendant's behaviour, its duration, its physical and mental consequences in relation to the child, the age and personal characteristics of the child and the reasons given by the defendant for administering punishment.[128]

It concluded that it was a proper incremental development of the common law for such a direction to be given.[129]

9. Social Security and Support

It is clear that, alongside Article 8, Article 3 can have some impact on the provision, or non-provision, of social security and support. However, the case law in this area is far from clear and offers little guidance. The failure to provide support may constitute a breach of the negative duty under Article 3 or the positive duty. As discussed in preceding paragraphs, in *Q*[130] the court found that the regime imposed on asylum seekers who were denied support engaged the negative duty and constituted treatment within the meaning of Article 3.[131] The problems inherent in this approach have already been discussed. However, it is clear that the court's finding does not mean that the state is never under a positive obligation to provide support insofar as it is necessary to prevent persons reaching that condition of degradation which would infringe Article 3.

---

[127] *R v H* [2001] EWCA Crim 1024, [2001] 2 FLR 431.
[128] *Ibid*, at [31].
[129] *Ibid*, at [35]. See further RKM Smith, 'Hands-off Parenting—Towards a Reform of the Defence of Reasonable Chastisement in the UK' (2004) 16 *CFLQ* 261.
[130] Above n 14.
[131] *Ibid*, at [56].

> There is a stage at which the dictates of humanity require the State to intervene to prevent any person within its territory suffering dire consequences as a result of deprivation of sustenance. If support is necessary to prevent a person in this country reaching the point of Art.3 degradation, then that support should be provided.[132]

Nevertheless, as yet there is no case law concerning the positive duty under Article 3 and state support.

Returning to *Q*, having determined that it was possible for a failure to provide support to constitute subjecting an asylum seeker to inhuman or degrading treatment,[133] the next question for the Court of Appeal was at what point the treatment became inhuman or degrading. It made clear that the requisite level of severity had to be reached[134] and, employing the test outlined in *Pretty v UK*,[135] held that some who applied for asylum would already be in a condition which engaged Article 3 and support would have to be provided.[136] With respect to others, it held that the Secretary of State had to be prepared to entertain further applications from those to whom he had refused support who had not been able to find any charitable support or other lawful means of fending for themselves.[137] In *Limbuela*[138] this was taken to mean the individual had done enough to show that he was 'verging on' the necessary degree of severity, and that Article 3 was accordingly engaged. There was no need to show the actual onset of severe illness or suffering.[139]

Unsurprisingly, a huge number of Article 3 applications were made to the courts by those asylum seekers who did not agree with the Home Secretary's assessment of their condition. In *T*[140] the Court of Appeal attempted to give further guidance. It held that the burden of satisfying the Secretary of State that support was necessary was on the applicant.

> Where the condition of an applicant verges on the degree of severity described in *Pretty* then the Secretary of State must act.[141]

With no reference to the absolute nature of the negative duty, the court held that, as the allocation of resources was involved, the court had to be careful not to set too low a threshold at which the duty to act arose.[142] The court applied the *Pretty* test, expanding a little on the meaning of degrading treatment. It is not enough for a victim to feel that he has suffered a loss of dignity.

> How he sees himself and how he is seen by others are matters which may be relevant, but they are not determinative.[143]

---

[132] *Anufrijeva v Southwark LBC* [2003] EWCA Civ 1406, [2004] QB 1124 at [35].
[133] Above n 14, at [46].
[134] *Ibid*, at [59]. Reference was made to *O'Rourke v UK*, 26 June 2001.
[135] Above n 32.
[136] *Ibid*, at [62]–[63].
[137] *Ibid*.
[138] Above n 4.
[139] *Ibid*, at [95] per Carnwath LJ. See A Bradley, 'Judicial Independence under Attack' [2003] *PL* 397 on the reaction of government to the judgment of the Court of Appeal and High Court.
[140] Above n 4.
[141] *Ibid*, at [10].
[142] *Ibid*, at [11].
[143] *Ibid*, at [12] in reliance upon *East African Asians* and *Lorsé*, above n 21.

It is relevant, but not requisite, that the purpose of the treatment is to debase or humiliate. What matters more is effect. Emotional distress of itself is not enough, but it is a factor.[144] Each case must be judged in relation to all the circumstances which are relevant to it.[145]

The court was required to reach a conclusion on the cases of S and T. S was a Somali who, although generally in good health, had no friends or family and no resources in the United Kingdom. Until NASS gave him interim support through the charity Migrant Help Line, he slept rough on the streets. The charity arranged for him to see a doctor, who reported symptoms of psychological disturbance and considerable malnutrition. On arriving in London, he slept rough again. He had to beg for money in order to eat, but received very little. He begged for shelter, but without success. His physical condition deteriorated and a further medical report from the hospital where he had gone because of abdominal pains confirmed his loss of weight. He became unable to eat more than a few mouthfuls of food when it was available. The court found that Article 3 was engaged here, although it stated that this did not mean that other cases had to reach the same or a similar degree of severity in order to engage Article 3.[146] Turning to T's case, the court commented that the boundary, which was not a 'fixed or bright line', lay somewhere between the two cases.[147]

T was sleeping and spending his days at Heathrow Airport. He claimed he found it difficult to rest or sleep because of the noise and the light, and because he was repeatedly moved on by the police. Any ablutions were confined to public lavatories, and he was unable to wash his hair or his clothes or to bathe or shower. He developed a problem with his left eye and also a cough. He carried his belongings around with him in holdalls and became increasingly worried. The court concluded that T's case did not reach the threshold.

> He had shelter, sanitary facilities and some money for food. He was not entirely well physically, but not so unwell as to need immediate treatment.[148]

However, the guidance given did little to help the lower courts. The Court of Appeal returned once again to this question in *Limbuela*,[149] reporting that although the lower courts had attempted to follow the guidance in *T*, all had found some difficulty in using it to arrive at a principled decision on the facts of the individual cases.[150] Carnwath LJ held that the factual circumstances were so varied and variable that it was practically meaningless to attempt to assess them by reference to a single test at a single point in time.

> They include the physical and mental resistance of the particular individual; the season of the year and the state of the weather; the incidence of any epidemics or illnesses affecting the area; the availability of medical help and drugs; the extent if any of the help available

---

144 *Ibid.*
145 *Ibid,* at [16].
146 *Ibid,* at [18].
147 *Ibid,* at [18].
148 *Ibid,* at [19].
149 Above n 4.
150 *Ibid,* at [86] per Carnwath LJ.

from other sources . . . and the degree of toleration or lack of it shown by other parties or the public at large.[151]

Simplifying matters, he concluded that if the evidence established clearly that charitable support was not available and the individual had no other means of fending for himself, the presumption would be that severe suffering would follow imminently and this was enough to engage Article 3.[152] Jacob LJ agreed, holding that if this sort of number were put on the streets, without money and with no entitlement to earn any, it was a near certainty that a substantial proportion would fall below the Article 3 threshold.[153] Individualised decision making disposed with, this was a clear message to the Home Secretary that the courts were very likely to find Article 3 violations in relation to all of the 600 plus cases waiting to be heard. Soon after this, the Immigration and Nationality Directorate issued a staff instruction stating that asylum seekers were not to be refused support unless it was clear that they had some alternative form of support, including night shelter, food and basic amenities.[154]

10. Deportation and Extradition

10.1 Nature of the Duty

Where there are strong grounds for believing that a person, if extradited or expelled, faces a real risk of being subjected to torture or to inhuman or degrading treatment or punishment in the destination state, it is unlawful to remove that person from the United Kingdom.[155] In *Soering v United Kingdom*,[156] which concerned extradition, the European Court explained the responsibility as follows:

> In sum, the decision by a Contracting State to extradite a fugitive may give rise to an issue under Article 3, and hence engage the responsibility of that State under the Convention, where substantial grounds have been shown for believing that the person concerned, if extradited, faces a real risk of being subjected to torture or to inhuman or degrading treatment or punishment in the requesting country. The establishment of such responsibility inevitably involves an assessment of conditions in the requesting country against the standards of Article 3 of the Convention. Nonetheless, there is no question of adjudicating on or establishing the responsibility of the receiving country, whether under general

---

[151] *Ibid*, at [89].
[152] *Ibid*, at [95].
[153] *Ibid*, at [148].
[154] See further P Billings and RA Edwards, 'Safeguarding Asylum Seekers' Dignity: Clarifying the Interface between Convention Rights and Asylum Law', (2004) 11 *JSSL* 83; K Puttick, 'Asylum Support and Limbuela: an End (Finally) to Section 55?' (2004) *IANL* 186.
[155] *Ullah*, above n 2, per Lord Bingham at [24] in reliance upon *Soering v United Kingdom* (1989) 11 EHRR 439 at [91]; *Cruz Varas v Sweden* (1991) 14 EHRR 1 at [69]; *Vilvarajah v United Kingdom* (1991) 14 EHRR 248 at [103]. However, it is important to note that the crucial issue in this case was whether reliance could be placed on any other Article of the Convention. The House of Lords concluded that it could. See also *Z*, above n 15 at [7].
[156] (1989) 11 EHRR 439.

international law, under the Convention or otherwise. In so far as any liability under the Convention is or may be incurred, it is liability incurred by the extraditing Contracting State by reason of its having taken action which has as a direct consequence the exposure of an individual to proscribed ill-treatment.[157]

The extension of the guarantee is not accompanied by a relaxation of its absolute nature,[158] and it applies however 'disgraceful, promiscuous or reprehensible' the claimant's conduct may have been.[159] The burden of proof is on the claimant, and the standard of proof is that there must be substantial grounds for believing that he or she is at real risk of prohibited ill-treatment contrary to Article 3.[160] A claimant may be able to meet this test either by referring to evidence specific to his own circumstances or by evidence applicable to a class of which he or she is a member. In the latter category, the claimant will only be able to demonstrate substantial grounds for believing that there is such a real risk if he or she can point to a consistent pattern of gross and systemic violation of rights under Article 3.[161] Nevertheless, it has been held that great care needs to be taken with such epithets which are intended to elucidate the jurisprudential concept of real risk, not to replace it. It is important not to assimilate risk to probability.[162] With respect to past events, it has been held that these can only cast light, as a matter of evidence, on what would happen if the claimant were returned.

> Such past events cannot of themselves constitute some part of the apprehended breach, which by definition lies in the future. That is not to say that evidence of these events may not be of great importance. They may cast much light on what will happen if the applicant is returned. They may, in some cases, show that by reason of his history the applicant's health or mental state is especially vulnerable.[163]

It is not clear whether the duty is negative or positive, and this is something that has not been addressed in the case law. As a UK public authority is not itself carrying out the torture or the inhuman or degrading treatment or punishment, it arguably falls within the category of positive obligation to protect. Given the real risk test is well established in this branch of Article 3 jurisprudence, it is questionable why it has not carried over to non-deportation/extradition cases. In *N*[164] Lord Brown did suggest, in the context of a deportation resisted on the ground of inadequate medical treatment in the receiving state, that it was actually a positive duty for which the claimant was contending.

> It is quite unreal to treat this article 3 complaint for all the world as if all that is required to safeguard the appellant's health is that the State refrain from deporting her. Realistically what she seeks is continuing treatment for her condition and is necessarily implicit in her

---

[157] *Ibid*, at [91].
[158] *N v Secretary of State for the Home Department* [2005] UKHL 31, [2005] 2 AC 296 at [28], [30] and [48] per Lord Hope.
[159] *Ibid*, at [27].
[160] *McPherson*, above n 47; *I v Secretary of State for the Home Department* [2005] EWCA Civ 886.
[161] *Batayav*, above n 51, at [7].
[162] *Ibid*, at [37]–[40].
[163] *Strbac v Secretary of State for the Home Department* [2005] EWCA Civ 848 at [43].
[164] Above n 158.

case that the State is bound to provide it. There would simply be no point in not deporting her unless her treatment here were to continue.[165]

However, this line of reasoning was not fully developed, his Lordship stating that the Strasbourg case law did not indicate that there was an absolute right for seriously ill persons to remain in the host country to get treatment.[166]

10.2 Application

This particular Article 3 obligation has generated a very large number of cases. It is common practice now for those claiming asylum in the UK to also claim protection on Article 3 grounds, even though the two claims remain very different.[167] Given that an individual may be deported or extradited from the UK to anywhere in the world, British courts and tribunals have had to consider the engagement of Article 3 in circumstances which would be very unlikely to arise in the domestic context. A number of categories have developed, and these are examined in the paragraphs below.

10.2.1 Illness

The illness of the individual subject to deportation may give rise to an Article 3 claim in two ways. First, the act of deportation itself may exacerbate an existing mental or physical illness. This may occur when the claimant is informed that a final decision has been made to remove or when he or she is physically removed.[168] For example, in *Lamanovs*[169] the claimant was liable to epileptic attacks and asked for a stay of his removal to France on the ground that it would be in breach of Article 3. The Court of Appeal considered medical evidence and also undertakings by the Secretary of State that he would be medically examined prior to removal; that he would be accompanied by a medical escort; and that the Home Office would inform the French immigration authorities of his medical condition. It concluded that what was proposed for the applicant was not of sufficient severity to breach Article 3.

> One has to remember that epilepsy is not a condition which is new to this applicant or by any means an unusual one for him or his family to deal with. What is threatened is a journey to France which will take less than an hour in the aeroplane, following a medical examination and in the presence of a medical escort. A journey moreover to French authorities who will have been warned of this man's condition.[170]

Whilst it has not yet occurred in practice, it has been held that, in principle, it is possible for an Article 3 claim to succeed where a claimant alleges that he or she would commit suicide if removed if it can be shown that there is a real risk of

---

[165] *Ibid*, at [88].
[166] *Ibid*, at [90].
[167] *R (on the application of Borak) v Secretary of State for the Home Department* [2005] EWCA Civ 110.
[168] *J v Secretary of State for the Home Department* [2005] EWCA Civ 629 at [17].
[169] *R (Lamanovs) v Secretary of State for the Home Department* [2001] EWCA Civ 1239.
[170] *Ibid*, at [16]. See also *X*, above n 7.

suicide.[171] A question of importance is whether the claimant's fear of ill-treatment in the receiving state upon which the risk of suicide is said to be based is objectively well founded.

> If the fear is not well-founded, that will tend to weigh against there being a real risk that the removal will be in breach of art 3.[172]

It is also relevant to consider whether the removing and/or the receiving state has effective mechanisms to reduce the risk of suicide. If there are effective mechanisms, that too will weigh heavily against a claim that removal will violate Article 3.[173]

Secondly, it may be that the medical treatment and care available in the destination state is inadequate. However, it has been held that Article 3 does not require contracting states to undertake the obligation of providing aliens indefinitely with medical treatment lacking in their home countries. This is so even where, in the absence of medical treatment, the life of the would-be immigrant would be significantly shortened.[174] The question which must be asked in such cases is whether the present state of the claimant's health is such that, on humanitarian grounds, he or she ought not to be expelled unless it can be shown that the medical and social facilities needed are actually available to him or her in the receiving state.[175]

This principle was established and applied by the House of Lords in N,[176] where the appellant had arrived in the United Kingdom from Uganda in 1998 and was shortly after diagnosed as HIV positive, with an AIDS-defining illness. As a result of medication and medical treatment over a lengthy period, her condition improved. Her doctors advised that if such treatment continued, she would remain well for decades. Following the refusal of her asylum application, she argued that to return her to Uganda would be a breach of her rights under Article 3. Their Lordships unanimously concluded that her removal to Uganda would not violate Article 3.

> So long as she continues to take the treatment she will remain healthy and she will have several decades of good health to look forward to. Her present condition cannot be said to be critical. She is fit to travel, and will remain fit if and so long as she can obtain the treatment that she needs when she returns to Uganda. The evidence is that the treatment she needs is available there, albeit at considerable cost. She also still has relatives there, although her position is that none of them would be willing and able to accommodate and take care of her.[177]

---

[171] *J*, above n 168, at [29].

[172] *Ibid*, at [30].

[173] *Ibid*, at [31]. See also *R (on the application of Kurtolli) v Secretary of State for the Home Department* [2003] EWHC (Admin) 2744.

[174] *N*, above n 158.

[175] *Ibid*. Their Lordships held that in *D v United Kingdom* (1997) 24 EHRR 425 it was the fact that the claimant was already terminally ill while still present in the territory of the receiving state that made his case exceptional; and in *BB v France*, 9 March 1998, Commission, it was the facts that the infection had already reached an advanced stage, necessitating repeated stays in hospital, and that the care facilities in the receiving country were precarious that made the case exceptional.

[176] *Ibid*.

[177] *Ibid*, at [51] per Lord Hope.

10.2.2 Conditions of Detention

If an individual subject to deportation is likely to be detained by the destination state on his or her return, the conditions of detention in the destination state may give rise to an Article 3 claim. Sometimes it is difficult for the claimant to satisfy the court that the law will be applied and imprisonment will result.[178] In *Mohammed Adam*[179] the Court of Appeal held that there must be a real risk that failure to do military service would be discovered on the claimant's return but also held that to place a burden on the claimant to show that there was a real risk of a fine and up to three years imprisonment was unfair. It held that the evidential burden had passed to the Home Office to produce the relevant evidence to show that there was no real risk that the penalties prescribed by law would be exacted.[180] Nevertheless, once it is established that imprisonment is a real risk, conditions in which a prisoner is detained can be so unsatisfactory as to constitute inhuman or degrading treatment within the meaning of Article 3 even though there is no intention on the part of the authorities to humiliate or debase the victim.[181] When assessing conditions of detention, account also has to be taken of the cumulative effect of these conditions.[182]

Conditions of detention in Russian prisons were at issue in *Batayav*.[183] It was necessary for the claimant to demonstrate substantial grounds for believing that there was a real risk of ill-treatment of the requisite degree of severity by pointing to a consistent pattern of gross and systemic violation of rights under Article 3.[184]

> To establish his case he does not need to refer to evidence specific to his own circumstances, but rather to the evidence bearing on the class of case of which he is a member; in other words . . . to the evidence showing the conditions faced generally by persons incarcerated in the Russian prison system.[185]

The Court of Appeal took particular note of the judgment of the European Court in *Kalashnikov v Russia*,[186] where a violation of Article 3 had been found in relation to conditions of detention and the Russian Federation had admitted that such conditions applied to most detainees in Russia. It concluded that this established that any person held in a Russian prison at this time was at real risk of degrading treatment and that there was a consistent pattern of gross and systemic, even if not intentional, violations of human rights of those detained in Russian prisons.[187] Therefore, there was a real risk the claimant would be subjected to degrading treatment and his return

---

[178] See, eg *Ngene v Secretary of State for the Home Department* [2002] EWCA Civ 185.
[179] *Mohammed Adam v Secretary of State for the Home Department* [2003] EWCA Civ 265.
[180] *Ibid*, at [12] and [14].
[181] *Batayav v The Secretary of State for the Home Department*, Court of Appeal, 5 November 2003 at [11] in reliance upon *Peers v Greece* (2001) 33 EHRR 1192.
[182] *Ibid*, at [13] in reliance upon *Dougoz v Greece* (2001) 34 EHRR 1480 at [45].
[183] Above n 51.
[184] *Ibid*, at [7].
[185] *Ibid*, at [23].
[186] (2002) 36 EHRR 587.
[187] *Ibid*, at [25].

to Russia was prima facie unlawful.[188] However, given the submission of fresh evidence concerning an improvement in conditions, the case was remitted to a freshly constituted tribunal. It found that conditions had improved to the extent that it was not necessarily a breach of Article 3 to return the claimant to the Russian Federation. This conclusion was upheld on appeal by the Court of Appeal.[189]

10.2.3 Legal Restrictions on Homosexuality

Returning a homosexual to a country where homosexuality is illegal has been held not to engage Article 3. In Z[190] the Court of Appeal explained that it was possible that treatment aimed at a particular sexual group could engage Article 3 but the mere existence of a law prohibiting particular types of sexual conduct in private amongst adults did not.[191] Similarly, in S,[192] which concerned return to Kosovo, the Administrative Court held that Article 3 could not be invoked as a guarantee against the risk that prejudice would occur. 'Social consequences will only occur if the claimant's sexual orientation becomes public.'[193]

10.2.4 Ill-treatment by Non-state Actors: Sufficiency of State Protection

In order for Article 3 to be engaged by a proposed deportation, it is not necessary for the real risk of ill-treatment in the destination state to emanate from state actors.[194] However, where the risk emanates from non-state actors, any harm inflicted by such actors will not constitute Article 3 ill-treatment unless, in addition, the state has failed to provide reasonable protection.[195] Article 3 requires a state to provide machinery to deter a violation of that article which attains a satisfactory degree of effectiveness. The reasoning in *Osman*[196] applies equally to Article 3. This does not require a state to guarantee safety, but it is expected to take reasonable measures to make the necessary protection available.[197] The focus must not just be on willingness to provide protection but also on the state's ability to do so.

> [I]t is no answer that a state is doing its incompetent best if it nevertheless falls below the appropriate standard. One has to ask whether the state is failing to perform its basic function of protecting its citizens. Does the writ of law run or not?[198]

---

[188] *Ibid*, at [27]. See also *R (on the application of Bahrami) v Secretary of State for the Home Department*, Administrative Court, 22 June 2003; *R (on the application of Mbanjabahizi) v Immigration Appeal Tribunal*, Administrative Court, 10 June 2004.
[189] *Batayav*, above n 51.
[190] Above n 15.
[191] *Ibid*, at [16]. The Court of Appeal also considered Art 8.
[192] *R (on the application of S) v Secretary of State for the Home Department* [2003] EWHC (Admin) 352.
[193] At [22]. See also *Mudarikwa v Secretary of State for the Home Department* [2003] EWCA Civ 583.
[194] *R (on the application of Bagdanavicius) v Secretary of State for the Home Department* [2005] UKHL 38, [2005] 2 WLR 1359.
[195] *Ibid*.
[196] Above n 52.
[197] *McPherson*, above n 47, at [36]–[39] per Arden LJ in reliance upon *X and Y v Netherlands* (1985) EHRR 235 at 241 and *A v United Kingdom* (1998) 27 EHRR 611 at 629 at [22].
[198] *Atkinson v Secretary of State for the Home Department* [2004] EWCA Civ 846, [2004] ACD 71.

Such claims have been made in a variety of contexts. In *McPherson*[199] the claimant's Article 3 argument related to her fear of renewed and serious personal violence on the part of a man who had repeatedly assaulted her in earlier years. The Court of Appeal held that it was not enough for the claimant to show that the sanctions imposed for offences against the person under the criminal law of Jamaica were ineffective as in the context of domestic violence a state can provide effective measures of a different nature.[200] Arden LJ concluded as follows:

> Accordingly, to be 'effective', measures for the purposes of art 3 must be those which attain an adequate degree of efficacy in practice as well as exist in theory. If the appellant were able to show to the requisite standard of proof that the remedies provided under the law of Jamaica against domestic violence are unlikely to be an effective deterrent, in my judgment she would have shown that her removal from the United Kingdom to Jamaica would violate her rights under art 3 . . .[201]

In *Bagdanavicius*[202] the claimants claimed persistent harassment in Lithuania due to the husband's Roma origin. They also claimed the police provided ineffective protection due to discrimination against Roma. The House of Lords unanimously found that, although the claimants were at real risk of serious injury by non-state agents, Lithuania provided a reasonable level of protection against violence of the sort threatened and there would be no violation of Article 3 if they were returned to Lithuania.

Gang-related violence was the subject of two cases concerning proposed deportations to Jamaica. In *A*[203] the Court of Appeal concluded that return of the claimant, a suspected informer, would involve a real risk of Article 3 treatment regardless of her efforts to relocate and protect her identity. In *Britton*[204] the Court of Appeal remitted the case to the Immigration Appeals Tribunal but observed that the fact that law enforcement and security forces in Jamaica were overzealous did not mean that they exerted effective control, nor did the fact that they used armed response when apprehending criminal suspects.[205]

---

[199] Above n 47.
[200] *Ibid*, at [32]–[35] per Arden LJ.
[201] *Ibid*, at [38]. Sedley LJ agreed at [22], as did Aldous LJ at [41]. The appeal was allowed and the case remitted to another adjudicator. See also *P v Secretary of State for the Home Department* [2004] EWCA Civ 1640.
[202] Above n 194.
[203] *A* [2003], above n 5.
[204] *Britton v Secretary of State for the Home Department* [2003] EWCA Civ 227.
[205] *Ibid*, at [20]. See also *Atkinson*, above n 198. As to other claims under this head, see *R (on the application of Tataw) v Immigration Appeal Tribunal* [2003] EWCA Civ 925 in which the claimant argued return to Cameroon to face female circumcision would engage Art 3; and *R (on the application of Bazdoaca) v Secretary of State for the Home Department* [2004] EWHC Admin 2054 in which the claimant argued the persecution he faced in Moldova as a homosexual engaged Art 3.

11. Duty to Investigate

Finally, it is clear that the positive duty under Article 3 also encompasses a procedural duty to investigate where it is arguable that there has been a breach of the article.[206] This ensures that accountability for a breach of Article 3 is established either in order that those who suffered thereby may be appropriately compensated, or in an attempt to ensure that such conduct does not reoccur.[207] It appears that the duty is similar, if not identical, to that under Article 2.[208] However, where the breach of Article 3 is continuing, the primary positive obligation of the state is to terminate the breach, the investigation to take place only when the breach has occurred and is over.[209]

Given that the duty to investigate under Article 2 arises where life-threatening injuries have occurred[210], the majority of claims have proceeded via the Article 2 route. For example, in *Wright*,[211] where a prisoner had died in his cell as a result of an asthma attack, the Administrative Court found Articles 2 and 3 engaged. With respect to Article 3, it found that the prisoner suffered from a serious asthmatic condition and that the medical treatment he had received was seriously deficient, and in the minutes leading up to his death he must have endured considerable pain and suffering.

> To leave a sick man locked in his cell and exposed to the risk of such pain and suffering might arguably be characterised as inhuman treatment.[212]

The Secretary of State was ordered to set up an independent investigation into the circumstances of the death.[213]

By contrast, in *Green*[214] only Lord Scott found that Article 2 was engaged. The majority proceeded on the assumption that Article 3 was engaged without exploring its precise ambit in this context or deciding whether Article 2 might also have been invoked. Briefly, the case concerned an investigation conducted by the Police Complaints Authority (PCA) following the claimant's serious injury when he was hit by an unmarked police car. The PCA originally informed the claimant that it did not propose to bring disciplinary proceedings against any officer. However, following an admission of error by the PCA, it undertook to look afresh at all the evidence. The claimant requested disclosure of all statements and evidence in possession of the

---

[206] *R (on the application of Green) v Police Complaints Authority* [2004] UKHL 6, [2004] 1 WLR 725; *R (on the application of Wright) v Secretary of State for the Home Department* [2001] EWHC (Admin) 520, (2001) 62 BMR 16; *R (on the application of Al-Skeini) v Secretary of State for Defence* [2004] EWHC (Admin) 2911; *Spinks*, above n 94.
[207] *Spinks, ibid*, at [31].
[208] *Green, Wright* and *Al-Skeini*, above n 206; *Spinks*, above n 94.
[209] *Spinks, ibid*, at [30].
[210] *R (on the application of Amin (Imtiaz) v Secretary of State for the Home Department* [2003] UKHL 51, [2004] 1 AC 653.
[211] Above n 206.
[212] *Ibid*, at [56].
[213] *Ibid*, at [67].
[214] Above n 206.

PCA. The PCA declined. The House of Lords held that an effective investigation required proper procedures for ensuring accountability of agents of the state so as to maintain public confidence and allay the legitimate concerns that arose from the use of lethal force.[215] However, it found the degree of the involvement of the claimant in the investigation sufficient to safeguard his legitimate interests and meet the requirements of Article 3.[216]

[215] *Ibid*, at [59] per Lord Rodger in reliance upon *Amin*, above n 210.
[216] *Ibid*, at [63] per Lord Rodger.

Article 5: The Right to Liberty and Security

1. Introduction

Article 5 is

> concerned that deprivation of liberty should be properly imposed, its lawfulness open to challenge so that a person unlawfully detained may be set free, and that the place of detention conforms to the purpose for which it is imposed.[1]

In addition to Article 5, the personal freedom of the individual is also reflected in the

> long libertarian tradition of English law, dating back to chapter 39 of Magna Carta 1215, given effect in the ancient remedy of habeas corpus, declared in the Petition of Right 1628, upheld in a series of landmark decisions down the centuries and embodied in the substance and procedure of the law to our own day.[2]

The importance of Article 5 is demonstrated by its absolute nature save only for the circumstances expressly provided for by Article 5(1) and also by the very limited deference the courts have afforded where this right is in issue.[3] Observations as to the prime importance of personal freedom are often made; for example, in *A v Secretary of State for the Home Department* Lord Hope commented that it was impossible ever to overstate the importance of the right to liberty in a democracy.[4]

Deference to the primary decision maker is something that is rarely mentioned in Article 5 cases. This reflects the importance with which the right is regarded, its

---

[1] *R (on the application of Munjaz) v Mersey Care NHS Trust* [2003] EWCA Civ 1036, [2004] QB 395 at [70]. See also *P v Nottinghamshire Healthcare NHS Trust* [2003] EWHC (Admin) 1782, [2003] ACD 403.
[2] *A v Secretary of State for the Home Department* [2004] UKHL 56, [2005] 2 AC 68 at [36] per Lord Bingham. See also *R v East London and the City Mental Health NHS Trust, ex p von Brandenburg* [2003] UKHL 58, [2004] 2 AC 280 at [6].
[3] See, eg the comments of Lord Hope in *A v Secretary of State, ibid*, at [108].
[4] *Ibid*, at [100]. See also Lord Nicholls at [74], Lord Hoffmann at [88] and Lord Bingham at [36].

narrow construction and the fact that many of its protections are absolute. In *Lichniak*[5] brief mention was made of the fact that the mandatory life sentence for murder represented the settled will of a democratic assembly and a degree of deference was due to the judgment of a democratic assembly on how a particular social problem was best tackled.[6] Occasionally there are also references to resources constraints. For example, in *Cawser*[7] the Court of Appeal held that the Home Secretary could not be under an absolute duty to provide particular courses to all prisoners who wanted them in order to maximise chances of release. However, as the case law under Article 5(4) demonstrates, resources arguments are generally given short shrift, the Court of Appeal holding in *Noorkoiv*[8] that if further resources were necessary to avert a breach of Article 5(4), these must be provided.

2. What Constitutes a Deprivation of Liberty?

It is usually clear whether or not there has been a deprivation of liberty to which Article 5 applies. Obvious examples include imprisonment following a conviction, arrest on reasonable suspicion of having committed an offence and detention in a secure hospital. However, occasionally it is difficult to discern on which side of the line facts fall.[9] Where the question is whether or not the detention falls within Article 5, the burden of proof is on the claimant.[10]

2.1 Restrictions on Liberty of Movement

It is clear that restrictions on liberty of movement fall within Article 2 of Protocol No.4 and do not engage Article 5.[11] The distinction is one of degree or intensity of restrictions, not of nature or substance. The court must start with the concrete or actual situation of the individual concerned and take account of a range of criteria such as type, duration, effects and manner of implementation of the measure in question. Account must also be taken of the cumulative effect of the various restrictions.[12] Finally, the purpose of any measures of restriction is a relevant consideration.

---

[5] *R v Lichniak* [2002] UKHL 47, [2003] 1 AC 903.
[6] *Ibid*, at [14] per Lord Bingham.
[7] *R (Cawser) v Secretary of State for the Home Department* [2003] EWHC Civ 1522, [2004] UKHRR 101.
[8] *R v Secretary of State for the Home Department, ex p Noorkoiv* [2002] EWCA Civ 770, [2002] 1 WLR 3284 at [44].
[9] In *R (on the application of Saadi) v Secretary of State for the Home Department* [2002] UKHL 41, [2002] 1 WLR 3131 it was held that asylum seekers at Oakington Reception Centre were deprived of their liberty as they could not leave the centre and had to conform to rules as to mealtimes and being in their rooms at night.
[10] *Austin v Metropolitan Police Commissioner* [2005] EWHC (QB) 480, [2005] HRLR 20.
[11] *Secretary of State for the Home Department v Mental Health Review Tribunal 'PH'* [2002] EWCA Civ 1868 at [14] in reliance upon *Guzzardi v Italy* (1980) 3 EHRR 333; *Ashingdane v United Kingdom* (1985) 7 EHRR 528; *HM v Switzerland*, Judgment of 26 February 2002.
[12] *Ibid*, at [15].

If the measures are taken principally in the interests of the individual who is being restricted, they may well be regarded as not amounting to a deprivation of liberty.[13]

An example of the distinction was shown in *PH*.[14] The Mental Health Review Tribunal had directed that PH be discharged subject to a number of conditions. The Secretary of State argued that the conditions imposed, in particular that he reside at specialist accommodation with security and not leave without an escort, were so restrictive as to deprive him of his liberty. The Court of Appeal held that the security measures and escorts were imposed to protect PH himself and it did not accept that the conditions inevitably meant that PH would be in a regime so restrictive that he would be deprived of his liberty.[15] However, the Administrative Court has been careful to confine this judgment to its own facts. In *G*[16] the court observed that any detention of a mentally ill person for treatment may be regarded as in his best interests, but that did not prevent such detention being a deprivation of liberty.[17]

2.2 Parents and Children

Commonly parents exercise restrictions upon the movement of their children and ordinary, acceptable parental restrictions do not engage Article 5.[18] By analogy with this principle, it was argued in *Re K*[19] that a secure accommodation order made in relation to a child under the Children Act 1989 did not engage Article 5. A majority of the Court of Appeal disagreed, holding that there was a point at which one had to stand back and ask whether or not this was within ordinary acceptable parental restrictions upon the movements of a child or whether it required justification.[20] It concluded that Article 5 was engaged, doubting whether the rights and responsibilities of a parent would cover such an exercise of parental authority for nearly two years.[21]

---

[13] *Ibid*, at [16] in reliance upon *Nielsen v Denmark* (1988) EHRR 175; *HM v Switzerland*, Judgment of 26 February 2002.

[14] *Ibid*.

[15] *Ibid*, at [23]–[25]. It was also suggested in *Austin*, above n 10, that if the police detention of a crowd during a demonstration had been for the protection of the members of the crowd themselves, this would not be a deprivation of liberty.

[16] *R (on the application of G) v Mental Health Review Tribunal*[2004] EWHC (Admin) 2193.

[17] at [13] in reliance upon *Ashingdane*, above n 11. See also *R (on the application of Secretary of State for the Home Department) v Mental Health Review Tribunal* [2004] EWHC (Admin) 2194. In *R (on the application of Davies) v South Devon Magistrates' Court*, Divisional Court, 21 December 2004, it was held that the condition of release on licence that the claimant reside at a bail hostel and only leave under escort or with express permission did not amount to a deprivation of liberty.

[18] *Re K (a child) (secure accommodation order: right to liberty)* [2001] 2 All ER 719 in reliance upon *Nielsen v Denmark* (1988) 11 EHRR 175 and *Family T v Austria* (1990) 64 DR 176 at 180.

[19] *Ibid*.

[20] *Ibid*, at [28] per Dame Butler Sloss.

[21] *Ibid*, at [29] per Dame Butler Sloss. See also the judgment of Judge LJ at [102]–[104]. Support for the conclusion was also found in *Koniarska v UK* 12 October 2000. Thorpe LJ dissented on this point, holding that the deprivation of liberty was a necessary consequence of an exercise of parental responsibility for the protection and promotion of his welfare. At [61].

2.3 Stop and Search

Whilst an arrest clearly triggers Article 5 protection, the exercise of police powers that fall short of arrest but nonetheless prevent an individual from doing what he or she likes, such as stop and search, fall into a grey area. In *Gillan*[22] the Court of Appeal concluded that it was not necessary to decide the point as what had occurred was justifiable under Article 5. Nevertheless, it held that, given the existence of Article 2 of Protocol No 4, the ambit of Article 5 should be construed strictly.[23] Taking into account the likely limited nature of any infringement of Article 5 in a normal stop and search, the fact that the main aim would not be to deprive an individual of his liberty but to effect a verification, and the existence of Article 2 of Protocol No 4, it concluded the better view was that a short detainment pursuant to a stop-and-search power would normally fall outside Article 5.[24]

In *Laporte*[25] the facts were significantly different. The claimant was one of about 120 passengers on one of three coaches travelling from London to RAF Fairford in Gloucestershire to join a demonstration there against the US-led war in Iraq. Some way short of Fairford the coaches were stopped by the police and searched. The coaches and passengers were then sent back to London under police escort without being allowed to stop on the way—a journey of two and a half hours. The Administrative Court held that this went far beyond transitory detention and was in violation of Article 5. The Court of Appeal dismissed the subsequent appeal without considering Article 5 as it found the detention to be unlawful by reference to the common law.[26]

Nevertheless, a similar issue arose in *Austin*[27] and the Divisional Court reached a positive conclusion on Article 5. The case concerned a demonstration organised in London on May Day 2001. At about 2 pm a crowd of demonstrators marched into Oxford Circus, central London, from Regent Street. Later in the afternoon others entered or tried to enter from all directions so that, by the end of the day, some 3,000 people were within the Circus. In addition, there were crowds of thousands outside it to the north of Oxford Street and on the west side in Oxford Street itself. The organisers had given no notice to police and refused to cooperate with them. The crowd who entered the Circus at 2 pm were, for the most part, prevented from leaving. The police stood in lines across the exits. From about 2.20 pm people could leave only with the permission of the police, but many were prevented from leaving for a period of over seven hours. The Divisional Court stated that if the only reason why the police had detained the crowd had been for the temporary protection of the members of the crowd themselves, this would not be a deprivation of liberty. However, it found that this was not the case and that there was a deprivation of liberty within the meaning of Article 5.

---

[22] *R (on the application of Gillan) v The Commissioner of Police for the Metropolis* [2004] EWCA Civ 1067, [2005] QB 388.
[23] *Ibid*, at [45]
[24] *Ibid*, at [46] in reliance upon *Guzzardi*, above n 11.
[25] *R (on the application of Laporte) v Chief Constable of Gloucestershire Constabulary* [2004] EWCA Civ 1639, [2005] QB 678.
[26] *Ibid*, at [56].
[27] Above n 10.

3. Article 5(1)

Article 5(1) guarantees liberty and security of person. The concepts of liberty and security are linked with the broad aim of protecting the person against an arrest or detention which is arbitrary.[28] Continued detention can be justified in a given case only if there are specific indications of a genuine requirement of public interest which, notwithstanding the presumption of innocence, outweighs the rule of respect for individual liberty.[29] To this end, Article 5(1) provides a right to liberty which is subject to six specified exceptions[30] and to two overriding requirements.[31] The first requirement is that any deprivation of liberty must be in accordance with a procedure prescribed by law. The second requirement is that it must be lawful.[32] If these requirements are met, Article 5(1) does not limit the period for which a person can be detained.[33]

3.1 Procedure Prescribed by Law

Any deprivation of liberty must be in accordance with a procedure prescribed by law. The notion underlying these words in Article 5(1) is one of fair and proper procedure, namely that any measure depriving a person of his liberty should issue from and be executed by an appropriate authority, and the procedure under which this is done should not be arbitrary.[34] Errors in what is said by counsel or a judge will not, of themselves, result in a procedure being unlawful. In contrast, defects such as a failure to give the individual an opportunity to be heard, or an opportunity properly to consider and to respond to the case or evidence against him, may lead to an infringement of Article 5(1).[35] Often this question is combined with the question of whether detention is lawful.

3.2 Lawful

Any deprivation of liberty under Article 5(1) must also be lawful. The first question is whether the detention is lawful under domestic law. Any detention which is unlawful in domestic law will automatically be unlawful under Article 5(1). The second question is whether, assuming that the detention is lawful under domestic law, it

---

[28] *R v Crown Court at Leeds, ex p Wardle* [2001] UKHL 12, [2001] 2 WLR 865 at [83] per Lord Hope in reliance upon *Bozano v France* (1986) 9 EHRR 297 at [54]; *Amuur v France* (1996) 22 EHRR 533 at [50].
[29] *Ibid.*
[30] This is an exhaustive list. See *Re K*, above n 18, at [33] per Dame Butler Sloss in reliance upon *Engel v Netherlands (No.1)* (1976) 1 EHRR 647 at [57].
[31] Where the detention falls within Art 5, the burden of proof is on the claimant to bring the facts within one of the exceptions. See *Austin*, above n 10.
[32] *Ibid*, in reliance upon *R v Governor of Brockhill Prison, ex p Evans (No.2)* [2001] 2 AC 19.
[33] *Flynn v HM Advocate* [2004] UKPC D1, [2004] HRLR 17.
[34] *Anderson v Scottish Ministers* [2001] UKPC D5, [2003] 2 AC 602 at [25] per Lord Hope in reliance upon *Winterwerp v The Netherlands* (1979) 2 EHRR 387 at 405.
[35] *R (on the application of A) v Harrow Crown Court* [2003] EWHC (Admin) 2020 at [16]. See also *Horgan v Horgan* [2002] EWCA Civ 1371; *Zakharov v White* [2003] EWHC (Ch) 2463.

nevertheless complies with the general requirements of the Convention. These are based upon the principle that any restriction on human rights and fundamental freedoms must be prescribed by law. This principle includes the requirements that the domestic law must be sufficiently accessible to the individual and that it must be sufficiently precise to enable the individual to foresee the consequences of the restriction. The third question is whether, again assuming that the detention is lawful under domestic law, it is nevertheless open to criticism on the ground that it is arbitrary because, for example, it was resorted to in bad faith or was not proportionate.[36]

3.2.1 Lawful under Domestic Law

Any detention which is unlawful in domestic law will automatically be unlawful under Article 5(1).[37] However, detention does not automatically become unlawful in domestic law merely because the European Court of Human Rights has found a particular domestic practice contrary to the Convention.[38] In addition, if an individual is committed to detention by an ultra vires order, it has been held that the order is legally effective unless and until it is set aside and the detention consequential on that order is lawful as a matter of domestic law.[39]

3.2.2 Prescribed by Law

Even if detention is lawful under domestic law, the domestic law must be sufficiently accessible to the individual and sufficiently precise to enable the individual to forsee the consequences of the restriction.[40] In *Wardle*[41] it was argued that the substitution of a fresh custody time limit in relation to a new charge was not prescribed by law. A majority of the House of Lords disagreed holding that if a fresh custody time limit was to be substituted, the procedure under which this was to be done was laid down by statute and the regulation defined the length of the substituted time limit.[42]

It may only be necessary to point to the empowering statute rather than any policy or procedure which has been derived from it. For example, in *Gillan*[43] the police had carried out their stop and search in reliance upon an authorisation made under section 44 of the Terrorism Act 2000 by the Assistant Commissioner of the Metropolitan Police and its subsequent confirmation by the Secretary of State. It was argued that what took place was not in accordance with a procedure prescribed by

---

[36] *Evans*, above n 32, per Lord Hope in reliance upon *Sunday Times v United Kingdom* (1979–80) 2 EHRR 245; *Zamir v United Kingdom* (1985) 40 DR 42 at [90]–[91]; *Engel v Netherlands* [1976] 1 EHRR 647 at [58]; *Tsirlis and Kouloumpas v Greece* [1997] 25 EHRR 198 at [56]. See also *Anderson*, above n 34, at [22] per Lord Hope.

[37] *Ibid.*

[38] *R (on the application of Middleton) v Secretary of State for the Home Department* [2003] EWHC (Admin) 315.

[39] *A*, above n 35.

[40] *Evans*, above n 32. See also *Nadarajah v Secretary of State for the Home Department* [2003] EWCA Civ 1768 at [64]–[65].

[41] Above n 28.

[42] *Ibid*, at [88] per Lord Hope. See also Lord Clyde at [107] and Lord Slynn at [34], and *Anderson*, above n 34.

[43] Above n 22.

law because the law was not published. The Court of Appeal did not agree, holding that the law that was under criticism was the statute, not the authorisation.

> [W]hile the authorisations and their confirmation are not published because not unreasonably it is considered publication could damage the effectiveness of the stop and search powers and as the individual who is stopped has the right to a written statement under s 45(5), in this context the lack of publication does not mean that what occurred was not a procedure prescribed by law.[44]

Nevertheless, it found that the use of the powers to police a protest was unlawful.[45]

However, the judgment of the Court of Appeal in *Nadarajah*[46] indicates that it is necessary for policies to be accessible and foreseeable. Here the policy of the immigration service was to not detain those to be imminently removed where proceedings challenging the right to remove had been instituted. However, it was also the policy to disregard information from those acting for asylum seekers that proceedings were about to be initiated. The latter aspect of the policy was not known or accessible, and the Court of Appeal therefore concluded that the detention was not lawful.[47]

3.2.3 Not Arbitrary

Finally, even if detention is lawful under domestic law, it is considered to be unlawful if it is arbitrary because, for example, it is resorted to in bad faith or is not proportionate.[48] In determining the arbitrariness of any detention, regard must be had to the legitimacy of the aim of detention and the proportionality of the detention in relation to that aim.[49] Detention does not become arbitrary simply because one cannot tell whether it will last longer than it would have done under the system that has been superseded.[50]

3.3 Article 5(1)(a): Conviction by a Competent Court

Article 5(1)(a) allows for the lawful detention of a person after conviction by a competent court.

3.3.1 Causal Link

There must be a causal link between the conviction and the subsequent detention. This has been of particular concern in relation to life sentences where the release date is not set by the sentencing court. Once the tariff period has expired, it is up to the Parole Board to decide whether or not the prisoner should be released. It has been held that the period of detention between the expiry of the tariff period and the

---

[44] *Ibid*, at [49].
[45] *Ibid*, at [56].
[46] Above n 40.
[47] *Ibid*, at [66]–[67].
[48] *Evans*, above n 32.
[49] *Lichniak*, above n 5, at [16] per Lord Bingham.
[50] *Flynn*, above n 33, at [87] per Lord Rodger.

decision of the Parole Board is not incompatible with Article 5(1)(a), although it must be subject to control through Article 5(4).[51]

The position is slightly more complicated where it is necessary for a prisoner to attend a treatment programme before the Parole Board will consider his or her release. For example, in *Cawser*[52] the prisoner complained that he had to wait a long time for his place on the Extended Sex Offender Treatment Programme and as a result his release date was substantially delayed because the Parole Board was precluded from directing a life prisoner's release unless it was satisfied that it was no longer necessary for the protection of the public that the prisoner should be confined.

The Court of Appeal concluded that detention would not become unlawful under Article 5(1)(a) even if no provision were made for such courses.[53] The causal link was not broken by the delay in providing (or a failure to provide) treatment which itself may or may not thereafter have served to establish the absence of continuing dangerousness.[54]

> The Secretary of State could hardly be under an absolute duty to devise and provide courses for all who want them, and, moreover, to do so early enough in the prisoner's sentence to maximise his hope of release on or very soon after his tariff expiry date.[55]

Laws LJ noted that there was a possibility that the Secretary of State might impose a condition so hard of fulfilment that continued detention for failure to meet the condition ought no longer to be regarded as justified by the original sentence, but this could not arise by reference to any judicial perception as to scarce resources.[56] Arden LJ dissented on this point, holding that in an exceptional case the failure by the Secretary of State to provide a particular prisoner with an appropriate treatment course which in practice is a condition of release may, if sufficiently prolonged, break the causal link and render the detention unlawful.[57]

Detention is no longer lawful once the date for release has passed. In *Evans*[58] the respondent was entitled to a reduction in the actual period to be served in prison due to the time she spent in prison before trial. The governor calculated the date in accordance with what he thought the law to be, but the High Court subsequently held that this was not the law and her release date should have been earlier. The House of Lords concluded that her detention after the correct date was unlawful and contrary to Article 5(1)(a).

3.3.2 Disproportionate Period of Detention

It has also been argued that the imposition of a life sentence in certain circumstances is contrary to Article 5(1)(a) because it is disproportionate. For example, in

---

[51] *Noorkoiv*, above n 8. See also *R (on the application of Smith) v Parole Board* [2005] UKHL 1, [2005] 1 WLR 350.
[52] Above n 7.
[53] *Ibid*, at [31] per Simon Brown LJ.
[54] *Ibid*, at [32] per Simon Brown LJ.
[55] *Ibid*, at [34] per Simon Brown LJ.
[56] *Ibid*, at [44].
[57] *Ibid*, at [45]–[54] in reliance upon *Van Droogenbroek v Belgium* (1982) 4 EHRR 443 at [40].
[58] Above n 32.

Lichniak[59] it was argued that the mandatory life sentence for murder[60] was arbitrary and disproportionate as it required the same sentence to be passed on all convicted murderers whatever the facts of the case or the circumstances of the offender, and irrespective of whether they were thought to present a danger to the public or not. The House of Lords held that if it was the case that, on imposition of a mandatory life sentence, the convicted murderer forfeited his liberty to the state for the rest of his days, this would violate Article 5 as being arbitrary and disproportionate.[61] However, it had been concluded in *Anderson*[62] that such was not the effect of the sentence. The punitive element of the sentence was represented by the tariff term, imposed as punishment for the serious crime. The preventative element was represented by the power to continue to detain until the Parole Board considered it safe to release him and also by the power to recall.[63]

Here, having regard to the legitimacy of the aim of the detention and the proportionality of the detention in relation to that aim, and viewing the complaints in the context of their treatment as a whole, the House of Lords concluded that the appellants were not sentenced to an arbitrary, rule-of-thumb term of imprisonment. Lord Bingham concluded as follows:

> Those responsible did their best to match the respective terms to the particular facts and circumstances of each case . . . There is, inevitably, a balance to be struck between the interest of the individual and the interest of society, and I do not think it objectionable, in the case of someone who has once taken life with the intent necessary for murder, to prefer the latter in case of doubt . . . But a prisoner recalled . . . should be in no danger of recall in the absence of any resort to violence.[64]

A different conclusion was reached in relation to the automatic life sentence in *Offen*.[65] This sentence must be imposed for a second serious offence unless the court is of the opinion that there are exceptional circumstances relating to either of the offences or to the offender which justify its not doing so.[66] The Court of Appeal held that there have been and will be cases where the automatic life sentence has and will operate in a disproportionate manner.

> It is easy to find examples of situations where two offences could be committed which were categorised as serious by the section but where it would be wholly disproportionate to impose a life sentence to protect the public.[67]

However, using section 3 of the HRA, this problem was avoided, the Court of Appeal concluding that the Act should be applied so that it did not result in offenders being

---

[59] Above n 5.
[60] Imposed under s 1(1) Murder (Abolition of Death Penalty) Act 1965.
[61] *Lichniak*, above n 5, at [8] per Lord Bingham.
[62] *R (on the application of Anderson) v Secretary of State for the Home Department* [2002] UKHL 46, [2003] 1 AC 837.
[63] *Ibid*, at [8] per Lord Bingham.
[64] *Ibid*, at [16] in reliance upon *V v United Kingdom* (1999) 30 EHRR 121. See also *R v Parchment* [2003] EWCA Crim 2428.
[65] *R v Offen* [2001] 1 WLR 253.
[66] Section 2, Crime (Sentences) Act 1997.
[67] *Ibid*, at [95].

sentenced to life imprisonment when they did not constitute a significant risk to the public.[68]

3.4 Article 5(1)(b): Non-compliance with the Lawful Order of a Court or to Secure the Fulfilment of any Obligation Prescribed by Law

Article 5(1)(b) permits the lawful arrest or detention of a person for non-compliance with the lawful order of a court or in order to secure the fulfilment of any obligation prescribed by law. It has been relied upon to justify arrest under a default warrant for non-payment of a fine,[69] detention for contempt of court[70] and a condition of bail requiring the defendant during the hours of curfew to present himself at the door of his home if required to do so by a police officer.[71] Although in *Gillan*[72] the Court of Appeal, without finally deciding, had indicated its opinion that stop and search did not engage Article 5, it nevertheless held that if it did, it would be possible for the police to rely upon 5(1)(b). Stopping and searching the two appellants, who were on their way respectively to join and film a demonstration against an arms fair, was in order to secure the fulfilment of any objective prescribed by law—here the prevention of acts of terrorism.[73]

With respect to arbitrariness, it was held in *Chorley Justices*[74] that a condition of bail requiring the defendant during the hours of curfew to present himself at the door of his home if requested to do so by a police officer struck the appropriate balance in the interests of both the individual and society.

> [T]here was a real risk that the Defendant would be deprived of his liberty; in other words, the justices would have been entitled to have him remanded in custody. The ability of the justices, therefore, to impose conditions appropriate to avoid the risks to the public . . . is one which is beneficial not only to the community, but also to the individual Defendant.[75]

3.5 Article 5(1)(c): Reasonable Suspicion of Having Committed an Offence

Article 5(1)(c) permits the lawful arrest or detention of a person effected for the purpose of bringing him before the competent legal authority on reasonable suspicion of having committed an offence or when it is reasonably considered necessary to prevent his committing an offence or fleeing after having done so. In order to have a reasonable suspicion, there must be facts or information to support the suspicion which

---

[68] *Ibid*, at [97]. See also *R v Kelly* [2001] EWCA Crim 1751, [2001] Crim LR 836; *R v Drew* [2003] UKHL 25, [2003] 1 WLR 1213.
[69] *Henderson v Chief Constable of Cleveland Constabulary* [2001] EWCA Civ 335. See generally D van Zyl Smit and A Ashworth, 'Disproportionate Sentences as Human Rights Violations' (2004) 67 *MLR* 541.
[70] *Horgan*, above n 35.
[71] *R (on the application of the Crown Prosecution Service) v Chorley Justices* [2002] EWHC (Admin) 2163.
[72] Above n 22.
[73] at [49].
[74] Above n 71.
[75] *Ibid*, at [33].

would satisfy an objective observer that the person concerned may have committed the offence.[76] 'Facts' must not be given a restrictive meaning, and clearly included is information and information obtained from a third party.[77] Opportunity can amount to reasonable grounds for suspicion, and more than one person can be arrested even if the crime could only have been committed by one person.[78] A person can be arrested and detained in good faith for questioning in order to obtain evidence.[79]

In a crowd situation, it appears there is no need for individual consideration. For example, in *Austin*[80] the police prevented a crowd of approximately 3,000 demonstrators from leaving Oxford Circus. Some were prevented from leaving for a period of over seven hours. The Divisional Court found that the detention fell within Article 5 but that it was also within Article 5(1)(c), as it was imposed with the conditional purpose of arresting those who it would be lawful and practicable to arrest and bring before a judge and to prevent such persons as might be so identified from committing offences of violence. In the opinion of the court, when each claimant came forward and asked to be released, it appeared to the police that all those present within the cordon, including each claimant, were demonstrators and, in the particular circumstances of the case, that meant they also appeared to the police to be about to commit that breach of the peace. However, the court noted that whilst this inference could be properly drawn in this case, it was unlikely to be capable of being drawn in all crowd cases.

At common law there is an additional requirement which must be satisfied even if there are reasonable grounds for suspicion. The officer must exercise his discretion in accordance with *Wednesbury* principles.[81] However, in *Cumming*[82] the Court of Appeal rephrased the test, holding that the court must consider whether or not the decision to arrest is one which no reasonable police officer, applying his mind to the matter, could reasonably take, bearing in mind the effect on the appellant's right to liberty.[83] The more substantial the interference with liberty, the narrower the otherwise generous *Wednesbury* ambit of reasonableness becomes.[84] It is possible that the test might approach one of necessity where the intrusion on a person's liberty is of an egregious or public nature and for a long period or accompanied by harsh treatment.[85] For example, in *Austin*[86] the Divisional Court held that the decision by the police to impose an absolute cordon to control demonstrators in Oxford Circus was a proportionate response by the police to the presence of the crowd.

---

[76] *Cumming v Chief Constable of Northumbria Police* [2003] EWCA Civ 1844, [2004] ACD 42 at [37] in reliance upon *Castorina v Chief Constable of Surrey* [1996] LG Rev Rep 241 and *Fox, Campbell and Hartley v United Kingdom* (1990) 13 EHRR 157.
[77] *Ibid*, at [40].
[78] *Ibid*, at [41] in reliance upon *Hussein v Chong Fook Kam* [1970] AC 942.
[79] *Al Fayed v Commissioner of Police of the Metropolis* [2004] EWCA Civ 1579 at [88] in reliance upon *Brogan v United Kingdom* (1988) 11 EHRR 117 and *Murray v United Kingdom* (1994) 19 EHRR 193.
[80] Above n 10.
[81] *Castorina*, above n 76, at 249.
[82] Above n 76.
[83] *Ibid*, at [43].
[84] *Al Fayed*, above n 79, at [83].
[85] *Ibid*, at [82].
[86] Above n 10.

3.6 Article 5(1)(d): Minors

Article 5(1)(d) permits the detention of a minor by lawful order for the purpose of educational supervision or his lawful detention for the purpose of bringing him before the competent legal authority. The meaning of educational supervision extends far beyond school.

> [I]t involves education in the broad sense, similar . . . to the general development of the child's physical, intellectual, emotional, social and behavioural abilities, all of which have to be encouraged by responsible parents, as part of his upbringing and education, and for this purpose, an appropriate level of supervision of the child to enhance his development, where necessary, by restricting his liberty is permitted.[87]

Education need not be demonstrated to be the sole purpose of the detention; Article 5(1)(d) is satisfied if it is just one of the purposes of the detention. Only where there is no present or reasonably imminent educational provision does the Article 5(1)(d) defence fail.[88]

In K[89] it was argued that a secure accommodation order imposed under section 25 of the Children Act 1989 did not fall within Article 5(1)(d). The Court of Appeal disagreed, holding that K was receiving education which was carefully supervised and from which he was clearly benefiting. In the opinion of the court, it was not necessary for section 25 to refer to education since, by the provisions of the Education Act 1996, education was compulsory for any child under 16, as K was.[90] Judge LJ held that the purpose of the order, and its implementation by the local authority, was to provide the best available environment to enable K's education, both in the narrow and broad senses, under the degree of supervision and control necessary to avoid harm or injury to himself, and to improve his prospects of avoiding both in the long term as well as in the immediate future.[91]

3.7 Article 5(1)(e): Persons of Unsound Mind

Article 5(1)(e) permits the lawful detention of persons for the prevention of the spreading of infectious diseases, and of persons of unsound mind, alcoholics, drug addicts or vagrants. However, it is only in relation the detention of persons of unsound mind that cases have been brought under the HRA.

3.7.1 Minimum Conditions

Three minimum conditions have to be satisfied for there to be lawful detention of persons of unsound mind within the meaning of Article 5(1)(e). These are commonly referred to as the 'Winterwerp criteria'.[92] The individual concerned must be reliably

---

[87] See Re K, above n 18, at [107] per Judge LJ in reliance upon Bouamar v Belgium (1989) 11 EHRR 1 and Koniarska v United Kingdom, Judgment of 12 October 2000.
[88] Ibid, at [64] per Thorpe LJ in reliance upon Bouamar, ibid.
[89] Ibid.
[90] Ibid, at [35]–[36] per Dame Butler-Sloss in reliance upon Koniarsaka v United Kingdom, Judgment of 12 October 2000.
[91] Ibid, at [107].
[92] Winterwerp, above n 34.

shown to be of unsound mind, that is to say, a true mental disorder must be established before a competent authority on the basis of objective medical expertise; the mental disorder must be of a kind or degree warranting compulsory confinement; and the validity of continued confinement depends upon the persistence of such a disorder.[93] It remains for domestic law to lay down the substantive and procedural rules which regulate the detention of persons of unsound mind.[94]

(a) Burden of Proof

The same approach must be applied when considering whether to admit a patient as that which has to be applied when considering discharge. The burden of proof in both instances is on those seeking to detain and can never be imposed on the patient.[95] In *H*[96] the Court of Appeal concluded that sections 72 and 73 of the Mental Health Act 1983 were incompatible with Article 5(1)(e) because the burden of proof was effectively placed on the patient who wished to be discharged to prove that the criteria for admission were not satisfied.[97]

(b) Discharge Subject to Supervision

Particular problems have arisen where a tribunal has ordered the discharge of a patient from detention subject to supervision in the community by a named social worker and named psychiatrist but no social worker or psychiatrist has been available. For example, in *IH*[98] a mental health review tribunal had decided that the appellant could be discharged from detention at a secure hospital provided, inter alia, there was supervision of him by a named social worker and named psychiatrist. The health authority was unable to find a psychiatrist willing to supervise and his detention continued. Although more than two years later another mental health review tribunal decided that it was still appropriate for him to be detained, he contended that his detention between these dates was in breach of Article 5.

The House of Lords held that there was no time when the appellant was unlawfully detained and no breach of Article 5(1)(e).

> There was never a medical consensus, nor did the tribunal find, that the *Winterwerp* criteria were not satisfied. The tribunal considered that the appellant could be satisfactorily treated and supervised in the community if its conditions were met, as it expected, but the alternative, if these conditions proved impossible to meet, was not discharge, either absolutely or subject only to a condition of recall, but continued detention. The appellant was never detained when there were no grounds for detaining him.[99]

---

93 *Anderson*, above n 34, at [26] per Lord Hope quoting from *X v United Kingdom* 4 EHRR 188 at [40]. See also *Luberti v Italy* (1984) 6 EHRR 440 at [27] and *Johnson v UK* (1997) 27 EHRR 296 at [60].
94 *Anderson, ibid*, at [23] per Lord Hope in reliance upon *Winterwerp*, above n 34.
95 *R (on the application of H) v Mental Health Review Tribunal, North & East London Region* [2001] EWCA Civ 415, [2002] QB 1.
96 *Ibid.*
97 The Mental Health Act 1983 (Remedial) Order 2001 came into force in 26 November 2001. Its effect is to reverse the burden of proof in ss 72 and 73 so that a tribunal is now obliged to direct the discharge of a patient unless satisfied that the relevant criteria for detention have been proved.
98 *R v Secretary of State for the Home Department, ex p IH* [2003] UKHL 59, [2004] 2 AC 253.
99 *Ibid*, at [28] per Lord Bingham. See also *H*, above n 95.

It concluded that the health authority only had to use its best endeavours to procure compliance with the conditions laid down by the tribunal and had no power to require any psychiatrist to act in a way which conflicted with the conscientious professional judgment of that psychiatrist.[100]

However, in W[101] the Court of Appeal held that if, although it has used its best endeavours, a health authority is unable to provide the necessary services, the tribunal must think again.

> If, as is likely in the circumstances, it concludes that it is necessary for the patient to remain detained in hospital in order to receive treatment it should record that decision.[102]

(c) Unfit to be Tried

There is a genuine concern that those determined unfit to be tried pursuant to section 4(5) of the Criminal Procedure (Insanity) Act 1964 but who are then found to have committed the act charged and admitted to hospital under a restriction order have not met the *Winterwerp* criteria. This was raised in *Grant*,[103] where the defendant, charged with murder, had been found unfit to be tried. A second jury found that she had committed the act charged and the judge ordered that she be admitted to hospital. Once a person is found to be unfit to be tried there is no further consideration of his or her mental condition. No one is required specifically to address, prior to the person's detention, the question of whether he suffers from a mental disorder sufficiently serious to warrant detention. The Court of Appeal appreciated that the question was one of some difficulty and concluded that, in the circumstances of the present case, it was unnecessary for it to reach any conclusions on the issue since it was satisfied on the facts that the conditions for detention were in fact met.[104]

3.7.2 Public Safety

The Convention allows the persons mentioned in Article 5(1)(e) to be deprived of their liberty because they are a threat to public safety and their own interests may necessitate their detention. The need to protect the public from serious harm is in itself a legitimate reason for the detention of persons of unsound mind, provided always that the conditions set out above are satisfied. In this context, the fair balance which is inherent in the whole of the Convention between the demands of the general interest of the community and the requirements of the protection of the individual's fundamental rights favours the general interests of the community.[105] In *Grant*[106] the Court of Appeal concluded that it was not unreasonable for Parliament to have laid down a mandatory requirement of admission to hospital for a person who has been charged with murder, has been found to have done the act charged but was under a

---

[100] *Ibid*, at [29] per Lord Bingham. This answered the question raised by the Court of Appeal in *R (K) v Camden and Islington Health Authority* [2001] EWCA Civ 240, [2002] QB 198.
[101] *W v Doncaster Metropolitan Borough Council* [2004] EWCA Civ 378, [2004] LGR 743.
[102] *Ibid*, at [50] per Baker LJ.
[103] *R v Grant* [2001] EWCA Crim 2611, [2002] 2 WLR 1409.
[104] *Ibid*, at [54].
[105] *Anderson*, above n 34, at [30] per Lord Hope in reliance upon *Guzzardi*, above n 11 at [98]; *Witold Litwa v Poland* (2000) 33 EHRR 1267 at [60].
[106] Above n 103.

disability so as to be unfit to be tried, and detention in those circumstances was not arbitrary.[107]

In certain circumstances, the objective may not be general public safety but the safety of a section of the public. For example, in *Anderson*[108] one appellant argued that he was a criminal who simply wished to go back to prison rather than remain in a secure hospital. The Privy Council held that detention could also be justified on the ground of protecting a section of the public—here those he would come into contact with in prison, such as prison officers, other inmates and those who visit prisons for religious, educational, social work or other purposes. It concluded that his continued detention in the hospital was not disproportionate to the legitimate aim of protecting that section of the public from serious harm.[109]

3.7.3 Treatment

A mental patient's right to treatment appropriate to his condition cannot as such be derived from Article 5(1)(e). Although there must be some relationship between the ground of permitted deprivation of liberty relied and the place and conditions of detention, the Article is not in principle concerned with suitable treatment or conditions. The fact that a mental disorder is not susceptible to treatment does not mean that continued detention in a hospital is arbitrary or disproportionate.[110] In *Anderson*[111] the Privy Council concluded that it was not incompatible with Article 5(1)(e) for the Scottish Parliament to require the continued detention of restricted patients in a hospital where this was necessary on grounds of public safety, whether or not their mental disorder was treatable.[112]

3.8 Article 5(1)(f): Unauthorised Entry, Action Taken with a View to Deportation or Extradition

Article 5(1)(f) permits the lawful arrest or detention of a person to prevent his effecting an unauthorised entry into the country or of a person against whom action is being taken with a view to deportation or extradition. It is clear that Article 5 affords those detained under this part no right to bail.[113]

3.8.1 Unauthorised Entry: Detention of Asylum Seekers

Courts considering Article 5(1)(f) often refer to the principle of international law that sovereign states can regulate the entry of aliens into their territory.[114] It has been held that, until the state has authorised entry, the entry is unauthorised and the state has the power to detain without violating Article 5 until the application has been

---

107 *Ibid*, at [51].
108 Above n 34.
109 *Ibid*, at [37]–[38] per Lord Hope and [65] per Lord Clyde.
110 *Ibid*, at [28]–[29] per Lord Hope in reliance upon *Winterwerp*, above n 34 at [51] and *Ashingdane*, above n 11, at [44].
111 *Ibid*.
112 *Ibid*, at [31] per Lord Hope and [60]–[64] per Lord Clyde. See also *von Brandenburg*, above n 2.
113 *R v Secretary of State for the Home Department, ex p Sezek* [2001] EWCA Civ 795, [2002] 1 WLR 348.
114 See, eg the comments of Lord Slynn in *Saadi*, above n 9, at [31].

considered and the entry is authorised.[115] In light of this view, in *Saadi*[116] the House of Lords concluded that the detention of asylum seekers at Oakington Reception Centre was compatible with Article 5(1)(f). This was detention for the purpose of inquiring whether the asylum seeker must or should be granted asylum, and it did not have to be shown that detention was necessary for that purpose.[117]

It must also be shown that detention in such instances is not arbitrary. In *Saadi*[118] it was argued that the detention was a disproportionate response to the reasonable requirements of immigration control. The House of Lords did not agree that the methods of selection of these cases (suitable for speedy decision), the objective (speedy decision) or the way in which people were held for short periods and in reasonable physical conditions, even if involving compulsory detention, could be said to be arbitrary or disproportionate.[119] Lord Slynn concluded as follows:

> It is regrettable that anyone should be deprived of his liberty other than pursuant to the order of a court but there are situations where such a course is justified. In a situation like the present with huge numbers and difficult decisions involved, with the risk of long delays to applicants seeking to come, a balancing exercise has to be performed. Getting a speedy decision is in the interests not only of the applicants but of those increasingly in the queue. Accepting as I do that the arrangements made at Oakington provide reasonable conditions, both for individuals and families and that the period taken is not in any sense excessive, I consider that the balance is in favour of recognising that detention under the Oakington procedure is proportionate and reasonable.[120]

3.8.2 Deportation: Detention of Deportees

Article 5(1)(f) also allows for the detention of those against whom action is being taken with a view to deportation. In *Nadarajah*[121] the Court of Appeal held that Article 5(1)(f) did not of itself import a test of proportionality so that it was necessary to balance the benefit of detention against the infringement of the right to personal liberty.[122] In the view of the court, it did not impose an obligation on states to give those whom they are in the process of removing a right to roam freely pending their removal whenever detention was not necessary to achieve ultimate removal.[123] This conclusion appears directly contrary to the approach taken in *Saadi*[124] and the fact that the prohibition of arbitrariness is an overarching requirement in relation to all Article 5(1) deprivations of liberty.[125]

---

[115] *Ibid*, at [35] per Lord Slynn.
[116] *Ibid*.
[117] *Ibid*, at [35] per Lord Slynn in reliance upon *Chahal v UK* (1996) 1 BHRC 405; *Conka v Belgium* (2002) 11 BHRC 555.
[118] *Ibid*.
[119] *Ibid*, at [45]–[46] per Lord Slynn.
[120] *Ibid*, at [47].
[121] Above n 40.
[122] *Ibid*, at [50] in reliance upon *Chahal v UK* (1996) 23 EHRR 413.
[123] *Ibid*, at [51].
[124] Above n 9.
[125] See *Evans*, above n 32, per Lord Hope in reliance upon *Sunday Times*, above n 36; *Zamir*, above n 36, at [90]–[91]; *Engel*, above n 36, at [58]; *Tsirlis and Kouloumpas* above n 36, at [56]. See also *Anderson*, above n 34, at [22] per Lord Hope.

The Court of Appeal also confused the question of lawfulness with arbitrariness, holding that the only question as to the policy on detention was whether it permitted arbitrary or irrational treatment.[126] It concluded that there was nothing arbitrary or irrational about a policy under which members of the immigration service would detain a person whom they were about to remove in circumstances where they had reason to doubt whether that person would provide the cooperation necessary for an orderly removal. It also found nothing arbitrary or irrational about a policy of not normally detaining an individual where removal was not imminent and the presumption that removal was not imminent if judicial proceedings had been commenced.[127] Although proportionality was not mentioned, it is likely that the Court of Appeal would have reached the same conclusion if the question of whether or not detention was a proportionate response to the reasonable requirements of immigration control had been asked. Nevertheless, the court eventually concluded that the detention was not lawful as it was not prescribed by law.[128]

3.8.3 Deportation: Length of Detention

With respect to the time an individual may be detained pending his or her removal or departure from the United Kingdom, Article 5 adds nothing to the common law.[129] The power of detention is limited to a period which is reasonably necessary for that purpose. The period which is reasonable will depend upon the circumstances of the particular case. Relevant considerations include

> the length of the period of detention; the nature of the obstacles which stand in the path of the Secretary of State preventing a deportation; the diligence, speed and effectiveness of the steps taken by the Secretary of State to surmount such obstacles; the conditions in which the detained person is being kept; the effect of detention on him and his family; the risk that if he is released from detention he will abscond; and the danger that, if released, he will commit criminal offences.[130]

The refusal of voluntary repatriation is also relevant but of little weight.[131]

A prolonged period of detention pending the final resolution of an asylum claim is sometimes permissible, but a detained asylum seeker cannot invoke the delay necessarily occasioned by his own asylum claim to contend that his removal was not going to be possible within a reasonable time.[132] If it is apparent to the Secretary of State that he is not going to be able to operate the machinery provided in the Act for removing persons who are intended to be deported within a reasonable period, the Secretary of State cannot seek to exercise his power of detention. Furthermore, the Secretary of State must exercise all reasonable expedition to ensure that the steps are

---

[126] *Nadarajah*, above n 40, at [61].
[127] *Ibid.*
[128] *Ibid*, at [64]–[67]. See also *Sezek*, above n 113.
[129] *Re Hardial Singh* [1984] 1 All ER 983 expressly adopted in *R (on the application of I) v Secretary of State for the Home Department* [2002] EWCA Civ 888.
[130] *R (on the application of I)*, *ibid*, at [48] per Dyson LJ.
[131] *Ibid*, at [50] per Dyson LJ.
[132] *Ibid*, at [36] per Simon Brown LJ in reliance upon *Chahal*, above n122.

taken which will be necessary to ensure the removal of the individual within a reasonable time.[133]

I[134] concerned an individual who had been in detention for nearly 16 months and there was no indication that enforced removal might become possible. Taking all the circumstances into account, a majority of the Court of Appeal held that he had been detained for a period that was longer than reasonable and ordered that he be released.

3.8.4 Extradition: Meaning of Lawfulness

In relation to extradition, it is not necessary, in order for the detention to be lawful in Convention terms, to establish that the ultimate trial in another country will be fair or that the motives of the requesting party in bringing the prosecution abroad are beyond reproach.[135]

4. Article 5(2): Reasons for Arrest

Article 5(2) is the first of the procedural rights set out in Article 5 for persons who have been arrested or are being detained. Most, if not all, are reflected in other laws such as the Police and Criminal Evidence Act 1984 (PACE). Article 5(2) provides that everyone who is arrested shall be informed promptly, in a language which he understands, of the reasons for his arrest and of any charge against him. It has its counterpart in section 28(3) of PACE and it has been held that, although the wording is not the same, the principles expressed are,[136] and in the vast majority of cases it will be sufficient to apply Article 5(2).[137] The underlying rationale is that a person is entitled to know why he is being arrested so that he has the opportunity, for example, of giving an explanation of any misunderstanding or of calling attention to others for whom he might have been mistaken.[138] It is also a matter of respect for the dignity of the individual—if the state is taking away your liberty, you are entitled to know why.[139]

Any person arrested must be told, in simple, non-technical language that he can understand, the essential legal and factual grounds for his arrest, so as to be able, if he sees fit, to apply to a court to challenge its lawfulness in accordance with Article 5(4). The question of whether or not the information given is adequate has to be assessed objectively, having regard to the information which is reasonably available to the officer.[140] Whilst this information must be conveyed promptly, it need not be

---

[133] *Ibid.*
[134] *Ibid.*
[135] *R (Kashamu) v Governor of Brixton Prison* [2001] EWHC (Admin) 980, [2002] 2 WLR 907.
[136] *Taylor v Chief Constable of Thames Valley Police* [2004] EWCA Civ 858, [2004] 1 WLR 3155 at [25].
[137] *Ibid*, at [26].
[138] *Ibid*, at [22].
[139] *Ibid*, at [58] per Sedley LJ.
[140] *Ibid*, at [30].

related in its entirety by the arresting officer at the very moment of the arrest. Whether the content and promptness of the information conveyed were sufficient is to be assessed in each case according to its special features.[141]

These principles were applied in *Taylor*,[142] which concerned the arrest of a ten-year-old boy at the site of one anti-vivisection protest for his activities at another. On his arrest, the officer informed him that he was arresting him on suspicion of violent disorder on 18 April 1998 at Hillgrove Farm. The Court of Appeal concluded that the reference to the farm and date gave clear information as to the event concerned.

> There can have been no reasonable doubt in his mind as to when and where the events occurred which led to his arrest. Despite the interval of time, there can have been no scope for confusion as to the incident to which WPC McKenzie was referring.

The court also pointed out that, even though he was only ten years old, his mother was present throughout.[143] It further held that there was no need to specify the precise way in which he was said to be taking part—violent disorder was a good enough description of what had happened on the occasion.[144] It concluded that Article 5(2) was satisfied.[145]

---

5. Article 5(3)

Article 5(3) provides that everyone arrested or detained in accordance with Article 5(1)(c) shall be brought promptly before a judge or other officer authorised by law to exercise judicial power and shall be entitled to trial within a reasonable time or to release pending trial. Release may be conditioned by guarantees to appear for trial. Three distinct rights are evident. These are:

1. the right to be brought promptly before a judge or other officer authorised by law to exercise judicial power;
2. the right to be released on bail, except where continued detention can be justified; and
3. the right to be tried within a reasonable period.[146]

The first has not yet arisen in a HRA case. The remaining two are examined in the following paragraphs.

---

[141] *Fox v United Kingdom* (1991) 13 EHRR 157 at [40] adopted in *Taylor, ibid.*
[142] *Ibid.*
[143] *Ibid,* at [36] per Clarke LJ.
[144] *Ibid,* at [38] per Clarke LJ.
[145] *Ibid,* at [40]. See also *Wilson v The Chief Constable of Lancashire Constabulary* [2001] 2 WLR 302.
[146] *Wardle,* above n 28, at [84] per Lord Hope.

5.1 The Right to be Released on Bail

The right to be released on bail is not absolute, but if bail is to be refused 'the refusal must be justified on the facts of each case to the satisfaction of the judge or other officer.'[147] Again, this aspect of Article 5 is already reflected in common law and statute such as the Bail Act 1976. However, the right to be released on bail has had some impact. For example, in *McKeown*[148] the Divisional Court concluded that if the Bail Act 1976 was interpreted so as to entitle a court to deny a defendant bail simply on the basis that he had been arrested for breaking conditions of bail, this may be incompatible with Article 5(3). It used section 3 of the HRA to hold that such an arrest should merely be taken into account in determining whether or not any of the grounds for refusing bail existed; it was not to be determinative.[149]

Similarly, in *O*[150] the question was the compatibility of section 25 of the Criminal Justice and Public Order Act 1994 with Article 5(3). Under Section 25 a judge could only grant bail if satisfied that there were exceptional circumstances which justified that course. The Divisional Court found it compatible, but noted that courts must be left free to examine all of the relevant circumstances and, in an appropriate case, override the presumption.[151] It held that it was important for the words 'exceptional circumstances' not to be too narrowly construed.

> If in fact, taking into account all the circumstances relating to a particular alleged offence and offender he does not create an unacceptable risk of that kind he is an exception to the norm, and in accordance with his individual right to liberty he should be granted bail.[152]

With respect to the question of whether or not the court was satisfied that there were exceptional circumstances, it held that this did not involve a standard of proof but was an exercise of judgment or evaluation.[153] In addition, Hooper J held that it was acceptable under Article 5(3) to place an evidential burden on the defendant to show exceptional circumstances. However, the burden remained upon the prosecution to satisfy the court that bail should not be granted.[154]

5.2 The Right to be Tried within a Reasonable Time

The purpose of the right to trial within a reasonable time under Article 5(3) is to ensure that no one spends too long in detention before trial. It therefore may be regarded as laying down a more exacting requirement than the Article 6(1) right to a hearing within a reasonable time.[155] However, usually the case law concerning both

---

[147] *Ibid*, at [85] per Lord Hope.
[148] *R (on the application of McKeown) v Wirral Borough Magistrates' Court* [2001] 1 WLR 805.
[149] *Ibid*, at [47]. See also *R (on the application of Vickers) v West London Magistrates' Court* [2003] EWHC (Admin) 1809, [2004] Crim LR 63, where it was held that breach of bail will be one factor as to whether or not the bailed person is admitted to bail again.
[150] *R (on the application of O) v Crown Court at Harrow* [2003] EWHC (Admin) 868.
[151] *Ibid*, at [28] per Kennedy LJ.
[152] *Ibid*, at [32] per Kennedy LJ.
[153] *Ibid*, at [33] per Kennedy LJ and at [64] per Hooper J.
[154] *Ibid*, at [99].
[155] *Wardle*, above n 28, at [85] per Lord Hope in reliance upon *Wemhoff v Germany* (1968) 1 EHRR 55 at [5] and *Tagci and Sargin v Turkey* (1995) 20 EHRR 505 at [50].

Articles is invoked and it is therefore important to consider the reasonable time provisions of Article 6 when considering this part of Article 5.[156]

The time span covered by Article 5(3) extends from the first remand into custody until the delivery of the judgment of the court.[157] What is a reasonable time depends on all the relevant circumstances of the case. It has been held that it is important to balance against the defendant's right to liberty the public interest in ensuring that those charged with serious offences are available to be tried, did not commit other offences whilst awaiting trial and did not interfere with witnesses.[158] Procedural time wasting in the part of the defendant and failure of the prosecution to show diligence can be taken into account.[159]

In *Wardle*[160] it was argued that allowing a fresh custody time limit to be applied in relation to each new charge was open to abuse and could result in detention for a time that was more than reasonable. Here, when the defendant appeared before the magistrates' court the prosecution offered no evidence on the murder charge but held that a new custody time limit should be applied to the manslaughter charge. A majority of the House of Lords held that the regulation which required that each offence charged attracted its own custody time limit had a legitimate purpose, which was to give sufficient time to the prosecutor to prepare the evidence relating to each offence for examination by the justices, and any abuse was subject to judicial control. No incompatibility with Article 5(3) was found.[161]

6. Article 5(4)

6.1 Introduction

Article 5(4) provides that everyone who is deprived of his liberty by arrest or detention shall be entitled to take proceedings by which the lawfulness of his detention shall be decided speedily by a court and his release ordered if the detention is not lawful. It is this part of Article 5 which has generated the most litigation under the HRA. It reflects principles long cherished in this country by lawyers and the public that no one shall be deprived of his liberty save on lawful authority; that anyone challenging the lawfulness of his detention shall have access to a court with power to decide whether his detention is lawful or not; and that if his detention is not held to be lawful his release shall be ordered.[162] It has been held that, where the requirements

---

[156] See, eg *Procurator Fiscal, Linlithgow v Watson* [2002] UKPC D1, [2004] 1 AC 379.
[157] *O*, above n 150, at [34].
[158] *Ibid.*
[159] *Ibid.*
[160] Above n 28.
[161] *Ibid*, at [89] per Lord Hope, with whom Lord Clyde agreed. Lord Slynn reached the same conclusion. See also *R (on the application of Gibson) v Winchester Crown Court* [2004] EWHC (Admin) 361, [2004] 1 WLR 1623.
[162] *R (Giles) v Parole Board* [2003] UKHL 42, [2004] AC 1 at [3] per Lord Bingham. See also *R (on the application of Sim) v Parole Board* [2003] EWCA Civ 1845, [2004] QB 1288 at [11].

of this part of Article 5 are clear, it is no answer that compliance would be burdensome, costly or difficult.[163] Compliance with Article 5(4) can only be assessed in retrospect by reference to the specific facts of an actual case. It cannot be said in advance that a breach of Article 5(4) is inevitable.[164]

6.2 Access

It has been held that Article 5(4) obliges the state to place the incompetent person in the same position as the competent person with regard to access to a review of the lawfulness of his or her detention.[165] In *MH*[166] the Court of Appeal declared sections of the Mental Health Act 1983 incompatible with Article 5(4) in that these did not make adequate provision for the reference to a court of the case of a patient detained in circumstances where the patient had a right to make an application to a mental health review tribunal but was incapable of exercising that right on his own initiative.

6.3 Review of Lawfulness

6.3.1 Introduction

The review of lawfulness by a court as required by Article 5(4) must encompass lawfulness on Convention grounds as well as lawfulness under domestic law.[167] In some cases the appeal process will satisfy the requirements of Article 5(4).[168] It has also been held that the power of the court on judicial review is sufficient to meet the standards of Article 5(4).[169] It does not appear to matter which court reviews lawfulness, as long as lawfulness is reviewed.[170] In *P*[171] it was argued by a life sentence prisoner also subject to the Mental Health Act 1983 that he was entitled to have the lawfulness of his detention reviewed by a single tribunal exercising the functions of both a Mental Health Review Tribunal and a Discretionary Lifer Panel. The Administrative Court rejected the argument holding that there was no reason to require that the same court determine each head of detention.[172]

---

[163] *R (on the application of P) v Secretary of State for the Home Department* [2003] EWHC (Admin) 2953 at [14].

[164] *Roberts v Parole Board* [2005] UKHL 45, [2005] 3 WLR 152; *R (on the application of Al-Jedda) v Secretary of State for Defence* [2005] EWHC (Admin) 1809 at [29].

[165] *R (on the application of MH) v Secretary of State for Health* [2004] EWCA Civ 1609, [2005] 1 WLR 1209.

[166] *Ibid.*

[167] *Anderson*, above n 34, at [39] per Lord Hope in reliance upon *Winterwerp*, above n 34, at [55]. See also *Smith*, above n 51, at [37].

[168] *Re Scriven*, Court of Appeal, 22 April 2004

[169] *R v An Immigration Officer, ex p Xuereb* [2000] 56 BMLR 180.

[170] See, eg *Kashamu*, above n 135.

[171] Above n 163.

[172] *Ibid*, at [34].

If a person is detained under more than one head . . . and a court decides that his continued detention under one of those heads is lawful, his continued detention is lawful, irrespective of the lawfulness of his detention under the other head or heads.[173]

In the case of those of unsound mind[174] and those serving indeterminate sentences,[175] what is required is review at reasonable intervals of the conditions which are essential for lawful detention.

6.3.2 Unsound Mind

In the case of those of unsound mind, there must be a review of the lawfulness of detention at reasonable intervals. The minimum for a judicial procedure is the right of the individual to present his own case and to challenge the medical and social evidence in support of his detention.[176] In *Anderson*[177] the appellants challenged a new piece of legislation which prevented their release on the ground of public safety. Medical knowledge had moved on and there was a strong body of opinion that their condition was not treatable. It was argued that, when applying the public safety test, the sheriff would not be conducting a review but exercising the function of primary decision maker. The Privy Council disagreed, holding that the exercise the sheriff was required to conduct was a review—a review of the patient's continued detention in the light of the new rules.[178]

6.3.3 Indeterminate Sentences

Where a prisoner has been lawfully detained within the meaning of Article 5(1)(a) following the imposition of a determinate sentence after his conviction by a competent court, the review which Article 5(4) requires is incorporated in the original sentence passed by the sentencing court. Once the appeal process has been exhausted, there is no right to have the lawfulness of the detention under that sentence reviewed by another court. However, where decisions as to the length of detention have passed from the court to the executive,[179] and there is a risk that the factors which informed the original decision will change with the passage of time, the review which Article 5(4) requires cannot be said to be incorporated into the original decision of the court. A further review in judicial proceedings is needed at reasonable intervals.[180] The underlying rationale is clear: a prisoner's danger to the public may diminish or disappear.[181]

---

[173] *Ibid*, at [36].
[174] *Anderson*, above n 34, at [39].
[175] *Giles* and *Sim*, above n 162.
[176] *Anderson*, above n 34, at [39] per Lord Hope.
[177] *Ibid*.
[178] *Ibid*, at [42].
[179] As in the case of life sentences, although it is important to note that this function is no longer performed by the Home Secretary but by the Parole Board.
[180] *Giles*, above n 162, at [51] per Lord Hope in reliance upon *De Wilde, Ooms and Versyp v Belgium (No.1)* (1971) 1 EHRR 373.
[181] *Ibid*, at [4] per Lord Bingham.

Sometimes it is difficult to determine on which side of the line a sentence falls. For example, in *Giles*[182] the appellant argued that, once he had served the part of his determinate sentence imposed for punishment and was about to begin serving the balance of the sentence imposed for public protection, Article 5(4) applied. The House of Lords disagreed, holding that his detention was in accordance with a determinate sentence imposed by a court and was justified under Article 5(1)(a) without the need for any further reviews under Article 5(4). The review required by Article 5(4) was incorporated in the sentence passed by the judge.

> He was able to take this decision in the light of the information before him and, in the exercise of his ordinary powers of sentencing, to decide on the total length of the sentence which in all the circumstances was appropriate.[183]

It was also held by a majority of the House of Lords in *McClean*[184] that Article 5(4) did not apply to the accelerated programme for the release of prisoners convicted of offences scheduled under the Northern Ireland (Emergency Provisions) Acts 1973, 1978, 1991 or 1996 as, very broadly, offences motivated by political or sectarian considerations. In the opinion of the majority, the prisoner's human rights did not entitle him to an early release scheme.

> He has been convicted of serious offences and sentenced to lengthy terms of imprisonment. There are many years to go before he could, absent the 1998 Act scheme, have any expectation of release. His continued incarceration does not infringe his human rights. The 1998 Act and its Rules constitute a statutory scheme of which the respondent was, and still is, a potential beneficiary.[185]

A different issue arose in *Sim*,[186] where the respondent had been recalled to prison while on licence under an extended sentence passed under section 85 of the Powers of Criminal Courts (Sentencing) Act 2000. This enabled the court to impose in cases of a sexual or violent offence a sentence which consisted of a custodial term and an extension period during which the offender would be on licence beyond the normal licence period. Whilst the Court of Appeal found that the overall period of the extended sentence had been determined by the court, this did not conclude the issue.[187] It found that with an extended sentence under section 85, once the custodial term had passed, no court had sentenced him to imprisonment but had authorised him to be imprisoned if his licence was revoked.[188] It observed that the extension period was designed to provide greater protection for the public and this put it into the category of case where there may need to be further assessments of risk.[189] It therefore concluded that, where an offender is detained during the extension period of a section 85 sentence, such detention must be subject to review by a judicial body.

---

182 *Ibid.*
183 *Ibid*, at [52] per Lord Hope. See also Lord Bingham [9]–[11] and the speech of Lord Hutton.
184 *In re McClean* [2005] UKHL 46.
185 Per Lord Scott at [51], with whom Lord Brown agreed. Lord Rodger agreed with Lord Brown.
186 Above n 162.
187 *Ibid*, at [28].
188 *Ibid*, at [33].
189 *Ibid*, at [35].

[I]t is the executive which decides upon an offender's recall during the extension period, and because that detention has not been ordered by a court it must be supervised by a judicial body.[190]

Here it was so supervised through the mechanism of the Parole Board.

6.4 Attributes of a Court

Article 5(4) specifies that the lawfulness of detention is to be decided by a court. It is clear that it is not necessary for the decision-making body to actually be labelled a 'court' as such. However, it must possess the attributes of a court, such as complying with the principles of natural justice, as discussed in the following paragraphs. In addition, there are a few other attributes of a court such as being competent to take a legally binding decision leading to a person's release. In *IH*[191] it was argued that a mental health review tribunal lacked the attributes of a court as it lacked coercive power. The tribunal had ordered the discharge of the appellant provided there was supervision of him by a named social worker and psychiatrist. The health authority was unable to find a psychiatrist willing to supervise and his detention continued. The House of Lords did not agree, holding that the power to discharge conditionally was not incompatible with Article 5(4).[192]

It is also possible, where a mental health review tribunal has ordered the discharge of a patient, that the patient is readmitted shortly after. This raises questions as to the power of the tribunal to order release. In *H*[193] the claimant had been discharged from detention by the tribunal but seven days later an approved social worker made an application for his admission and detention, and since that date he had been detained for treatment. The Court of Appeal held that, in the absence of material circumstances of which the tribunal was not aware when it ordered discharge, it was not open to the professionals, until the tribunal's decision had been quashed by a court, to resection a patient.

> To countenance such a course as lawful would be to permit the professionals and their legal advisers to determine whether a decision by a court to discharge a detained patient should have effect.

In the opinion of the court, this would not be compatible with Article 5(4).[194] However, the court was willing to countenance a stay if there was strong evidence to justify it, the majority finding that this could even require a forcible return to hospital.[195] In the present case it concluded that the principal ground on which the professionals relied in deciding to resection was one which had been rejected by the

---

190 *Ibid*, at [36].
191 Above n 98.
192 *Ibid*, at [26]. This judgment answered questions raised in *K*, above n 100.
193 *R (on the application of H) v Ashworth Hospital Authority* [2002] EWCA Civ 923.
194 *Ibid*, at [56].
195 *Ibid*, Dyson LJ at [57] and Mummery LJ at [94]. Simon Brown LJ took a stricter view at [105]–[106].

tribunal. Therefore, even if the tribunal's decision was unlawful, there were not sufficient reasons to resection.[196]

Whilst conditional discharge in *IH*[197] was found acceptable, another aspect of the
decision in this case was found to be unacceptable. Once the tribunal had made its
original order, it was not lawful for it to reconsider it. In the view of the House of
Lords, this left the appellant in limbo for a period much longer than was compatible
with Article 5(4).[198] It concluded that tribunals should no longer proceed on the basis
that they cannot reconsider a decision to direct a conditional discharge on specified
conditions where, after deferral and before directing discharge, there is a material
change of circumstances.[199]

6.5 Independence and Impartiality

It is beyond question that the court reviewing the lawfulness of detention must be
independent and impartial. Although it has not been confirmed as such, it is likely
that the test for independence and impartiality would be same as that adopted under
Article 6.

Particular problems have arisen in relation to the role of the Home Secretary, an
office which does not embody the qualities of independence or impartiality.[200] Whilst
many of the questions concerning the Home Secretary's role in sentencing have now
been resolved,[201] some issues still remain. For example, *D*[202] concerned a discretionary life prisoner who was also the subject of a transfer and restriction direction under
the Mental Health Act 1983. His detention was subject to two statutory
regimes—mental health and penal. His case for discharge had to be considered by
both the mental health tribunal and the Parole Board. However, if the tribunal
decided he was no longer detainable under the Mental Health Act, the intervention
of the Home Secretary was required for his case to be referred to the Parole Board.

Although it was the Home Secretary's policy to always refer, the Administrative
Court appreciated that there was no right to require the Home Secretary to refer.[203] It
concluded that the present arrangement was not compatible with Article 5(4).

> The word 'entitled' in Article 5(4) is not satisfied unless there is a legal right of access to a
> court that can determine the lawfulness of detention and direct the prisoner's release if his
> detention is not justified.[204]

---

[196] *Ibid*, at [64]. See also *von Brandenburg*, above n 2; and *R (on the application of RA) v Secretary of State
for the Home Department* [2002] EWHC (Admin) 1618, which concerned the Secretary of State's power to
give or refuse his consent to community leave under the Mental Health Act 1983.
[197] Above n 98.
[198] *Ibid*, at [27].
[199] *Ibid*, at [27]. See also *R (on the application of C) v Secretary of State for the Home Department* [2002]
EWCA Civ 647.
[200] *Kashamu*, above n 135.
[201] See, eg *Anderson*, above n 62.
[202] *D v Secretary of State for the Home Department* [2002] EWHC Admin 2805, [2003] 1 WLR 1315.
[203] *Ibid*, at [18].
[204] *Ibid*, at [24] in reliance upon *Benjamin and Wilson v United Kingdom*, Judgment of 26 September 2002.

The Court declared the provisions incompatible with Article 5(4). However, not all of the Home Secretary's functions run the risk of violating Article 5(4). In *Day*[205] the Administrative Court held that it was acceptable for the Secretary of State to fix the date for the next review by the Parole Board of the claimant's application for release under a mandatory life sentence licence.[206]

The existence of directions by the Home Secretary to the Parole Board in the discharge of its functions under section 28 of the Crime (Sentences) Act 1997 has also been the subject of challenge on independence grounds. In *Girling*[207] the Administrative Court observed that directions purporting to govern how the Board actually decided cases involved what would ordinarily be regarded as a trespass into the judicial sphere.

> Political accountability for the penal system is of great importance. It does not, however, entail that the Home Secretary should give directions as to judicial functions: on the contrary, when the Parole Board is exercising judicial functions the common law and recognised principles of political accountability both require that the Home Secretary and other members of the executive respect the judicial nature of those functions.[208]

However, it concluded that the problem could be resolved if section 32(6) of the Criminal Justice Act 1991, concerning directions which could be given by the Secretary of State, were read as inapplicable to the Parole Board's judicial functions, and in particular its functions under section 28 of the 1997 Act.[209] In the present case, it concluded that whilst there had been an inadvertent trespass on the Parole Board's independence, the content of the directions was innocuous and the trespass was not so substantial as to deprive the Parole Board of its true character as a judicial body. No breach of Article 5(4) was found.

In addition to the role of the Home Secretary, questions have also arisen in relation to the role of the medical member of mental health review tribunals. In *S*[210] the claimant challenged rule 11 of the tribunal rules, which required that he be seen by the medical member before the hearing of his application. The Administrative Court held that care was required if rule 11 was not to result in unfairness.[211] However, it noted that the rule did not require the medical member to form an opinion as to the patient's mental condition, and therefore this would not give rise to unfairness.[212] It also held that there was normally no objection to members of a tribunal or court forming or discussing their provisional view of a case before the hearing. This would only be objectionable if the view formed was firm and concluded, in which case the hearing would be a charade.[213] Therefore, there was no objection to the expression of a provisional opinion by the medical member before the hearing provided other

---

[205] *R (on the application of Day) v Secretary of State for the Home Department* [2004] EWHC (Admin) 1742, [2004] ACD 78.
[206] See also *Girling v Parole Board* [2005] EWHC (Admin) 5469.
[207] *Ibid.*
[208] at [70].
[209] at [78].
[210] *R (on the application of S) v Mental Health Review Tribunal* [2002] EWHC (Admin) 2522.
[211] *Ibid*, at [15].
[212] *Ibid*, at [21].
[213] *Ibid*, at [22].

members were aware that this was only provisional and understood that they were free to disagree if the evidence and submissions led to a different conclusion.[214]

6.6 Fairness

6.6.1 Introduction

Article 5(4) requires there to be in place a judicial procedure which not only meets the criterion of being in accordance with law, but which also provides the basic protection for a defendant inherent in the concept of judicial proceedings. In short, a person liable to detention is entitled to natural justice.[215] Although some of the general concepts of fairness in judicial proceedings have been borrowed from Article 6, this does not mean that the process required for conformity with Article 5 must also be in conformity with Article 6.

> That would conflate the convention's control over two separate sets of proceedings, which have different objects. Article 5, in the present context, is concerned to ensure that the detention of an accused person before trial is only justified by proper considerations relating to the risk of absconding, and of interfering with witnesses, or the commission of other crimes. Article 6 is concerned with the process of determining the guilt or otherwise of a person who if found guilty would be subject to criminal penalties.[216]

It is also important to note that Article 6 may not apply to some proceedings where guarantees of fairness may be important, such as proceedings before a Parole Board.[217]

As with Article 6, the constituent elements of fairness under Article 5(4) are not considered to be absolute. Fairness and its ingredients need to be judged in context. The formulation of hard-edged principles is eschewed. Qualifications are justified provided they are necessary and proportionate. In considering whether qualification to the right is proportionate, consideration must be given to ways of mitigating or counterbalancing the restriction so as to achieve substantial fairness. The extent to which qualification or flexibility is permitted depends upon the context. A greater degree of latitude is permitted in cases concerning civil rights than in criminal cases. In deciding what is necessary, it is legitimate to have regard to the interest of others, including the public if they are affected. The interaction of these interests is a matter of degree, to be judged on a case-by-case basis.

6.6.2 Burden of Proof and Evidence

The burden of justifying a person's detention lies on the person detaining.[218] In *Sim*[219] the Court of Appeal concluded that a conventional interpretation of section

---

[214] *Ibid*, at [23]. This was also found to be compatible with Convention jurisprudence in particular *DN v Switzerland* Judgment of 29 March 2001.
[215] *McKeown*, above n 148, at [27].
[216] *Ibid*, at [35].
[217] See, eg *Roberts*, above n 164.
[218] *Sim*, above n 162.
[219] *Ibid*.

44A(4) of the Criminal Justice Act 1991 would be incompatible with Article 5(4) as detention was to continue unless the Parole Board was satisfied that it was not necessary. However, using section 3 of the HRA, it construed the word 'necessary' in a flexible way so that the Board had to be positively satisfied that continued detention was necessary in the public interest.[220]

In a number of cases, questions have arisen as to particular types of evidence affecting the fairness of Article 5(4) proceedings. It has been held that the court, when forming its opinion, must take proper account of the quality of the material upon which it is asked to adjudicate.

> This material is likely to range from mere assertion at the one end of the spectrum which may not have any probative effect, to documentary proof at the other end of the spectrum.[221]

The court must take proper account of the quality of the material and ensure that the defendant has a full and fair opportunity to comment on and answer that material.[222] There is no requirement that the underlying facts relevant to detention are to be proved to the criminal standard of proof.[223]

Hearsay evidence is not in principle inadmissible. However, the fact that it is hearsay should be borne in mind when determining the weight which is attached to it. If the evidence is fundamental to the decision, fairness may require that the offender is given the opportunity to test it by cross-examination before it is taken into account.[224] In *Sim*[225] the Court of Appeal concluded that the disputed matters were not the key factors in the decision and it did not accept that the admission of hearsay evidence about those disputed matters rendered the proceedings unfair or in breach of Article 5(4).[226] Similarly, there is no rule against the admission of evidence from an anonymous witness. In *Eidarous*[227] the House of Lords concluded that it was no violation of Article 5(4) for the magistrate, when deciding a request for extradition, to take into account the affidavit of an anonymous witness. It observed that the principles of a fair trial require that, in appropriate cases, the interests of the defence are balanced against those of witnesses or victims called upon to testify. Here there were real grounds to fear for the safety of the witness.[228]

6.6.3 Oral Hearing

There is no duty under Article 5(4) to afford an oral hearing in every case. Article 5(4) is satisfied provided that the review is conducted in a manner which meets the

---

[220] *Ibid*, at [51]. See also *R (on the application of Jarvis) v The Parole Board* [2004] EWHC (Admin) 872; *H*, above n 95; *Hirst v Parole Board*, Court of Appeal, 25 September 2002; and *McClean*, above n 184.
[221] *McKeown*, above n 148, at [41].
[222] *Ibid*.
[223] *Ibid*, at [39]–[40].
[224] *Sim*, above n 162, at [57].
[225] *Ibid*.
[226] *Ibid*, at [59].
[227] *R (Eidarous) v Governor of Brixton Prison* [2001] UKHL 69, [2002] 2 WLR 101.
[228] Per Lord Rodger at [166]. See also Lord Slynn at [44] and Lord Hutton at [85]–[88]. Reliance was placed on *Doorson v The Netherlands* (1996) 22 EHRR 330.

requirements of common law procedural fairness. In some instances, this may require an oral hearing. Even if important facts are not in dispute,

> they may be open to explanation or mitigation, or may lose some of their significance in the light of other new facts.[229]

In *Smith*[230] the House of Lords had to determine whether or not the procedure to be followed by the Parole Board should include an oral hearing when a determinate sentence prisoner released on licence sought to resist revocation of his licence. It stated that the Board may be assisted by exposure to the prisoner or those who had dealt with him.

> The prisoner should have the benefit of a procedure which fairly reflects, on the facts of his particular case, the importance of what is at stake for him, as for society.[231]

Where there were issues of fact or explanations put forward to justify actions said to be in breach of licence conditions, or where the officer's assessment needed further probing, fairness may well require an oral hearing.[232] A breach of Article 5(4) was found in relation to each appellant, their Lordships concluding that their challenges could not be fairly resolved without an oral hearing.[233]

6.6.4 Equality of Arms

The principle of equality of arms undoubtedly applies in Article 5(4) proceedings. Article 5(4) prohibits interference with the administration of justice designed to influence the judicial determination of a dispute other than on compelling grounds of the general public interest.[234] In *Anderson*[235] the Privy Council found that the purpose of the legislation was to protect the public and it was necessary for the Scottish Parliament to address the serious risk to public safety which would arise if others whose mental disorder was regarded as untreatable were to apply to the sheriff for their discharge. It concluded that this was a compelling ground of the public interest.[236]

Similarly, in *Roberts*[237] a majority of the House of Lords held that the fact that information is withheld from a prisoner in Parole Board proceedings does not mean that there is automatically a breach of the prisoner's rights under Article 5(4).

> There can be an infinite variety of circumstances as to the degree of information that is withheld completely or partially without any significant unfairness being caused. The responsibility of the panel is to ensure that any unfairness is kept to a minimum while balancing the triumvirate of interests . . . There may need initially to be a total withholding of

---

[229] *Smith*, above n 51, at [35] and [37] per Lord Bingham.
[230] *Ibid.*
[231] *Ibid*, at [35] per Lord Bingham.
[232] *Ibid*, at [50] per Lord Slynn.
[233] See also *R (on the application of Williams) v Secretary of State for the Home Department* [2002] EWCA Civ 498, [2002] 1 WLR 2264.
[234] *Anderson*, above n 34 at [43] per Lord Hope in reliance upon *National and Provincial Building Society v United Kingdom* (1997) 25 EHRR 127 at [112] and *Zielinski v France* (2001) 31 EHRR 532.
[235] *Ibid.*
[236] *Ibid*, at [44].
[237] Above n 164.

information, but at an early stage of the hearing the prisoner may be able to be informed of the gist of what is relied on against him. Documents can be edited. There has to be detailed management of the hearing to ensure that the prisoner has the widest information possible. In relation to this management the [specially appointed advocate] can have a critical role to play on the prisoner's behalf.[238]

It concluded that, where the Parole Board was confronted with a situation where a specially appointed advocate may be appointed to receive material withheld from the prisoner and to represent the prisoner at a closed hearing before the Board, it was necessary for the Board to balance carefully the conflicting interests involved in protecting the prisoner's right to be treated fairly.[239]

However, whilst the majority held that, in principle, to withhold material from the prisoner and his representatives and to disclose that material to the specially appointed advocate who would represent the prisoner in his absence at a closed hearing before the Board was not in violation of Article 5(4) per se, it was also held that it was not possible to reach a final conclusion on Article 5(4) without examining the facts as a whole, including any appellate process.[240]

To make rulings in advance of the actual hearing would be to introduce a rigidity that would make the task of the Board extraordinarily difficult. The position has to be looked at in the round examining the proceedings as a whole with hindsight and taking into account the task of the Board.[241]

Nevertheless, their Lordships also pointed out that the members of the public who could be affected by a decision of the Board have human rights as well as the prisoner.

If the Board releases a prisoner when it is unsafe to do so, the public's individual rights can be grievously affected. In addition in a situation where the Board has to consider whether to withhold evidence from a prisoner, for example to protect an individual whose life could be threatened if his identity were revealed, the Board is under a duty to protect this individual's interests. Not to do so could involve the breach of art 2 or 3 of the ECHR.[242]

6.7 Decided Speedily

6.7.1 Principles

Article 5(4) also provides that the proceedings testing the lawfulness of detention are to be decided speedily. As with the reasonable time requirement in Article 6, there are no hard-and-fast rules about whether or not a period of time is speedy enough. However, there is a distinction between the articles. The fact that the state is dealing with people who are at least presumptively detained unlawfully, and the legality of whose detention is controlled by Article 5(4), imposes a more intense obligation than that

---

[238] *Ibid*, at [76] per Lord Woolf.
[239] *Ibid*, at [82] per Lord Woolf.
[240] *Ibid*, at [77] per Lord Woolf, [19] per Lord Bingham, [112] per Lord Rodger and [144] per Lord Carswell.
[241] *Ibid*, at [77] per Lord Woolf.
[242] *Ibid*, at [80] per Lord Woolf. See also *McClean*, above n 184.

entailed by the need for a prompt trial of people who are not in custody.[243] Delay may result in unjustified detention and prolongs the period of uncertainty, often causing distress and disappointment.[244]

To comply with Article 5(4), efforts must be made to see that the individual application is heard as soon as reasonably practicable having regard to the relevant circumstances of the case.[245] Such time must be allowed as is reasonably necessary to ensure that the tribunal is in a position, adequately and fairly, to adjudicate on the issues before it.[246] This may be affected by the nature and importance of the subject matter of the case, the complexity of the issues, the preparation required before the hearing and the evidence considered. The fact that a case may be considered unmeritorious does not deprive the applicant of the right to a speedy hearing.[247] Automatically listing an application for hearing within a particular period of time without considering individual circumstances is not generally compatible with Article 5(4) unless this is the only practical way of ensuring that individual cases are determined as speedily as their individual circumstances reasonably permit.[248]

Considerations such as constraint of resources or administrative convenience are not relevant.[249] It is the obligation of the state to organise its legal system to enable it to comply with the Convention requirements. General faults in or underfunding of the system will provide no defence, but the practical realities of litigious life will.[250] There may be adjournments or cancelled hearings for a number of reasons, such as the illness of a judge, the unavailability of necessary witnesses, the overrunning of an earlier hearing or the need to accommodate an urgent case.[251] However, the excessive workload of the judge cannot be prayed in aid, nor can the fact that the judge is on holiday.[252] In K[253] the Administrative Court held that the correct approach was to consider first whether the delays in question were inconsistent with the requirement of a speedy hearing. If they were, the onus was on the state to excuse the delay.

> It may do so by establishing, for example, that the delay has been caused by a sudden and unpredictable increase in the workload of the tribunal, and that it has taken effective and sufficient measures to remedy the problem. But if the State fails to satisfy that onus, the Claimant will have established a breach of his right under Article 5(4).[254]

It is clear that it is for the state to ensure speedy hearings and it is irrelevant which government department or other public authority was at fault.[255]

---

[243] *Noorkoiv*, above n 8.
[244] *R (on the application of K) v Mental Health Review Tribunal* [2002] EWHC (Admin) 639 at [8].
[245] *R (on the application of C) v The Mental Health Review Tribunal London and South West Region* [2001] EWCA Civ 1110, [2002] 1 WLR 176 at [66] in reliance upon *Winterwerp*, above n 110, *E v Norway* (1990) 17 EHRR 30 and *Sanchez-Reiss v Switzerland* (1986) 9 EHRR 71.
[246] *C, ibid*, at [52].
[247] *K*, above n 244, at [31].
[248] *C*, above n 245, at [45].
[249] *Ibid*, at [45] and [64] in reliance upon *Bezicheri v Italy* (1989) 12 EHRR 210.
[250] *Noorkoiv*, above n 8, at [25].
[251] *K*, above n 244 at [38] in reliance upon *Dyer v Watson* [2002] UKPC D1, [2002] 1 AC 379.
[252] *Noorkoiv*, above n 8, at [24] in reliance upon *Bezicheri*, above n 249 and *E*, above n 245.
[253] Above n 244.
[254] *Ibid*, at [47] in reliance upon *Koendjbiharie v The Netherlands* (1990) 13 EHRR 820; *Musial v Poland* (2001) 31 EHRR 29.
[255] *Noorkoiv*, above n 8, at [31]; *K*, above n 244, at [112].

Speediness is also an issue with respect to the period between reviews of the detention of those serving life sentences. In determining whether the interval complies with Article 5(4) on the facts of a particular case, the court asks itself whether the interval was reasonable.[256]

6.7.2 Application: Mental Health

The question of speediness of determination has arisen on a number of occasions in the context of mental health. In C[257] the claimant applied to the tribunal for discharge and in accordance with current practice, his case was listed for hearing eight weeks later. The Court of Appeal first noted that the practice of automatically listing an application for hearing eight weeks after the date of application was not compatible with Article 5(4) unless this was the only practical way of ensuring that individual cases were determined as speedily as their individual circumstances reasonably permitted.[258] It did not accept that it was impossible to tailor lead times inside the eight-week target to suit particular cases[259] and concluded that the practice was bred of administrative convenience, not of administrative necessity. Whilst there was nothing wrong with having a target date of eight weeks maximum, to comply with Article 5(4) efforts had to be made to see that the individual application was heard as soon as reasonably practicable.[260]

In K[261] the issue was repeated adjournments rather than an inflexible policy. The eight claimants had applied to the mental health review tribunal for a review of their detention and it each case the hearing was repeatedly adjourned. The hearings took place between nine weeks and over 22 weeks after the dates of their respective applications. The Administrative Court appreciated that it was not possible to have an effective tribunal hearing immediately after a patient makes an application for the review of his detention,[262] but held that the listing of cases must be considered on an individual basis and that it should be practicable for the hearings to take place within eight weeks of the application.[263]

In response to the argument that the state was doing all that could reasonably be done to remedy the problem, the court held that the onus was on the state to excuse the delay, which it may do by establishing that there was a sudden and unpredictable increase in workload but that it had taken effective and sufficient measures to remedy the problem.[264] It found here that the state should have taken the likelihood of continuing increases in applications, as well as the experience of actual increases, into account in deciding on the allocation of resources to the tribunals.[265] It also found that the lack of medical tribunal members that caused cancellations was due in part

---

[256] *R (on the application of Spence) v Secretary of State for the Home Department* [2003] EWCA Civ 732; *Murray v Parole Board* [2003] EWCA Civ 1561; *D v Secretary of State for the Home Department* [2002] EWHC (Admin) 2805, [2003] 1 WLR 1315.
[257] Above n 245.
[258] *Ibid*, at [45].
[259] *Ibid*, at [60].
[260] *Ibid*, at [64]–[66].
[261] Above n 244.
[262] *Ibid*, at [31].
[263] *Ibid*, at [37].
[264] *Ibid*, at [47] in reliance upon *Koendjbiharie* and *Musial*, above n 254.
[265] *Ibid*, at [56].

to the previous inadequate rates of pay.[266] It was also not satisfied that the shortage of appropriately qualified legal tribunal members had occurred without responsibility on the part of the state.[267] In addition, to the extent that failures to provide speedy hearings were due to shortages of staff, pressure of work on staff or the lack of suitably trained staff, it was not satisfied that these were not due to matters that were the responsibility of the state.[268]

The court concluded that the principal causes of cancellations and delays were the shortage of tribunal members, particularly medical members, and shortage and lack of training of staff. Inadequate IT provision was also a contributory factor.[269] A violation of Article 5(4) was found in relation to all of the claimants.[270]

6.7.3 Application: Life Sentence Prisoners

In *Noorkoiv*[271] the claimant received an automatic life sentence in 1998. His tariff expired in April 2001 but his hearing before the Parole Board to determine whether he should continue to be detained was not held until June 2001. It was the policy of the Board to only schedule hearings for a date after the expiry of the tariff period and it was the position of the Secretary of State that a lack of resources prevented any improvement on the present procedures. The Court of Appeal held that there was no general principle that administrative necessity excuses. It noted that here all cases were treated the same irrespective of preparation time and the authorities had the case under consideration for many months before expiry of the tariff. It could not therefore be suggested that delay after expiry of the tariff was necessary to give proper consideration to an difficult individual case.[272]

The court concluded that the arrangements infringed Article 5(4) and that it was infringed in the present case. The arrangements envisaged a delay of up to three months.[273] When the prisoner reached the end of his tariff period the authorities did not then start on consideration of his case with no prior knowledge of his situation. He was within the custody of and well known to the authorities.[274] The full penal regime was imposed on him and this was seen to be a strong reason for determining the lawful status of that treatment sooner rather than later.[275] Resources constraints did not offset what was objectively a breach on the part of the state.[276] The scheme treated every case alike and imposed delays for reasons that were unrelated to the nature or difficulty of the particular case.[277] The court found no support for the argument that the final decision must be delayed to a date after

---

[266] *Ibid*, at [74].
[267] *Ibid*, at [79].
[268] *Ibid*, at [83].
[269] *Ibid*, at [87].
[270] See also *MH*, above n 165.
[271] Above n 8.
[272] *Ibid*, at [26].
[273] *Ibid*, at [33].
[274] *Ibid*, at [34].
[275] *Ibid*, at [36].
[276] *Ibid*, at [36].
[277] *Ibid*, at [37].

the end of the tariff period.[278] It concluded that it was for the Secretary of State to consider in detail how to proceed, and if further resources were seen as necessary, these must be provided.[279] The following observation was made:

> Given the imperative need to release from prison any post-tariff prisoner who no longer remains a danger (not least in these days of acute prison overcrowding), any system tending to delay such release (as the Board's present system does) requires the most compelling justification. Although by no means unsympathetic to the Board's difficulties, at the end of the day I am not persuade that any such compelling justification exists, or at any rate that it need continue to exist.[280]

Speediness is also an issue with respect to the period between reviews of the detention of those serving life sentences. For example, in *Spence*[281] the prisoner challenged the decision of the Secretary of State to extend the nine months recommended by the Parole Board which should be passed in open prison conditions before the next review substitute to a period of 18 months. In light of the circumstances of the case, the Court of Appeal concluded that the interval was reasonable.[282] However, in *Murray*,[283] taking into account Strasbourg jurisprudence, the Court of Appeal held that an interval of up to a year has ordinarily to be shown to be in breach of Article 5(4) on some particular ground whilst an interval of more than a year has generally to be shown not to be in breach of it.[284] Here a delay of 15 months was not held to be excessive.[285]

---

7. Article 5(5): Enforceable Right to Compensation

7.1 Principles

Article 5(5) provides that everyone who has been the victim of arrest or detention in contravention of the provisions of Article 5 shall have an enforceable right to compensation. The provisions of Article 5(5) are mandatory—if there has been a breach of Article 5, there is an enforceable right to compensation.[286] However, it is possible in some instances for no compensation to be awarded. For example, in *IH*[287] the

---

[278] *Ibid*, at [39]–[40].
[279] *Ibid*, at [44].
[280] *Ibid*, at [58] per Simon Brown LJ.
[281] Above n 256.
[282] *Ibid*, at [30] in reliance upon *Oldham v UK* Judgment of 26 September 2000. See also *MacNeill v Parole Board* [2001] EWCA Civ 448 and *R (on the application of Clough) v Secretary of State for the Home Department* [2003] EWHC (Admin) 597.
[283] Above n 256.
[284] *Ibid*, at [14] in reliance upon *Oldham v UK* Judgment of 26 September 2000 and *Hirst v United Kingdom* 24 October 2001.
[285] *Ibid*, at [5]. See also *King v Secretary of State for the Home Department* [2003] EWHC (Admin) 2831, [2004] HRLR 9; *D*, above n 256; *Day*, above n 205.
[286] *Evans*, above n 32, per Lords Hope, Steyn and Hobhouse.
[287] Above n 98.

House of Lords, although finding a violation of Article 5(4), did not consider that an award of compensation was required. This was because the violation had been publicly acknowledged and the appellant's right thereby vindicated; the law had been amended in a way which should prevent similar violations in future; and the appellant had not been the victim of unlawful detention, which Article 5 was intended to avoid.[288]

With respect to the award of compensation, to date there has been little guidance as to determining the appropriate amount, but certain matters are clear. First, the award of damages under Article 5(5) depends on there being proof of damage. Damage may be pecuniary or non-pecuniary,[289] and account can be taken of the scale of damages awarded by the ECHR, although UK courts are free to depart from this in order to award adequate compensation in UK terms.[290] The object of the award is to provide compensation for injury, not to mark the court's disapproval of the conduct complained of, to compel future compliance with the Convention or to reflect the importance of the right infringed.[291] There is no justification for an award being lower than it would be for a comparable tort.[292] If there is no comparable tort or other wrong, damages should reflect as far as possible the English level of damages.[293] Section 9(3) of the HRA prevents the award of exemplary damages.[294]

In *KB*[295] the Administrative Court had to assess the damages to be awarded to individuals who had had their rights under Article 5(4) breached due to delays in the hearing of the applications by a mental health review tribunal. The court held that a claimant who sought damages on the basis of an allegation that he would have had a favourable decision at an earlier date if his Convention rights had been respected had to prove this on the balance of probabilities.[296] The period to which any award of damages related was that from the time when the tribunal should have determined a patient's application to the date when it was actually determined. The court noted that the assessment of the period of delay was bound to be somewhat impressionistic.[297]

Whilst noting that every disappointment and feeling of distress did not constitute compensable damage, the court held that full account had to be taken of the fact that the claimants were patients detained on account of the state of their mental health and thus in a vulnerable mental condition. Damages could be awarded to such persons even though in analogous circumstances no award would be made to a healthy person. The frustration and distress must be significant, of such intensity that it would in itself justify an award of compensation for non-pecuniary damage. It noted that an important touchstone of that intensity in cases such as the present was that hospital staff considered it to be sufficiently relevant to the mental state of the

---

[288] *Ibid*, at [30].
[289] *R (on the application of KB) v Mental Health Review Tribunal* [2003] EWHC (Admin) 193, [2004] QB 936.
[290] *Ibid*, at [47].
[291] *Ibid*, at [50].
[292] *Ibid*, at [53].
[293] *Ibid*, at [54]–[55].
[294] *Ibid*, at [60].
[295] Above n 289.
[296] *Ibid*, at [64].
[297] *Ibid*, at [65].

patient to warrant its mention in clinical notes.[298] For some of the claimants the court held that a finding of violation was sufficient. For others, amounts ranging between £1,000 and £4,000 were awarded.

7.2 Relationship with the HRA

The relationship between Article 5(5) and the rest of the HRA is not yet clear. A particularly difficult question arose in *Richards*.[299] The claimant was serving a mandatory life sentence for murder. The Parole Board recommended him for release on 16 November 2001, but he was not released by the Home Secretary until 12 August 2002. On 28 May 2002, in a different case, the European Court of Human Rights found that the role of the Home Secretary was in violation of Article 5(4). It was clear that the claimant could not recover damages under section 6 of the HRA, as subsection 6(2) provides that subsection (1) does not apply to an act if the authority could not have acted differently as a result of one or more provisions of primary legislation. The claim for damages was therefore based on Article 5(5).

The Administrative Court concluded that Article 5(5) conferred a Convention right to enable victims of wrongful detention to have an enforceable right to compensation in the English courts. It reached this conclusion for a number of reasons. First, the Strasbourg court considers that the right given by Article 5(5) is to pursue an enforceable claim for compensation in the domestic courts.[300] Secondly,

> the words used in Article 5(5) stating that those victims of breaches of Article 5 shall have an enforceable right to compensation clearly entail the conferment of a right to obtain an enforceable award and that this should be in the local courts.[301]

Thirdly, it was difficult to understand why Article 5(5) was needed if Contracting States could refuse to give an enforceable right to compensation for detention contrary to Article 5.[302] In its view, the effect of Article 5(5) was to require an enforceable claim to compensation before the national courts whenever a breach of the other paragraphs of Article 5 had occurred.[303]

The court also found that the right under Article 5(5) was a Convention right, as specified in section 1 of the HRA, and will be triggered if there has been a declaration by the domestic courts either expressly or impliedly that Article 5 has been contravened.[304]

> Thus if the continued detention of the claimant at any time after 17 November 2001 was a breach of art 5 because of the decision in *Stafford* and the claimant can establish a right to

---

[298] *Ibid*, at [72]–[73].
[299] *R (on the application of Richards) v Secretary of State for the Home Department* [2004] EWHC (Admin) 93, [2004] ACD 69.
[300] *Ibid*, at [40] in reliance upon *Brogan v United Kingdom* (1998) 11 EHRR 117, 138 at [67]; *Fox, Campbell and Hartley*, above n 76 at [46].
[301] *Richards, ibid*, at [41].
[302] *Ibid*, at [42].
[303] *Ibid*, at [44].
[304] *Ibid*, at [45]–[46].

damages or compensation, then the defendant will have been in breach of art 5(5) of the Convention by not paying compensation or damages.[305]

Section 6(2) of the HRA did not assist the defendant, as a payment of compensation could have lawfully been made.[306]

The court concluded that the judgment in *Stafford* governed periods of detention that occurred both before and after the date of the decision.[307] Therefore, his Article 5 rights were infringed so that, pursuant to Article 5(5), he could obtain either an assessment by the court of an appropriate level of compensation payable by the defendant or a mandatory order that it must pay such sums or damages.[308] The main issue was to consider what would have happened to the claimant between November 2001 and his release in August 2002 if the Parole Board's recommendation in November 2001 that he should be released had taken effect.[309] Here the claim failed because no loss could be established. Even if the Parole Board recommendation had taken effect as an instruction to release him, the court concluded that the claimant would still have been detained from the time of the Parole Board recommendation in November 2001 until his actual release on 12 August 2002.[310]

The possible ramifications of this judgment are enormous as it essentially allows those who have suffered a breach of Article 5 to get around all of the difficulties presented by the HRA, such as retrospective effect and declarations of incompatibility. A less controversial approach would have been to hold that the breach of Article 5 must have been established in domestic law under the HRA. Here the role of the Home Secretary was not found to be incompatible with a Convention right until the Home Secretary declared it as such on 25 November 2002 in the case of *Anderson*.[311] Even then the Convention right utilised was Article 6, not Article 5(4), and the declaration did not affect the continuing validity of the empowering primary legislation.

The wider ramifications of the judgment have already been tested. In *Wright*[312] the Administrative Court held that compensation was not payable to the claimant as his detention occurred before the HRA came into force. However, it also noted that compensation was payable under Article 5(5) provided there had been a breach of Articles 5(1) or 5(4), whether or not any cause of action under section 6(1) of the HRA could be defeated by the operation of section 6(2). It remains to be seen what approach the higher courts will take.

---

[305] *Ibid*, at [46].
[306] *Ibid*, at [47].
[307] *Ibid*, at [81].
[308] *Ibid*, at [87].
[309] *Ibid*, at [92] in reliance upon *Anufrijeva v London Borough of Southwark* [2003] EWCA Civ 1406, [2004] QB 1124.
[310] *Ibid*, at [139].
[311] Above n 62.
[312] *R (on the application of Wright) v Secretary of State for the Home Department* [2004] EWHC (Admin) 3084.

10

Article 6: The Right to a Fair Trial

1. Introduction

The first sentence of Article 6(1) provides that in the determination of his civil rights and obligations, or of any criminal charge against him, everyone is entitled to a fair and public hearing within a reasonable time by an independent and impartial tribunal established by law. The Article also provides that judgment shall be pronounced publicly, and in Articles 6(2) and 6(3) protects a range of other rights in relation to those who have been charged with a criminal offence. The core right guaranteed is the right to a fair trial, and the focus of the Article is on achieving a result which is, and is seen to be, fair. Most of the other rights singled out for mention relate to the fairness and perceived fairness of the trial process.[1] However, it is clear that each of the rights protected by Article 6 must be considered separately. A complaint that one of these rights was breached cannot be answered by showing that the other rights were not breached. Furthermore, the consequences of a breach are not necessarily the same for each right protected.[2]

The Article was conceived primarily as a 'bulwark to protect private citizens against the abuse of power by state and public authorities.'[3] The importance of the rights with which it deals is reflected in the fact that on its face the Article permits no restriction the only express qualification relating to the requirement of a public hearing. There is 'nothing to suggest that the fairness of the trial itself may be qualified, compromised or restricted in any way, whatever the circumstances and whatever the

---

[1] *Attorney General's Reference No.2 of 2001* [2003] UKHL 68, [2004] 2 AC 72 at [10].
[2] *Porter v Magill* [2001] UKHL 67, [2002] 2 WLR 37 at [87] and [108]. See also *Millar v Dickson* [2002] 1 WLR 1615; *Procurator Fiscal, Linlithgow v Watson* [2002] UKPC D1, [2004] 1 AC 379 at [73]; *Mills v HM Advocate (No.2)* [2002] UKPC D2, [2004] 1 AC 441 at [9]–[12]; *Attorney General's Reference No.2 of 2001, ibid*, at [12].
[3] *R v Weir* [2001] 1 WLR 421.

public interest in convicting the offender.'[4] In addition, the Article does not just protect those rights which appear on its face. A number of other rights have been implied by the ECHR including the right not to incriminate oneself, the right of access to a court and equality of arms. Their purpose is to give effect in a practical way to the fundamental and absolute right to a fair trial.[5] However, these implied rights are not absolute. Modification or restriction is possible if it has a legitimate aim in the public interest, and there is a reasonable relationship of proportionality between the means employed and the aim sought to be realised.[6]

Most of the rights protected by Article 6, both express and implied, will be familiar to British lawyers, and the observation is often made that the principles which are enshrined in Article 6 have long been a part of the common law.[7] However, it is important not to be too complacent as it has also been recognised that some re-examination and revision of these principles in the light of the Article may be necessary.

> The scheme of the articles involves the application of different tests at each stage of the inquiry from those applied by the common law. It requires that a more structured approach be taken when the overriding test of fairness is applied to the facts.[8]

Article 6 has been considered in almost every context possible. However, it is rare for a court to refer to the principle of deference when adjudicating upon this Article. This may be due to the absolute nature of many of the guarantees, but could also have something to do with the fact that British courts are used to dealing with natural justice at common law. In the area of criminal justice, the affording of deference is rare although not unknown. For example, in *Kebilene*[9] Lord Hope noted that in some circumstances it will be appropriate for the courts to recognise that there is an area of judgment within which the judiciary will defer, on democratic grounds, to the considered opinion of the elected body or person whose act or decision was said to be incompatible with the Convention:

> [E]ven where the right is stated in terms which are unqualified the courts will need to bear in mind the jurisprudence of the European Court which recognises that due account should be taken of the special nature of terrorist crime and the threat which it poses to a democratic society.[10]

In *McIntosh*[11] Lord Bingham noted that the statutory scheme regarding confiscation of the assets of those convicted of drug trafficking offences was one approved by a democratically elected Parliament and should not be at all readily rejected.[12] An

---

[4] *Brown v Stott (Procurator Fiscal, Dunfermline)* [2001] 1 AC 681 per Lord Bingham. See also *Watson*, above n 2, at [73].

[5] *Ibid*, per Lord Hope.

[6] *Ibid*, per Lord Hope.

[7] See, eg the comments of Lord Hope in *R v A* [2001] UKHL 25, [2002] 1 AC 45 at [51].

[8] *Brown*, above n 4, per Lord Hope.

[9] *R v Director of Public Prosecutions, ex p Kebilene* [1999] 3 WLR 972.

[10] In reliance on *Murray v United Kingdom* (1994) 19 EHRR 193 at [47].

[11] *McIntosh v Lord Advocate* [2001] 1 AC 1078.

[12] *Ibid*, at [36].

appeal for deference was also made in *R v A*,[13] but was only considered by Lords Steyn and Hope. Lord Steyn noted that clearly the House must give weight to the decision of Parliament.

> On the other hand, when the question arises whether in the criminal statute in question Parliament adopted a legislative scheme which makes an excessive inroad into the right to a fair trial the court is qualified to make its own judgment and must do so.[14]

Lord Hope took the opposite position, noting that there were areas of law which lay within the discretionary area of judgment which the court ought to accord to the legislature.

> [I]t is appropriate in some circumstances for the judiciary to defer, on democratic grounds, to the considered opinion of the elected body as to where the balance is to be struck between the rights of the individual and the needs of society.[15]

His Lordship saw the essential question as whether Parliament acted within its discretionary area of judgment when it was choosing the point of balance.[16] He continued:

> The area is one where Parliament was better equipped than the judges are to decide where the balance lay. The judges are well able to assess the extent to which the restrictions will inhibit questioning or the leading of evidence. But it seems to me in this highly sensitive and carefully researched field an assessment of the prejudice to the wider interests of the community if the restrictions were not to take that form was more appropriate for Parliament. An important factor for Parliament to consider was the extent to which restrictions were needed in order to restore and maintain public confidence.[17]

Outside of the criminal justice sphere, it appears that there is a little more scope for deference, particularly in the context of administrative decision making. This was particularly clear from the speeches made in *Alconbury*.[18] Finding that the Secretary of State in his planning capacity was not independent and impartial but that this could be overcome by the jurisdiction of the High Court to exercise judicial review, all of their Lordships referred to the inappropriateness of allowing a court to substitute its decision for that of the administrative authority in questions of planning policy. Lord Slynn noted that the adoption of planning policy and its application to particular facts was quite different from the judicial function.

> It is for elected Members of Parliament and ministers to decide what are the objectives of planning policy, objectives which may be of national, environmental, social or political significance and for these objectives to be set out in legislation, primary and secondary, in ministerial directions and planning policy guidelines.[19]

---

[13] Above n 7.
[14] *Ibid*, at [36].
[15] *Ibid*, at [58].
[16] *Ibid*.
[17] *Ibid*, at [99].
[18] *R v Secretary of State for the Environment, Transport and the Regions, ex p Alconbury Developments Ltd* [2001] UKHL 23, [2001] 2 WLR 1389.
[19] *Ibid*, at [48].

In Lord Nolan's view, to

> substitute for the Secretary of State an independent and impartial body with no central electoral accountability would not only be a recipe for chaos: it would be profoundly undemocratic.[20]

Lord Hoffmann also pointed out that the question of what the public interest requires for the purpose of property rights can and should be determined according to the democratic principle—by elected local or central bodies, or by ministers accountable to them subject to the rule of law.[21]

> [P]olicy decisions within the limits imposed by the principles of judicial review are a matter for democratically accountable institutions and not for the courts.[22]

Lord Clyde also found that planning was a matter of the formation and application of policy, and that the policy was not a matter for the courts but for the executive.[23]

> Once it is recognised that there should be a national planning policy under a central supervision, it is consistent with democratic principle that the responsibility for that work should lie on the shoulders of a minister answerable to Parliament.[24]

2. Article 6(1) Application: Determination of Civil Rights and Obligations

The first sentence of Article 6(1) provides that a person is only entitled to the rights there enshrined 'in the determination of his civil rights and obligations or of any criminal charge against him.' The meaning of the phrase 'determination of civil rights and obligations' is autonomous[25] and has given rise to a great deal of litigation from those seeking to bring themselves within the protection of Article 6(1). It has been held that a narrow view is inappropriate[26] and pragmatically, in *Beeson*,[27] the Court of Appeal recognised that it should lean towards finding that civil rights were engaged, given that, at common law, whether or not executive action touched the

---

[20] *Ibid*, at [60].
[21] *Ibid*, at [72]–[73].
[22] *Ibid*, at [76].
[23] *Ibid*, at [139].
[24] *Ibid*, at [141]. See also *Begum (Runa) v Tower Hamlets London Borough Council* [2003] UKHL 5, [2003] 2 AC 430.
[25] *Alconbury, ibid*, at [148] per Lord Clyde in reliance upon *König v Germany* (1978) 2 EHRR 170; *H v France* (1989) 12 EHRR 74.
[26] *Ibid*, at [146] per Lord Clyde in reliance upon *X v United Kingdom* (1998) 28 D&R 177; *Ringeisen v Austria (No.1)* (1971) 1 EHRR 455; *Golder v United Kingdom* (1975) 1 EHRR 524; *Le Compte, Van Leuven and De Meyere v Belgium* (1981) 4 EHRR 1.
[27] *R (on the application of Beeson) v Secretary of State for Health* [2002] EWCA Civ 1812, [2003] HRLR 345.

citizen's rights in private law was irrelevant to the availability of judicial review.[28] Nevertheless, a number of rules and restrictions apply.[29]

2.1 Civil Rights and Obligations

Civil rights and obligations are rights and obligations which can be said, at least on arguable grounds, to be recognised under domestic law.[30] It is not open to a court when applying Article 6 to create a substantive right which has no legal basis in the domestic system at all.[31] For example, in *Alconbury*,[32] which concerned the role of the Secretary of State in referring planning applications to himself and appointing inspectors to hold public planning inquiries, the House of Lords held that the rights with which the appeals were concerned were rights of property and clearly fell within the scope of civil rights. By contrast, in *Kehoe*[33] a majority of their Lordships held that, as the Child Support Act 1991 did not confer on the caring parent a right of recovering or enforcing a claim to child maintenance against an absent or non-resident parent, the caring parent had no civil right within the meaning of Article 6. Other examples of civil rights include the right to practise a profession[34]; rights under family law[35]; rights under tort law[36]; and rights under employment law.[37] Due to the Human Rights Act, Convention rights are also considered to be civil rights within the meaning of Article 6(1). For example, in *Re S*[38] the House of Lords concluded that the making of a care order, which endowed a local authority with parental responsibility for a child, affected Article 8 rights of parents and children. Concluding that these were now civil rights, Article 6(1) was held to apply.[39] Similarly, in *McCann*[40] the House of Lords held that proceedings for an anti-social behaviour order under section 1 of the Crime and Disorder Act 1998 engaged rights under Articles 8, 10 and 11, and therefore Article 6(1) applied.[41]

---

[28] *Ibid*, at [17] and [19].

[29] It is important to remember that even if Art 6 does not apply, the common law may provide a remedy. See, eg *R (on the application of Smith) v Parole Board* [2005] UKHL 1, [2005] 1 WLR 350 and the comments of the Court of Appeal in *Beeson*, above n 27, at [17].

[30] *Alconbury*, above n 18, at [148] in reliance upon *James v United Kingdom* (1986) 8 EHRR 123 at [81].

[31] *R (on the application of Kehoe) v Secretary of State for Work and Pensions* [2005] UKHL 48, [2005] 3 WLR 252 at [41] per Lord Hope.

[32] Above n 18.

[33] Above n 31.

[34] *Preiss v General Dental Council* [2001] UKPC 36, [2001] 1 WLR 1926.

[35] *Re S* [2002] UKHL 10, [2002] 2 WLR 720.

[36] *Polanski v Condé Nast Publications* [2005] UKHL 10, [2005] 1 WLR 637.

[37] *Stansbury v Datapulse plc* [2003] EWCA Civ 1951, [2004] ICR 523.

[38] Above n 35.

[39] *Ibid*, at [69]–[72].

[40] *R (on the application of McCann) v Crown Court at Manchester* [2002] UKHL 39, [2003] 1 AC 787.

[41] *Ibid*, at [29] per Lord Steyn and [80] per Lord Hope. Other examples include *R (on the application of Thompson) v Law Society* [2004] EWCA Civ 167, [2004] 1 WLR 2522, where it was accepted by the Court of Appeal that an order by the Office for Supervision of Solicitors that the claimant refund costs was a determination of civil rights and obligations as he was deprived of a possession, at [107]; *R (on the application of Q) v Secretary of State for the Home Department* [2003] EWCA Civ 364, [2004] QB 36, where, without finally determining the issue, the Court of Appeal proceeded on the basis that the decision concerning entitlement of an asylum seeker to support engaged civil rights because of the gravity of such a decision, in human rights terms, for the individual, at [115]–[116]; and *S T and P v London Borough of Brent* [2002] EWCA Civ 693, [2002] ACD 90, where the Court of Appeal held Art 6 was engaged by a school exclusion given its impact on the right to education.

It is clear that Article 6(1) can also apply to administrative decisions on the ground that these can determine or affect rights in private law.[42] The European Court of Human Rights has also extended Article 6(1) to public law rights, such as entitlement to social security or welfare benefits under publicly funded statutory schemes, on the ground that they closely resemble rights in private law.[43] The position under the HRA is not yet clear. In *Begum*,[44] whilst not finally deciding the issue, the House of Lords found the reasoning of Hale LJ in *Adan*[45] persuasive. Hale LJ had held that, once the local authority were satisfied that the statutory criteria for providing accommodation existed, they had no discretion and had to provide it irrespective of local conditions of demand and supply. She therefore concluded that this was more akin to a claim for social security benefits than a claim for social or other services where the authorities had a greater degree of discretion, and was therefore a determination of a civil right within the meaning of Article 6(1).[46] In *Begum*, the appellant was homeless and the Council owed her a duty under section 193 of the Housing Act 1993 to ensure that accommodation was available to her. Despite the comments on *Adan*, their Lordships noted that to apply Article 6(1) to the provision of benefits in kind, involving the amount of discretion which was inevitably needed in such cases, would be to go further than Strasbourg had gone.[47] However, they found no violation of the independence and impartiality guarantee without determining whether Article 6 actually applied to the decision.[48]

Despite the possible extension of the Article to public law rights, it still remains the position that the disputes of individuals in the public service sector who wield a portion of the state's sovereign power are outside the protection of Article 6(1).[49] For example, in *Mangera*[50] the Court of Appeal concluded that Article 6 had no application to a case brought by a serving soldier under the Race Relations Act 1976.[51] However, the lower the grade of public servant, the more likely it is that Article 6(1) will apply. In *Heath*[52] the Court of Appeal held that a civilian police station reception officer was unlikely to meet the test of 'wielding a portion of the State's sovereign power' and therefore, whilst not finally determining the issue, held that it was likely Article 6(1) applied.[53]

---

[42] See, eg *Alconbury*, above n 18, and *R (on the application of McLellan) v Bracknell Forest Borough Council* [2002] 1 All ER 899.

[43] *Begum*, above n 24, at [30] in reliance upon *Salesi v Italy* (1993) 26 EHRR 187.

[44] *Ibid.*

[45] *Adan v Newham London Borough Council* [2001] EWCA Civ 1916, [2002] 1 WLR 2120.

[46] *Ibid*, at [55].

[47] *Begum*, above n 24, per Lord Hoffmann at [69], Lord Bingham at [6], Lord Millett at [94] and Lord Walker at [115].

[48] In *Beeson*, above n 27, the Court of Appeal held that the decision of a county council that an elderly man had deprived himself of certain property belonging to him in circumstances such that the value of the property fell to be taken into account in assessing his ability to pay for residential accommodation arranged for him by the Council engaged his civil rights. See generally P Craig, 'The Human Rights Act, Article 6 and Procedural Rights' [2003] *PL* 753; I Loveland, 'Does Homelessness Decision-making Engage Article 6(1) of the European Convention on Human Rights?' [2003] *EHRLR* 176.

[49] *Heath v Commissioner of Police for the Metropolis* [2004] EWCA Civ 943, [2005] ICR 329 in reliance upon *Devlin v UK* (2002) EHRR 43. See further G Morris, 'Public Employment and the Human Rights Act 1998' [2001] *PL* 442.

[50] *Mangera v Ministry of Defence* [2003] EWCA Civ 801.

[51] In reliance upon *Pellegrin v France* (1999) 31 EHRR 651.

[52] Above n 49.

[53] *Ibid*, at [60]–[61].

2.2 Determination

For Article 6(1) to apply, it must also be shown that civil rights and obligations are being determined. In order for there to be a determination, there must be a dispute of a genuine and serious nature,[54] though it need not be a dispute in any formal sense.[55] The decision must directly affect civil rights and obligations by determining the existence of a right or the scope of manner in which it may be exercised.[56] For example, in *Alconbury*[57] the House of Lords found that the role of the Secretary of State in referring planning applications to himself, and appointing inspectors to hold public planning inquiries, fell within the meaning of determination of civil rights even though there was no issue about the existence of those rights and no determination of those rights in the strict sense. However, civil rights were directly affected and the dispute was of a genuine and serious nature.[58]

By contrast, in *Smith*[59] a majority of the House of Lords concluded that proceedings before the Parole Board where a determinate sentence prisoner released on licence sought to resist subsequent revocation of his licence did not constitute a determination of civil rights and obligations. What the Board was doing was giving effect, in the performance of functions given to it by statute, to the sentences which had previously been imposed by the judge when the appellants were convicted. None of the elements that were inherent in the sentence from the beginning were being enlarged or altered.[60] Similarly, in *Harrison*[61] the Court of Appeal concluded that Article 6 did not apply because the legislation conferred no jurisdiction on the Secretary of State to determine in any authoritative way whether a person was a British citizen—this was something for the courts to decide.[62]

It is unlikely for interim orders to constitute determinations. For example, in *M*[63] the Court of Appeal held that, because an application for an interim anti-social behaviour order under the Crime and Disorder Act 1998 without notice could only be made when the justices' clerk was satisfied that it was necessary for the application to be made without notice, and because the order could only be made for a limited period, when the court considered that it is just to make it, and in circumstances where it could be reviewed or discharged, it was impossible to say that it determined civil rights.[64] It has also been held that disciplinary proceedings resulting in severe

---

[54] *Alconbury*, above n 18, at [149]. See also *R v Lord Chancellor, ex p Lightfoot* [2000] QB 597.

[55] *Ibid*, at [147] per Lord Clyde in reliance upon *Le Compte*, above n 26, and *Moreira de Azevedo v Portugal* (1990) 13 EHRR 721.

[56] *Ibid*, at [149] in reliance upon *Le Compte, ibid; Balmer-Schafroth v Switzerland* (1997) 25 EHRR 598.

[57] Above n 18.

[58] at [150] per Lord Clyde. See also *R v Secretary of State for Health, ex p C* [2000] 1 FCR 471, where the Court of Appeal held that inclusion on the Department of Health's list of people about whom there were doubts about their suitability to work with children was not determinative of anything.

[59] Above n 29.

[60] *Ibid*, at [81] per Lord Hope. Lord Carswell agreed and Lord Slynn reached a similar conclusion. See also *St Brice v London Borough of Southwark* [2001] EWCA Civ 1138, [2002] 1 WLR 1537, where the Court of Appeal held that enforcement of a judgment did not involve a separate determination of civil rights and obligations.

[61] *Harrison v Secretary of State for the Home Department* [2003] EWCA Civ 432.

[62] *Ibid*, at [31]–[32].

[63] *R (on the application of M) v Secretary of State for Constitutional Affairs and Lord Chancellor* [2004] EWCA Civ 312, [2004] 1 WLR 2298.

[64] *Ibid*, at [39].

reprimand rather than the loss of the right to continue to practise a profession do not determine civil rights and obligations.[65]

2.3 Administrative Decisions: the Two-stage Process

Despite the speeches in *Begum*,[66] the higher judiciary does not appear favourably disposed to the extension of Article 6(1) to administrative decision making. In *Alconbury*[67] Lord Hoffmann noted that, were it not for Strasbourg authority, he would have concluded that a decision as to what the public interest required in the planning context was not a determination of civil rights or obligations.[68] But whilst Article 6(1) may apply to the decision, this does not mean that the administrative decision maker must himself or herself comply with its requirements. In determining whether the requirements of Article 6(1) have been met, regard must be had to all stages of the process.[69] In the case of administrative decisions, it is possible for a breach by the primary decision maker to be cured by the availability of judicial review. However, from Strasbourg case law, it is not clear whether the reviewing court must exercise 'full jurisdiction' or 'full decision making power'. In *Alconbury*[70] the House of Lords concluded that full jurisdiction meant full jurisdiction in the context of the case, and that here a full merits review was not necessary and judicial review was sufficient.[71]

In determining the context of the case it is necessary to have regard to matters such as the subject matter of the decision, the manner in which that decision was arrived at and the content of the dispute, including the actual and desired grounds of appeal.[72] In the context of disciplinary proceedings, a more exhaustive remedy may be required to satisfy Article 6[73] and judicial review may not suffice for a decision on the factual question of whether or not there has been a breach of planning control.[74] Indeed, the more any given statutory scheme is likely to give rise to fact-laden issues, the more Article 6 will require independent adjudication on the facts.[75]

In *Re S*[76] the House of Lords held that judicial review would meet the demands of Article 6 in some instances but held that there were important decisions for which the Children Act 1989 made no provision. Cited as an example were questions for the local authority regarding a child's future, such as whether rehabilitation was a realistic possibility. Their Lordships were doubtful whether judicial review would meet the

---

[65] *Thompson*, above n 41.
[66] Above n 24.
[67] Above n 18.
[68] *Ibid*, at [74].
[69] *Ibid*, at [29] per Lord Slynn in reliance upon *Albert and Le Compte v Belgium* (1983) 5 EHRR 533; *Le Compte*, above n 26; *Golder*, above n 26; *Kaplan v United Kingdom* 4 EHRR 64; *ISKCON v United Kingdom*, 8 March 1994; *Bryan v United Kingdom* (1995) 21 EHRR 342; *Chapman v United Kingdom*, 18 January 2001; *Howard v United Kingdom*, 16 July 1987; *Varey v United Kingdom*, 27 October 1999.
[70] *Ibid*.
[71] *Ibid*, at [87] per Lord Hoffmann, [154] per Lord Clyde and [189] per Lord Hutton.
[72] *Ibid*, at [154] per Lord Clyde.
[73] *Ibid*, at [154] per Lord Clyde.
[74] *Ibid*, at [100] per Lord Hoffmann.
[75] *Beeson*, above n 27, at [23].
[76] Above n 35.

high degree of judicial control required in such circumstances.[77] In *Beeson*[78] the Court of Appeal held that the question of whether a person was in need of care and attention for the purposes of section 21 of the National Assistance Act 1948 was not a hard-edged issue of fact. It concluded that the scheme was exactly of the kind where the first decisions were properly confined within the public body having responsibility for the scheme's administration and, given the availability of judicial review, the requirements of Article 6 were met.[79]

2.4 Examples

It has been held that there is a determination of civil rights and obligations in the following instances: decision of a professional tribunal affecting the right to practise a profession[80]; proceedings conducted by an auditor under section 20 of the Local Government Finance Act 1982[81]; the making of a confiscation order as a result of convictions for certain types of offences[82]; the role of the Secretary of State in referring planning applications to himself and appointing inspectors to hold public planning inquiries[83]; the making of a care order which endows a local authority with parental responsibility for a child[84]; care proceedings under Part IV of the Children Act 1989[85]; proceedings for an anti-social behaviour order under section 1 of the Crime and Disorder Act 1998[86]; the making of a secure accommodation order[87]; a decision to forcibly treat a patient detained under the Mental Health Act 1983[88]; a decision of the Disciplinary Appeals Tribunal of the Securities and Futures Authority finding an individual guilty of improper conduct as a trader in securities[89]; proceedings for possession[90]; an order for residential assessment under section 38(6) of the Children Act 1989[91]; proceedings of the Special Immigration Appeals Commission[92]; the obligation to pay VAT and penalties associated with its non-payment[93]; notification of a site as a site of special scientific interest under section 28 of the Wildlife and Countryside Act 1981.[94]

---

[77] *Ibid*, at [81].
[78] Above n 27.
[79] *Ibid*, at [33]–[34]. See also *R (on the application of Adlard) v Secretary of State for Environment, Transport & Regions* [2002] EWCA Civ 735, [2002] 1 WLR 2515; *Q*, above n 41, at [115]–[117]; *R (on the application of Whitmey) v The Commons Commissioners* [2004] EWCA Civ 951, [2005] QB 282. See generally, Craig, 'The Human Rights Act', above n 48.
[80] *Preiss*, above n 34.
[81] *Porter*, above n 2.
[82] *McIntosh*, above n 11; *R v Rezvi* [2002] UKHL 1, [2003] 1 AC 1099.
[83] *Alconbury*, above n 18.
[84] *Re S*, above n 35.
[85] *Re V (a child) (care proceedings: human rights claims)* [2004] EWCA Civ 54, [2004] 1 All ER 997.
[86] *McCann*, above n 40.
[87] *Re M (A child) (secure accommodation)* [2001] EWCA Civ 458, [2001] 1 FCR 692.
[88] *R (on the application of Wilkinson) v The Responsible Medical Officer, Broadmoor Hospital* [2001] EWCA Civ 1545, [2002] 1 WLR 419.
[89] *R (on the application of Fleurose) v Securities and Futures Authority Ltd* [2002] EWCA Civ 2015, [2002] IRLR 297.
[90] *Sheffield City Council v Smart* [2002] EWCA Civ 4, [2002] ACD 56.
[91] *Re G (a child: residential assessment)* [2004] EWCA Civ 24, [2004] 1 FCR 317.
[92] *A v Secretary of State for the Home Department* [2002] EWCA Civ 1502, [2004] QB 335.
[93] *Begum v The Commissioners of Customs and Excise*, VADT, 30 May 2002.
[94] *R v English Nature ex p Aggregate Industries UK Ltd* [2002] EWHC (Admin) 908, [2003] Env LR 3.

It has also been held that there has not been a determination of civil rights and obligations in the following instances: the procedure followed by the Parole Board when a determinate sentence prisoner, released on licence, seeks to resist the subsequent revocation of his licence[95]; inclusion on the Department of Health's list of people about whom there are doubts as to their suitability to work with children[96]; a tax appeal claiming error or mistake relief as opposed to a private law claim against the Revenue based on unjust enrichment[97]; proceedings relating to the entry, stay or deportation of aliens[98]; proceedings concerning a right to citizenship[99]; decision by the Office for the Supervision of Solicitors to severely reprimand a solicitor[100]; a petitioner seeking a bankruptcy order under the Insolvency Act 1986 but unable to pay the deposit.[101]

3. Article 6(1) Application: Determination of Any Criminal Charge

Establishing that there has been a determination of a criminal charge makes a great difference to the range of protections available to an individual under Article 6. In *McCann*[102] the House of Lords confirmed that the concept of 'charged with a criminal offence' under Articles 6(2) and 6(3) was coextensive with the concept of 'determination of any criminal charge'.[103] Therefore, bringing oneself within the definition means that, in addition to the protections of Article 6(1), Articles 6(2) and 6(3) are also available. Further, it has also been held that states have far greater latitude when dealing with civil cases than when dealing with criminal cases.[104] Given this is the position, the case law concerning the meaning of 'charged with a criminal offence' is also considered in this part.

3.1 Determination

The determination of a criminal charge, to be properly so regarded, must expose the subject of the charge to the possibility of punishment, whether in the event punishment is imposed or not. A process which can only culminate in measures of a

---

[95] *Smith*, above n 29.
[96] *C*, above n 58.
[97] *Eagerpath Ltd v Edwards (Inspector of Taxes)* [2001] STC 26.
[98] *R (on the application of Ullah) v Secretary of State for the Home Department* [2003] EWCA Civ 1366.
[99] *Harrison*, above n 61.
[100] *Thompson*, above n 41.
[101] *R v Lord Chancellor, ex p Lightfoot* [1999] 4 All ER 583.
[102] Above n 40.
[103] *Ibid*, at [28] in reliance upon *Lutz v Germany* (1987) 10 EHRR 182.
[104] *Ibid*, at [7] per Lord Steyn in reliance upon *Dombo Beheer v The Netherlands* (1993) 18 EHRR 213 at [32].

preventative, curative, rehabilitative or welfare-promoting kind will not ordinarily be the determination of a criminal charge.[105]

3.1.1 Pre-trial Decisions

Before considering the meaning of 'criminal charge' it must first be established that there has been a determination to which Article 6 can apply. This has caused particular difficulties with respect to decisions that have been made before a criminal trial has actually commenced. For example, in *Kebilene*[106] the claimants sought judicial review of the Director of Public Prosecution's consent to their prosecutions for offences under terrorism legislation as it was alleged that the legislation was incompatible with Article 6(2). The House of Lords held that it was rightly conceded that, once the HRA was fully in force, it would not be possible to apply for judicial review on the ground that a decision to prosecute was in breach of a Convention right and that the only available remedies would be in the trial process or on appeal.[107] Whilst it was not fully explained in the speeches given, it would appear this conclusion was reached because the DPP did not actually 'determine' the charge against the accused—that was a matter for the court.[108]

However, whilst this may be the position in England and Wales, it appears that, due to the Scotland Act 1998, once again a different position has been reached in Scotland. *Brown*[109] concerned Mrs Brown's challenge under the Scotland Act 1998 to the intention of the procurator fiscal to rely at trial on her admission obtained under the Road Traffic Act 1988 that she was driving her car when it was alleged that the driver of the car had committed certain specified offences. It was argued that use of this admission in evidence would infringe her right to a fair hearing. The Privy Council concluded that, under the Scotland Act 1998, the right of the accused to a fair trial was a responsibility of the Lord Advocate in the prosecution of offences as well as of the court. If this was not the case, the Privy Council saw much force in the argument that, as the determination during a criminal trial of the criminal charge in all its aspects was a matter for the court and not the prosecutor, the acts of the Lord Advocate lay outside the scope of the Article.[110]

It is also possible for a criminal charge to be determined without the matter reaching trial. In *R (on the application of R) v Durham Constabulary*[111] the House of Lords considered the procedure for warning young offenders under sections 65 and 66 of the Crime and Disorder Act 1988. Although expressing considerable doubt, given the concession by the Secretary of State, it assumed that the appellant faced a criminal charge once he had been formally notified by the police that allegations of

---

[105] *R (on the application of R) v Durham Constabulary* [2005] UKHL 21, [2005] 1 WLR 1184 at [12] per Lord Bingham.

[106] Above n 9.

[107] Per Lord Steyn with whom Lords Slynn and Cooke agreed.

[108] See also *Lai v Commissioners of Customs & Excise*, VADT, 1 July 2002, where it was held that the steps leading up to the issue of assessment and a penalty notice were not the determination of a criminal charge.

[109] Above n 4.

[110] By contrast Lord Clyde held that even without the Scotland Act, Art 6 applied to activities occurring during the criminal trial which had a bearing on the fairness of the proceedings. See also *Montgomery v HM Advocate* [2003] 1 AC 641.

[111] *R (on the application of R) v Durham Constabulary*, above n 105.

criminal conduct against him were being investigated.[112] However, it concluded that the criminal charge ceased to exist when a firm decision was made not to prosecute.[113] This was despite the fact that the warning would be recorded on the Police National Computer and the Sex Offenders Register.

3.1.2 Sentencing

It is clear that sentencing is within the meaning of 'determination of a criminal charge' and therefore covered by Article 6 as it is part of the trial and the same procedural protections apply to the imposition of sentence as to the determination of guilt.[114] In *Anderson*[115] the House of Lords concluded that, in fixing a convicted murderer's tariff, the Home Secretary was assessing the term of imprisonment which the convicted murderer should serve as punishment for his crime.[116] Article 6(1) applied and the Home Secretary's role was declared incompatible with the guarantee of independence and impartiality.

3.2 Criminal Charge

The meaning of 'criminal charge' is autonomous. Under the HRA the courts have adopted the *Engel*[117] criteria formulated by the ECHR. When determining whether there has been a determination of any criminal charge, the domestic classification, the nature of the offence and the severity of the potential penalty are taken into account.[118] These criteria are alternative and not cumulative. One criterion cannot be applied so as to divest an offence of a criminal character if that has been established under another criterion. However, a cumulative approach can be adopted if the separate analysis of each does not lead to a clear conclusion.[119]

3.2.1 Domestic Classification

The first test is the category into which the proceedings are placed by domestic law. Whilst this test is generally regarded as far from decisive, it is a starting point.[120] Regarding the test as such largely renders irrelevant the rationale underlying a national law which seeks to decriminalise conduct which would otherwise be treated, or generally regarded, as criminal in nature.[121] It is necessary to look at the substance of the matter rather than its form, and to look behind appearances and investigate the realities of the procedure.[122] Indications of classification as criminal may be: the

---

[112] *Ibid*, at [11]–[12] per Lord Bingham.

[113] *Ibid*, at [12] per Lord Bingham in reliance upon *X v United Kingdom* (1979) 17 DR 122 and *S v Miller* 2001 SC 977.

[114] *R v Secretary of State for the Home Department, ex p Anderson* [2002] UKHL 46, [2003] 1 AC 837 at [22] per Lord Bingham, [50]–[51] per Lord Steyn and [67] per Lord Hutton.

[115] *Ibid.*

[116] *Ibid*, at [13] per Lord Bingham, [39] and [52] per Lord Steyn and [75] per Lord Hutton.

[117] *Engel v The Netherlands (No.1)* (1976) 1 EHRR 647 at [82].

[118] See, eg *McCann*, above n 40.

[119] *Ibid*, at [65] per Lord Hope in reliance upon *Lauko v Slovakia* (1998) 33 EHRR 994 at [57]; *Ozturk v Germany* 6 EHRR 409 at [54].

[120] *McIntosh v Lord Advocate* [2003] 1 AC 1078 at [16] per Lord Bingham..

[121] *Customs and Excise Commissioners v Han* [2001] EWCA Civ 1040, [2001] 1 WLR 2253 at [68].

[122] *Porter*, above n 2, at [84] per Lord Hope in reliance upon *Deweer v Belgium* (1980) 2 EHRR 439.

involvement of the Crown Prosecution Service; a formal accusation of breach of the criminal law; the need to prove *mens rea*; and entry on the record as a conviction or a recordable offence for the purpose of taking fingerprints.[123] If the purpose of the proceedings is to punish rather than to protect or prevent, this is also an indication of classification as criminal.[124]

In *McCann*[125] the House of Lords had to determine whether the proceedings leading to the making of an anti-social behaviour order under the Crime and Disorder Act 1998 involved the determination of a criminal charge. Their Lordships were particularly influenced by Parliament's intention that the proceedings be civil and not attract the rigour of the hearsay rule.[126] Taking into account the facts that the CPS was not involved, there was no formal accusation of a breach of the criminal law, *mens rea* did not need to be proved and that the purpose of the proceedings was preventative not to obtain a conviction, the House of Lords concluded that the proceedings were civil proceedings under domestic law.[127]

In *McIntosh*[128], a case brought under the Scotland Act 1998 concerning the application of Article 6(2) to confiscation proceedings under section 3(2) of the Proceedings of Crime (Scotland) Act 1995, the Privy Council concluded that the respondent would not be considered to be a person charged with a criminal offence as that expression was understood in these jurisdictions. The following considerations were taken into account:

(1) The application is not initiated by complaint or indictment and is not governed by the ordinary rules of criminal procedure. (2) The application may only be made if the accused is convicted, and cannot be pursued if he is acquitted. (3) The application forms part of the sentencing procedure. (4) The accused is at no time accused of committing any crime other than that which permits the application to be made. (5) When, as is standard procedure in anything other than the simplest case, the prosecutor lodges a statement under section 9, that statement (usually supported by detailed schedules) is an accounting record and not an accusation. (6) The sum ordered to be confiscated need not be the profit made from the drug trafficking offence of which the accused has been convicted, or any other drug trafficking offence. (7) If the accused fails to pay the sum he is ordered to pay under the order, the term of imprisonment which he will be ordered to serve in default is imposed not for the commission of any drug trafficking offence but on his failure to pay the sum ordered and to procure compliance. (8) The transactions of which account is taken in the confiscation proceedings may be the subject of a later prosecution, which would be repugnant to the rule against double jeopardy if the accused were charged with a criminal offence in the confiscation proceedings. (9) The proceedings do not culminate in a verdict which would (in

---

123 *McCann*, above n 40, at [22] per Lord Steyn.
124 *Ibid*, at [22]. See also *R v H* [2004] UKHL 3, [2004] 2 AC 134, where the House of Lords concluded that the procedure under s 4A of the Criminal Procedure (Insanity) Act 1964 which provided for a finding that the accused did the act which constituted the *actus reus* of the crime did not involve the determination of a criminal charge as the provision was designed to protect the public and not to punish the subject of the order.
125 Above n 40.
126 *Ibid*, at [18] per Lord Steyn.
127 *Ibid*, at [22]–[27] per Lord Steyn, who placed reliance on *B v Chief Constable of Avon and Somerset Constabulary* [2001] 1 WLR 340 and *Gough v Chief Constable of the Derbyshire Constabulary* [2002] EWCA Civ 351, [2002] QB 459. See also Lord Hutton at [94]–[98].
128 Above n 120.

proceedings on indictment) be a matter for the jury if the accused were charged with a criminal offence.[129]

In *Han*[130] a majority of the Court of Appeal was not convinced by the classification of the penalties for tax evasion as civil. In the opinion of the court, the levying and enforcement of the penalty concerned was designed to punish and deter members of the public at large in respect of dishonest conduct. It was also possible for the Commissioners to decide in the course of an investigation to switch from the civil regime to the criminal.[131]

3.2.2 Nature of the Offence

The second test is the nature of the offence, and again it is necessary to look behind appearances and investigate the reality of the procedure.[132] If the 'offence' applies to the public at large rather than a specific group it is likely to be regarded as criminal.[133] Proceedings which are punitive or disciplinary rather than compensatory, regulatory or preventative are likely to be considered more in the nature of a criminal charge. It has been held that the distinguishing feature of a criminal charge is that it may lead to punishment[134] even if the penalty is in the nature of a fine rather than imprisonment[135] and even if the fine is minor.[136] In *Porter*[137] it was argued that the proceedings under the Local Government Finance Act 1982 were in the nature of a criminal charge. The House of Lords disagreed, holding that these were compensatory and regulatory, not punitive. No fine was involved, nor was there provision for any penalty by way of imprisonment.[138]

In *McCann* it was noted that the person against whom an anti-social behaviour order was sought was not being charged with an offence and the conduct required to be demonstrated was not conduct which would be capable of being treated as criminal. Proceedings were preventative, not punitive or disciplinary. There was no power of arrest and proceedings could not result in the immediate imposition of a penalty.[139] Similarly, in *R v H*[140] the House of Lords held that the procedure under the Criminal Procedure (Insanity) Act 1964 allowing for a finding that the accused committed the *actus reus* of the crime was not in the nature of a criminal charge as it could not result in conviction or punishment.[141] The absence of punishment was also

---

[129] *Ibid*, at [14] per Lord Bingham.
[130] Above n 121.
[131] *Ibid*, at [75].
[132] *McCann*, above n 40, at [99] in reliance on *Deweer*, above n 122.
[133] *Han*, above n 121.
[134] *Smith*, above n 29, at [40] per Lord Bingham.
[135] *Han*, above n 121, at [66].
[136] *R (on the application of Mudie) v Kent Magistrates' Court* [2003] EWCA Civ 237, [2003] 2 WLR 1344.
[137] Above n 2.
[138] *Ibid*, at [85] per Lord Hope.
[139] *Ibid*, at [71]–[74] per Lord Hope in reliance upon *Lauko*, above n 119; *Guzzardi v Italy* (1980) 3 EHRR 333; *Raimondo v Italy* (1994) 18 EHRR 237; *M v Italy* (1991) 70 DR 59; *Gough*, above n 127. See also the speech of Lord Hutton at [102]–[108].
[140] Above n 124.
[141] *Ibid*, at [18] per Lord Bingham. See also *R v Grant*, Court of Appeal, 22 November 2001 [2001] EWCA Crim 2611, [2002] 2 WLR 1409.

the key to the House of Lords conclusion in *Smith*[142] that Parole Board proceedings determining whether or not a prisoner's licence should be revoked and he be recalled to prison did not constitute the determination of a criminal charge.[143] 'Recall of a prisoner on licence is not a punishment. It is primarily to protect the public against further offences.'[144]

3.2.3 Severity of the Potential Penalty

The final test is the severity of the potential penalty. Here the question is whether, by reason of its nature and degree of severity, the penalty or sanction amounts to a penalty in the sense of punishment.[145] Outside the context of disciplinary proceedings and, in particular, in the field of tax evasion, it appears that a substantial financial penalty which is imposed by way of punishment and deterrence may render the charges criminal in nature.[146] By contrast, the imposition of no penalty may indicate the opposite conclusion.[147]

In *McCann*[148] the House of Lords concluded that the anti-social behaviour order itself involved no penalty and that the proceedings were not in respect of a criminal charge.[149] In *R v H*[150] the House of Lords held that it was difficult, if not impossible, to conceive of a criminal proceeding which did not culminate in the imposition of any penalty.[151] Here there was no criminal charge as the statute merely sought to strike a fair balance between protecting a defendant who was unfit to plead and protecting the public from a defendant who had committed an injurious act.[152] However, in *Napier*[153] the Administrative Court concluded that it was the imposition of additional days to be served in prison that carried prison disciplinary proceedings over the line from civil to criminal.[154] This will never be the case with respect to life sentence prisoners as they cannot be subject to the punishment of additional days. In *Tagney*[155] the Court of Appeal held that in such instances it would be rare for the proceedings to constitute the determination of a criminal charge although it did not rule this out, suggesting that the Secretary of State may wish to consider amending the Prison Rules to give the governor the power to refer an adjudication to an

---

[142] Above n 29.
[143] *Ibid*, at [40] per Lord Bingham in reliance upon *Ganusaukas v Lithuania*, Application No. 47922/99 and *Brown v United Kingdom*, Judgment of 26 October 2004.
[144] *Ibid*, at [56] per Lord Slynn. See also *Re M*, above n 87.
[145] *Porter*, above n 2, at [84] per Lord Hope in reliance upon *Engel*, above n 117, at [82]–[83]; *Lutz*, above n 103, at [54]; *Democoli v Malta* (1991) 14 EHRR 47 at [34].
[146] *Han*, above n 121, at [67].
[147] *Mudie*, above n 136.
[148] Above n 40.
[149] *Ibid*, at [30] per Lord Steyn. For a critique of this judgment see S Macdonald, 'The Nature of the Anti-Social Behaviour Order—R (McCann & Others) v. Crown Court at Manchester', (2003) 66 *MLR* 630; A Ashworth, 'Social Control and "Anti-Social Behaviour": The Subversion of Human Rights?' (2004) 120 *LQR* 263.
[150] Above n 124.
[151] *Ibid*, at [19].
[152] *Ibid*, at [20] per Lord Bingham in reliance upon *R v Antoine* [2000] 2 All ER 208 at 221.
[153] *R (on the application of Napier) v Secretary of State for the Home Department* [2004] EWHC (Admin) 936, [2004] 1 WLR 3056.
[154] In reliance upon *Ezeh and Connors v United Kingdom*, Judgment of 15 July 2002.
[155] *Tangney v The Governor of HMP Elmley* [2005] EWCA Civ 1009.

independent adjudicator if, in the exceptional circumstances of the case, it was necessary to do so.[156]

3.3 Examples

It has been held that there is a determination of a criminal charge in the following instances: sentencing[157]; an application under the Debtors Act 1869[158]; the imposition of penalties for alleged dishonest evasion of pursuant to s 60(1) of the Value Added Tax Act 1994 and section 8(1) of the Finance Act 1994[159]; the regime under the Immigration and Asylum Act 1999 by which drivers and others bringing clandestine entrants into the United Kingdom in a vehicle are liable to a fixed penalty of £2,000 for each person transported[160]; committal for breach of an order or for telling lies in the face of the court[161]; prison disciplinary proceedings where the sanction of additional days of imprisonment is imposed.[162]

It has also been held that there has not been a determination of a criminal charge in the following instances: proceedings for making an anti-social behaviour order[163]; confiscation proceedings[164]; proceedings conducted by an auditor under the Local Government Act 1982[165]; procedures under the Criminal Procedure (Insanity) Act 1964[166]; Parole Board proceedings determining whether or not a prisoner's licence should be revoked[167]; proceedings for making a secure accommodation order under section 25 of the Children Act 1989[168]; decisions of the Disciplinary Appeals Tribunal of the Securities and Futures Authority finding an individual guilty of improper conduct as a trader in securities[169]; proceedings leading to the making of banning orders under the Football Spectators Act 1989[170]; condemnation proceedings pursuant to schedule 3 and section 139 of the Customs and Excise Management Act 1979[171]; proceedings before the VAT and Duties Tribunal under the Customs and Excise Management Act 1979 and the Finance Act 1994 for restoration of condemned goods[172]; disqualification proceedings under the Company Directors Disqualification Act 1986[173]; proceedings before the Special Immigration Appeals Commission[174]; the procedure for warning young offenders under sections 65 and 66

---

[156] *Ibid*, at [33].
[157] *Anderson*, above n 114.
[158] *Murbarak v Murbarak* [2001] 1 FCR 193.
[159] *Han*, above n 121.
[160] *International Transport Roth GmbH v Secretary of State for the Home Department* [2002] EWCA Civ 158, [2002] 3 WLR 344.
[161] *Berry Trade Ltd v Moussavi* [2002] WLR 1910.
[162] *Napier*, above n 153. But see *Tangney*, above n 155, in relation to life sentence prisoners.
[163] *McCann*, above n 40.
[164] *McIntosh*, above n 120.
[165] *Porter*, above n 2.
[166] *R v H*, above n 124.
[167] *Smith*, above n 29.
[168] *Re M*, above n 87, although the Court of Appeal did conclude that at common law the child should be afforded the rights set out in Art 6(3).
[169] *Fleurose*, above n 89.
[170] *Gough*, above n 127.
[171] *Mudie*, above n 136.
[172] *Gora v Customs and Excise Commissioners* [2003] EWCA Civ 525, [2004] QB 93.
[173] *Re Westminster Property Management Ltd* [2001] 1 WLR 2230.
[174] *A v Secretary of State for the Home Department*, above n 92.

of the Crime and Disorder Act 1988[175]; the default surcharge VAT penalty and penalties for misdeclaration and late registration.[176]

4. Access to Court

The first of the Article 6 rights is the implied right of access to court, which has its roots in the policy which has first claim on the loyalty of the law that wrongs should be remedied.[177] It requires the maintenance of fair and public judicial processes and forbids the state from denying individuals access to those processes for the determination of their civil rights.[178] However, it does not confer on the state adjudicative powers which it does not possess.[179] In particular, the right of access to court does not confer a right of appeal although, where such a right exists, Article 6 does apply to it.[180] Essentially the question is whether an issue which ought to be decided by a court is being prevented from being so decided.

> The touchstone in this regard is the proper role of courts in a democratic society. A right of access to a court is one of the checks on the danger of arbitrary power.[181]

As this is an implied right, it is not absolute and may be made subject to procedural restrictions. However, these must not so restrict or reduce the litigant's right of access as to impair the essence of the right and must satisfy the test of proportionality.[182]

> It must pursue a legitimate aim, it must be necessary and suitable for the attainment of that aim and must not restrict the right of access to the court disproportionately in relation to the importance of the aim it pursues.[183]

---

[175] *R (on the application of R) v Durham Constabulary*, above n 105.
[176] *Begum*, above n 93.
[177] *Holland v Lampen-Wolfe* [2000] 1 WLR 1573 per Lord Bingham quoting from *X v Bedfordshire County Council* [1995] 2 AC 633 at 663. The right is also a common law constitutional right. See, eg *R v Lord Chancellor, ex p Witham* [1997] 2 All ER 779 and *Lightfoot*, above n 101.
[178] Such a denial may arise, for example, from the compulsion of alternative dispute resolution. See *Halsey v Milton Keynes General NHS Trust* [2004] EWCA Civ 576, [2004] 1 WLR 3002.
[179] *Lampen-Wolfe*, above n 177.
[180] *R (on the application of Aru) v Chief Constable of Merseyside* [2004] EWCA Civ 199, [2004] 1 WLR 1697; *BLCT (13096) Limited v J Sainsbury plc* [2003] EWCA Civ 884, [2004] 2 P&CR 32.
[181] *Wilson v Secretary of State for Trade and Industry* [2003] UKHL 40, [2003] 3 WLR 568 at [35] per Lord Nicholls. In *Sinclair Garden Investments (Kensington) Ltd v Lands Tribunal* [2004] EWHC (Admin) 1910 the court held that the Lands Tribunal had the qualities of a court for the purposes of Art 6. Therefore, no special factors would justify a practice of entertaining claims for judicial review of refusals of leave to appeal by the Tribunal in the absence of special circumstances.
[182] *Matthews v Ministry of Defence* [2003] UKHL 4, [2003] 1 AC 1163 at [121] per Lord Walker in reliance upon *Golder v UK* (1975) 1 EHRR 524 at [35]–[38]; *Stubbings v UK* (1996) 23 EHRR 213 at [48].
[183] *Ibid*, at [33].

It is clear that the right of access is available to everyone, including serving prisoners conducting their own litigation[184] and illegal immigrants seeking access to the divorce courts.[185] In *Polanski*[186] a majority of the House of Lords held that a fugitive from justice, not willing to enter the United Kingdom to give evidence in his libel proceedings due to the risk of extradition to the United States, could give evidence by video link from France.

4.1 Substantive and Procedural Bars

The right of access to court for the determination of civil rights does not guarantee any particular content of those rights.[187] '[O]ne must take the domestic law as one finds it, and apply to it the autonomous Convention concept of civil rights.'[188] Therefore, if a restriction on access can be classified as a substantive element of national law, it is beyond the reach of Article 6. It is only if it can be classified as a procedural bar that it must satisfy the test of proportionality. The difficulty lies in distinguishing between substantive and procedural bars. The distinction is debatable close to the borderline,[189] and it has been held that the Strasbourg case law in this area remains uncertain.[190] In order to determine whether or not Article 6 is engaged, often the question is asked of whether or not the legislature or executive has encroached on territory which ought properly to be the province of courts in a democratic society.[191]

The most common examples of purely procedural bars are those which have no connection with the substance of the would-be litigant's claim, such as security for costs[192], obtaining the court's permission to continue or commence proceedings, statutes of limitation, and state and diplomatic immunity.[193] These are substantive rules of law which, because they can be described as conferring immunity on a particular class of potential defendants may also be perceived as objectionable restrictions on a claimant's access to court, even though they cannot fairly be described as procedural bars.[194] Many of these bars to access are examined in the following paragraphs.

---

[184] See, eg *R (on the application of Ponting) v Governor of HMP Whitemoor* [2002] EWCA Civ 224.

[185] *Mark v Mark* [2005] UKHL 42, [2005] 3 WLR 111. The House of Lords upheld the conclusion that the wife had access to the English divorce court although not legally resident in the jurisdiction.

[186] *Polanski v Condé Nast Publications Limited* [2005] UKHL 10, [2005] 1 WLR 637.

[187] *Matthews*, above n 182, at [121] per Lord Walker in reliance upon *James v UK* (1986) 8 EHRR 123 at [81]; *Powell and Rayner v UK* (1990) 12 EHRR 355 at [36]. See also *Wilson*, above n 181, at [32] per Lord Nicholls.

[188] *Matthews*, ibid, at [3] per Lord Bingham.

[189] *Ibid*, at [127] per Lord Walker, with whom all agreed apart from Lord Hoffmann. See also *Wilson*, above n 181, at [35] per Lord Nicholls.

[190] *Matthews*, ibid, per Lord Walker at [130]–[143]. The cases cited were *Ashingdane v United Kingdom* (1983) 6 EHRR 69; *Pinder v United Kingdom* (1984) 7 EHRR 464; *Powell and Rayner*, above n 187; *Fayed v United Kingdom* (1994) 18 EHRR 393; *Stubbings*, above n 182; *Tinnelly & Sons Ltd v United Kingdom* (1998) 27 EHRR 249; *Osman v United Kingdom* (1998) 29 EHRR 245; *Waite and Kennedy v Germany* (1999) 30 EHRR 261; *Z v United Kingdom* (2002) 34 EHRR 3; *Fogarty v United Kingdom* (2002) 34 EHRR 13.

[191] See the comments of Lord Hoffmann in *Matthews*, ibid, at [29] and [39] and Lord Nicholls in *Wilson*, above n 181, at [36]–[37].

[192] See, eg *Federal Bank of the Middle East v Hadkinson*, Court of Appeal, 5 November 1999.

[193] Cited in *Matthews*, above n 182, at [128].

[194] *Ibid*, at [129] citing *Osman*, above n 190, as an example, although noting that the Court had withdrawn from this position in *Z*, above n 190.

In *Matthews*[195] the House of Lords considered section 10 of the Crown Proceedings Act 1947 which provided, inter alia, that, on certification by the Secretary of State that a member of the armed forces was entitled to a pension by reason of suffering attributable to service in the armed forces, the Crown was not subject to liability in tort. Their Lordships unanimously characterised this as a substantive bar which substituted a no-fault system of compensation for a claim for damages.

> This was and is a matter of substantive law and the provision for an official certificate (in order to avoid or at least minimise the risk of inconsistent decisions on causation) does not alter that. Section 10(1)(b), taken on its own, is a provision for the protection of persons with claims against the Ministry.[196]

In *Wilson*[197] the question before their Lordships was whether section 127(3) of the Consumer Credit Act 1974 was a procedural or substantive bar. This section meant that the agreement between the pawnbroker and Ms Wilson was unenforceable as it did not contain all the prescribed terms. Their Lordships concluded it was a substantive bar as it did not bar access to court to decide whether the case was caught by the restriction but it did bar a court from exercising any discretion over whether to make an enforcement order.

> [I]n taking that power away from a court the legislature was not encroaching on territory which ought properly to be the province of the courts in a democratic society.[198]

In the view of their Lordships, it no more offended the rule of law or the separation of powers than would be the case if Parliament had said that such an agreement was void.[199]

4.2 Limitation Periods

In order to be compatible with the right of access to court, limitation periods must pursue a legitimate aim and be proportionate to the aim sought to be achieved.[200] It is in the interests of the state that there should be a finality to litigation.[201]

> For any criminal appellate system to operate efficiently there has to be a time limit specifying the period within which the conviction or sentence must ordinarily be challenged.[202]

---

[195] *Ibid.*
[196] *Ibid*, at [143] per Lord Walker. See also [15] per Lord Bingham.
[197] Above n 181.
[198] *Ibid*, at [36] per Lord Nicholls.
[199] *Ibid*, at [37] per Lord Nicholls, [105] per Lord Hope and [165] per Lord Scott. However, even if Art 6 is not engaged, the law may deprive a person of his or her possessions, therefore Art 1 Protocol No 1 must also be considered. Other examples of substantive bars include *D'Souza v Lambeth London Borough* [2001] EWCA Civ 794 and *Laws v Society of Lloyd's* [2003] EWCA Civ 1887; *Pennycook v Shaws (EAL) Ltd* [2004] EWCA Civ 100, [2004] Ch 296. See further TR Hickman, 'The "Uncertain Shadow": Throwing Light on the Right to a Court under Article 6(1) ECHR', [2004] *PL* 122.
[200] *Goode v Martin* [2001] EWCA 1899, [2002] 1 WLR 1828.
[201] *R (on the application of Blackett) v The Nursing and Midwifery Council* [2004] EWHC (Admin) 1494.
[202] *R v Ballinger* [2005] EWCA Crim 1060.

In *Anderton*[203] the Court of Appeal held that the fact that Civil Procedure Rule 6.7 concerning the calculation of a deemed day of service of a claim form sent by first class post or by fax was not rebuttable by evidence proving the claim form had actually been received on an earlier day was compatible with the right of access to court.

> Procedural rules are necessary to achieve justice. Justice and proportionality require that there are firm procedural rules which should be observed, not that general rules should be construed to create exceptions and excuses whenever those, who could easily have complied with the rules, have slipped up and mistakenly failed to do so.[204]

By contrast, in *Goode v Martin*[205] the claimant sought to amend her statement of claim after the period of limitation had expired. Using section 3 of the HRA, the Court of Appeal interpreted Civil Procedure Rule 17.4(2) so as to allow her to do so, detecting no sound policy reason what she should not add to her claim the alternative plea she proposed.

> No new facts are being introduced: she merely wants to say that if the defendant succeeds in establishing his version of the facts, she will still win because those facts, too, show that he was negligent.[206]

In the view of the Court of Appeal, to prevent her from putting this case before the court would impose an impediment on her access to the court which would require justification.[207]

4.3 Security for Costs

An order of security for costs can give rise to a breach of the right of access to court. Again, it all depends upon the circumstances of the case.[208] Closely analogous is the requirement under the Insolvency Act 1986 when petitioning for bankruptcy to pay a deposit of £250 as security against the fees which the official receiver would incur. In *Lightfoot*,[209] although the Court of Appeal had concluded that Article 6 did not actually apply to such a situation, on the assumption that it did, it held that, insofar as the deposit precondition constituted a restriction upon the appellant's right to petition the court, it had a legitimate aim and by its nature was proportionate to that aim.

---

[203] *Anderton v Clwyd County Council* [2002] EWCA Civ 933, [2002] 1 WLR 3174.
[204] *Ibid*, at [36]. In *Akram v Adam* [2005] 1 All ER 741 the Court of Appeal held that service by post to an individual's last known residence was compatible with the right of access to court. See also *Young v Western Power Distribution (South West) plc* [2003] EWCA Civ 1034; *Rowe v Kingtson-Upon-Hull City Council and Essex County Council* [2003] EWCA Civ 1281; *J & PM Dockeray (a firm) v Secretary of State for the Environment, Food & Rural Affairs* [2002] EWHC (Admin) 420, [2002] HLR 27.
[205] *Goode v Martin*, above n 200.
[206] *Ibid*, at [42].
[207] *Ibid*, at [43].
[208] *Hadkinson*, above n 192. See also *Nasser v United Bank of Kuwait* [2001] EWCA Civ 556, [2002] 1 WLR 1868, which concerned Art 14 and the right of access to court.
[209] Above n 101.

Its legitimacy lies in an aspiring bankrupt's need to have the bankruptcy administered by a third party and the state's entitlement to require some payment at least in respect of the cost of that third party's service. The fee represents but a modest proportion of that cost and can hardly therefore be judged disproportionate.

4.4 Vexatious Litigants

It is well established that any court has an inherent jurisdiction to protect itself from abuse. So long as the very essence of a litigant's right to access the court is not extinguished, a court has a right to regulate its processes as it thinks fit so long as its remedies are proportionate to the identified abuse.[210] There are two methods generally utilised by the courts to protect proceedings against abuse. The first is by the route of the Attorney-General seeking an order under section 42 of the Supreme Court Act that a litigant be declared a vexatious litigant. It has been held that an order under this section is compatible with the right of access to court. It is made after a detailed inquiry. The individual is able to revisit the issue in the context of new facts and of new complaints that he wishes to make. Each step is the subject of a separate judicial decision. Furthermore, the procedures respect proportionality in the general access to public resources in that they seek to prevent the monopolisation of court services by a few litigants.[211]

The second means of protection is what is known as a *Grepe v Loam* order (civil restraint order) within the four corners of the particular proceedings. This requires a litigant who has abused his or her rights to obtain the permission of the court before any further applications are issued and served.[212] There is also the possibility of a general civil restraint order, which lasts for two years and restrains the litigant from commencing any action or making any application in that court without the prior permission of the court. Any application for permission must be made in writing and will be dealt with in writing. It has been held that, if proportionate to the identified abuse, such orders are also compatible with the right of access to court.[213]

4.5 Immunity from Suit

Any immunity from suit must pursue a legitimate aim and satisfy the test of proportionality.[214] For example, in *Heath*[215] the Court of Appeal held that judicial immunity extended to proceedings before a Policy Disciplinary Board, thereby prohibiting claims of unlawful sex discrimination committed in the course of such proceedings. Its purpose was held to be legitimate and necessary and proportionate in the public

---

210 *Bhamjee v Forsdick (No.2)* [2003] EWCA Civ 1113.
211 *Ebert v Official Receiver* [2001] EWCA Civ 340, [2002] 1 WLR 320 at [9] in reliance upon *Golder*, above n 182; *H v UK* (1985) 45 DR 281; *Ashingdane v UK* (1985) 7 EHRR 528. See also *Attorney General v Covey* [2001] EWCA Civ 254; *Attorney General v Wheen* [2001] IRLR 91.
212 *Parkins v Westminster City Council*, Court of Appeal, 20 March 2000.
213 *Bhamjee*, above n 210, at [54]; *Mahajan v Department of Constitutional Affairs* [2004] EWCA Civ 946. There is also the possibility of an extended civil restraint order restraining all activity in the Court of Appeal, High Court and any county court for a period of two years unless permission is obtained following a written application.
214 *Arthur J S Hall & Co (a firm) v Simons* [2000] 2 FCR 673 at 718–19 per Lord Hope.
215 *Heath v Commissioner of Police for the Metropolis* [2000] EWCA Civ 943, [2005] ICR 329.

interest for the protection of the integrity of the judicial system.[216] By contrast, in relation to witness immunity, the House of Lords held in *Darker*[217] that, although the absolute immunity from action given in the interests of the administration of justice to a party or witness, including a police witness, in respect of what he said or did in court extended to statements made for the purpose of court proceedings, and to prevent him from being sued for conspiracy to give false evidence, public policy did not require it to be extended to things done by the police during the investigative process which could not fairly be said to form part of their participation in the judicial process as witnesses. In particular, the immunity did not extend to cover the fabrication of false evidence.[218]

Such considerations do not apply to state immunity. An assertion by a foreign state of immunity before the English courts does not infringe the right of access to court. In *Holland v Lampen-Wolfe*[219] the House of Lords described state immunity as a creature of customary international law, not a self-imposed restriction on the jurisdiction of its courts which the United Kingdom had chosen to adopt.

> The United Kingdom cannot, by its own act of acceding to the Convention and without the consent of the United States, obtain a power of adjudication over the United States which international law denies it.[220]

However, different considerations apply where the immunity is claimed in respect of a state official alleged to have committed acts of systemic torture. In *Jones*[221] the Court of Appeal held that there was no settled international practice in relation to serious international crimes of that nature.[222] Therefore, unlike a claim of immunity asserted in respect of the state itself, or its head or diplomats, a different approach was required.[223] Two possible analyses of the State Immunity Act 1978 were put forward. The first would require the court to determine whether it was in pursuit of a legitimate aim and proportionate to recognise state immunity in respect of the particular claim. The second would be to simply recognise that states have no right to claim state immunity in respect of civil claims against their officers arising from the alleged commission of an international crime such as systemic torture, and the involvement of a foreign state would be no more than a factor in considering whether or not to exercise jurisdiction.[224] The court did not choose between the alternatives but held that

---

[216] *Ibid*, at [70] Auld LJ commented that this particular immunity was more in the nature of a substantive than procedural bar although this is not in keeping with the judgment of the House of Lords in *Darker v Chief Constable of the West Midlands Police* [2000] 3 WLR 747.

[217] *Ibid.*

[218] *Ibid*, per Lord Hope at 752 and Lord Hutton at 773. See also *L v Reading Borough Council* [2001] 1 WLR 1575; *D v East Berkshire Community NHS Trust* [2003] EWCA Civ 1151, [2004] QB 558.

[219] Above n 177.

[220] Cf. the speeches of Lords Hope and Clyde. See also *Jones v Ministry of the Interior* [2004] EWCA Civ 1394, [2005] QB 699. See further M Tomonori, 'One Immunity Has Gone . . . Another . . . Holland v. Lampen-Wolfe' (2001) 64 *MLR* 472.

[221] *Ibid.*

[222] *Ibid*, at [83].

[223] *Ibid*, at [92].

[224] *Ibid*, at [93]–[94].

any absolute view of immunity must at the very least yield in the face of assertions of systemic torture to a more nuanced and proportionate approach . . . the permissibility, appropriateness and proportionality of exercising jurisdiction ought to be determine at one and the same time. Such a conclusion reflects the importance attaching in today's world and in current international thinking and jurisprudence to the recognition and effective enforcement of individual human rights.[225]

4.6 Prisoners

It is clear that convicted prisoners also have a right of access to court, although obstacles imposed primarily in the interests of security and safety considerations mean that this is generally not an unimpeded right. For example, in *Ponting*[226] the Court of Appeal considered whether limitations imposed on a dyslexic prisoner litigant's use of a computer and printer were legitimate and proportionate. It is important to note that the question of whether or not access to computers by prisoners was required in order to meet the obligation imposed by the right of access to court was not considered, the court proceeding on the basis that access to court in at least one of the four cases the prisoner was pursuing would be impaired if he did not have a computer.

Briefly, the conditions imposed restricted the use of the computer to the prisoner's cell, limited the times during which the computer could be in the prisoner's possession, prescribed conditions in which it and all disks were to be stored, and made various provisions for the supervision of use and inspection of materials. They were imposed in the interests of safety and security. A majority of the court found the conditions legitimate and proportionate, in particular the denial of 24 hour access to the computer.[227]

4.7 Absence of Legal Representation

Whilst the absence of legal representation in civil proceedings would appear to sit more happily in the context of denial of a fair hearing, it has been held that access to the court must be effective access, and in some instances this may require legal representation.[228] However, it has also been held that a litigant who wishes to argue that without legal aid his right of effective access will have been violated has a relatively high threshold to cross.[229]

> The test . . . is whether a court is put in a position that it really cannot do justice in the case because it has no confidence in its ability to grasp the facts and principles of the matter on which it has to decide. In such a case it may well be said that a litigant is deprived of effective access; deprived of effective access because, although he can present his case in person,

---

[225] *Ibid*, at [96]. See further H Fox, 'Where Does the Buck Stop? State Immunity from Civil Jurisdiction and Torture' (2005) 121 *LQR* 353.

[226] Above n 184.

[227] Clarke LJ dissented on this point, although his judgment was based more on equality of arms than access to court.

[228] *Perotti v Collyer-Bristow (a firm)* [2003] EWCA Civ 1521, [2004] 2 All ER 189 in reliance upon *Airey v Ireland* (1979) 2 EHRR 305.

[229] *Ibid*, at [31].

he cannot do so in a way which will enable the court to do its paramount and over-arching function of reaching a just decision.[230]

In *Perotti*,[231] given that the applications were for permission to appeal, the Court of Appeal held that the scope for advocacy was relatively limited and the absence of legal representation did not deprive the litigant of effective access to justice.[232]

4.8 Striking Out

Where the legal position is clear and an investigation of the facts would provide no assistance, a court may take the step of striking out the claim. It has been held that there is no question of any contravention of Article 6 in doing so as

> defendants as well as claimants are entitled to a fair trial and it is an important part of the case management function to bring proceedings to an end as expeditiously as possible.[233]

Particular issues have arisen in relation to the striking out of claims in negligence. In *Osman v UK*[234] the ECHR held that it was a breach of the right of access to court for the Court of Appeal to strike out a claim in negligence against the police in light of the clearly established principle that the police owed no duty of care to individual citizens in relation to the vigour with which they carried out their duties.

> [T]he applicants must be taken to have had a right, derived from the law of negligence, to seek an adjudication on the admissibility and merits of an arguable claim that they were in a relationship of proximity to the police, that the harm caused was foreseeable and that in the circumstances it was fair, just and reasonable not to apply the exclusionary rule.[235]

This decision 'perplexed' common law judges and jurists[236] and led to a considerable reluctance on the part of English courts to use the striking out procedure in negligence proceedings.[237] However, in *Z v United Kingdom*[238] the ECHR reversed the trend, holding that the inability of the applicants to sue the local authority in negligence flowed not from an immunity but from the applicable principles governing the substantive right of action in domestic law. There was no restriction on access to court.[239] If a court concludes that it is not fair, just and reasonable to impose a duty of care, striking out the claim is no longer considered with the same reluctance.[240]

---

[230] *Ibid*, at [32].
[231] *Ibid*.
[232] *Ibid*, at [37]. In *Alliss v Legal Services Commission* [2002] EWHC (Admin) 2079 the court found that the withdrawal of legal aid denied the claimant effective access to the court in breach of Art 6(1).
[233] *Kent v Griffiths* [2001] QB 36. See also *Outram v Academy Plastics* [2000] IRLR 499; *Terry v Hoyer (UK) Limited* [2001] EWCA Civ 678; *Rampal v Rampal (No.2)* [2001] EWCA Civ 989, [2001] 3 WLR 795.
[234] (1998) 29 EHRR 245
[235] *Ibid*, at [139].
[236] *D*, above n 218, at [14].
[237] See, eg *Barrett v Enfield London Borough Council* [2001] 2 AC 550; *Griffiths*, above n 233.
[238] (2001) 34 EHRR 97.
[239] *Ibid*, at [101]–[102]. See also *TP and KM v United Kingdom* (2001) 34 EHRR 42.
[240] See, eg *D*, above n 218. See generally J Wright, *Tort Law and Human Rights* (Oxford, Hart Publishing, 2001).

5. Fair Hearing

The first right expressly protected by Article 6(1) is the right to a fair hearing which must be upheld in the determination of civil rights and criminal charges. The Article does not spell out in any detail what a fair hearing requires, and it has been held that this cannot be the subject of a single, unvarying rule or collection of rules: the facts and circumstances of the case must be taken into account.[241] Nevertheless, a number of subsidiary rights have emerged from the case law, such as the right to equality of arms, the presumption of innocence and the privilege against self-incrimination. Whist the right to a fair hearing is an absolute right, irregularities or breaches of these subsidiary rights along the way is possible as long as, taking all the facts and circumstances into account, there has on the whole been a fair hearing. The fairness of the trial may not be qualified, compromised or restricted in any way whatever the circumstances and whatever the public interest in convicting the offender.[242]

The right to a fair hearing is a separate and distinct right. Therefore the consequences of a breach, or a threatened or prospective breach, need to be considered separately.[243] Difficult questions have arisen in relation to criminal proceedings. One breach of the right to a fair hearing along the way may not necessarily mean that a conviction is unsafe.[244] However, if, on consideration of all the facts and the whole history of the proceedings, it is concluded that the right to fair trial has been infringed, a conviction must be held to be unsafe within the meaning of section 2 of the Criminal Appeal Act 1968.[245] For example, in *Lambert*[246] the House of Lords held that a breach of the right to be presumed innocent by a direction to the jury that the accused was under a persuasive rather than evidential burden would not necessarily lead to an unsafe conviction.

> There will be cases where a conviction cannot stand and must be quashed irrespective of the strength of the evidence against the defendant because the trial as a whole is judged to be unfair. But . . . where the unfairness is claimed to arise from the transfer of the onus and it was open to the appellant to seek to rebut the presumption, and where there can be no doubt that the jury would have convicted if only an evidential burden had rested on the appellant, then the imposition of a persuasive burden as to knowledge resulted in no injustice and . . . no breach of art 6(2).[247]

---

[241] *Brown*, above n 4, per Lord Bingham.
[242] *Ibid*. See also *Watson*, above n 2, at [73] per Lord Hope.
[243] *Porter*, above n 2; *Attorney General's Reference No.2 of 2001*, above n 1.
[244] The same applies where the ECHR has found a violation of Art 6. See *R v Lewis* [2005] EWCA Crim 859.
[245] *R v Forbes* [2001] UKHL 40, [2001] 3 WLR 428, endorsing the judgment of the Court of Appeal in *R v Togher* [2001] 3 All ER 463.
[246] *R v Lambert* [2001] UKHL 37, [2002] 2 AC 545.
[247] *Ibid*, at [202]. See also Lord Clyde at [159], Lord Steyn at [43], Lord Hope at [117] and Lord Slynn at [18]. Also *R v Davis* [2001] 1 Cr App Rep 115, where the Court of Appeal held that the question to be asked was would a reasonable jury, after a proper summing up, convict the appellant on the rest of the evidence to which no objection could be taken.

5.1 Equality of Arms

The first subsidiary right derived from the right to a fair hearing is the right to equality of arms. There must be a fair balance between the parties. In civil cases the accused must be afforded an opportunity to present his case under conditions which do not place him at a substantial disadvantage as compared with his opponent. In criminal cases the requirement that there be a fair balance is no less important. The purpose of Article 6 is not to make it impractical to bring those accused of crime to justice. The essential question is whether the alleged inequality of arms is such as to deprive the accused of his right to a fair trial.[248] What has to be demonstrated is that the prosecutor will enjoy some particular advantage that is not available to the defence or that would otherwise be unfair.[249] For example, it has been held that limited provision of computer facilities to a prisoner representing himself in proceedings could engage the principle of equality of arms.[250] In *D*[251] it was argued that requiring the evidence of child witnesses to be given by video recording and/or video link, while not affording a similar facility to child defendants, was in breach of the principle of equality of arms. The House of Lords disagreed and also noted that the court had the power, in the exercise of its inherent jurisdiction, to make such an order in relation to a child defendant if necessary.[252]

A number of claims have been made concerning legal representation and equality of arms. For example, in *McLean*[253] it was argued under the Scotland Act 1998 that regulations fixing payments to which solicitors were entitled was in breach of the principle of equality of arms. The Privy Council rejected the argument as it was not demonstrated that any inequality there may be was of such a character that the legal assistance provided would be ineffective and the trial unfair.[254] There was no reason to doubt that the solicitors would conduct the case for the defence according to the required standards.[255] In *Attorney General's Reference No.82a of 2000*[256] the appellants contended that, because the Crown had instructed leading counsel, it was in violation of the principle of equality of arms for them to be represented by junior counsel. The Court of Appeal disagreed, holding that a fair trial did not necessarily entail representation by a Queen's Counsel merely because the Crown were represented by Queen's Counsel.

> The importance is to have an advocate, whether he be a barrister or a solicitor, who can ensure that a defendant's defence is properly and adequately placed before the court.[257]

---

[248] *McLean v Procurator Fiscal* [2001] 1 WLR 2425 at [39] per Lord Hope in reliance upon *Dombo Beheer*, above n 104, at [33]; *De Haes and Gijsels v Belgium* (1997) 24 EHRR 1 at [53]; *Montgomery*, above n 110.
[249] *McLean*, ibid, at [40]. Equality of arms does not apply to the role played by a clerk when giving legal advice to a justice in private as the clerk functions on the same side of the court as the justice. See *Clark (Procurator Fiscal) v Kelly* [2003] UKPC D1, [2004] 1 AC 681.
[250] *Ponting*, above n 184.
[251] *R v Camberwell Green Youth Court, ex p D* [2005] UKHL 4, [2005] 1 WLR 393.
[252] *Ibid*, at [16]–[17] per Lord Rodger.
[253] *McLean v Procurator Fiscal, Fort William* [2001] 1 WLR 2425.
[254] *Ibid*, at [41] per Lord Hope.
[255] *Ibid*, at [43] per Lord Hope.
[256] [2002] EWCA Crim 215.
[257] *Ibid*, at [14].

With respect to unrepresented litigants, it has been held that where there is an application made for the assistance of a McKenzie friend, there is a strong presumption in favour of granting such an application.[258]

A far more common example of breach of the right to equality of arms is failure on the part of the prosecution to disclose to the defence a relevant piece of evidence.[259]

[T]he prosecution is under a duty to disclose to the defence all material evidence in its possession for or against the accused. For this purpose any evidence which would tend to undermine the prosecution's case or to assist the case for the defence is to be taken as material. [But] the defence does not have an absolute right to the disclosure of all relevant evidence. There may be competing interests which it is in the public interest to protect. But decisions as to whether the withholding of relevant information is in the public interest cannot be left exclusively to the Crown. There must be sufficient judicial safeguards in place to ensure that information is not withheld on the grounds of public interest unless this is strictly necessary.[260]

In *Sinclair*[261] the Privy Council held that it was incompatible with Article 6(1) for the Lord Advocate to bring proceedings and seek a conviction without having produced or disclosed the existence and contents of statements made to the police by a witness who was to corroborate the complainer's account of the incident. It was held that this was information that was plainly likely to be of material assistance to the defence. Their Lordships confirmed that the fact that the statements were not made available could not be attributed to any failure in duty on the part of the defence.

The duty of disclosure was on the Crown, and it was a breach of that duty for these statements not to have been provided to the defence before the trial.[262]

It was also held that the police statements of all the witnesses who were to be called at the trial were to be regarded as containing material evidence either for or against the accused, and the Crown were therefore under an obligation in terms of Article 6(1) to disclose their statements to the defence.[263]

The issue also arose in *Holland*,[264] where the Privy Council held that it was in principle wrong that at trial the prosecutor should have official information about the witnesses' previous convictions which has been withheld from the defence.

The presentation of the defence case is liable to be less effective if the accused's counsel and agents do not have the information in advance of the trial.[265]

Information about previous convictions of any witnesses to be led at the trial is likely to be of material assistance to the proper preparation or presentation of the accused's defence, and under Article 6(1) the accused's agents and counsel are accordingly

---

[258] *Re O (children) (representation: McKenzie friend)* [2005] EWCA Civ 759.
[259] *R v Bishop*, Court of Appeal, 10 November 2003.
[260] *Sinclair v HM Advocate* [2005] HRLR 26 at [33] per Lord Hope.
[261] *Ibid.*
[262] *Ibid*, at [34] per Lord Hope.
[263] *Ibid*, at [49] per Lord Rodger.
[264] *Holland v HM Advocate* [2005] HRLR 25.
[265] *Ibid*, at [70] per Lord Rodger.

entitled to have that information disclosed so that they can prepare his defence.[266] However, given that details of outstanding charges are more difficult to discover, there is no general duty to search for outstanding charges.

> If Crown officials are asked about a particular witness, they need only take such steps to search for any outstanding charges as are appropriate, having regard to any indications given in the defence request.[267]

A claim of public interest immunity raises serious problems with equality of arms, particularly in a criminal case where the prosecution seeks to withhold documents on this ground. Circumstances may arise in which material held by the prosecution and tending to undermine the prosecution or assist the defence cannot be disclosed to the defence fully, or even at all, without the risk of serious prejudice to an important public interest.[268] The public interest most regularly claimed is in the effective investigation and prosecution of serious crime. The courts have accepted that, in such circumstances, some derogation from the golden rule of full disclosure may be justified, though such derogation must always be the minimum necessary to protect the public interest in question and must never imperil the overall fairness of the trial.[269]

In *R v H*[270] both of the appellants had been charged with conspiracy to supply a class A drug. The prosecution sought to withhold documents on the ground of public interest immunity. The appellants argued that it was incompatible with Article 6 for a judge to rule on a claim to public interest immunity in the absence of adversarial argument on behalf of the accused where the material which the prosecution was seeking to withhold was, or may be, relevant to a disputed issue of fact which the judge had to decide in order to rule on an application which would effectively determine the outcome of the proceedings. The House of Lords held that this would place the trial judge in a straightjacket and the best approach was on a case-by-case basis, avoiding rigid or inflexible rules.[271] It concluded that, when any issue of derogation from the golden rule of full disclosure came before it, the court must address a series of questions, and if scrupulous attention was paid to these and the proper interests of the defendant, there should be no violation of Article 6.[272] The series of questions was as follows:

> (1) What is the material which the prosecution seek to withhold? This must be considered by the court in detail. (2) Is the material such as may weaken the prosecution case or strengthen that of the defence? If, No, disclosure should not be ordered. If, Yes, full disclosure should (subject to (3), (4) and (5) below) be ordered. (3) Is there a real risk of serious prejudice to an important public interest (and, if so, what) if full disclosure of the material is ordered? If, No, full disclosure should be ordered. (4) If the answer to (2) and (3) is, Yes, can the defendant's interest be protected without disclosure or disclosure be ordered to an extent or in a way which will give adequate protection to the public interest in question and also afford adequate protection to the interests of the defence? This question requires the

---

[266] *Ibid*, at [72] per Lord Rodger.
[267] *Ibid*, at [74] per Lord Rodger.
[268] See, eg *R v H*, above n 124.
[269] See, eg *R v H ibid* at [18].
[270] *Ibid*.
[271] *Ibid*, at [33].
[272] *Ibid*, at [39].

court to consider, with specific reference to the material which the prosecution seek to withhold and the facts of the case and the defence as disclosed, whether the prosecution should formally admit what the defence seek to establish or whether disclosure short of full disclosure may be ordered. This may be done in appropriate cases by the preparation of summaries or extracts of evidence, or the provision of documents in an edited or anonymised form, provided the documents supplied are in each instance approved by the judge. In appropriate cases the appointment of special counsel may be a necessary step to ensure that the contentions of the prosecution are tested and the interests of the defendant protected . . . In cases of exceptional difficulty the court may require the appointment of special counsel to ensure a correct answer to questions (2) and (3) as well as (4). (5) Do the measures proposed in answer to (4) represent the minimum derogation necessary to protect the public interest in question? If, No, the court should order such greater disclosure as will represent the minimum derogation from the golden rule of full disclosure. (6) If limited disclosure is ordered pursuant to (4) or (5), may the effect be to render the trial process, viewed as a whole, unfair to the defendant? If, Yes, then fuller disclosure should be ordered even if this leads or may lead the prosecution to discontinue the proceedings so as to avoid having to make disclosure. (7) If the answer to (6) when first given is, No, does that remain the correct answer as the trial unfolds, evidence is adduced and the defence advanced? It is important that the answer to (6) should not be treated as a final, once-and-for-all, answer but as a provisional answer which the court must keep under review.[273]

5.2 Self-incrimination

The right not to incriminate oneself is also an implied right, even though it is based on the presumption of innocence in Article 6(2) as well as the fair hearing guarantee in Article 6(1).[274] It is not an absolute right and an interference with it may be justified if it pursues a legitimate aim and if the scope of the interference is necessary and proportionate to the achievement of the aim.[275] The right is firmly anchored to the fairness of the trial and not concerned with extra-judicial inquiries.[276] For example, in *Green*[277] a company which was alleged to have unlawfully deposited waste refused to provide information about its activities on the ground that the answers may incriminate it. The House of Lords concluded that the right was not applicable as no answer had actually been tendered in evidence against the company.[278] The right is also primarily concerned with respecting the will of an accused person to remain silent and does not extend to the use in criminal proceedings of material which may be obtained from the accused through the use of compulsory powers but which has an existence independent of the will of the subject, such as documents delivered under compulsion pursuant to the Insolvency Act 1986.[279] It is also not infringed by

---

273 *Ibid*, at [36]. See also *R v Smith* [2002] EWCA Crim 2561; *R v Brushett* [2001] Crim LR 471; *R v Botmeh* [2001] EWCA Crim 2226, [2002] 1 WLR 531; *Chief Constable of the Greater Manchester Police v McNally* [2002] EWCA Civ 14, [2002] Cr LR 832; *R v Templar* [2003] EWCA Crim 3186. As to the appointment of 'special advocates' see generally *Roberts v Parole Board* [2005] UKHL 45, [2005] 3 WLR 152.

274 *R v Hertfordshire County Council, ex p Green Environmental Industries Ltd* [2000] 2 AC 483; *Brown*, above n 4.

275 *Brown ibid* per Lord Steyn.

276 *Green*, above n 274.

277 *Ibid*.

278 See also *R v Kearns* [2002] EWCA Crim 748, [2002] WLR 2815.

279 *Attorney General's Reference No.7 of 2000* [2001] EWCA Crim 888, [2001] 1 WLR 1879. See also *R v Hundal; R v Dhaliwal* [2004] EWCA Crim 389.

requiring an accused to be present at his or her trial where he may be identified by a witness.[280]

Under the HRA, interferences with the right have arisen in the context of compulsorily obtained admissions which are then sought to be relied upon at trial. For example, in *Brown*[281] Ms Brown had been required by police, exercising their powers under section 172(2)(a) of the Road Traffic Act 1988, to say who had been driving her car when she would have travelled in it to the store car park. She replied 'it was me' and the prosecution later sought to rely on this admission at her trial for driving a car after having consumed excessive alcohol. Her objection to the reliance on her admission was raised as a devolution issue under the Scotland Act 1998.

The Privy Council concluded that section 172 was a proportionate response to a serious social problem and that reliance on her admission would not undermine her right to a fair trial. In particular, Lord Hope found that the system of regulation and the provisions which the legislation contained for the detection and prosecution of road traffic offences served a legitimate aim.

> The purpose which these offences are designed to serve would be at risk of being defeated if no means were available to enable the police to trace the driver of a vehicle who, as so often happens, had departed from the place where the offence was committed before he or she could be identified.

With respect to the question of proportionality or fair balance, Lord Hope took into account the limited incursion presented by the section and the use made of the response—under Scottish law at trial the admission had to be corroborated and there had to be other evidence to show beyond reasonable doubt that the driver committed the offence. 'All the usual protections against unreliable evidence and evidence obtained by oppression or other improper means remained in place.'

It is not only the legitimate aim of road safety that can justify incursions into the right against self-incrimination. In *R v Allen*[282] the appellant's argument that the Revenue had breached his right against self-incrimination by compulsorily obtaining from him the schedule of assets upon which the prosecution case was based was dismissed by the House of Lords, which held that it was 'self-evident that the payment of taxes, fixed by the legislature, is essential for the functioning of any democratic state.' Furthermore, to ensure due payment of taxes, the House of Lords pointed out that the state had to have the power to require its citizens to inform it of the amount of their annual income and to have sanctions available to enforce the provision of that information.[283] Such provisions could not constitute a violation of the right against self-incrimination.[284]

The right also extends to confession evidence, as obtaining a confession by oppression is a form of compulsion which constitutes a breach of the right of an accused

---

[280] *Holland*, above n 264.
[281] Above n 4.
[282] *R v Dimsey; R v Allen* [2001] UKHL 46, [2001] 3 WLR 843.
[283] *Ibid*, at [29] per Lord Hutton.
[284] *Ibid*, at [30] in reliance upon *Brown*, above n 4, and distinguishing *Saunders v UK* (1996) 23 EHRR 313. Their Lordships did note that the appellant's would have had a much stronger argument if, in response to the Hansard statement, he had given true and accurate information which disclosed that he had earlier cheated the Revenue and had then been prosecuted for that earlier dishonesty. See also *Westminster Property*, above n 173; *Kearns*, above n 278.

person not to incriminate himself.[285] In *Mushtaq*[286] the House of Lords held that the logic of section 76(2) of the Police and Criminal Evidence Act 1984 required that the jury should be directed that, if they consider that the confession was, or may have been, obtained by oppression, or in consequence of anything said or done which was likely to render it unreliable, they should disregard it.[287] It is incompatible with Article 6 for a judge to direct a jury that they are entitled to take into account a confession which he considered was, or might have been, obtained by oppression or any other improper means in violation of the defendant's right against self-incrimination.[288]

5.3 Right to Silence

The right to a fair hearing also encompasses a defendant's right to silence, although it is clear that this is not an absolute right.[289] Considerable incursions on the right to silence are made by section 34 of the Criminal Justice and Public Order Act 1994 which, inter alia, allows the court or jury, in determining guilt, to draw such inferences as appear proper from the accused's failure to mention any fact relied on in his or her defence at the time of being charged which he or she could reasonably have been expected to mention. As the drawing of an adverse inference may infringe the right to a fair hearing, an appropriate balance must be struck between the accused's right to silence and the fair drawing of an adverse inference by the jury.[290] Provided the trial judge directs the jury in the required terms,[291] it has been held that section 34 is compatible with the right to a fair hearing under Article 6.[292]

Each case depends upon its own facts, and the failure to direct the jury in a particular way may in some circumstances amount to a breach of Article 6 whereas the same failure in other circumstances may not.[293] It does not necessarily follow from the fact that a direction which should have been given was not given that there has been a breach of Article 6 or that the convictions are unsafe.[294] For example, in *R v Chenia*[295] the Court of Appeal concluded that there was no breach in the fraud trial. The appellant did not refuse to answer questions in reliance upon a solicitor's advice.[296] The case against him was very strong, and the judge gave a clear and accurate direction under section 35 of the Criminal Justice and Public Order Act 1994 in relation to his failure to give evidence. This direction is almost in identical terms to

---

[285] *R v Mushtaq* [2005] UKHL 25, [2005] 1 WLR 1513 at [73] per Lord Carswell.
[286] *Ibid.*
[287] *Ibid*, at [47] per Lord Rodger.
[288] *Ibid*, at [53].
[289] *R v Francom* [2001] 1 Cr App Rep 237 at [42] in reliance upon *Murray v United Kingdom* (1996) 22 EHRR 29.
[290] *R v Betts; R v Hall* [2001] 2 Cr App R 257 at [34] in reliance upon *Condron v UK* (2002) 31 EHRR 1.
[291] In accordance with the latest Judicial Studies Board Specimen Direction.
[292] *Francom*, above n 289.
[293] *R v Chenia* [2002] EWCA Crim 2345, [2004] 1 All ER 543 at [58] in reliance upon *Beckles v UK* (2002) 13 BHRC 522.
[294] *Ibid*, at [59].
[295] *Ibid.*
[296] See further *R v Howell* [2003] EWCA Crim 01, [2005] 1 Cr App Rep 1, where the Court of Appeal held that it is not the case that if a suspect remains silent on legal advice he may systematically avoid adverse comment at his trial.

the Judicial Studies Board section 34 direction. There was no realistic possibility that the jury drew an adverse inference while at the same time thinking the appellant's statement of his reasons for silence might be true. The jury must have excluded both the reason for silence offered and the possibility of an innocent explanation before drawing any inference adverse to the appellant.[297]

However, in the same case the court reached a different conclusion in relation to the appellant's drugs trial. The Court of Appeal found that the judge did not identify any of the facts relied upon at the trial which the prosecution said that the appellant could reasonably have been expected to mention.[298] It also found that the direction was insufficient because it may have given the impression that the jury might draw an adverse inference because the appellant was sheltering behind his solicitor's advice. It was only possible for the jury to draw such an inference if they were sure, not only that his failure to mention facts was the result of the advice, however adequate or inadequate that explanation might be, but also that the appellant had at that stage no explanation to offer or none that would stand up to questioning or investigation.[299] The Court concluded that the appellant did not receive a fair hearing and the convictions were unsafe notwithstanding the strength of the prosecution case.[300]

5.4 Presumption of Innocence

As well as being an express right under Article 6(2), the presumption of innocence is also an implied right as part of the fair hearing guarantee under Article 6(1).[301] However, the right is not absolute and may be subject to interferences which pursue a legitimate aim and are proportionate.[302] The fact that the presumption of innocence forms part of the fair hearing guarantee is particularly important where Article 6(2) does not apply, such as in relation to the making of a confiscation order.

However, although the right applies, it has had little impact. For example, in *R v Rezvi*[303] the House of Lords noted that effective but fair powers of confiscating the proceeds of crime were essential—it is a 'notorious fact that professional and habitual criminals frequently take steps to conceal their profits from crime.'[304] It concluded that the statutory measures, which allowed the court to assume that the property held by the defendant within the relevant period was received by him in connection with the commission of offences, was a proportionate response to the problem addressed.[305] In particular, Lord Steyn noted that Parliament had attempted to balance the interests of the defendant against that of the public in the following respects: it was only after conviction that the question of confiscation arose; the

---

[297] *R v Chenia*, above n 293, at [60]–[64].
[298] *Ibid*, at [89].
[299] *Ibid*, at [92].
[300] *Ibid*, at [93]. See also *Francom*, above n 289; *R v Betts* [2001] 2 Cr App R 257; *R v Robinson* [2003] EWCA Crim 2219. In relation to s 36 of the Criminal Justice and Public Order Act 1994 see *R v Compton* [2002] EWCA Crim 2835.
[301] *Rezvi*, above n 82, in reliance upon *Phillips v United Kingdom*, 5 July 2001. See also *McIntosh*, above n 120.
[302] *Rezvi*, ibid, at [11] per Lord Steyn; *McIntosh*, ibid.
[303] *Rezvi*, ibid.
[304] *Ibid*, at [14] per Lord Steyn.
[305] *Ibid*, at [16] per Lord Steyn.

prosecution had the responsibility for initiating the confiscation proceedings unless the court regarded them as inappropriate; the court must not make a confiscation order if there was a serious risk of injustice; and the role of the court on appeal was to ensure there was no unfairness.[306]

5.5 Representation

The absence of legal representation may have an adverse affect on the fairness of proceedings. However, there is no absolute right to legal representation. Provided that the tribunal is aware of and constantly reminds itself of the duty of fairness, it is very much a matter for the tribunal whether it is able to discharge the case fairly if the parties are not represented.[307] In *Pine*[308] the Court of Appeal held that the absence of legal representation before the Solicitors' Disciplinary Tribunal did not lead to unfairness.

> The procedure was not complex. The relevant facts were within the knowledge of Mr Pine. Mr Pine was a solicitor experienced in commercial litigation. Mr Pine had ample opportunity to indicate any defences he might wish to advance.[309]

It is also important to note that, in addition to the absence of representation, it is possible for inadequate representation to also result in a denial of a fair hearing.[310]

5.6 Oral Hearing

In civil cases it has been held that, in order to determine whether an oral hearing is required for a fair hearing, the nature of the application must be examined. In *BLCT (13096) Limited*[311] the Court of Appeal held that Article 6 did not require an oral hearing of an application for leave to appeal. The question was a question of law, there was no question of any decision on the facts and there was no question as to a party's credibility.[312]

Similarly, in criminal matters there is not absolute right to a public hearing at every stage in the proceedings at which the claimant and his or her representatives are heard orally.[313]

> Account must be taken of the entirety of the proceedings of which they form part, including those at first instance. Account must also be taken of the role of the person or persons

---

[306] *Ibid*, at [86]. See also *R v Benjafield* [2002] UKHL 2, [2003] 1 AC 1099 and *R v Barnham* [2005] EWCA Crim 1049.

[307] *Re B and T (care proceedings: legal representation)* [2001] 1 FCR 512.

[308] *Pine v Solicitors' Disciplinary Tribunal* [2001] EWCA Crim 1574, [2002] UKHRR 81.

[309] *Ibid*, at [39]. See also *Perotti*, above n 228, where the absence of legal representation was considered in the context of denial of access to court.

[310] *R v Thakrar* [2001] EWCA Crim 1096.

[311] Above n 180.

[312] *Ibid*, at [37]–[38].

[313] *R (on the application of Dudson) v Secretary of State for the Home Department* [2005] UKHL 52 at [34] per Lord Hope.

conducting the proceedings that are in question, the nature of the system within which they are being conducted and the scope of the powers that are being exercised. The overriding question, which is essentially a practical one as it depends on the facts of the case, is whether the issues that had to be dealt with at the stage could properly, as a matter of fair trial, be determined without hearing the applicant orally.[314]

Applying these principles in *Dudson*,[315] the House of Lords concluded that it was not obvious, given the comparatively limited nature of the exercise, that an oral hearing was needed to equip the Lord Chief Justice with the information that he needed for the proper conduct of setting the minimum term of the appellant, convicted of murder and sentenced to be detained at Her Majesty's pleasure. It was particularly important that it was not suggested by the appellant's solicitors that an oral hearing was required so that the appellant could appeal in person before the Lord Chief Justice and give evidence. In their Lordships' view, all the signs were that an oral hearing would have been a formality as all relevant material was being disclosed and a sufficient opportunity was being given for representations to be made in writing.

5.7 Conducting a Proper Examination

The duty to afford a fair hearing also requires the decision maker to conduct a proper examination of the submissions, arguments and evidence adduced by the parties without prejudice to its assessment of whether they are relevant to its decision.[316] Appearances are important, as is public confidence in the administration of justice. In *Stansbury*[317] the Court of Appeal found on the balance of probabilities that a lay member of an Employment Tribunal had consumed alcohol prior to, and fallen asleep during, an unfair dismissal hearing. It therefore concluded that the appellant could not have had the fair hearing to which he was entitled.

5.8 Evidence

It is clear that the right to a fair hearing can also have an impact on the rules of evidence. What Article 6 does is guarantee a fair trial and so, when the introduction of some form of evidence is said to have infringed the accused's Article 6 rights, the question always is whether admitting the evidence has resulted in the accused not having a fair trial in the circumstances of the particular case.[318] Under the HRA a number of cases have been brought concerning illegally obtained evidence, evidence obtained by entrapment and hearsay evidence. These are examined in the following paragraphs.

---

[314] *Ibid.*
[315] *Ibid.*
[316] Above n 37, at [28] in reliance upon *Kraska v Switzerland* (1993) 18 EHRR 188.
[317] *Ibid.*
[318] *Holland*, above n 264, at [39] per Lord Rodger.

5.8.1 Evidence Obtained by Entrapment

Entrapment occurs when an agent of the state[319] causes someone to commit an offence in order that he should be prosecuted. It is widely accepted by the courts that there are occasions when it is necessary for the police to resort to investigatory techniques in which the police themselves are the reporters and the witnesses of the commission of a crime. However, it is also widely accepted that the use of evidence obtained by entrapment may deprive a defendant of the right to a fair trial. Although entrapment is not a substantive defence under English law, the court may stay the proceedings and exclude the evidence under section 78 of the Police and Criminal Evidence Act 1984. This gives the court the power to exclude evidence on which the prosecution proposes to rely if, having regard to all the circumstances, the court considers the admission of the evidence would have such an adverse effect on the fairness of the proceedings that the court ought not to admit it. The grant of a stay is normally regarded as the appropriate response. It has been held that this approach is compatible with Article 6.[320]

Whilst no two cases are ever likely to be the same, it has been held that a stay should be granted where there has been an abuse of executive power or an affront to public conscience, or where the court's participation in such proceedings would bring the administration of justice into disrepute.[321] The court must balance the competing requirements that those who commit crimes should be convicted and punished and that there should not be an abuse of process which would constitute an affront to public conscience. English courts have placed particular emphasis on

> the need to consider whether a person has been persuaded or pressurised by a law enforcement officer into committing a crime which he would not otherwise had committed, or whether the officer did not go beyond giving the person an opportunity to break the law, when he would have behaved in the same way if some other person had offered him the opportunity to commit a similar crime, and when he freely took advantage of the opportunity presented to him by the officer.[322]

In *R v Loosley*[323] the House of Lords held that the undercover officer and his superiors had reasonable cause to suspect that the defendant was a dealer and that the offer to purchase was in the course of a legitimate undercover purchase and not calculated to cause him to do anything which he would not have done in response to a similar request from any customer. The police did not have to take any steps to persuade him which might have taken them across the boundary between giving him the opportunity to commit the offence and causing him to do so, and the trial judge was right to reject the section 78 application.[324] However, in *Attorney General's Reference No.3 of 2000*, the House of Lords held that the trial judge was right to stay the proceedings. The defendant had never dealt in heroin.

---

[319] Whilst generally such evidence is obtained by undercover police officers, an agent of the state may also be someone else such as an investigative journalist. See, eg *R v Shannon* [2001] 1 WLR 51.
[320] *Attorney General's Reference No.3 of 2000* [2001] UKHL 53, [2001] 1 WLR 2060.
[321] *Ibid*, at [47] per Lord Hoffmann.
[322] *Ibid*, at [101] per Lord Hutton.
[323] *R v Loosley* [2001] UKHL 53, [2001] 1 WLR 2060.
[324] *Ibid*, at [78] per Lord Hoffmann.

He was induced to procure heroin for the undercover officer by the prospect of a profitable trade in smuggled cigarettes. The judge was entitled to take the view that even if this was an authorised operation, the police had caused him to commit an offence which he would not otherwise have committed.[325]

5.8.2 Illegally Obtained Evidence

Section 78 of the Police and Criminal Evidence Act 1984 also applies to the admission of illegally obtained evidence and it has been confirmed that this approach is compatible with Article 6.[326] A defendant is not entitled to have the illegally obtained evidence excluded simply because it has been illegally obtained. What he is entitled to is an opportunity to challenge its use and admission, and a judicial assessment of the effect of its admission upon the fairness of the trial as provided for by section 78.[327] The same considerations apply to evidence obtained in violation of Article 8.[328]

It was held by a majority of the Court of Appeal in *A v Secretary of State for the Home Department*[329] that Articles 3 and 6, and the common law, do not prevent the admission in evidence by the Special Immigration Appeals Commission of statements made by a person, who is not a party to the proceedings, as a result of torture inflicted by the agents of a foreign state. However, it was unanimously held that it is not possible to admit statements which a United Kingdom public authority has procured by torture.

5.8.3 Hearsay Evidence

Whilst Article 6(3)(d) effectively prohibits the admission of hearsay evidence in criminal proceedings, this does not affect its admission in civil proceedings. However, it appears its admission is not automatic and must be proportionate in the circumstances.[330] In *McCann*,[331] although the House of Lords characterised the application for an anti-social behaviour order under the Crime and Disorder Act 1998 as determination of civil rights rather than a criminal charge, it held that, given the seriousness of the matters involved, the criminal standard of proof had to be applied. Nevertheless, this did not prevent the admission of hearsay evidence.

> [T]he striking of a fair balance between the demands of the general interest of the community (the community in this case being represented by weak and vulnerable people who claim that they are the victims of anti-social behaviour which violates their rights) and the requirements of the protection of the defendants' rights requires the scales to come down in

---

[325] *Ibid*, at [81] per Lord Hoffmann. See also *Shannon*, above n 319; *Lewis*, above n 244. See further A Ashworth, 'Re-drawing the Boundaries of Entrapment' [2002] *CLR* 161; S McKay, 'Entrapment: Competing Views on the Effect of the Human Rights Act on English Criminal Law' [2002] *EHRLR* 764.
[326] *R v P* [2001] 2 WLR 463 in reliance upon *Schenk v Switzerland* (1988) 13 EHRR 242; *Teixeira de Castro v Portugal* (1998) 28 EHRR 101; *Khan v United Kingdom* (2000) 8 BHRC 310.
[327] See also *R v Bailey* [2001] EWCA Crim 733; *R v Everson* [2001] EWCA Crim 896.
[328] *R v P*, above n 326; *R v Loveridge* [2001] 2 Cr App R 591; *R v Mason* [2002] 2 Cr App R 628; *R v Button* [2005] EWCA Crim 516.
[329] *A v Secretary of State for the Home Department*, above n 92.
[330] *McCann*, above n 40, at [113].
[331] *Ibid*.

favour of the protection of the community and of permitting the use of hearsay evidence in applications for anti-social behaviour orders.[332]

5.8.4 Dock Identification Evidence

The use of dock identification evidence must not always be regarded as incompatible with the accused's Article 6(1) right to a fair trial.[333] However, particular care must be taken where identification is likely to be a real issue in the case to ensure that the way the evidence is obtained and presented is compatible with Article 6(1).[334] The proper approach is to consider whether, having regard to all the elements of the proceedings, including the way in which the identification evidence was obtained, the accused had a fair trial in terms of Article 6.[335] It has been held that, where such evidence has been admitted, two factors which will weigh in favour of the conclusion that an accused did have a fair trial will be the fact that he was legally represented and that the rights of the defence were respected, with the accused's representative being able to challenge the admissibility of the evidence, to cross-examine the witness and then to address the jury on the weakness of the evidence.

> It will also be important to consider any directions which the judge gave to the jury about the identification evidence. The significance of the contested evidence in the context of the prosecution case as a whole will also be relevant. In particular, was it one of the principal planks in the case against the accused or was there a substantial body of other evidence pointing to his guilt?[336]

5.8.5 Exclusionary Rules

Anything which may prevent an accused person from putting forward evidence critical to his defence is likely to be incompatible with the right to a fair hearing. However, exclusionary rules are possible if these pursue a legitimate aim and are proportionate.[337]

In *R v A*[338] the respondent was due to stand trial for rape. He alleged that, for approximately three weeks prior to the date of the alleged rape, he and the complainant had had a sexual relationship. His defence was that sexual intercourse took place with the complainant's consent or, alternatively, that he believed she consented. At a preparatory hearing, counsel for the respondent applied for leave to cross-examine the complainant about the alleged previous sexual relationship between the complainant and the respondent and to lead evidence about it. Relying on section 41 of the Youth Justice and Criminal Evidence Act 1999, the judge ruled that the complainant could not be cross-examined, nor could evidence be led, about her alleged sexual relationship with the defendant and that the prepared statement could not be put in evidence.

---

[332] *Ibid*, at [113].
[333] *Holland*, above n 264, at [5] per Lord Hope.
[334] *Ibid*, at [6] per Lord Hope.
[335] *Ibid*, at [41] per Lord Rodger.
[336] *Ibid*, at [42] per Lord Rodger.
[337] *R v A*, above n 7.
[338] *Ibid*.

The House of Lords held that, on ordinary principles of construction, section 41 was prima facie capable of preventing an accused person from putting forward evidence critical to his defence and, thus construed, was incompatible with Article 6. In Lord Steyn's view, the question was whether, measured against the guarantee of a fair trial, the breadth of exclusionary provisions of section 41 in respect of sexual experience between a complainant and the defendant were justified and proportionate.[339] He concluded that 'Whilst the statute pursued desirable goals, the methods adopted amounted to legislative overkill.'[340] However, a majority agreed that a declaration of incompatibility could be avoided by applying the interpretative obligation under section 3 of the HRA. In their Lordships' view, with due regard always being paid to the importance of seeking to protect the complainant from indignity and from humiliating questions, the test of admissibility under section 41(3)(c) was whether the evidence (and questioning in relation to it) was nevertheless so relevant to the issue of consent that to exclude it would endanger the fairness of the trial under Article 6. If this test was satisfied, the House held that the evidence should not be excluded.[341]

In *R v Connor*[342] it was argued before the House of Lords that the common law rule which prevents evidence about the deliberations of a jury which reveal a lack of impartiality from being admissible, however compelling the evidence may be and however grave the circumstances of the lack of impartiality, was incompatible with Article 6. A majority found the rule proportionate and consistent with Article 6, holding that the rationality of the rule was incontrovertible.

> The objects of the rule . . . provide essential assistance for the jury to operate as a collective body independently of outside influences and be impartial. It helps them to reach a determination of the criminal charge within a reasonable time without the need for retrials every time a juror wanted to change his mind or express his or her dissatisfaction with the reasoning of the majority.[343]

Lord Steyn dissented, holding that there was a positive duty on judges, when things had gone seriously wrong in the criminal justice system, to do everything possible to put them right.[344]

> If there are substantial reasons to doubt the impartiality of the tribunal, the matter must be examined in order to determine whether there has been a breach of this fundamental guarantee.[345]

In his view, in exceptional circumstances, Article 6 required that the evidence be admitted.[346]

---

[339] *Ibid*, at [35].
[340] *Ibid*, at [43]. See also Lord Clyde at [122] and [137].
[341] See also *R v T; R v H* [2001] EWCA Crim 1877, [2001] 1 WLR 632. See further D Birch, 'Rethinking Sexual History Evidence: Proposals for Fairer Trials' [2002] *CLR* 531; A Kavanagh, 'Unlocking the Human Rights Act: The "Radical" Approach to Section 3(1) Revisited' [2005] *EHRLR* 259.
[342] *R v Connor; R v Mirza* [2004] UKHL 2, [2004] 1 AC 118.
[343] *Ibid*, at [145]–[147] per Lord Hobhouse. See also Lord Slynn at [50]–[51], Lord Hope at [129] and Lord Rodger at [168].
[344] *Ibid*, at [4].
[345] *Ibid*, at [5].
[346] *Ibid*, at [20] in reliance on *Remli v France* (1996) 22 EHRR 252.

5.8.6 Trial in Absentia

In criminal cases, whilst a defendant has, in general, a right to be present at his trial and a right to be legally represented, these rights can be waived, separately or together, wholly or in part, by the defendant himself. They may be wholly waived if, knowing, or having the means to know, when and where his trial is to take place, he deliberately and voluntarily absents himself and/or withdraws instructions from those representing him. They may be waived in part if, being present and represented at the outset, the defendant, during the course of the trial, behaves in such a way as to obstruct the proper course of the proceedings and/or withdraws his instructions from those representing him.[347] The trial judge has discretion as to whether a trial should take place or continue in the absence of a defendant and/or his legal representatives. That discretion must be exercised with great care, and it is only in rare and exceptional cases that it should be exercised in favour of a trial taking place or continuing, particularly if the defendant is unrepresented.[348] It is generally desirable that a defendant be represented even if he has voluntarily absconded.[349] In exercising that discretion, fairness to the defence is of prime importance but fairness to the prosecution must also be taken into account.[350]

The judge must have regard to all the circumstances of the case, including

- the nature and circumstances of the defendant's behaviour in absenting himself from the trial or disrupting it and whether, in so doing, his behaviour was deliberate, voluntary or as such that he plainly waived his right to appear;
- whether an adjournment might result in the defendant being caught or attending voluntarily and/or not disrupting the proceedings;
- the likely length of such an adjournment;
- whether the defendant, though absent, is, or wishes to be, legally represented at the trial or has, by his conduct, waived his right to representation;
- whether an absent defendant's legal representatives are able to receive instructions from him during the trial and the extent to which they are able to present his defence;
- the extent of the disadvantage to the defendant in not being able to give his account of events, having regard to the nature of the evidence against him;
- the risk of the jury reaching an improper conclusion about the absence of the defendant;
- the general public interest and the particular interest of victims and witnesses that a trial should take place within a reasonable time of the events to which it relates;
- the effect of delay on the memory of the witnesses;

---

[347] *R v Hayward; R v Jones* [2001] EWCA Crim 168, [2001] 3 WLR 125 at [22] as approved in *R v Jones* [2002] UKHL 5, [2002] 2 WLR 524. It is important to note that the question of waiver was not raised before the House of Lords. However, their Lordships did offer their views, the majority concluding that waiver was possible even if there was no direct evidence to show that the accused knew what the consequences of his absconding would be.
[348] *Ibid.*
[349] *Jones*, above n 347, at [15].
[350] *Hayward; Jones*, above n 347, at [22] as approved in *Jones, ibid.*

- where there is more than one defendant and not all have absconded, the undesirability of separate trials, and the prospects of a fair trial for the defendants who are present.[351]

If the judge decides that a trial should take place or continue in the absence of an unrepresented defendant, he must ensure that the trial is as fair as the circumstances permit. In particular, he must take reasonable steps, both during the giving of evidence and in the summing up, to expose weaknesses in the prosecution case and to make such points on behalf of the defendant as the evidence permits. In summing up he must warn the jury that absence is not an admission of guilt and adds nothing to the prosecution's case.[352]

In civil cases it has been held that a litigant whose presence is needed for the fair trial of a case, but who is unable to be present through no fault of his own, will usually have to be granted an adjournment, however inconvenient it may be to the tribunal or court and to the other parties.[353] However, the tribunal or court is entitled to be satisfied that the inability of the litigant to be present is genuine, and the onus is on the applicant for an adjournment to prove the need for such an adjournment.[354]

5.9 Reasons

Finally, the right to a fair hearing generally carries with it an obligation to give reasons, although a detailed answer to every argument is not required. The judgment must contain reasons that are sufficient to demonstrate that the essential issues that have been raised by the parties have been addressed by the court and how those issues have been resolved. It is not necessary to go further and explain why one contention, or piece of evidence, has been preferred to another.[355] The extent to which the duty to give reasons applies varies according to the nature of the decision.[356] Where a judicial decision affects the substantive rights of the parties, the decision should be reasoned. However, there are some judicial decisions where fairness does not demand reasons, such as interlocutory decisions in the course of case management. There are also some circumstances in which the reason for the decision will be implicit from the decision itself.[357] Where there are conflicts of expert evidence, the judge should explain why he accepted the evidence of one and rejected the evidence of the other.[358] Where the reason for an order as to costs is not obvious, the judge should explain why he or she has made the order. The explanation can usually be brief.[359]

---

[351] *Ibid.*

[352] *Ibid.* See also *R v Singh* [2003] EWCA Crim 3712. See further PW Ferguson, 'Trial in Absence and Waiver of Human Rights', [2002] *CLR* 554.

[353] *Teinaz v London Borough of Wandsworth* [2002] EWHC Civ 1040, [2002] ICR 1471.

[354] *Ibid.* See also *Andreou v Lord Chancellor's Department* [2002] EWCA Civ 1192, [2002] IRLR 728; *Re S (a child) (adoption: order made in father's absence)* [2001] 2 FCR 148; *Pine*, above n 308.

[355] *English v Emery Reimbold & Strick Ltd* [2002] EWCA Civ 605 at [12] in reliance upon *Torija v Spain* (1994) 19 EHRR 553; *Van de Hurk v The Netherlands* (1994) 18 EHRR 481; *Helle v Finland* (1997) 26 EHRR 159.

[356] *North Range Shipping Ltd v Seatrans Shipping Corporation* [2002] EWHC Civ 405, [2002] 1 WLR 2397 at [20] in reliance upon *Hiro Balani v Spain* (1995) 19 EHRR 566 at [27].

[357] *English*, above n 355, at [13].

[358] *Ibid*, at [20].

[359] *Ibid*, at [14].

It has been held that the reasoning of the ECHR goes no further that that which is required under domestic law.[360] At common law, the adequacy of reasons depends on the nature of the case.[361] If the appellate process is to work satisfactorily, the judgment must enable the appellate court to understand why the judge reached his decision.

> [T]he issues the resolution of which were vital to the judge's conclusion should be identified and the manner in which he resolved them explained.[362]

In *North Range Shipping*[363] the Court of Appeal held that the practice of not giving reasons for granting or refusing leave to appeal from an arbitration award under the Arbitration Act 1996 was incompatible with Article 6. However, whilst it agreed that the judge should inform the unsuccessful applicant for leave about which of the statutory tests he failed, it did not think it necessary for the judge to go further and explain in every case why the relevant threshold test had been failed. Further reasons may be necessary where the issue is whether the tribunal's decision was wrong or not open to serious doubt. However, these need only be brief to show the losing party why he lost.[364]

6. Public Hearing and Public Pronouncement

In the determination of civil rights and obligations or a criminal charge, Article 6 also requires a public hearing. Such a hearing is of benefit to the individual litigants and the wider public interest.[365] The public nature of the proceedings deters inappropriate behaviour on the part of the members of the court; maintains the public's confidence in the administration of justice by enabling the public to know that justice is being administered impartially; and can result in evidence becoming available which would not be available if the proceedings were conducted behind closed doors or with one or more of the parties' or witnesses' identity concealed.[366] Although it is possible to waive this right, waiver must not run counter to any important public interest.[367]

It is clear that the right to a public hearing is not absolute. In Article 6 itself it is recognised that the press and public may be excluded in the interests of morals, public order or national security; where the interest of juveniles or the protection of the

---

[360] *Ibid*, at [12].
[361] *Ibid*, at [17].
[362] *Ibid*, at [19].
[363] *North Range Shipping*, above n 356.
[364] *Ibid*, at [27]. See also *Threlfall v General Optical Council* [2004] EWHC (Admin) 2683, [2005] Lloyd's Rep Med 250; *R (on the application of Luthra) v General Dental Council* [2004] EWHC (Admin) 458.
[365] *R (on the application of Mersey Care Trust) v Mental Health Review Tribunal* [2004] EWHC (Admin) 1749, [2005] 1 WLR 2469 at [13].
[366] *Ibid*.
[367] *Ibid*.

private life of the parties so require[368]; or 'to the extent strictly necessary in the opinion of the court in special circumstances where publicity would prejudice the interests of justice.' The latter has been held to apply to a situation where a witness refused to give evidence unless the public gallery was cleared.[369] Certain hearings, such as hearings before mental health review tribunals, are always held in private. In such circumstances, it is for the individual who desires a public hearing to demonstrate why the normal rules should not be followed. In *Mersey Care Trust*[370] the patient, Ian Brady, requested that his statutory review before the mental health tribunal be in public. The Divisional Court held that the tribunal had failed to take account of considerations of public order and security and whether a public hearing would impose a disproportionate burden on the state.[371] It remitted the request to it for rehearing. Prison disciplinary proceedings are also held in private in the prison. In *Bannatyne*[372] the Administrative Court held that this practice was justified given the considerations of public order and the security problems that would be involved if the proceedings were conducted in public.[373]

Violations of the right to a public hearing are rare and have only been found where the judge has received some advice or information in private which has not been repeated in open court. For example, in *Kelly*[374] a majority of the Privy Council held that, in order to comply with Article 6, the advice of the clerk of the Scottish district court to the justice should be disclosed in open court and the parties given the opportunity to comment on it.[375]

Article 6(1) also provides that 'judgment shall be pronounced publicly,' and it has been held that it is not possible for a court to simply apply by analogy the same restrictions as are available in relation to holding the trial in public.[376] However, if it is impossible to produce an anonymised or abridged version of the judgment, the interests of justice may permit pronouncement in private.[377]

---

7. Reasonable Time

Article 6 also provides that the hearing determining civil rights and obligations or a criminal charge must be held within a reasonable time. This requirement is of benefit both to the individual and to the legal system. In criminal matters it is important that

---

[368] See, eg *Arundel Corporation v Khokher* [2003] EWCA Civ 491.
[369] *R v Richards* [1999] Crim LR 764.
[370] *Mersey Care Trus*, above n 365.
[371] *Ibid*, at [64] in reliance on *Campbell and Fell v UK* (1985) 7 EHRR 165.
[372] *Bannatyne v Secretary of State for the Home Department* [2004] EWHC (Admin) 1912.
[373] *Ibid*, at [52] in reliance on *Campbell and Fell*, above n 371, and *Ezeh and Connors v United Kingdom* Judgment of 15 July 2002. Affirmed by Grand Chamber, 9 October 2003.
[374] *Clark (Procurator Fiscal) v Kelly* [2003] UKPC D1, [2004] 1 AC 681.
[375] *Ibid*, at [69] per Lord Hope and [7] per Lord Bingham. See also *The Bow Spring and the Manzanillo II* [2004] EWCA Civ 1007, [2005] 1 Lloyd's Rep 1.
[376] *In the Matter of the Trusts of the X Charity* [2003] EWHC (Ch) 1462, [2003] 1 WLR 2751. See also *Pelling v Bruce-Williams* [2004] EWCA Civ 845, [2004] Fam 155.
[377] *Ibid*.

an accused person does not lie under a charge for too long in a state of uncertainty. Delays might jeopardise the effectiveness and credibility of the administration of justice.[378] For example, too long a delay may result in the loss of exculpatory evidence or a deterioration in the quality of evidence generally. The safety of a verdict reached a considerable time after the offence often becomes the subject of controversy and undermines public confidence in the criminal justice system.[379]

The reasonable time requirement is a separate guarantee and is not to be seen as part of the overriding right to a fair trial. It does not require the person concerned to show that he has been prejudiced by the delay.[380] The right is not subject to any words of limitation, nor is it capable of modification on the ground of proportionality. The only question is whether, having regard to all the circumstances of the case, the time taken to determine the person's rights and obligations or criminal charge is unreasonable.[381] The question of remedy is complicated and is considered in detail at the end of this section.

One final point to note is that Article 5(3) also provides for trial within a reasonable time and the Strasbourg case law concerning both Articles has often been considered together.[382]

7.1 Criminal Proceedings

7.1.1 Start of the Time Period

When considering the start of the relevant time period, regard must be had to the purpose of the reasonable time requirement—which is to ensure that criminal proceedings, once initiated, are prosecuted without undue delay so as to protect defendants from the trauma of awaiting trial for inordinate periods.[383] As a general rule, with respect to criminal matters the relevant time period begins at the earliest time at which a person is officially alerted to the likelihood of criminal proceedings against him. Ordinarily this will be when a defendant is formally charged or served with a summons, but this rule is not inflexible.[384] Interviewing for the purposes of a regulatory inquiry in England and Wales will not meet this test.[385] Nor, ordinarily, will time begin to run until after the suspect has been interviewed under caution. Arrest will not ordinarily mark the beginning of the period, but an official indication that a person will be reported with a view to prosecution may do so.[386] The period ends when there is a determination of the charge and it includes the time taken by any appeal.[387]

---

[378] *Watson*, above n 2, at [50] per Lord Bingham in reliance upon *Wemhoff v Federal Republic of Germany* (1968) 1 EHRR 55 at [18]; *Stögmuller v Austria* (1969) 1 EHRR 155; *H v France*, above n 25, at [58]. See also *Mills*, above n 2.

[379] *Mills, ibid*, at [14]. See also *Attorney General's Reference No.2 of 2001*, above n 1, at [16].

[380] *Porter*, above n 2, at [109].

[381] *Ibid*. See also *Watson*, above n 2, at [50] per Lord Bingham and [73] per Lord Hope; *Mills*, above n 2, at [9] per Lord Steyn.

[382] *Watson, ibid*, at [30].

[383] *Attorney General's Reference No.2 of 2001*, above n 1, at [27] per Lord Bingham.

[384] *Ibid*.

[385] See, eg *R v James* [2002] EWCA Crim 119.

[386] *Attorney General's Reference No.2 of 2001*, above n 1, at [28] per Lord Bingham.

[387] *HM Advocate v R* [2002] UKPC D3, [2004] 1 AC 462.

7.1.2 Determining a Reasonable Time

It is not possible to identify from the case law a tariff by reference to which decisions may be taken as to whether a given period of delay is or is not acceptable. Each case must be judged according to its own facts and circumstances.[388] Whilst this right is important and should not be watered down or weakened, it has been held that the

> individual does not enjoy these rights in a vacuum. He is a member of society and other members of society also have interests deserving of respect.[389]

There is a public interest in the bringing to trial of those reasonably suspected of committing crimes and, if they are not convicted, in their being appropriately sentenced.[390]

The threshold of proving a breach of the reasonable time requirement is a high one, not easily crossed. The first step is to consider the period of time which has elapsed.

> Unless that period is one which, on its face and without more, gives grounds for real concern it is almost certainly unnecessary to go further, since the convention is directed not to departures from the ideal but to infringements of basic human rights.[391]

Next it is necessary for the court to look into the detailed facts and circumstances of the particular case, and for the state to explain and justify any lapse of time which appears to be excessive.[392]

In accordance with Strasbourg case law, three areas call for particular inquiry. The first is the complexity of the case.

> It is recognised, realistically enough, that the more complex a case, the greater the number of witnesses, the heavier the burden of documentation, the longer the time which must necessarily be taken to prepare it adequately for trial and for any appellate hearing. But with any case, however complex, there comes a time when the passage of time becomes excessive and unacceptable.[393]

The second matter is the conduct of the defendant.

> In almost any fair and developed legal system it is possible for a recalcitrant defendant to cause delay by making spurious applications and challenges, changing legal advisers, absenting himself, exploiting procedural technicalities, and so on. A defendant cannot properly complain of delay of which he is the author. But procedural time-wasting on his

---

[388] *Watson*, above n 2, at [74] per Lord Hope in reliance upon *Stögmuller*, above n 378; *Obermeier v Austria* (1990) 13 EHRR 290.

[389] *Watson, ibid*, at [51] per Lord Bingham in reliance upon *Sporrong and Lönnroth v Sweden* (1982) 5 EHRR 35; *Soering v United Kingdom* (1989) 11 EHRR 439; *B v France* (1992) 16 EHRR 1; *Doorson v The Netherlands* (1996) 22 EHRR 330.

[390] *Watson, ibid*, at [51] per Lord Bingham.

[391] *Watson, ibid*, at [52] per Lord Bingham.

[392] *Ibid*, at [52] per Lord Bingham.

[393] *Ibid*, at [53] per Lord Bingham.

part does not entitle the prosecuting authorities themselves to waste time unnecessarily and excessively.[394]

The third matter is the manner in which the case has been dealt with by the administrative and judicial authorities. It is generally incumbent on contracting states to organise their legal systems so as to ensure that the reasonable time requirement is honoured.

But nothing in the convention jurisprudence requires courts to shut their eyes to the practical realities of litigious life even in a reasonably well-organised legal system.

However,

a marked lack of expedition, if unjustified, will point towards a breach of the reasonable time requirement, and the authorities make clear that while, for the purposes of the reasonable time requirement, time runs from the date when the defendant is charged, the passage of any considerable period of time before charge may call for greater than normal expedition thereafter.[395]

7.1.3 Application

Given that each case is judged on its own facts and circumstances, what was a reasonable time in one case may not necessarily be reasonable in another. However, to understand the process of determining a reasonable time, it is useful to consider some examples, such as the appeals determined by the Privy Council in *Watson*.[396] In the first case, police officers had been charged with perjury and 20 months had elapsed between charge and trial, although they were not in custody over this period. The Privy Council held that, although a shorter period would be desirable, this was not a period which caused real concern 'such as to suggest that a basic human right of the officers may have been infringed.'[397] It found a strong public interest in the integrity of the police and the interest of individual officers in vindicating their reputations, which required a careful and independent investigation. This inevitably took time and no violation was found.[398]

In the second case, 27 months had elapsed between the charge and the service of the indictment and 28 months would have elapsed had the trial proceeded as planned. During the period JK was not in custody, but he was a child at the time of the alleged offences. The Privy Council held that, when dealing with children, the reasonable time requirement had to be read in light of the UN Convention on the Rights of the Child, which required all due expedition.[399] In particular, delay may prejudice the fairness of the trial as a more mature accused may make a different impression. Delay prolongs the stress to which a vulnerable accused is inevitably subject, and puts off

---

[394] *Ibid*, at [54] per Lord Bingham.
[395] *Ibid*, at [55] per Lord Bingham. See also Lord Hope at [76]–[77]. Lord Hope also noted that the reasonable time guarantee should not be seen as an impediment to maintaining high standards in the system of public prosecution, at [83].
[396] Above n 2.
[397] *Ibid*, at [56] per Lord Bingham.
[398] *Ibid*, at [58] per Lord Bingham.
[399] *Ibid*, at [61] per Lord Bingham.

the date at which his problems can be addressed and full counselling given.[400] The Privy Council found that this was not a complex case and it was not suggested that JK was responsible for the delay. There was no attempt to treat the case with the urgency which it deserved. A breach of the reasonable time requirement was found.[401]

7.2 Civil Proceedings

7.2.1 Start of the Time Period

With respect to civil proceedings, time usually begins to run from the date when the proceedings in question are initiated.[402] In *Porter*[403] it was held that the time began to run from the date when the objections which gave rise to the investigation were received by the auditor.[404] What is of concern is procedural delay in the course of proceedings, not the delay between the commission of the allegedly wrongful actions and the commencement of proceedings.[405]

7.2.2 Determining a Reasonable Time

When determining the reasonableness of the duration of the proceedings, the same criteria as used in criminal proceedings apply.[406] Again, it all depends on the facts and circumstances of the case, but some examples are useful. In *Porter*[407] the House of Lords concluded that there was no basis for the suggestion that there was an unreasonable delay at the Divisional Court stage, having regard to the complexity of the issues and the volume of evidence that had to be prepared and presented.[408] Similarly, the 65 months which elapsed before the auditor issued his decision and certificates of surcharge was found to be reasonable. The House of Lords found that his investigation was vast and that he was constantly in action.[409]

In *Haikel*,[410] although no explanation was offered for the period of 22 months between the letter from the General Medical Council to the appellant and the commencement of the hearing, the Privy Council concluded it was reasonable.

> There was no evidence or suggestion by the Appellant that he had suffered any material prejudice in addition to the lapse of time. There was no complaint that witnesses were no

---

[400] *Ibid*, at [62] per Lord Bingham.
[401] *Ibid*, at [63]–[64] per Lord Bingham. See also *HM Advocate v R*, above n 387, where the appellant was charged in 1995 and not indicted for trial until 2001. A breach of the reasonable time guarantee was assumed. See also *James*, above n 385; *R v Coates* [2004] EWCA Crim 3049.
[402] *Porter*, above n 2, at [107] in reliance upon *Ausiello v Italy* (1996) 24 EHRR 568 at [18].
[403] *Ibid*.
[404] *Ibid*, at [107].
[405] *Haikel v The General Medical Council* [2002] UKPC 37, [2002] Lloyd's Rep 415 at [14].
[406] *Porter*, above n 2, at [107] per Lord Hope in reliance upon *König*, above n 25, at [99].
[407] *Ibid*.
[408] *Ibid*, at [111].
[409] *Ibid*, at [112]–[114].
[410] *Haikel*, above n 404.

longer available who would have been but for the delay. The records of the patients were available and full'.[411]

7.3 Remedy

The reasonable time requirement is a separate guarantee which is not to be seen simply as part of the overriding right to a fair trial.[412] A violation may be found in the absence of any prejudice to the fairness of the defendant's trial.[413] Therefore, the consequences of any breach or threatened breach need to be considered separately. There has been little discussion in cases brought under the HRA of the appropriate remedy in civil proceedings.[414] However, the question of remedy in criminal proceedings has received detailed consideration.

7.3.1 Criminal Proceedings: Pre-conviction

The question of the appropriate remedy where there has been a breach of the reasonable time guarantee before a case has even been brought to trial has caused considerable difficulty and even led to a split between Scottish and English jurisprudence. In Scotland, a majority of the Privy Council held in *HM Advocate v R*[415] that, as a result of section 57(2) of the Scotland Act 1998, once it had been established that a proposed or continuing act was incompatible with a person's Article 6(1) rights, the Lord Advocate was prohibited from doing that act. In the context of the reasonable time guarantee, this meant that it would be incompatible with Article 6 for the Lord Advocate to prosecute an individual because to do so would violate his right to a hearing within a reasonable time. Therefore, the proceedings had to be stayed as the Lord Advocate had no power to proceed with the prosecution.[416]

Under the HRA in England and Wales, a majority of the House of Lords held in *Attorney General's Reference No.2 of 2001*[417] that if, through the action or inaction of a public authority, a criminal charge was not determined at a hearing within a reasonable time, there must be afforded such remedy as may be just and appropriate:

> The appropriate remedy will depend on the nature of the breach and all the circumstances, including particularly the stage of the proceedings at which the breach is established. If the breach is established before the hearing, the appropriate remedy may be a public

---

[411] *Ibid*, at [14].
[412] *Porter, Watson* and *Mills*, above n 2.
[413] *Watson, ibid*, at [50] per Lord Bingham.
[414] In *R v Gorman*, 2 April 2004 the Court of Appeal held that a delay of over seven years in granting leave to appeal against a confiscation order violated the reasonable time guarantee and resulted in the quashing of the order. See also *R v Goring* [2004] EWCA Crim 969 and *In the Matter of Saggar*, Court of Appeal [2005] EWCA Civ 174. In *Bangs v Connex South Eastern Ltd* [2005] EWCA Civ 14, [2005] 2 All ER 316, in the context of an Employment Tribunal's delay, the Court of Appeal held that the question was whether, due to the delay, there was a real risk of denial of a fair trial and whether it was unjust or unfair to allow the decision to stand.
[415] Above n 387.
[416] In *Attorney General's Reference No.2 of 2001*, above n 1, at [83] Lord Hope held that the Human Rights Act did not require such an approach as it enabled one to say that the proposed act of bringing the defendant to trial after an unreasonable time had elapsed was unlawful, and then to provide a just and appropriate remedy. Lord Rodger agreed at [167].
[417] *Ibid*.

acknowledgement of the breach, action to expedite the hearing to the greatest extent practicable and perhaps, if the defendant is in custody, his release on bail. It will not be appropriate to stay or dismiss the proceedings unless (a) there can no longer be a fair hearing or (b) it would otherwise be unfair to try the defendant. The public interest in the final determination of criminal charges requires that such a charge should not be stayed or dismissed if any lesser remedy will be just and proportionate in all the circumstances.[418]

The majority confirmed that to hold a trial after the lapse of a reasonable time would not in itself be a breach of a Convention right and therefore it would not in itself comprise unlawful conduct under section 6 of the HRA.[419] Lord Bingham appreciated that it was a powerful argument that, if a public authority caused or permitted such delay to occur that a criminal charge could not be heard against a defendant within a reasonable time, so breaching his right under Article 6(1), any further prosecution or trial of the charge must be unlawful within the meaning of the Article. But he cited four reasons which compelled its rejection.

First, it would be anomalous if breach of the reasonable time requirement had an effect more far-reaching than breach of the defendant's other Article 6 rights when the breach did not taint the basic fairness of the hearing at all, and even more anomalous that the right to a hearing should be vindicated by ordering that there be no trial at all.[420] Secondly, he pointed out that a rule of automatic termination of proceedings on breach of the reasonable time requirement could not sensibly be applied in civil proceedings.

> [T]ermination of the proceedings would defeat the claimant's right to a hearing altogether and seeking to make good his loss in compensation from the state could well prove a very unsatisfactory alternative.[421]

Thirdly, a rule of automatic termination had been shown to have the effect in practice of emasculating the right which the guarantee was designed to protect.

> There is, however, a very real risk that if proof of a breach is held to require automatic termination of the proceedings the judicial response will be to set the threshold unacceptably high.[422]

---

[418] *Ibid*, at [24] per Lord Bingham, with whom Lords Nicholls, Steyn, Hoffmann, Hobhouse and Scott agreed. Lord Bingham thought it unwise to attempt to describe the category of cases in which it may be unfair to try a defendant but did cite as possible examples bad faith, unlawfulness, executive manipulation or extreme breach of prosecutor's professional duty. Lords Hope and Rodger agreed that the remedy must be that which was just and appropriate, but held that to hold the trial after a lapse of a reasonable time was itself a breach of Art 6. For application of this principle, see *R v Wheeler* [2004] EWCA Crim 572.
[419] Per Lord Nicholls at [38]–[39]. Lords Hope and Rodger dissented on this point. The majority pointed out that, if the very holding of the trial by the court would be unlawful, the trial must be stayed. Lord Bingham could not accept that it could ever be proper for a court, whose purpose was to uphold, vindicate and apply the law, to act in a manner which a statute declared to be unlawful. At [30].
[420] *Ibid*, at [20].
[421] *Ibid*, at [21].
[422] *Ibid*, at [22].

Fourthly, his Lordship found that the Strasbourg jurisprudence gave no support to the contention that there should be no hearing of a criminal charge once a reasonable time had passed.[423]

Finally, his Lordship did not accept that 'compatible' bore a different meaning under the HRA to the Scotland Act,

> even though the statutory consequence is unlawfulness in the one instance and lack of power in the other. In each case the act is one that may not lawfully be done.[424]

7.3.2 Criminal proceedings: post conviction

Where there has been a breach of the reasonable time guarantee, setting aside a conviction is not a necessary consequence.[425] The appropriate remedy may be a public acknowledgement of the breach, a reduction in the penalty imposed on a convicted defendant or the payment of compensation to an acquitted defendant.[426] For example, in *Mills*[427] the appellant complained of a breach of the guarantee where there had been a delay in the hearing of his appeal of about 12 months for which the Crown was unable to give any explanation. The Privy Council found no precedent in domestic law for the setting aside of a conviction which had been upheld on appeal as a sound conviction on the ground that there was an unreasonable delay between the date of the conviction and the hearing of the appeal.[428] Taking into account the anxiety resulting from prolongation of the proceedings, and the fact that his life had changed during the period of the delay, the Privy Council concluded that the decision of the High Court of Justiciary to reduce his sentence by nine months in order to compensate him for the effects of the delay was an appropriate and sufficient remedy.[429]

---

8. Independent and Impartial Tribunal

When civil rights and obligations, or a criminal charge, are being determined, Article 6(1) also provides that the hearing must be conducted by an independent and impartial tribunal. Justice must not only be done, it must be seen to be done. The function of this right is not only to ensure that the tribunal is free from any actual or personal bias or prejudice; it also requires this matter to be viewed objectively so as to exclude

---

[423] *Ibid*, at [23] citing *X v Germany* (1980) 25 DR 142; *Eckle v Germany* (1982) 5 EHRR 1; *Neuback v Germany* (1983) 41 DR 13; *Bunkate v Netherlands* (1995) 19 EHRR 477; *Beck v Norway*, Judgment of 26 June 2001.
[424] *Ibid*, at [30]. The majority held that *R v Lord Advocate* was wrongly decided. See further J Jackson and J Johnstone, 'The Reasonable Time Requirement: an Independent and Meaningful Right?' [2005] *CLR* 3.
[425] *Mills*, above n 2, at [41] per Lord Hope in reliance upon *Bunkate*, above n 422.
[426] *Attorney General's Reference No.2 of 2001*, above n 1, at [24] per Lord Bingham.
[427] Above n 2.
[428] *Ibid*, at [52] per Lord Hope.
[429] *Ibid*, at [55] per Lord Hope in reliance upon *Bunkate*, above n 422; *Eckle v Germany* (1983) 13 EHRR 556; *Beck v Norway*, Judgment of 26 June 2001. See also Lord Steyn at [16].

any legitimate doubt as to the tribunal's independence and impartiality.[430] This part of Article 6(1) is not subject to any words of limitation and does not require or permit a balance to be struck between the right to an independent and impartial tribunal and other considerations, such as the public interest.[431] Independence and impartiality is an essential element if the trial is to satisfy the overriding requirement of fairness.[432] Nevertheless, it has been held that the rule of law lies at the heart of the Convention and it is not the purpose of Article 6 to make it impracticable to bring those who are accused of crime to justice.[433]

In common with the rights already examined, this right is separate and there is no room for the argument that the question of whether there was a breach could be tested after the event by asking whether the proceedings overall were fair.[434] To remedy a breach, a declaratory judgment and damages are possible. In criminal cases, if there has been a breach, a conviction must be quashed although it is possible to order a retrial.[435]

8.1 Test for Independence and Impartiality

There is a close relationship between the concept of independence and that of impartiality.

> In both cases the concept requires not only that the tribunal must be truly independent and free from actual bias, proof of which is likely to be very difficult, but also that it must not appear in the objective sense to lack these essential qualities.[436]

8.1.1 Subjective Test

The tribunal must actually be independent and impartial. Proof of actual lack of impartiality or independence is usually very difficult and such cases are unusual. Some examples would be if a judge has a personal interest, which is not negligible, in the outcome of the case; is a friend or relation of a party or a witness; or is disabled by personal experience from bringing an objective judgment to bear on the case in question.

> What disqualifies the judge is the presence of some factor which could prevent the bringing of an objective judgment to bear, which could distort the judge's judgment.[437]

---

[430] *Millar v Procurator Fiscal* [2001] 1 WLR 1615 at [63] per Lord Hope in reliance upon *McGonnell v United Kingdom* (2000) 30 EHRR 289; *Findlay v United Kingdom* (1997) 24 EHRR 221; *Rimmer v HM Advocate*, 23 May 2001.
[431] *Montgomery*, above n 110; *Baragiola v Switzerland* (1993) 75 DR 76 distinguished.
[432] *Millar*, above n 429, at [52] per Lord Hope.
[433] *Montgomery*, above n 110, per Lord Hope in reliance upon *Pullar v United Kingdom* (1996) 22 EHRR 391. See also *Preiss*, above n 34, and the comments of Lord Hope in *Davidson v Scottish Ministers* [2004] UKHL 34, [2004] HRLR 34 at [49].
[434] *Millar*, above n 429, at [66] per Lord Hope.
[435] *HM Advocate v R*, above n 387, at [8] per Lord Steyn. See also *Attorney General's Reference No.2 of 2001*, above n 1.
[436] *Porter*, above n 2, at [88] in reliance on *Findlay*, above n 429, at [73].
[437] *Davidson*, above n 432.

8.1.2 Objective Test

The objective test for independence and impartiality exists because the appearance of independence and impartiality is just as important as the question of whether those qualities exist in fact. Justice must not only be done, it must be seen to be done.[438] The common law test for bias originally formulated in *R v Gough*[439] has now been modified. Under Article 6, the court must ascertain all the circumstances which have a bearing on the suggestion that the judge was biased. It must then ask whether those circumstances would lead a fair-minded and informed observer to conclude that there was a real possibility that the tribunal was biased.[440] It is unnecessary to delve into the characteristics to be attributed to the observer. One is entitled to conclude that such an observer will adopt a balanced approach, neither complacent nor unduly sensitive or suspicious.[441] This test applies to both independence[442] and impartiality.[443]

When applying the test it is important that account is taken of all the circumstances. For example, in *Montgomery*[444] it was argued that there could not be a fair trial because of the impact pre-trial publicity would have on a jury. The Privy Council noted that the question was not confined to the residual effect of the publicity on the minds of each of the jurors. Account also had to be taken of the part the judge would play in order to ensure, so far as possible, that the defendants would receive a fair trial.[445]

8.1.3 Rehearing: Generally

The prospect of a complete rehearing of the case must also be taken into account. For example, in *Preiss*[446] the Privy Council, acting in the capacity of hearing appeals from decisions of the Professional Conduct Committee of the General Dental Council, held that the points taken under Article 6(1) could not succeed if the Privy Council was prepared to conduct a complete rehearing of the case, including a full reconsideration of the facts and of the question of whether the facts amounted to serious professional misconduct. Similarly, in *Porter*,[447] in relation to the multiplicity of roles performed by the auditor[448], the House of Lords held that there was no breach of Article 6(1) if the proceedings were subject to subsequent control by a judicial body that had full jurisdiction and did provide the guarantees of Article 6(1).[449]

---

[438] *Millar*, above n 429, at [63] per Lord Hope, in reliance upon *McGonnell v United Kingdom*, *Findlay*, above n 429; *Rimmer v HM Advocate*, 23 May 2001.
[439] [1993] AC 646.
[440] *Porter*, above n 2, at [103] per Lord Hope. See also *Director General of Fair Trading v The Proprietary Association of Great Britain* [2001] 1 WLR 700.
[441] *Lawal v Northern Spirit Ltd* [2003] UKHL 35, [2004] 1 All ER 187.
[442] *Boyd v The Army Prosecuting Authority* [2002] UKHL 31, [2003] 1 AC 734.
[443] *Porter*, above n 2.
[444] Above n 110.
[445] Per Lord Hope in reliance upon *Pullar*, above n 432.
[446] Above n 34.
[447] *Porter*, above n 2.
[448] He conducted the investigation, took the decision whether there was a case to answer, tried the case, assessed the loss and then appeared in the Divisional Court to defend his decision and his conduct.
[449] *Ibid*, at [93] in reliance upon *Kingsley v United Kingdom*, 7 November 2000 at [51] and [58]; *Bryan*, above n 69, at [44] and [46].

Here the powers of the Divisional Court fully satisfied the requirements. It had the power to quash the decision taken by the auditor, to rehear the case and to take a fresh decision itself in the exercise of the powers given to the auditor.[450]

However, it is not clear whether a rehearing can cure a breach in criminal proceedings. To date the issue has only arisen in cases under the Scotland Act 1998. *Millar*[451] concerned four individuals who were the subject of criminal proceedings before temporary sheriffs, although the Scottish High Court had held that temporary sheriffs were not independent and impartial within the meaning of Article 6.[452] The Privy Council held that independence and impartiality of the tribunal in criminal cases was not a matter that could be cured by the existence of a right of appeal to a court which itself satisfied the requirements of Article 6(1).[453] The appearance that justice was being done was as important as the actual doing of justice.

> The independence of the judiciary is not an empty principle which can be forgotten simply because one thinks that a correct conclusion has been reached.[454]

The opposite conclusion appears to have been reached in *Clark*,[455] which concerned the role of the clerk of the Scottish district court in criminal proceedings. It was alleged that, in trials in the district court, legal decisions were effectively taken by the clerk, who lacked the necessary independence for the purposes of Article 6(1). Finding that the clerk was a part of the court, the Privy Council held that, in order to determine whether the court lacked independence and impartiality due to the role of the clerk, it had to be looked at as a whole in the context of the procedures available for appeal and for the review of its decisions on the ground of alleged miscarriages of justice.[456] Even though the High Court did not have power to rehear the case, it had full power to re-examine all questions of law, practice and procedure, and to substitute its own decision on these matters for decisions taken by the justice on the advice of the clerk. The Privy Council held that this was sufficient to meet the requirements of Article 6(1).[457]

8.1.4 Rehearing: Administrative Decisions

Rehearing is particularly important in the context of administrative decision making, where it has been held that a breach of the guarantee of independence and impartiality can be overcome by the existence of a sufficient opportunity for appeal or review.[458] It is often held that such an approach takes into account democratic

---

[450] *Ibid*, at [93] per Lord Hope.
[451] Above n 429.
[452] *Starrs v Ruxton* [2000] JC 208.
[453] *Ibid*, at [81] per Lord Clyde in reliance upon *De Cubber v Belgium* (1984) 7 EHRR 236; *Findlay*, above n 429.
[454] *Ibid*, at [83].
[455] *Kelly*, above n 374.
[456] *Ibid*, at [55] per Lord Hope.
[457] *Ibid*, at [58] per Lord Hope in reliance upon *Albert and Le Compte*, above n 69, at [29]; *Bryan v UK* (1995) 21 EHRR 342.
[458] *Alconbury*, above n 18.

accountability, efficient administration and the sovereignty of Parliament.[459] What is required is sufficient judicial control to ensure a determination by an independent and impartial tribunal subsequently. This does not necessarily mean jurisdiction to re-examine the merits of the case but jurisdiction to deal with the case as the nature of the decision requires.[460]

In *Alconbury*,[461] although it had been concluded that the Secretary of State in his planning capacity was not an independent and impartial tribunal for the purposes of Article 6(1) due to the jurisdiction of the High Court to exercise judicial review, the House of Lords concluded that there was sufficient judicial control to ensure a subsequent determination by an independent and impartial tribunal.[462] In *Begum*[463] the question was whether the provision of an appeal to the county court on a point of law from a review of a council housing decision conducted by the council's rehousing manager was sufficient. The House of Lords noted that the appeal against the enforcement notice was closely analogous to a criminal trial.[464] However, it also had regard to democratic accountability, efficient administration and the sovereignty of Parliament.[465] It noted that Parliament was entitled to take the view that it was not in the public interest that an excessive proportion of the funds available for a welfare scheme should be consumed in administration and legal disputes.[466] Nothing was found to recommend recourse to contracting out,[467] and the House of Lords concluded that, in the case of a Part VII Housing Act decision involving no human rights other than Article 6, a conventional judicial review was sufficient and the right of appeal to the county court was sufficient to satisfy Article 6.[468]

8.2 Separation of Powers

Beyond the objective and subjective tests for independence and impartiality, it is possible that the principle of separation of powers has also found expression via Article 6. In *Anderson*,[469] in addition to the application of Article 6 to the facts, many references were also made to the separation of powers. Lord Bingham, commenting on

---

[459] *Begum (Runa) v Tower Hamlets London Borough Council* [2003] UKHL 5, [2003] 2 AC 430 at [35] per Lord Hoffmann.
[460] *Ibid*, at [33] and [35] per Lord Hoffmann and his Lordship's comments in *Alconbury*, above n 18, at [129].
[461] *Alconbury*, ibid.
[462] Whilst Lord Slynn agreed that the current scope of judicial review was sufficient to comply with Art 6(1), he also held that the time had come to recognise that the principle of proportionality was part of English administrative law and that the court also had jurisdiction to quash for a misunderstanding or ignorance of an established and relevant fact. See [51] and [53]. See also the comments of Lord Nolan at [61], Lord Hoffmann at [128] and Lord Clyde at [159].
[463] Above n 458.
[464] *Ibid*, at [42] per Lord Hoffmann in reliance upon *De Cubber*, above n 452.
[465] *Ibid*, at [43] per Lord Hoffmann.
[466] *Ibid*, at [44] per Lord Hoffmann.
[467] *Ibid*, at [46] per Lord Hoffmann.
[468] *Ibid*, at [50] and [58] per Lord Hoffmann. See also Lord Bingham at [9]–[10]. In *Adan*, above n 45, the Court of Appeal noted that if, on such a review, there was a dispute about the primary facts of a kind which had to be resolved because it was material to the decision making process, there was a danger the proceedings as a whole would not be Convention compliant. At [42] per Brooke LJ. See further *R (on the application of McLellan) v Bracknell Forest Borough Council* [2001] EWCA Civ 1510, [2002] QB 1129; *Beeson*, above n 27.
[469] Above n 114.

the European Court of Human Rights' conclusion in *Stafford*, noted that it was right to describe the complete functional separation of the judiciary from the executive as fundamental 'since the rule of law depends on it.'[470] Lord Steyn made it clear that the principle of separation of powers was not something that arrived in our legal system at the same time as the HRA:

> [T]he separation of powers between the judiciary and the legislative and executive branches of government is a strong principle of our system of government. The House of Lords and Privy Council have so stated . . . It is reinforced by constitutional principles of judicial independence, access to justice, and the rule of law.[471]

His Lordship pointed out that the decision to punish an offender by ordering him to serve a period of imprisonment was historically a decision which may only be made by the courts, and this idea was a principle feature of the rule of law on which the unwritten constitution was based. Although it had been overridden by Parliament, in his view the courts now had the ability to determine the compatibility of that statute with Article 6(1).[472] He also noted that in *Stafford* the European Court of Human Rights was rightly influenced by the strengthening of the principle of separation of powers between the executive and judiciary which underlies Article 6(1).[473]

However, it is not clear whether a court would find a violation of Article 6(1) if there were no legitimate doubt as to independence or impartiality but simply a violation of the separation of powers. In *Davidson*[474] Lord Hope stated that arguments based on the theory of the separation of powers alone would not suffice[475] and this is in keeping with Strasbourg authority. In *Kleyn v The Netherlands*[476] the ECHR held that, although the notion of separation of powers had assumed growing importance in the Court's case law, neither Article 6 nor any other provision of the Convention required states to comply with any theoretical constitutional concepts regarding the permissible limits of the powers' interaction.[477]

Regardless of whether or not the European Court of Human Rights continues to develop the principle of separation of powers, under the HRA British judges now have a far greater opportunity to uphold the principle than they have had in the past.[478] If the courts of the United Kingdom were to continue to develop and apply

---

[470] *Ibid*, at [27].
[471] *Ibid*, at [39].
[472] *Ibid*, at [51].
[473] *Ibid*, at [54]; per Lord Hutton at [76]. See also *Millar*, above n 429.
[474] Above n 432.
[475] *Ibid*, at [53].
[476] Judgment of 6 May 2003.
[477] *Ibid*, at [193]. The applicants alleged that the Administrative Jurisdiction Division of the Netherlands Council of State was not independent and impartial in that the Council exercised both advisory and judicial functions. It was also alleged that the procedure for appointment to the Council of State meant that it had to be regarded as part of the legislature and executive. All Councillors are appointed by Royal Decree (*Koninklijk Besluit*) following nomination by the Minister of the Interior and Kingdom Relations in agreement with the Minister of Justice. The Court (Grand Chamber) held by 12 votes to five that there had been no violation of Art 6(1). See also *McGonnell v United Kingdom* (2000) 30 EHRR 289; *Pabla Ky v Finland*, 22 June 2004.
[478] The independence and impartiality of the judiciary has been upheld via the principles of natural justice. Separation of powers principles have influenced the conclusions of the court in several cases. See, eg *Gouriet v Union of Post Office Workers* [1978] AC 435; *Duport Steels Ltd v Sirs* (1980) 1 WLR 142; *M v Home Office* [1994] 1 AC 377; *R v Secretary of State for the Home Department, ex p Fire Brigades Union* [1995] 2 AC 513.

the principle via Article 6, it would of course be necessary to find a workable definition and decide what degree of overlap was acceptable—a far from simple task.[479] The most obvious starting points would be the Lord Chancellor[480] and the Law Lords.[481] Writing extra-judicially, Lord Steyn has made clear his view that

> nowhere outside Britain, even in democracies with the weakest forms of separation of powers, is the independence of the judiciary potentially compromised in the eyes of citizens by relegating the status of the highest court to the position of a subordinate part of the legislature. And nowhere outside Britain is the independence of the judiciary potentially compromised in the eyes of citizens by permitting a serving politician to sit as a judge at any level, let alone in the highest court which fulfils constitutional functions.[482]

8.3 Waiver

It is possible to waive the entitlement to a determination by an independent and impartial tribunal.[483] Waiver results from a voluntary, informed and unequivocal election by a party not to claim a right or raise an objection which it is open to that party to claim or raise. The waiver must be voluntary, and it cannot be meaningfully said that a party has voluntarily elected not to claim a right or raise an objection if he was unaware that it was open to him to make the claim or raise the objection. For a waiver to be effective it must be unequivocal, which means clear and unqualified. Ignorance of the law does not suffice to found a plea of waiver.[484] Waiver was argued in *Millar*,[485] but the Privy Council held that it was impossible to accept that the qualification of temporary sheriffs was generally known to be open to serious question or that the representatives of the accused were subject to no misapprehension attributable to some established view of what the law was.[486]

8.4 Application

As with other Article 6 rights, whether or not the rights to independence and impartiality are satisfied depends very much on the circumstances of the case. Precedent can be helpful in focusing the mind on the relevant issues and producing consistency of approach. However, it is important to remember that the search is for the reaction of the fair-minded and informed observer.

---

[479] See N Barber, 'Prelude to the Separation of Powers' [2001] *CLJ* 59.
[480] Cabinet Minister, Speaker in the House of Lords, President of the Supreme Court, ex officio judge of the Court of Appeal and President of the Chancery Division.
[481] The Appellate Committee of the House of Lords is the highest court as well as a committee of the legislature.
[482] Lord Steyn, 'The Case for a Supreme Court' [2002] 118 *LQR* 382, 383. See also R Cornes, 'McGonnell v. United Kingdom, the Lord Chancellor and the Law Lords' [2000] *PL* 166; and ME Amos, 'R v. Secretary of State for the Home Department, ex p Anderson—Ending the Home Secretary's Sentencing Role' (2004) 67 *MLR* 108.
[483] *Millar*, above n 429.
[484] *Ibid*, at [31] per Lord Bingham in reliance upon *Deweer*, above n 122; Pfeifer and *Plankl v Austria* (1992) 14 EHRR 692. See also Lord Hope at [53]–[58] and Lord Clyde at [81].
[485] *Ibid*.
[486] at [38] per Lord Bingham.

The court has to apply an objective assessment as to how such a person would react to the material facts. There is a danger when applying such a test that citation of authorities may cloud rather than clarify perception. The court must be careful when looking at case precedent not to permit it to drive common sense out of the window.[487]

The following selected examples illustrate the impact of this part of Article 6 in a number of key areas.

8.4.1 Judiciary

The independence of the judiciary is viewed with particular seriousness and is often said to be of fundamental constitutional importance.

We are fortunate in this country that for a very considerable length of time this principle has never been lost, although through the annals of history there may have been times when its light burned less brightly.[488]

A number of issues have arisen under the HRA concerning independence of the judiciary.

(a) Part-time and Temporary Judges

In *Starrs v Ruxton*[489] the High Court in Scotland held that temporary sheriffs were not an independent and impartial tribunal. They were appointed for one year only and were subject to recall during that period at the instance of the Lord Advocate. In *Millar*[490] the Privy Council considered the argument that the Lord Advocate and procurators fiscal who conducted the prosecutions were acting incompatibly with Article 6 by prosecuting before temporary sheriffs. Whilst there was nothing to suggest that the outcome would have been any different had the prosecution been before a permanent sheriff, the Privy Council concluded that the right could not be compromised or eroded.[491] It found that the Lord Advocate had infringed the right of the accused to have the criminal charges against them determined by an independent and impartial tribunal contrary to section 57(2) of the Scotland Act 1998.[492]

The question of part-time judges was considered by the House of Lords in *Lawal*.[493] The issue was whether, in circumstances in which a Queen's Counsel appearing on an appeal before the Employment Appeal Tribunal (EAT) had sat as a part-time judge in the EAT with one or both of the lay members ('wing members') hearing that appeal, the hearing before the EAT was compatible with Article 6. The House of Lords considered that the observer was likely to approach the matter on the basis that the lay members look to the judge for guidance on the law, and can be

---

[487] *R (on the application of PD) v West Midlands and North West Mental Health Review Tribunal* [2004] EWCA Civ 311.
[488] *Millar*, above n 429, at [80] per Lord Clyde.
[489] 2000 JC 208.
[490] Above n 429.
[491] at [16] per Lord Bingham.
[492] at [27] per Lord Bingham.
[493] Above n 440.

expected to develop a fairly close relationship of trust and confidence with the judge. Furthermore, the observer was credited with knowledge that a Recorder, who in a criminal case had sat with jurors, may not subsequently appear in a case in which one or more of those jurors serve and the knowledge that part-time judges in the Employment Tribunal are forbidden from appearing as counsel before an Employment Tribunal which includes lay members with whom they had previously sat.[494] Their Lordships concluded that the present practice undermined public confidence in the system and there should be a restriction on part-time judges appearing as counsel before a panel of the EAT consisting of one or two lay members with whom they had previously sat.[495]

(b) Extra-judicial Activities

All members of the judiciary have a past. In some instances, their past can raise concerns about their independence and impartiality. For example, *Davidson*[496] concerned Lord Hardie, who had previously held the office of Lord Advocate. In this role he piloted the Scotland Bill through the House of Lords and advised the House of Lords on the effect of section 21 of the Crown Proceedings Act 1947 on the remedies which might be available to the courts in Scotland against the Scottish Ministers. In particular, he advised that the effect of section 21 was to preclude the grant of any coercive order against the Scottish Ministers. He later became a judge in the Scottish Court of Session. In this role he refused leave to appeal to Mr Davidson. Part of Mr Davidson's claim was for an order requiring the Scottish Ministers to secure his transfer to prison conditions which would comply with Article 3. The lower court had refused the order, relying, inter alia, on section 21.

On becoming aware of Lord Hardie's role in the House of Lords, Mr Davidson argued that the refusal of leave was vitiated for want of independence and impartiality. Applying the objective test, the House of Lords noted that rarely, if ever, in the absence of injudicious or intemperate behaviour, can a judge's previous activity as such give rise to an appearance of bias. Adherence to an opinion expressed judicially in an earlier case does not of itself denote a lack of open-mindedness. However, their Lordships also recognised that problems are liable to arise where the exercise of judicial functions is preceded by the exercise of legislative functions.[497] Here it concluded that the fair-minded and informed observer, having considered the facts, would conclude that there was a real possibility that Lord Hardie, sitting judicially, would subconsciously strive to avoid reaching a conclusion which would undermine the very clear assurances he had given to Parliament.[498] In reaching this conclusion the judicial oath was not overlooked, their Lordships holding that the observer would regard it as important protection but not as a sufficient guarantee to exclude all legitimate

---

[495] At [21].
[495] At [23]. See also *PD*, above n 486, where it was held not to be incompatible with Art 6 for a consultant psychiatrist, employed by an NHS Trust party to the proceedings, to sit on the Mental Health Review Tribunal. In *Scanfuture UK Ltd v Secretary of State for Trade and Industry* [2001] IRLR 416 the Employment Appeal Tribunal held that it was incompatible with Art 6(1) for lay members to sit on cases where the Secretary of State was a party.
[496] Above n 432.
[497] *Ibid*, at [10] per Lord Bingham.
[498] *Ibid*, at [17] per Lord Bingham.

doubt.[499] It was also noted that a failure to disclose prior activities in a case which calls for it must inevitably colour the thinking of the observer.[500]

(c) Clerks of the Court

In Clark[501] the Privy Council agreed that the clerk of the Scottish district court in criminal proceedings was part of the court but lacked the necessary independence for the purposes of Article 6. However, in the context of the procedures available for appeal and review on the ground of alleged miscarriage of justice, it concluded that there was sufficient protection to satisfy Article 6 even though the High Court did not have the power to rehear the case.[502]

8.4.2 Juries

In Montgomery[503] it was argued that there could not be a fair trial of the two defendants for the murder of a young Asian man because of the publicity which the case and facts had already received. Applying the objective test and considering the part the judge would play, the Privy Council concluded that the acts of the Lord Advocate in bringing the prosecution were not incompatible with Article 6(1) as the careful direction which the judge may be expected to give the jury in the course of the trial would be sufficient to remove any legitimate doubt that may exist about the objective impartiality of the tribunal.[504]

8.4.3 Courts Martial

A number of aspects of the court martial procedure were considered by the House of Lords in Boyd.[505] At the outset, the House of Lords confirmed that Article 6 did not require that the members of the tribunal should not share the values of the military community to which they belong.[506] With respect to the position of permanent presidents, it was held that the absence of a formal recognition of irremovability did not in itself imply a lack of independence provided that it was recognised in fact and that other necessary guarantees were present.[507] However, it was noted that the practice of

---

[499] Ibid, at [18] per Lord Bingham.

[500] Ibid, at [20] per Lord Bingham. See also the speech of Lord Hope and R v Secretary of State for the Home Department, ex p Al-Hasan [2005] UKHL 13, [2005] 1 WLR 688. Other examples include Taylor v Lawrence [2001] EWCA Civ 119 (affirmed on a reopened appeal at [2002] EWCA Civ 90, [2003] QB 528), where no violation of Art 6 was found and where the deputy judge was a client of the claimant's solicitors. In Wilkinson v S [2003] EWCA Civ 95, [2003] 1 WLR 1254 no violation of Art 6 was found where the judge who found the appellant guilty of contempt had witnessed the contempt herself. In Birmingham City Council v Yardley [2004] EWCA Civ 1756 no violation of Art 6 was found where the Recorder and counsel for one of the parties were members of the same chambers. Considerable guidance is also contained in Locabail (UK) Ltd v Bayfield Properties Ltd [2000] 1 All ER 65, although it is important to note the pre-HRA 'real danger' test applied in this judgment is not compliant with Art 6.

[501] Kelly, above n 374.

[502] Ibid, at [55] and [58] per Lord Hope in reliance upon Albert and Le Compte, above n 69, at [29]; Bryan, above n 456.

[503] Above n 110.

[504] See also R v Thoron [2001] EWCA Crim 1797 and R v Smith (No.2) [2005] UKHL 12, [2005] 1 WLR 704. See further K Quinn, 'Jury Bias and the ECHR: a Well Kept Secret?' [2004] Crim LR 998.

[505] Above n 441.

[506] Ibid, at [57] per Lord Rodger in reliance upon Morris v United Kingdom (2002) 34 EHRR 1253 at [58].

[507] Ibid, at [69] per Lord Rodger in reliance on Morris, ibid, at [68]–[69].

the Air Force of preparing reports on officers who were serving as permanent presidents was undesirable and unnecessary, and it would be better if it were discontinued.[508]

The position of other officers in courts martial was a little more complicated, as in *Morris*[509] the European Court had found a violation of Article 6 in relation to the two serving officers who sat on the applicant's court martial, primarily due to the insufficiency of safeguards against outside pressures. The House of Lords found that the European Court had been given less information about the safeguards than the House of Lords. These included selection of officers ad hoc; the oath taken by members; the directions of the judge advocate; the fact that officers were always taken from another unit; the briefing notes; and the list of witnesses. The House of Lords found it hard to see how anyone, either in the court or outside it, could improperly influence the members' decision. It saw no reason to think that, when duly directed by the judge advocate, officers sitting on a court martial could not properly assess the evidence and return a true verdict based on it.[510]

With respect to sentencing, it was argued that, as the members would have regard to such issues as the impact of the offence on Service morale and discipline, and would be more aware of these effects than a civil judge, the sentences may therefore not coincide exactly with the sentences which a civil judge would pass. The House of Lords held that this did not call the decisions of the courts martial into question. The judge advocate advised on sentencing, and the sentence imposed was subject to review and appeal.[511] The House of Lords also dispensed with remaining arguments. It found that the absence of legal training did not undermine independence and impartiality.[512] The fact that the officers were subject to Army discipline and reports did not mean that they were under the command of any higher authority in their function as members of the courts martial and did not compromise their independence and impartiality.[513]

8.4.4 Government Ministers

As part of the executive, it is clear that government ministers do not satisfy the test of independence. In *Anderson*[514] the House of Lords confirmed that it was incompatible with Article 6 for the Secretary of State for the Home Department to exercise the judicial function of fixing the tariff of a convicted murderer. However, in *Smith*[515] the House of Lords held that this constraint only applied to the setting of the minimum term and where the term of imprisonment was to be increased by executive decision.

---

[508] *Ibid*, at [62] per Lord Rodger.
[509] Above n 505.
[510] *Ibid*, at [85] per Lord Rodger.
[511] *Ibid*, at [86] per Lord Rodger.
[512] *Ibid*, at [88] per Lord Rodger.
[513] *Ibid*, at [89]–[90] per Lord Rodger. The House of Lords also found that the role played by the reviewing authority was not incompatible with Art 6—also contrary to the conclusion of the European Court in *Morris*, above n 505. See [94] per Lord Rodger and [13] per Lord Bingham. See also *R v Skuse* [2002] EWCA Crim 991 concerning the independence of the judge advocate at a naval court martial; *R v Dundon* [2004] EWCA Crim 621, [2004] UKHRR 717; *R v Dudley* [2005] EWCA Crim 719; and *R v Stow* [2005] EWCA Crim 1157.
[514] Above n 114.
[515] *R (on the application of Smith) v Secretary of State for the Home Department* [2005] UKHL 51.

While it would obviously be wrong for that term to be subsequently increased by executive decision, it does not follow that the same considerations necessarily apply to a reduction, even if pursuant to a review mandated by domestic law. A reduction in the sentence imposed by a court is a well-recognised exercise of executive clemency.[516]

In the civil context, in *Alconbury*[517] the House of Lords concluded that the Secretary of State for the Environment, Transport and the Regions, when exercising his planning powers, was not an independent and impartial tribunal. The Secretary of State himself had accepted that he made policy and applied that policy in particular cases and that was sufficient to prevent him from being either independent or impartial for the purposes of Article 6.[518]

8.4.5 Local Authorities

Using a member of staff of a local authority to conduct review of particular decisions will sometimes involve a breach of Article 6, although it is important to note that this breach may be cured by the availability of judicial review or appeal to a court on a point of law. For example, in *Begum*[519] the House of Lords held that the council's rehousing manager, who had conducted a review of the council's decision to offer particular accommodation to Ms Begum under the Housing Act 1996, was not an independent tribunal as she was an administrator and could not be described as part of the judicial branch of government[520]:

> One of the purposes of Art.6, in requiring that disputes over civil rights should be decided by or subject to the control of a judicial body, is to uphold the rule of law and the separation of powers . . . If an administrator is regarded as being an independent and impartial tribunal on the ground that he is enlightened, impartial and has no personal interest in the matter, it follows there need not be any possibility of judicial review of his decision. He is above the law. That is a position contrary to basic English constitutional principles. It is also something which the Strasbourg court has been unable to accept.[521]

8.4.6 Professional Bodies

Finally, professional bodies also have the potential to fall foul of the requirements of independence and impartiality. For example, in *Preiss*[522] the appellant objected to the role of the President in the disciplinary system of the General Dental Council. As Preliminary Screener, he had the function of setting in train proceedings before the Preliminary Proceedings Committee (PPC) unless he considered that the matter need not proceed further. It was the function of the PPC to decide whether the case should be referred to the Professional Conduct Committee (PCC). The Privy Council

---

[516] *Ibid*, at [13] per Lord Bingham.
[517] Above n 18.
[518] *Ibid*, at [45] per Lord Slynn and [124] per Lord Hoffmann. It is important to note that this breach was cured by the availability of judicial review.
[519] Above n 458.
[520] *Ibid*, at [27].
[521] *Ibid*, in reliance upon *Golder*, above n 182, and *Alconbury*, above n 18. See also *McLellan*, above n 467; *Adan*, above n 45; *Beeson*, above n 27.
[522] Above n 34.

concluded that, when the participation of the President both as Preliminary Screener and as Chairman of the PCC was seen in conjunction with the predominance of Council members in both the PPC and the PCC, and in conjunction moreover with the fact that the disciplinary charge was brought on behalf of the the the council, the cumulative result was a real danger that the PCC lacked the necessary independence and impartiality.[523]

9. Tribunal Established by Law

The final right protected by Article 6(1) in relation the determination of civil rights and obligations or any criminal charge is the right to a tribunal established by law. There is very little case law on this part of Article 6, either under the HRA or before the European Court of Human Rights. In criminal trials it has been confirmed that it is appropriate to treat the court made up of both judge and jury as the tribunal for the purposes of Article 6—it is not possible to regard the jury as a separate entity.[524] This part of Article 6 was considered in detail by the Court of Appeal in *Coppard*,[525] where it was discovered following judgment that the judge was not actually authorised to sit as a judge of the High Court. As the judge did not know, nor ought to have known, that he was not so authorised, the court found that at common law he was a judge-in-fact of the High Court and his judgment therefore was a judgment of the High Court.[526]

But this did not get around the problem presented by the right to a tribunal established by law. The court went on to find that, at common law, a person who is believed and believes himself to have the necessary judicial authority would be regarded in law as possessing such authority and the judge in fact was a tribunal whose authority was established by the common law.[527] The next question was whether this met the Article 6 standard. The court noted that the purpose of this right was to ensure that justice was administered by, and only by, the prescribed exercise of the judicial power of the state, not by ad hoc 'people's courts' and the like.

> Such a principle must be fundamental to any concept of the rule of law. Implicit in it is that the composition and authority of a court must not be arbitrary.[528]

---

[523] The breached was cured by the availability of appeal to the Privy Council. See also *R (on the application of Mahfouz) v Professional Conduct Committee of the General Medical Council* [2004] EWCA Civ 233, [2004] Lloyd's Rep Med 389; *R (on the application of Panjawani) v Royal Pharmaceutical Society of Great Britain* [2002] EWHC (Admin) 1127; *P, a barrister v The General Council of the Bar* [2005] 1 WLR 3019; *Shrimpton v The General Council of the Bar*, The Visitors to the Inns of Court, 6 May 2005; *Pine*, above n 308; *Holder v Law Society* [2000] EWHC (Admin) 2023.
[524] *Mushtaq*, above n 285.
[525] *Coppard v HM Customs and Excise* [2003] EWCA Civ 511, [2003] QB 1428.
[526] *Ibid*, at [24].
[527] *Ibid*, at [32].
[528] *Ibid*, at [34].

A particular problem was presented by the word 'established', which, it was argued, required a tribunal to have been established by the time the individual's civil rights and obligations came before it.[529] However, the court reminded itself that it should be less concerned with close analysis of the language of the Convention than with the principles which animate it. It concluded that

> [p]rovided the United Kingdom's legal response . . . is not such as to ratify the acts of usurpers or to operate arbitrarily and is limited, in effect, to the correction of mistakes of form rather than of substance—and in our judgment it meets all these tests—we do not consider that the Convention requires the disqualification of a judge purely because his authority was not formally established before he sat.[530]

10. Article 6(2): Presumption of Innocence

Starting with Article 6(2), the remaining rights set out in Article 6 only apply to those who have been charged with a criminal offence. It has been held that the meaning of 'charged with a criminal offence' is coextensive with the meaning of 'determination of any criminal charge' in Article 6(1).[531] With respect to the application of these rights, it is therefore important to consider that section of this chapter.

Article 6(2) provides that everyone charged with a criminal offence shall be presumed innocent until proved guilty according to law. It is often noted by the courts that this Article reflects a fundamental common law principle.

> Throughout the web of the English criminal law one golden thread is always to be seen, that it is the duty of the prosecution to prove the prisoner's guilt.[532]

The underlying rationale is

> that it is repugnant to ordinary notions of fairness for a prosecutor to accuse a defendant of a crime and for the defendant to then be required to disprove the accusation on pain of conviction and punishment if he fails to do so.[533]

However, it is clear that Article 6(2) is not an absolute right and is subject to modifications or limitations which pursue a legitimate aim and satisfy the principle of proportionality.[534] Furthermore, a breach of Article 6(2) does not necessarily mean a

---

[529] *Ibid*, at [37].
[530] *Ibid*, at [39].
[531] *McCann*, above n 40.
[532] *Woolmington v Director of Public Prosecutions* [1935] AC 462 at 481 per Viscount Sankey LC as quoted by Lord Hope in *Kebilene*, above n 9. See also the comments of Lord Steyn in *Lambert*, above n 246, at [32].
[533] *Attorney General's Reference No.4 of 2002* [2004] UKHL 43, [2005] 1 AC 264 at [9] per Lord Bingham.
[534] *Lambert*, above n 246, at [88] per Lord Hope in reliance upon *Ashingdane*, above n 211, and *Brown*, above n 4. See also *Kebilene*, above n 9, and *McIntosh*, above n 120.

conviction is unsafe, particularly if a jury would have reached the same conclusion notwithstanding the breach.[535]

10.1 Burden of Proof

Under the HRA, Article 6(2) has primarily arisen in relation to the burden of proof. In *Kebilene*[536] Lord Hope gave detailed and useful consideration to this question. In his Lordship's view the first step is to identify the nature of the provision which is said to transfer the burden of proof from the prosecution to the accused. This involves distinguishing between the evidential burden—the burden of introducing evidence in support of a case—and the persuasive or legal burden—the burden of persuading the jury as to guilt or innocence. A persuasive burden of proof requires the accused to prove, on a balance of probabilities, a fact which is essential to the determination of his guilt or innocence. It reverses the burden of proof by removing it from the prosecution and transferring it to the accused. An evidential burden requires only that the accused must adduce sufficient evidence to raise an issue before it has to be determined as one of the facts in the case. The prosecution does not need to lead any evidence about it, so the accused needs to do this if he wishes to put the point in issue. But if it is put in issue, the burden of proof remains with the prosecution. The accused need only raise a reasonable doubt about his guilt.[537]

Lord Hope stated that statutory presumptions which place an evidential burden on the accused, requiring the accused to do no more than raise a reasonable doubt on the matter with which they deal, do not breach the presumption of innocence and are not incompatible with Article 6(2). However, statutory presumptions which transfer the persuasive burden to the accused require further examination. In his Lordship's view, there are three categories. First, the mandatory presumption of guilt as to an essential element of the offence. This is inconsistent with the presumption of innocence. Second is the presumption of guilt as to an essential element which is discretionary—the tribunal of fact may or may not rely on the presumption, depending upon its view as to the cogency or weight of the evidence. If a presumption is of this kind, it may be necessary for the facts of the case to be considered before a conclusion can be reached as to whether the presumption of innocence has been breached. The third category is provisions which relate to an exemption or proviso which the accused must establish if he wishes to avoid conviction but which are not an essential element of the offence. These may or may not violate the presumption of innocence, depending on the circumstances.[538]

In relation to this last category, Lord Hope was careful to note that this was not an exact science and that the provisions vary widely in their detail as to what the prosecutor must prove before the onus shifts—and these matters may not be capable of being fully assessed until after the trial. More importantly, his Lordship stated that, even if the conclusion is reached that prima facie the provision breaches the presumption of innocence, this will not lead inevitably to the conclusion that the provision

535 *Lambert, ibid.*
536 Above n 9. Lord Hope's comments were *obiter* as their Lordships had concluded that the DPP's consent to a prosecution was not amenable to judicial review.
537 See also *Attorney General's Reference No.4 of 2002*, above n 532, at [1] per Lord Bingham.
538 See also the comments of Lord Steyn in *Lambert*, above n 246, at [37].

was incompatible with Article 6(2). As stated above, although Article 6(2) is in absolute terms, it is not regarded as imposing an absolute prohibition on reverse onus clauses, whether they be evidential (presumptions of fact) or persuasive (presumptions of law).

In striking the balance, his Lordship adopted the questions posed by counsel: (1) what does the prosecution have to prove in order to transfer the onus to the defence? (2) What is the burden on the accused—does it relate to something which is likely to be difficult for him to prove, or does it relate to something which is likely to be within his knowledge or to which he readily has access? (3) What is the nature of the threat faced by society which the provision is designed to combat? [539] Later judgments have expanded on this. In *R v Johnstone*[540] the House of Lords held that the more serious the punishment which may flow from conviction, the more compelling must be the reasons.

> The extent and nature of the factual matters required to be proved by the accused, and their importance relative to the matters required to be proved by the prosecution, have to be taken into account. So also does the extent to which the burden on the accused relates to facts which, if they exist, are readily provable by him as matters within his own knowledge or to which he has ready access.[541]

Furthermore, it was stated that the court would reach a different conclusion from the legislature only when it was apparent that the legislature had attached insufficient importance to the fundamental right of an individual to be presumed innocent until proved guilty.[542] In *Attorney General's Reference No.4 of 2002*[543] the House of Lords held that relevant to any judgment on reasonableness or proportionality

> will be the opportunity given to the defendant to rebut the presumption, maintenance of the rights of the defence, flexibility in application of the presumption, retention by the court of a power to assess the evidence, the importance of what is at stake and the difficulty which the prosecutor may face in the absence of a presumption.[544]

10.2 Application

It is clear that the

> justifiability of any infringement of the presumption of innocence cannot be resolved by any rule of thumb, but on examination of all the facts and circumstances of the particular provision as applied in the particular case.[545]

---

[539] In *McIntosh*, above n 120, Lord Hope stated that the questions he posed in this judgment were not presented as a set of rules. 'They were no more than an indication of an approach which it might be useful to adopt when the interest of the individual are being balanced against those of society. Each case will vary, and they may be more helpful in some cases than others.'

[540] [2003] UKHL 28, [2003] 1 WLR 1736.

[541] *Ibid*, at [50] per Lord Nicholls.

[542] *Ibid*, at [51].

[543] Above n 532.

[544] *Ibid*, at [21] per Lord Bingham. See generally P Roberts, 'The Presumption of Innocence Brought Home? Kebilene Deconstructed' (2002) 118 *LQR* 41; V Tadros and S Tierney, 'The Presumption of Innocence and the Human Rights Act' (2004) 67 *MLR* 402.

[545] *Attorney General's Reference No.4 of 2002*, above n 532, at [21] per Lord Bingham.

It is therefore instructive to consider the application of Article 6(2) in a number of key areas.[546]

10.2.1 Confiscation Orders

Although in *McIntosh*[547] the Privy Council concluded that Article 6(2) did not apply to a confiscation order, it did go on to consider its application to section 3 of the Proceeds of Crime (Scotland) Act 1995. Section 3 provided, inter alia, that, in making an assessment of the value of the proceeds of the person's drug trafficking, the court may assume that any property appearing to the court to have been held by him at any time since his conviction, or to have been transferred to him at any time since a date six years before his being indicted or being served with the complaint, was received by him as a payment or reward in connection with drug trafficking carried on by him. The court had a discretion whether to make the statutory assumptions or not; the assumptions were rebuttable by the accused on a balance of probabilities; the proceedings in question related to drug trafficking and not the commission of drug-trafficking offences; and the assumptions related to property which appeared to the court to meet the conditions specified and to expenditure of the accused during the relevant period.[548]

Concluding that reliance on the assumption permitted under section 3 struck the appropriate balance between conflicting interests and would not violate Article 6(2), even if it did apply, the Privy Council identified the nature of the public threat to which the legislation was directed as the punishment and deterrent from drug trafficking given that the unlawful consumption of drugs was a very 'grave, far-reaching and destructive social evil.'[549] It also found it significant that the United Nations Convention against Illicit Traffic in Narcotic Drugs and Psychotropic Substances 1998,[550] ratified by the UK in 1991, provided that state parties may consider a reverse onus of proof regarding the lawful origin of alleged proceeds or other property liable to confiscation.[551] It also took into account the fact that the confiscation order

---

[546] Other examples include: *R v Carass* [2001] EWCA Crim 2845, [2002] 1 WLR 1714, where the court that the persuasive burden imposed by s 206(4) of the Insolvency Act 1986 was not justified and read it down under s 3 HRA to impose an evidential burden. It is important to note that in *Attorney General's Reference No.4 of 2002, ibid*, the House of Lords held that this judgment was wrongly decided; *International Transport Roth GmbH v Secretary of State for the Home Department* [2002] EWCA Civ 158, [2003] QB 728, which concerned the fixed penalty regime for carriers liability for clandestine entrants under the Immigration and Asylum Act 1999. Only Jonathan Parker LJ held that the s 34 defence was incompatible with Art 6(2). Simon Brown LJ found it incompatible only in conjunction with other features of the scheme. Laws LJ held that the regime was not criminal; in *Davies v Health and Safety Executive* [2002] EWCA Crim 2949 the court concluded that the legal burden imposed by s 40 of the Health and Safety at Work Act 1974 was justified, necessary and proportionate; in *R v Matthews* [2003] EWCA Crim 813, [2004] QB 690 the court concluded that ss 139(4) and 139(5) of the Criminal Justice Act 1988 were proportionate; see also *Attorney General's Reference No.1 of 2004* [2004] EWCA Crim 1025, where the Court of Appeal considered s 352 Insolvency Act 1986, s 1(2) Protection from Eviction Act 1977, s 4(2) Homicide Act 1957 and s 51(7) Criminal Justice and Public Order Act 1994. The House of Lords held in *Attorney General's Reference No.4 of 2002, ibid*, that the conclusions of the Court of Appeal were correct in each case.
[547] Above n 120.
[548] *Ibid*, at [8].
[549] *Ibid*, at [4] per Lord Bingham.
[550] (1992) Cm 1927.
[551] Article 5(7) at [32]. The PC also referred to a 1991 report of the Irish Law Reform Commission, *The Confiscation of the Proceeds of Crime* LRC 35 (1991), in which the Commission recommended the adoption of such a presumption.

procedure could only be initiated if the accused was convicted of a drug-trafficking offence. It was then incumbent on the prosecutor to prove the amount of property held by the accused and his expenditure. It was only if a significant discrepancy was shown between the property and expenditure of the accused on the one hand and his known sources of income on the other that the court would think it right to make the section 3 assumptions.[552]

10.2.2 Drugs Offences

Although a majority of the House of Lords in *Lambert*[553] held that the HRA had no application to the appeal as the trial had taken place before the HRA came into force, their Lordships commented on section 28(3) of the Misuse of Drugs Act 1971. The appellant had been convicted of possession of a controlled drug contrary to the Act. He relied upon section 28(3)(b)(i) of the Act, asserting that he did not believe or suspect, or have reason to suspect, that the bag which he carried contained a controlled drug. The trial judge directed the jury that the prosecution only had to prove that he had and knew that he had the bag in his possession and that the bag contained a controlled drug. To establish the defence under section 28(3) he had to prove on the balance of probabilities that he did not know that the bag contained a controlled drug. This was the legal rather than the evidential burden.

Their Lordships found that the defence put forward by the appellant under section 28 was an ingredient of the offence. Therefore, section 28 derogated from the presumption of innocence.[554] With respect to the question of justification, it was held that there was an objective justification for some interference with the burden of proof in prosecutions under the Act.

> The basis of this justification is that sophisticated drug smugglers, dealers and couriers typically secrete drugs in some container, thereby enabling the person in possession of the container to say that he was unaware of the contents. Such defences are commonplace and they pose real difficulties for the police and prosecuting authorities.[555]

With respect to the question of proportionality, it was noted that a guilty verdict may be returned in respect of an offence punishable by life imprisonment even though the jury may consider that it is reasonably possible that the accused has been duped.[556] Taking into account domestic, Canadian and South African authorities, and also the fact that a number of factors have now significantly reduced the difficulties of the prosecution in drugs cases, it was concluded that a reverse legal burden was a disproportionate means of addressing the legislative goal of easing the task of the

---

[552] *McIntosh*, above n 120, at [35]–[36] per Lord Bingham. See also *Hughes v Customs and Excise Commissioners* [2002] EWCA Civ 670, [2002] 4 All ER 633, where the Court of Appeal held that it was compatible with Art 6(2) for a receiver appointed by a court pursuant to the Criminal Justice Act 1988 or Drug Trafficking Act 1994 to use the defendant's assets under his control to meet the costs of the receivership whether or not the defendant had been convicted or a confiscation order made against him. See also *R v Goodenough* [2004] EWCA Crim 2260, [2005] 1 Cr App R (S) 88.

[553] Above n 246.

[554] *Ibid*, at [35] per Lord Steyn.

[555] *Ibid*, at [36] per Lord Steyn.

[556] *Ibid*, at [38] per Lord Steyn.

prosecution. However, using section 3 of the HRA, their Lordships read the sections to create an evidential burden only.[557]

10.2.3 Road Traffic Offences

In *Director of Public Prosecutions v Sheldrake*[558] the appellant challenged section 5(2) of the Road Traffic Act 1988, which provided that it was a defence to prove that, at the time he was alleged to have committed the offence, the circumstances were such that there was no likelihood of his driving the vehicle whilst the proportion of alcohol in his breath, blood or urine remained likely to exceed the prescribed limit. Assuming that section 5(2) infringed the presumption of innocence, the House of Lords held that the provision was directed to a legitimate object: the prevention of death, injury and damage caused by unfit drivers. Furthermore, it found that the burden was not beyond reasonable limits or arbitrary.

> The defendant has full opportunity to show that there was no likelihood of his driving, a matter so closely conditioned by his own knowledge and state of mind at the material time as to make it much more appropriate for him to prove on the balance of probabilities that he would not have been likely to drive than for the prosecutor to prove, beyond reasonable doubt, that he would.[559]

10.2.4 Trade Marks Offences

Section 92 of the Trade Marks Act 1994 was considered by the House of Lords in *R v Johnstone*.[560] The defendant had been convicted of possessing some 500 bootleg recordings to which had been applied a sign identical to, or likely to be mistaken for, a registered trade mark. Section 92(5) provided a defence if the accused could show that he believed on reasonable grounds that the use of the sign in the manner in which it was used was not an infringement of the registered trade mark. The House of Lords accepted that this subsection imposed a legal burden on the defendant and prima facie derogated from the presumption of innocence.[561] However, it concluded that there were compelling reasons for the imposition of the legal burden, including international pressure in the interests of consumers and traders to restrain fraudulent trading in counterfeit goods, the framing of section 92 offences as offences of near absolute liability and the dependence of the subsection (5) defence on facts within the defendant's own knowledge.[562] Also taken into consideration was the fact that those who trade in brand products are aware of the need to be on guard against counterfeit goods, the need to deal with reputable suppliers and the risks they take if they do not; and the fact that those who supply traders are unlikely to be cooperative. If the

---

[557] *Ibid*, at [41]–[42] per Lord Steyn. See also Lord Slynn at [17], Lord Hope at [87]–[91] and Lord Clyde at [133], [150] and [153]–[157]. Lord Hutton, whilst agreeing that a persuasive burden was imposed, did not find this incompatible with Art 6(2) at [190]–[197].
[558] *DPP v Sheldrake* [2004] UKHL 43, [2005] 1 AC 264.
[559] *Ibid*, at [41] per Lord Bingham. In *R v Drummond* [2002] EWCA Crim 527, [2002] 2 Cr Ap R 25, the court held that the persuasive burden imposed by s 15 of the Road Traffic Offenders Act 1988 was justified and necessary. See also *Director of Public Prosecutions v Ellery*, Divisional Court, 14 July 2005.
[560] *R v Johnstone* [2003] UKHL 28, [2003] 1 WLR 1736.
[561] *Ibid*, at [47] per Lord Nicholls.
[562] *Ibid*, at [52].

prosecution had to prove that a trader acted dishonestly, fewer prosecutions would take place.[563]

10.2.5 Terrorism Offences

In *Kebilene*,[564] although the House of Lords concluded that the Director of Public Prosecution's consent to a prosecution was not amenable to judicial review, Lord Hope commented on section 16A of the Prevention of Terrorism (Temporary Provisions) Act 1989. Section 16A provided that a person was guilty of an offence if he had any article in his possession in circumstances giving rise to a reasonable suspicion that the article was in his possession for a purpose connected with the commission, preparation or instigation of acts of terrorism. Under section 16A(3) it was a defence for a person charged under the section to prove that at the time of the alleged offence the article was not in his possession for such a purpose. Lord Hope characterised this section as imposing a persuasive burden of proof on the accused. If that burden was not discharged, subsection (1) contained a mandatory presumption that the article was in his possession for a purpose connected with terrorism which was applied if the prosecutor proved that it was in his possession in circumstances giving rise to a reasonable suspicion that it was in his possession for that purpose. Subsection (4) also imposed a persuasive burden on the accused that he did not know that the article was in the premises or, if he did, that he had no control over it. If that burden was not discharged, or the accused elected not to undertake it, the subsection contained a discretionary presumption that he was in possession of the article.

His Lordship noted that the legislative problem which these provisions sought to address was how to curb a grave evil which postulated a guilty mind or mental element on the part of the offender when proof of that guilty mind or mental element was likely to be a matter of inherent difficulty. He concluded that the discretionary presumption in subsection (4) could not be objected to at this stage. With respect to subsections (1) and (3), he found good reasons for thinking that they might not be as damaging to the presumption of innocence as might at first sight appear, and stated that account may legitimately be taken of the problems which the legislation was designed to address, noting that society has a strong interest in preventing acts of terrorism before they are perpetrated. He concluded that a sound judgment on this question was unlikely to be possible until the facts were known, but it was not immediately obvious to him that

> it would be imposing an unreasonable burden on an accused who was in possession of articles from which an inference of involvement in terrorism could be drawn to provide an explanation for his possession of them which would displace that inference.

In *Attorney General's Reference No.4 of 2002*[565] the House of Lords considered section 11(2) of the Terrorism Act 2000. Section 11(1) made it an offence to belong or

---

[563] *Ibid*, at [53]. In *Attorney General's Reference No.4 of 2002*, above n 532, the House of Lords answered the comment that there was significant difference between the approach in *Lambert* and *Johnstone* stating that the justifiability and fairness of the respective exoneration provisions had to be judged in the particular context of each case, at [30] per Lord Bingham.
[564] Above n 9.
[565] Above n 532.

profess to belong to a proscribed organisation. Section 11(2) provided a defence if the accused could prove that the organisation was not proscribed on the last (or only) occasion on which he became a member or began to profess to be a member and that he had not taken part in the activities of the organisation at any time while it was proscribed. Their Lordships concluded that section 11(2) imposed a legal burden on the accused in breach of the presumption of innocence[566] but that this was directed to a legitimate end: deterring people from becoming members and taking part in the activities of proscribed terrorist organisations.[567] However, a majority of their Lordships concluded that imposition of a legal burden in this particular situation was not a proportionate and justifiable legislative response to an undoubted problem.[568]

A number of factors led to this conclusion. A person who was innocent of any blameworthy or properly criminal conduct could fall within section 11(1), and there would be clear breach of the presumption of innocence and a real risk of unfair conviction if such persons could exonerate themselves only by establishing the defence provided on the balance of probabilities; it might be impossible for a defendant to show that he had not taken part in the activities of the organisation at any time while it was proscribed; the subsection provided no flexibility and there was no room for the exercise of discretion; the potential consequences were severe, with the possibility of imprisonment for up to ten years; security considerations do not absolve states from their duty to ensure that basic standards of fairness are observed; and little significance could be attached to the fact that the requirement that the Director of Public Prosecutions give his consent to a prosecution.[569] Section 3 of the HRA was employed to read down the subsection so that it only imposed an evidential burden.

11. Article 6(3)(a): Informed of the Nature and Cause of the Accusation

Article 6(3) sets out minimum rights for everyone charged with a criminal offence. The first of these contained in Article 6(3)(a) is the right to be informed promptly, in a language which the accused understands and in detail, of the nature and cause of the accusation against him.[570]

---

[566] *Ibid*, at [50] per Lord Bingham.
[567] *Ibid*.
[568] *Ibid*.
[569] *Ibid*, at [51] per Lord Bingham. Lords Rodger and Carswell dissented on this point.
[570] See *Newman v Modern Bookbinders Ltd* [2000] 2 All ER 814.

12. Article 6(3)(b): Adequate Time and Facilities for Preparation of Defence

Article 6(3)(b) provides for the right to have adequate time and facilities for the preparation of a defence. 'Facilities' is not satisfied simply by the provision of money; the paragraph is

> principally directed to the securing for an accused person the opportunity and the services necessary for the preparation of his defence. It strikes at the imposition of restraints on his freedom to organise the preparation of his defence. A refusal of access to his lawyer while he is detained pending trial would be an obvious example.[571]

Another example may be failure to grant an adjournment so as to allow an accused to obtain expert reports[572] or call witnesses.[573] In *McLean*[574] the Privy Council held that a fixed fee system was not incompatible with this right, although Lord Clyde commented that, whilst the provision of funding was not immediately a facility for the preparation of the defence, it may be the means of providing those facilities.[575]

13. Article 6(3)(c): Legal Assistance

Article 6(3)(c) provides that everyone charged with a criminal offence has the right to defend himself in person or through legal assistance of his own choosing, or, if he has not sufficient means to pay for legal assistance, to be given it free when the interests of justice so require. It is clear that this forms an important part of the guarantee of 'equality of arms'. The paragraph identifies three distinct rights for the accused: to defend himself in person,[576] to defend himself through legal assistance of his own choosing[577] and, under certain conditions, to be given free legal assistance. The three rights are not alternatives[578]; therefore the accused cannot be forced to defend himself.[579] The paragraph guarantees the right to an adequate defence either in person or through a lawyer, the right being reinforced by an obligation on the part of the state to provide free legal assistance in certain cases.[580]

---

[571] *McLean v Procurator Fiscal Fort William* [2001] 1 WLR 2425 per Lord Clyde at [56].
[572] See, eg *R v Porter* [2001] EWCA Crim 2699.
[573] *R v Haslam* [2003] EWCA Crim 3444.
[574] *Ibid.*
[575] *Ibid.*
[576] See, eg *Raja v van Hoogstraten* [2004] EWCA Civ 968, [2004] 4 All ER 793.
[577] See *Berry Trade Ltd v Moussavi*, Court of Appeal, 21 March 2002 and *R (on the application of Van Hoogstraten) v Governor of Belmarsh Prison* [2002] EWHC (Admin) 1965, [2003] 4 All ER 309.
[578] *McLean*, above n 570, per Lord Clyde, with whom Lords Nicholls and Millet agreed, in reliance on *Pakelli v Germany* (1983) 6 EHRR 1.
[579] *Ibid*, at [59] per Lord Clyde.
[580] *Ibid.*

13.1 Process of Investigation

The right applies to the process of investigation, although it does not impose a blanket requirement that each time a person is detained legal advice must be obtained for him before he can do or say anything. However, any restriction on the right must be proportionate to the aim sought to be achieved.[581] Evidence obtained in breach of this right may be excluded at any subsequent trial pursuant to section 78 of the Police and Criminal Evidence Act 1984.

13.2 Effective Representation

The representation to which an accused is entitled must be an effective representation.

> The right to an effective representation should be satisfied by the services of a lawyer actually exercising the ordinary professional skill and care in the interests of the defence of his client.[582]

The principle of equality of arms provides one way of formulating the breach of the Convention which can occur through the absence of a competent and effective representation.[583] It is not necessary for a contravention of Article 6(3)(c) that the accused should have suffered injury as a result of the contravention:

> He need not show that with an effective representative the trial would have gone differently or that the outcome would have been different. Where in a serious case an accused has no effective representation that fact may be enough to constitute a contravention . . . The appearance of fairness may be a relevant consideration in this context. That justice should not only be done but should be seen to be done is a principle often referred to in relation to cases of bias or partiality, but it may also be applied to an absence of effective representation.[584]

Where an accused represents himself, it has been held that he cannot pray in aid the ordinary and anticipated disadvantages of his choice in support of the argument that there was inequality of arms which renders his conviction unsafe.[585] Where no defence is put forward at a trial in consequence of the defendant's deliberate decision not to be present, there is no violation of the right as the defendant has chosen not to exercise it.[586]

---

[581] *Campbell v Director of Public Prosecutions* [2002] EWHC (Admin) 1314. See also *Causey v Director of Public Prosecutions* [2004] EWHC (Admin) 3164.

[582] *McLean*, above n 570, at [60] per Lord Clyde in reliance on *Artico v Italy* (1980) 3 EHRR 1; *Goddi v Italy* (1984) 6 EHRR 457.

[583] *Ibid*, at [61] per Lord Clyde.

[584] *Ibid*, at [62] per Lord Clyde in reliance on *S v Switzerland* (1991) 14 EHRR 670; *Artico*, above n 581; *Boner v United Kingdom* (1994) 19 EHRR 246

[585] *R v Brown* [2001] EWCA Crim 1771.

[586] Per Lord Hutton at [36]. *Jones*, above n 347.

13.3 Legal aid

The right is not an absolute one and in the context of civil proceedings there may be reasonable grounds for refusing legal aid.[587] In criminal proceedings consideration of the cost-effective use of funds has been recognised by the European Commission of Human Rights as an appropriate consideration in determining the work for which payments may be made.

> But in such proceedings, particularly where there is a risk of a loss of liberty, it would be far more difficult to find examples where legal aid might be refused, particularly at first instance.[588]

Even in relation to an appeal the interests of justice may require the state to grant legal assistance in the light of such considerations as the severity of the sentence, the need for professional skill in handling the case and the complexity of the issues.[589] In some instances, proceedings may change from civil to criminal, such as where, in disobedience of an order of the Family Court, an individual faces committal proceedings for contempt of court.[590] At least in the context of legal aid, the accused may not be absolutely entitled to a representative of his own choice.[591]

13.4 Application

This particular aspect of Article 6 has arisen rarely under the HRA. However, it was considered in detail by the Privy Council in the devolution case of *McLean*.[592] In April 1999 the appellants were charged with racially aggravated assault and breach of the peace. They were granted criminal legal aid pursuant to section 24 of the Legal Aid (Scotland) Act 1986. They instructed two Glasgow firms of solicitors to conduct their defence. The payments to which the solicitors were entitled for conducting the proceedings were set out in the Criminal Legal Aid (Fixed Payments) (Scotland) Regulations 1999. In July 1999 the solicitors lodged pleas in bar of trial on the appellants' behalf raising two devolution issues. The first issue was whether the act of the Lord Advocate in continuing to prosecute the appellants was incompatible with Article 6 of the ECHR. The second issue was whether the failure of the Scottish Executive to repeal or amend the Criminal Legal Aid (Fixed Payments) (Scotland) Regulations 1999 was incompatible with Article 6.

The Privy Council unanimously held that what must be shown to support a plea in bar of trial was that some form of actual or inevitable prejudice would result so that

---

[587] *McLean*, above n 570, at [63] per Lord Clyde in reliance on *Thaw v UK* (1996) 22 EHRR CD 100; *S & M v UK* (1993) 18 EHRR CD 172.

[588] See, eg *Newman v Modern Bookbinders*, above n 569.

[589] *McLean*, above n 570, at [63] per Lord Clyde in reliance on *M v UK* (1983) 6 EHRR 345; *Monnell & Morris v UK* (1987) 10 EHRR 205; *Pakelli*, above n 577; *Granger v UK* (1990) 12 EHRR 469. In *R v Oates*, Court of Appeal, 25 April 2002 the court, in reliance on *Monnell, ibid*, held that representation was not required on an application for leave to appeal.

[590] *In the Matter of K (children)* [2002] EWCA Crim 1071, [2002] 1 WLR 2833. See also *In the Matter of G (a child)* [2003] EWCA Civ 489, [2003] 1 WLR 2051 and *Begum v Anam* [2004] EWCA Civ 578.

[591] *McLean*, above n 570, at [64] per Lord Clyde in reliance on *Croissant v Germany* (1992) 16 EHRR 135 at [29].

[592] *Ibid*.

the Sheriff could not be expected to reach a fair verdict in all the circumstances.[593] The principle that there must be equality of arms on both sides required that there must be a fair balance between the parties. However, the purpose of Article 6 was not to make it impractical to bring those accused of crime to justice. The essential question was whether the alleged inequality of arms was such as to deprive the accused of his right to a fair trial. The majority concluded that in the present case it was not shown that the fixed fee regime would give rise to any actual or inevitable prejudice at the appellants' trial. It was wrong to assume that the solicitors who were instructed would reduce their standards of preparation simply because they considered that they would not receive adequate remuneration for their work when they were paid the fixed fee. In the absence of any contrary evidence, the assumption was that they would conduct the defence according to the standards which are expected of their profession as they were required to do by the codes.[594]

However, it was pointed out that different considerations would arise were the solicitors to withdraw and the appellants were unable to find replacement solicitors because of the inflexibility of the Regulations. Lord Clyde in particular held that there was a real likelihood that in another case a serious risk of a contravention of Article 6 may arise. If the result of the Regulations was that no legal representative was available for an accused in a case where the ECHR requires that he should be represented, a breach would occur.[595]

14. Article 6(3)(d): Witnesses

Article 6(3)(d) provides that everyone charged with a criminal offence has the right to examine or have examined witnesses against him and to obtain the attendance and examination of witnesses on his behalf under the same conditions as witnesses against him. This right does not guarantee the accused a right to be in the same room as the witness giving evidence[596] and does not prevent evidence being given by live television link or video recording as long as the defence has an adequate and proper opportunity to challenge and question a witness on his statement at some stage.[597]

It is not necessarily incompatible with this article for depositions to be read even if there has been no opportunity to question the witness at any stage of the proceedings. However, the trial must be fair, and the quality of the evidence and its inherent reliability plus the degree of caution exercised in relation to reliance on it will be relevant to this question.[598] Where that witness provides the sole or determinative evidence against the accused, permitting the statement to be read may risk infringing this

---

[593] *Ibid*, at [37] per Lord Hope, with whom Lords Nicholls and Millet agreed.
[594] *Ibid*, at [38]–[43] per Lord Hope.
[595] *Ibid*, at [32]. Lord Hobhouse did not accept that the regulations as they stood were fully compatible with Art 6 at [75]–[81].
[596] *R v Camberwell Green Youth Court ex p D* [2005] UKHL 4, [2005] 1 WLR 393 at [15] per Lord Rodger.
[597] *Ibid*, at [12] per Lord Rodger. See also *R v Radak* [1999] 1 Cr App Rep 187
[598] *R v Sellick* [2005] EWCA Crim 651 at [50]. See also *R v Denton* [2001] 1 Cr App Rep 227; *R v Abiodun* [2003] EWCA Crim 2167.

right.[599] Much depends on whether or not the witness has been intimidated by the defendant. It has been held that, where the court is sure that the sole witness has been kept away by the defendant or persons acting for him, there would be no breach of the article if

> care has been taken to see that the quality of the evidence was compelling, if firm steps were taken to draw the jury's attention to aspects of that witnesses' credibility and if a clear direction was given to the jury to exercise caution.[600]

More difficulty arises where it is not quite so clear-cut, but it has also been held that where there is a high probability of witness intimidation on behalf of the defence, and where the court is sure to the criminal standard of proof that witnesses cannot be traced or brought before the court, there is no absolute rule that, where compelling evidence is the sole or decisive evidence, admission of a statement would infringe the article.[601]

---

15. Article 6(3)(e): Interpreter

Finally, Article 6(3)(3) protects the right to have the free assistance of an interpreter if the accused cannot understand or speak the language used in court. Provided that the interpreter is competent, the right is not infringed.[602] If an interpreter is required to be present during an interview between a solicitor and his client, the interpreter is subject to exactly the same duties in relation to confidentiality as the solicitor who is giving the advice.[603]

---

[599] *R v Arnold* [2004] EWCA Crim 1293.
[600] *Sellick*, above n 597, at [52].
[601] *Ibid*, at [53].
[602] *R v Ungvari* [2003] EWCA Crim 2346.
[603] *R (on the application of Bozkurt) v South Thames Magistrates Court* [2001] EWHC (Admin) 400.

11

Article 8: The Right to Respect for Private Life

1. Introduction

Article 8(1) provides that everyone has the right to respect for his private and family life, his home and his correspondence. It has been held that the nature of this right, in essence, is the right to live one's personal life without unjustified interference; the right to one's personal integrity.[1] It is clear that these are not absolute rights, and Article 8(2) provides that the rights contained in Article 8(1) may be subject to interference provided the interference is in accordance with law and necessary in one of the interests there set out. It is the first of the Convention rights drafted in this manner, the others being Articles 9 (freedom of thought, conscience and religion), 10 (freedom of expression) and 11 (freedom of assembly and association).

Apart from the right to respect for correspondence, the rights contained in Article 8(1) have generated a considerable amount of litigation and are therefore considered separately in this and the following two chapters. By far the greatest amount of litigation has been generated by the right to respect for private life, the subject of this chapter. But despite this judicial attention, in contrast to other Convention rights, the importance of the right to respect for private life is rarely commented on, although it has been recognised that a 'proper degree of privacy is essential for the well-being and development of an individual' and that 'restraints imposed on government to pry into the lives of citizens go to the essence of a democratic state.'[2]

Prior to the HRA, the right to respect for private life was relatively underdeveloped in English law. At common law, the courts have been unwilling, or unable, to formulate a tort of invasion of privacy. However, that is not to say that the concepts examined in this chapter were completely unknown to English law prior to the HRA.

---

[1] *Anufrijeva v Southwark LBC* [2003] EWCA Civ 1406, [2004] QB 1124.
[2] *Campbell v MGN Ltd House of Lords* [2004] UKHL 22, [2004] 2 AC 457 at [12] per Lord Nicholls.

There are a

number of common law and statutory remedies of which it may be said that one at least of the underlying values they protect is a right of privacy.[3]

These include the torts of trespass, nuisance, defamation and malicious falsehood, breach of confidence and the statutory remedies under the Protection from Harassment Act 1997 and the Data Protection Act 1998.[4]

The affording of deference to the primary decision maker and the legislature is not uncommon in private life cases under the HRA. Given the facts that the right is subject to exceptions, the subject matter raised by many private life claims and that UK courts were not used to dealing with a right to respect for private life at common law pre-HRA, this is not surprising.

Particular deference has been shown to the legislature. For example, in *Bellinger*[5] the House of Lords was not prepared to recognise the appellant as a female for the purposes of the Matrimonial Causes Act, holding that the issues were ill-suited for determination by the courts and pre-eminently a matter for Parliament. This was particularly so given the government's intention to bring forward legislation on the subject.[6] Similarly, in *Evans*[7] the Court of Appeal was not prepared to dispense with a biological father's consent under the Human Fertilisation and Embryology Act 1990. In *Pretty*[8] Lord Steyn pointed out that that such a fundamental change could not be brought about by judicial creativity. 'Essentially, it must be a matter for democratic debate and decision making by legislatures.'[9] In *S*[10] the House of Lords virtually gave Parliament free rein to utilise new technologies in the pursuit of the guilty.

Deference to primary decision makers is also common. For example, in *Woolgar*[11] the Court of Appeal held that the primary decision as to disclosure should be made by the police, not the court. In *N*[12] the Administrative Court held that the secure hospital was entitled to a margin of appreciation in recording and listening to the incoming and outgoing phone calls of patients. In *E*[13] the Administrative Court held that the starting point for determining whether a particular interference was necessary was the view taken by those responsible for the claimant in the hospital.

However, it is clear that the courts have not abdicated their responsibility under Article 8. Even where deference has been afforded, the courts have gone on to balance the interference against the justification. As the approach taken by the House of Lords in *Razgar* illustrates, individual fundamental rights are still protected.

---

[3] *Wainwright v Home Office* [2003] UKHL 53, [2004] 2 AC 406 at [18] per Lord Hoffmann.
[4] *Ibid.*
[5] *Bellinger v Bellinger* [2003] UKHL 21, [2003] 2 AC 467.
[6] *Ibid*, at [37] per Lord Nicholls.
[7] *Evans v Amicus Healthcare Ltd* [2004] EWCA Civ 727, [2004] 3 WLR 681.
[8] *R v Director of Public Prosecutions, ex p Pretty* [2001] UKHL 61, [2001]3 WLR 1598.
[9] *Ibid*, at [58].
[10] *R (on the application of S) v Chief Constable of South Yorkshire Police* [2004] UKHL 39, [2004] 1 WLR 2196.
[11] *Woolgar v Chief Constable of Sussex Police* [2000] 1 WLR 25.
[12] *R (on the application of N) v Ashworth Special Hospital Authority* [2001] EWHC (Admin) 339, [2001] 1 WLR 25.
[13] *R (on the application of E) v Ashworth Hospital Authority* [2001] EWHC (Admin) 1089, [2002] ACD 149.

Decisions taken pursuant to the lawful operation of immigration control will be proportionate in all save a small minority of exceptional cases, identifiable only on a case by case basis.[14]

In these types of cases it has been held that the court or adjudicator is not called upon to judge policy and therefore no question of deference arises.[15] Their duty is to see to the protection of individual fundamental rights, which is the particular territory of the courts.[16]

---

2. Private Life

It is clear that private life is a broad term and there has been no real attempt to define it comprehensively.[17] 'An interference with privacy is not even like the elephant, of which it can be said it is at least easy to recognise if not to define.'[18] At a very general level it covers all aspects of a person's physical identity and thus freedom to live life as he or she chooses.[19] Others have attempted more comprehensive definitions.

[T]he privacy of a human being denotes at the same time the personal 'space' in which the individual is free to be itself, and also the carapace, or shell, or umbrella, or whatever other metaphor is preferred, which protects that space from intrusion. An infringement of privacy is an affront to the personality, which is damaged both by the violation and by the demonstration that the personal space is not inviolate.[20]

Some matters are clearly not within the private sphere. For example, in *Orejudos*[21] the Court of Appeal held that the terms on which a homeless person was provided with accommodation by a public authority were not within his private sphere. Other matters, such as information, identity, physical and psychological integrity and autonomy, are undoubtedly included within the concept of private life. Other aspects of private life, such as sexual behaviour and private space, which have generated a significant amount of case law before the European Court and Commission of Human Rights, have not given rise to much litigation under the HRA. But that is not to say that these do not also form part of private life.

---

[14] *R (on the application of Razgar) v Secretary of State for the Home Department* [2004] UKHL 27, [2004] 2 AC 368 at [20].
[15] *Huang v Secretary of State for the Home Department* [2005] EWCA Civ 105, [2005] 3 All ER 435 at [62].
[16] *Ibid*, at [55].
[17] *Razgar*, above n 14, at [9] per Lord Bingham.
[18] *R v Broadcasting Standards Commission ex p BBC* [2001] QB 885 at [14] per Lord Woolf MR.
[19] *Orejudos v Royal Borough of Kensington and Chelsea* [2003] EWCA Civ 1967 at [20].
[20] *BBC*, above n 18, at [48] per Mustill LJ.
[21] *Orejudos*, above n 19.

2.1 Information

Private information concerning an individual is clearly within the protection of Article 8. The holding, disclosure and refusal to allow access to such information may all constitute interferences with this right.[22] Liability is not dependent on carelessness or bad faith and a breach may be committed unwittingly.[23] Photographs also convey information and are similarly protected if the activity photographed is private.[24] Filming a private activity may also constitute a violation of Article 8(1).[25] However, it is important to note that if photography or filming takes place without consent, this may also constitute an interference with autonomy.[26]

The difficulty lies in determining whether or not the information or activity is private and not public. Article 8 is engaged if the person publishing the information knows or ought to know that there is a reasonable expectation that the information in question will be kept confidential[27] (or private).[28] Where information is generally accessible, it is not private. However, the fact that it is known to a limited number of members of the public does not prevent it having and retaining the character of privacy, or even that it has previously been widely available.[29] It may also be necessary to take into account the use to which the information will be put. For example, in *Robertson*[30] the Divisional Court held that the sale of the Electoral Register to commercial organisations engaged Article 8.[31] If a public figure has made untrue pronouncements about the information which has been revealed, this does not make the information any less private[32] but will ultimately affect the balance struck between private life and freedom of expression. Where a public figure makes untrue pronouncements about his or her private life, the press is normally entitled to put the record straight.[33]

Certain types of information are obviously private. These include information about a person's health and treatment for ill-health[34]; private conversations[35] and

[22] *Baker v Secretary of State for the Home Department* [2001] UKHRR 1275.
[23] *W v Westminster City Council* [2005] EWHC (QB) 102, [2005] 4 All ER 96.
[24] *Campbell*, above n 2, per Baroness Hale at [154]. Baroness Hale commented that, in this case, the photographs by themselves were not objectionable but became so with the accompanying text. It is clear that photographs taken without consent do not amount to an interference with private life per se.
[25] See, eg *Jones v University of Warwick* [2003] EWCA Civ 151, [2003] 1 WLR 954.
[26] *Douglas v Hello! Ltd* [2001] QB 967 per Sedley LJ at [139] and Keene LJ at [165].
[27] In *Campbell v MGN Ltd* [2004] UKHL 22, [2004] 2 AC 457 Lord Nicholls commented that the essence of the tort was now better encapsulated as misuse of private information.
[28] *Ibid*, per Lord Nicholls at [21], Lord Hope at [85] and Baroness Hale at [134]. Doubt was cast on the test proposed by Gleeson CJ in *Australian Broadcasting Corporation v Lenah Game Meats Pty Ltd* (2001) 185 ALR 1 at [42].
[29] *Mills v News Group Newspapers Ltd* [2001] EMLR 41 at [25]. In *R (on the application of Pearson) v Driving & Vehicle Licensing Agency* [2002] EWHC (Admin) 2482, [2003] Crim LR 199 the court held that the endorsement of driving licences with road traffic offences was not an interference.
[30] *R (Robertson) v Wakefield Metropolitan District Council* [2001] EWHC (Admin) 915, [2002] 2 WLR 889.
[31] *Ibid*, at [34]. However, in *Farrer v Secretary of State* [2002] EWHC (Admin) 1917 the court held that the supply by the DVLA of vehicle registration details to detective agencies and others was a moderate interference and proportionate to the legitimate aim of the enforcement of fines.
[32] *Campbell*, above n 27, at [147] per Baroness Hale.
[33] *Ibid*, at [82] per Lord Hope.
[34] *Ibid*, at [145] per Baroness Hale. See also *R (on the application of S) v Plymouth City Council* [2002] EWCA Civ 388, [2002] 1 WLR 2583; *H (A Healthcare Worker) v Associated Newspapers Ltd* [2002] EWCA Civ 195, [2002] EMLR 23.
[35] *R v Mason* [2002] EWCA Crim 385, [2002] 2 Cr App R 38.

private telephone conversations[36]; the information contained in a DNA sample[37]; and documents subject to legal professional privilege.[38] In other instances, the courts proceed on a case-by-case basis. For example, in *Campbell*[39] a majority of the House of Lords found that Miss Campbell would have had a reasonable expectation of privacy in relation to the fact that she was receiving treatment at Narcotics Anonymous, the details of the treatment and the photograph (visual portrayal) of her leaving a specific meeting with other addicts.

> [I]t related to an important aspect of Miss Campbell's physical and mental health and the treatment she was receiving for it. It had also been received from an insider in breach of confidence.[40]

In *Douglas*[41] the Court of Appeal held that the wedding was not private, attended by a few members of family and friends.[42] Furthermore, the appellants had sold their privacy to the magazine *OK!* for a handsome sum.[43] The only aspect of private life which remained was not information but autonomy, in particular, their right of veto over publication of the photographs in order to maintain the kind of image professionally and personally important to them. In *B&C v A*[44] the Court of Appeal held that there is a difference between the confidentiality which attaches to permanent relationships and that which attaches to affairs.[45] Nevertheless, there was still a modest degree of confidentiality (or privacy) concerning these relationships to which A was entitled.[46]

The information contained in an enhanced criminal record certificate issued under section 115 of the Police Act 1997 has also been held to be private. The certificate contains information in addition to that which is recorded in central records. It may concern offences of which the person is suspected of committing even though his responsibility has not been and cannot be proved.[47] It has also been held that prior convictions, spent for the purposes of the Rehabilitation of Offenders Act 1974, are private information,[48] as are unspent convictions.[49] The conclusion in *X v Y*[50] that a caution received by an individual for committing a sex offence with another man in a

---

[36] *R v P* [2001] 2 WLR 463; *N*, above n 12.

[37] *Attorney General's Reference (No.3 of 1999)* [2001] 2 AC 91.

[38] *R (on the application of Morgan Grenfell & Co Ltd) v Special Commissioners of Income Tax* [2002] UKHL 21, [2003] 1 AC 563.

[39] Above n 27.

[40] *Ibid*, at [147] per Baroness Hale. See also Lord Hope at [95] and Lord Carswell at [165].

[41] Above n 26.

[42] *Ibid*, at [95] per Brooke LJ and [168]–[169] per Keene LJ.

[43] *Ibid*, at [140] per Sedley LJ.

[44] *B & C v A* [2002] EWCA Civ 337, [2002] 3 WLR 542.

[45] *Ibid*, at [43](ii).

[46] *Ibid*, at [44]. See also *Theakston v MGN Limited* [2002] EWHC (QB) 137, [2002] EMLR 22; *R (on the application of Ford) v The Press Complaints Commission* [2001] EWHC (Admin) 683, [2002] EMLR 5.

[47] *R (on the application of X) v Chief Constable of West Midlands Police* [2004] EWCA Civ 1068, [2005] 1 WLR 65. See also *Woolgar*, above n 11, and *R v A Local Authority in the Midlands, ex p LM* [2000] 1 FCR 736.

[48] *N v Governor of HM Prison Dartmoor*, Administrative Court, 13 February 2001. But see *Pearson*, above n 29.

[49] *R (Ellis) v Chief Constable of Essex Police* [2003] EWHC (Admin) 1321, [2003] 2 FLR 566; *R (on the application of A) v National Probation Service* [2003] EWHC (Admin) 2910.

[50] [2004] EWCA Civ 662, [2004] ICR 1634.

transport café lavatory, to which the public had access, was not private as in committing the offence the individual would not have had a reasonable expectation of privacy does not sit easily with this line of authority. The better view would be that the caution needs to be considered apart from the details of the offence. And the caution itself is private information.

Privacy of information is also important in the corporate world. In *Banque Internationale à Luxembourg*[51] it was accepted without question by the High Court that notices issued by the Commissioners of the Inland Revenue to the bank requiring specific classes of documents in relation to named taxpayers as part of an investigation into a large-scale corporate tax avoidance scheme impinged on the confidentiality and rights of privacy of the bank and the targets.[52] In *Newman*[53] it was accepted by the Lands Tribunal that sale price information contained in Particulars Delivered Forms (provided to the Inland Revenue for stamp duty purposes) were private.[54]

2.2 Identity

The right to respect for private life protects a person's identity—how they see themselves and how others see them. Respect for this aspect of private life also requires that everyone should be able to establish details of their identity as individual human beings. This includes their origins and the opportunity to understand them.[55] In *Rose*[56] the Administrative Court considered the application of individuals born as a result of artificial insemination by donor who wished to obtain identifying and non-identifying information about the donor. It concluded that Article 8 was engaged, stating that

> [a] human being is a human being whatever the circumstances of his conception and an AID child is entitled to establish a picture of his identity as much as anyone else.[57]

A number of cases have also been brought under the HRA concerning the failure of United Kingdom law to recognise a transsexual's change in sex from their sex at birth. The test for determining a person's sex set out in *Corbett v Corbett*[58] is purely biological. If the gonodal, chromosomal and genital tests are congruent, that determines the person's sex and psychological factors are not taken into account. A person's sex is fixed at birth and cannot be changed.

In *Bellinger*[59] the appellant, a male to female transsexual, argued that her marriage to a man was a valid marriage under the Matrimonial Causes Act 1973 although this Act provided that the marriage would be void if the parties were not male and female.

---

[51] *R v Inland Revenue Commissioners, ex p Banque Internationale à Luxembourg SA* [2000] STC 708.
[52] See also *Guyer v Walton (Inspector of Taxes)* [2001] STC (SCD) 75.
[53] *Newman (Inspector of Taxes) v Hatt* [2002] 04 EG 175.
[54] See also *Igroup Ltd v Ocwen* [2003] EWHC (Ch) 2431, [2004] 1 WLR 451.
[55] *R (on the application of Rose) v Secretary of State for Health* [2002] EWHC (Admin) 1593, [2002] 3 FCR 731 at [45]. See also *Re T (a child) (DNA tests: paternity)* [2001] 3 FCR 577.
[56] *Ibid.*
[57] *Ibid,* at [47].
[58] [1970] 2 All ER 33.
[59] Above n 5.

The House of Lords was not prepared to recognise the appellant as a female for the purposes of the Matrimonial Causes Act, holding that the issues were ill-suited for determination by the courts and pre-eminently a matter for Parliament. This was particularly so given the government's intention to bring forward legislation on the subject.[60] However, their Lordships did declare that, in so far as section 11(c) of the Matrimonial Causes Act 1973 made no provision for the recognition of gender reassignment, it was incompatible with Articles 8 and 12.[61]

The position is different when the individual is not a transsexual but is of indeterminate sex or 'physical inter-sex'. In *W v W*[62] the Family Court held that, as the person was not a transsexual, the purely biological test in *Corbett v Corbett* did not apply. It concluded that, when determining whether such an individual was male or female for the purposes of marriage, it was necessary to take into account chromosomal factors, gonodal factors, genital factors, psychological factors, hormonal factors and secondary sexual characteristics. Furthermore, the decision could be made with the benefit of hindsight looking back from the date of the marriage. Whilst not explicitly mentioned, it is clear that identity played a part in the conclusion reached.[63]

2.3 Physical and Psychological Integrity

Private life includes the physical and psychological integrity of a person.[64] It extends to those features which are integral to a person's identity or ability to function socially as a person.[65] However, to qualify as an interference with psychological integrity, the interference must be serious. For example, Article 8 is not engaged every time a public body informs someone that it has decided to take some formal step which is the precursor to some active and potentially unpleasant means of enforcement.[66]

Any medical treatment, including the taking of samples, without consent is an interference with the right to respect for physical integrity.[67] It does not matter if the patient is capacitated or incapacitated, although it has been held that the degree of interference is greater where there is a capacitated refusal because not only is their privacy being invaded but also their ability to make decisions, though not impaired, is nevertheless being overridden. In such instances there is also an interference with

---

[60] *Ibid*, at [37] per Lord Nicholls

[61] *Ibid*, at [53] per Lord Nicholls in reliance upon *Goodwin v United Kingdom* (2002) 35 EHRR 18. See also [70] per Lord Hope and [79] per Lord Hobhouse. See further S Cowan, 'That Woman is a Woman! The Case of Bellinger v. Bellinger and the Mysterious (Dis)appearance of Sex' (2004) 12 *FLS* 79. See also *Chief Constable of West Yorkshire Police v A* [2004] UKHL 21, [2005] 1 AC 51, but note that this judgment turned on rights under the Equal Treatment Directive 1976, not Art 8.

[62] [2001] 2 WLR 674.

[63] See also *E*, above n 13.

[64] *Razgar*, above n 14, at [9] per Lord Bingham in reliance upon *Pretty v United Kingdom* (2002) 35 EHRR 1 at [61]. See also *NHS Trust A v Mrs M* [2001] 2 WLR 942 at [41].

[65] *Ibid*.

[66] *R (on the application of Denson) v Child Support Agency* [2002] EWHC (Admin) 154, [2002] 1 FCR 460 at [43]. See also *Brumfitt v Ministry of Defence* [2005] IRLR 4.

[67] *Whitefield v General Medical Council* [2002] UKPC 62, [2003] HRLR 243 at [31]; *R (Wooder) v Feggetter* [2002] EWCA Civ 554, [2003] QB 219; *R (on the application of Wilkinson) v The Responsible Medical Officer Broadmoor Hospital* [2001] EWCA Civ 1545, [2002] 1 WLR 419 at [14]; *R (on the application of Burke) v The General Medical Council* [2005] EWCA Civ 1003 at [30].

autonomy.[68] It has been held that treatment of patients in permanent vegetative states which is not in their best interests would be an intrusion into bodily integrity which would have to be justified under Article 8(2).[69] It has also been held that to become infected with a sexually transmissible disease such as Hepatitis C is a violation of physical integrity which the state has a positive obligation to prevent.[70] However, Article 8 imposes no positive obligation to provide medical treatment.[71]

The taking of fingerprints and DNA samples undoubtedly involves an interference with private life.[72] However, the retention of fingerprints and samples does not.[73] This is because a person can only be identified by fingerprint or DNA sample either by an expert or with the use of sophisticated equipment, or both. In both cases it is essential to have some sample with which to compare the retained data. Further, in the context of the storage of this type of information within records retained by the police, the material stored says nothing about the physical makeup, characteristics or life of the person to whom they belong.[74]

Seclusion of prisoners and psychiatric patients undoubtedly impacts on physical and psychological integrity.[75] Stop and search also engages Article 8.[76] It has also been held that the denial of welfare support may impact on a person's autonomy and physical and psychological integrity to such an extent as to amount to an interference under Article 8.[77] However, as discussed in the chapter on Article 3 and in the following paragraphs, failure to provide support would be better considered as a failure to fulfil a positive obligation rather than a negative duty.

It is also possible for environmental pollution to constitute an interference with physical integrity. In *Furness*[78] it was argued that the conditions of authorisation granted by the Environment Agency for the incineration of municipal waste were insufficient to protect the claimant's right to information. The Divisional Court held that, since the threat to health and property was not of a substantial kind, there was no necessity for the information to be made available before it was placed in the register.[79] However, in *Andrews*[80] the court held that the increase in road and traffic noise

---

[68] *R (on the application of B) v Responsible Medical Officer, Broadmoor Hospital* [2005] EWHC (Admin) 1936 at [75]. Whether an interference with Art 8(1) in such circumstances may be justified turns on the orthodox test under Art 8(2)—see [82].

[69] *Mrs M*, above n 64, at [28] and [41].

[70] *R (on the application of H) v Ashworth Hospital Authority* [2001] EWHC (Admin) 872, [2002] 1 FCR 206 at [124] in reliance upon *Guerra v Italy* (1998) 4 BHRC 63; *Lopez Ostra v Spain* (1994) 20 EHRR 277.

[71] *R (on the application of A) v North West Lancashire Health Authority* [2000] 1 WLR 977; *R (on the application of Watts) v Bedford Primary Care Trust* [2003] EWHC (Admin) 2228, [2004] Lloyd's Rep Med 113.

[72] *S*, above n 10; *Attorney General's Reference (No.3 of 1999)*, above n 37.

[73] *S, ibid*, at [31] per Lord Steyn.

[74] *Ibid*, at [29] per Lord Steyn quoting from the judgment of the Divisional Court.

[75] *R (on the application of Munjaz) v Mersey Care NHS Trust* [2003] EWCA Civ 1036, [2004] QB 395. See also *R (on the application of P) v Secretary of State for the Home Department* [2003] EWHC (Admin) 1963.

[76] *R (on the application of Gillan) v The Commissioner of Police for the Metropolis* [2004] EWCA Civ 1067, [2005] QB 388 at [47].

[77] *R (on the application of Q) v Secretary of State for the Home Department* [2003] EWCA Civ 364, [2004] QB 36; *R (on the application of Bernard) v London Borough of Enfield* [2002] EWHC (Admin) 2282, [2003] HRLR 4.

[78] *Furness v Environment Agency* [2002] Env. LR 26.

[79] *Ibid*, at [26]. *Guerra v Italy* (1998) 26 EHRR 357 was distinguished.

[80] *Andrews v Reading Borough Council* [2005] EWHC (QB) 256.

on the road in which the claimant lived constituted a violation of his rights under Article 8.

In the immigration context, the rights protected by Article 8 can be engaged by the foreseeable consequences for health of removal from the United Kingdom pursuant to an immigration decision, even where removal does not violate Article 3, if the facts relied upon by the applicant are sufficiently strong.[81] In some instances, where a family is being deported, it may be necessary to look at the family as a whole. The mental health or condition of one member may have relevance to that of another.[82] In *Razgar*[83] the main emphasis was not on the severance of family and social ties but on the consequences for the applicant's mental health of removal to the receiving country. A majority of the House of Lords concluded that a decision which, if implemented, might lead to Mr Razgar taking his own life could not be dismissed as of insufficient gravity.[84] Prior to removal, the possibility of 'dispersal' of an asylum seeker impacting on psychological integrity has also been considered.[85]

2.4 Autonomy (Self-determination)

Article 8(1) also protects personal autonomy or self-determination. However, this aspect of Article 8 can only be taken so far and does not, for example, incorporate an individual's choice to live no longer.[86]

It is clear that to film or photograph a person without his or her consent is an interference with private life because it interferes with personal autonomy or the control every person has over his own identity.[87] In *R v Loveridge*[88] the police had arranged for the appellants to be filmed by video camera, without their knowledge, while they were at a magistrates court. The Court of Appeal held that secret filming was objectionable in terms of Article 8(1) per se.[89] Similarly, in *Douglas*[90] Sedley LJ

---

[81] *Razgar*, above n 14, at [10] per Lord Bingham in reliance upon *Bensaid v United Kingdom* (2001) 33 EHRR 205.

[82] *R (on the application of Ahmadi) v Secretary of State for the Home Department* [2002] EWHC (Admin) 1897 at [52].

[83] Above n 14.

[84] *Ibid*, at [23] per Lord Bingham, with whom Lords Steyn and Carswell agreed. See also *Djali v Immigration Appeal Tribunal* [2003] EWCA Civ 1371; *R (on the application of Kastrati) v Special Adjudicator* [2002] EWHC (Admin) 415; *R (on the application of Bardiqi) v Secretary of State for the Home Department* [2003] EWHC (Admin) 1788; *R (on the application of Mehmeti) v Secretary of State for the Home Department* [2004] EWHC (Admin) 2999; *R (on the application of Ali) v Secretary of State for the Home Department*, Administrative Court, 21 January 2005.

[85] See, eg *R (on the application of Blackwood) v Secretary of State for the Home Department* [2003] EWHC (Admin) 98, [2003] HLR 638; *R (on the application of Muwangusi) v Secretary of State for the Home Department* [2003] EWHC (Admin) 813.

[86] *Pretty*, above n 8, at [26] per Lord Bingham, [61] per Lord Steyn, [112] per Lord Hobhouse and [124] per Lord Scott. Lord Hope held that the way Ms Pretty chose to pass the closing moments of her life was part of the act of living and she had a right to ask that this be respected. See [100]. See further A Pedain, 'The Human Rights Dimension of the Diane Pretty Case' (2003) 62 *CLJ* 181.

[87] *BBC*, above n 18, although it is important to note that in this case the Court of Appeal was considering a complaint under the Broadcasting Act 1996 where 'privacy' is not expressed identically to Art 8.

[88] [2001] EWCA Crim 1034, [2001] 2 Cr App R 29.

[89] *Ibid*, at [30].

[90] Above n 26.

perceived the unauthorised photographs of the wedding as an interference with the fundamental value of personal autonomy.[91]

There are few other examples of interferences with autonomy. In M[92] it was held by the Administrative Court that the absence of any possibility of changing the nearest relative under the Mental Health Act 1983 was incompatible with Article 8. In *Evans*[93] the Court of Appeal held that the refusal of a fertility clinic to continue her treatment using frozen embryos created from her and her former partner was an interference with her autonomy.[94] In *Roddy*[95] the Family Division held that the personal autonomy protected by Article 8 embraced the right to decide who was to be within the inner circle—the right to decide whether that which was private should remain private or whether it should be shared with others.

> Article 8 thus embraces both the right to maintain one's privacy and, if this is what one prefers, not merely the right to waive that privacy but also the right to share what would otherwise be private with others or, indeed, with the world at large.[96]

If the person is a child, the older the child, it has been held, the greater the weight the court should give to his or her wishes.[97] In *Roddy*, the court concluded that a 17-year-old woman who had a baby when she was aged 13 was of an age and of sufficient understanding and maturity to decide for herself whether that which was private, personal and intimate should remain private or whether it should be shared with the whole world.[98]

2.5 Social Life

The capacity to enter into social relationships with others is included within the concept of private life. There is a right to establish and develop relationships with other human beings, and the fact that there is no existing relationship does not prevent the engagement of Article 8.[99] It is possible that being able to communicate functionally may also come within the scope of Article 8.[100] In *Whitefield*[101] the Privy Council was not satisfied that the ban on the consumption of alcohol imposed by the General

---

[91] *Ibid*, at [126]. See also *Ford*, above n 46; *BBC*, above n 18.
[92] *R (on the application of M) v Secretary of State for Health* [2003] EWHC (Admin) 1094, [2003] ACD 389. See also *R (on the application of E) v Bristol City Council* [2005] EWHC (Admin) 74.
[93] Above n 7.
[94] *Ibid*, at [60]. See further S Sheldon, 'Evans v. Amicus Healthcare; Hadley v. Midland Fertility Services—revealing cracks in the "twin pillars"'? (2004) 16 *CFLQ* 437.
[95] *Re Roddy (a child) (identification: restriction on publication)* [2003] EWHC (Fam) 2927, [2004] FCR 481.
[96] *Ibid*, at [36].
[97] *Ibid*, at [55].
[98] *Ibid*, at [56]. However in *E v Director of Public Prosecutions* [2005] EWHC (Admin) 147 the court concluded that to proscribe sexual intercourse between 15 year olds did not interfere with private life having regard to the tender age of those involved. See also *E (by her litigation friend the Official Solicitor) v Channel Four* [2005] EWHC (Fam) 1144, [2005] EMLR 30 concerning the consent of a woman with a learning disability to the broadcast of a documentary about her.
[99] *Rose*, above n 55, at [45]. See also *R (on the application of J) v Southend Borough Council*, Administrative Court, 5 August 2005 concerning the right to maintain relationships.
[100] *R (on the application of Jegatheeswaran) v Secretary of State for the Home Department* [2005] EWHC (Admin) 1131.
[101] Above n 67.

Medical Council on the appellant in order to retain his registration was an interference. In its view, he was not prevented from going to his local public house or engaging in his social life while drinking non-alcoholic drinks.[102]

2.6 Correspondence

Finally, whilst correspondence is protected separately under Article 8(1), it is examined in this chapter as it is often considered by the courts within the context of 'private life' rather than correspondence. Correspondence includes legal correspondence between a prisoner and legal advisor. A custodial order does not wholly deprive a prisoner of all the rights enjoyed by other citizens.[103]

---

3. Positive Duties

The state must itself refrain from interference with private life, but in addition it must provide for an effective respect for private life.[104] In certain circumstances, Article 8(1) may also impose a positive duty to act. For example, the House of Lord's declaration in *Bellinger*[105] that section 11(c) of the Matrimonial Causes Act 1973, which made no provision for the recognition of gender reassignment, was incompatible with Articles 8 and 12 was obviously based on a failure of the state to act in this area with respect to private life. In *Wooder*[106] Sedley LJ appeared to suggest that the interference with private life involved in medical treatment for a psychiatric condition against a patient's will was such that Article 8 may require written and adequate reasons to be given.[107] However, the principle of autonomy, or self-determination, does not entitle a patient to insist on receiving a particular medical treatment regardless of the nature of the treatment.

> Insofar as a doctor has a legal obligation to provide treatment this cannot be founded simply upon the fact that the patient demands it. The source of the duty lies elsewhere.[108]

It has been suggested that the test to be applied to an allegation that the state has failed to respect private life is in principle the same test as that to be applied to an allegation that the state has failed to protect life in breach of Article 2. If there is a

---

[102] *Ibid*, at [27].
[103] *R (on the application of Daly) v Secretary of State for the Home Department* [2001] UKHL 26, [2001] 2 AC 532. See also *R (on the application of Ponting) v Governor of HMP Prison Whitemoor* [2002] EWCA Civ 224; *R (on the application of Szuluk) v The Governor of HMP Full Sutton* [2004] EWCA Civ 1426.
[104] *Hadiova v Secretary of State for the Home Department* [2003] EWCA Civ 701.
[105] Above n 5.
[106] Above n 67. See also *R (on the application of B) v Haddock* [2005] EWHC (Admin) 921.
[107] Wooder, *ibid*, at [48]–[49]. See also *Rose*, above n 55.
[108] *Burke*, above n 67, at [31].

risk to respect for private life of which a public authority knows or ought to know, it must take reasonable measures within the scope of its powers to obviate that risk.[109]

Difficult questions have arisen in the context of welfare support. It has been recognised that there are some circumstances in which a public authority will be required to devote resources to make it possible for individuals to enjoy the rights that they are entitled to respect for under Article 8.[110]

> While it is possible to identify a degree of degradation which demands welfare support, it is much more difficult to identify some other basic standard of private and family life which Art.8 requires the State to maintain by the provision of support.[111]

Often it is noted that it is hard to conceive of a situation in which the predicament of an individual will be such that Article 8 requires him to be provided with welfare support but will not be sufficiently severe to engage Article 3.[112]

In so far as Article 8 does impose positive obligations, it has been held that these are not absolute. Before inaction can amount to a lack of respect for private and family life, there must be some ground for criticising the failure to act.

> There must be an element of culpability. At the very least there must be knowledge that the claimant's private and family life were at risk.[113]

Reference has been made to the test set out in *Osman v United Kingdom*[114] in relation to Article 2.

> Where the domestic law of a State imposes positive obligations in relation to the provision of welfare support, breach of those positive obligations of domestic law may suffice to provide the element of culpability necessary to establish a breach of Art.8, provided that the impact on private or family life is sufficiently serious and was foreseeable.[115]

Where the complaint is one of delay, there is no infringement unless substantial prejudice has been caused to the applicant. There is a need to have regard to resources, and the demands on resources would be significantly increased if states were to be faced with claims for breaches of Article 8 simply on the ground of administrative delays.[116] Maladministration will only infringe Article 8 where the consequence is serious. The

> more glaring the deficiency in the behaviour of the public authority, the easier it will be to establish the necessary want of respect. Isolated acts of even significant carelessness are unlikely to suffice.[117]

---

[109] *H*, above n 70. See also *Anufrijeva*, above n 1.
[110] *Anufrijeva, ibid*, at [28] and [33].
[111] *Ibid*, at [37].
[112] *Ibid*, at [43].
[113] *Ibid*, at [45].
[114] (1998) 29 EHRR 245
[115] *Anufrijeva*, above n 1, at [45].
[116] *Ibid*, at [46] and [47].
[117] *Ibid*, at [48].

Applying these principles to two appeals, the Court of Appeal concluded in *Anufrijeva*[118] that the accommodation provided was not ideal but fell far short of placing the family in the type of conditions that would impose a positive obligation under Article 8 to install them in superior accommodation.[119] In *N* it concluded that the maladministration in determining his asylum claim did not breach Article 8 simply because it led a particularly susceptible individual to suffer harm in circumstances where this was not reasonably to be anticipated.[120]

---

4. Deportation and Extradition: 'Foreign' Cases

It is clear that the right to respect for private life can be engaged by the deportation or extradition of an individual. In a domestic case, the contracting state is directly responsible, because of its own act or omissions, for the breach of Convention rights. Here it is possible to consider Article 8(2). Therefore these cases are considered below in the section concerning permitted interferences. In foreign cases the contracting state is not directly responsible; its responsibility is engaged because of the real risk that its conduct in expelling the person will lead to a gross invasion of his most fundamental rights.[121] With respect to these cases, to successfully resist deportation or extradition it must be shown that Article 8(1) rights will be subject to flagrant denial or gross violation in the destination country. In short, it must be shown that the right will be completely denied or nullified.[122] As it was only finally determined in June 2004 that Article 8 applied to these types of cases,[123] many of the earlier cases are now of dubious authority and are only examined in the paragraphs below if the test applied was the same as the test now established.

4.1 Medical Treatment

In *Razgar*[124] Lord Bingham commented *obiter* that, under Article 8, removal cannot be resisted merely on the ground that medical treatment or facilities are better or more accessible in the removing country than in that to which the applicant is to be removed.

> It would indeed frustrate the proper and necessary object of immigration control in the more advanced member states of the Council of Europe if illegal entrants requiring

---

[118] *Ibid.*
[119] *Ibid,* at [115].
[120] *Ibid,* at [143]. See also *R (on the application of Khan) v Oxfordshire County Council* [2004] EWCA Civ 309, [2004] BLGR 257.
[121] *Razgar*, above n 14, at [41] per Baroness Hale.
[122] *R (on the application of Ullah) v Special Adjudicator* [2004] UKHL 26, [2004] 2 AC 323 at [24] per Lord Bingham.
[123] *Ibid.*
[124] Above n 14.

medical treatment could not, save in exceptional cases, be removed to the less developed countries of the world where comparable medical facilities were not available.[125]

He also commented that the Convention is directed to the protection of fundamental human rights, not the conferment of individual advantages or benefits.[126] He applied this to welfare, noting that an applicant could never hope to resist an expulsion decision without showing something very much more extreme than relative disadvantage as compared with the expelling state.[127]

4.2 Homosexuality

Often deportation is resisted on the ground that homosexuality is illegal in the destination state. In Z[128] the Court of Appeal held that the tribunal's view that laws against sodomy, even if not enforced, were a breach of the right to respect for private life was too wide. It held that it was necessary for the tribunal to go further and examine whether there would be any possibility of a prosecution.[129] Furthermore, the court held it should also have examined whether, and in what circumstances, any criminal investigation short of prosecution might be embarked upon.[130]

5. Who Has a Private Life?

Article 8(1) provides that 'everyone' has the right to respect for his private life. Whilst it is clear that this extends to all persons, it is sometimes questioned whether 'everyone' includes legal persons such as companies. In relation to the meaning of privacy under the Broadcasting Act 1996, the Court of Appeal has held that it was clear that a company could make a complaint about infringement of its privacy.[131]

> [A] company does have activities of a private nature which need protection from unwarranted intrusion. It would be a departure from proper standards if, for example, the BBC without any justification attempted to listen clandestinely to the activities of a board meeting . . . The company has correspondence which it could justifiably regard as private.[132]

A similar view has been reached in HRA Article 8 cases, although no discussion of the issue has arisen.[133]

---

[125] *Ibid*, at [4]. Lords Steyn, Walker and Carswell agreed. See also Baroness Hale at [59].
[126] *Ibid*.
[127] *Ibid*, at [10].
[128] *Secretary of State for the Home Department v Z* [2002] EWCA Civ 952, [2002] Imm AR 560.
[129] *Ibid*, at [29].
[130] *Ibid*, at [30]. See also *Hadiova*, above n 104; *Z v The Secretary of State for the Home Department* [2004] EWCA Civ 1578; *R (on the application of S) v Secretary of State for the Home Department* [2003] EWHC (Admin) 352; *R (on the application of M) v Immigration Appeal Tribunal* [2005] EWHC (Admin) 251.
[131] *BBC*, above n 18.
[132] *Ibid*, at [33] per Lord Woolf MR and [42] and [44] per Hale LJ. Cf Mustill LJ at [45]–[50].
[133] See, eg *Banque Internationale à Luxembourg SA*, above n 51.

However, a company's privacy may not extend as far as an individual's. For example,

> the reading and copying of personal diaries, letters to relatives or lovers, poems and so on . . . Such conduct is specially objectionable . . . because of the insult done to the person as a person.[134]

It may be that no such complaint would be feasible when made by a company because

> an intrusion into such matters has an extra dimension, in the shape of the damage done to the sensibilities of a human being by exposing to strangers the inner workings of his or her inward feelings, emotions, fears and beliefs, a damage which an artificial 'person', having no sensibilities, cannot be made to suffer.[135]

---

6. Who Must Respect Private Life?

Even though the HRA does not apply directly to private bodies, courts, as public authorities, must act compatibly with Convention rights when adjudicating on existing remedies such as the tort of breach of confidence. Modification of this tort in the light of Articles 8 and 10 has had a considerable impact on some parts of the private sector, in particular media companies.

> The values embodied in Arts 8 and 10 are as much applicable in disputes between individuals or between an individual and a non-governmental body such as a newspaper as they are in disputes between individuals and a public authority.[136]

There is no logical ground for saying that a person should have less protection against a private individual than he would have against the state for the publication of personal information for which there is no justification.[137]

As examined in the paragraphs above, it is clear that, for private bodies, a duty of confidence arises whenever the party subject to the duty is in a situation where he knows or ought to know that the other person can reasonably expect his privacy to be protected.[138] An intrusion in such a situation will be capable of giving rise to liability in an action for breach of confidence unless the intrusion can be justified.[139] In

---

[134] *BBC*, above n 18, at [49] per Mustill LJ.
[135] *Ibid*.
[136] *Campbell*, above n 27, at [17] per Lord Nicholls
[137] *Ibid*, at [50] per Lord Hoffmann.
[138] *Ibid*, at [85] per Lord Hope. See also *Douglas*, above n 26; *Theakston*, above n 46; *B & C v A*, above n 44; *Douglas v Hello! Ltd (No.3)* [2003] EWHC (Ch) 786, [2003] 3 All ER 996; *Archer v Williams* [2003] EWHC (QB) 1670, [2003] EMLR 38.
[139] *B & C v A, ibid*, at [11(ix)]—[11(x)]. See generally G Phillipson, 'Transforming Breach of Confidence? Towards a Common Law Right of Privacy under the Human Rights Act' (2003) 66 *MLR* 726; J Morgan, 'Privacy, Confidence and Horizontal Effect: "Hello" Trouble' (2003) 62 *CLJ* 444; A Sims, 'A Shift in the Centre of Gravity: the Dangers of Protecting Privacy through Breach of Confidence' (2005) *IPQ* 27.

addition, Article 8 has also had an impact on the inherent jurisdiction of the High Court to protect the children for whom it is responsible.[140]

However, the judicial creation of a general 'privacy tort' appears a long way off. As the HRA did not apply to the facts of the case, it was argued before the House of Lords in *Wainwright*[141] that there was, and always has been, a tort of invasion of privacy. The House of Lords disagreed, holding that the courts have so far refused to formulate a general principle of invasion of privacy[142] and finding no suggestion that they should do so.[143] It found a great difference between identifying privacy as a value which underlay the existence of a rule of law and privacy as a principle of law in itself.[144] Furthermore, it saw nothing in the jurisprudence of the European Court of Human Rights which suggested that the adoption of some high-level principle of privacy was necessary to comply with Article 8.[145] It concluded that this was an area which required a detailed approach that could be achieved only by legislation rather than the 'broad brush of the common law principle.'[146] Finally, it noted that the coming into force of the HRA weakened the argument even further. The creation of a general tort would preempt the controversial question of the extent, if any, to which the Convention required states to provide remedies for invasions of privacy by persons who were not public authorities.[147]

7. Permitted Interferences

It is clear that the right to respect for private life is not an absolute right. Article 8(2) provides that interferences are permissible if they are in accordance with the law and necessary in a democratic society

> in the interests of national security, public safety or the economic well-being of the country, for the prevention of disorder or crime, for the protection of health or morals, or for the protection of the rights and freedoms of others.

Each of these interests is examined in the following paragraphs. However, it is first necessary to consider some general factors which may affect any balancing process engaged in by a court.

It is important to appreciate that, just as a freedom of expression claim is affected by the subject matter of the expression, so too there are strong and weak claims to

---

[140] See, eg *Re S (A Child)* [2004] UKHL 47, [2004] 1 AC 593 at [22]–[23] per Lord Steyn; *Roddy*, above n 95. In *Local Authority v Health Authority* [2003] EWHC (Fam) 2746, [2004] 1 All ER 480 this was extended to adults under a disability and vulnerable adults.

[141] Above n 3.

[142] *Ibid*, at [19] per Lord Hoffmann.

[143] *Ibid*, at [26] per Lord Hoffmann.

[144] *Ibid*, at [32] per Lord Hoffmann.

[145] *Ibid*, in reliance upon *Earl Spencer v UK* (1998) 25 EHRR CD 105; *Peck v UK* (2003) 13 BHRC 669.

[146] *Ibid*, at [33] per Lord Hoffmann.

[147] *Ibid*, at [34] per Lord Hoffmann. See also *Theakston*, above n 46, at [27] and *B & C v A*, above n 44, at [11(vi)]. See generally NW Barber, 'A Right to Privacy?' [2003] *PL* 602.

respect for private life. The strength or otherwise of such a claim will have a considerable impact on the balancing processes carried out by a court when determining whether or not an interference is justified. It is therefore essential to consider how the courts go about determining the strength of such claims. The first factor taken into account appears to be the level of harm which the interference will cause. The more harm caused, the stronger the private life claim. For example, in *Campbell*,[148] picking up on the comments of Keene LJ in *Douglas v Hello! Ltd*,[149] Lord Hope held that there are different degrees of privacy and, in the present context, the potential for disclosure of the information to cause harm was an important factor to be taken into account in the assessment of the extent of the restriction that was needed to protect Ms Campbell's right to privacy.[150] Here he found that the publication of the details of her treatment at Narcotics Anonymous had the potential to cause harm to her, so he attached a 'good deal of weight to this factor.'[151] He commented that for someone in her position

> there are few areas of the life of an individual that are more in need of protection on the grounds of privacy than the combating of addiction to drugs or to alcohol.[152]

He noted that it was

> hard to break the habit which has led to the addiction. It is all too easy to give up the struggle if efforts to do so are exposed to public scrutiny. The struggle, after all, is an intensely personal one.[153]

Baroness Hale also commented that the risk of harm was important.

> People trying to recover from drug addiction need considerable dedication and commitment, along with constant reinforcement from those around them.[154]

She reached a similar conclusion to Lord Hope, although she also noted that the interests involved in *Re S*, which concerned the private life of a child whose mother was being tried for the murder of his brother, were far more serious than those of a 'prima donna celebrity against a celebrity-exploiting tabloid newspaper.'[155] Lord Carswell reached a similar conclusion. However, it is interesting to note that, in *Re S* itself, the House of Lords found that the interference with the Article 8 rights of the boy were not of the same order when compared with cases of juveniles who were directly involved in criminal trials.[156]

Secondly, where different pieces of information are published together, or where there are a number of interferences, considering them as a whole may significantly

---

[148] Above n 27.
[149] [2001] QB 967 at [168].
[150] *Ibid*, at [118].
[151] *Ibid*, at [119].
[152] *Ibid*, at [81].
[153] *Ibid*.
[154] *Ibid*, at [157].
[155] *Ibid*, at [143].
[156] *Ibid*, at [27] per Lord Steyn. See also *Theakston*, above n 46; *B & C v A*, above n 44; *X (a woman merly known as Mary Bell) v O'Brien* [2003] EWHC (QB) 1101, [2003] 2 FCR 686.

bolster the strength of a private life claim. For example, in *Campbell*[157] Lord Hope commented that, were it not for the photographs, he would have regarded the balance between private life and freedom of expression as even.[158]

> But these were not just pictures of a street scene where she happened to be when the photographs were taken. They were taken deliberately, in secret and with a view to their publication in conjunction with the article.[159]

Similarly, Baroness Hale commented that

> [a] picture is 'worth a thousand words' because it adds to the impact of what the words convey; but it also adds to the information given in those words . . . it also added to the potential harm, by making her think that she was being followed or betrayed, and deterring her from going back to the same place again.[160]

Finally, it is not clear whether or not the strength of a claim to privacy is affected by the fact that a person, in particular a public figure, has previously lied about the information sought to be kept private, or whether a person's right to privacy may be limited by the public's interest in knowing about certain traits of her personality and certain aspects of her private life. The better view is that this only affects the freedom of expression side of the equation. For example, where a public figure has lied, it may be a matter of public interest that the record is set straight.[161] This is examined in more detail in the chapter concerning freedom of expression.

---

8. National Security

Interferences with private life in accordance with the law may be permitted if necessary in the interests of national security. This was the justification pleaded by the Secretary of State in *Baker*,[162] where, under the Data Protection Act 1998, the claimant, a serving member of Parliament, contended that the Security Service held or had held personal information about him. He required them to say whether or not that was correct and to disclose the data to him. The Secretary of State signed a certificate purporting to exempt the Service from complying with Part II of the Act. Reading the Act in a manner which protected Article 8,[163] the Information Tribunal, whilst affording considerable deference, concluded that the Secretary of State did not have reasonable grounds for providing the Service with a blanket exemption. The blanket

---

[157] Above n 27.
[158] *Ibid*, at [121].
[159] *Ibid*, at [123].
[160] *Ibid*, at [155]. See also *Theakston*, above n 46; *B & C v A*, above n 44. See further NA Moreham, 'Privacy in the Common Law: a Doctrinal and Theoretical Analysis' (2005) 121 *LQR* 628.
[161] This was the view adopted by Baroness Hale in *Campbell*, *ibid*. See also *Theakston* and *B & C v A*, *ibid*.
[162] *Baker*, above n 22.
[163] *Ibid*, at [57].

exemption was wider than necessary to protect national security; some personal data relating to individuals could be released to them without endangering national security; there was no reason to suppose that the burden of dealing with claimants individually would be unduly onerous; and evidence as to practice in other countries did not show an identical unchallengeable provision. It concluded that the proportionate and reasonable response was to consider each request on its merits.[164]

9. Economic Well-being of the Country

Interferences with private life in accordance with the law are permitted if necessary in the interests of the economic well-being of the country. A variety of interferences have sought to be justified on this basis. It is clear that, whilst not all deportations will be justified on the ground of economic well-being, the majority are sought to be justified as such—and deportations are therefore considered in this section.

9.1 Deportation and Extradition: 'Domestic' Cases

It is clear that the right to respect for private life can be engaged by the deportation or extradition of an individual. In a domestic case, the contracting state is directly responsible, because of its own act or omissions, for the breach of Convention rights. In foreign cases the contracting state is not directly responsible, its responsibility being engaged because of the real risk that its conduct in expelling the person will lead to a gross invasion of his most fundamental rights.[165] In a domestic case where removal is resisted in reliance on Article 8, questions which are likely to be important are as follows:

(1)   Will the proposed removal be an interference by a public authority with the exercise of the applicant's right to respect for private or (as the case may be) family life?

(2)   If so, will such interference have consequences of such gravity as potentially to engage the operation of Article 8?[166]

(3)   If so, is such interference in accordance with the law?

(4)   If so, is such interference necessary in a democratic society in the interests of national security, public safety or the economic well-being of the country, for the prevention of disorder or crime, for the protection of health or morals, or for the protection of the rights and freedoms of others?

(5)   If so, is such interference proportionate to the legitimate public end sought to be achieved?[167]

---

[164] *Ibid*, at [113].
[165] *Razgar*, above n 14, at [41] per Baroness Hale.
[166] It is important to note that domestic cases are not governed by a flagrancy threshold. See *Huang*, above n 15.
[167] *Razgar*, above n 14, at [17] per Lord Bingham.

It has been held that interferences are always likely to be in accordance with law and, where removal is proposed in pursuance of lawful immigration policy, question (4) will almost always fall to be answered affirmatively.

> This is because the right of sovereign states, subject to treaty obligations, to regulate the entry and expulsion of aliens is recognised in the Strasbourg jurisprudence . . . and implementation of a firm and orderly immigration policy is an important function of government in a modern democratic state. In the absence of bad faith, ulterior motive or deliberate abuse of power it is hard to imagine an adjudicator answering this question other than affirmatively.'[168]

With respect to question (5) this involves the striking of a fair balance between the rights of the individual and the interests of the community. The Secretary of State must exercise his judgment in the first instance. On appeal the adjudicator must exercise his or her own judgment.[169] A reviewing court must assess the judgment which would or might be made by an adjudicator on appeal.

> Decisions taken pursuant to the lawful operation of immigration control will be proportionate in all save a small minority of exceptional cases, identifiable only on a case by case basis.[170]

In these types of cases it has been held that the court or adjudicator is not called upon to judge policy therefore, no question of deference arises.[171] Their duty is to see to the protection of individual fundamental rights, which is the particular territory of the courts.[172]

In *Razgar*[173] a majority of the House of Lords found that there was a threat to the private life of the applicant in that, if the decision was implemented, it might lead him to take his own life. As the Secretary of State had not considered the proportionality of the interference, the majority concluded that he could not certify the claim as manifestly unfounded.[174] In *Ay*,[175] decided before *Razgar*, the Court of Appeal considered the claim that to remove four children to Germany would have a significant impact on their physical and psychological development. It held that it was possible to take into account the message that would be sent if the court decided against the Secretary of State. Considering the medical evidence that the impact would only be for a confined period, it held the Secretary of State was entitled to certify the case that the family's appeal to the adjudicator was bound to fail.[176]

---

[168] *Ibid*, at [19] per Lord Bingham.
[169] The adjudicator must decide for himself or herself, on the merits, whether the removal would be proportionate or not. See *Huang*, above n 15.
[170] *Razgar*, above n 14, at [20].
[171] *Huang*, above n 15, at [62].
[172] *Ibid*, at [55]. In the context of Art 8 private life, *Huang* was applied in *Jegatheeswaran*, above n 100; *Dbeis v Secretary of State for the Home Department* [2005] EWCA Civ 584.
[173] Above n 14.
[174] at [24] per Lord Bingham
[175] *R (on the application of Ay) v Secretary of State for the Home Department* [2003] EWCA Civ 1012.
[176] See also *Djali* and *Mehmeti*, above n 84.

9.2 Other

Also justified on the ground of economic well-being are interferences in the area of taxation. For example, in *Banque Internationale à Luxembourg*[177] the High Court held that, although notices issued by the Inland Revenue requiring specific classes of documents did impinge on private life, there was ample justification

> [f]or the notices were issued according to law, in pursuit of a legitimate aim and necessary in a democratic society for protecting the taxation system and revenue.[178]

The argument in *Robertson*[179] that the supply of the electoral register to commercial interests who utilise it for marketing purposes was justified as the benefits reflect on the economy, was ultimately unsuccessful, the court holding that the sale of the register, absent an individual right of objection, was disproportionate.[180]

---

10. Prevention of Disorder or Crime

Interferences with the right to respect for private life which are in accordance with law and necessary in a democratic society are also possible for the prevention of disorder or crime.

10.1 Evidence Obtained by Secret Filming or Recording

It is not uncommon for evidence to be obtained for criminal and civil trials by secret filming. For example, in *Jones*,[181] in a personal injury claim, the claimant was filmed in her home without her knowledge after the person taking the film obtained access to her home by deception. The Court of Appeal found that there is usually no question of justification in such cases and a breach of Article 8 was found.[182] However, as discussed in the preceding chapter, this does not necessarily mean the evidence will be excluded from the trial.

In criminal proceedings, the court considers whether such evidence adversely affects the fairness of the proceedings and, if it does, may exclude it under section 78 of the Police and Criminal Evidence Act 1984.[183] In civil cases, the breach of Article 8 is a relevant circumstance for the court to weigh in the balance when coming to a decision as to how it should properly exercise its discretion in making orders as to the

---

[177] See, eg *Banque Internationale à Luxembourg*, above n 51.
[178] at [17] in reliance upon *Funke v France* (1993) 16 EHRR 297 and *Chappell v United Kingdom* (1989) 12 EHRR 1. See also *Guyer*, above n 52; *Morgan Grenfell*, above n 38, at [39].
[179] Above n 30.
[180] *Ibid*, at [36]–[39].
[181] Above n 25.
[182] *Ibid*.
[183] *R v P*, above n 36; *R v Loveridge* [2001] 2 Cr App R 591; *R v Mason* [2002] 2 Cr App R 628. See also *R v E* [2004] EWCA Crim 1234, [2004] 1 WLR 3279; *R v Allsopp* [2005] EWCA Crim 703.

management of proceedings.[184] The significance of the evidence will differ according to the facts of the particular case, as will the gravity of the breach of Article 8. The decision will depend on all the circumstances. In *Jones*[185] the Court of Appeal concluded that the conduct was not so outrageous that the defence should be struck out.[186] However, it did note that its disapproval of the conduct of the insurers could be reflected in the orders for costs.[187]

10.2 Fingerprints and DNA Samples

It has been held that the taking of fingerprints and DNA samples from persons suspected of having committed relevant offences is a reasonable and proportionate response to the scourge of serious crime.[188] Although the retention of fingerprints and samples has been held not to engage Article 8(1), on the assumption that it does it has been held that, as Parliament had decided to provide for retention, this legislative choice had to be approached with deference[189] and retention was proportionate. In *S* they were kept only for the limited purpose of the detection, investigation and prosecution of crime. The fingerprints and samples were not of any use without a comparator fingerprint or sample from the crime scene. The fingerprints and samples would not be made public. A person was not identifiable to the untutored eye simply from the profile on the database. Any interference was minimal when compared with the enormous advantages in the fight against serious crime.[190] Furthermore, it was observed that the legislative aim could not be achieved by less intrusive means.[191]

With respect to new technologies which impact on private life in the pursuit of the guilty, the comment has been made that it is of paramount importance that law enforcement agencies should take full advantage of the available techniques of modern technology and forensic science.[192]

10.3 Stop and Search

It is clear that stop and search constitutes an interference with private life. In *Gillan*,[193] in a rather unclear judgment, the Court of Appeal held that the stops and searches carried out were in accordance with law as the Terrorism Act 2000, which allowed the Assistant Commissioner to make the authorisation relied upon, was a

---

[184] *Jones*, above n 25, at [25].
[185] *Ibid*.
[186] *Ibid*, at [28].
[187] *Ibid*, at [30]. See also *McGowan v Scottish Water* [2005] IRLR 167 concerning evidence covertly obtained for the purpose of disciplinary proceedings against an employee. See further D Ormerod, 'ECHR and the Exclusion of Evidence: Trial Remedies for Article 8 Breaches?' [2003] *CLR* 61.
[188] *S*, above n 10, at [3] per Lord Steyn.
[189] *Ibid*, at [33] per Lord Steyn.
[190] *Ibid*, at [38] per Lord Steyn.
[191] *Ibid*, at [40] per Lord Steyn. See further A Roberts and N Taylor, 'Privacy and the DNA Database', [2005] EHRLR 373. See also *Attorney General's Reference (No.3 of 1999)*, above n 37, which concerned a sample which should have been destroyed but eventually resulted in the conviction of the defendant for a serious crime. The House of Lords found no violation of Art 8 and, even assuming there was, held that the evidence was admissible under s 78 of the Police and Criminal Evidence Act 1984.
[192] *R (on the application of S)*, ibid, at [1] per Lord Steyn.
[193] Above n 76.

matter of public record even thought the authorisations were not published.[194] However, the court went on to hold that the onus on the Commissioner of Police to show that the interference with the appellants was lawful was not discharged as the powers were used to police a protest and this was not a lawful use of the power.[195]

10.4 Disclosure of Allegations

Enhanced criminal record certificates issued under section 115 of the Police Act 1997 raise particular issues. They contain information about offences of which the person is suspected of committing even though his responsibility has not been proved. The Chief Constable must be of the opinion that the information might be relevant to a position which involves regularly caring for, training, supervising or being in sole charge of persons under 18 or vulnerable persons aged 18 or over. The information can be highly prejudicial and could 'blight an individual's opportunity to obtain employment in his chosen field.'[196]

The Court of Appeal held in X[197] that the legislation itself did not contravene Article 8.[198] However, it also considered proportionality in relation to the individual claimant. Here the certificate contained allegations of indecent exposure. The claimant had applied for a job which would involve work with those under 18. The court stated that, as long as the Chief Constable was entitled to form the opinion that the information disclosed might be relevant, absent any untoward circumstance, it was difficult to see that there could be any reason why the information that might be relevant ought not to be included in the certificate. But it did accept that it might be disproportionate to include information as to some trifling matter or information which evidence made unlikely to be correct.[199] It also stated that responsibility for forming an opinion was on the Chief Constable, and if that opinion was formed properly it was not for the courts to interfere.[200] It concluded that disclosure was proportionate, holding that if

the claimant was guilty of the conduct alleged, then that conduct would be highly relevant to the question of his employment with children or vulnerable adults. It was information of which the prospective employer should be aware.[201]

10.5 Offender Naming Schemes

Whilst not finally determining the lawfulness or otherwise of the scheme, in $Ellis$[202] the Divisional Court considered an offender naming scheme devised by Essex Police. The scheme involved displaying posters at train stations and other travel locations

---

[194] *Ibid*, at [49].
[195] *Ibid*, at [56].
[196] Above n 47.
[197] *Ibid*.
[198] *Ibid*, at [20].
[199] *Ibid*, at [41].
[200] *Ibid*, at [47].
[201] *Ibid*, at [43]. See also *Maddock v Devon County Council*, Divisional Court, 13 August 2003.
[202] Above n 49.

where it was thought they would have the greatest effect on the itinerant criminal. The first poster would have a picture of an individual who was not recognisable and was not an offender. Above the photograph would appear the words 'If you commit a crime in Brentwood' and below 'Your name and image will be on this poster'. The other poster would contain a photograph of the face of a selected offender and above the photograph would appear the name of the offender, the nature of his offence and the sentence he was serving. Below the picture would appear the words 'If you come to Brentwood to commit crime, expect to do the time'. Offenders selected would be given seven days to register a legal objection to their inclusion, and selection would only follow a risk assessment.

The court pointed out that the lawfulness or otherwise of the scheme would depend on the circumstances of the offender selected. However, it stated that it had in mind that it should not declare unlawful a genuine initiative on the part of the police to reduce crime.[203]

> [W]e have not only to take into account the rights of the offender . . . but those of the public as well.[204]

However, it noted that there was a real question about whether it would ever be appropriate to select a father of young children;[205] further, there was a need for appraisal and monitoring, and a need for a structured assessment of the risks involved.[206] The court was not prepared to declare that the scheme could not be operated lawfully during the trial period.[207]

Similarly, in *Stanley*[208] it was argued that for the police to distribute leaflets and publicise other material carrying the claimants' images, names and ages, and details of anti-social behaviour orders issued against them, was a breach of Article 8. Although noting that those considering post-order publicity in future should have in mind the Convention rights of those against whom orders were made, the court concluded here that the interference was proportionate.

> [W]hether publicity is intended to inform, to reassure, to assist in enforcing the existing orders by policing, to inhibit the behaviour of those against whom the orders have been made, or to deter others, it is unlikely to be effective unless it includes photographs, names and at least partial addresses. Not only do the readers need to know against whom orders have been made, but those responsible for publicity must leave no room for misidentification.[209]

---

[203] *Ibid*, at [32].
[204] *Ibid*, at [33].
[205] *Ibid*, at [35].
[206] *Ibid*, at [37].
[207] *Ibid*, at [39].
[208] *R (on the application of Stanley, Marshall and Kelly) v Metropolitan Police Commissioner* [2004] EWHC (Admin) 2229, [2005] EMLR 3.
[209] *Ibid*, at [40].

10.6 Prisoners

Article 8 does not render unlawful that interference with private life which inevitably follows from a lawfully imposed custodial sentence.[210] However, a custodial order does not wholly deprive a prisoner of all rights enjoyed by other citizens.[211]

In *Daly*[212] the House of Lords held that a blanket policy which required the absence of prisoners when their legally privileged correspondence was opened interfered with Article 8 rights to a much greater extent than necessity required. However, it was possible for a rule to provide for the exclusion of a prisoner while the examination took place if there was reasonably believed to be good cause for excluding him to safeguard the efficacy of the search.[213] In *Ponting*[214] the Court of Appeal held that it was proportionate to require a prisoner not to password-protect the files on his computer and to only print documents in the presence of an appointed member of staff.[215] In *Szuluk*[216] the Court of Appeal held that it was proportionate for the prison medical officer to read the correspondence between a prisoner and his NHS consultant. The need for order and prevention of crime in prisons and secure hospitals also has been held to permit the random recording of and subsequent listening to the outgoing and incoming telephone calls of patients and inmates.[217]

Whilst the seclusion of secure psychiatric patients undoubtedly engages Article 8, it has been held to be justified under Article 8(2) as long as it is carried out in accordance with the Code of Practice issued by the Secretary of State for Health under section 118 of the Mental Health Act 1983. In *Munjaz*[218] the Court of Appeal held that departures from the Code meant that the necessary requirement of legality was not fulfilled.

11. Protection of Health

Interferences with the private lives of those working in the health sector in the interests of health is common and usually proportionate. For example, in *Whitefield*[219] the Privy Council found that the conditions imposed by the General Medical Council on the appellant general practitioner, in order for him to keep his registration, were

---

[210] *R (on the application of Morley) v Nottinghamshire Health Care NHS Trust* [2002] EWCA Civ 1728, [2003] 1 All ER 784.
[211] *Daly*, above n 103, at [5] per Lord Bingham.
[212] *Ibid.*
[213] *Ibid*, at [22] per Lord Bingham
[214] Above n 103.
[215] *Ibid*, at [38] and [40].
[216] Above n 103.
[217] *N*, above n 12. In *R (on the application of Taylor) v The Governor of Her Majesty's Prison Risley*, Administrative Court, 20 October 2004, the court found a call enabling system, requiring the prisoner to makes calls through the use of a PIN number and the prior notification of outside numbers desired to be called, to be compatible with Art 8.
[218] *Munjaz*, above n 75.
[219] Above n 67.

necessary and proportionate. The conditions included a complete ban on the consumption of alcohol, blood and urine testing, and attending Alcoholic Anonymous meetings. In *Woolgar*[220] the court held that it was proportionate for the police to disclose to the UK Central Council for Nursing, Midwifery and Health Visiting the contents of an interview between the claimant and the police. Allegations had been made, including an allegation of overadministration of diamorphine, about the claimant, following the death of a patient in her care.[221]

---

12. Protection of Rights and Freedoms of Others

As with other similarly drafted Convention rights, the 'rights and freedoms of others' is fairly open ended. Nevertheless, the majority of claims have fallen within the purview of another Convention right. These are examined in the following paragraphs.

12.1 Fair Trial

Where the necessity for a fair trial is at issue, this will usually justify interferences with Article 8(1) by requiring, for example, the disclosure of medical records.[222] This is particularly so in relation to Children Act 1989 proceedings.[223] The interests of a fair trial may also require one of the parties to submit to a medical examination, particularly where what is at issue is compensation for physical or psychological injury.[224]

In certain circumstances, an interference with private life may be necessary in order to provide access to court pursuant to Article 6. For example, in *S*[225] the Court of Appeal concluded that a mother should have access to confidential information concerning her son, who was in the local social services authority's guardianship under the Mental Health Act 1983. As his nearest relative she wished to have access to enough information about him to exercise her statutory functions under the Act.

> Proper access to the court therefore requires that she have proper access to legal advice before she sets that process in motion. Proper access to legal advice requires that she have access to the information which will be relevant to the court's decision.[226]

---

[220] *Woolgar v Chief Constable of Sussex Police* [1999] 3 All ER 604.
[221] See also *A Health Authority v X* [2001] EWCA Civ 2014, [2002] 2 All ER 780.
[222] See, eg *B R & C (Children)* [2002] EWCA Civ 1825; *A v X* [2004] EWHC (QB) 447.
[223] *Ibid.* See also *A Health Authority v X* [2001] EWCA Civ 2014, [2002] 2 All ER 780.
[224] See, eg *De Keyser Ltd v Wilson* [2001] IRLR 324. With respect to a fair trial generally and the right to respect for private life, see *Newman*, above n 53.
[225] Above n 34.
[226] *Ibid*, at [41].

12.2 Right to Life

In *Pretty*[227] it was argued that Article 8 conferred a right to self-determination, and the refusal of the Director of Public Prosecutions to undertake that he would not, under section 2(4) of the Suicide Act 1961, consent to the prosecution of Mr Pretty under section 2(1) if he were to assist his wife to commit suicide was incompatible with this right. The House of Lords doubted that Mrs Pretty's rights under Article 8 were engaged at all.[228] Nevertheless, assuming there was an infringement, it went on to consider whether the infringement was justifiable under Article 8(2) and concluded that it was.[229] The basis of the justification was the protection of the vulnerable.

> It is not hard to imagine that an elderly person, in the absence of any pressure, might opt for a premature end to life if that were available, not from a desire to die or a willingness to stop living, but from a desire to stop being a burden to others.[230]

12.3 Private Life

In certain circumstances, it may be necessary to balance the private life of one individual against that of another. For example, in *Evans*,[231] affording considerable deference to Parliament, the Court of Appeal held that the refusal of a fertility clinic, in accordance with the Human Fertilisation and Embryology Act 1990, to treat a woman following the withdrawal of her former partner's consent to the storage and use of the frozen embryos was proportionate.

> The need, as perceived by Parliament, is for bilateral consent to implantation, not simply to the taking and storage of genetic material, and that need cannot be met if one half of the consent is no longer effective. To dilute this requirement in the interests of proportionality, in order to meet Ms Evans' otherwise intractable biological handicap, by making the withdrawal of the man's consent relevant but inconclusive, would create new and even more intractable difficulties or arbitrariness and inconsistency.[232]

12.4 Freedom of Expression

Where respect for private life is asserted via the tort of breach of confidence against a media organisation, the right to freedom of expression is the opposing right placed in the balance.

> [T]he right to privacy which lies at the heart of an action for breach of confidence has to be balanced against the right of the media to impart information to the public. And the right

---

[227] Above n 8.
[228] *Ibid*, at [26] per Lord Bingham.
[229] *Ibid*, at [30] per Lord Bingham, [62] per Lord Steyn, [102] per Lord Hope, [112] per Lord Hobhouse and [112] per Lord Scott.
[230] *Ibid*, at [29] per Lord Bingham and [50] per Lord Steyn. See further D Morris, 'Assisted Suicide under the European Convention on Human Rights: a Critique' [2003] *EHRLR* 65.
[231] Above n 7.
[232] *Ibid*, at [69]. See also *Roddy*, above n 95, where the right to autonomy of one individual was balanced against he rights of others to keep their identities secret.

of the media to impart information to the public has to be balanced in its turn against the respect that must be given to private life.[233]

The same applies where an injunction is sought under the inherent jurisdiction of the High Court to protect identity.[234]

It is clear that one article does not have priority over the other even taking into account section 12(4) of the HRA.[235]

> Any restriction of the right to freedom of expression must be subjected to very close scrutiny. But so too must any restriction of the right to respect for private life. Neither Art.8 nor Art.10 has any pre-eminence over the other in the conduct of this exercise. As Resolution 1165 of the Parliamentary Assembly of the Council of Europe (1998), para. 11, pointed out, they are neither absolute nor in any hierarchical order, since they are of equal value in a democratic society.[236]

Both Articles 8 and 10 are qualified, and the proportionality of interfering with one has to be balanced against the proportionality of restricting the other. 'As each is a fundamental right, there is evidently a "pressing social need" to protect it.'[237] A basic approach is to first examine the comparative importance of the actual rights being claimed in the individual case; then look at the justifications for interfering with or restricting each of those rights; and then apply the proportionality test to each.[238] The means chosen to limit the Article 10 right must be rational, fair and not arbitrary, and impair the right as minimally as is reasonably possible.[239] It is clear that weighing and balancing these factors is a process which may well lead different people to different conclusions.[240]

If the invasion of private life is held to be a matter of legitimate public interest because, for example, a public figure has previously lied about the matter, the claim to freedom of expression will be particularly strong and will often defeat the strongest privacy claim.[241]

> [W]here a public figure chooses to make untrue pronouncements about his or her private life, the press will normally be entitled to put the record straight.[242]

For example, in *Campbell*[243] the House of Lords concluded unanimously that Ms Campbell had no claim in relation to the fact of her drug addiction or to the fact that she was receiving treatment as she had lied about these facts and also sought to

---

[233] *Campbell*, above n 27, at [105] per Lord Hope.
[234] See, eg *Re S*, above n 140.
[235] *Campbell*, above n 27, at [106] and [111] per Lord Hope.
[236] *Ibid*, at [113] per Lord Hope. See also Lord Nicholls at [12]. Also *Re S*, above n 140, at [17] per Lord Steyn.
[237] *Campbell ibid*, at [140] per Baroness Hale.
[238] *Ibid*, at [141] per Baroness Hale. This test was employed by the House of Lords in *Re S*, above n 140 at [17] per Lord Steyn.
[239] *Campbell*, *ibid*, at [115] per Lord Hope with whom Lord Carswell agreed at [167].
[240] *Ibid*, at [168] per Lord Carswell.
[241] See, eg *Campbell*, *ibid*, where the House of Lords unanimously held that Ms Campbell could not seek a remedy in relation to the disclosure of the fact of her drug addiction and the fact that she was receiving treatment as she had previously lied about both.
[242] *Campbell*, *ibid*, at [82] per Lord Hope.
[243] *Ibid*.

benefit from this by comparing herself with others in the fashion business who were addicted. However, in relation to the fact that she was receiving treatment at Narcotics Anonymous, the details of the treatment and the visual portrayal (photograph) of her leaving specific meeting, the majority concluded that the balance was in favour of respect for her private life and the invasion of that right entitled her to damages.[244]

Whilst a public figure was not seeking protection in *Re S*,[245] the House of Lords was required to balance the freedom of the press to report on everything that took place in a criminal court against the right to respect for private life of an eight-year-old boy whose mother was being tried for the murder of his older brother. An order had been granted to prohibit publication of any information which might lead to his identification or that of the mother or deceased child. The House of Lords held that the Article 8 right was not of the same order when compared with the cases of juveniles who were directly involved in criminal trials.[246] Balanced against the importance of the press to report the progress of a criminal trial without restraint, it concluded that injunction should not be granted.

The following five reasons were given. First, adult non-parties to a criminal trial would be added to the prospective pool of applicants who could apply for such injunctions confronting newspapers with an ever wider spectrum of potentially costly proceedings.[247] Secondly, further exceptions to the principle of open justice would be encouraged and would gain in momentum.[248] Thirdly, a report of a sensational trial without revealing the identity of the defendant would be a disembodied trial and informed debate about criminal justice would suffer.[249] Fourthly, it was costly for newspapers to contest an application for an injunction.[250] Finally, local newspapers threatened with the prospect of an injunction were likely to be silenced and this would seriously impoverish public discussion of criminal justice.[251]

12.5 Children

Finally, a number of Article 8 cases have been brought concerning disclosure of information private to an individual concerning allegations of sexual abuse of children. In some cases, the allegation has been investigated and then no further action taken. In others, criminal charges have been brought and the defendant later acquitted. Local authorities have been found to have a power to disclose such information arising by implication from their responsibilities for the welfare and protection of

---

[244] See also *Douglas*, above n 26; *Theakston*, above n 46; *B & C v A*, above n 44; *X v O'Brien*, above n 156. See further discussion of this issue in the chapter concerning freedom of expression.
[245] Above n 140.
[246] *Ibid*, at [27] per Lord Steyn.
[247] *Ibid*, at [32] per Lord Steyn.
[248] *Ibid*, at [33] per Lord Steyn.
[249] *Ibid*, at [34] per Lord Steyn.
[250] *Ibid*, at [35] per Lord Steyn.
[251] *Ibid*, at [36] per Lord Steyn. See also *R v Teeside Crown Court, ex p Gazette Media Co. Ltd* [2005] EWCA Crim 1983; *E v Channel Four*, above n 98; and *Pelling v Bruce-Williams* [2004] EWCA Civ 845, [2004] Fam 155, where the Court of Appeal held that, in Children Act 1989 cases, the time had come for the court to consider in each case whether a proper balance of competing rights required the anonymisation of any report of the proceedings and judgment following a hearing that was conducted in public. See further H Fenwick, 'Clashing Rights, the Welfare of the Child and the Human Rights Act' (2004) 67 *MLR* 889.

children.[252] Nevertheless, such disclosure must still meet the requirements of Article 8. The necessity for disclosure has been considered under a variety of interests listed in Article 8(2), including public safety and prevention of crime. The majority, however, have been considered as an aspect of the protection of the rights of the child.

In *LM*[253] the High Court held that a blanket approach was impermissible and disclosure should only be made if there was a pressing need.

> Disclosure should be the exception, and not the rule. That is because the consequences of disclosure of such information for the subject of the allegations can be very damaging indeed.[254]

The court stated that it was important to take into account its own belief as to the truth of the allegation. At one end of the spectrum is the person who has actually been convicted. At the other is the situation where the allegation has been investigated but it has been concluded that there is no substance to it. The interest of the third party in obtaining the information must also be considered.

> The more intense the legitimacy of the interest in the third party in having the information, the more pressing the need to disclose is likely to be. Thus, at one extreme are local authorities with a statutory responsibility for the protection of children. At the other are members of the public whose sole interest is to expose those whom they consider to be child sex abusers.[255]

The degree of risk posed by the person if disclosure is not made should also be taken into account.

In the present case, the court concluded that a pressing need for disclosure had not been demonstrated. In particular, LM had no criminal record. There had been an internal investigation into the allegations of the first child at the end of which the evidence was destroyed. The allegation of his daughter was not proved. He had worked on a school bus run for the past 12 years and it had never been alleged that he used his position as a school bus driver to indecently assault a child. Similarly he had been involved in teaching children archery for the past 18 years and no allegations had been made.[256]

By contrast, *N v Governor of HM Prison Dartmoor*[257] concerned an actual prior conviction for gross indecency with a child. N challenged the decision of the prison governor to notify local authority social services departments and the probation service that a prisoner who had been in the past convicted of an offence against a child had been received into custody notwithstanding that this conviction was spent for the purposes of the Rehabilitation of Offenders Act 1974. The court concluded that the governor was entitled to communicate this information to the appropriate department of social services.

---

[252] See *R (on the application of A) v Hertfordshire CC* [2001] EWHC (Admin) 211, [2001] ACD 469.
[253] Above n 47.
[254] In reliance upon *R v Chief Constable of North Wales, ex p AB* [1998] 3 FCR 371.
[255] *Ibid*, at 746.
[256] See also *Re S* [2001] EWHC (Admin) 334, [2001] FLR 776.
[257] Administrative Court, 16 February 2001.

[C]hildren are accorded a special place in terms of international Conventions (both UN and ECHR). It is their human rights which have a high need of domestic protection. Against that is the impact of the Governor's decision which would not necessarily lead to any adverse effect on the prisoner's rights. If there is then aggregated with those internationally recognised rights, the state's obligation to afford children every protection, the balance is ineluctably in terms of necessity on the side of the Governor's decision.[258]

The rights of the victims of child abuse may also, in certain circumstances, outweigh any Article 8 right asserted against disclosure of information. For example, in X[259] leave was sought to disclose two documents—the transcript of the judgment given by the judge and the local authority's statement of the threshold criteria in respect of X, who had been accused of child abuse by the local authority, and M, his wife. It was sought to disclose the material to the victims of X's abuse and a limited class of people standing in a close and confidential relationship with them. It was recognised by the court that there would be no further dissemination and no breach of the curtain of privacy, and the disclosure would be for the positive benefit of the children.[260] Particular emphasis was placed on the fact of limited disclosure.[261]

The court accepted that X's rights under Article 8 were implicated; however, these rights were subject to the rights of the victims of his abuse. In particular, the court noted the child's right to obtain from public records information necessary to know and understand their childhood and early development.[262] It concluded that, in a case such as the present, the Article 8 rights of the child victims of sexual and other abuse outweighed the conflicting Article 8 rights of the perpetrator.

There are . . . clear and compelling reasons why these children, the victims of X's abuse, should, by being afforded the disclosure which is sought, be placed in a position where they will be better able to know and to understand their childhood, development and history.[263]

---

[258] *Ibid*, at [26]. See also *R v Smethurst* [2001] EWCA Crim 772, [2002] 1 Cr App R 6.
[259] *In the Matter of X*, Family Division, 21 February 2001.
[260] *Ibid*, at [20].
[261] *Ibid*, at [26].
[262] *Ibid*, at [34] relying on *Gaskin v United Kingdom* (1989) 12 EHRR 36.
[263] *Ibid*. See also *Maddock v Devon County Council*, Divisional Court, 13 August 2003.

Article 8: The Right to Respect for Family Life

1. Introduction

The second right protected by Article 8 is the right to respect for family life. As with the right to respect for private life, this is also not an absolute right and may be subject to interferences in accordance with law and necessary in one of the interests listed in Article 8(2). Prior to the HRA, in the United Kingdom there was an array of laws relating to children and families, but there was no overriding legal principle of respect for family life or a duty to ensure that decisions impacting on family life were proportionate. However, now that the principle of respect for family life is actually part of UK law, it is questionable what impact it has actually had on child and family law—it is often held by the courts that Article 8 has made no difference at all to the approach they take.[1] Nevertheless, this right has had significant impact in other areas, in particular immigration and prisoners' rights, and has the potential for impact in even more, including social security and support. As the meaning of 'family' develops, so too will the reach of this part of Article 8.

2. Family Life

2.1 Definition

Such is the diversity of forms that the family takes in contemporary society that it is impossible to define what it meant by family life.[2] The existence of family life within

---

[1] See, eg *Payne v Payne* [2001] EWCA Civ 166, [2001] 2 WLR 1826.
[2] *Singh v Entry Clearance Officer New Delhi* [2004] EWCA Civ 1075, [2005] QB 608 at [72] per Munby J.

the meaning of Article 8 is essentially a question of fact, depending upon the real existence in practice of close personal ties. Typically the question is whether there is a close personal relationship, one which has sufficient constancy and substance to create de facto family ties.[3]

It is clear that the notion of family life is not confined to families based on marriage and may encompass other relationships, such as those between grandparents and grandchildren[4], uncle and nephew[5], siblings[6] and cousins.[7] In determining whether or not family life exists, it is important to appreciate that there have been profound changes in family life in recent decades.

> [M]any adults and children, whether through choice or circumstance, live in families more or less removed from what until comparatively recently would have been recognised as the typical nuclear family.[8]

2.2 Parents and Children

Close personal ties are usually presumed to exist between children and their natural parents, although exceptionally this presumption may be displaced[9] and does not apply when the child reaches adulthood.[10] A mere time gap in contact between child and parent is not in itself sufficient to indicate that the normal family tie has been broken.[11]

Applications have been brought concerning biological fathers who have no relationship with their child. For example, in *Re J*[12] the Family Division found that D, the biological father of J, of whom he was not aware, did not have a right to respect for his family life with J. His relationship with J's mother was not one of cohabitation and there were no exceptional facts to show that their relationship had sufficient constancy to create de facto family ties.[13] Similarly, in *Leeds Teaching Hospital*,[14] where, following a mix up, Mrs A's eggs had been fertilised with Mr B's sperm rather than that of Mr A her husband, the Divisional Court concluded that Mr B had no right to respect for family life. He was the biological father of the twins but had had no opportunity to forge any relationship with them.[15] By contrast, Mr A had rights

---

[3] *Ibid*, at [79] per Munby J.
[4] *Ibid*, per Dyson LJ in reliance upon *Marckx v Belgium* (1979) 2 EHRR 330. See also Munby J at [58]–[62].
[5] See, eg *R (on the application of L) v Secretary of State for Health*[2001] 1 FLR 406.
[6] See, eg *Senthuran v Secretary of State for the Home Department* [2004] EWCA Civ 950, [2004] 4 All ER 365.
[7] *Singh*, above n 2 per Munby J at [58] in reliance upon *Abdulaziz v UK* (1985) 7 EHRR 471; *Berrehab v Netherlands* (1988) 11 EHRR 322; *Marckx*, above n 4; *Boyle v UK* [1994] 2 FCR 822,.
[8] *Ibid* per Munby J at [63].
[9] *Ibid*, per Dyson LJ at [21].
[10] *Kugathas v Secretary of State for the Home Department* [2003] EWCA Civ 31. In *Evans v Amicus Healthcare Ltd* [2004] EWCA Civ 727, [2005] Fam 1 it was held that a potential mother could not assert a right to family life with a future child whose embryo had not yet been transferred to her.
[11] *R (on the application of Doka) v Immigration Appeal Tribunal* [2004] EWHC (Admin) 3072, [2005] 1 FCR 180.
[12] *Re J (Adoption: Contacting Father)* [2003] EWHC (Fam) 199, [2003] 1 FLR 933.
[13] *Ibid*, at [23].
[14] *Leeds Teaching Hospital NHS Trust v A* [2003] EWHC (QB) 259.
[15] *Ibid*, at [48] in reliance upon *M v Netherlands* (1993) 74 D&R 120.

under Article 8 as he was in the position of father and had established a close relationship with the twins.[16]

However, the situation may be different where a biological father does have a relationship with the child, even if that relationship is not particularly strong. For example, in *Re H*[17] the question was whether or not the natural fathers should be joined as respondents to the adoption proceedings. In each case the mother was unmarried and did not wish to disclose the identity of the father. The Family Division held that not every natural father had a right to respect for family life with regard to every child of whom he may be the father and the application of Article 8 would depend upon the facts of each case.[18]

In the case of H the court found that the parents had a relationship, including cohabitation, that lasted for several years. It broke down before the birth of S but was resumed with a view to reconciliation. Unfortunately the reconciliation failed and the relationship came to an end. The mother of H said that the father was a good dad to S, but a part-time dad, and had no wish to take on a more involved role. However, the father had shown a continuing commitment to S and the fact of the attempted reconciliation underlined to the court that there had also been a genuine commitment to each other, even though the attempt failed. The father had two children by the mother and was in regular contact with one of them. The decision of the mother to bring up S herself and to involve the father in the life of S demonstrated a continuing relationship between them for the benefit of S and was an important factor in illuminating the question of whether there were family ties. The court was satisfied that H was part of a family unit with her father, with the consequence that it gave the father a right under Art 8(1).[19] However, in the joined case of *Re G*, the court concluded that the facts were far less strong—the parents had never cohabited and, their relationship having faded and died, they had lost touch—and there were no exceptional factors to show that the relationship had sufficient constancy to create de facto family ties.[20]

2.3 Adoptive Relationships

The relationship between adoptive parent and child can also give rise to family life within the meaning of Article 8,[21] although it is clear that Article 8 does not guarantee a right to adopt a child.[22] A particularly difficult issue arose in *Singh*,[23] where a six-year-old Indian boy had been adopted by a couple in the United Kingdom. The

---

[16] *Ibid*, at [49]. See also *Re R (a child)* [2003] EWCA Civ 182, [2003] Fam 129, where the court concluded that a man who was neither biological father nor had a relationship with the child but had participated as the mother's partner during IVF treatment had no right to respect for family life.

[17] *Re H; Re G (adoption: consultation of unmarried fathers)* [2001] 1 FLR 646.

[18] *Ibid*, at [38] per Butler-Sloss P in reliance upon *B v UK* [2000] 1 FLR 1; *McMichael v UK* (1995) 20 EHRR 205; *K v UK* (1987) 50 D&R 199; *Keegan v Ireland* (1994) 18 EHRR 342; *Kroon v The Netherlands* (1994) 17 EHRR 263.

[19] *Ibid*, at [44].

[20] *Ibid*, at [51]. See also *Re T (a child) (DNA tests: paternity)* [2001] 2 FLR 1190; *Re M (adoption: rights of natural father)* [2001] 1 FLR 745.

[21] See, eg *Gunn-Russo v Nugent Care Society* [2001] EWHC (Admin) 566, [2002] 1 FLR 1.

[22] *R (on the application of Thomson) v Secretary of State for Education and Skills* [2005] EWHC (Admin) 1378.

[23] Above n 2.

adoption was valid according the law of India but was not recognised by the United Kingdom. He was therefore refused entry clearance to join his adoptive parents.

The adoptive father and natural father were cousins. His natural parents and the sponsors agreed that the appellant should be adopted by the sponsors. The sponsors travelled to India and a religious ceremony took place, as a result of which he was adopted according to the religious laws and practices of the Sikh faith. The arrangement for the transfer of parental responsibility was made at the appellant's birth because the sponsors were unable to have any more children. It was a genuine transfer of responsibility in the sense that it was not an arrangement of convenience to facilitate the appellant's entry into the United Kingdom. There was a genuine change in the appellant's status following his adoption, so that, for example, he had no right to inherit his natural parents' estate. He was cared for by the sponsors when they were in India. They had made all the major decisions about his care and future, including the decision to send him to boarding school when he was five. Since his birth, one or other or both of them have visited India two or three times each year in order to see him. The sponsors communicated with the appellant frequently by telephone, and supported him financially. The appellant was unaware of the adoption and called his natural parents 'uncle' and 'aunt', and was brought up to regard the sponsors as his real parents.[24]

The Court of Appeal unanimously held that family life was established between the child and his adoptive parents in the United Kingdom. Whilst the failure to satisfy the requirements of international instruments was taken into account, it was not decisive. However, it was noted that, if the departure was one of substance rather than procedure and went to the heart of the safeguards the instrument was intended to promote, it may be appropriate to give the adoption order little weight.[25]

3. Interference

Considering that respect for family life entails members of a family being able to share family life together,[26] an interference with this right can arise in a variety of ways, ranging from the imposition of a custodial sentence[27] to the allocation of public housing.[28] It is clear that public authorities are under a negative duty not to interfere with this right as well as a positive duty to ensure that family life is respected. The right also carries with it procedural rights—proceedings engaging the right must be conducted fairly to ensure due respect to the interests protected by

---

[24] *Ibid*, at [40].
[25] *Ibid*, at [33] per Dyson LJ.
[26] *Anufrijeva v Southwark LBC* [2003] EWCA Civ 1406, [2004] QB 1124 at [12] per Lord Woolf CJ.
[27] *R (on the application of P & Q) v Secretary of State for the Home Department* [2001] EWCA Civ 1151; *R (on the application of Stokes) v Gwent Magistrates' Court* [2001] EWHC (Admin) 569.
[28] *Yumsak v London Borough of Enfield* [2002] EWHC (Admin) 280.

Article 8.[29] From the case law, the areas where interferences commonly arise can be identified. These are examined in the following paragraphs.

3.1 Children

3.1.1 Generally

A court order placing a child in care undoubtedly interferes with the right of the child and his or her parents to respect for family life.[30] An order giving permission to a local authority to refuse contact between parents and children taken into care is a further interference.[31] If matters go seriously awry, the manner in which a local authority discharges its parental responsibilities to a child in its care may violate the rights of the child or its parents.[32]

Adoption orders,[33] dispensing with a natural father's consent to an adoption order[34] and orders allowing one parent to remove a child permanently from the jurisdiction[35] also constitute interferences, as may an order to pay child support if it impacts on family relationships with others.[36] Finally, prohibiting babies from remaining with their mothers in prison after they have reached the age of 18 months may also impact on family life. This is not a right which a prisoner should necessarily lose by reason of his or her incarceration.[37]

3.1.2 Procedural Rights

The procedural rights also protected by Article 8 require local authorities to conduct their decision-making processes in relation to children in care fairly and so as to afford due respect to the interests protected by Article 8. '[T]he parents should be involved to a degree which is sufficient to provide adequate protection for their interests.'[38] The protection afforded by Article 8 is not just confined to the trial process and guarantees fairness in the decision-making process at all stages of child protection. The requirements of fairness apply to the other persons and agencies involved in child protection work just as they apply to the local authority.[39] It is also important

---

[29] *Re S* [2002] UKHL 10, [2002] 2 WLR 720.
[30] *Lancashire County Council v Barlow* [2002] 2 AC 147; *Re S, ibid.*
[31] *Re C and B (children) (care order: future harm)* [2002] 2 FCR 614.
[32] *Re S*, above n 29 at [54].
[33] *Re B (a child) (sole adoption by unmarried father)* [2001] UKHL 70, [2002] 1 WLR 258.
[34] *Re B (a child) (adoption order)* [2001] EWCA Civ 347, [2001] 2 FCR 89. But see *Re J*, above n 12.
[35] *Re A (permission to remove child from jurisdiction: human rights)* [2000] 2 FLR 225; *Payne v Payne*, above n 1.
[36] *R (on the application of Denson) v Child Support Agency* [2002] 1 FLR 938; *R (on the application of Plumb) v Secretary of State for Work and Pensions* [2002] EWHC (Admin) 1125.
[37] *P & Q*, above n 27. See also *L*, above n 5, which concerned restrictions on visits by children to patients in high security hospitals; and *R v Secretary of State for the Home Department, ex p Mellor* [2001] EWCA Civ 472, [2002] QB 13 where the court held that in exceptional circumstances denial of access to a life sentence prisoner of facilities for artificial insemination may constitute a breach.
[38] *Re S*, above n 29 at [55] in reliance upon *W v United Kingdom* (1987) 10 EHRR 29. See also *P & Q*, above n 27; *R (on the application of S) v Plymouth City Council* [2002] EWCA Civ 388, [2002] 1 WLR 2583.
[39] *Re C (care proceedings: disclosure of local authority's decision making process)* [2002] EWHC (Fam) 1379, [2002] 2 FCR 673 at [88]–[90].

to remember that Article 6 applies to such proceedings and that many of these rights are absolute, unlike Article 8.[40]

These principles have been applied in many cases. For example, it has been held that, if the parents are to have a fair and adequate opportunity to make representations to the court on whether a care order should be made, the care plan must be appropriately specific.[41] Far more detailed guidance in relation to care proceedings was given in *Re C*.[42] The Family Division held, inter alia, that social workers should, as soon as practicable, notify parents of criticisms of their parenting and advise them how to improve. All professionals involved should keep clear and accurate notes of conversations and meetings. The local authority should make a full and frank disclosure of all key documents at an early stage in the proceedings. Where it was proposed that social workers and/or guardian should meet with expert witnesses, clear written notice of the meeting must be given. The parent must be given the opportunity to make representations, and should be able to attend or be represented at the meeting.[43] It has also been held that Article 8 affords children procedural rights in relation to decision-making processes which fundamentally affect their family life. If the child has sufficient understanding, and direct participation in such proceedings would not pose an obvious risk of harm, separate representation may be required.[44]

Finally, it is important to note that the procedural guarantees are not just limited to care proceedings. The principles also apply in other areas, such as mental health, where, for example, a mother requires access to information about her son in order to exercise her powers as the nearest relative under the Mental Health Act 1983.[45]

3.1.3 Positive Duties

Particularly in relation to children, it is clear that failures on the part of public authorities to act may constitute interferences with the right to respect for family life. For example, failure on the part of a court to join the natural father as a respondent to adoption proceedings even if he has played no part in the child's care or upbringing may constitute an interference.[46] Similar considerations may apply in relation to other biological relatives. In *R*[47] the Family Division held that it would constitute an interference to fail to contact the biological relatives of a small child who did not know of his existence and see if they could offer him a suitable home prior to him being freed for adoption. It has also been held that failure on the part of the court to

---

[40] *Ibid*, at [113].
[41] *Ibid*, at [99]. In *Re D (Children) (care order)* [2003] EWCA Civ 1592 it was held that the irregularities in the proceedings did not justify the unravelling of the care order. See also *Claire F v Secretary of State for the Home Department* [2004] EWHC (Fam) 111, [2004] 2 FLR 517.
[42] Above n 39.
[43] *Ibid*, at [154]. In *C v Bury Metropolitan Borough Council* [2002] EWHC (Fam) 1438, [2003] 2 FLR 868, whilst the Family Division found procedural irregularities, it granted no remedy in relation to the finding that, even if the mother had been informed and involved, the local authority would have reached the same conclusion.
[44] *Mabon v Mabon* [2005] EWCA Civ 634, [2004] 3 WLR 460.
[45] *S*, above n 38.
[46] *Re S (a child) (adoption proceedings: joinder of father)* [2001] 1 FCR 158. See also *Re P (care proceedings: father's application to be joined as a party)* [2001] FLR 781; *Re H*, n 17 above; *Re M (adoption: rights of a natural father)* [2001] FLR 745.
[47] *Z County Council v R* [2001] 1 FLR 365.

order blood and DNA tests to show who is the father of a child, may constitute an interference with the right to respect for family life of the child.[48]

It is under the banner of the positive duty to respect family life that attacks have been directed at specific deficiencies in the system of child protection and family law. For example, in *Re S*[49] it was argued that the Children Act 1989 did not contain an adequate remedy if the local authority failed to discharge its parental responsibilities properly by, for example, failing to implement a care plan, and therefore the rights of the child or parents under Article 8 were violated. The House of Lords did not agree, holding that the possibility that something may go wrong with the local authority's discharge of its parental responsibilities or its decision-making processes and that this would be a violation of Article 8 so far as the child or parent was concerned did not mean that the legislation itself was incompatible or inconsistent with Article 8.[50]

> There is no suggestion in the Strasbourg jurisprudence that absence of court supervision of a local authority's discharge of its parental responsibilities is itself an infringement of Article 8.[51]

However, the House of Lords did state that if a local authority fails to discharge its parental responsibilities properly, and in consequence the rights of parents under Article 8 are violated, 'the parents may, as a longstop, bring proceedings against the authority under section 7 [of the HRA].'[52] It also drew attention to the case where there is no parent able and willing to become involved.

> In this type of case the Article 8 rights of a young child may be violated by a local authority without anyone outside the local authority becoming aware of the violation. In practice, such a child may not always have an effective remedy.[53]

But, in the opinion of their Lordships, this did not mean that the Children Act was incompatible with Article 8.[54]

In relation to contact orders, a concerted effort was made in *F v M*[55] to use Article 8 to bolster the right of a father to contact with his daughter and also her right to contact with him. The Family Division recognised the positive obligation of the court in protecting those rights and noted that the positive obligations extended in principle to the taking of coercive measures not merely against the recalcitrant parent but even against the children.[56] It was also held that the national authorities could not

---

[48] *Re T*, above n 20. In *Leeds Teaching Hospital*, above n 14, it was held that the presumption in the Human Fertilisation and Embryology Act that Mr A was not the father of the twins (his wife had been inseminated with Mr B's semen by mistake) was an interference with his right to respect for family life but his position was safeguarded by the remedies of residence order and adoption. See also *R (on the application of Rose) v Secretary of State for Health* [2002] EWHC (Admin) 1593, [2002] 3 FCR 731, which concerned children conceived by artificial insemination seeking information about donors. The Administrative Court saw the issue as one of identity and private life rather than strictly family life.
[49] Above n 29.
[50] *Ibid*, at [56].
[51] *Ibid*, at [57].
[52] *Ibid*, at [62]–[63].
[53] *Ibid*, at [63] and [113].
[54] *Ibid*, at [64]. See further J Herring, 'The Human Rights of Children in Care' [2002] 118 *LQR* 534.
[55] *F v M* [2004] EWHC (Fam) 727.
[56] *Ibid*, at [30].

shelter behind the applicant's lack of action[57] and that there was no room for complacency about the way in which the courts handle these cases.[58] Although no findings of breach were made, it was observed that the two great vices of the present system were the fact that the system was still almost exclusively court based and that the court's procedures were not working—or not working as speedily and efficiently as they could, and therefore should, be.[59]

3.2 Social Security and Support

It has been held that the right to respect for family life is capable of imposing on the state a positive obligation to provide support. For example, where the welfare of children is at stake, Article 8 may require the provision of welfare support in a manner which enables family life to continue.[60] In J[61] the Divisional Court accepted that, whilst Article 8 did not require the provision of accommodation for a family, if the failure to provide support resulted in a child being taking away from her mother and put into care this would violate Article 8. It concluded that, if all other possible routes to providing accommodation or financial support were inapplicable, the local authority would not be able to justify taking the child into care, thereby separating mother and child, because of difficulties in acquiring accommodation.

> Typically it will be cheaper to provide accommodation (or the finance to acquire it) for the family than to take the child into care, and moreover that step will keep the family together.[62]

However, insofar as any obligation is imposed, it is not absolute.

> Before inaction can amount to a lack of respect for private and family life, there must be some ground for criticising the failure to act. There must be an element of culpability. At the very least there must be knowledge that the claimant's private and family life were at risk.[63]

Breach of a positive legal obligation to provide welfare support may provide the element of culpability necessary to establish a breach of Article 8 provided that the impact on family life is sufficiently serious and foreseeable.[64] Where the complaint is one of delay, an infringement will not be found unless substantial prejudice has been caused to the applicant.[65] There is a need to have regard to resources when considering the obligations imposed.[66]

---

[57] *Ibid*, at [33].
[58] *Ibid*, at [35].
[59] *Ibid*, at [36].
[60] *Anufrijeva*, above n 26, at [43] in reliance upon *J v London Borough of Enfield* [2002] EWHC (Admin) 735, [2002] 2 FLR 1; and *Bernard v London Borough of Enfield* [2002] EWHC (Admin) 2282, [2003] HRLR 4.
[61] *Ibid.*
[62] *Ibid*, at [48].
[63] *Ibid*, at [45] in reliance upon *Osman v UK* (1998) 29 EHRR 245.
[64] *Ibid.*
[65] *Ibid*, at [46].
[66] *Ibid*, at [47].

Clearly, where one is considering whether there has been a lack of respect for Art.8 rights, the more glaring the deficiency in the behaviour of a public authority, the easier it will be to establish the necessary want of respect. Isolated acts of even significant carelessness are unlikely to suffice.[67]

Such glaring deficiency was found by the Administrative Court in the case of *Bernard*.[68] The court held that, following assessments, the defendant local authority was under an obligation to take positive steps, including the provision of suitably adapted accommodation, to enable the claimants and their children to lead as normal a family life as possible, bearing in mind the second claimant's severe disabilities.

Suitably adapted accommodation would not merely have facilitated the normal incidents of family life, for example the second claimant would have been able to move around her home to some extent and would have been able to play some part, together with the first claimant, in looking after their children. It would also have secured her 'physical and psychological integrity'. She would no longer have been housebound, confined to a shower chair for most of the day, lacking in privacy in the most undignified of circumstances, but would have been able to operate again as part of her family and as a person in her own right, rather than being a burden, wholly dependent upon the rest of her family. In short, it would have restored her dignity as a human being.[69]

3.3 Deportation and Entry Clearance

Removal or exclusion or one family member from a state where other members of the family are lawfully resident will not necessarily infringe Article 8 provided that there are no insurmountable obstacles to the family living together in the country of origin of the family member excluded, even where this involves a degree of hardship for some or all members of the family.[70] However, Article 8 is likely to be violated by the expulsion of a member of a family that has been long established in a state if the circumstances are such that it is not reasonable to expect the other members of the family to follow that member expelled.[71] With regard to married couples, Article 8 does not impose any general obligation on a state to respect their choice of residence. Knowledge on the part of one spouse at the time of marriage that the rights or residence of the other were precarious militates against a finding that an order excluding the latter spouse violates Article 8.[72]

Whilst it has not been finally determined whether or not the right to respect for family life applies to entry clearance, in a number of judgments this has been assumed to be the case—it often being characterised as a positive obligation to permit family

---

[67] *Ibid*, at [48]. See also *R (on the application of Q) v Secretary of State for the Home Department* [2003] EWCA Civ 364, [2004] QB 36 at [64]; *Greenfield v Irwin* [2001] EWCA Civ 113, [2001] 1 WLR 1279.
[68] Above n 60.
[69] *Ibid*, at [33].
[70] *R v Secretary of State for the Home Department, ex p Mahmood* [2001] 1 WLR 840 at [55] per Lord Phillips MR. See also *R v Secretary of State for the Home Department, ex p Isiko* [2001] 1 FLR 930; *R (on the application of Samaroo) v Secretary of State for the Home Department* [2001] EWCA Civ 1139; *R (on the application of L) v Secretary of State for the Home Department* [2003] EWCA Civ 25, [2003] 1 All ER 1062; *R (Sandhu) v Secretary of State for the Home Department* [2003] EWHC (Admin) 2152.
[71] *Mahmood, ibid*, at [55].
[72] *Ibid*.

reunion.[73] However, it does not require a state to permit a claimant seeking to enter for family reasons to be permitted to enter, or to remain in the state on public support pending resolution of a disputed claim.[74] Furthermore, considerable delay in the process of family reunion will not necessarily lead to a breach of Article 8. For example, in M[75] the claimant arrived in the United Kingdom from Angola in May 1996 and claimed asylum. His claim was allowed on appeal in January 2001. M then wished to start proceedings for family reunion; however, the letter confirming his grant of refugee status was not received until August 2001. The issue of visas for his family, who were then in Kinshasa, did not take place until November 2002. The Court of Appeal held that, although there were enormous administrative failings, what had happened did not entail a lack of respect for the claimant's family life.[76]

4. Permitted Interferences

The right to respect for family life is not an absolute right and, under Article 8(2), interferences by a public authority with the exercise of the right are possible if they are in accordance with the law and necessary in a democratic society in the interests of national security, public safety or the economic well-being of the country, for the prevention of disorder or crime, for the protection of health or morals, or for the protection of the rights and freedoms of others. Not all of these justifications have been examined under the HRA. Those which have are discussed in the following paragraphs.

5. Economic Well-being of the Country

5.1 Deportation

If there are insurmountable obstacles to the family living together in the country of origin of the family member excluded, or it is not reasonable to expect the other members of the family to follow the family member expelled,[77] the right to respect for

---

[73] See, eg, *Singh*, above n 2; *R (Suresh) v Secretary of State for the Home Department* [2001] EWHC (Admin) 1028; *Sayania v Immigration Appeal Tribunal*, Administrative Court, 5 April 2001; *R (on the application of Singh) v Immigration Appeal Tribunal* [2002] EWHC (Admin) 2096.

[74] *R (on the application of K) v Lambeth London Borough Council* [2003] EWCA Civ 1150, [2004] 1 WLR 272.

[75] one of the appeals considered by the Court of Appeal in *Anufrijeva*, above n 26.

[76] *Ibid*, at [165]. See also *R (on the application of A) v National Asylum Support Service* [2003] EWCA Civ 1473, [2004] 1 WLR 752 at [82]–[83]. In *R (on the application of Montana) v Secretary of State for the Home Department* [2001] 1 WLR 552 it was held that the refusal of British citizenship could not in itself be an interference with family life.

[77] *Mahmood*, above n 70, at [55].

family life will be engaged. In order for the deportation to take place, it must then be shown that the interference is in accordance with the law, necessary in one of the interests set out in Article 8(2) and proportionate to the legitimate public end sought to be achieved.[78] In such cases the interest pursued under Article 8(2) is not usually made clear, the argument being made that removal is simply in the interests of main-taining firm immigration control. In *Isiko*[79] the Court of Appeal stated that the mere fact that the presence of an individual and his family in this country did not in itself constitute a threat to one of the interests enumerated in Article 8(2) did not prevent a decision to enforce a lawful immigration policy from being lawful.[80] Nevertheless, deportation is examined under the heading of economic well-being of the country as, in a few cases, this has been the justification given.[81]

As discussed in the preceding chapter, interferences are always likely to be in accordance with law and where removal is proposed in pursuance of lawful immigra-tion policy and necessary in one of the interests set out in Article 8(2).

> This is because the right of sovereign states, subject to treaty obligations, to regulate the entry and expulsion of aliens is recognised in the Strasbourg jurisprudence . . . and imple-mentation of a firm and orderly immigration policy is an important function of government in a modern democratic state. In the absence of bad faith, ulterior motive or deliberate abuse of power it is hard to imagine an adjudicator answering this question other than affirmatively.[82]

When determining proportionality, the Secretary of State must exercise his judg-ment in the first instance. On appeal the adjudicator must exercise his or her own judgment.[83] A reviewing court must assess the judgment which would or might be made by an adjudicator on appeal.

> Decisions taken pursuant to the lawful operation of immigration control will be propor-tionate in all save a small minority of exceptional cases, identifiable only on a case by case basis.[84]

In these types of cases it has been held that the court or adjudicator is not called upon to judge policy and therefore no question of deference arises.[85] Their duty is to see to the protection of individual fundamental rights, which is the particular terri-tory of the courts.[86]

When applying these principles it is important to note that, in many of the earlier cases, a different test was applied. In the light of the judgments of the House of

---

[78] *R (on the application of Razgar) v Secretary of State for the Home Department* [2004] UKHL 27, [2004] 2 AC 368 at [17] per Lord Bingham.
[79] Above n 70.
[80] *Ibid*, at [36].
[81] See, eg *Samaroo*, above n 70, where it was held that the maintenance of a firm but fair immigration policy was necessary for the economic well-being of the UK and for the prevention of disorder and crime.
[82] *Razgar*, above n 78, at [19] per Lord Bingham.
[83] The adjudicator must decide for himself or herself, on the merits, whether the removal would be propor-tionate or not. See *Huang v Secretary of State for the Home Department* [2005] EWCA Civ 105, [2005] 3 All ER 435.
[84] *Razgar*, above n 78, at [20].
[85] *Huang*, above n 83, at [62].
[86] *Ibid*, at [55].

Lords in *Razgar*[87] and the Court of Appeal in *Huang*,[88] these cases are now of doubtful authority.[89] When determining whether a family life argument will succeed against a proposed deportation, what must be shown is an exceptional case such that the requirement of proportionality requires a departure from the relevant Immigration Rule in the particular circumstances.[90] In *Huang*[91] the Court of Appeal considered three appeals, but it was only in relation to Huang that the court concluded that a tribunal might find her case truly exceptional. Her case was based on the bond between herself and her daughter, who was lawfully settled in the United Kingdom, and her daughter's own family. She had lived in her daughter's household since 2000. The adjudicator found that she was 60 years of age and could not be expected to make the long journey from China to visit her family. Furthermore, her family in the United Kingdom could not be expected to move to China or make trips to visit her.[92]

Whilst it has been held that in the majority of cases there is no need to judge policy and therefore no question of deference arises, there remains a small number of instances where policy does arise and deference is due. *Samaroo*[93] was identified as one of these cases by the Court of Appeal in *Huang*.[94] What made *Samaroo* different was that he was being deported following his conviction for a serious drugs offence. He was married to a British citizen and had been granted indefinite leave to remain as a foreign spouse. There was also one son born to the marriage. It was accepted that a deportation order made in respect of a person convicted of a serious criminal offence was a measure taken in pursuance of a legitimate aim,

> namely the prevention of crime and disorder, and (in the case of serious drug trafficking offences) the protection of the health, rights and freedoms of others.[95]

The remaining question was whether deportation had a disproportionate effect on Samaroo's rights under Article 8(1). As to the test to be applied, the Court of Appeal held that the task for the decision-maker, when deciding whether to interfere with the right, was to strike a fair balance between the legitimate aim on the one hand and the

---

[87] Above n 78.
[88] Above n 83.
[89] See, eg *Mahmood*, above n 70; *Isiko*, above n 70; *Edore v Secretary of State for the Home Department* [2003] EWCA Civ 716, [2003] 1 WLR 2979.
[90] *Huang*, above n 83, at [56].
[91] *Ibid.*
[92] See also *Shala v Secretary of State for the Home Department* [2003] EWCA Civ 233, where what made the case exceptional was the fact that, had the appellant's asylum application been dealt with reasonably efficiently, he would have been likely to have obtained at least exceptional leave to remain as a Kosovo refugee, thereby giving him the ability to apply from within the United Kingdom for a variation in that leave on the grounds of his marriage. The delay meant he had to make his application for leave from outside the UK. However, it was held by the Court of Appeal in *Strbac v Secretary of State for the Home Department* [2005] EWCA Civ 848 that delay is not determinative but only a factor which the decision makier is obliged to consider. See also *Secretary of State for the Home Department v Akaeke* [2005] EWCA Civ 947. Examples where *Huang* has been applied include *R (on the application of Ahmadi) v Secretary of State for the Home Department* [2005] EWHC (Admin) 687; *R (on the application of Lekstaka) v Immigration Appeal Tribunal* [2005] EWHC (Admin) 745; *Mongoto v Secretary of State for the Home Department* [2005] EWCA Civ 751; *Betts v Secretary of State for the Home Department* [2005] EWCA Civ 828.
[93] Above n 70.
[94] Above n 83, at [61].
[95] *Ibid*, at [13] per Dyson LJ, with whom the others agreed.

affected person's Convention rights on the other.[96] It noted that, in reaching its decision, the court must recognise and allow to the Secretary of State a discretionary area
of judgment.[97] And in a case such as the present, it noted that a significant margin of
discretion was required.

> The Convention right engaged is not absolute. The right to respect for family life is not
> regarded as a right which requires a high degree of constitutional protection. It is true that
> the issues are not technical as economic and social issues often are. But the court does not
> have expertise in judging how effective a deterrent is a policy of deporting foreign nationals
> who have been convicted of serious drug trafficking offences once they have served their
> sentences.[98]

It was not incumbent on the Secretary of State to prove that the withholding of a
deportation order in any particular case would seriously undermine his policy of
deterring crime and disorder. What was required was for the Secretary of State to justify a derogation from a Convention right and for that justification to be convincingly
established.[99]

> In asking whether the justification has been convincingly established, the domestic court . . .
> should consider the matter in a realistic manner, and always keep in mind that the
> decision-maker is entitled to a significant margin of discretion . . . The court will interfere
> with the weight accorded by the decision-maker if, despite an allowance for the appropriate
> margin of discretion, it concludes that the weight accorded was unfair and unreasonable.[100]

It concluded that in the present case the interference with Article 8 rights was justified.[101]

5.2 Dispersal of Asylum Seekers

In *Yumsak*[102] the Administrative Court was not satisfied that the decision of the local
authority to place the claimant and her children in temporary accommodation in
Birmingham was a proportionate response to the interference with her family life
that this would entail. There was no evidence that the only way of meeting the
statutory obligation was to send the claimant and her children to Birmingham, 100
miles away.

---

[96] *Ibid*, at [25] in reliance upon *Boughanemi v France* (1996) 22 EHRR 228; *Bouchelkia v France* (1997) 25
EHRR 228; *Mehemi v France* Judgment of 26 September, 1997
[97] *Ibid*, at [35].
[98] *Ibid*, at [36].
[99] *Ibid*, at [39] in reliance upon *Barthold v Germany* (1985) 7 EHRR 383, 403.
[100] *Ibid*, at [39].
[101] *Ibid*, at [40]. See also *R (on the application of Kenya) v SS for the HD* [2004] EWCA Civ 1094; and
Machado v Secretary of State for the Home Department [2005] EWCA Civ 597, which had the added factor
that the claimant was also the husband of an EU national with right of establishment in the United
Kingdom.
[102] Above n 28.

6. Prevention of Disorder or Crime

6.1 Prisoners

The right to respect for family life is not a right necessarily lost by reason of incarceration. However, the desire to avoid disorder in prisons, or the perpetration of crime, usually leads to interferences with the right to respect to family life of prisoners being justified, although there are some exceptions. The case of *P & Q*[103] concerned the challenge of two mothers, both serving substantial prison sentences, to the lawfulness of the formulation and application of the policy of the Prison Service which prohibited babies from remaining with their mothers in prison after they had reached the age of 18 months. The Court of Appeal saw the issue before it as the state's justification for the violations of the right to respect for family life that would be inherent not only in the separation of these two mothers from their 18-month-old children but also in the separation of those children from their mothers.[104]

The court saw the intervention with the right to respect for family life here to be a serious one which required a compelling justification.[105] It found a number of interests to be balanced: those of the state in the proper management of prisons; of the mothers in their family life; and of the children in the protection, not only of their family life but also of their best interests.[106] It held that section 1(1) of the Children Act 1989, making the welfare of the child the paramount consideration, did not govern the court's decision as this dispute was not about separating children from their mothers but about separating mothers from their children.[107] It also took into account the responsibilities of local service authorities to provide a range of services for children in need.[108]

The court concluded that the Prison Service was entitled to have a policy.[109] However, it was not entitled to operate its policy in a rigid fashion however catastrophic the separation may be in the case of a particular mother and child, however unsatisfactory the alternative placement available for the child, and however unattractive the alternative solution of combining day care outside prison compared with remaining in prison with the mother.[110] The policy needed to be flexible to meet its own aims of promoting the welfare of the child and striking a fair balance in accordance with Article 8(2).[111] The court noted that in the great majority of cases the mother and child should be separated at or before the age of 18 months. But it also pointed out that there would be rare exceptions where the interests of the mother and child outweighed other considerations.[112] In the case of P it concluded that the harm done to P's child by separation would not outweigh all the other relevant considerations. In

---

[103] Above n 27.
[104] *Ibid*, at [61].
[105] *Ibid*, at [78].
[106] *Ibid*, at [88].
[107] *Ibid*, at [91].
[108] *Ibid*, at [92].
[109] *Ibid*, at [99].
[110] *Ibid*, at [100].
[111] *Ibid*, at [101]–[102].
[112] *Ibid*, at [106].

the case of Q it found that this might be such an exceptional case as to justify a departure from the policy.[113]

A completely different issue arose in *Mellor*.[114] The appellant was serving a life sentence for murder. He was married and wished to found a family, but the Secretary of State denied his request to have access to facilities for artificial insemination. The Court of Appeal held that the qualifications on the right to respect for family life recognised in Article 8(2) applied equally to the right under Article 12 to found a family. Whilst imprisonment was incompatible with the exercise of conjugal rights and involved an interference with family life and the right to found a family, this was found to be ordinarily justifiable under Article 8(2) taking into account the consequences of imprisonment, public concern and the disadvantage of single parent families. It did appreciate that in exceptional circumstances it may be necessary to relax the imposition of detention in order to avoid a disproportionate interference with a human right. However, it found that a prisoner was not entitled to assert the right to found a family by the provision of semen for the purpose of artificially inseminating his wife.[115] Here, as there were no exceptional circumstances, the court concluded that the prison authorities were not in breach of Articles 8 or 12 by failing to provide assistance with artificial insemination.[116]

6.2 Parenting Orders

In making a parenting order under section 8 of the Crime and Disorder Act 1998, a magistrate must be satisfied that the order is desirable in the interests of preventing any further offence by the child. An order requires the parent in respect of whom it is made to comply with requirements specified in the order and attend counselling and guidance services specified. It is designed to prevent repetition of behaviour in the child which led to a safety order, anti-social behaviour order or sex offender order being made. Such orders have been held to constitute an interference with family life.[117] In *M*[118] the Divisional Court found that such orders were achieving the aim of cutting youth crime and were necessary.[119] In considering proportionality, the court held that deference had to be shown to Parliament as parenting orders were designed to balance the community's right to protection of life, limb and property against the parent's rights to respect for private and family life. The court concluded that sections 8–10 of the Act were compatible with Article 8[120] but found the making of the order in the present case to be irrational, not disproportionate.[121]

---

[113] *Ibid*, at [115]. See also *Claire F*, above n 41.
[114] Above n 37.
[115] *Ibid*, at [39] in reliance upon *X v Switzerland* (1978) 13 D&R 241; *Hamer v UK* (1979) 4 EHRR 139; *Draper v UK* (1980) 24 DR 72; *ELH v UK* (1997) 91A DR 61.
[116] See also *L*, above n 5, which concerned a challenge to the guidance for visits by children to patients in high security hospitals; and *R (on the application of Kpandang) v Secretary of State for the Home Department* [2004] EWHC (Admin) 2130, which concerned detention in order to process an asylum claim.
[117] *R (M) v Inner London Crown Court* [2003] EWHC (Admin) 301, [2003] 1 FLR 994.
[118] *Ibid*.
[119] *Ibid*, at [22] and [61].
[120] *Ibid*, at [67].
[121] *Ibid*, at [74].

6.3 Compellable Witnesses

Only the wife or husband of a person charged is prevented from being a compellable witness under section 80(1) of the Police and Criminal Evidence Act 1984. In *Pearce*[122] it was accepted that to compel the defendant's cohabitee to give evidence against him was an interference with family life but necessary for the prevention of crime.[123] The argument in relation to his daughter was found to be even weaker.[124]

7. Protection of the Rights and Freedoms of Others

The final interest which may justify an interference with the right to respect for family life is the protection of the rights and freedoms of others. It is clear that the 'rights' of others is not limited to Convention rights,[125] and it has been held that too close a definition of the rights and freedoms of others may be too difficult and too restrictive of the variety and development of human interests.[126] Such rights have been held to include the right of a crime victim's family to go about their business with a minimum of anxiety, and without undue restriction on their own movements. This right was held to justify the restriction on the perpetrator for the duration of his release on life licence.[127]

However, the most common justification put forward within this category for interferences with the right to respect for family life is the rights of children—in particular, their right to protection from harm. In addition to the rights of the child protected under Article 8(2), when determining cases where children are involved a court must also have in mind section 1(1) of the Children Act 1989, which provides that, when a court determines any question with respect to the upbringing of a child, the child's welfare shall be the court's paramount consideration. It has been held that where this principle is in conflict with a parent it is overriding.[128] Cases concerning children where the right to respect for family life has been engaged are considered in the following paragraphs.

7.1 Children: Care Orders

It has been held that the provisions of the Children Act 1989 generally and Part IV (care and supervision orders) in particular are compatible with Article 8.[129] It has

---

[122] *R v Pearce* [2001] EWCA Crim 2834, [2002] 1 WLR 1553.
[123] *Ibid*, at [12].
[124] *Ibid*, at [13].
[125] *R (on the application of Craven) v Secretary of State for the Home Department* [2001] EWHC (Admin) 813.
[126] *Ibid*, at [35].
[127] *Ibid*, at [43].
[128] *Payne v Payne*, above n 1, at [82] per Butler-Sloss P in reliance upon *Johansen v Norway* (1996) 23 EHRR 33. See also *Re S (a child) (contact)* [2004] EWCA Civ 18, [2004] 1 FLR 1279 at [15].
[129] *Re V (a child) (care proceedings: human rights claims)* [2004] EWCA Civ 54, [2004] 1 WLR 1433.

also been held that Article 8 is to a lesser or greater extent engaged in each and every application issued by a local authority under Part IV of the Act. In every case where the threshold criteria under section 31 of the 1989 Act are established, the court, in deciding what (if any) order to make, is required to apply the welfare checklist under section 1(3) of the 1989 Act; to balance the competing Article 8 rights to respect for family life of the parties and the child; and to achieve a result which is both proportionate and in the best interests of the child.[130] Furthermore, every court hearing proceedings under Part IV has a duty under section 3 of the HRA to give effect to the provisions of the 1989 Act in a way which is compatible with Convention rights.[131]

Any allegation made in care proceedings pursuant to section 6(1) of the HRA that a local authority has acted in a way which is incompatible with a Convention right, including any allegation which involves a breach of a party's rights under either Article 6 or Article 8 of the Convention, can and should be dealt with in the care proceedings by the court hearing those proceedings under section 7(1)(b) of the HRA. It has been held that it is neither necessary nor desirable to transfer proceedings to a superior level of court merely because a breach of Convention rights is alleged,[132] although it has been recognised that post-care order challenges under the HRA are different.[133]

Cutting off all contact and relationship between a child and his or her family is rarely justified. The principle is that the local authority works to support and eventually to reunite the family unless the risks are so high that the child's welfare requires alternative family care.[134] For example, in Re C and B[135] the Court of Appeal found that care orders in relation to two of the children were disproportionate as the local authority could not justify the early removal and complete severance of all ties between the children and their parents. The court accepted that there were cases where the local authority was not bound to wait until the inevitable harm happened but could intervene to protect a child long before that, but the cases where it was appropriate to do so were likely to involve long-standing problems which interfered with the capacity to provide even 'good enough' parenting in a serious way, such as serious mental illness, a serious personality disorder, intractable substance abuse, evidence of past chronic neglect or abuse, or evidence of serious ill-treatment and physical harm.[136] The court also held that it did not follow that every case where there was a significant risk of harm to a young child should result in a care order in which the care plan was adoption.[137]

It is also clear that a local authority's intervention in the life of a child, although justified at the outset when the care order was made, may cease to be justifiable under

---

[130] Ibid, at [8].
[131] Ibid.
[132] Ibid.
[133] Ibid, at [107] in reliance upon Re L (care proceedings: human rights claims) [2003] EWHC (Fam) 665, [2004] 1 FCR 289.
[134] Re C and B (children) (care order: future harm) [2000] 2 FCR 614.
[135] Ibid.
[136] Ibid, at [30]. See also Re H (a child) (interim care order) [2002] EWCA Civ 1932, [2003] 1 FLR 350. In Barlow, above n 30, the House of Lords held that, where a court was not able to identify whether the parents or the childminder was responsible for the child suffering harm, it was still proportionate to make the care order given the need for caution and restraint.
[137] Ibid, at [30].

Article 8(2).[138] For example, a care order which keeps a child away from his family for purposes which, as time goes by, are not being realised will sooner or later become a disproportionate interference with the child's primary Article 8 rights.[139]

7.2 Children: Contact Orders

When considering a contact order, again the court must take into account the rights of each parent and of the child under Article 8. The court must have the greatest flexibility in deciding on the type and amount of contact allowed according to the circumstances of each individual case.[140] Cutting off all contact and relationship between a child and his or her family is only justified by the overriding necessity of the interests of the child. The aim should be to reunite the family when the circumstances enable it, and the effort should be devoted towards that end.[141] Whilst permission to refuse contact was granted in relation to two of the children in *Re C and B*,[142] the Court of Appeal noted that the local authority would still have a duty to try to promote contact unless this was not reasonably practicable or consistent with the welfare of the children.[143]

7.3 Children: Adoption

Adoption orders also engage the Article 8 rights of the child and his or her parents. The adoption order must meet a pressing social need and be a proportionate response to that need. It has been held that the balancing exercise required by Article 8 does not differ in substance from that undertaken by a court when deciding whether adoption would be in the best interests of the child.[144]

In *Re B*[145] the natural father sought an adoption order with the consent of the mother. Since birth the mother had never met the child nor, save at a distance, seen her. The father had been looking after the child since she was two months old. He sought an adoption order primarily because he was anxious to secure the child's future in his sole care and he would feel more secure knowing that the mother's parental responsibility had been removed. This could only be achieved by an adoption order, and an adoption order would mean that the child was treated in law as if she were not the child of her mother.

The House of Lords held that there must be some reason justifying the exclusion of the other natural parent.

> The reason must be sufficient to outweigh the adverse consequences such an order may have by reason of the exclusion of one parent from the child's life.[146]

---

[138] *Re S*, above n 29, at [54].
[139] *Ibid*
[140] *Re S*, above n 128, at [27].
[141] *Re C and B (children) (care order: future harm)* [2000] 2 FCR 614 at [34]
[142] *Ibid.*
[143] *Ibid*, at [39].
[144] *Re B (sole adoption)*, above n 33, at [31]. See also *Re B (adoption order)*, above n 34; and *Re M (a child) (adoption)* [2003] EWCA Civ 1874, [2004] 1 FCR 157.
[145] *Ibid.*
[146] *Ibid*, at [22].

It pointed out that the circumstances in which it would be in the best interests of a child to make an adoption order in favour of one natural parent alone, thereby taking away one half of the child's legal family, are likely to be exceptional.[147] It upheld the decision of the judge of first instance to make the order as it was in the child's best interests and therefore could not infringe the child's rights under Article 8.

Although in R[148] the Family Division held that it would be an interference with family life to fail to contact the biological relatives of a small child who did not know of his existence and see if they could offer him a suitable home prior to him being freed for adoption, the court held that, as his mother did not want them informed, failing to inform them was necessary and proportionate in the present case for the protection of the child, who could gain nothing from them being informed and who could lose the longer term cooperation and involvement of the mother. Furthermore, the court pointed out that the mother has her own right to respect for her private life and it would be a grave interference to impart this information to people from whom she wanted to keep it secret.

Similarly, in *Re M*[149] the Family Division held that there was no need to inform the natural father regarding the child's adoption. He had no knowledge of the existence of the child and had a history of violence towards the mother. There was

> every reason to be concerned that he has the temperament to cause considerable disruption not only to the stability of the mother's caring for their mutual child F, but also for the prospects of speedy 'home-finding' regarding M.

However, in *Re H*[150] the Family Division held that, balancing the rights of all the parties, the father should be made aware of the proceedings and given an opportunity to take part.[151]

7.4 Children: Removing a Child from the Jurisdiction

Where one parent seeks to remove a child from the jurisdiction, the right to respect for family life of the child and the other parent are engaged, as is often the right to respect for private life of the parent wishing to move. For example, in *Re A*[152] a mother sought the permission of the court to permanently remove the child from the jurisdiction in order to take up a life in New York as she had been offered work there. The Court of Appeal stated that, whilst the child and father had a right to family life, Article 8 also gave the mother a right to her private life.

> In this case it is the right and freedom of the mother and her freedom to live her private life as she wishes and to have the freedom to work where reasonably she chooses to do so.[153]

It concluded permission had been correctly granted by the lower court.

---

[147] *Ibid*, at [27].
[148] Above n 47.
[149] Above n 20.
[150] Above n 17.
[151] *Ibid*, at [48].
[152] *Re A (permission to remove child from jurisdiction: human rights)* [2001] 1 FCR 43.
[153] *Ibid*, at [5].

It has also been held in this area that Article 8 has not necessitated a revision of the fundamental approach to relocation applications formulated by the court. The approach has always been to apply child welfare as the paramount consideration.

[E]ach member of the fractured family has rights to assert and that in balancing them, the court must adhere to the paramountcy of the welfare principle.[154]

In *Payne v Payne*[155] Butler-Sloss P suggested that the following considerations should be in the forefront of the mind of a judge.

(a) The welfare of the child is always paramount. (b) There is no presumption created by s 13(1)(b) in favour of the applicant parent. (c) The reasonable proposals of the parent with a residence order wishing to live abroad carry great weight. (d) Consequently the proposals have to be scrutinised with care and the court needs to be satisfied that there is a genuine motivation for the move and not the intention to bring contact between the child and the other parent to an end. (e) The effect upon the applicant parent and the new family of the child of a refusal of leave is very important. (f) The effect upon the child of the denial of contact with the other parent and in some cases his family is very important. (g) The opportunity for continuing contact between the child and the parent left behind may be very significant.[156]

7.5 Children: Paternity

Whilst the right to respect for family life of a child may extend to him or her discovering his or her true paternity, this must be balanced against the rights of others—particularly rights to respect for private life. For example, in *Re T*[157] the Family Division held that failure on the part of the court to order blood and DNA tests to establish who was the father of the child could constitute an interference with the right to respect for family life of the child. However, it also appreciated that the mother and her husband had a right to respect for their private and family life. Balancing the rights, it held that weightiest was that of the child, namely that he should have the possibility of knowing his true roots and identity.

[A]ny such interference as would occur to the right to respect for family/private life of the mother and her husband, to be proportionate to the legitimate aim of providing T with the possibility of certainty as to his real paternity, a knowledge which would accompany him throughout his life.

A slightly different issue arose in *Leeds Teaching Hospital*.[158] The Divisional Court found that the presumption in the Human Fertilisation and Embryology Act that Mr

---

[154] Above n 1, at [37] in reliance upon *Johansen v Norway* (1996) 23 EHRR 33; *L v Finland* [2000] 3 FCR 219; *Scott v UK* [2000] 2 FCR 560.
[155] *Ibid.*
[156] *Ibid*, at [85]. See also *Re S (a child) (residence order: condition) (No.2)* [2002] EWCA Civ 1795, [2003] 1 FCR 138, where the Court of Appeal held that the exceptional circumstances justified the imposition of a condition on a residence order prohibiting the mother from moving the daughter to live in Cornwall. See also *S v B (a child) (abduction: objections to return)* [2005] EWHC 733.
[157] Above n 20.
[158] Above n 14.

A was not the father of the twins (Mrs A had been inseminated with Mr B's semen by mistake) was an interference with his right to respect for family life.[159] However, it concluded that within the domestic family legislation there were remedies which could underpin and protect the position of Mr A with respect to the twins,[160] namely a residence order to give him parental responsibility[161] and adoption.[162] The court found this remedy to be proportionate to the aim of providing necessary protection to the twins whose rights and welfare must predominate.[163] Although they lost the immediate certainty of the irrebuttable presumption that Mr A was their legal father, they remained within a stable and secure home and retained the great advantage of preserving the reality of their paternal identity.[164]

[159] *Ibid*, at [49].
[160] *Ibid*, at [51].
[161] *Ibid*.
[162] *Ibid*, at [52].
[163] *Ibid*, at [54].
[164] *Ibid*, at [56]–[57].

Article 8: The Right to Respect for Home

1. Introduction

The final right protected by Article 8 considered here is the right to respect for home. In common with other Article 8 rights, this is not an absolute right and can be subject to interference such as in accordance with the law and necessary in one of the interests set out in Article 8(2).

It has been held that 'few things are more central to the enjoyment of human life than having somewhere to live.'[1] It has also been held that the essence of the right lies in the concept of respect for the home as one among various things that affect a person's right to privacy.

> The emphasis is on the person's home as a place where he is entitled to be free from arbitrary interference by the public authorities. Article 8(1) does not concern itself with the person's right to the peaceful enjoyment of his home as a possession or as a property right.[2]

As will be examined later in this book, the latter rights are protected by Article 1 of Protocol No 1, which is often raised in conjunction with the right to respect for home.

As discussed later in this chapter, when considering the right to respect for home the courts have directed particular attention to the word 'respect'. A right to respect for home has been held to be an entirely different concept to a right to a home.[3] The comment has also been made that, at the time of the drafting of the Convention, the intention was to enshrine fundamental rights and freedoms, not to 'engage in social engineering in the housing field.'[4] It is interesting that it is only in relation to this part of Article 8 that the courts have chosen to focus on the qualification made by the addition of 'respect' to the right.

[1] *Harrow London Borough Council v Qazi* [2003] UKHL 43, [2004] AC 983 at [8] per Lord Bingham.
[2] *Ibid*, at [50] per Lord Hope in reliance upon *Marckx v Belgium* (1979) 2 EHRR 330.
[3] See, eg the comments of Lord Home in *Qazi, ibid*, at [69].
[4] *Qazi, ibid*, at [123] per Lord Scott. See also the comments of Lord Millett at [100].

2. Home

The meaning of 'home' is autonomous. What is required is a down-to-earth, pragmatic consideration of whether the place in question is that where a person lives and to which he returns and which forms the centre of his existence. A simple, factual and untechnical test must be applied, taking full account of the factual circumstances and very little of the legal niceties.[5] The meaning of home is not defined by the particular building which a person owns or occupies. As stated above, a person's home is the place where he and his family are entitled to be left in peace free from interference by the state or agents of the state.

> It is an important aspect of his dignity as a human being, and is protected as such and not as an item of property.[6]

In order for premises to be a home, it is not necessary for a person to have a proprietary interest in them. A person may make his home where he has no right to be; and a person may choose not to make his home where he does have a right to live.[7] In *Qazi*[8] the House of Lords held that that the premises were the claimant's home, even though his former wife, a joint tenant, had served a notice to quit on the landlord, thereby terminating the tenancy. He had lived at the premises for eight years. The house had been his home and he had no other.

> The expiry of his wife's notice to quit brought his right to occupy the house as a tenant to an end, but it did not bring his occupation to an end. The house continued to be the place where he lived and so his home.[9]

A home includes a caravan occupied by a gypsy regardless of whether or not the gypsy is living in the caravan on a site in breach of planning control.[10] It also includes the site occupied by travelling show-people and travellers.[11] A NHS facility for the long-term disabled constitutes a home.[12] In *C*[13] the Administrative Court held that, for many patients, accommodation provided by a health authority frequently constituted their only home.[14] Business premises may also come within the meaning of

---

[5] *Qazi, ibid*, at [8]–[10] per Lord Bingham in reliance upon *Gillow v UK* (1986) 11 EHRR 335 and *Buckley v UK* (1996) 23 EHRR 101.

[6] *Qazi, ibid*, at [89] per Lord Millett.

[7] *Qazi, ibid*, at [97] per Lord Millett. See also *Royal Borough of Kensington and Chelsea v O'Sullivan* [2003] EWCA Civ 371, [2003] 2 FLR 459.

[8] *Ibid*.

[9] *Ibid*, at [11] per Lord Bingham. See also [29] per Lord Steyn and [68] per Lord Hope.

[10] *South Bucks District Council v Porter* [2003] UKHL 26, [2003] 2 AC 558..

[11] *Davis v Tonbridge & Malling Borough Council* [2004] EWCA Civ 194; *R (Fuller) v Chief Constable of the Dorset Police* [2001] EWHC (Admin) 1057, [2003] QB 480.

[12] *R v North and East Devon Health Authority, ex p Coughlan* [2001] QB 213. See also *R (on the application of Phillips) v Walsall Metropolitan Borough Council* [2001] EWHC (Admin) 789.

[13] *R (on the application of C) v Brent, Kensinton, Chelsea and Westminster Mental Health NHS Trust* [2002] EWHC (Admin) 181, [2002] Lloyd's Med Rep 321.

[14] at [38] per Newman J.

home. It was accepted with no argument in *Miller Gardner*[15] that Article 8 was engaged by a search of the solicitor's premises for material relating to a particular client.[16] Home may also constitute a hotel room where someone is continuing their private life away from their normal residence.[17]

It is possible for premises to cease being a home. In *Le Roi*[18] the appellant had erected two buildings on agricultural land, adapted these to residential purposes and from time to time lived there. The Court of Appeal pointed out that, at the time of the enforcement action under planning legislation, he was not actually living on the premises and

> therefore the effect of having to demolish will not in fact be that he is deprived of accommodation, even though he may be forced to live in less agreeable circumstances than he otherwise would.[19]

3. Interference

An interference with the right to respect for home can arise in a variety of ways. The main categories into which interferences fall are examined in the following paragraphs.

3.1 Planning

It is clear that decisions within the planning field have the potential to interfere with the right to respect for home. For example, enforcement action by the local planning authority to secure the removal of a gypsy from a site involves an interference with the gypsy's right to respect for home.[20] A measure which prevents a traveller from residing in his vehicle on identified land also interferes with the right.[21] However, the loss in value of a home as a result of a planning decision has been held not to constitute an interference.[22]

It has also been held that not every loss of amenity involves a breach of Article 8. In *Lough*[23] a group of residents complained that the development of a site in the Bankside area would lead to a loss of privacy, a loss of light, a loss of a view and interference with television reception. The Court of Appeal held that, whilst Article 8

---

15 *R (on the application of Miller Gardner Solicitors) v Minshull Street Crown Court* [2002] EWHC (Admin) 3077.
16 See also *Office of Fair Trading v X* [2003] EWHC (Comm) 1042, [2004] ICR 105.
17 *R v Hardy* [2003] EWCA Crim 3092.
18 *Salisbury District Council v Le Roi* [2001] EWCA Civ 1490.
19 *Ibid*, at [31] per Buxton LJ.
20 *Porter*, above n 10, in reliance upon *Buckley*, above n 5, and *Chapman v UK* (2001) 33 EHRR 399.
21 *Fuller*, above n 11.
22 *Lough v First Secretary of State* [2004] EWCA Civ 905, [2004] 1 WLR 2557 at [51].
23 *Ibid*.

required respect for the home and protection for the environment of the home, it created no absolute right to amenities currently enjoyed.

> Its role though important, must be seen in the context of competing rights, including rights of other landowners and of the community as a whole.[24]

It further held that the contents of Article 8(2) threw light on the extent of the right in Article 8(1) and concluded that the degree of seriousness required to trigger a lack of respect for the home depended on the circumstances but had to be substantial.[25]

> [T]he reasonableness and appropriateness of measures taken by the public authority are relevant in considering whether the respect required by Article 8(1) has been accorded.[26]

In the present case it found no interference with the right to respect for home.[27]

3.2 Proceedings for Possession

Difficult issues have arisen in relation to the question of whether or not Article 8(1) is engaged by proceedings to recover possession of a home. In *Qazi*[28] a majority of the House of Lords concluded that any attempt to evict a person, whether directly, indirectly or by process of law, from his or her home was 'a derogation from the respect to which the home is prima facie entitled'[29] and therefore Article 8 was engaged.[30] However, as discussed later in this chapter, a different majority[31] determined that it was not necessary for a court to consider whether the making of an order for possession would be proportionate.[32]

3.3 Care Homes

A number of cases have been brought concerning respect for home and the proposed closure of care homes. Prior to the coming into force of the HRA, it was held in *Coughlan*[33] that the closure of an NHS facility for the long-term disabled constituted

---

[24] *Ibid*, at [41].

[25] *Ibid*, at [43].

[26] *Ibid*.

[27] *Ibid*, at [46]. Other planning decisions include *Vallen International Limited v Secretary of State for Transport, Local Government and the Regions* [2002] EWHC (Admin) 1107, [2002] 21 EG 145 (CS); *R (on the application of Morgan) v Secretary of State for Transport, Local Government and the Regions* [2002] EWHC (Admin) 2652; *Massingham v Secretary of State for Transport, Local Government and the Regions* [2002] EWHC (Admin) 1578; *Cranage Parish Council v First Secretary of State* [2004] EWHC (Admin) 2949.

[28] Above n 1.

[29] *Ibid*, at [70] per Lord Hope.

[30] *Ibid*, per Lord Hope at [71], Lord Millett at [103], Lord Bingham at [23] and Lord Steyn at [27].

[31] Lords Hope, Millett and Scott.

[32] See also *Mayor and Burgesses of the London Borough of Lambeth v Howard* [2001] EWCA Civ 468; *Poplar Housing and Regeneration Community Association v Donoghue* [2001] EWCA Civ 595, [2001] QB 48; *Sheffield City Council v Hopkins* [2001] EWCA Civ 1023, [2001] 26 EG 163 (CS); *St Brice v London Borough of Southwark* [2001] EWCA Civ 1138, [2002] 1 WLR 1537; *R (McLellan) v Bracknell Forest Borough Council* [2001] EWCA Civ 1510, [2002] QB 1129.

[33] Above n 12.

an interference with the right to respect for home. However, in *Phillips*[34] the Administrative Court held that, whilst it was ready to assume that in the present context Article 8 required the council permanently to provide a home for the applicants, this did not mean that the council could not substitute one home for another and this would not constitute an interference.[35] This reasoning was doubted in *C*,[36] where it was held by the Administrative Court in relation to the closure of a hospital for the mentally ill that it was plain that a health authority having the responsibility for the long-term care of mental patients and their placement in appropriate accommodation was required to act compatibly with Article 8.[37] Similarly, in *Madden*,[38] which concerned a challenge to the proposed closure of two residential homes, the Administrative Court held that Article 8 was engaged.[39]

Even though a local authority has contracted out its obligations to a private company, in certain circumstances its actions could still be construed as involving a lack of respect for the right to home. For example, in *Haggerty*[40] proceedings were brought against a council in relation to its decision not to enter into a new contract with a private company which operated a private nursing home. It was argued that this decision had led to the private company deciding to close the home. However, the Administrative Court was not satisfied that Article 8 was engaged, holding that there was no cogent evidence of disruption.[41] A great deal had been done to ensure the move was as undisruptive as possible.

> [T]he individual assessments of all residents have been carried out . . . the Council has agreed to liase with the claimants' expert consultant psychiatrist on the best ways of moving the claimants so as to reduce any risk to them.[42]

3.4 Environmental Pollution

Whilst there have been very few cases decided on this basis under the HRA, it is clear that environmental pollution can also constitute an interference with respect for home. For example, in *Dennis*[43] it was held that the effect of noise from Harrier jet fighters on the claimant's estate constituted an interference with Article 8 rights.[44] However, the argument in *Westminster City Council*[45] by a group of residents that the congestion charge would result in an increase in traffic in their area with consequential noise and air pollution would constitute a violation of Article 8 was not

---

[34] Above, n 12.
[35] *Ibid*, at [11] per Lightman J.
[36] Above n 13.
[37] *Ibid*, at [38] per Newman J.
[38] *R (on the application of Madden) v Bury Metropolitan Borough Council*[2002] EWHC (Admin) 1882.
[39] *Ibid*, at [68] per Richards J.
[40] *R (on the application of Haggerty) v St Helens Council*[2003] EWHC (Admin) 803.
[41] *Ibid*, at [58] per Silber J.
[42] *Ibid*, at [59] per Silber J. See also *McKellar v Mayor & Burgesses of the London Borough of Hounslow* [2003] EWHC (QB) 3145.
[43] *Dennis v Ministry of Defence* [2003] EWHC (QB) 793, [2003] 19 EG 118 (CS).
[44] *Ibid*, at [61].
[45] *R (on the application of Westminster City Council) v Mayor of London*[2002] EWHC (Admin) 2440.

successful. The Administrative Court held that evidence of such effects had to be reasonable and convincing, and here it was not.[46]

3.5 Criminal Justice

It is also possible for interferences to arise in the field of criminal justice. For example, a police search of premises constituting a home undoubtedly engages Article 8(1).[47] A condition of bail requiring an accused person to present himself at the door of his home if required to by a police officer has been held to constitute an interference,[48] as has a licence condition preventing an individual access to his home.[49] A confiscation order may also result in an interference if it results in the sale of a home. For example, in Re A[50] it was held that the sale of a home to satisfy a criminal confiscation order made against her husband was an interference with the wife's Article 8 rights.[51]

---

4. Positive Duties

The right to respect for home does not just entail refraining from interference; in certain circumstances a positive duty of respect may arise—although there are limits. For example, there is no positive right to require the state to provide a home,[52] nor is the state required to provide housing benefit.[53] It has also been held that Article 8 imposes no duty on a council to exercise its powers so as to provide an adequate number of gypsy sites.[54]

---

[46] *Ibid*, at [115] per Maurice Kay. See also *Andrews v Reading Borough Council* [2005] EWHC (QB) 256, where it was held that an increase in road and traffic noise constituted an interference with the right to respect for private life; and *Arscott v The Coal Authority* [2004] EWCA Civ 892, [2005] Env LR 6, where it was held that developing land so that floodwater damaged someone else's property constituted an interference.

[47] *R (on the application of Rottman) v Commissioner of Police of the Metropolis* [2002] UKHL 20, [2002] 2 WLR 1315.

[48] *R (on the application of CPS) v Chorley Justices* [2002] EWHC (Admin) 2162.

[49] *R (on the application of Davies) v Secretary of State for the Home Department* [2004] EWHC (Admin) 1512.

[50] [2002] EWHC (Admin/Fam) 611, [2002] 2 FCR 481.

[51] See also *R v Goodenough* [2004] EWCA Crim 2260, [2005] 1 Cr App R (S) 88; and *R v Ahmed* [2004] EWCA Crim 2599, [2005] 1 WLR 122.

[52] *Wandsworth LBC v Michalak* [2002] EWCA Civ 271, [2003] 1 WLR 617 at [18]; *R (on the application of W) v Lambeth London Borough Council* [2002] EWCA Civ 613, [2002] 2 All ER 901 at [85]; *O'Sullivan*, above n 7, at [46]; *R (on the application of J) v Enfield London Borough Council* [2002] EWHC (Admin) 432, [2002] 2 FLR 1.

[53] *R (on the application of Painter) v Carmarthenshire County Council Housing Benefit Review Board* [2001] EWHC (Admin) 308.

[54] *Chichester District Council v The First Secretary of State*, Administrative Court, 29 July 2003 at [36]; *Codona v Mid-Bedfordshire District Council* [2004] EWCA Civ 925, [2005] HLR 1.

A failure to grant planning permission may amount to an interference with the right to respect for home,[55] as may failures to act resulting in pollution and damage to a home. In *Marcic*[56] it was held by the House of Lords that the failure to construct new sewers with a greater capacity, leading to serious and repeated external flooding of a person's home, constituted an interference. The courts are wary of judicial creativity in the field of social housing responsibilities. Nevertheless, it has been held that local authority landlords are obliged to take steps to ensure that the condition of houses let for social housing are such that Article 8 rights are not infringed.[57]

Where local authorities have contracted out functions to a private company, positive obligations under Article 8 may require them to ensure the ongoing protection of the right to respect for home. In *Heather*[58] the Court of Appeal held that, if the local authority had made the arrangements with the private company after the HRA had come into force, it would arguably be possible for a resident to require the local authority to enter into a contract with its provider which fully protected the resident's Article 8 rights.[59] Finally, it is important to remember that, as Article 8 protects both substantive and procedural rights, an interference can also arise from a failure to consult.[60]

5. Permitted Interferences

In common with the other rights protected by Article 8, it is possible to interfere with the exercise of the right to respect for home if such interference is in accordance with the law and necessary in a democratic society in the interest of national security, public safety or the economic well-being of the country, for the prevention of disorder or crime, for the protection of health or morals, or for the protection of the rights and freedoms of others. The justifications that have been put forward under the HRA for interferences with respect for home are examined in the following paragraphs.

6. For the Prevention of Disorder or Crime

Searches of a home by police following arrest are generally sought to be justified on the ground of prevention of crime. In *Rottman*[61] a majority of the House of Lords

---

[55] See, eg *Chichester District Council v The First Secretary of State* [2004] EWCA Civ 1248, [2005] 1 WLR 279.
[56] *Marcic v Thames Water Utilities Ltd* [2003] UKHL 66, [2004] 2 AC 42.
[57] *Lee v Leeds City Council* [2002] EWCA Civ 6, [2002] 1 WLR 1488.
[58] *R (on the application of Heather) v Leonard Cheshire* [2002] EWCA Civ 366, [2002] HLR 893.
[59] *Ibid*, at [34].
[60] See, eg *C*, above n 13.
[61] Above n 47.

concluded that the common law power of police to search for and seize any goods or documents following an arrest under section 8 of the Extradition Act 1989 had the legitimate aim in a democratic society of preventing crime, and was necessary in order to prevent the disappearance of material evidence after the arrest of a suspect.

> The power is proportionate to that aim because it is subject to the safeguards that it can only be exercised after a warrant of arrest has been issued by a magistrate or a justice of the peace in respect of an extradition crime and where the evidence placed before him would, in his opinion, justify the issue of a warrant for the arrest of a person accused of a similar domestic offence.[62]

Confiscation orders have raised issues under a number of Convention rights, including Article 6 and Article 1 of Protocol No 1. Where it is necessary to sell a home to satisfy a criminal confiscation order, Article 8 rights may also be involved. In *Re A*[63] it was argued that it was a disproportionate interference with a wife's Article 8 rights to sell the matrimonial home to satisfy a criminal confiscation order made against her husband. The court held that it must exercise its powers in a way which was compatible with the Convention and having regard to a number of potentially conflicting rights and interests: the wife's right to respect for her private life and her home under Article 8; the husband's right to liberty under Article 5 and his right under Article 1 of Protocol No 1 to use his assets to discharge his liabilities; and the interests of the prosecutor, representing the public's interest in the prevention of crime, the protection of health and the protection of the rights and freedoms of potential victims of drug traffickers.[64] It concluded that there was a compelling case for making an order that would allow the wife to go on living in the house.[65]

Finally, an unusual bail condition which required the accused to present himself at the door of his accommodation if required to do so by a police officer has also been held to be necessary for the prevention of crime.[66]

7. Economic Well-being of the Country

7.1 Care Home Closures

Resources arguments feature heavily in HRA cases concerning care home closures. Usually such arguments are successful, although in *Coughlan*[67], a pre-HRA case, such arguments did not prevail. In this case, the Court of Appeal concluded that the price of the saving was to be

---

[62] *Ibid*, at [80] per Lord Hutton. See also *Miller Gardner*, above n 15.
[63] Above n 50.
[64] *Ibid*, at [171].
[65] *Ibid*, at [221].
[66] *CPS*, see above n 48, at [32].
[67] Above n 12.

not only the breach of a plain promise made to Miss Coughlan but, perhaps more importantly, the loss of her only home and of a purpose-built environment which had come to mean even more to her than a home does to most people.[68]

Post-HRA, it appears that this outcome was unusual. For example, in C,[69] which concerned the closure of a hospital for the mentally ill, it was appreciated that the NHS Trust, in accordance with the principle of proportionality, had to strike a fair balance between the interference with the claimants' Convention rights in connection with Harefield Lodge and the requirements of other patients for whom the Trust was responsible, and to involve the claimants in the process of making the decision so that it was sensitive to the needs of the claimants.[70] No breach of Article 8 was found. Similarly, in *Haggerty*,[71] when considering Article 8(2), the Administrative Court pointed out that the financial resources of the council were an important element to be considered in the balancing exercise and justified the decision here not to enter into a new contractual arrangement with the private company. The court noted that a local authority was obliged by statute and entitled to take into consideration resources when deciding how to meet individual needs.[72] It also found that the council was entitled to a substantial degree of deference relating to the way in which it allocated its resources and provided services.

These are matters very much within the expertise of a local authority and with which a court should only interfere where the evidence is very clear.[73]

7.2 Standards of Public Housing

Whilst it has been held that a local authority landlord is under a positive obligation to keep houses which it has let for social housing in such a condition that Article 8 rights are not infringed, resources considerations are still important. In *Lee*[74] the Court of Appeal held that the steps which a public authority will be required to take in order to ensure compliance with Article 8 'must be determined, in each case, by having due regard to the needs and resources of the community and of individuals.'[75] The allocation of resources to meet the needs of social housing was seen as very much a matter for democratically determined priorities. The court found no support in domestic or Strasbourg jurisprudence for the proposition that Article 8 imposed some general and unqualified obligation on local authorities in relation to the condition of their housing stock.[76] However, the court was careful to point out that this did not mean that there would never be cases where a local authority, as the landlord of a dwelling house let for the purpose of social housing which was unfit for human

---

[68] *Ibid*, at [92].
[69] Above n 13.
[70] *Ibid*, at [39].
[71] *Haggerty*, above n 40.
[72] *Ibid*, at [60].
[73] *Ibid*, at [61]. See also *Phillips*, above n 12; *R (on the application of Cowl) v Plymouth City Council* [2001] EWCA Civ 1935, [2002] 1 WLR 803; *Madden*, above n 38; *R (on the application of Dudley) v East Sussex County Council* [2003] EWHC (Admin) 1093; *McKellar*, above n 42.
[74] Above n 57.
[75] *Ibid*, at [49].
[76] *Ibid*.

habitation or in a state prejudicial to health, would be in breach of the positive duty. But it had not been shown that there had been a breach in the present cases.[77]

7.3 Management of Sewage and Drainage

Whilst flooding arising from overloaded sewers undoubtedly has the potential to interfere with someone's respect for their home, resources considerations play a considerable role in determining whether or not such interference is justified. For example, in *Marcic*[78] the House of Lords accepted that the repeated and serious external sewer flooding arising from overloaded sewers endured by Mr Marcic was prima facie a violation of Article 8. However, it saw the issue as whether or not the statutory scheme as a whole was Convention compliant. In its view, the role of the domestic policy maker should be given special weight and a fair balance struck between the interests of the individual and those of the community as a whole. In the present case

> the interests Parliament had to balance included, on the one hand, the interests of customers of a company whose properties are prone to sewer flooding and, on the other hand, all the other customers of the company whose properties are drained through the company's sewers. The interests of the first group conflict with the interest of the company's customers as a whole in that only a minority of customers suffer sewer flooding but the company's customers as a whole meet the cost of building more sewers.[79]

Their Lordships concluded that the scheme whereby a general drainage obligation was imposed on a sewerage undertaker but enforcement of this obligation was entrusted to an independent regulator and decisions of the Director General of Water Services were subject to judicial review struck a reasonable balance.[80]

> [T]he malfunctioning of the statutory scheme on this occasion does not cast doubt on its overall fairness as a scheme. A complaint by an individual about his particular case can, and should, be pursued with the Director pursuant to the statutory scheme, with the long stop availability of judicial review. That remedial avenue was not taken in this case.[81]

There was some concern about the uncertain position regarding payment of compensation to those who suffer flooding while waiting for flood alleviation works to be carried out.

> [I]n principle, if it is not practicable for reasons of expense to carry out remedial works for the time being, those who enjoy the benefit of effective drainage should bear the cost of paying some compensation to those whose properties are situated lower down in the catchment area and, in consequence, have to endure intolerable sewer flooding, whether internal or external . . . the flooding is the consequence of the benefit provided to those making use

---

[77] *Ibid*, at [50]. See also *Fuller*, above n 11, where the court held that the eviction of travellers from a site was necessary in the interests of the economic well-being of the country as the council wished to have a contract for the conversion of compost carried out there.
[78] Above n 56.
[79] *Ibid*, at [42].
[80] *Ibid*, at [43].
[81] *Ibid*.

of the system . . . The minority who suffer damage and disturbance as a consequence of the inadequacy of the sewerage system ought not to be required to bear an unreasonable burden.[82]

However, not finding a violation, their Lordships merely stated that this was a matter for the Director and others to reconsider in the light of the facts of the present case.[83]

---

8. Protection of the Rights and Freedoms of Others

8.1 Generally

Similarly to other Convention rights, the 'rights and freedoms of others' is interpreted broadly. In the context of respect for home, the 'rights of the community' generally or the 'public interest' feature heavily as justifications. For example, in *Dennis*[84] it was held that the noise of Harrier jets flying over the claimant's estate was justifiable in the public interest but that a fair balance could not be struck without the payment of compensation to the claimants.[85] In *Lough*[86] it was argued that the development of a site in the Bankside area would interfere with the Article 8 rights of residents. Although holding that there was no interference, the Court of Appeal went on to consider questions of proportionality, noting that Article 8 had to be seen in the context of competing rights, including rights of other landowners and the community as a whole.[87] It also noted that a certain margin of appreciation was to be granted to the public authority.[88] Here the court found that the correct balance had been struck by the Inspector, taking into consideration such matters as the removal of an unsightly building, the provision of affordable housing and the contribution to the regeneration of this area of London.[89]

Included within the concept of 'rights of others' are two categories where a number of applications have been brought. The first is concerned with preservation of the environment and the second with proceedings for recovering possession and the allocation of public housing. These are considered in the paragraphs below.

---

[82] *Ibid*, at [45].
[83] *Ibid*. In *Arscott*, above n 46, the Court of Appeal held that the common enemy rule, which in this case prevented an action in nuisance being brought where land had been developed so that floodwater flooded someone else's property, was compatible with Art 8 as it struck the correct balance between the interests of persons whose homes and property were affected.
[84] Above n 43.
[85] *Ibid*, at [63].
[86] Above n 22.
[87] *Ibid*, at [41].
[88] *Ibid*, at [43].
[89] *Ibid*, at [47]. See also *Mountney v Treharne* [2002] 2 FLR 406 and *Barca v Mears* [2004] EWHC (Ch) 2170, [2005] 2 FLR 1, where it was held the rights of others included the rights of a bankrupt's creditors; *Westminster City Council*, above n 45, concerning the legitimate aim of reducing congestion in central London; and *Davies*, above n 49, where it was held that the rights of the victims of a perpetrator of sexual abuse justified a licence condition excluding him from his own home on his release.

8.2 Public Interest in Preserving the Environment

The enforcement of planning laws often involves interfering with the right to respect for someone's home. When determining whether or not such interferences are justified, usually it is argued that the interference is proportionate to the public interest in preserving the environment. For example, in *Porter*[90] the House of Lords considered the grant of injunctions against gypsies on the application of local planning authorities under section 187B of the Town and Country Planning Act 1990 ordering the removal of mobile homes occupied on sites in breach of planning permission. The House of Lords concluded that, when asked to grant injunctive relief under section 187B, the court must consider whether, on the facts of the case, such relief was proportionate in the Convention sense and grant relief only if it judges it to be so.[91]

> Proportionality requires not only that the injunction be appropriate and necessary for the attainment of the public interest objective sought—here the safeguarding of the environment—but also that it does not impose an excessive burden on the individual whose private interests—here the gipsy's private life and home and the retention of his ethnic identity—are at stake.[92]

In striking the balance, the House of Lords held that a number of factors were present and again endorsed the approach of the Court of Appeal.[93] The Court of Appeal had held that the judge should not grant injunctive relief unless he would be prepared, if necessary, to contemplate committing the defendant to prison for breach of the order, and that he would not be of this mind unless he had considered for himself all questions of hardship for the defendant and his family if required to move, including the availability of alternative sites, the family's health and education. Countervailing considerations were also important, such as the need to enforce planning control in the general interest, the planning history of the site, the degree and flagrancy of the postulated breach of planning control, considerations of health and safety, and previous planning decisions.[94] The Court of Appeal also highlighted the relevance of the local authority's decision to seek injunctive relief. 'They, after all, are the democratically-elected and accountable body principally responsible for planning control in their area.'[95]

A similar approach in relation to travelling show-people was taken by the Court of Appeal in *Davis*,[96] the court confirming that this was a two-stage process. First, the court must look at the planning merits of the matter and accord respect to the local planning authority's conclusions. And secondly, it should consider for itself, in the light of the planning merits and any other circumstances, whether to grant injunctive relief.[97] Here the court held that the lower court was entitled to reach the conclusion

---

[90] Above n 10.

[91] *Ibid*, at [37] per Lord Bingham and [53] per Lord Steyn.

[92] *Ibid*, quoting from the judgment of the Court of Appeal [2001] EWCA Civ 1549, [2002] 1 WLR 1359 at [41].

[93] *Ibid*, at [38]–[42].

[94] *Ibid*, at [38]. See also *Clarke v Secretary of State for Transport, Local Government and the Regions* [2002] EWCA Civ 819.

[95] *Ibid*, at [39]. See also *Coates v South Bucks DC* [2004] EWCA Civ 1378, [2005] BLGR 626.

[96] Above n 11.

[97] *Ibid*, at [37].

that the combination of the seriousness of the environmental damage caused by the planning violation in respect of this highly sensitive site and the appellant's deliberately unlawful conduct in commencing and persisting in it for some three years outweighed the hardship that they would suffer in having to leave it.[98]

This approach applies not only where injunctive relief is sought, but also at the stage of planning permission. For example, in *Chichester District Council*[99] the claimant gypsies sought planning permission to use land they owned as a private gypsy site with mobile homes and associated outbuildings. A majority of the Court of Appeal held that the inspector was entitled to take account of the limited environmental harm caused by the presence of the caravan sites in this location, and to balance that limited harm against the factors that weighed in the gypsies' favour.

> The latter properly included the fact that the council had, on the inspector's findings, failed to fulfil its role as local planning authority for Chichester, in pursing the national planning objective of seeking to meet the accommodation needs of gypsies.[100]

8.3 Proceedings for Possession

As discussed in the paragraphs above, it has been established that any attempt to evict a person, whether directly, indirectly or by process of law, from his or her home is an interference with the right to respect for home.[101] However, the correct approach to the application of Article 8(2) in such cases is far from clear. At the heart of the case in *Qazi*[102] was the question of whether, having regard to the provisions of Article 8(1), it was lawful for a public authority to recover possession from a former tenant by a procedure which led to possession being granted automatically, or whether the court must always be given an opportunity to consider whether the making of an order for possession would be proportionate.[103] Mr Qazi had stayed on in the house after his former wife, a joint tenant, had served a notice to quit on the landlord, thereby terminating the tenancy.

Lord Hope stated that the joint tenancy had been brought to an end by the service of a tenant's notice to quit and that the position in domestic law was that, in these circumstances, the whole of the joint tenancy was terminated. Therefore, the county court had no discretion as to whether or not it should grant an order for possession and the making of an order for possession followed automatically.[104] His Lordship's understanding of European jurisprudence led him to the conclusion that Article 8(2) was met where the law afforded an unqualified right to possession on proof that the tenancy had been terminated. He held that such interference with the right to respect

---

[98] *Ibid*, at [64]. See also *South Buckinghamshire District Council v Cooper* [2004] EWHC (QB) 155; *Brazil v Secretary of State for Transport, Local Government and the Regions* [2001] EWHC (Admin) 991; and *Lee v Secretary of State for Local Government, Transport and the Regions*, Administrative Court, 13 March 2003, regarding Art 8 considerations at the stage of grant of planning permission.
[99] Above n 55.
[100] *Ibid*, at [91]. See also *R (on the application of Evans) v First Secretary of State* [2005] EWHC (Admin) 149.
[101] *Qazi*, above n 1.
[102] *Ibid*.
[103] *Ibid*, at [36] per Lord Hope.
[104] *Ibid*, at [74].

for home which came from the application of the law enabling the public authority landlord to recover possession did not violate the essence of the right to respect for the home.[105]

Similarly, Lord Millett held that, whilst Article 8(2) might call for a balance to be struck, no such balancing exercise need be conducted where the outcome was a forgone conclusion.[106] In his view, the fact that a person could not be evicted without a court order did not mean that the court, as a public authority, was bound in each case to consider whether an order for possession would be disproportionate.[107]

> In most cases the statutory scheme established by Parliament will provide the objective justification for the council's decision to seek possession, which need not be demonstrated on a case by case basis.[108]

Lord Scott, having concluded that there was no interference with Article 8(1), did not discuss Article 8(2) but agreed with Lords Hope and Millett that the case should not be remitted to the County Court. Both Lords Bingham and Steyn dissented on this point, holding that the domestic law procedures should be subjected to scrutiny for conformity with the Article 8(2) standards and the issue of justification remitted to the county court. Therefore, whilst a majority determined that the appeal should be dismissed, there was no majority decision on whether or not Article 8(2) should be considered.[109]

The conclusion of Lords Hope and Millett that there is no need to consider Article 8(2) on a case-by-case basis as the balance has already been struck by the legislature is problematic. Although Mr Qazi's application to the European Court of Human Rights was declared inadmissible, in *Price*[110] the Court of Appeal held that this did not implicitly endorse the reasoning of the House of Lords.[111] Furthermore, the Court of Appeal held that the conclusion in *Qazi* was incompatible with the judgment of the European Court of Human Rights in *Connors v United Kingdom*.[112]

> The decision in *Connors* is unquestionably incompatible with the proposition that the exercise by a public authority of an unqualified proprietary right under domestic law to repossess its land will never constitute an interference with the occupier's right to respect for his home, or will always be justified under Article 8(2). To that extent *Connors* is incompatible with *Qazi*.[113]

---

[105] *Ibid*, at [83].
[106] *Ibid*, at [103].
[107] *Ibid*, at [108].
[108] *Ibid*, at [109]. See also the comments of Lord Bingham in *Porter*, above n 10, at [37] and Lord Clyde at [90].
[109] For a critique of this judgment see I Loveland, 'The Impact of the Human Rights Act on Security of Tenure in Public Housing' [2004] *PL* 594. See also M Davis and D Hughes, 'An End of the Affair—Social Housing, Relationship Breakdown, and the Human Rights Act 1998' (2004) *CPL* 19.
[110] *Price v Leeds City Council* [2005] EWCA Civ 289, [2005] 1 WLR 1825.
[111] *Ibid*, at [15].
[112] Judgment of 27 May, 2004.
[113] *Ibid*, at [26].

However, despite this conclusion, the Court of Appeal held that it was bound to follow *Qazi* even though it also stated that it would give permission, if sought and not successfully opposed, to appeal to the House of Lords.[114]

Although difficult to follow, it appears that the judgment of the majority in *Qazi* is in keeping with judgments in the Court of Appeal. For example, in *Howard*[115] the Court of Appeal considered a possession order sought against a secure tenant under section 84 and Part I of Schedule 2 to the Housing Act 1985 on the ground of nuisance or annoyance to neighbours. Such ground, if it is reasonable to do so, allows an outright or suspended possession order. The court recognised that, in situations where the law affords an unqualified right to possession on proof of entitlement, it may be that Article 8(2) is met, but held that the present case was not of this class.[116] Here it concluded that an outright possession order was necessary to protect the tenant's neighbour and her daughter.

> It meets a pressing social need. It is proportionate to that need in the straightforward sense that nothing less will do and that it is an acceptable means of achieving a legitimate aim.[117]

By contrast, in *Donoghue*[118] a claim for possession had been made by a housing association on termination of an assured shorthold tenancy. Under section 21 of the Housing Act 1988 the court has to make an order for possession if there is a tenancy to which the subsection applies and the appropriate notice has been given. There was no requirement for the court to be satisfied that it was reasonable to make the order. Although Article 8(2) was not applied to the circumstances of the case, unlike the House of Lords in *Qazi*, the Court of Appeal did consider the compatibility of section 21(4) with Article 8.

First, it paid considerable attention to the fact that Parliament intended, when enacting section 21(4),

> to give preference to the needs of those dependent on social housing as a whole over those in the position of the defendant. The economic and other implications of any policy in this area are extremely complex and far-reaching. This is an area where, in our judgment, the courts must treat the decisions of Parliament as to what is in the public interest with particular deference.[119]

It concluded that the defendant's lack of security was due to her low priority under the legislation because she was found to be intentionally homeless.

---

[114] *Ibid*, at [33]. But see *Kay v London Borough of Lambeth* [2004] EWCA Civ 926, [2005] QB 352, where the Court of Appeal held that *Qazi*, above n 1, was compatible with *Connors*, above n 112.

[115] Above n 32.

[116] *Ibid*, at [32].

[117] *Ibid*, at [39]. In *St Brice*, above n 32, the Court of Appeal considered a secure tenancy under s 82(1) of the Housing Act 1985 on which, before and order for possession could be made, the court had to be satisfied that there existed one of the specified grounds for making the order and that it was reasonable to make the order. The court concluded that proportionality was to be considered when the order was made and there was no burden on the local authority or court to ensure that each step taken towards eviction was also proportionate. See also *Hopkins*, above n 32.

[118] Above n 32.

[119] *Ibid*, at [69].

She was and must be taken to be aware that she was never more than a tenant as a temporary measure. In the case of someone in her position, even if she is a mother of young children, it is perfectly understandable that Parliament should have provided a procedure which ensured possession could be obtained expeditiously and that Poplar should have availed itself of that procedure.[120]

Furthermore, the court pointed out that tenants in the position of the defendant had remedies other than under section 21(4) which were relevant when considering Article 8.

There are provisions for appeal against the decision that a person is intentionally homeless. There is the regulatory role of the Corporation and there is the ombudsman. There is also the fact that RSLs are subject to considerable guidance as to how they use their powers.[121]

It concluded that, despite its mandatory terms, section 21(4) did not conflict with her right to family life.[122]

Similarly, in *McLellan*[123] the Court of Appeal considered the 'macro' question of whether or not section 127 of the Housing Act 1996 was incompatible with Article 8. Provided that a local authority followed the correct procedure for terminating an introductory tenancy under section 127, the county court was obliged to make a possession order. Finding that it was very much for Parliament to make the relevant judgments in the area, the court found the scheme justified under Article 8(2).[124] It concluded that the review procedure (the tenant has the right to a review of that decision by the authority) and judicial review provided adequate protection for a possible breach of Article 8.[125]

Finally, in *Smart*[126] the Court of Appeal summarised the competing approaches, noting that, in relation to secure tenancies and planning control, the court possessed a discretion and therefore in such cases had to make a decision as to whether, based on the particular facts, the authority's actions were necessary or proportionate to the statutory aim in view.[127] However, it also noted that not all statutory regimes were like that, and some gave the court no discretion but required the order to be made against the tenant or occupant upon certain conditions being satisfied.[128] It stated that, where Parliament has established, in the context of a particular sector in the public housing field, a scheme for the creation and distribution of housing authorities' duties such that the authority was entitled (on certain conditions being met) to demand possession of let property from a tenant,

---

[120] *Ibid*, at [70].
[121] *Ibid*, at [71].
[122] *Ibid*, at [72]. Although the case was determined on the basis of the right to respect for family life, it would appear to fit more comfortably with the right to respect for home.
[123] Above n 32.
[124] *Ibid*, at [47].
[125] *Ibid*, at [64]. See also *Somerset County Council v Isaacs* [2002] EWHC (Admin) 1014, [2002] 25 EG 151 (CS), concerning proceedings for possession under the Caravan Sites Act 1968; and *The Mayor and Burgesses of the London Borough of Merton v Williams* [2002] EWCA Civ 980, [2002] 30 EG 133 (CS).
[126] *Sheffield City Council v Smart* [2002] EWCA Civ 4, [2002] ACD 56.
[127] *Ibid*, at [31].
[128] *Ibid*, at [32]. *Donoghue* and *McLellan*, above n 32, were cited as examples.

art 8(2) exonerates the authority of any liability under art 8(1) arising from the tenant's eviction if it has acted fairly and reasonably in conformity with the scheme.[129]

In the present case, possession proceedings had been brought against non-secure tenants following complaints of nuisance from the neighbours. The court concluded that, if it were here to hold that, by force of Article 8(2), the appellants were entitled to have the county court judge or judicial review court decide on the facts whether the eviction was disproportionate, 'we would in effect thereby convert the non-secure tenancies enjoyed by homeless persons into a form of secure tenancy.'[130] It held that such a state of affairs would not be consistent with the scheme of Part VII of the Housing Act 1996 for the assistance of homeless persons:

> [S]o long as she remains housed as a homeless person, the policy of the scheme is to allow the council to obtain her eviction upon service of a good notice to quit.[131]

A sharp distinction has been drawn between 'unqualified' rights to possession, at issue in *Qazi*, *Donoghue*, *McLellan* and *Smart*, and 'qualified' rights to possession where the court possesses a discretion, or margin of judgment, as to what order should be made. It is only in relation to qualified rights that the court must apply Article 8(2) and decide whether or not the authority's actions are proportionate. In relation to unqualified rights, although it did not happen in *Qazi*, it is possible to question whether or not the statutory regime itself is compatible with Article 8. It is also important to note that, even where an unqualified right to possession is at issue, there may be an exceptional case where it might be permissible to raise Article 8 grounds by way of defence to possession proceedings in the county court.[132] In *Smart* the Court of Appeal recognised that, at the stage of the trial of the possession proceedings, there might be the rare case where something wholly exceptional had happened since service of the notice to quit which fundamentally altered the rights and wrongs of the proposed eviction and the court judge might be obliged to address it in deciding whether or not to make an order for possession.[133] It concluded that, in these extremely limited circumstances in which an Article 8(2) point may arise at the stage of trial of the possession proceedings, the trial judge must deal with it, and it was not necessary for the county court judge to adjourn for application to be made by the tenant for relief by way of judicial review in the Administrative Court.[134]

---

[129] *Ibid*, at [35].

[130] *Ibid*, at [37].

[131] *Ibid*. See also *Michalak*, above n 52; *O'Sullivan*, above n 7; *R (on the application of Gangera) v London Borough of Hounslow* [2003] EWHC (Admin) 794. Whilst none of these cases has concerned private parties, the observation was made by Lord Millett in *Qazi*, above n 1, at [109], that it made no difference that the landlord was a public authority.

[132] *Qazi, ibid*, per Lord Hope. Lord Millett held that in the exceptional case, judicial review proceedings could be brought, at [110]. See also *Hounslow LBC v Adjei* [2004] EWHC (Ch) 207.

[133] *Ibid*, at [40].

[134] at [45]. See also *Michalak*, above n 52; *O'Sullivan*, above n 7; *Gangera*, above n 131.

14

Article 10: The Right to Freedom of Expression

1. Introduction

Article 10 provides that everyone has the right to freedom of expression. This right includes freedom to hold opinions and to receive and impart information and ideas without interference by public authority and regardless of frontiers. Furthermore, Article 10 does not prevent states from requiring the licensing of broadcasting, television or cinema enterprises. The right to freedom of expression is not an absolute right and, under Article 10(2), it may be subject to such formalities, conditions, restrictions or penalties as are prescribed by law and are necessary in a democratic society in one of the interests there set out.

Before the Human Rights Act 1998 came into force, the right to freedom of expression enjoyed considerable protection in the context of particular torts and statutory wrongs and via the common law. In early cases, freedom of expression or freedom of speech was referred to exclusively as a liberty or freedom, and although the term 'right' was used, it was clear that it was actually 'liberty' that was meant.[1] In the late 1970s there was a change in terminology and judges began referring to the 'right' to freedom of expression, sometimes the 'constitutional right' to freedom of expression.[2] In many cases, Article 10 was also mentioned.[3] Now that the HRA is in

---

[1] See, eg *R v Secretary of State for Home Affairs, ex p O'Brien* [1923] 2 KB 361; *Silkin v Beaverbrook Newspapers Ltd* [1958] 2 All ER 516; *Webb v Times Publishing Co. Ltd* [1960] 2 QB 535.

[2] See, eg *Cassell & Co v Broome* [1972] 2 WLR 645 per Lord Kilbrandon at 726; *Harman v Secretary of State for the Home Department* [1982] 2 WLR 338 per Lord Scarman at 351; *Secretary of State for Defence v Guardian Newspapers Ltd* [1984] 3 WLR 986 per Lord Fraser at 1001.

[3] See, eg *R v Lemon* [1979] 2 WLR 281 at 315 per Lord Scarman; *Associated Newspapers Group Ltd v Wade* [1979] 1 WLR 697 at 708–9 per Lord Denning; *A-G v BBC* [1980] 3 WLR 109 at 130 per Lord Scarman; *Schering Chemicals Ltd v Falkman Ltd* [1981] 2 WLR 848 at 862, 864 per Lord Denning. It is possible that this development was driven by the finding of a violation of Art 10 by the European Court of Human Rights in *Sunday Times v UK* (1979) 2 EHRR 245.

force, it is widely thought that Article 10 reinforces and gives greater weight to the principles already established in our case law.[4]

Unlike other Convention rights, when considering Article 10 it is important to remember the common law protection which operates alongside the HRA. Section 11 of the HRA makes it clear that a person's reliance on a Convention right does not restrict any other right or freedom conferred on him. Where freedom of expression is threatened, as Lord Steyn noted in *Reynolds*,[5] there are now actually three routes to protection: first is the principle of liberty—that individuals are free to do whatever is not specifically forbidden by law[6]; secondly, there is a constitutional right to freedom of expression[7]; and thirdly, there is Article 10, which is given further effect in domestic law by the HRA. In this chapter the focus will be predominantly on the interpretation of Article 10.

Finally, by way of introduction it is essential to note the importance with which the right to freedom of expression is regarded by the courts. It is widely recognised that there is a public interest per se in freedom of expression and freedom of the press.[8] Judicial observations are often made as to why the right is fundamental. One example is the comments of Lord Bingham in *R v Shayler*[9]:

> Modern democratic government means government of the people by the people for the people. But there can be no government by the people if they are ignorant of the issues to be resolved, the arguments for and against different solutions and the facts underlying those arguments.

The importance with which freedom of expression is regarded is reflected in the fact that, where freedom of expression is at issue, deference to the primary decision maker is rarely shown. However, it is important to note that this may also be influenced by the fact that cases concerning freedom of expression are less controversial and generally do not involve difficult moral questions or difficult political questions such as immigration[10] or the allocation of resources. Furthermore, given the pre-HRA protection afforded to freedom of expression, it is possible that judges are simply more comfortable with upholding this right despite the views of the primary decision maker.

---

[4] *Venables v News Group Newspapers Ltd* [2001] WLR 1038 at [36].
[5] *Reynolds v Times Newspapers Ltd* [1999] 4 All ER 609.
[6] See, eg *R v Secretary of State for the Home Department, ex p Simms* [2000] 2 AC 115 and *Redmond-Bate v Director of Public Prosecutions* [2000] HRLR 249.
[7] See, eg *Simms, ibid.*
[8] See, eg *Ashdown v Telegraph Group Ltd* [2001] EWCA Civ 1142, [2001] 3 WLR 1368.
[9] [2002] UKHL 11, [2002] 2 WLR 754 at [21].
[10] Except in *R v Secretary of State for the Home Department, ex p Farrakhan* [2002] EWCA Civ 606, [2002] 3 WLR 481.

2. Expression

The term 'expression' includes a wide range of material and actions, such as the written word, spoken word, web pages,[11] photographs,[12] archived material[13] and advertisements.[14] Also included is behaviour. For example, in *Percy*[15] the Divisional Court confirmed that it was protected expression for the appellant, whilst protesting at an American airbase, to deface the American flag with the words 'Stop Star Wars' and stand on it.[16] Behaviour may take the form of a performance. In *Pay*[17] it was held that the claimant's hobby of a circus-related fire act was protected expression within Article 10.

In order to be protected, the expression does not have to pass a test of quality or truth.[18] There is no need for there to be an identifiable special public interest in any particular material being published, and it is not for the courts to act as censors or arbiters of taste.[19] Article 10 protects in substance and in form a right to freedom of expression which others may find insulting.[20] For example, in *O'Shea*[21] the Divisional Court held that a pornographic advertisement, which may have been regarded by many as squalid and degrading to women and distasteful, was a form of protected expression. In *Perrin*[22] the Court of Appeal held that a web page showing people covered in faeces, coprophilia or coprophagia and men involved in fellatio was protected expression. In *Norwood*[23] the Divisional Court held that a poster containing the words 'Islam out of Britain' with a photograph of the World Trade Centre in flames was protected expression.[24]

Whist it is rare for a court to find that expression is not protected under Article 10, it is possible. In *Thomas*[25] the Court of Appeal considered whether or not to strike out the particulars of a claim under the Protection from Harassment Act 1997 on the ground that the course of conduct did not constitute harassment within the meaning

---

[11] *R v Perrin* [2002] EWCA Crim 747.

[12] *Douglas v Hello! Ltd* [2001] QB 967.

[13] *Loutchansky v Times Newspapers Ltd (No.2)* [2001] EWCA Civ 1805, [2002] 2 WLR 640.

[14] *Smithkline Beecham plc v Advertising Standards Authority* [2001] EWHC (Admin) 6, [2001] EMLR 23; *R (on the application of British American Tobacco UK Ltd) v The Secretary of State for Health* [2004] EWHC (Admin) 2493.

[15] *Percy v DPP* [2001] EWHC (Admin) 1125, [2002] Crim LR 835.

[16] See also *R (on the application of Laporte) v Chief Constable of Gloucestershire Constabulary* [2004] EWCA Civ 1639, [2005] QB 678 and R (on the application of Brehony) v Chief Constable of Greater Manchester Police [2005] EWHC (Admin) 640.

[17] *Pay v Lancashire Probation Service* [2004] ICR 187.

[18] *Reynolds*, above n 5.

[19] *B & C v A* [2002] EWCA Civ 337, [2002] 3 WLR 542 at [11].

[20] *Percy*, above n 15, at [27].

[21] *O'Shea v MGN Ltd* [2001] EMLR 40 at [37].

[22] *Perrin*, above n 11. For the purposes of s 1(3) of the Obscene Publications Act 1959 the court held that a person publishes an article who transmits data: 'there is publication for the purposes of section 1(3) both when images are uploaded and when they are downloaded' at [18].

[23] *Norwood v Director of Public Prosecutions* [2003] EWHC (Admin) 1564, [2003] Crim LR 888.

[24] See also *Re Roddy (a child) (identification: restriction on publication)* [2003] EWHC (Fam) 2927, [2004] 2 FLR 949; *Hammond v Director of Public Prosecutions* [2004] EWHC (Admin) 69. See generally A Geddis, 'Free Speech Martyrs or Unreasonable Threats to Social Peace?—Insulting Expression and Section 5 of the Public Order Act 1986' [2004] *PL* 853.

[25] *Thomas v News Group Newspapers* [2001] EWCA Civ 1233, [2002] EMLR 4.

of the Act. The parties agreed that the publication of press articles calculated to incite racial hatred of an individual provided an example of conduct which was capable of amounting to harassment under the Act.[26] It was also agreed that the right to freedom of expression did not extend to protect remarks directly against the Convention's underlying values.[27] Whilst the court did not comment on this the discussion indicated its approval particularly its observation that such publications constitute an abuse of the freedom of the press.[28]

A claim to freedom of expression may also be weakened where someone is seeking entry clearance to the United Kingdom to express their views. In *Farrakhan*[29] the Court of Appeal held that, whilst Article 10 required the authorities of a state to permit those within its boundaries freely to express their views, even if these are deeply offensive to the majority of the community, it did not believe that it followed that those authorities should be obliged to allow into the state a person bent on giving its citizens such offence.[30]

---

3. Medium, Manner and Timing of Communication

Also protected by Article 10 are the medium, manner and timing of communication. Often the medium of communication is of particular importance. In *Hirst*[31] the Home Secretary had denied a serving prisoner's request that he be entitled, in certain circumstances, to speak to the media by telephone on matters of legitimate public interest relating to prisons and prisoners. In the Home Secretary's view, he could exercise his right to freedom of expression by expressing his views in writing. The Administrative Court disagreed and found the blanket ban to be a disproportionate interference.[32] However, a different approach was taken by the Court of Appeal in *Farrakhan*.[33] When concluding that Mr Farrkhan's exclusion from the United Kingdom was proportionate, the court took into account the very limited extent to which his right to freedom of expression was restricted as he remained free to disseminate information and opinions within the United Kingdom by any means of communication other than his presence in the country.[34]

---

[26] *Ibid*, at [37].
[27] *Ibid*.
[28] *Ibid*, at [50]. The court referred to *Jersild v Denmark* (1994) 19 EHRR 1 at [35] and *Lehideux and Isorni v France* (1998) 5 BHRC 540. It found little assistance in First Amendment jurisprudence from the United States. It is possible for other forms of harassment under the Act to constitute protected expression. See, eg *Silverton v Gravett*, Divisional Court, 19 October 2001 and *Emerson Developments Ltd v Avery* [2004] EWHC (QB) 194.
[29] Above n 10.
[30] *Ibid*, at [33].
[31] *Hirst v Secretary of State for the Home Department* [2002] EWHC (Admin) 602, [2002] 1 WLR 2929.
[32] *Ibid*, at [88].
[33] Above n 10.
[34] *Ibid*, at [77].

Whilst in certain circumstances the manner of communication may be protected, in *Percy*[35] the Divisional Court noted that the appellant could have demonstrated her message in a way which did not involve the use of a national flag of symbolic significance to her target audience. Nevertheless, this was only one factor and was not decisive.[36] Finally, the perishable nature of news is often referred to in the context of protecting the timing of a communication. It has been held that an important aspect of freedom of speech is that one should be able to publish what one wishes but also to do so when one wishes.[37] 'News is a perishable commodity. Public and media interest in topical issues fades.'[38]

---

4. Freedom to Receive and Impart Information and Ideas

Expressly included in the right to freedom of expression set out in Article 10(1) is the freedom to receive and impart information and ideas. However, this aspect of Article 10 has been the subject of little litigation under the HRA. In *Ashdown*[39] the court made clear that the freedom to convey information and ideas extended to the freedom to convey ideas and information using the form of words devised by someone else.[40] However, in *Marmont*[41] the Divisional Court was not convinced that the compulsory television licence fee was an interference with the right to receive commercial programmes although it did consider the question of justification, assuming that the licence was at least a 'condition' attached to the exercise of Article 10 freedoms which needed justification.

The right to receive information was briefly considered by the Court of Appeal in *Farrakhan*,[42] the court recognising that, if it upheld the Home Secretary's exclusion order, it would impinge on the freedom of those who wished to hear Mr Farrakhan speak to receive his views and information face to face.[43] But it is in relation to the holding of public inquires that this aspect of Article 10 has received the most attention and produced conflicting High Court decisions. In *Persey*[44] the claimants challenged the government's decision to set up three separate private inquiries into the 2001 foot and mouth outbreak rather than a full-scale open public inquiry. By contrast to the judgment of the Divisional Court in *Wagstaff*,[45] the Divisional Court

---

[35] Above n 15.
[36] *Ibid*, at [31]. See also *Hutchinson v Newbury Magistrates Court*, Divisional Court, 9 October 2000; *Re Roddy*, above n 24.
[37] *R v Sherwood, ex p The Telegraph Group plc* [2001] EWCA Crim 1075, [2001] 1 WLR 1983 at [16].
[38] *Attorney General v Punch Ltd* [2002] UKHL 50, [2003] 1 AC 1046 at [31].
[39] Above n 8.
[40] *Ibid*, at [31].
[41] *Marmont v Secretary of State for Culture, Media and Sport* [2003] EWHC (QB) 2300.
[42] Above n 10.
[43] *Ibid*, at [77].
[44] *Persey v Secretary of State for Environment, Food and Rural Affairs* [2002] EWHC (Admin) 371, [2003] QB 794.
[45] *R (on the application of Wagstaff) v Secretary of State for Health* [2001] 1 WLR 292.

here concluded that Article 10 was simply not engaged by a decision to hold a closed public inquiry and that it did not confer the right of access to information.[46]

> It is not a corollary of the right to freedom of expression that public authorities can be required to put in place additional opportunities for its exercise. Article 10 imposes no positive obligation on government to provide, in addition to existing means of communication, an open forum to achieve the yet wider dissemination of views.[47]

5. Interference

An interference with the right to freedom of expression may arise in any number of ways. An injunction restraining publication or further publication is obviously an interference.[48] Awards of damages and costs against newspapers can generally impinge upon and have a chilling effect upon freedom of expression.[49] A blanket exemption from orders for costs for charitable donors to a litigant running a defamation case has been held to constitute an interference,[50] as has a requirement that a newspaper editor seek confirmation from the Attorney General or court that the facts are not confidential prior to publication.[51] Proceedings for defamation,[52] an order that the identity of parties to an action not be disclosed,[53] an order requiring a journalist to disclose his or her source,[54] reporting restrictions,[55] proceedings for contempt of court[56] and advertising restrictions[57] can all interfere with freedom of expression.

An interference may also arise from a conviction under the Public Order Act 1986,[58] Official Secrets Act 1989,[59] Obscene Publications Act 1959,[60] Protection of

---

[46] *Ibid*, at [50] and [52] in reliance upon *Leander v Sweden* (1987) 9 EHRR 433; *Gaskin v United Kingdom* (1990) 12 EHRR 36; *Taylor v United Kingdom* (1994) 18 EHRR CD 215; *Guerra v Italy* (1998) 26 EHRR 357.

[47] *Ibid*, at [53]. The court added that, even if it had found Art 10(1) engaged, it would have concluded that the interference was justified. In *R (on the application of Howard) v Secretary of State for Health* [2002] EWHC (Admin), [2003] QB 830 the court distinguished Wagstaff on the ground that in the present case the claimants were entitled to be present and the media were not parties. Nevertheless, it was also stated that the judgment in Wagstaff was wrong as it was not supported by jurisprudence of the European Court of Human Rights.

[48] See, eg *Douglas*, above n 12.

[49] See, eg *Ashdown*, above n 8, at [52].

[50] *Hamilton v Al Fayed* [2002] EWCA Civ 665, [2003] QB 1175.

[51] *Attorney General v Times Newspapers Ltd* [2001] EWCA Civ 97, [2001] 1 WLR 885.

[52] *Reynolds*, above n 5.

[53] *H (A Healthcare Worker) v Associated Newspapers Ltd* [2002] EWCA Civ 195, [2002] EMLR 23.

[54] *Ashworth Hospital Authority v MGN Ltd* [2002] UKHL 29, [2002] 1 WLR 2033.

[55] See, eg *Briffet v DPP* [2001] EWHC (Admin) 841, [2002] EMLR 12; *McKerry v Teesdale & Wear Valley Justices* [2001] EMLR 5.

[56] *Punch*, above n 38.

[57] *British American Tobacco*, above n 14.

[58] *Percy*, above n 15.

[59] *Shayler*, above n 9.

[60] *Perrin*, above n 11.

Children Act 1978,[61] Contempt of Court Act 1981,[62] sections of the Terrorism Act 2000 which penalise the profession of membership of a proscribed organisation[63] or a conviction for the common law offence of causing a public nuisance.[64] It has been held that preventing demonstrators from proceeding to a demonstration then escorting their coach back to London constituted an interference,[65] as did dismissing a probation officer from his employment because his hobby was a circus-related fire act which he performed in hedonist and fetish clubs.[66] It has also been held that requiring journalists' interviews with Category A prisoners to be conducted within earshot of officials and tape recorded constituted a interference.[67] However, hypothetical interferences are not sufficient. For example, in *Rusbridger*[68] it was held that the mere existence of section 3 of the Treason Act 1848 was not an interference.[69]

Sometimes the interference is not so obvious. In relation to the laws of copyright, it has been argued that these do not constitute an interference with freedom of expression as the information can still be conveyed. This argument was dismissed by the Court of Appeal in *Ashdown*,[70] the court finding that copyright was antithetical to freedom of expression as it prevented all, save the owner of the copyright, from expressing information in the form of the literary work protected by the copyright.[71] One was prevented from conveying ideas and information using the form of words devised by someone else. However, as copyright does not normally prevent the publication of the information, the court concluded that it would not normally constitute a significant encroachment.[72]

Difficult questions have also arisen in relation to entry clearance. In *Farrakhan*,[73] relying on Strasbourg authorities, the Court of Appeal held that, where the authorities of a state refuse entry to or expel an alien from their territory solely for the purpose of preventing the alien from exercising a Convention right within the territory, or by way of sanction for the exercise of a Convention right, the Convention would be directly engaged.[74] Therefore, where the authorities refused entry to an alien solely to prevent his expressing opinions within its territory, Article 10 would be engaged.[75] However, in the case of Mr Farrakhan the court observed that the reason for his exclusion was the risk that his presence in this country might prove a catalyst for disorder.[76] Therefore, preventing Mr Farrakhan from expressing his views was not

---

61 *R v Smethurst* [2001] EWCA Crim 772, [2002] 1 Cr App R 6.
62 *Attorney General v Scotcher* [2005] UKHL 36, [2005] 1 WLR 1867.
63 *Attorney General's Reference No.4 of 2002* [2004] UKHL 43, [2005] 1 AC 264 at [54].
64 *R v Goldstein* [2003] EWCA Crim 3450, [2004] WLR 2878.
65 *Laporte*, above n 16.
66 *Pay*, above n 17.
67 *R (on the application of A) v Secretary of State for the Home Department* [2003] EWHC (Admin) 2846, [2004] HRLR 12.
68 *R (on the application of Rusbridger) v Attorney General* [2003] UKHL 38, [2004] 1 AC 357.
69 *Ibid.*
70 Above n 8.
71 *Ibid*, at [30].
72 *Ibid*, at [31]. See also *Imutran Ltd v Uncaged Campaigns Ltd* [2001] 2 All ER 385 and *Levi Strauss & Co v Tesco Stores Ltd* [2002] EWHC (Ch) 1556, [2003] RPC 18 concerning trade marks.
73 Above n 10.
74 *Agee v United Kingdom* (1976) 7 D&R 164; *Piermont v France* (1995) 20 EHRR 301; *Swami Omkarananda and the Divine Light Zentrum v Switzerland* (1997) 25 D&R 105; *Adams and Benn v United Kingdom* (1997) 88A D&R 137.
75 *Ibid*, at [55]–[56].
76 *Ibid*, at [58].

the primary object of his exclusion. However, in contrast to the Strasbourg authorities reviewed, the Court concluded that it was clear that one object of his exclusion was to prevent him from exercising the right of freedom of expression in this country, and therefore Article 10 was in play.[77]

6. Positive Duties

Positive duties under Article 10 before either the European Court of Human Rights or British courts are not yet well developed. In fact, there have been a number of observations made in HRA cases that Article 10 does not impose positive duties. For example, in *Smeaton*[78] the Administrative Court held that Article 10 does not require the public subsidy of campaigning free speech. In *Persey*[79] the Divisional Court held that Article 10 prohibited interference with expression, rather than requiring its facilitation.[80] Similarly, it was held by a majority of the House of Lords in *Prolife Alliance*[81] that Article 10 did not entitle the Prolife Alliance or anyone else to make free television broadcasts.[82] Nevertheless, it concluded that the principle underlying Article 10 required that access to an important public medium of communication should not be refused on discriminatory, arbitrary or unreasonable grounds. Nor should access be granted subject to discriminatory, arbitrary or unreasonable conditions.

> A restriction on the content of a programme, produced by a political party to promote its stated aims, must be justified. Otherwise it will not be acceptable.[83]

The only sign that there may be a positive aspect to Article 10 is to be found in the judgment of the Court of Appeal in *Laporte*.[84] Here the court recognised that interferences with the rights of those seeking to demonstrate may be necessary as otherwise the conduct of those intent on creating unlawful disturbances could undermine the ability of others lawfully to exercise their rights, including their rights to protest.

> [I]mportant protection for the rights contained in Arts 10 and 11 is provided by the duty of the police, which is shared by members of the public, to take reasonable steps to prevent a breach of the peace occurring.[85]

---

[77] *Ibid*, at [62].
[78] *R (on the application of Smeaton on behalf of the Society for the Protection of Unborn Children) v The Secretary of State for Health* [2002] EWHC (Admin) 886, [2002] 2 FLR 146.
[79] Above n 44.
[80] *Ibid*, at [53].
[81] *R (on the application of Prolife Alliance) v British Broadcasting Corporation* [2003] UKHL 23, [2004] 1 AC 185.
[82] *Ibid*, at [8] per Lord Nicholls and at [56] per Lord Hoffmann.
[83] *Ibid*, at [8] per Lord Nicholls and at [58] per Lord Hoffmann.
[84] Above n 16.
[85] *Ibid*, at [37].

7. Permitted Interferences

The right to freedom of expression is not an absolute right. Article 10(2) provides that the exercise of these freedoms,

> since it carries with it duties and responsibilities, may be subject to such formalities, conditions, restrictions or penalties as are prescribed by law and are necessary in a democratic society, in the interests of national security, territorial integrity or public safety, for the prevention of disorder or crime, for the protection of health or morals, for the protection of the reputation or rights of others, for preventing the disclosure of information received in confidence, or for maintaining the authority and impartiality of the judiciary.

The notion of the right carrying with it duties and responsibilities is not found in any other Convention right, but it has played little part in Article 10 case law to date. Only in *Shayler*[86] did Lord Hutton lay particular emphasis on the special conditions attached to life in the security service and the special duties and responsibilities incumbent on the defendant whereby he was prohibited by statute from disclosing information about his work. Moreover, these duties and responsibilities were specifically acknowledged and accepted.[87]

As an aspect of necessity, the most important question in the freedom of expression cases brought under the HRA has been whether or not the interference is proportionate to the legitimate aim pursued. The important differences between this principle and traditional grounds of review were outlined in *Daly*.[88] The reviewing court may be required to assess the balance which the decision maker has struck. Secondly, the proportionality test may go further than the traditional grounds of review inasmuch as it may require attention to be directed to the relative weight accorded to interests and considerations. When this process is carried out in a freedom of expression case, it appears that, in addition to the considerations peculiar to each objective or interest listed in Article 10(2), certain general principles affect the balancing process. Although alone it is difficult for any one principle to tip the scales too far, when combined these represent a formidable argument against countervailing interests. These general principles are examined in the following paragraphs.

---

[86] Above n 9.
[87] *Ibid*, at [95].
[88] *R v Secretary of State for the Home Department, ex p Daly* [2001] UKHL 26, [2001] 2 AC 532 per Lord Steyn. See further I Leigh, 'Taking Rights Proportionately: Judicial Review, the Human Rights Act and Strasbourg' [2002] *PL* 265.

8. General Principles

8.1 Section 12 HRA

The first general principle is section 12 of the HRA. Section 12 was inserted during the parliamentary debates on the Bill in response to press fears that the HRA, in particular the right to respect for private life, would lead to untrammelled restrictions on freedom of expression and the freedom of the press. It was the wish of the government,

> [s]o far as we are able, in a manner consistent with the convention and its jurisprudence . . .[to say] to the courts that whenever there is a clash between article 8 rights and article 10 rights, they must pay particular attention to the article 10 rights.[89]

The section applies if a court is considering whether to grant any relief which, if granted, might affect the exercise of the Convention right to freedom of expression. Section 12(2) relates to unrepresented defendants, section 12(3) to prior restraints and section 12(4) to the importance of freedom of expression.

It is becoming increasingly clear that section 12 adds very little to existing UK or ECHR jurisprudence. In *Ashdown*, the Court of Appeal held that section 12 does no more

> than underline the need to have regard to contexts in which . . . [Strasbourg] jurisprudence has given particular weight to freedom of expression, while at the same time drawing attention to considerations which none the less justify restricting that right.[90]

It does not give Article 10 presumptive priority.[91] Nevertheless, some small changes have occurred.

Section 12(3) imposes a threshold test which has to be satisfied before a court may grant interlocutory injunctive relief. It provides that no such relief (which might affect the exercise of the Convention right to freedom of expression) is to be granted so as to restrain publication before trial unless the court is satisfied that the applicant is likely to establish that publication should not be allowed. There has been considerable litigation as to the meaning of 'likely' in this context. In *Cream Holdings Ltd*[92] the House of Lords held that it did not mean 'more likely than not' or 'probably'.[93] In the opinion of their Lordships, that, as a test of universal application, would set the degree of likelihood too high and some flexibility was essential.[94] It concluded that the effect of section 12(3) was that the court was not to make an interim restraint order unless satisfied that the applicant's prospects of success at the trial were sufficiently favourable to justify such an order being made in the particular circumstances

---

[89] HC Deb, Vol 315, col 543 (2 July 1998), Secretary of State for the Home Department, Mr Jack Straw.
[90] *Ashdown*, above n 8, at [27]. See also *Imutran*, above n 72, at [18]–[19].
[91] *Douglas*, above n 12, at [135] per Sedley LJ and [150] per Keene LJ.
[92] *Cream Holdings Ltd v Banerjee* [2004] UKHL 44, [2005] 1 AC 253.
   Ibid, at [16].
   Ibid, at [20].

of the case.[95] As to what degree of likelihood made the prospects of success sufficiently favourable, it held that the general approach should be that courts will be
exceedingly slow to make interim restraint orders where the applicant has not satisfied the court that he will probably (more likely than not) succeed at the trial.
However, it appreciated that there would be cases where it would be necessary for a
court to depart from this general approach and where a lesser degree of likelihood
would suffice. This may apply where the potential adverse consequences of the disclosure are particularly grave or where a short-lived injunction was needed to enable the
court to hear and give proper consideration to an application for interim relief pending the trial or any relevant appeal.[96]

With respect to section 12(4), the press may well have shot itself in the foot. The
section elevates the Press Complaints Commission (PCC) Code of Practice to a position it has not occupied previously. This is of particular relevance in respect to private
life cases, where it has been held that, where the Code has been flouted and no public
interest claim is asserted, a claim to freedom of expression is likely to be trumped by
Article 10(2).[97]

8.2 Importance of Freedom of Expression

Given that section 12 has proved largely irrelevant, it is important to consider the
principles established at common law and under the ECHR which are now utilised by
the courts. The first is the importance of freedom of expression. Of all the Convention rights given further effect by the HRA, freedom of expression was the most
developed in UK law prior to the HRA coming into force. UK courts have generally
given great respect to freedom of expression. In *Douglas*, Brooke LJ stated that,
although the

> right to freedom of expression is not in every case the ace of trumps, it is a powerful card to
> which the courts of this country must always pay appropriate respect.[98]

It is widely recognised that there is a public interest per se in freedom of expression.[99]
By contrast to other Convention rights, frequent judicial explanations are given as to
why it is important to protect freedom of expression.[100]

---

[95] *Ibid*, at [22].
[96] *Ibid*. Section 12(3) does not apply to defamation cases, where the rule remains that claimants will be
unable to obtain an interim injunction to restrain the publication of an allegedly defamatory statement
unless it is plain that the plea of justification is bound to fail. See *Greene v Associated Newspapers Ltd*
[2004] EWCA Civ 1462, [2005] 3 WLR 281.
[97] *Douglas*, above n 12, at [94] per Brooke LJ; *Theakston v MGN Ltd* [2002] EWHC (QB) 137, [2002]
EMLR 22 at [26]; *Campbell v Mirror Group Newspapers Ltd* [2004] UKHL 22, [2004] 2 AC 457; and *X (a
woman formerly known as Mary Bell) v O'Brien* [2003] EWHC (QB) 1101, [2003] 2 FCR 686.
[98] *Ibid*, at [49].
[99] *Ashdown*, above n 8, at [66].
[100] See, eg *R v Secretary of State for the Home Department, ex p Simms* [1999] 3 WLR 328 at 337 per Lord
Steyn.

8.3 Importance of Freedom of the Press

The importance of freedom of expression in the minds of the judiciary cannot be underestimated. However, as the majority of cases to date have involved the press, the importance of the freedom of the press has begun to eclipse the importance of freedom of expression. It is generally recognised that the media have a positive duty to act as a watchdog or as the eyes and ears of the general public and to inform their readers about matters of public interest.[101] It has been held that the existence of a free press is in itself desirable and in the public interest[102] irrespective of whether a particular publication is in the public interest.[103] It has also been held that the press are entitled to a reasonable margin of appreciation in taking decisions as to what details need to be included in an article to give it credibility as this is an essential part of the journalistic exercise.[104]

> [J]ournalists need to be permitted a degree of exaggeration even in the context of factual assertions not only when making comments or voicing their opinions.[105]

Whilst freedom of the press was recognised in the House of Lords' pre-HRA decision in *Reynolds*, it was not held to be outweigh other interests where a claim of qualified privilege was made and had to be balanced against protection of reputation. Incursions into press freedom in order to ensure responsible journalism were held to be necessary.[106] Post-HRA the message still appears to be that freedom of a *responsible* press is what is important. This is reflected in the approach taken by the courts to disclosure of journalists' sources. Although the *Norwich Pharmacal*[107] jurisdiction to order disclosure has now expanded,[108] any order made must still conform to section 10 of the Contempt of Court Act 1981 and Article 10 of the ECHR. In both the *Ashworth*[109] and *Interbrew*[110] cases, the importance of the protection of sources to press freedom was recognised, as was the importance of freedom of the press. Nevertheless, in both cases disclosure was found to be proportionate—in *Ashworth* because the confidentiality of psychiatric medical records was at issue and in *Interbrew* because the expression was of low value, designed to wreck legitimate commercial activity. The public interest in protecting the source of information was found in both cases to be very low, insufficient to outweigh countervailing considerations.

---

[101] *Sherwood*, above n 37, at [17]–[18]. See also *Re S (A Child) (Identification: Restriction on Publication)* [2004] UKHL 47, [2005] 1 AC 593 concerning the freedom of the press to report a criminal trial.
[102] *Ashdown*, above n 8, at [66]. *Financial Times v Interbrew* [2002] EWCA Civ 274, [2002] EMLR 446 at [52] per Sedley LJ.
[103] *B & C v A*, above n 19, at [11(iv)].
[104] *Campbell*, above n 97, at [112] per Lord Hope and [143] per Baroness Hale.
[105] *Turcu v News Group Newspapers Ltd* [2005] EWHC (QB) 799 at [108].
[106] *Reynolds*, above n 5, per Lord Nicholls.
   Norwich Pharmacal Co v Customs and Excise Commissioners [1973] 2 All ER 943.
   See *Ashworth*, above n 54; Interbrew, above n 102.
   shworth, ibid.
   bove n 102.

8.4 The Public Interest

As noted already, it has been held that there is a public interest in freedom of expression and freedom of the press per se. In addition, it may be in the public interest for particular material to be published. Of all the general considerations taken into account by a court considering the application of Article 10, the public interest in publication appears to be the most important. However, it is not yet possible to state with certainty that where there is a public interest in publication this will outweigh other interests and publication will be allowed. Much still depends on countervailing public interests, such as the protection of reputation,[111] maintenance of national security[112] and protection of property interests,[113] and also the category of public interest the information falls into given that there appear to be different gradations, starting with political information and ending with public figure information.

8.4.1 Defining the Public Interest

The greatest problems arise from the question of when, exactly, it is in the public interest for material to be published. In *B&C v A,* the Court of Appeal stated that in the majority of situations, whether the public interest is involved or not will be obvious.[114] Furthermore, it was thought impossible to define the public interest as the 'circumstances in any particular case under consideration can vary so much that a judgment in one case is unlikely to be decisive in another case.'[115]

However, despite these protestations, the Court of Appeal went on to essentially define the public interest as what the public is interested in:

> The courts must not ignore the fact that if newspapers do not publish information which the public are interested in, there will be fewer newspapers published, which will not be in the public interest.[116]

Such a perspective is greatly at odds with other UK jurisprudence, ECHR jurisprudence,[117] even the PCC Code of Practice, and cannot be correct. It is also at odds with the eventual conclusion of the Court of Appeal in the case that there was a public interest in the material not because it will sell newspapers but because the footballer was a role model for young people and it was important his undesirable behaviour and unfortunate example be exposed.[118]

The best starting point, given it now has legislative force via section 12(4) of the HRA, is the PCC Code. In the Code, the public interest is defined to include detecting or exposing crime or a serious misdemeanour; protecting public health and safety, preventing the public from being misled by some statement or action of an individual

---

[111] *Reynolds,* above n 5.
[112] *Shayler,* above n 9.
[113] *Ashdown,* above n 8.
[114] *B & C v A,* above n 19, at [11(viii)].
[115] *Ibid.*
[116] *Ibid,* at [11(xii)].
[117] See further S Tierney, 'Press Freedom and the Public Interest: the Developing Jurisprudence of the European Court of Human Rights' [1998] 4 *EHRLR* 419.
[118] *B & C v A,* above n 19, at [43(vi)].

or organisation.[119] The next step is to examine the case law. At one end of the spectrum is 'political information', where a public interest in publication is generally always found to exist. It has been held that freedom of political speech

> is a freedom of the very highest importance in any country which lays claim to being a democracy. Restrictions on this freedom need to be examined rigorously by all concerned, not least the courts.[120]

With respect to the meaning of political speech, in *Campbell*[121] Baroness Hale stated that this included information and ideas on matters relevant to the organisation of the economic, social and political life of the country, which included information about public figures, especially those in elective office, that would otherwise be private but was relevant to their participation in public life. One example is *Ashdown*, where it was held that information about a meeting between the Prime Minister and an opposition party leader to discuss possible close cooperation between those parties was very likely to be of legitimate and continuing public interest.[122] Another is *Rusbridger*,[123] where the House of Lords indicated that a press campaign advocating the peaceful and constitutional replacement of the monarchy by a republican form of government would be considered political speech.

Also at the high end of the spectrum is information concerning activities in the public sector. In *Shayler*, Lord Hope suggested that Shayler might have had good grounds for his claim that it was in the public interest for him to disclose what he perceived to be the unlawfulness, irregularity, incompetence, misbehaviour and waste of resources in the security service.[124] In *H (A Healthcare Worker)* the Court of Appeal considered that the story that Associated Newspapers wished to publish had a number of features of considerable public interest. These included whether N, the health authority, should have reacted swiftly and forcefully when faced with a healthcare worker who was challenging the Department of Health Guidelines with regard to the fact that there were no guidelines in place covering notification to patients that a healthcare worker with a particular speciality who is or was treating them is HIV-positive.[125] In *London Regional Transport* the decision to allow publication of a redacted version of a report concerning the public–private partnership for London Underground was particularly influenced by the strong public interest in publication.[126] It has also been held that there is a public interest in the process of rehabilitation of offenders, including details of how former serious offenders have succeeded in re-establishing themselves in society.[127]

---

[119] See http://www.pcc.org.uk/cop/cop.asp.
[120] *Prolife Alliance*, above n 81, at [6] per Lord Nicholls.
[121] Above n 97.
[122] *Ashdown*, above n 8, at [64]. See further I Hare, 'Is the Privileged Position of Political Expression Justified?' in J Beatson and Cripps (eds) *Freedom of Expression and Freedom of Information* (Oxford University Press, 2000).
[123] *R (on the application of Rusbridger) v Attorney General* [2003] UKKHL 38, [2004] 1 AC 357.
[124] Above n 9, at [51].
[125] *H*, above n 53, at [24].
[126] *London Regional Transport v The Mayor of London*, Divisional Court, 31 July 2001 at [40]. The conclusion of the High Court was later upheld on appeal; see *London Regional Transport v The Mayor of London* [2001] EWCA Civ 1491, [2003] EMLR 4. See also *Re X* [2001] 1 FCR 541; *Medway Council v BBC* [2002] 1 FLR 104; and *Ackroyd v Mersey Care NHS Trust* [2003] EWCA Civ 663, [2003] EMLR 36.
[127] *Mary Bell*, above n 97, at [58].

8.4.2 Public Figures

Further down the spectrum is information concerning public figures. These are defined in Resolution 1165 of the Parliamentary Assembly of the Council of Europe (1998) as

> persons holding public office and/or using public resources and, more broadly speaking, all those who play a role in public life, whether in politics, the economy, the arts, the social sphere, sport or in any other domain.[128]

Post-HRA, the courts have been faced with a variety of claims concerning respect for private life from public figures working in the arts and sport. Generally the claim of respect for private life is lessened by the individual's status as a public figure. However, the situation is made slightly worse for the individual by the tendency of the courts to find the Article 10 claimed strengthened by a public interest in what can only be described as exposing the perceived duplicity of public figures. The duplicity is 'perceived' as, in the majority of cases, the individual concerned has not given any firm indication that they do not participate in the undesirable behaviour at issue. As role models for young people, they are expected by the courts not to visit brothels[129] or have extra-marital affairs,[130] and it has been held to be in the public interest for them to be exposed.

It is not really correct to say that these individuals have misled the public to the extent that there is a public interest in the truth being revealed. It is more accurate to say that the public are interested in learning about such activities as it satisfies our innate curiosity about the lifestyles of the rich and famous. This is a factor which should definitely not weigh in on the side of freedom of expression where it is sought to protect private life. In the latest of these cases, a majority of the House of Lords appears to have adopted a more moderate approach, holding that the public had a need to know that Naomi Campbell had been misleading them by her denials of drug addiction and that she was receiving therapy for her drug addiction. However, other confidential details she had chosen not to put in the public domain were off limits, including the fact that she was receiving treatment at Narcotics Anonymous, the details of the treatment and the visual portrayal of her leaving a specific meeting with other addicts.[131] Baroness Hale commented that it might be questioned why

> if a role model has adopted a stance which all would agree is beneficial rather than detrimental to society, it is so important to reveal that she has feet of clay.[132]

However, in the present case she concluded that the possession and use of illegal drugs was a criminal offence and a matter of serious public concern.[133]

---

[128] *Ibid*, at [7]. In *Archer v Williams* [2003] EWHC (QB) 1670, [2003] EMLR 38 the court held that Mary Archer was not a public figure and there was therefore no public interest in the matters she sought to keep confidential.
[129] *Theakston*, above n 97.
[130] *B & C v A*, above n 19.
[131] *Campbell*, above n 97. See generally R Singh and J Strachan, 'The Right to Privacy in English Law' [2002] 2 *EHRLR* 129.
[132] *Ibid*, at [151].
[133] *Ibid*.

8.4.3 Commercial Expression

Even further down the scale of protected expression is commercial expression such as advertising, which has traditionally been treated as of less significance than freedom of political or artistic expression.[134]

9. National Security

Following the consideration of general principles, it is necessary to turn to consideration of the permitted interferences as set out in Article 10(2). The first is national security. Whilst this interest has not arisen often in proceedings under the HRA, when it has, it is taken very seriously by the courts, although the comment has been made that the Security Service is not entitled to immunity from criticism.[135] *Shayler*[136] concerned a former member of the security services who had been indicted on three counts of unlawful disclosure contrary to sections 1(1)(a), 4(1) and 4(3)(a) of the Official Secrets Act 1989. At a preparatory hearing, the questions were whether the sections under which the defendant was charged afforded him a public interest defence and, if not, whether those sections were compatible with Article 10. The defendant argued that he believed it to be in the public interest to disclose what he perceived to be unlawfulness, irregularity, incompetence, misbehaviour and waste of resources in the security service.

The House of Lords concluded that a defendant prosecuted under sections 1(1)(a), 4(1) and 4(3)(a) of the Act was not entitled to be acquitted

> if he shows that it was or that he believed that it was in the public or national interest to make the disclosure.[137]

It then considered whether or not this was in breach of Article 10. The need to preserve the secrecy of information was recognised, the real question in the opinion of the House of Lords was whether the

> interference with the individual's convention right prescribed by national law is greater than is required to meet the legitimate object which the state seeks to achieve.[138]

In reaching its conclusion that the interference was proportionate, the House of Lords was particularly influenced by the fact that the ban was not an absolute ban—it was a ban on disclosure 'without lawful authority.'[139] Under section 7(3)(a) a former member may make disclosure to a Crown servant for the purposes of his

---

[134] *British American Tobacco*, above n 14, at [28].
[135] *Punch*, above n 38, at [29].
[136] Above n 9.
[137] *Ibid*, at [20] per Lord Bingham.
[138] *Ibid*, at [26] per Lord Bingham.
[139] *Ibid*, at [27] per Lord Bingham and [70]–[71] per Lord Hope.

functions as such. It is also open to a former member to seek official authorisation to make a disclosure to a wider audience.[140] If such authority is refused, in the opinion of the House of Lords, a former member is entitled to seek judicial review of the decision to refuse and, as freedom of expression is at issue, 'the court will now conduct a much more rigorous and intrusive review than was once thought to be permissible.'[141] Furthermore, a fair hearing would require disclosure to a qualified lawyer from whom the former member wished to seek advice. If the material was too sensitive, 'arrangements could be made.'[142]

Taking into account these safeguards, and the further safeguard that section 9(1) of the Official Secrets Act 1989 required the consent of the Attorney General before any prosecution, the House of Lords concluded that there were sufficient and effective safeguards.

> It is, however, necessary that a member or former member of a relevant service should avail himself of the procedures available to him under the Act.[143]

Sections 1(1), 4(1) and 4(3) were found to be compatible with Article 10.[144]

---

10. Prevention of Disorder or Crime

It is clear that expression has the potential to provoke disorder, although, again, consideration of this interest under the HRA has been rare. In *Farrakhan*[145] the Home Secretary argued that his decision to exclude Mr Farrakhan from the United Kingdom turned on his evaluation of the risk that, because of his notorious opinions, a visit by him might provoke disorder. In evaluating the risk, the Home Secretary had regard to tensions in the Middle East current at the time of his decision, the 'fruits of widespread consultation' and sources of information available to him not available to the court. He chose not to describe his sources of information or the purport of that information.[146] Nevertheless, the Court of Appeal held that this was sufficient explanation, although commenting

> it would have been better had he been less diffident about explaining the nature of the information and the advice that he had received.[147]

---

140 *Ibid*, at [29] per Lord Bingham.
141 *Ibid*, at [33] per Lord Bingham, [72], [75], [77]–[78] per Lord Hope and [107] per Lord Hutton.
142 *Ibid*, at [34] per Lord Bingham, [73]–[74] per Lord Hope and [111]–[114] per Lord Hutton.
143 *Ibid*, at [36] per Lord Bingham and [83]–[85] per Lord Hope.
144 See also *Secretary of State for Defence v Times Newspapers Ltd*, Divisional Court, 28 March 2001; A, above n 67.
145 Above n 10.
146 *Ibid*, at [78].
147 *Ibid*.

As a result of this decision, the level of proof required to show that disorder would result from the exercise of the right to freedom of expression appears very low. It is not clear whether the absence of proof will apply only in cases where the decision of the executive are an issue or generally to all decisions, such as decisions of police under the Public Order Act in relation to marches and assemblies. There was no conclusive evidence in *Farrakhan* that disorder would result from his visit. In fact, in his decision letter of 20 November 2000 the Home Secretary noted that, apart from one incident, there was no record of violent disorder associated with the group in the United Kingdom, that Farrakhan was not excluded from any other country, that nothing objectionable occurred during his visits to Israel, Australia and Canada, that he has signed assurances as to his behaviour and that his current message was one of reconciliation. Nevertheless, the Home Secretary remained satisfied that Mr Farrakhan has expressed anti-semitic and racially divisive views. Therefore, a visit would pose a threat to public order and stir up racial hatred contrary to the Public Order Act 1986.[148]

The potential for disorder, along with administrative difficulties, was also the justification put forward in *Hirst*[149] to limit the prisoner's telephone contact with the media. The Administrative Court found that the limitation on telephone contact with the media was not part of the sentence of imprisonment itself and therefore Article 10(2) had to be considered. It concluded that the administrative difficulties presented and the alleged potential for prison disorder did not justify what was effectively a blanket ban on media interviews, particularly as the conditions proposed on the exercise of the right went a considerable way towards meeting the concerns of the prison authorities.[150] Along with national security, this justification was also employed in *A*,[151] where, affording considerable deference, the Divisional Court held that it was proportionate for the Secretary of State's to permit Category A prisoners detained under section 21 of the Anti-Terrorism Crime and Security Act 2001 only to be interviewed by journalists if the interviews were conducted within the earshot of officials and tape recorded.

---

11. Protection of Health or Morals

It is clear that legislation such as the Obscene Publications Act 1959 has the potential to interfere greatly with the right to freedom of expression. Nevertheless, in the interests of the protection of morals, the courts are willing to grant the legislature and

---

[148] However, in *Laporte*, above n 16, the Court of Appeal concluded that, although it was not a disproportionate interference with Arts 10 and 11 to stop demonstrators proceeding to a demonstration, it became disproportionate when their coach was escorted back to London and was not within the ambit of action reasonably taken to prevent a breach of the peace at common law. See also *Brehony*, above n 16.

[149] *Hirst*, above n 31.

[150] *Ibid*, at [78]–[84].

[151] Above n 67.

police a wide margin of discretion. In *R v Perrin*,[152] dismissing an appeal against a conviction under the Act, the Court of Appeal commented that

> there was no public interest to be served by permitting a business for profit to supply material which most people would regard as pornographic or obscene

and further that there was 'no reason why a responsible government should abandon that protection in favour of other limited remedies.'[153]

Similarly, where the protection of health is put forward as the justification, the courts appear willing to grant the decision maker some latitude. In *British American Tobacco*[154] six corporations in the tobacco industry challenged the lawfulness of new advertising regulations which provided for a total ban on the advertising of tobacco products with limited exceptions relating to the display of products at points of sale. The Administrative Court held that the protection of public health was a very important counterbalance to unrestricted commercial expression[155] and it was principally for the decision maker to resolve how best the aim of protecting health could be achieved by restricting promotion of extremely harmful but lawful products.[156] It concluded that the regulations were proportionate, noting that, given

> the enormous health risks and economic costs to society caused by smoking tobacco and a substantial weight of expert opinion as to the effects of advertising . . . upon the levels of consumption, I believe it to have been a responsible and proportionate step to have regulated as the Minister has now done.[157]

---

12. Protection of the Reputation of Others

The law of defamation constitutes an undoubted interference with the right to freedom of expression, although in many instances its application to particular facts is justified in the interests of the protection of the reputation of others. Prior to the HRA coming into force, the common law constitutional right to freedom of expression had already had some impact on the law of defamation, and the comment was often made that no different conclusion would have been reached had Article 10 been applied.[158] Under the HRA, Article 10 has continued to shape the law of defamation,

---

[152] Above n 11.
[153] *Ibid*, at [49] in reliance upon *Muller v Switzerland* (1991) 13 EHRR 212 and *Wingrove v United Kingdom* (1997) 24 EHRR 1.
[154] Above n 14.
[155] *Ibid*, at [32].
[156] *Ibid*, at [37].
[157] *Ibid*, at [52].
[158] See, eg *Derbyshire County Council v Times Newspapers Ltd* [1993] AC 534.

ensuring in particular that the interference posed by this law is proportionate to the aim of protecting reputation.[159]

A particular impact of the right to freedom of expression in this area has been on the defence of qualified privilege. The limits of this defence were the subject of the House of Lords judgment in *Reynolds*,[160] which concerned an article published in the British mainland edition of the *Sunday Times* about the resignation of Mr Reynolds as Prime Minister of Ireland. Mr Reynolds alleged that the sting of the article was that he had deliberately and dishonestly misled the Dail and his cabinet colleagues.

The *Sunday Times* argued that the defence of qualified privilege applied to the article. In particular, relying on the right to freedom of expression, the *Sunday Times* sought the incremental development of the common law by the creation of a new category of occasion when privilege derives from the subject matter alone: political information. The House of Lords rejected this development. Although the importance of the role discharged by the media 'in the expression and communication of information and comment on political matters'[161] was recognised, the public interest that the 'reputation of public figures should not be debased falsely'[162] was also taken into account. With respect to defamatory imputations of fact, as was at issue here, it was concluded that the established common law approach was essentially sound. Where publication is to the world at large, the publication will be privileged if the public is entitled to know the particular information. However, all the circumstances must be taken into account in determining whether the test is satisfied.

> The duty–interest test, or the right to know test, cannot be carried out in isolation from these factors and without regard to them. A claim to privilege stands or falls according to whether the claim passes or fails this test.[163]

By way of illustration, Lord Nicholls listed ten matters which may be taken into account, depending on the circumstances:

> (1) The seriousness of the allegation. The more serious the charge, the more the public is misinformed and the individual harmed, if the allegation is not true. (2) The nature of the information, and the extent to which the subject matter is a matter of public concern. (3) The source of the information. Some informants have no direct knowledge of the events. Some have their own axes to grind, or are being paid for their stories. (4) The steps taken to verify the information. (5) The status of the information. The allegation may have already been the subject of investigation which commands respect. (6) The urgency of the matter. News is often a perishable commodity. (7) Whether comment was sought from the plaintiff. He may have information others do not possess or have not disclosed. An approach to the plaintiff will not always be necessary. (8) Whether the article contained the gist of the

---

[159] The only case to arise under this ground outside of the defamation context has been *Pay*, above n 17, where the Employment Appeal Tribunal decided that the dismissal of the claimant because of his hobby of a circus-related fire act which he performed in fetish and hedonist clubs was not disproportionate to protecting the reputation of the Probation Service.
[160] Above n 5. Although this judgment actually pre-dated the coming into force of the HRA, their Lordships indicated that no different conclusion would have been reached under the HRA.
[161] *Ibid*, per Lord Nicholls.
[162] *Ibid*, per Lord Nicholls.
[163] *Ibid*, per Lord Nicholls.

plaintiff's side of the story. (9) The tone of the article. A newspaper can raise queries or call for an investigation. It need not adopt allegations as statements of fact. (10) The circumstances of the publication, including the timing.

A majority concluded that, given the article made no mention of Reynold's explanation, this was not information the public had a right to know and was not protected by privilege.[164]

As the Court of Appeal pointed out in *Loutchansky*,[165] the modifications made by the judgment in *Reynolds* to the defence of qualified privilege are significant. First, it was established that privilege attaches to the publication itself rather than the occasion of the publication. Secondly, once it attaches, there is little scope for any subsequent finding of malice.[166] The Court of Appeal also further explained the interest and duty underlying the privilege:

> The interest is that of the public in a modern democracy in free expression and, more particularly, in the promotion of a free and vigorous press to keep the public informed ... The corresponding duty on the journalist (and equally his editor) is to play his proper role in discharging that function. His task is to behave as a responsible journalist. He can have no duty to publish unless he is acting responsibly any more than the public has an interest in reading whatever may be published irresponsibly ... Unless the publisher is acting responsibly privilege cannot arise.[167]

It concluded that the question to be posed is whether it was in the public interest to publish the article, true or false, rather than whether it was in the public interest to publish an untruth.[168] It is clear that, post-HRA, the key questions when qualified privilege is claimed are whether responsible journalism has been exercised and whether the subject matter of the publication is such that it is in the public interest that it be published.[169]

Although the greatest impact has been on qualified privilege, Article 10 does apply to other aspects of the law of defamation. It has been held that the rule that each individual publication of libel gives rise to a separate cause of action is compatible with Article 10,[170] as is requiring a defendant who relies on the defence of justification to justify the essence or sting of an assault on reputation rather than a diminished version of it.[171] It has also been held that a defence of justification based

[164] See further K Williams, 'Defaming Politicians: The Not So Common Law' (2000) 63 *MLR* 748; I Loveland, 'Freedom of Political Expression: Who Needs the Human Rights Act?' [2001] *PL* 233.

[165] Above n 13.

[166] *Ibid*, at [33].

[167] *Ibid*, at [36].

[168] *Ibid*, at [41]. Prior to this judgment there were a number of different interpretations of the House of Lords judgment in Reynolds. See, eg *Al-Fagihv HH Saudi Research & Marketing (UK) Ltd* [2001] EWCA Civ 1634, [2002] EMLR 13; *Lukowiak v Unidad Editorial SA* [2001] EMLR 46; *Baldwin v Rusbridger* [2001] EMLR 24.

[169] *Jameel v Wall Street Journal Europe SPRL (No.3)* [2005] EWCA Civ 74, [2005] HRLR 10 at [87]. See also *Al Misnad v Azzaman Ltd* [2003] EWHC (QB) 1783.

[170] *Loutchansky*, above n 13.

[171] *Berezovsky v Forbes* [2001] EWCA Civ 1251, [2001] EMLR 45.

upon reasonable grounds for suspicion which focuses on some conduct of the individual claimant that itself gives rise to the suspicion is compatible with Article 10.[172]

However, in *O'Shea*[173] the Divisional Court concluded that the strict liability principle which applied to cases of 'look alike' defamation, making the intention of the publisher irrelevant, was a disproportionate interference with freedom of expression. The court reasoned that it would impose an impossible burden on a publisher if he were required to check if the true picture of someone resembled someone else who because of the context of the picture was defamed.[174]

13. Protection of the Rights of Others

The 'rights of others' has the potential to justify a wide range of interferences with freedom of expression. However, most interferences on this basis have sought to be justified by reference to another Convention right, in particular Article 8.

13.1 Articles 2 and 3

In certain circumstances, the disclosure of information may lead to someone being killed or seriously injured. In such circumstances the right to life and the right to freedom from torture or inhuman or degrading treatment or punishment fall to be considered. The issue arose in *Venables*,[175] where the claimants sought injunctions to restrain the publication of information relating to their identities and whereabouts. They had both been convicted of the murder of two-year-old James Bulger in 1993 when they were ten years old, a case which was widely publicised in the media. Although only three news groups were named as defendants, the injunction was sought *contra mundum*—against the world at large.

The Family Division found that it had the jurisdiction, in exceptional cases, to extend the protection of confidentiality of information where not to do so would be likely to lead to serious physical injury, or to the death, of the person seeking that confidentiality.[176] Here the court was satisfied that, if the claimant's identities were discovered, neither of them would have the chance of a normal life and there was a real and strong possibility that their lives would be at risk.[177] It concluded that the

---

[172] *Chase v Newsgroup Newspapers Ltd* [2002] EWCA Civ 1772, [2003] EMLR 11. See also *Jameel*, above n 169, concerning the rule that a corporation need not prove special damage in order to establish a cause of action; *Dow Jones & Co Inc v Jameel* [2005] EWCA Civ 75, [2005] EMLR 16, concerning the presumption of damage and abuse of process; and *Pedder v News Group Newspapers Ltd* [2003] EWHC (QB) 2442, [2004] EMLR 19, concerning abuse of process.
[173] Above n 21.
[174] *Ibid*, at [43]–[45].
[175] Above n 4, at [80].
[176] *Ibid*, at [81].
[177] *Ibid*, at [94].

extension of the tort here was proportionate to the legitimate aim of protecting the claimants from serious and possibly irreparable harm.[178]

13.2 Article 8

As discussed in the chapter concerning the right to respect for private life, freedom of expression and the right to respect for private life are commonly balanced against each other where the media seeks to publish details of the private life of a public figure. The values enshrined in these rights are now part of the cause of action for breach of confidence[179] and are

> as much applicable in disputes between individuals or between an individual and a non-governmental body such as a newspaper as they are in disputes between individuals and a public authority.[180]

It is often stated that both are vitally important rights and neither has precedence over the other.[181]

> [W]here the values under the two articles are in conflict, an intense focus on the comparative importance of the specific rights being claimed in the individual case is necessary . . . the justifications for interfering with or restricting each right must be taken into account. Finally, the proportionality test must be applied to each.[182]

As discussed at the start of this section, various factors affect the balancing process, in particular the question of whether or not the information is of public interest, the importance of freedom of expression and the importance of freedom of the press. In these types of cases, these factors have a tendency to skew the result of the balancing exercise in favour of freedom of expression. For example, in *Campbell*[183] it was accepted by the claimant and not commented upon by the House of Lords that, as she had lied about the fact of her drug addiction and the fact that she was receiving treatment, this gave the press the right to put the record straight[184] as this was a matter of legitimate public comment.[185]

> [W]here a public figure chooses to make untrue pronouncements about his or her private life, the press will normally be entitled to put the record straight.[186]

---

[178] *Ibid*, at [86].
[179] *Campbell*, above n 97.
[180] *Ibid*, at [17] per Lord Nicholls. See also *Re S*, above n 101, concerning the inherent jurisdiction of the court.
[181] See, eg the comments of Lord Nicholls in *Campbell*, above n 97, at [12], Lord Hoffmann at [55], Lord Hope at [111], [113], Baroness Hale at [138].
[182] *Re S*, above n 101, at [17].
[183] Above n 97.
[184] *Ibid*, per Lord Nicholls at [24].
[185] *Ibid*, per Lord Hope at [82].
[186] *Ibid*.

However, this did not affect three other pieces of information: the fact that she was receiving treatment at Narcotics Anonymous; the details of the treatment; and the visual portrayal of her leaving a specific meeting.

A majority in *Campbell*[187] concluded that the protection of Ms Campbell's rights under Article 8 was sufficiently important to justify limiting the fundamental right to freedom of expression which the press asserted on behalf of the public.[188]

> [T]he right of the public to receive information about the details of her treatment was of a much lower order than the undoubted right to know that she was misleading the public when she said that she did not take drugs.[189]

Furthermore, it was noted that the political and social life of the community, and the intellectual, artistic or personal development of individuals, were not obviously assisted by poring over the intimate details of a fashion model's private life.[190]

The case law in this area is not just all about celebrities and newspapers. Cases have also been brought by those who have not courted publicity as part of their career but are the subject of public interest nonetheless. For example, in *X (a woman formerly known as Mary Bell)* the claimant and her daughter sought lifetime anonymity from the intrusions of the media and any disclosures of their identifies, their addresses or any details about their lives which might identify them. The Family Division found that, whilst neither had courted publicity, Mary Bell remained a legitimate subject of public interest.[191] However, it concluded that there were special features of the case which required the balance between Articles 8 and 10 to be resolved in favour of recognising the confidentiality of some information to protect them. Injunctions *contra mundum* were granted to protect their anonymity.[192]

A number of cases have also related to the jurisdiction of a court under section 1(1) of the Children Act 1989 to restrain publication of material relating to a child's upbringing where the child's welfare would be affected. For example, *Re X*[193] concerned the policy of a local authority in relation to transracial placements of foster children. The Family Division held that it was important to respect private life but that the public importance of the story and the freedom of the press necessitated a modification of the injunction.[194] In *Re S*[195] the House of Lords considered whether the right to freedom of expression outweighed the request for an injunction protecting his identity of a boy whose mother was to be tried for the murder of his older brother. Their Lordships held that the interference with Article 8 rights was not of the same order when compared with cases of juveniles who were directly involved in

---

[187] Above n 97.

[188] *Ibid*, per Lord Hope at [115].

[189] *Ibid*, per Lord Hope at [117].

[190] *Ibid*, per Baroness Hale at [149]. See also *Douglas*, above n 12; and the judgment on liability, *Douglas v Hello! Ltd* [2005] EWCA Civ 595; *B & C v A*, above n 19; *Theakston*, above n 97.

[191] *Mary Bell*, above n 97, at [30].

[192] *Ibid*, at [60]. See also *Carr v News Group Newspapers*, Divisional Court, 24 February 2005; *Archer v Williams*, above n 128; *Re Roddy*, above n 24; *E (by her litigation friend the Official Solicitor) v Channel Four* [2005] EWHC (Fam) 1144, [2005] EMLR 30. In *Chancellor, Masters and Scholars of the University of Oxford v Broughton* [2004] EWHC (QB) 2543, balancing Art 8 rights of employees against Art 10 rights of animal rights protesters, the court granted an injunction under the Protection from Harassment Act 1997.

[193] Above n 126.

[194] See also *BBC*, above n 126.

[195] Above n 101.

criminal trials.[196] Furthermore, it found the freedom of the press to report the progress of a criminal trial to be of considerable importance.[197] It concluded that the rights under Article 8 were not sufficient to outweigh those under Article 10. A number of factors led to this conclusion. First, it would seriously inhibit the freedom of the press to report criminal trials. Secondly, it would be a further exception to the principle of open justice. Thirdly, informed debate about criminal justice would suffer. Fourthly, it was a costly process for newspapers to contest an application for an injunction and often it would be too late. Finally, it was thought that such injunctions would have a particularly chilling effect on local newspapers.[198]

13.3 Article 1 Protocol No 1

As copyright constitutes a possession within the scope of Article 1 of Protocol No 1, where the courts are considering the remedy for infringement of copyright, it has been held that Article 10 must be balanced against Article 1 Protocol No 1.[199] In *Ashdown*[200] the Court of Appeal considered itself bound to apply the Copyright, Designs and Patents Act 1988 in a manner that accommodated the right of freedom of expression.[201] Applying the Act in this way, it declined the discretionary relief of an injunction but required the newspaper to indemnify the author for any loss caused or alternatively account to him for any profit.[202]

It also considered the defence of public interest preserved by section 171(3) of the Act. The courts have an inherent jurisdiction to refuse to allow their process to be used in certain circumstances—here, to refuse to enforce copyright.[203] Following a review of the authorities, the court concluded that the circumstances in which public interest may override copyright are not capable of precise categorisation or definition.[204]

> Now that the Human Rights Act 1998 is in force, there is the clearest public interest in giving effect to the right of freedom of expression in those rare cases where this right trumps the rights conferred by the 1988 Act. In such circumstances, we consider that section 171(3) of the Act permits the defence of public interest to be raised.[205]

---

[196] *Ibid*, at [27].
[197] *Ibid*, at [31].
[198] *Ibid*, at [36]. See also *Pelling v Bruce-Williams* [2004] EWCA Civ 845, [2004] Fam 155; *A Local Authority v A Health Authority* [2003] EWHC (Fam) 2746, [2004] Fam 96; *Blunkett v Quinn* [2004] EWHC (Fam) 2816, [2005] 1 FLR 648; *R v Teeside Crown Court, ex p Gazette Media Co. Ltd* [2005] EWCA Crim 1983. See also *O'Riordan v Director of Public Prosecutions* [2005] EWHC (Admin) 1240, where the court held that the statutory prohibition on a child's name imposed by the Sexual Offences (Amendment) Act 1982 was compatible with Art 10. See further H Fenwick, 'Clashing Rights, the Welfare of the Child and the Human Rights Act' (2004) 67 *MLR* 889.
[199] *Ashdown*, above n 8.
[200] *Ibid*.
[201] *Ibid*, at [45].
[202] *Ibid*, at [46].
[203] *Ibid*, at [44].
[204] Thereby overruling the interpretation of *Lion Laboratories* [1985] QB 526, adopted by the Court of Appeal in *Hyde Park Residence Ltd v Yelland* [2001] Ch 143.
[205] *Ibid*, at [58].

In the opinion of the court, this would not lead to a flood of cases where freedom of expression was invoked as a defence to a claim for breach of copyright.

> It will be very rare for the public interest to justify the copying of the form of a work to which copyright attaches.[206]

The court then considered section 30(2), the defence of fair dealing for the purpose of reporting current events. Interpreting the expression 'reporting current events' liberally, and without articulated resort to the HRA, the court concluded that information about a meeting between the Prime Minister and an opposition party leader during the then current Parliament to discuss possible close cooperation between the parties was likely to be of legitimate and continuing public interest. Noting that the section was 'clearly intended to protect the role of the media in informing the public about matters of current concern,'[207] it concluded that the publication was arguably for the purpose of reporting current events.[208] This was despite the fact that the meeting took place in October 1997 but the report did not appear in the *Sunday Telegraph* until November 1999.

It was then for the court to determine whether what had occurred was in fact 'fair dealing'. It noted that, where part of a work is copied in the course of a report on current events, this defence will normally afford the court all the scope that it needs properly to reflect the public interest in freedom of expression and freedom of the press. There was no need to give separate consideration to the section 171 public interest defence.[209] Relying on pre-HRA authorities, the court concluded that there was no realistic prospect that a defence of fair dealing would be made out.[210] Furthermore, the facts of the case post-HRA were not such that the importance of freedom of expression outweighed the conventional considerations so as to afford a defence of fair dealing. There was no justification found for the extent of reproduction of Mr Ashdown's own words.[211]

13.4 Right Not to be Insulted and Distressed

Finally, also considered to be within the category of 'rights of others' is the right not to be insulted and distressed, although this is clearly not a Convention right. This particular interest was at issue in *Percy*,[212] where the Divisional Court considered whether the conviction of a protester under section 5 of the Public Order Act 1986 for defacing then standing on the American flag at an American airbase struck the appropriate balance between freedom of expression and the right not to be insulted and distressed. The court found that

---

[206] *Ibid*, at [59].
[207] *Ibid*, at [64].
[208] *Ibid*, at [65].
[209] *Ibid*, at [66].
[210] *Ibid*, at [77].
[211] *Ibid*, at [82]. Also raising issues under Art 1 Protocol No 1 are breach of contract cases, eg *Psychology Press Limited v Flanagan* [2002] EWHC (QB) 1205, and trade mark cases, eg *Levi Strauss v Tesco*, above n 72.
[212] Above n 15.

[s]ome people will be more robust than others. What one person finds insulting and distressing may be water of a duck's back to another. A civilised society must strike an appropriate balance between the competing rights of those who may be insulted by a particular course of conduct and those who wish to register their protest on an important matter of public interest.[213]

Taking into consideration the fact that the appellant could have demonstrated her message in a way which did not involve use of the national flag and the fact that her actions were deliberate with consequences of which she was well aware, the court nevertheless concluded that the conviction was disproportionate.[214]

Questions of taste and decency also raise issues in relation to the right not to be insulted and distressed and from the judgment of the House of Lords in *Prolife Alliance*,[215] it appears the judiciary will be particularly deferential where an expert body, in this case various broadcasters, has come to a conclusion on whether material is distasteful or indecent. The Prolife Alliance was a political party registered under Part II of the Political Parties, Elections and Referendums Act 2000. It was opposed to abortion, euthanasia, destructive embryo research and human cloning. It participated in the general election in 2001 and thereby qualified for a party election broadcast in accordance with the rules of allocation agreed by all broadcasters. It was to produce and edit the programme at its own expense but transmission was provided free of charge by the broadcasters. It submitted a tape of its proposed broadcast to broadcasters, including the appellant. The major part of the proposed programme was devoted to explaining the processes involved in different forms of abortion, including prolonged and graphic images of the product of suction abortion.

In accordance with section 6(1)(a) of the Broadcasting Act 1990 and paragraph 5.1(d) of the BBC's agreement with the Secretary of State for National Heritage, the broadcasters declined to transmit the programme on the grounds that it offended good taste, decency and public feeling. Although a majority of the House of Lords found that Article 10 did not entitle Prolife to make a free television broadcast, it accepted that access should not be refused on discriminatory, arbitrary or unreasonable grounds. Nor should access be granted subject to discriminatory, arbitrary or unreasonable conditions. It held that the restriction had to be justified.[216] No challenge had been brought to the statutory offensive material restriction itself, and only Lord Hoffmann considered it in detail, concluding that it was compatible with Article 10.[217] The real focus was on whether the broadcasters' decisions were arbitrary, discriminatory or unreasonable—the question of proportionality was not considered.[218] The majority concluded that the broadcasters' application of the statutory criteria could not be faulted[219] and the Court of Appeal had fallen into error by carrying out their own balancing exercise between the requirements of freedom of

---

[213] *Ibid*, at [28].
[214] See also Norwood, above n 23; Hammond, above n 24.
[215] Above n 81.
[216] *Ibid*, at [8] per Lord Nicholls.
[217] *Ibid*, at [65]–[77].
[218] *Ibid*, at [10] per Lord Nicholls and [58] per Lord Hofmann.
[219] *Ibid*, at [13] per Lord Nicholls, [80] per Lord Hoffmann and [141] per Lord Walker.

political speech and the protection of the public from being unduly distressed in their own homes.[220]

14. Preventing the Disclosure of Information Received in Confidence

14.1 Generally

Interferences with the right to freedom of expression may also be justified on the ground of preventing the disclosure of information received in confidence. Where the tort of breach of confidence is at issue, it is important to note the modifications made by Article 8, the right to respect for private life, to this tort. As discussed in the preceding paragraphs, where 'modified breach of confidence' constitutes the interference, the court will most likely consider whether the interference is justified by balancing Article 8 against Article 10 rather than considering this part of Article 10(2).[221]

However, where the right to respect for private life is not at issue, there is some scope for the application of this part of Article 10(2). For example, in *London Regional Transport v The Mayor of London*[222] the Divisional Court considered a report by Deloitte & Touche which criticised the value for money calculations that had been undertaken by London Underground Limited as part of the public–private partnership appraisal process. London Underground had obtained an interim injunction restraining the Mayor of London and Transport for London from releasing the report on the basis that it contained confidential information. It was proposed to publish a redacted version of the report, omitting detailed information which might be of assistance to bidders.

In deciding whether to lift the injunction, the court held that it had a discretion and would carry out a balancing exercise having regard to the public interest.[223] It confirmed that it was impossible to assert, in the face of Article 10, that confidentiality must be regarded as an absolute requirement and that the court had no discretion but to enforce a confidentiality agreement. Nevertheless, the court decided that, in the circumstances of the case, the defendants had to show an exceptional case to justify publication.[224] Finding it genuinely in the public interest that the material be

---

[220] *Ibid*, at [16] per Lord Nicholls. For a critique of this judgment see E Barendt, 'Free Speech and Abortion' [2003] *PL* 580. See also *Nilsen v Governor of HMP Full Sutton* [2004] EWCA Civ 1540, [2005] 1 WLR 1028, which concerned the rights of the victims of Dennis Nilsen not to be distressed by publication of his autobiography. See generally A Geddis, 'Free Speech Martyrs or Unreasonable Threats to Social Peace?—Insulting Expression and Section 5 of the Public Order Act 1986 [2004] *PL* 853.
[221] See, eg *Campbell*, above n 97.
[222] *London Regional Transport v The Mayor of London*, Divisional Court, 31 July 2001.
[223] *Ibid*, at [11].
[224] *Ibid*, at [39].

made available, and that LRT had failed to put forward a very persuasive case of harm, publication of the redacted report was permitted.[225]

Although in *H*[226] the right to respect for private life could have been argued, it was not, and the matter was considered on the justification of confidentiality. The case concerned an HIV-positive healthcare worker's attempts to maintain his anonymity whilst he challenged the legality of the health authority's actions in response to his disclosure. The Court of Appeal recognised that this was an issue of confidentiality: 'H disclosed to N the fact that he was HIV-positive in confidence.'[227] In bolstering the claim to confidence there was an

> obvious public interest in preserving the confidentiality of victims of the AIDS epidemic and, in particular, of healthcare workers who report the fact that they are HIV-positive.[228]

Furthermore, it was accepted that the health authority had a legitimate interest in striving to protect the information, which they had obtained in confidence, that one of their healthcare workers was HIV-positive.[229] However, the court did not accept that it was possible to grant an injunction restraining freedom of expression merely on the ground that the release of the information would give rise to 'administrative problems and a drain on resources.'[230]

Weighing these considerations against freedom of expression, freedom of the press and the public interest, the court concluded that the order that the health authority and health worker only be identified by initials was appropriate.[231] However, it was not acceptable to restrain the disclosure of the health worker's speciality or to restrain the newspaper from soliciting information which may lead to the disclosure of the identity of the health worker or his patients.[232]

Confidence was also at issue in *Scotcher*,[233] which concerned a disclosure by a juror of what was said or done by the jury during the course of their deliberations. The House of Lords emphasised that the secrecy of jury deliberations was a crucial and legitimate feature of English trial law and the objective of section 8 of the Contempt of Court Act 1981 in punishing disclosures by jurors was sufficiently important to justify limiting freedom of expression.[234]

> The provision is rationally connected to its aim and the means adopted are no more than is reasonably necessary, since the restriction does not apply to bona fide disclosures to the court authorities.[235]

---

[225] An appeal against this order was dismissed by the Court of Appeal on 24 August 2001. See also *Imutran*, above n 72, where disclosure of confidential documents on public interest grounds was not permitted; and *Tillery Valley Foods v Channel Four Television* [2004] EWHC (Ch) 1075.
[226] Above n 53.
[227] *Ibid*, at [26].
[228] *Ibid*, at [27].
[229] *Ibid*, at [32].
[230] *Ibid*, at [41].
[231] *Ibid*, at [58].
[232] *Ibid*, at [61].
[233] Above n 62.
[234] *Ibid*, at [29] in reliance upon *Gregory v United Kingdom* (1997) 25 EHRR 577.
[235] *Ibid*, at [29]. See also *Archer v Williams*, above n 128.

14.2 Disclosure of a Journalist's Source

Whilst the justification for ordering the disclosure of a journalist's source need not lie in the category of preventing the disclosure of information received in confidence, two important cases concern this interest and therefore it is considered here. It has been held that an order for a journalist to disclose his or her source has a chilling effect on freedom of the press[236] and that there is a public interest not only in the freedom of the press per se but also in the confidentiality of their sources.[237] However, in accordance with the principle in *Norwich Pharmacal*,[238] it is possible for a court to order that a source be disclosed. Essentially, where a person, albeit innocently and without incurring any personal liability, becomes involved in a wrongful act of another, that person thereby comes under a duty to assist the person injured by those acts by giving him any information which he is able to give by way of discovery that discloses the identity of the wrongdoer.[239] The principle is not confined to cases in tort and is of general application.[240]

However, any order must still conform to section 10 of the Contempt of Court Act 1981 and Article 10, which have a 'common purpose in seeking to enhance the freedom of the press by protecting journalistic sources.'[241] Section 10 provides that

> no court may require a person to disclose, nor is any person guilty of contempt of court for refusing to disclose, the source of information contained in a publication for which he is responsible, unless it be established to the satisfaction of the court that disclosure is necessary in the interests of justice or national security or for the prevention of disorder or crime.

The 'interests of justice' exception is not limited to cases where disclosure is required for existing or intended proceedings[242] and may also encompass disclosure to facilitate the detection of crime.[243]

These principles were applied by the House of Lords in *Ashworth Hospital Authority v MGN Ltd*.[244] In 1999 MGN had published in the *Daily Mirror* an article written by a journalist about Ian Brady. The article included a series of verbatim extracts from information held on a database maintained by staff of Ashworth Hospital Authority. The journalist had received these extracts from one of his regular sources (the intermediary), who had in turn received the information from a member of staff at Ashworth (the source). Ashworth wished the identity of the intermediary to be disclosed as a means of identifying the source.

The House of Lords concluded that, given the probability that the source was a member of staff, they were undoubtedly wrongdoers as they were acting in breach of their contract of employment or in breach of confidence.[245] Furthermore, it did not matter if the wrongdoing was tortious or in breach of contract: all that mattered was

---

[236] *Ashworth*, above n 54, at [61].
[237] *Interbrew*, above n 102, at [54].
[238] Above n 107.
[239] *Ashworth*, above n 54, at [61].
[240] *Ibid*.
[241] *Ibid*, at [38].
[242] *Ibid*, at [39].
[243] *Ibid*, at [53], expressly disagreeing with the conclusion of the Court of Appeal in *Interbrew*, above n 102.
[244] *Ibid*.
[245] *Ibid*, at [31]–[32].

that there was involvement or participation on the part of the journalist and/or news-paper. This requirement was undoubtedly satisfied in the view of the House of Lords as the information wrongfully obtained was published.[246] Furthermore, the jurisdiction applied whether or not the victim intended to pursue action in the courts against the wrongdoer.[247] Taking into consideration the importance of maintaining confidentiality in medical records, particularly in the case of the class of patients that the authority is responsible for caring for at Ashworth, the House of Lords concluded that the situation was exceptional and orders to disclose were necessary and justified.[248]

In *Interbrew*[249] a Norwich Pharmacal order had been made against five media companies requiring them to preserve and deliver up to the claimant their original copies of a leaked and partially forged document concerning a contemplated take-over by the claimant, a major brewer, of another brewery company. Entitlement to delivery up was established by the existence of a breach of confidence.[250] The Court of Appeal then considered whether the public interest in doing justice was sufficient to make disclosure necessary drawing particular attention to the purpose of the leak.

> If it is to bring wrongdoing to public notice it will deserve a high degree of protection . . . If the purpose is to wreck legitimate commercial activit . . . it will be less deserving of protection.[251]

If the falsehood of the nub of the story has been established, this is an additional reason for overriding the protection accorded to the source.[252] In the present case, it concluded that the order for disclosure was rightly made against all the defendants.[253]

These two judgments have caused particular disquiet in media circles. Prior to the HRA coming into force, there was some expectation on the part of the media that it would lead to greater protection for journalists' sources. However, all is not lost. In both cases, Article 10 was applied with considerable regard to the public interest in the freedom of the press and also in the confidentiality of their sources.[254] It has also been recognised that any disclosure of a journalist's source does have a chilling effect on the freedom of the press.[255] Although the jurisdiction is now easier to invoke, it will still not be exercised unless in conformity with Article 10. The decision in both cases came down to whether or not the disclosure was necessary. The circumstances in both were exceptional: in *Ashworth* the confidentiality of psychiatric medical records was at issue, whilst in *Interbrew* the key factor was that the expression was of low value, designed to 'wreck' legitimate commercial activity. The public interest in

---

[246] *Ibid*, at [34].
[247] *Ibid*, at [49] in reliance on *British Steel Corp v Granada Television Ltd* [1981] AC 1096.
[248] *Ibid*, at [63] and [66] taking into account *Goodwin v United Kingdom* 22 EHRR 123 and *Z v Finland* (1998) 25 EHRR 371. It was also noted that the fact that Ian Brady had himself disclosed his medical history did not detract from the need to prevent staff from revealing medical records of patients. His conduct did not damage the integrity of Ashworth's patients' records; see [66]. See also *Ackroyd*, above n 126.
[249] Above n 102.
[250] *Ibid*, at [28].
[251] *Ibid*, at [42] and [55].
[252] *Ibid*, at [57].
[253] *Ibid*, at [49].
[254] *Interbrew*, above n 102, at [54].
[255] *Ashworth*, above n 54, at [61].

protecting the source of such information was found in both cases to be very low, insufficient to outweigh countervailing considerations. Although not stated as such, it is clear that the courts were continuing the 'responsible journalism' line of reasoning of *Reynolds*.[256] Responsible journalism concerning matters in the public interest is generally protected whilst irresponsible journalism concerning matters not in the public interest is not.

The media should take comfort in the fact that it all depends on the facts and context. No insurmountable precedents have been established by either case. Indeed, the media have won the war to protect sources, it having been clearly recognised that there is a public interest in freedom of the press and protection of sources. To reach any different result, the media organisations will have to convince the courts that the public interest in protection of journalistic sources is so great that it is tantamount to an absolute right—an unlikely prospect.

15. Maintaining the Authority and Impartiality of the Judiciary

Finally, an interference with freedom of expression may be justified in the interests of maintaining the authority and impartiality of the judiciary. Under the HRA this justification has been invoked only in relation to the laws of contempt of court—in particular, third-party contempt, which was applied by the House of Lords in the 'Spycatcher' case[257] but has been rarely invoked since. Nevertheless, it remains part of the common law and was invoked by the Attorney General in *Attorney General v Punch Ltd*[258] in relation to an article by David Shayler, formerly an officer in the security service.

In 1997 an order had been made against Mr Shayler and Associated Newspapers restraining disclosure or publication of information obtained by Mr Shayler in the course of or by virtue of his employment in and position as a member of the security service. In 1998, Mr Shayler started writing a regular column in *Punch*. In July 2000 *Punch* notified the Treasury Solicitor that it intended to publish an article by Mr Shayler relating to the Bishopsgate bombing. The article was published, amended from the draft version, but did not reflect all of the amendments which had been notified to *Punch* by the Treasury Solicitor. The Attorney-General brought proceedings for contempt at common law.

It is a contempt of court for a third party, with the intention of impeding or prejudicing the administration of justice by the court in an action between two other parties, to do the acts which the injunction restrains the defendant in that action from committing if the acts done have some significant and adverse affect on the adminis-

---

[256] Above n 5.
[257] *A-G v Times Newspapers Ltd* [1992] 1 AC 191.
[258] Above n 38.

tration of justice in that action.[259] In short, it must be proved that the individual did the relevant act (*actus reus*) with the necessary intent (*mens rea*).[260] In *AG v Punch Ltd*[261] *actus reus* was admitted and the House of Lords found that there was no doubt with respect to *mens rea*, holding that the editor

> must, inevitably, have appreciated that by publishing the article he was doing precisely what the order was intended to prevent, namely, pre-empting the court's decision on these confidentiality issues. That is knowing interference with the administration of justice.[262]

Little comment was made in the speeches given as to the impact of Article 10. Lord Hope held that in the present context, when determining proportionality, three requirements had to be met: first, that there was a genuine dispute as to whether the information was confidential because its publication might be a threat to national security; secondly, that there were reasonable grounds for thinking that publication of the information before trial would impede or interfere with the administration of justice; and thirdly, that the interference with the right of free speech was no greater than was necessary.[263]

It was observed that the proviso in the original order that those seeking to publish should seek the consent of the Attorney General was acceptable as it set out a

> simple, expeditious and inexpensive procedure which avoids the necessity of an application to the court whose outcome would not be in dispute.[264]

Nevertheless, it was also observed that this type of proviso should make plain that it was also possible to apply to the court for a variation in the terms of the order.[265] A warning was also given about overly wide interlocutory injunctions which, although not disproportionate in the present case, had the potential to have a chilling effect on the press and the media generally, and were better avoided.[266]

Orders made under the Contempt of Court Act 1981 postponing the reporting of court cases also raise issues under Article 10. In *ex p The Telegraph Group plc*[267] the Court of Appeal determined an appeal against an order made under section 4(2) of the Act postponing any reporting of a case until after the conclusion of another trial arising out of the same or closely related facts. It was held that the phrase 'authority and impartiality of the judiciary' should be given a broad interpretation and was 'certainly wide enough to embrace the concept of a fair trial.'[268] Orders under section 4(2) were found to fulfil the criteria of prescribed by law and necessary in a democratic society but it was held should only be made if the court is persuaded that it is necessary in the interests of justice.[269] The court noted that 'necessary' is used in two

---

[259] *Ibid*, at [4].
[260] *Ibid*, at [20].
[261] *Ibid*.
[262] *Ibid*, at [52].
[263] *Ibid*, at [114].
[264] *Ibid*, at [59].
[265] *Ibid*, at [60].
[266] i, at [62]–[63].
[267] *R v Sherwood, ex p The Telegraph Group* [2001] EWCA Civ 1075, [2001] 1 WLR 1983.
[268] *Ibid*, at [13].
[269] *Ibid*, at [18].

senses in this context. First, the statute requires the court to address the question of whether a ban is necessary to avoid prejudice. Secondly, the order must be necessary in the sense contemplated by Article 10(2). At this stage, 'wider considerations of public policy will come into play'.[270] It must be considered whether there is a way to overcome the risk of prejudice to the administration of justice by less restrictive means. It may be that the degree of risk is tolerable in the sense of being the 'lesser of two evils.'[271] It was concluded in the present case that the evidence in the two trials was going to be inextricably linked and the problems were incapable of being overcome by judicial directions to the second jury. The order was upheld as unavoidable

in order to ensure that the three defendants in the second trial have a fair hearing in accordance with the rights guaranteed under article 6 of the Convention.[272]

---

[270] *Ibid*, at [20].
[271] *Ibid*, at [22].
[272] *Ibid*, at [34].

Article 14: Prohibition of Discrimination

1. Introduction

Article 14 provides that the enjoyment of the rights and freedoms set forth in the Convention shall be secured without discrimination on any ground. Unlike Article 1 of Protocol No 12 to the Convention, Article 14 does not confer a free-standing right of non-discrimination but precludes discrimination in the enjoyment of Convention rights. For this Article to be applicable, the facts at issue must fall within the ambit of one or more of the Convention rights.[1]

The observation is often made that Article 14 is very important. For example, in *Ghaidan* Lord Nicholls commented that discrimination was an insidious practice and that

> [d]iscriminatory law undermines the rule of law because it is the antithesis of fairness. It brings the law into disrepute. It breeds resentment. It fosters an inequality of outlook which is demeaning alike to those unfairly benefited and those unfairly prejudiced.[2]

In a similar vein, Baroness Hale noted that

> [t]reating some as automatically having less value than others not only causes pain and distress to that person but also violates his or her dignity as a human being . . . such treatment is damaging to society as a whole. Wrongly to assume that some people have talent and others do not is a huge waste of human resources, it also damages social cohesion, creating not only an under-class, but an under-class with a rational grievance . . . it is the reverse of the rational behaviour we now expect of the government and the state . . . Finally, it is a

---

[1] *Ghaidan v Godin-Mendoza* [2004] UKHL 30, [2004] 2 AC 557 at [10].
[2] *Ibid*, at [9].

purpose of all human rights instruments to secure the protection of the essential rights of members of minority groups, even when they are unpopular with the majority.[3]

Despite the brevity of its expression, applying Article 14 to a factual situation is a matter of some complexity. To make this task easier, in a number of judgments the Court of Appeal adopted what it labelled the 'structured approach' and posed a series of questions to be answered. The most well known is the list formulated by Brooke LJ in *Michalak*,[4] later modified by the Court of Appeal in *Carson*.[5] The questions formulated were as follows:

(1) Do the facts fall within the ambit of one or more of the Convention rights? (2) Was there a difference in treatment in respect of that right between the complainant and others put forward for comparison? (3) If so, was the difference in treatment on one or more of the proscribed grounds under article 14? (4) Were those others in an analogous situation? (5) Was the difference in treatment objectively justifiable in the sense that it had a legitimate aim and bore a reasonable relationship of proportionality to that aim?[6]

However, this approach is not to be employed without caution. In *Ghaidan*[7] Baroness Hale noted that there was a considerable overlap between the questions,

in particular between whether the situations to be compared were truly analogous, whether the difference in treatment was based on a proscribed ground and whether it had an objective justification.

In her view, a rigid formulaic approach was to be avoided.[8] Nevertheless, noting this caveat, in its judgment shortly after in *S*[9] the House of Lords followed the five questions without comment, as did their Lordships in *A v Secretary of State*.[10] It was not until its judgment in *Carson*[11] that the House of Lords suggested avoiding the structured approach altogether, Lord Nicholls stating that the issues in Article 14 cases should be kept as simple and non-technical as possible[12] and Lord Hoffmann noting that the questions were not always helpful as a framework of reasoning,[13] in particular because of the overlap between analogous situation and justification.[14] However,

---

[3] *Ibid*, at [132]. See also the comments of Lord Bingham in *A v Secretary of State for the Home Department* [2004] UKHL 56, [2005] 2 AC 68 at [46] and Baroness Hale at [237]; and the comments of Lord Walker in *R (on the application of Carson) v Secretary of State for Work and Pensions* [2005] UKHL 37, [2005] 2 WLR 1369 at [49].
[4] *Wandsworth London Borough Council v Michalak* [2002] EWCA Civ 271, [2003] 1 WLR 617. These questions were actually first formulated in *St Brice v London Borough of Southwark* [2001] EWCA Civ 1138, [2002] 1 WLR 1537.
[5] *R (on the application of Carson) v Secretary of State for Work and Pensions* [2003] EWCA Civ 797, [2003] 3 All ER 577.
[6] As set out by Lord Steyn in *R (on the application of S) v Chief Constable of South Yorkshire* [2004] UKHL 39, [2004] 1 WLR 2196 at [42].
[7] Above n 1.
[8] *Ibid*, at [134].
[9] Above n 6.
[10] Above n 3, at [50] per Lord Bingham.
[11] *Carson*, above n 3.
[12] *Ibid*, at [3].
[13] *Ibid*, at [29].
[14] See also the doubts expressed by Simon Brown LJ in *R (on the application of Purja) v Ministry of Defence* [2003] EWCA Civ 1345, [2004] 1 WLR 289 at [44]–[47].

whilst their Lordships did not use the framework, it is clear that by doing so they could have reached exactly the same conclusion.[15]

Rather than abandoning the structured approach altogether, it may be best to follow the advice of Baroness Hale in *Ghaidan*. The questions are a useful tool for analysis but should not be applied rigidly. The advice of Lord Nicholls in *Carson* is also helpful. Once ambit, difference in treatment and ground are established, the question for the court is whether the alleged discrimination can withstand scrutiny.

> Sometimes the answer to this question will be plain. There may be such an obvious, relevant difference between the claimant and those with whom he seeks to compare himself that their situations cannot be regarded as analogous. Sometimes, where the position is not so clear, a different approach is called for. Then the court's scrutiny may best be directed at considering whether the differentiation has a legitimate aim and whether the means chosen to achieve the aim is appropriate and not disproportionate in its adverse impact.[16]

Despite the doubts expressed in *Carson*, the structured approach is followed in this chapter but with the caveats set out in the paragraph above.

---

2. Application: No Independent Existence

For Article 14 to be applicable, the facts at issue must fall within the ambit of one or more of the Convention rights.

> Article 14 comes into play whenever the subject matter of the disadvantage 'constitutes one of the modalities' of the exercise of a right guaranteed or whenever the measures complained of are 'linked' to the exercise of a right guaranteed.[17]

There is no need to demonstrate that another right has actually been breached.[18] Furthermore, whilst a particular Convention right may not require the state to act so as to secure that right, if it does do so, it must do so without discrimination.[19] In the case of legislation, it is necessary to look at both the purpose and the effect of the legislation. It does not have to be enacted for the purpose of promoting a Convention right, but it must have as its purpose the furthering of a right which is in fact guaranteed by the Convention.[20]

This aspect of Article 14 is very fact sensitive and it is difficult to draw out principles of general applicability. Usually a generous approach is taken, although there are

---

[15] See also the comments of Lord Walker, *ibid*, at [61]–[70].
[16] *Ibid*, at [3].
[17] *Ghaidan*, above n 1, at [10] per Lord Nicholls in reliance upon *Petrovic v Austria* (2001) 33 EHRR 307.
[18] *R (on the application of Montana) v Secretary of State for the Home Department* [2001] 1 WLR 552 at [21] in reliance upon *Abdulaziz v United Kingdom* (1985) 7 EHRR 471.
[19] *Nasser v United Bank of Kuwait* [2001] EWCA Civ 1454 at [51].
[20] *R (on the application of Erskine) v London Borough of Lambeth* [2003] EWHC (Admin) 2479 at [33]–[34].

exceptions, and there is debate as to how slender the link can legitimately be.[21] In *T*[22] the claimant asylum seeker, who was HIV-positive, with a daughter born HIV-negative, sought two additional benefits, including the entitlement for a child under the age of one year to receive a given weekly quantity of dried milk or liquid milk. The court accepted that a mother who was HIV-positive should not breastfeed her baby for fear of passing on her condition to it but held that her claim did not come within the ambit of Article 2 (right to life) or Article 8 (private life).[23] It is also possible for there to be some link with another Convention right, but for that link to be considered too remote to engage Article 14. For example, in *Douglas*[24] the claimant was denied a student loan because he was over the age of 55 on the first day of the course. The Court of Appeal concluded that the loan arrangements could be described as a facilitator of education but they were one stage removed from the education itself.

> The absence of funding arrangements may make it difficult for a student to avail himself of his Article 2 Protocol No 1 rights but they are not so closely related as to prevent him from doing so.[25]

Almost every Convention right given further effect under the HRA has been raised in conjunction with Article 14—some successfully, some not.[26] For example, in *Ghaidan*[27] it was concluded that paragraph 2 of Schedule 1 to the Rent Act 1977, which enabled the survivor of a heterosexual couple, but not the survivor of a homosexual couple, to become a statutory tenant by succession, fell within the ambit of the right to respect for home guaranteed by Article 8.[28] In *A v Secretary of State*[29] it was held that the facts fell within the ambit of Article 5. The appellants were being detained without charge or trial under the Anti-Terrorism, Crime and Security Act 2001. However, in *S*[30] the House of Lords held that the retention of fingerprints and samples did not fall within the ambit of Article 8 and in *Hooper*[31] it found that the willingness of the government to reach a friendly settlement with those who petitioned the European Court of Human Rights before the HRA came into force, but

---

[21] See the comments of Lord Nicholls in *Ghaidan*, above n 1, at [11] and Sedley LJ in *Secretary of State for Work and Pensions v M* [2004] EWCA Civ 1343, [2005] 2 WLR 740 at [34].

[22] *R (on the application of T) v Secretary of State for Health*, Court of Appeal, 29 July 2002.

[23] See also *X v Y* [2004] EWCA Civ 662, [2004] IRLR 625.

[24] *R (on the application of Douglas) v North Tyneside Metropolitan Borough Council* [2003] EWCA Civ 1847.

[25] *Ibid*, at [57]. See also the judgment of Sedley LJ in *R (on the application of Hindawi) v Secretary of State for the Home Department* [2004] EWCA Civ 1309, [2005] 1 WLR 1102. Other claims concerning Art 2 Protocol No 1 and Art 14 include *R (on the application of Hounslow London Borough Council) v Schools Admissions Appeal Panel for Hounslow* [2002] EWCA Civ 900.

[26] See, eg: Art 6 (access to court) *Nasser v United Bank of Kuwait* [2001] EWCA Civ 1454, (fair trial) *E v Director of Public Prosecutions* [2005] EWHC (Admin) 147; Art 8 (private life) *Evans v Amicus Healthcare Ltd* [2004] EWCA Civ 727; Art 8 (family life) *Montana*, above n 18, *R (on the application of L) v Manchester City Council* [2001] EWHC (Admin) 707, [2002] FLR 43, and *M*, above n 21.

[27] Above n 1.

[28] *Ibid*, at [12] per Lord Nicholls.

[29] *A v Secretary of State*, above n 3. See also *R (on the application of Clift) v Secretary of State for the Home Department* [2004] EWCA Civ 514 concerning the role of the Secretary of State in determining when prisoners should be released from prison on licence.

[30] Above n 6.

[31] *R (on the application of Hooper) v Secretary of State for Work and Pensions* [2005] UKHL 29, [2005] 1 WLR 1681.

not those who petitioned after, did not come close to the ambit of any Convention right.[32]

By far the greatest number of applications has concerned the right to respect for home protected under Article 8 and the right to protection of property protected by Article 1 of Protocol No 1. In *Michalak*[33] the claimant sought to overcome an order for possession of the council flat he occupied by arguing that he was a member of the deceased former tenant's family. The Court of Appeal was satisfied that the complaint was within the ambit of the right to respect for home. Similarly, in *O'Sullivan*,[34] seeking an order for possession against a wife who carried on living in the premises following her husband's determination of the tenancy without disclosing to the local authority that she was still living in the premises engaged Article 8. However, Arden LJ pointed out that Article 8 was not engaged when the tenancy was granted to her husband in 1970 as Article 8 did not confer a right to be provided with a home.[35] But not all claims concerning housing engage Article 8. In *Erskine*[36] the Administrative Court held that the legislation subject to challenge must have as its purpose the furthering of a right which was in fact guaranteed by the Convention. Here it concluded that the purpose of section 189 of the Housing Act 1985 was to protect and promote public health and to improve the condition of low-cost housing stock. Therefore, the differences in the enforcement regime applicable to different categories of tenant did not fall within Article 14.[37]

With respect to the protection of property, it has been held that widow's bereavement allowance by way of deduction from liability for income tax which was not available for widowers comes within the ambit of Article 1 Protocol No 1,[38] as does widow's payment, widowed mother's allowance and widow's pension.[39] Not paying annual increases to pensioners ordinarily resident abroad also comes within the ambit of Article 1 Protocol No 1.[40] However, *ex gratia* payments, unenforceable by action under domestic law, have been held to be outside the scope of the Article.[41] Welfare benefits have also been found to come within the ambit of the right to respect for

---

[32] *Ibid*, at [66] per Lord Hoffmann. See also *R (on the application of Pretty) v Director of Public Prosecutions* [2001] UKHL 61, [2001] 3 WLR 1598. Although their Lordships found no other Convention right engaged, the European Court of Human Rights found Art 8 engaged as she was prevented by law from exercising her choice to avoid an undignified and distressing end to her life. See *Pretty v United Kingdom*, 29 April 2002 at [67].

[33] Above n 4.

[34] *Royal Borough of Kensington and Chelsea v O'Sullivan* [2003] EWCA Civ 371, [2003] 2 FLR 459.

[35] *Ibid*, at [48]. Other claims concerning the right to respect for home and Art 14 include *Clarke v Secretary of State for Transport, Local Government and the Regions* [2002] EWCA Civ 819; *Waite v London Borough of Hammersmith & Fulham* [2002] EWCA Civ 482; *St Brice*, above n 4; *Tucker v Secretary of State for Social Security* [2001] EWCA Civ 1646.

[36] Above n 20.

[37] *Ibid*, at [43]–[44].

[38] *R (on the application of Wilkinson) v Inland Revenue Commissioners* [2005] UKHL 30, [2005] 1 WLR 1718.

[39] *Hooper*, above n 31.

[40] *Carson*, above n 3, at [12] per Lord Hoffmann. See also *Purja*, above n 14.

[41] *Association of British Civilian Internees—Far East Region, v Secretary of State for Defence* [2003] EWCA Civ 473, [2003] QB 1397. Other claims concerning Art 1 Protpcol No 1 include: *Lloyds UDT Finance Ltd v Chartered Finance Trust Holdings plc* [2002] EWCA Civ 806, [2002] STC 956; *Waite*, above n 35; and *R (on the application of Middlebrook Mushrooms Ltd) v The Agricultural Wages Board of England & Wales* [2004] EWHC (Admin) 1447, where it was held that legislation fixing minimum wages came within the ambit of Art 1 Protocol No 1.

family life. For example, in *Morris*[42] the Administrative Court concluded that the purpose of section 189(1)(b) of the Housing Act 1996, which related to the priority need for accommodation of those with dependent children, was to ensure families would not be split up. Therefore the alleged discrimination in determining who was in priority need was within the ambit of Article 8.

> Even if there had been a final safety net elsewhere to prevent them from being split up or on the streets, the existence of such a safety net would not have prevented the relevant provisions in Pt VII of the Housing Act 1996 from being regarded as having been intended to promote family life.[43]

---

3. Without Discrimination

Article 14 provides that the enjoyment of the Convention rights and freedoms must be secured without discrimination. It is clear that the meaning of discrimination under Article 14 encompasses both direct and indirect discrimination. Direct discrimination occurs where there is a failure to 'treat like cases alike'. Indirect discrimination occurs when there is a failure to treat differently persons whose situations are significantly different.[44] Furthermore, the concept of discrimination involves less favourable treatment,[45] and it is not possible to argue that one has been discriminated against directly or indirectly unless one has been subjected to less favourable treatment.

For example, in *St Brice*[46] the claimant argued that he was discriminated against on the ground of status in that he was a defendant in the County Court rather than the High Court, where he would have had notice of an application for a warrant of possession. The Court of Appeal concluded that in fact he was not treated less favourably than a defendant in the High Court. He had an equal opportunity to require the court to hear him before eviction.[47] Sometimes the fact of less favourable treatment may not be clear. For example, in *Hindawi*[48] it was argued that the exclusion of the Parole Board from decisions on release made by the Home Secretary was not necessarily less favourable treatment. This was not accepted by the Court of Appeal, it noting that the Parole Board brought an independent body into the process.[49]

> The Secretary of State is likely to find a recommendation for release persuasive, coming as it does from an independent body rather than direct from those acting on behalf of the prisoner.[50]

---

[42] *R (on the application of Morris) v Westminster City Council* [2004] EWHC (Admin) 2191, [2005] 1 WLR 865.
[43] *Ibid*, at [14].
[44] *Carson*, above n 3, at [14] per Lord Hoffmann.
[45] *St Brice*, above n 4.
[46] *Ibid*.
[47] See also *O'Sullivan*, above n 34, at [64].
[48] Above n 25.
[49] *Ibid*, at [25].
[50] *Ibid*, at [27].

3.1 Difference in Treatment: Direct Discrimination

In order to determine whether or not there has been a difference in treatment, or a failure to treat like cases alike, there must be a comparator person or group. Usually this is easy to identify. For example, in *Ghaidan*[51] it was clear that there was a difference in treatment in respect of the right to respect for home between survivors of heterosexual relationships and survivors of homosexual relationships. Under the Rent Act 1977, only the former could become a statutory tenant by succession.[52] In *A v Secretary of State*[53] the comparison was between suspected international terrorists who were not UK nationals and suspected international terrorists who were UK nationals. However, in *S*[54] it was not so straightforward. The appellants complained that, by retaining their fingerprints and DNA samples, the police were discriminating against them as compared with the general body of persons who had not had fingerprints and samples taken by the police in the course of a criminal investigation.[55]

3.2 No Difference in Treatment: Indirect Discrimination

Indirect discrimination has not yet been considered in detail in an HRA case. In *S*[56] the claim was characterised by the House of Lords as one of direct discrimination although their Lordships clearly did not rule out the fact that Article 14 also applied to claims of indirect discrimination. However, whilst not appreciated as a claim of indirect discrimination, in *Clarke*[57] the Court of Appeal essentially determined a question of indirect discrimination by holding that, in certain circumstances, it could amount to a breach of Article 8 with Article 14 to weigh in the balance and hold against a gypsy applying for planning permission or resisting eviction that he or she has refused conventional housing accommodation as being contrary to his or her culture.[58]

---

4. Positive Duty

In common with indirect discrimination, the question of whether or not Article 14 imposes a positive duty on the state to act so as to avoid discrimination is not yet well developed in HRA case law. It is likely that the strength of any argument concerning positive duties and Article 14 would be linked closely to whether or not the Article it

---

[51] Above n 1, at [10].
[52] See also *M*, above n 21, concerning the calculation of child support liability for those living in same sex relationships.
[53] Above n 3.
[54] Above n 6.
[55] *Ibid*, at [45] per Lord Steyn.
[56] Above n 6.
[57] Above n 35.
[58] *Ibid*, at [9]. See also *Codona v Mid-Bedfordshire District Council* [2004] EWCA Civ 925, [2005] HLR 1.

is taken in conjunction with imposes a positive duty on the facts. Nevertheless, that is not to say that the positive duties and Article 14 have never been considered.

In *O'Sullivan*[59] it was argued that the respondent local authority had an obligation to offer to make the female claimant a joint tenant, given that it had granted a sole tenancy to her husband in 1970 as at that time it was common practice to grant tenancies to husbands alone. Arden LJ stated that the question of whether the positive obligation arose entailed an inquiry into whether the imposition of such an obligation on the respondent would fairly balance the parties' respective interests:

> It must be accepted in answering this question (a) that as a matter of law the consent of the tenant would be necessary; (b) that the positive obligation could not be limited to female spouses: it would have to extend to male spouses and also analogous relationships, whether heterosexual or not; and (c) that it would not be enough simply to write a few letters: other inquiries would have to be made. The appellant, on the other hand, could have initiated the process herself and she would receive a measure of protection on the alternative basis of being treated as the remaining joint tenant for the purpose of the Housing Allocation Scheme policy.[60]

Arden LJ concluded that such a positive obligation would impose an excessive burden on the respondent in practice which would result in the balance being swung unfairly in the appellant's direction. Therefore, she concluded that no such obligation was imposed.[61]

---

5. Grounds

Various grounds of prohibited discrimination are set out in Article 14 itself. These are sex, race, colour, language, religion, political or other opinion, national or social origin, association with a national minority, property, birth and other status. Whilst the list of grounds is not exhaustive, it is limited, and the limit depends upon the meaning of 'other status'.[62] Despite some earlier conflicting authority in the Court of Appeal,[63] it was held by the House of Lords in *S*[64] that 'other status' means a personal characteristic[65] analogous to the grounds expressed in the Article itself.[66] '[I]t has to do with who people are, not with what their problem is.'[67] In *S* their Lordships concluded that the difference in treatment between those who had to provide

[59] Above n 34.
[60] *Ibid*, at [60].
[61] *Ibid*, at [61]. See also *L*, above n 26, and *Campbell v South Northamptonshire District Council* [2004] EWCA Civ 409, [2004] 3 All ER 387.
[62] *S*, above n 6, at [48] per Lord Steyn.
[63] *Michalak*, above n 4; *Waite*, above n 35.
[64] Above n 6.
[65] *Ibid*, at [48] per Lord Steyn.
[66] *Ibid*, at [51] per Lord Steyn.
[67] *C v Secretary of State for the Home Department* [2004] EWCA Civ 234 at [36].

fingerprints and DNA samples pursuant to a criminal investigation as compared with the rest of the public who had not was not on the grounds of status.

> The fact that the police are now in possession of fingerprints and samples which were previously lawfully acquired as a result of a criminal investigation does not give rise to a 'status' within the meaning of article 14. The appellants, and other individuals in their position, are as fully entitled to the presumption of innocence as the general body of citizens.[68]

Similarly, in *Hooper*[69] the House of Lords held that being a person who had started legal proceedings did not qualify as a status.[70] It is not clear how the requirement for a personal characteristic affects a corporate entity claiming a violation of Article 14. In *Middlebrook Mushrooms*[71] it was held by the Administrative Court that discrimination between growers and harvesters based on type of crop was a status within the meaning of Article 14, even though this post-dated the judgment of the House of Lords in *S*.[72]

It has been accepted by UK courts determining claims under the HRA that Article 14 precludes discrimination on the grounds of sexual orientation[73]; nationality[74]; sex[75]; residence[76]; age[77]; physical or mental capacity[78]; residence[79]; distance of family relationship[80]; ethnicity[81]; family relationship[82]; and status as an asylum seeker.[83] It is clear that certain grounds of discrimination are regarded more seriously by the courts, requiring more intense scrutiny and more cogent reasons if differential treatment is to be justified. Included in this list are differences in treatment based on race, sex and sexual orientation[84] and nationality or national origin,[85] but not age.[86] In *Carson*[87] Lord Hoffmann made a distinction between two categories of grounds. In the first, which he labelled 'values', he included race, caste, noble birth, membership of a political party and gender, and stated that such characteristics are seldom, if ever, acceptable grounds for differences in treatment. Furthermore, in his view,

---

[68] *Ibid.*
[69] Above n 31.
[70] *Ibid*, at [65] per Lord Hoffmann. See also *St Brice*, above n 4, where the Court of Appeal held that the landlord's choice of forum for a possession action was not based on any personal characteristic of the tenant; and *Lancashire County Council v Taylor* [2005] EWCA Civ 284, [2005] HRLR 17. It is doubtful whether the conclusions in *Michalak*, above n 4, concerning public sector tenants and private sector tenants and *Waite*, above n 35 concerning the appellant's status as an HMP detainee would be decided in the same way post the judgments of the House of Lords in these cases.
[71] *Middlebrook Mushrooms*, above n 41.
[72] *Ibid*, at [82].
[73] *Ghaidan*, above n 1, and *M*, above n 21.
[74] *A v Secretary of State*, above n 3; *Morris*, above n 42.
[75] *Wilkinson*, above n 38; *Hooper*, above n 31.
[76] *Carson*, above n 3 at [13] per Lord Hoffmann.
[77] *R (on the application of Reynolds) v Secretary of State for Work and Pensions* [2005] UKHL 37, [2005] 2 WLR 1369; *Douglas*, above n 24.
[78] *Pretty*, above n 32, at [105]; *B v Secretary of State for Work and Pensions* [2005] EWCA Civ 929.
[79] *Nasser*, above n 19.
[80] *Michalak*, above n 4.
[81] *Clarke*, above n 35.
[82] *L*, above n 26.
[83] *R (on the application of G) v Immigration Appeal Tribunal* [2004] EWCA Civ 173, [2005] 1 WLR 1445.
[84] *Ghaidan*, above n 1, at [19] per Lord Nicholls.
[85] *Morris*, above n 42 at [32].
[86] *Carson*, above n 3, at [59]–[60] per Lord Walker.
[87] *Ibid.*

discrimination on such grounds could not be justified merely on utilitarian grounds and would be carefully examined by the courts.

In the second category, which he labelled 'questions of rationality', he included grounds such as ability, education, wealth and occupation. He stated that differences in treatment here usually depend upon considerations of the general public interest and that decisions which underpinned differences in treatment in this category were very much a matter for the elected branches of government.[88] He also noted that there may be borderline cases in which it is not easy to allocate a ground to one category or the other and, citing sexual orientation discrimination, that there may be shifts in the values of society in these matters.[89]

---

6. Analogous Position

There may be such an obvious, relevant difference between the claimant and those with whom he seeks to compare himself that their situations cannot be regarded as analogous[90] and Article 14 does not apply. When determining whether the claimant and those put forward for comparison are in an analogous position, Laws LJ suggested in his judgment in *Carson*[91] in the Court of Appeal that the question should be whether the circumstances of X and Y are so similar as to call (in the mind of a rational and fair-minded person) for a positive justification for the less favourable treatment of Y in comparison with X.[92] This was adopted by Lord Bingham in *A v Secretary of State*,[93] his Lordship finding that suspected international terrorists who were UK nationals were in a situation analogous with the appellants (suspected international terrorists who were non-UK nationals) because they shared the most relevant characteristics of the appellants. However, in the House of Lords' judgment in *Carson*[94] considerable doubt was cast on this approach, Lord Hoffmann suggesting a single question: 'is there enough of a relevant difference between X and Y to justify different treatment?'[95]

Whatever way the question is approached, it appears that there is the potential for overlap between this question and the following question of justification. However, as the judgments of the House of Lords in *A v Secretary of State for the Home Department* and *Ghaidan* show, where the questions are applied correctly, there is room for both. It was clear in *Ghaidan*[96] that the survivors of unmarried heterosexual couples and homosexual couples were in an analogous situation. 'Homosexual relationships can have exactly the same qualities of intimacy, stability and inter-dependence that

---

[88] *Ibid*, at [15]–[16].
[89] *Ibid*, at [17]. See also the comments of Lord Walker at [55]–[60].
[90] *Carson*, above n 3, per Lord Nicholls at [3].
[91] Above n 5, at [61].
[92] See also *Purja*, above n 14.
[93] Above n 3, at [53].
[94] Above n 3.
[95] *Ibid*, at [31].
[96] Above n 1.

heterosexual relationships do.'[97] Furthermore, the capacity to have children was irrelevant, as it was the long-standing social and economic interdependence which qualified for the protection of the Rent Act 1977.[98]

> [A] homosexual couple whose relationship is marriage-like in the same ways that an unmarried heterosexual couple's relationship is marriage-like are indeed in an analogous situation.[99]

Their Lordships then went on to consider whether the aim of preserving the traditional family unit was legitimate, and justified this difference in treatment as discussed in the following paragraphs. Questions of analogous situation rightly did not enter this discussion. Similarly, in *A v Secretary of State*, once it had been determined that the two groups were in an analogous situation, the question of justification centred on whether the legitimate aim of the prevention of terrorist acts justified the difference in treatment. The issue in *Carson* could have been resolved simply by their Lordships finding that UK resident pensioners and UK non-resident pensioners were not in an analogous position.[100] If it had been necessary to consider justification, the legitimate aim would most likely have been the economic well-being of the United Kingdom.

As with other aspects of Article 14, determining whether or not those put forward are in an analogous situation to the claimant is fact-sensitive and the case law cannot be easily categorised. In some instances it is obvious that an analogy can be drawn. In *Wilkinson*[101] and *Hooper*[102] the House of Lords confirmed that widows and widowers were in an analogous position in relation to bereavement allowance by way of deduction from liability for income tax and in relation to widow's pension, widow's payment and widowed mother's allowance. In *Nasser*[103] the Court of Appeal concluded that claimants and appellants before English courts not resident in a contracting state to the Brussels or Lugano Conventions were in an analogous position to all other personal claimants or appellants before the English courts when it came to awarding security for costs.[104] In *Middlebrook Mushrooms*[105] the Administrative Court held that mushroom growers and harvesters were in an analogous position to growers and harvesters of other crops when it came to the determination of minimum wages. Finally, in *Morris*[106] the Administrative Court held that an applicant for housing assistance under the Housing Act 1996 who was a British citizen and who had a dependent child subject to immigration control was in an analogous position to an applicant British citizen whose child was not subject to immigration control.[107]

---

97 *Ibid*, at [139] per Baroness Hale.
98 *Ibid*, at [141] per Baroness Hale.
99 *Ibid*, at [143] per Baroness Hale.
100 *Carson*, above n 3.
101 Above n 38.
102 Above n 31.
103 Above n 19.
104 *Ibid*, at [58].
105 Above n 41.
106 Above n 42.
107 *Ibid*, at [26].

In other cases it will be obvious that analogous circumstances are not conceivable. In S^{108} the House of Lords found no analogous position to exist between individuals who have had their fingerprints and DNA samples lawfully taken in consequence of being charged with a recordable offence and those who have not.[109] In *Michalak*[110] the Court of Appeal found too many differences between the regimes for private sector tenants and public sector tenants to conclude that the two groups were in an analogous situation with respect to successor tenancies. However, it did find in favour of the claimant on his alternative argument that distant relatives were in a relevantly similar situation to close relatives entitled to succeed to a tenancy under section 113 of the Housing Act 1985. In *Waite*[111] the Court of Appeal held that the positions of the HMP detainee and remand prisoner were not sufficiently analogous to make an Article 14 case in the light of the differential treatment of those two classes for the purposes of housing benefit.

> The HMP detainee has been convicted of murder. The remand prisoner has not been convicted of anything. He enjoys the presumption of innocence.[112]

However, more often than not it is not obvious on which side of the line a particular case falls. This was clear from the judgment of the Court of Appeal in *Purja*,[113] which concerned allegations of the Gurkha Brigade of the British Army that terms as to pension rights, pay whilst on long leave in Nepal and accompanied service discriminated against Gurkhas on the ground of their nationality. With respect to pension rights and pay whilst on long leave, looking at the basis and circumstances of the Gurkhas' recruitment, service and discharge, the court unanimously held that the Gurkhas were not in an analogous position to British soldiers. Gurkhas leave the UK and return to Nepal, where their pensions will be paid and where conditions are markedly different from those in the UK. Pensions are also payable to Gurkhas from a much earlier age.[114]

The question of accompanied service was more difficult. The majority took into account the fact that Gurkhas could return to Nepal for five months' long leave every third year, which made it more tolerable for them to be separated from their families.[115] Also considered were the need to maintain linkages with Nepal and the fact that they tended to marry at a younger age and therefore the provision of considerably more married quarters would have a tangible impact on effectiveness and

---

[108] Above n 6.
[109] *Ibid*, at [53] per Lord Steyn.
[110] Above n 4.
[111] *Waite*, above n 35.
[112] *Ibid*, at [30]. See also *Montana*, above n 18, where the Court of Appeal concluded that those who acquired citizenship under s 2 of the British Nationality Act 1981 as of right at birth were not true comparators with those who may apply for it under s 3; *R v Kirk* [2002] EWCA Crim 1580, [2002] Crim LR 756, where the Court of Appeal held that a woman who had sexual intercourse with a boy aged under 16 years was not in an analogous position with a man who had sexual intercourse with a girl aged under 16 years; and *G*, above n 83, where the Court of Appeal held that asylum seekers were not in an analogous position to others seeking to appeal from decisions of tribunals.
[113] Above n 14.
[114] *Ibid*, at [60] per Simon Brown LJ.
[115] *Ibid*, at [62] per Simon Brown LJ.

deployability.[116] Although the majority concluded that the Gurkha and British soldiers were not in an analogous position with regard to accompanied service, this was not without reservations, Chadwick LJ commenting that the decision of the court should not be taken to suggest that Gurkha soldiers do not have a legitimate grievance about the limited provision of married accommodation.[117]

7. Objective and Reasonable Justification

Article 14 is not an absolute right. Differences in treatment can be justified if these pursue a legitimate aim and there is a reasonable relationship of proportionality between the means employed and the aim sought to be realised.[118] Unlike Articles 8 and 10, the interests which may be put forward to justify an interference are not set out in the Article. It is therefore possible for any legitimate aim to be put forward. For example, it has been held to be justified to reach a friendly settlement with those who petitioned the European Court of Human Rights before the HRA came into force but not with those who petitioned it after.

> The Government is entitled to have its domestic obligations under the 1998 Act clarified by this court before the Strasbourg court considers whether the domestic system, taken as a whole, complies with the Convention.[119]

However, as with other Convention rights, from the case law certain categories emerge. These are discussed in the following paragraphs.

7.1 Social and Economic Factors

A number of claims have been made concerning the provision of welfare benefits. Usually the justification put forward for paying one group but not another, or paying different rates to different groups, includes social and economic factors. For example, in *Hooper*[120] it was argued that the preservation of widow's pension for widows bereaved before 9 April 2001 discriminated against widowers contrary to Article 14 taken together with Article 1 of Protocol No 1. The House of Lords appreciated that the pension was not means tested but paid upon the perception that older widows as a class were likely to be needier than older widowers as a class or younger widows as a class.[121] Furthermore,

---

116 *Ibid*, at [66] per Simon Brown LJ.
117 *Ibid*, at [90].
118 *Ghaidan*, above n 1, at [18] per Lord Nicholls.
119 *Hooper*, above n 31, at [67] per Lord Hoffmann.
120 *Ibid*.
121 *Ibid*, at [16] per Lord Hoffmann.

in the social conditions which prevailed for most of the last century, it was unusual for married women to work and . . . it was unreasonable to expect them to be equipped to earn their own living if they were widowed in middle age. This argument self-evidently did not apply to men.[122]

Noting that the question of the precise moment at which special treatment was no longer justified was a social and political question within the competence of Parliament,[123] their Lordships concluded that the preservation of widow's pension for widows bereaved before 9 April 2001 was objectively justified.[124]

Social and economic factors were also at issue in *Carson*.[125] Mrs Carson had been denied the annual increase payable to pensioners living in the UK because she lived in South Africa. Whilst their Lordships did not find the formulaic approach to Article 14 helpful, its conclusion in short was that the discrimination was justified. In its view, discrimination on the ground of residence did not require intensive scrutiny on the part of the court, unlike discrimination on the ground of race, sex or sexual orientation.[126] Furthermore, it was found that she moved to South Africa voluntarily and thereby placed herself outside of the UK social security system[127] and that she was not in the same position as a UK resident.[128] Furthermore, it was found that this was very much a case in which Parliament was entitled to decide whether the differences justify a difference in treatment.

And in deciding what expatriate pensions should be paid, Parliament must be entitled to take into account competing claims on public funds.[129]

Similarly, in *Reynolds*[130] their Lordships concluded that it was justified to pay those under the age of 25 income support at a reduced rate.

[O]nce it is accepted that the necessary expenses of young people, as a class, are lower than those of older people, they can properly be treated differently for the purpose of social security payments. No doubt there are different ways of giving effect to the distinction, but that is a matter for Parliament to chose.[131]

---

[122] *Ibid*, at [17] per Lord Hoffmann.
[123] *Ibid*, at [32] per Lord Hoffmann.
[124] *Ibid*, at [40] per Lord Hoffmann.
[125] Above n 3.
[126] *Ibid*, at [18] per Lord Hoffmann.
[127] *Ibid*, at [18] per Lord Hoffmann.
[128] *Ibid*, at [25] per Lord Hoffmann.
[129] *Ibid*, at [25] per Lord Hoffmann.
[130] Above n 77.
[131] *Ibid*, at [40] per Lord Hoffmann.

Furthermore, although the 25th birthday was accepted to be a very arbitrary line, their Lordships held that the justification was also the need for legal certainty and a workable rule.[132]

From these cases it appears that, where economic or social factors are raised as a justification for different treatment, the courts are more willing to defer to judgment of the legislature or executive. This may not be the case if the discrimination is regarded as particularly invidious. For example, in *Ghaidan*[133] it was stated by their Lordships that national housing policy was a field where the court would be less ready to intervene, but as the alleged violation comprised differential treatment based on the ground of sexual orientation, it scrutinised with intensity the reasons said to constitute justification. 'The reasons must be cogent if such differential treatment is to be justified.'[134] It concluded that the distinction here fell outside the discretionary area of judgment.[135] However, in *Michalak*[136] the Court of Appeal noted that determining who should succeed to a secure tenancy was pre-eminently a matter for Parliament, 'which has to determine the manner in which public resources should be allocated for local authority housing on preferential terms.'[137]

7.2 Protection of the Traditional Family Unit

Justifications based on protection of the traditional family unit are usually not successful. For example, in *Ghaidan*[138] it was argued that the difference in treatment between heterosexual and same-sex partnerships was to provide protection for the traditional family as same-sex partners were unable to have children with each other and there was a reduced likelihood of children being part of such a household. This was rejected by the House of Lords, their Lordships finding no reason for believing these factual differences had any bearing on why succession rights had been conferred on heterosexual couples but not on homosexual couples.

> Protection of the traditional family unit may well be an important and legitimate aim in certain contexts . . . Marriage is not now a prerequisite to protection . . . Nor is parenthood, or the presence of children in the home . . . Nor is procreative potential a prerequisite.[139]

---

[132] *Ibid*, at [41] per Lord Hoffmann. Social and economic justifications were also successful in *Tucker*, above n 35, which concerned a challenge to the regulation preventing a tenant, who was responsible for a child of the landlord, from being paid housing benefit; *Michalak*, above n 4, concerning the justification for only allowing close relatives to succeed to a secure tenancy under the Housing Act 1985; and *Douglas*, above n 24, concerning an age bar in relation to the provision of student loans. However, in *L*, above n 26, the Administrative Court held that paying short-term foster carers who were friends or relatives of the child at a different rate to other foster carers was not justified. The Administrative Court also found in *Morris*, above n 42, that failing to give priority under the Housing Act 1996 to a homeless British citizen with a child because her child was subject to immigration control was not proportionate to the aims of discouraging benefit tourism and encouraging illegal entrants to regularise their status.
[133] Above n 1.
[134] *Ibid*, at [19] per Lord Nicholls.
[135] *Ibid*, at [23] per Lord Nicholls.
[136] Above n 4.
[137] *Ibid*, at [41].
[138] Above n 1.
[139] *Ibid*, at [16] per Lord Nicholls.

Furthermore, it was noted that a homosexual couple, as much as a heterosexual couple, share each other's life and make their home together.[140] Here no legitimate aim was found, and their Lordships used section 3 of the HRA to read the legislation in such a way that cohabiting heterosexual couples and cohabiting homosexual couples would be treated alike for the purposes of succession as a statutory tenant.[141]

7.3 Detection and Prevention of Serious Crime

Although the House of Lords had already found in S[142] that the Article 14 claim failed for a number of other reasons, it went on to consider whether the retention of the fingerprints and DNA samples of those who had had these taken lawfully in the consequence of being charged with a recordable offence was justified. It concluded that it was as it promoted the public interest by the detection and prosecution of serious crime and by exculpating the innocent, and was proportionate to this aim, affording due deference to Parliament in the fight against serious crime.[143]

Discrimination has also been claimed in relation to the role of the Secretary of State in determining when prisoners should be released from prison on licence. He still has jurisdiction, together with the Parole Board, in relation to those serving a determinate sentence of 15 years or more. In *Clift*[144] it was argued that the difference in treatment between such prisoners and those serving determinate sentences of less than 15 years, in relation to whom the Parole Board's decision would be final, was not justified. The Court of Appeal disagreed, holding that the Secretary of State's involvement existed because of the gravity of the crime committed.

> [I]t is perfectly reasonable for the Secretary of State to draw a line and say that in relation to those prisoners who will, in the case of those sentenced to a determinate sentence, generally have committed the most serious crimes or have the worse record (or both), he should remain democratically accountable.[145]

7.4 Protection against Terrorist Acts

Finally, the legitimate aim put forward to justify the detention of suspected international terrorists who were not UK nationals in *A v Secretary of State*[146] was protection against terrorist acts. Their Lordships did not find this sufficient justification as the threat was also presented by UK nationals, who were not so detained.

> The comparison contended for by the Attorney General might be reasonable and justified in an immigration context, but cannot in my opinion be so in a security context, since the

---

[140] *Ibid*, at [17] per Lord Nicholls. See also the comments of Baroness Hale at [143].
[141] *Ibid*, at [35] per Lord Nicholls.
[142] Above n 6.
[143] *Ibid*, at [55] per Lord Steyn.
[144] Above n 29.
[145] *Ibid*, at [26]. See also *R v Witchell*, Court of Appeal, 15 September 2005 concerning the fact that a suspended sentence was not available for a young offender.
[146] Above n 3.

threat presented by suspected international terrorists did not depend on their nationality or immigration status.[147]

Their Lordships declared section 23 of the Anti-Terrorism Crime and Security Act 2001 incompatible with Article 14.

---

8. Remedy for Breach

8.1 Just Satisfaction

In addition to the usual constraints regarding remedies under the Human Rights Act, particular considerations apply to any remedy for breach of Article 14. A general principle applied to affording just satisfaction is to put the applicant so far as possible in the position in which he would have been if the state had complied with its obligations under the Act.

> In a discrimination case, in which the wrongful act is treating A better than B, this involves forming a view about whether the State should have complied by treating A worse or B better. Normally one would conclude that A's treatment represented the norm and that B should have been treated better. In some cases, however, it will be clear that A's treatment was an unjustifiable anomaly.[148]

Although the House of Lords found the respondent protected by section 6(2)(a) of the HRA in *Wilkinson*,[149] their Lordships went on to indicate what remedy they would have awarded if the claimant did have a cause of action. Mr Wilkinson, a widower, claimed that, if he had been a widow, he would have been entitled to a widow's bereavement allowance by way of deduction from his liability for income tax. Their Lordships held that there was no justification for extending the widow's allowance to men.

> If, therefore, Parliament had paid proper regard to Article 14, it would have abolished the allowance for widows. Mr Wilkinson would not have received an allowance and no damages are therefore necessary to put him in the position in which he would have been if there had been compliance with his Convention rights.[150]

---

[147] *Ibid*, at [54] per Lord Hoffmann.
[148] *Wilkinson*, above n 38, per Lord Hoffmann at [26]. See also the comments of Lord Brown at [47]–[52].
[149] *Ibid*.
[150] *Ibid*, at [28] per Lord Hoffmann. See also *Langley v Bradford Metropolitan District Council* [2004] EWCA Civ 1343, [2005] 2 WLR 740.

8.2 Reasonable Time for Change

As society changes, it is often the case that discrimination which was previously accepted is no longer justified.[151] It has been held that, where this is the case, a period of consultation, drafting and debate must be included in the time which the legislature may reasonably consider appropriate for making a change. Up to the point at which that time is exceeded, there is no violation of a Convention right.[152]

---

[151] See, eg the comments made concerning discrimination on the ground of sexual orientation on *Ghaidain*, above n 1.

[152] *Hooper*, above n 31, at [62] per Lord Hoffmann.

Article 1 Protocol No 1: Protection of Property

1. Introduction

The Human Rights Act also gives further effect to the rights contained in Protocol No 1 to the European Convention on Human Rights. The rights protected are the right to education (Article 2), the right to free elections (Article 3) and the subject of this chapter, Article 1, the right to peaceful enjoyment of possessions. Article 1 is the only Protocol No 1 right examined in this book primarily because it has generated an enormous amount of litigation under the Human Rights Act and its importance cannot be underestimated.

It has been held that Article 1 contains three distinct rules.

> The first rule is set out in the first sentence, which is of a general nature and enunciates the principle of the peaceful enjoyment of property. It then deals with two forms of interference with a person's possessions by the state: deprivation of possessions which it subjects to certain conditions, and control of the use of property in accordance with the general interest. In each case a balance must be struck between the rights of the individual and the public interest to determine whether the interference was justified. These rules are not unconnected as, before considering whether the first rule has been complied with, the court must first determine whether the last two rules are applicable . . . the second and third rules are concerned with particular instances of interference with the right to peaceful enjoyment of property. They should be construed in the light of the general principle enunciated in the first rule.[1]

---

[1] *Aston Cantlow and Wilmcote with Billesley Parochial Church Council v Wallbank* [2003] UKHL 37, [2004] 1 AC 546 at [67] per Lord Hope in reliance upon *Sporrong and Lonnroth v Sweden* (1982) 5 EHRR 35 and *James v United Kingdom* (1986) 8 EHRR 123. See also *R v Secretary of State for Health, ex p Eastside Cheese Co.* [1999] 3 CMLR 12.

2. Possessions

2.1 Generally

The meaning of 'possessions' is autonomous and wide,[2] and it is clear that a variety of things can come within the scope of Article 1. General principles applicable when determining the existence of a possession are difficult to extract, although it has been held many times that only existing possessions are protected and the Article does not guarantee the right to acquire possessions.[3] For example, in *Re A*[4] the court held that Article 1 only protected the wife's existing interest in the house and not anything she might hope to acquire from her husband in the future pursuant to her claim under the Matrimonial Causes Act 1973.[5] Therefore, when a confiscation order was made against her husband under the Drug Trafficking Act 1994, she had no right to protection from the prosecutor's claim to the husband's interest in the house.[6]

It is therefore difficult to describe anything as a possession where there is a discretion in the decision maker as to whether or not to make the claimed possession available. For example, *Association of British Civilian Internees*[7] concerned the British government's decision to make an *ex gratia* payment of £10,000 to those who had been interned by the Japanese during the Second World War who were born in the United Kingdom or had a parent or grandparent born there. The claimant association represented a number of British citizens interned during their war and their surviving spouses who did not meet these criteria and had therefore been refused an *ex gratia* payment. The Court of Appeal held that claims which had been held to be without foundation could not be possessions within the meaning of Article 1. There was no right to judicial review of the scheme to vindicate their public law rights to receive compensation.[8]

The only possible way a future possession may become a possession within the meaning of Article 1 is if the claimant has a legitimate expectation in relation to it. In *Rowland*[9] it was confirmed by the Court of Appeal that a legitimate expectation, even if arising from ultra vires acts by a public authority, can constitute a possession for the purposes of Article 1.[10] In *National Farmers Union*[11] the issue was a legitimate expectation not as to payment but as to a particular level of payment. It had been

---

[2] *Davies v Crawley Borough Council* [2001] EWHC (Admin) 854.
[3] See, eg *R (on the application of the National Farmers Union) v Secretary of State for the Environment, Food and Rural Affairs*, Administrative Court, 6 March 2003 at [65].
[4] [2002] 2 FCR 481.
[5] *Ibid*, at [164].
[6] See also *Ram v Ram* [2004] EWCA Civ 1452, [2004] 3 FCR 425.
[7] *Association of British Civilian Internees—Far East Region v Secretary of State for Defence* [2003] EWCA Civ 473, [2003] QB 1397.
[8] *Ibid*, at [82]. See also *R (on the application of Toovey) v The Law Society* [2002] EWHC (Admin) 391, where the court held that an application for a discretionary discount was not capable of being a possession; and *Shaw (Inspector of Taxes) v Vicky Construction Ltd* [2002] EWHC (Ch) 5659, [2002] STC 1544, where the court held that the refusal to grant a fresh certificate to a taxpayer under s 561 of the Income and Corporation Taxes Act 1988 was not an interference with the peaceful enjoyment of a possession.
[9] *Rowland v Environment Agency* [2003] EWCA Civ 1885, [2005] Ch 1.
[10] See *ibid*, [66]–[68], for an explanation of the circumstances in which a legitimate expectation may arise.
[11] *National Farmers Union*, above n 3.

argued that merely having made an application to enter the scheme for compensation for the slaughter of livestock as a result of the outbreak of foot and mouth prior to 30 April did not confer any right to payment at the originally agreed higher rates. However, it was held to be arguable that there was a legitimate expectation as to payment at the rates prevailing at the time and this was considered to be possession within the meaning of Article 1.[12]

2.2 Personal Possessions

A range of personal possessions have been held to be within the scope of Article 1, including money[13]; copyright[14]; shares[15]; the rights to a retirement annuity and associated benefits under an annuity contract or personal pension arrangement[16]; an unregistered interest in land even if not in possession[17]; a home[18]; and land.[19] However, the right to be employed or not to have a contract of employment terminated have been held to be outside its scope.[20] Contributory benefits, such as the state pension, have generally been considered in the context of Article 14, where it has been held that such benefits are within the ambit of Article 1.[21] It has also been held that non-contributory rights under a pension scheme may be considered possessions if they are part of a package of remuneration which, unlike a non-contributory social security benefit, the individual has earned by service.[22] However, Article 1 does not guarantee a right to a pension of a particular amount or payment of it at a particular time.[23]

2.3 Business Possessions

Many more claims under Article 1 have concerned possessions necessary to run a business. It has been held that a business itself is a possession,[24] as are licences such as

---

12 See also *PW & Co v Milton Gate Investments Ltd* [2003] EWHC (Ch) 1994, [2004] Ch 142; *Re an application to vary the undertakings of A* [2005] STC (SCD) 103; and *Re West Norwood Cemetery* [2005] 1 WLR 2176.

13 *R v Dimsey; R v Allen* [2001] UKHL 46, [2001] 3 WLR 843; *R v Benjafield* [2002] UKHL 2, [2003] 1 AC 1099; *R (on the application of Denson) v Child Support Agency* [2002] EWHC (Admin) 154, [2002] 1 FLR 938.

14 *Ashdown v Telegraph Group Ltd* [2001] EWCA Civ 1142, [2001] 3 WLR 1368.

15 *Ibid.* However, here the court held that the alleged violation of the company's rights leading to a diminution in the value of the shares would only give a shareholder cause for complaint if there was a factual or legal impossibility preventing the company suing for the loss.

16 *Krasner v Dennison* [2000] 3 WLR 720.

17 *Kingsalton Ltd v Thames Water Developments Ltd* [2001] EWCA Civ 20.

18 *Marcic v Thames Water Utilities Ltd* [2003] UKHL 66, [2004] 2 AC 42.

19 *Beaulane Properties Limited v Palmer* [2005] HRLR 19.

20 *A v Hounslow London Borough Council,* Employment Appeal Tribunal, 11 July 2001.

21 *R (on the application of Hooper) v Secretary of State for Work and Pensions* [2005] UKHL 29, [2005] 1 WLR 1681; *R (on the application of Carson) v Secretary of State for Work and Pensions* [2005] UKHL 37, [2005] 2 WLR 1369. In relation to non-contributory benefits, see *Campbell v South Northamptonshire District Council* [2004] EWCA Civ 409, [2004] 3 All ER 387. It was held in *B v Secretary of State for Work and Pensions* [2005] EWCA Civ 929 that overpaid non-contributory benefits were outwith with scope of Art 1 Protocol No 1.

22 *R (Smith) v Secretary of State for Defence and Secretary of State for Work and Pensions* [2004] EWHC (Admin) 1797, [2005] 1 FLR 97 at [27].

23 *Ibid.*

24 *R (on the application of Kelsall) v Secretary of State for the Environment, Food and Rural Affairs* [2003] EWHC (Admin) 459 at [62].

a telecommunications licence[25] or an operator's licence for goods vehicles,[26] and a contractual right to receive payment as well as the money paid when received.[27] A trade mark is also considered to be a possession,[28] as is a claim for repayment of VAT paid in error.[29]

It is not clear whether planning permission to run a particular type of business can be considered a possession. In *Davies*[30] the claimants each owned a mobile catering van. One had obtained planning permission for her van, the other had obtained a certificate of lawful use. In 2001 the streets where the vans were located were designated as prohibited and both were offered a site on a 'consent street' for £5,000 per year. It was argued that the claimants had an economic interest in their vans and that the planning permission was a component of that. The Administrative Court held that it was doubtful that the definition of possessions was as wide as contended but it did not finally decide the issue, proceeding on the assumption that their possessions had been subject to interference.[31]

State regulatory approval for a product can clearly have an effect on the ability of a company to sell the product; however, it is not clear whether such approval can be considered to be a possession. *Amvac Chemicals UK Ltd*[32] concerned a decision to suspend regulatory approvals for dichlorvos, a chemical used in pesticides. The claimant manufactured dichlorvos for non-agricultural uses and supplied it to the distributors of such products. The Administrative Court noted that such approvals may have an economic value to a person or company and that the withdrawal of such approval may have serious economic effects. Without finally deciding, it was inclined to the view that regulatory approval could not be a possession.[33] However, in the present case, where only provisional approval had been granted, it concluded that this was definitely not a possession.[34]

3. Interferences with the Peaceful Enjoyment of Possessions

When determining whether or not there has been an interference with the peaceful enjoyment of possessions, it is important to look behind appearances and investigate the realities of the situation complained of.[35] The most common interferences with

[25] *R (on the application of Orange Personal Communications Ltd) v Secretary of State for Trade and Industry*, Administrative Court, 25 October 2000.

[26] *Crompton v Department of Transport North Western Area* [2003] EWCA Civ 64.

[27] *Vicky Construction*, above n 8.

[28] *Levi Strauss and Co v Tesco Stores Ltd* [2002] EWHC (Ch) 1556.

[29] *Local Authorities Mutual Investment Trust v Customs and Excise Commissioners* [2003] EWHC (Ch) 2766, [2004] STC 246.

[30] Above n 2.

[31] *Ibid*, at [129].

[32] *R (on the application of Amvac Chemicals UK Ltd) v Secretary of State for the Environment, Food and Rural Affairs* [2001] EWHC (Admin) 1011, [2002] ACD 219.

[33] *Ibid*, at [94].

[34] *Ibid*, at [95]–[96].

[35] *Eastside Cheese*, above n 1, in reliance upon *Sporrong and Lonnroth*, above n 1, at [63].

peaceful enjoyment arise from deprivation or control of possessions, although it is possible for an interference to not constitute either. Possible interferences are examined in the following paragraphs.

3.1 Deprivation

In some situations the fact that a deprivation of a possession has occurred is clear. For example, a transfer in the ownership of a possession is undoubtedly a deprivation within the meaning of Article 1,[36] as is the imposition of taxes and duties,[37] a compulsory purchase order,[38] an order of the court declining rectification of the Land Registry if the order fails to give effect to the substantive property rights of a party,[39] the vesting in the trustee in bankruptcy of the bankrupt's rights to a retirement annuity or personal pension,[40] a confiscation order under the Drug Trafficking Act 1994[41] and an infringement of copyright.[42] A reduction in market value also amounts to a deprivation. In *Dennis v Ministry of Defence*[43] it was held that the noise from Harrier jets flying over the claimant's estate significantly reduced its market value and thus constituted an interference with Article 1 rights. In *Marcic*[44] the House of Lords held that serious flooding of a person's home was an interference with his Article 1 rights.[45] However, it is clear that claimants have a high threshold to surmount when a claim is based on environmental impact and a reduction in property values.[46] It is also possible that a legal requirement to pay a minimum wage constitutes a deprivation, although this has only been considered in the context of Article 14.[47]

It is possible that there can be no deprivation if the interference is simply an incident of ownership of the possession. Whilst the House of Lords has considered the issue in two cases, its observations have been *obiter* and the issue is still to be determined conclusively. In the first case of *Wallbank*[48] the respondents were freeholders of a farm which included rectorial property, constituting them as lay rectors and subjecting them to the liability of paying for all and necessary repairs to the chancel of St John the Baptist church, the parish church of Aston Cantlow. When the Parochial

---

[36] *Ibid.*
[37] *Lydiashourne Ltd v The Commissioners of Customs & Excise*, Court of Appeal, 1 November 2000; *Dimsey; Allen*, above n 13; *Lindsay v Customs and Excise Commissioners* [2002] EWCA Civ 267, [2002] 1 WLR 1766.
[38] *R (on the application of Aina) v London Borough of Hackney*, Court of Appeal, 24 November 2000; *London Borough of Bexley v Secretary of State for the Environment, Transport and the Regions* [2001] EWHC (Admin) 323; *R (on the application of Peart) v The Secretary of State for Transport, Local Government and the Regions* [2002] EWHC (Admin) 2964.
[39] *Kingsalton*, above n 17, at [45].
[40] *Krasner vDennison* [2000] 3 WLR 720.
[41] *Benjafield*, above n 13 at [17].
[42] *Ashdown*, above n 14, at [28].
[43] [2003] EWHC (QB) 793, [2003] 19 EG 118 (CS).
[44] Above n 18.
[45] *Ibid*, at [37] per Lord Nicholls.
[46] *R (on the application of Westminster City Council) v Mayor of London* [2002] EWHC (Admin) 2440 in reliance upon S v France (1990) 65 D&R 250. See also *Lough v First Secretary of State* [2004] EWCA Civ 905, [2004] 1 WLR 2557; *R (on the application of Trailer & Marina (Leven) Ltd) v Secretary of State for the Environment, Food & Rural Affairs* [2004] EWCA Civ 1580, [2005] 1 WLR 1267.
[47] *R (on the application of Middlebrook Mushrooms Ltd) v The Agricultural Wages Board of England and Wales* [2004] EWHC (Admin) 1447.
[48] *Wallbank*, above n 1.

Church Council served notices on the respondents requiring them to put the chancel in proper repair, they disputed their liability. The House of Lords did not need to deal with the question of Article 1 as it had decided that the Parochial Church Council was not a public authority and, not exercising a public function, was therefore not bound by the Human Rights Act. However, Lords Hope, Scott and Hobhouse did consider the application of Article 1 to the facts. Their Lordships concluded that the respondents were not being deprived of their possessions or being controlled in the use of their property. The liability was simply an incident of the ownership of the land which gave rise to it. The peaceful enjoyment of the land involved the discharge of burdens which were attached to it as well as the enjoyment of its rights and privileges.

> This is a burden on the land, just like any other burden that runs with the land. It is, and has been at all times, within the scope of the property right which she acquired and among the various factors to be taken into account in determining its value. She could have divested herself of it at any time by disposing of the land to which it was attached. The enforcement of the liability under the general law is an incident of the property right . . . It is not . . . an outside intervention by way of a form of taxation.[49]

A similar issue arose in *Wilson*[50] concerning a loan agreement regulated by the Consumer Credit Act 1974. However, the reasoning of their Lordships on the issue was not clear. Mrs Wilson argued that, as the agreement did not contain all the prescribed terms, by reason of section 127(3) of the Act the court would not be able to make an enforcement order. As the case was determined on the issue of retrospective effect, there was actually no need for their Lordships to comment on the Article 1 issue. However, all apart from Lord Rodger did. Lord Nicholls and Lord Hobhouse found that the relevant provisions of the Consumer Credit Act constituted a statutory deprivation of the lender's rights of property.

> The lender's rights were extinguished in favour of the borrower by legislation for which the state was responsible. This was a deprivation of possessions within the meaning of article 1.[51]

By contrast Lord Hope and Lord Scott, taking a similar line to that in *Wallbank*, did not find Article 1 engaged. Lord Hope pointed out that the agreement which was entered into was improperly executed from the outset, so it was always subject to the restrictions on its execution in the Act. The lender

> never had an absolute and unqualified right to enforce this agreement or to enforce the rights arising from the delivery of the motor car.[52]

---

[49] *Ibid*, at [71] per Lord Hope. See also Lord Hobhouse at [91] and Lord Scott at [92] and [133].
[50] *Wilson v First County Trust* [2003] UKHL 40, [2003] 3 WLR 568.
[51] *Ibid*, at [44] per Lord Nicholls in reliance upon James, above n 1, at [38]. See also Lord Hobhouse at [136].
[52] *Ibid*, at [108]. See also Lord Scott at [168]. On this issue see also *Mills v MI Developments (UK) Ltd* [2002] EWCA Civ 1576 concerning the creation of an easement over a property; *Local Authorities Mutual Investment Trust*, above n 29, concerning a limitation period within with to reclaim VAT paid in error; *Pennycook v Shaws (EAL) Ltd* [2004] EWCA Civ 100, [2004] Ch 296 concerning the statutory right to renew a business tenancy under the Landlord and Tenant Act 1954; *Kay v London Borough of Lambeth* [2004] EWCA Civ 926, [2004] 3 WLR 1396 concerning secure tenancies under Part IV. of the Housing Act 1985; and *Soteriou v Ultrachem Ltd* [2004] EWHC (QB) 983, [2004] IRLR 870 concerning a contract unenforceable for illegality.

In *Beaulane Properties*[53] the Chancery Division attempted to get around this line of reasoning by holding that Article 1 was engaged where a property right was acquired which was subject to a law with the potential for depriving the owner of it if and when this subsequently happened.[54] It held that, in *Wilson*, the reason why there was a delimitation of rights and not a deprivation was that the legislation did not bite subsequently but at the moment the transaction took effect. Therefore the lender never had a right of which he could be deprived. In the present case it concluded that the effect of section 17 of the Limitation Act 1980 and section 75 of the Land Registration Act 1925 was to deprive the owner of the land of all his rights to it and of any means, whether by taking direct action or by going to the law, of recovering possession of it, and thus to transfer the right to possession and title to the trespasser—a deprivation of possessions within the meaning of Article 1.[55]

3.2 Control

Even if there is no transfer of ownership and therefore no deprivation, there may still be an interference with peaceful enjoyment if control is exercised over possessions. Control can take many forms. It has been held that both planning laws[56] and housing laws[57] can amount to 'controls' over possessions, as do the powers retained by public authorities to enter land for the purpose of carrying out land drainage works,[58] laws preventing trade and business vehicles being driven in certain areas,[59] the conditions imposed by a professional body which had to be complied with by the individual in order for him to continue in practice,[60] notification of a site as being of special scientific interest under the Wildlife and Countryside Act 1981[61] and a requirement to pay child support.[62]

In *Eastside Cheese*[63] an emergency control order under section 13 of the Food Safety Act 1990 was made in relation to cheese following a boy becoming seriously ill with *E. coli*. The effect of the order was to prohibit the carrying out of any commercial operation in relation to cheese originating from a particular company. It paralysed that company's cheese-making business and also paralysed the business of cheese processers and maturers to the extent that they depended on supplies from this

---

[53] Above n 19.
[54] *Ibid*, at [146].
[55] *Ibid*, at [136].
[56] *Waltham Forest London Borough Council v Secretary of State for Transport, Local Government and the Regions* [2002] EWCA Civ 330, [2002] 13 EG 99 (CS). See also *R (on the application of Fuller) v Chief Constable of Dorset Police* [2001] EWHC Admin 1057, [2003] QB 480, in which it was held that a direction to travellers to leave land under s 61 of the Criminal Justice and Public Order Act 1994 was a control on property.
[57] *Stanley v London Borough of Ealing*, Court of Appeal, 16 April 2003.
[58] *R (on the application of MWH & H Ward Estates Ltd) v Monmouthshire CC* [2002] EWCA Civ 1915, [2003] ACD 115.
[59] *Phillips v DPP* [2002] EWHC (Admin) 2903, [2003] RTR 8.
[60] *Whitefield v General Medical Council* [2002] UKPC 62, [2003] HRLR 243.
[61] *R (on the application of Fisher) v English Nature* [2004] EWCA Civ 663, [2005] 1 WLR 147. See also *Leven*, above n 46.
[62] *Denson*, above n 13. See also *Secretary of State for Work and Pensions v M* [2004] EWCA Civ 1343, [2005] 2 WLR 740, in which a majority of the Court of Appeal held that the requirement to pay child support was within the ambit of Art 1 for the purposes of a claim under Art 14.
[63] Above n 1.

company. Rather than a deprivation of possessions, the Court of Appeal concluded that the order was an instance where the state had deemed it necessary to control the use of possessions in accordance with the general interest. Similarly, the Administrative Court concluded in *Davies*[64] that the council's new street trading scheme which required the claimant owners of mobile catering vans to pay £5,000 per year for a new site was not a deprivation of possessions but a measure of control of the use of property.

> The claimants never had security of tenure. They retain their vans. They did not lose an ability to trade from them. They could trade from a position nearby on the same industrial estate.[65]

4. Justifying Interferences

4.1 Generally

The right to the peaceful enjoyment of possessions is not an absolute right. However, the question of justifying interferences with the peaceful enjoyment of possessions is complicated by the drafting of Article 1. The Article provides that

> no one shall be deprived of his possessions except in the public interest and subject to the conditions provided for by law and by the general principles of international law.

In relation to control, it provides that the right to the peaceful enjoyment of possessions shall not

> in any way impair the right of a State to enforce such laws as it deems necessary to control the use of property in accordance with the general interest.

Despite the different wording in relation to deprivation and control, it has been established by the case law that any interference with the peaceful enjoyment of possessions, whether by deprivation or control, must achieve a fair balance between the demands of the general interest of the community and the requirements of the protection of the individual's fundamental rights. There must therefore be a reasonable relationship of proportionality between the means employed and the aim pursued.[66]

It has been held that the point at which the line is drawn is quite different from that established in proportionality decisions under Articles 8(2), 9(2), 10(2) and 11(2).

> These articles place on the court the obligation to decide whether an interference with the primary right has been 'necessary in a democratic society', and a sophisticated

---

[64] Above n 2.
[65] *Ibid*, at [135].
[66] *Dimsey; Allen*, above n 13 in reliance upon *Gasus Dosier-und Fordertecknik GmbH v The Netherlands* (1995) 20 EHRR 403 at [62]; *Marcic*, above n 18. See also *Eastside Cheese*, above n 1.

jurisprudence . . . now exists in this regard. When, however, the court speaks of proportionality under art 1 of the First Protocol, its starting point is an extant judgment by the state signatory as to what is necessary in the public interest. The court's duty is to gauge whether the state has nevertheless gone beyond what the article will tolerate.[67]

However, this view is by no means universal. In *Clays Lane Housing*[68] the Court of Appeal held that there was no real difference on the test to be applied between the jurisprudence of the European Court of Human Rights[69] and the conclusion of the House of Lords in *Daly*.[70]

They both allow 'necessary', where appropriate, to mean 'reasonably', rather than 'strictly' or 'absolutely' necessary. Everything then depends on the context.[71]

This approach by far reflects more accurately the approach the courts have taken to the application of this Article under the HRA.

Although it is specified in Article 1 that a deprivation must be subject to the conditions provided for by law, there has been little mention in the case law of legality forming part of the test for a justified interference.[72] In common with Article 14, legitimate aims are not set out in Article 1. However, certain categories appear from the case law, including consumer protection,[73] public health,[74] prevention of crime[75] and the economic well-being of the country.[76] These are examined in the next section.

4.2 Compensation

Where there has been a deprivation of possessions without compensation of an amount reasonably related to the value of the possessions, this will normally constitute a disproportionate interference. A total lack of compensation is justifiable under Article 1 only in exceptional circumstances.[77]

[S]ome public interest is necessary to justify the taking of private property for the benefit of the state and . . . when the public interest does so require, the loss should not fall upon the individual whose property has been taken but should be borne by the public as a whole.[78]

---

[67] *R (on the application of Hamilton) v United Kingdom Central Council for Nursing, Midwifery and Health Visiting* [2003] EWCA Civ 1600, [2004] 79 BMLR 30 at [33] per Sedley LJ.
[68] *R (on the application of Clays Lane Housing Co-Operative Limited) v The Housing Corporation* [2004] EWCA Civ 1658, [2005] 1 WLR 2229.
[69] *James*, above n 1.
[70] *R (on the application of Daly) v Secretary of State for the Home Department* [2001] UKHL 26, [2001] 2 AC 532.
[71] *Ibid*, at [23].
[72] Two exceptions are *Krasner*, above n 16, and *Al-Kishtaini v Shanshal* [2001] EWCA Civ 264, [2001] 2 All ER (Comm) 601.
[73] See, eg *Wilson*, above n 50.
[74] See, eg *Eastside Cheese*, above n 1; *Amvac Chemicals*, above n 32; and *Stanley*, above n 57.
[75] See, eg *Benjafield*, above n 13.
[76] See, eg *Lindsay*, above n 37.
[77] *Eastside Cheese*, above n 1, in reliance upon *Holy Monasteries v Greece* (1994) 20 EHRR 1 at [71]. See also *Kingsalton*, above n 17; *MWH & H Ward*, above n 58; *Corton Caravans and Chalets Limited v Anglian Water Services Limited* [2003] RVR 323.
[78] *Davies*, above n 2, quoting from *Grape Bay Ltd v AG of Bermuda* [2000] 1 WLR 574 at 583 per Lord Hoffmann.

However, in relation to a control on the use of possessions, the payment of compensation is not normally required for the interference to be justifiable.

> This is so even if, as will inevitably be the case, the legislation in general terms affects some people more than others.[79]

The question of compensation arose in *Kelsall*,[80] which concerned a challenge by 10 mink farmers to the compensation scheme designed to compensate them for the effects of the Fur Farming Prohibition Act 2000. The Secretary of State accepted that their businesses were possessions and that they were deprived of these possessions by the Act. The Administrative Court held that the compensation should be reasonably related to the value of the property taken[81] and that the provisions for compensation must not be so inflexible that they fail to take account of substantially different situations.[82] Here it concluded that the scheme did not comply with the requirements of Article 1.

> The provisions of the Order as to compensation . . . fail on every count . . . they operate unfairly as between different farmers and generally; they fail to take account of the different values of premium breeds . . . and they produce arbitrary effects. Reasons have been put forward to justify provisions of the order that do not bear scrutiny and are irrational. The consequences of the defects in the Order are too great to be contained within a permissible margin for workability or approximation.[83]

The question of compensation also arose in *Dennis*,[84] which concerned the effect of noise from Harrier jet fighters on the market value of the estate. The Divisional Court concluded that a fair balance could not be struck in the absence of compensation.

> [C]ommon fairness demands that where the interests of a minority, let alone an individual, are seriously interfered with because of an overriding public interest, the minority should be compensated.[85]

It held that damages fell to be considered under three heads: past and future loss of amenity; past and future loss of use; loss of capital value. The overall figure arrived at was £950,000. Whilst this was an assessment of damages for nuisance at common law, the court made it clear that, if nuisance had not provided a remedy, the claim would have succeeded under Article 1 and compensation in the same sum would have been awarded to enable a fair balance to be struck.[86]

---

[79] *Leven*, above n 46, at [58].
[80] Above n 24.
[81] *Ibid*, at [62] in reliance upon *Lithgow v UK* (1986) EHRR 329.
[82] *Ibid*, at [62] in reliance upon *Papachelas v Greece* Judgment, 25 March 1999.
[83] *Ibid*, at [63].
[84] Above n 43.
[85] *Ibid*, at [63] in reliance upon *S v France*, above n 46.
[86] *Ibid*, at [88]–[92]. See also *Marcic*, above n 18, where it was held that those who enjoyed the benefit of effective drainage should bear the cost of paying compensation to those whose properties are situated lower down in the catchment area and who, in consequence, have to endure intolerable sewer flooding; *R (on the application of London and Continental Stations and Property Ltd) v Rail Regulator* [2003] EWHC (Admin) 2607, concerning compensation for the deprivation of property resultant from the redevelopment of St Pancras Station; and *Beaulane Properties*, above n 19, which concerned the acquisition of land by adverse title.

4.3 Procedural Rights

Finally, where there has been deprivation or control, it may not be possible for a fair balance to be struck unless certain procedural rights have been afforded. For example, in *Orange Personal Communications Ltd*[87] telecommunications licence holders objected to regulations made by the Secretary of State which inserted a raft of new conditions into existing licences. Declaring certain conditions in the regulations unlawful, the court held that, in practice, most enactments try to ensure that a fair balance is struck and proportionality observed by providing the licence holder with an opportunity to appeal against, or to object to, proposed mechanisms.[88] However, Article 1 does not extend to setting up an inquiry.[89]

5. Consumer Protection

An objective put forward in a number of cases to justify an interference with the peaceful enjoyment of possessions is the objective of consumer protection. Although in *Wilson*[90] the case was determined by the issue of retrospective effect, four of their Lordships considered the question of the application of Article 1 to the facts. As discussed in preceding paragraphs, the lender could not enforce a loan agreement as the agreement did not contain all the prescribed terms required by the Consumer Credit Act 1974. Assuming this did amount to a deprivation of the lender's possessions, Lord Nicholls held that the Act pursued a legitimate aim in that it protected persons wishing to borrow money from exploitation.[91] Furthermore, in his view, Parliament was charged with the primary responsibility for deciding whether the means chosen to deal with a social problem were both necessary and appropriate.[92] He concluded that the response of Parliament was proportionate. Lords Hope[93], Hobhouse[94] and Scott[95] reached similar conclusions.

The protection of the consumer is also the objective of laws regulating competition. *Interbrew SA v Competition Commission*[96] concerned a challenge to the Competition Commission's recommendation that Interbrew should be ordered to divest itself of the entire United Kingdom beer business of Bass Brewers which it had recently acquired. The Administrative Court concluded that the divestment of Bass

---

[87] Above n 25.
[88] *Ibid*, at [82].
[89] *Persey v Secretary of State for Environment, Food and Rural Affairs* [2002] EWHC (Admin) 371, [2003] QB 794.
[90] Above n 50.
[91] *Ibid*, at [68].
[92] *Ibid*, at [70].
[93] *Ibid*, at [109].
[94] *Ibid*, at [138].
[95] *Ibid*, at [169].
[96] [2001] EWHC (Admin) 367.

was strictly necessary and there was no other effective remedy available to restore effective competition to the market.[97]

The regulation of various professions also has at its heart the protection of those using the services provided. A number of complaints under Article 1 have been raised in relation to interventions by the Law Society into solicitors' practices. In *Wright*[98] the Chancery Division held that the public interest required a balance to be struck between the draconian effect of intervention and the protection of clients, other solicitors, and the general reputation of the profession.[99] In the view of the court, it was not possible to devise a different and less draconian remedy, and the balance came down in favour of protecting the public.[100]

6. Planning and the Environment

Planning and environmental rules and regulations often interfere with the peaceful enjoyment of possessions. However, given the beneficial consequences of these measures, such interferences are generally found to be justified. For example, in *Davies*[101] the Administrative Court stated that Article 1 bestowed a very wide margin of appreciation. It concluded that the Council's adoption of a street trading scheme, meaning that certain streets, including those where the claimants traded, were prohibited and charging £5,000 per year for a consent site, was proportionate and struck a fair balance.[102]

> All that happened was that in the public good, and in common with others, they were required to move to a different position in the same general location. A system of appeals was set up. A fee, payable by instalments, was reasonably decided upon. The fact that Mrs Atkins ceased to trade does not, I am afraid, make the use of the Act disproportionate.[103]

Similarly, in *Phillips*[104] the Divisional Court held that the Royal Parks and Other Open Spaces Regulations 1997 which made it an offence to drive or ride any trade or business vehicle in specified areas were proportionate.

---

[97] Nevertheless the decision was struck down as unfair as Interbrew were not given a proper opportunity to deal with a particular issue. See also *R (on the application of Pow Trust) v The Chief Executive and Registrar of Companies* [2002] EWHC (Admin) 2783, [2004] BCC 268, in which the court held that penalties under the Companies Act 1985 for non-compliance with requirements for delivery of accounts and reports were proportionate.

[98] *Wright v Law Society*, Chancery Division, 4 September 2002.

[99] *Ibid*, at [61].

[100] *Ibid*. See also *Holder v Law Society* [2003] EWCA Civ 39, [2003] 1 WLR 1059; *Law Society v Sritharan* [2005] EWCA Civ 476; and Hamilton, above n 67, which concerned the suspension of the appellant from practice as a state-registered nurse and midwife.

[101] Above n 2.

[102] *Ibid*, at [100]–[105].

[103] *Ibid*, at [139].

[104] *Phillips*, above n 59.

The areas covered by the Regulations are areas of particular historical and patrimonial significance and also of natural beauty. It seems clear that the Secretary of State has considered it appropriate to proscribe, so far as is possible, trade activities within these areas, no doubt with a view to preserving their status . . . for the benefit of society as a whole.[105]

Compulsory purchase orders also raise issues under Article 1. In *London Borough of Bexley*[106] the Administrative Court considered a compulsory purchase order under section 226(1) of the Town and Country Planning Act 1990 which had been confirmed by the Secretary of State. The court noted that the right to peaceful enjoyment of possessions was a qualified rather than an absolute right and involved a balancing exercise between the 'public interest and the individual's right whereby any interference with the individual's right must be necessary and proportionate.'[107] The court was not persuaded that there was anything materially different between those principles and the principles applied by the Secretary of State under Circular 14/94 whereby a compulsory purchase order was not to be made unless there was a compelling case in the public interest as such an approach 'necessarily involves weighing the individuals rights against the public interest.'[108] The court concluded that there was a compelling case in the public interest and that a fair balance had been struck between the rights of the individual and the public interest.[109]

7. The Rights of Others

7.1 Freedom of Expression

Occasionally the rights of others are claimed to justify an interference with the peaceful enjoyment of possessions. In *Ashdown*[110] the Court of Appeal considered an infringement of the copyright held by the former leader of the Liberal Democrats, Paddy Ashdown, by the *Sunday Telegraph*. A major part of the defence was the right to freedom of expression. The court concluded that it was not arguable that Article 10 required the Telegraph Group should be able to profit from this use of Mr Ashdown's copyright without paying compensation.[111]

---

[105] *Ibid*, at [20]. See also: *Kingsalton*, above n 17; *Waltham Forest*, above n 56; *Rowland*, above n 9; *Fisher*, above n 61; *Leven*, above n 46; and *Young v First Secretary of State* [2004] EWHC (Admin) 2167. It is also possible for a tax or levy to have an environmental rationale. See, eg *R (on the application of British Aggregates Associates) v Her Majesty's Treasury* [2002] EWHC (Admin) 926.
[106] Above n 38.
[107] *Ibid*, at [46].
[108] *Ibid*.
[109] *Ibid*, at [48]. See also *Clays Lane*, above n 68, concerning the compulsory transfer of land under s 27 of the Housing Act 1996 following mismanagement on the part of a registered social landlord; and *Alliance Spring Co Ltd v First Secretary of State* [2005] EWHC (Admin) 18.
[110] Above n 14.
[111] *Ibid*, at [82].

Mr Ashdown's work product was deployed in the way that it was for reasons that were essentially journalistic in furtherance of the commercial interests of the Telegraph Group.[112]

7.2 Peaceful Enjoyment of Possessions

It many HRA cases, one person's Article 1 rights have to be balanced against the Article 1 rights of another. For example, in *Levi Strauss*[113] the court recognised that there were competing property rights: Tesco's interest in the jeans which it had acquired from outside the European Economic Area and Levi's interest in the trade marks. It found that the balance which the European Community legislature and the domestic legislature had decided to hold between them prohibited parallel importation from outside the European Economic Area of trade marked goods. Noting that the scope of discretion conferred on the legislature was wide, it concluded that the prohibition was proportionate.[114]

The Article 1 rights of creditors are also considered where a bankruptcy order is made. It was argued in *Krasner*[115] that it was incompatible with a bankrupt's rights for rights to a retirement annuity and associated benefits under an annuity contract or personal pension arrangements to vest in the trustee in bankruptcy in circumstances which excluded the power of the court to make an income payment order under section 310 of the Insolvency Act 1986. The Court of Appeal noted that a wide margin of appreciation was available to the legislature here. It concluded that it was not a violation of Article 1 for annuity and pension benefits to be used in this way.

> Clearly Parliament has been responding to a perception of what the public interest requires in this field. It has done so against a background of judicial decisions, over very many years, that that public interest requires, generally, that a bankrupt's property should be available to answer the claims of his creditors.[116]

Whilst it was not entirely clear from the judgments given, it could also be argued that in *Marcic*[117] the House of Lords was essentially balancing the property rights of one group against those of another. As Lord Nicholls expressed it, the balance was between

> the interests of customers of a company whose properties are prone to sewer flooding and, on the other hand, all the other customers of the company whose properties are drained through the company's sewers. The interests of the first group conflict with the interests of the company's customers as a whole in that only a minority of customers suffer sewer flooding but the company's customers as a whole meet the cost of building more sewers.[118]

---

[112] *Ibid.*
[113] Above n 28.
[114] *Ibid*, at [40]. See also *MWH & H Ward*, above n 58, which concerned an interference with property in order to alleviate a long-standing flooding problem relating to other properties.
[115] Above n 16.
[116] *Ibid*, at [74]. See also *Fuller*, above n 56, which concerned a direction under s 61 of the Criminal Justice and Public Order Act 1994 requiring travellers to leave land.
[117] Above n 18.
[118] *Ibid*, at [42].

Affording a broad discretion to Parliament, their Lordships concluded that the balance struck by the statutory scheme to impose a general drainage obligation on a sewerage undertaker but to entrust enforcement of this obligation to an independent regulator who had regard to all the different interests involved struck a reasonable balance and that Parliament had acted well within its bounds as policy maker.[119] The claimant here had not taken this remedial avenue and that is why his claim failed. Nevertheless, their Lordships did point to one item of concern with the present scheme concerning the payment of compensation to those suffering external sewer flooding. It recommended that, if it was not practicable to carry out remedial works, those who enjoy the benefit of effective drainage should bear the cost of paying some compensation.

> The minority who suffer damage and disturbance as a consequence of the inadequacy of the sewerage system ought not to be required to bear an unreasonable burden.[120]

Finally, in *Beaulane Properties*[121] the Chancery Division considered the difficult question of the acquisition of adverse title. Pursuant to section 17 of the Limitation Act 1980 and section 75 of the Land Registration Act 1925, the defendant had acquired adverse title to the land of the claimant by enclosing it and by allowing cattle and horses to graze on it for in excess of 12 years. Having concluded that this constituted a deprivation of possessions within the meaning of Article 1, the court considered the policy aims put forward for the statutory provisions, including the prevention of stale claims, the promotion of social stability, the facilitation of conveyancing, the promotion of certainty of title, the avoidance of hardship to the adverse possessor and discouraging the waste of land as a resource.

The court concluded that the taking of property without payment of an amount reasonably related to its value was normally disproportionate interference. '[I]f an expropriation without compensation is to be justified, it must be by reference to "the public interest".'[122] In the present case, it found no public interest.

> There is no social evil. There has been no careful consideration of the matter in parliament. The registered owner does not lose his title as a result of failing to carry out any express provision of law to protect his property. He might be forgiven for thinking that he had a clearly established registered title which required no protection. There is no limit on the loss which he may suffer, and the law applies in any event to individuals or companies which do not carry on a property business; even if the land is of not great value, it may be of great financial importance to the individual company involved.[123]

Concluding that the operation of the legislation was disproportionate, the court used section 3 of the HRA to reinterpret the legislation so that the defendant's claim to have acquired the disputed land failed.[124]

---

[119] *Ibid*, at [43] per Lord Nicholls, [71] per Lord Hoffmann and [87] per Lord Hope.
[120] *Ibid*, at [45] per Lord Nicholls. See also *Arscott v The Coal Authority* [2004] EWCA Civ 892, [2005] Env. LR 6.
[121] Above n 19.
[122] *Ibid*, at [192].
[123] *Ibid*, at [195].
[124] *Ibid*, at [224].

7.3 Other

The unenforceability of a claim on the ground of illegality may also be justified as being in the interests of the rights of others. *Al-Kishtaini*[125] concerned a claimant prevented from recovering damages for breach of contract as, in order to prove his rights under the contract, he had to rely on his own illegal act. The Court of Appeal found that the public interest reflected by the doctrine of illegality weighed particularly heavily in the scales. It was also influenced by two further factors. First, the secondary legislation which resulted in the illegality on which the claim was based originated in the resolutions of the UN Security Council in an international emergency—implementation of the UN sanctions against Iraq following the invasion and occupation of Kuwait.

> If a public interest of this degree does not fall within the exception in art 1, it is difficult to conceive of any other matters which would fall within it.[126]

Secondly, the prohibition was not an absolute one. It was open to the claimant to obtain advance clearance from the Treasury, so that he could find out precisely where he stood before entering into and carrying out a potentially illegal transaction.

> In such a case it does not offend the principle of proportionality invoked by the claimant to apply to its full extent the high public policy applicable to this case, so as to prevent the enforcement of his claim.[127]

---

8. Prevention of Crime

Court orders to confiscate the proceeds of crime have raised issues under Article 1. In *Benjafield*[128] the House of Lords considered the proportionality of a confiscation under section 72AA of the Criminal Justice Act 1988 and section 4 of the Drug Trafficking Act 1994. It concluded that the legislation was a precise, fair and proportionate response to the important need to protect the public.[129] Similarly, in *Hughes*[130] the Court of Appeal stated that there was a significant public interest in ensuring that criminals do not profit from their crimes and that the proceeds of crime are confiscated in the event of conviction.[131]

---

[125] *Al-Kishtaini v Shanshal*, above n 72.
[126] *Ibid*, at [58] per Mummery LJ.
[127] *Ibid*, at [59] per Mummery LJ. Holman J and Rix LJ expressly stated that the 'fair balance' test was met respectively at [68] and [96]. See also *Soteriou*, above n 52.
[128] Above n 13.
[129] *Ibid*, at [17] in reliance upon *Phillips v UK* [2001] Crim LR 817.
[130] *Hughes v Customs and Excise Commissioners* [2002] EWCA Civ 670.
[131] *Ibid*, at [52] in reliance upon *Raimondo v Italy* (1994) 18 EHRR 237. See also *R v Goodenough* [2004] EWCA Crim 2260; *In the Matter of D (Interim Receiver Order: Proceeds of Crime Act 2002)*, Administrative Court, 7 December 2004; and *R v May* [2005] EWCA Crim 97, [2005] 1 WLR 2902.

9. Economic Well-being of the Country

The final justification to be considered is that of the economic well-being of the country. Whilst a number of interests come under this category, the most important is the payment of taxes and duties.

9.1 Taxes and Duties

It is expressly stated in Article 1 that the right to peaceful enjoyment of possessions shall not impair the right of a state to enforce such laws as it deems necessary to secure the payment of taxes or other contributions or penalties. As for other interferences with peaceful enjoyment, taxes and duties must meet the fair balance test. However, as the Court of Appeal noted in *Lydiashourne Ltd*,[132] attempts to challenge fiscal measures in the Strasbourg Court have failed almost without exception. This is an area where considerable deference is afforded and a challenge to tax laws as infringing Article 1 is a very steep hill to climb.[133]

In *R v Dimsey*[134] the House of Lords considered sections 739–46 of the Income and Corporations Taxes Act 1988, which concerned provisions designed to counter tax avoidance by the transfer of assets abroad. The appellant argued that to use section 739(2) to deem the income of the offshore companies to be the income of an individual for tax purposes and also for it to remain for tax purposes the income of the companies was inconsistent with Article 1 as it amounted to double taxation. The House of Lords made clear that it regarded the section as a penal one intended to be an effective deterrent which would put a stop to practices considered to be against the public interest.[135] It concluded that the section was well within the margin of appreciation allowed to member states in respect of tax legislation.

> The public interest requires that legislation designed to combat tax avoidance should be effective. That public interest outweighs, in my opinion, the objections, mainly theoretical.[136]

With respect to duties, a number of claims have been brought under the HRA particularly in relation to forfeiture provisions. *Lindsay v Customs and Excise Commissioners*[137] concerned the alleged importation of excise goods without paying duty. Section 49 of the Customs and Excise Management Act 1979 provided that goods imported without payment of duty chargeable on them were subject to forfeiture. Section 141 provided that, where anything became liable to forfeiture, any vehicle which had been used for its carriage also became liable to forfeiture. Mr Lindsay had been stopped by British Customs just as he was about to drive onto the Shuttle in

---

[132] Above n 37.
[133] *Ibid*, at [21]. See also *Vicky Construction*, above n 8.
[134] Above n 13.
[135] *Ibid*, at [66].
[136] *Ibid*, at [71]. See also *Greengate Furniture Ltd v The Commissioners of Customs and Excise*, VAT and Duties Tribunals, 11 August 2003; Re A, above n 12.
[137] [2002] 3 All ER 118.

Calais to return to England. The officer found that he was carrying a substantial quantity of cigarettes and tobacco. He said that he had purchased some of this for members of his family with money provided by them. The officer informed him that he should have paid duty on the goods and proceeded to forfeit both the dutiable goods and his car in which those goods were being carried. This was in accordance with the Commissioners' policy that any car used for smuggling would be seized and not restored.

The Court of Appeal agreed that the decision of the Commissioners had to comply with Article 1.[138] The court understood the issue before it to be whether the current policy of the Commissioners so fettered their discretion when reviewing decisions taken to forfeit vehicles of those who evaded duty on cigarettes tobacco and alcohol as to prevent them from considering proportionality and thus to render their decisions unlawful.[139] It noted that the prevention of the evasion of excise duty that was imposed in accordance with EC law was a legitimate aim. The question was whether the policy was liable to result in the imposition of a penalty in the individual case that was disproportionate with regard to that aim.[140] The Court noted that the policy did not suggest that any regard should be paid to the value of the car. And it did not suggest that it was relevant to consider whether the goods were being imported to be distributed between family and friends or whether the importation was pursuant to a commercial venture under which the goods were to be sold at a profit.[141] The Court quoted from the comments of the European Court of Human Rights in *Allgemeine Gold-und Silverscheideanstalt v UK*[142] that, when striking a fair balance, the behaviour of the owner of the property had to be taken into account.[143] It also held that it was appropriate to consider the scale of evil against which the policy was directed: 'the trade that is carried on in smuggled cigarettes is massive'[144]; the fact that free movement of persons within the internal market greatly facilitated illicit importation; and the fact that notice was given that smuggling could lead to forfeiture of vessels.[145]

The court concluded that the policy was disproportionate as it did not draw a distinction between the commercial smuggler and the driver importing goods for social distribution to family or friends in circumstances where there was no attempt to make a profit:

> But where the importation is not for the purpose of making a profit, I consider that the principle of proportionality requires that each case should be considered on its particular facts, which will include the scale of importation, whether it is a 'first offence', whether there was an attempt at concealment or dissimulation, the value of the vehicle and the degree of hardship that will be caused by forfeiture. There is open to the commissioners a wide range of lesser sanctions that will enable them to impose a sanction that is proportionate where forfeiture of the vehicle is not justified.[146]

---

138 *Ibid*, at [40].
139 *Ibid*, at [45].
140 *Ibid*, at [55].
141 *Ibid*, at [57].
142 (1986) 9 EHRR 1 at [54].
143 *Ibid*, at [58].
144 *Ibid*, at [60].
145 *Ibid*, at [61]–[62].
146 *Ibid*, at [64].

As the Customs officers had drawn no distinction between the true commercial smuggler and the driver importing goods for family and friends, the court concluded that the decision could not stand.[147]

It is clear that the judgment of the Court of Appeal in *Lindsay* opened up a new route for those who wished to challenge the application of the forfeiture provisions to them. In *Fox*[148] the Administrative Court held that, in order to establish that the goods owned by Fox were liable to forfeiture, it was necessary to prove that the goods owned by Everett (part of the share load) were liable to forfeiture rather than simply deeming these as such. In *Newbury*[149] the Divisional Court confirmed that the court considering whether goods were liable to forfeiture was under a duty to consider Convention rights.[150]

> The right to peaceful enjoyment is engaged from the moment of seizure and continues thereafter. The initial act of seizure may not be disproportionate because the Commissioners are entitled to investigate. But the interference should cease once an opportunity is available properly to consider whether it complies with Convention rights. The court should not be asked or expected to make an order which is not only in breach of those rights in itself but also legitimates continuing breach by the Commissioners unless and until the review process takes place.[151]

9.2 Clandestine Entrants

Harsh penalties are imposed on those who intentionally or negligently allow clandestine entrants into the United Kingdom. In *International Transport Roth*[152] a challenge was brought to Part II of the Immigration and Asylum Act 1999 which created a new penalty regime. Those responsible, generally the owner, hirer or driver, were liable for each such entrant to a fixed penalty of £2,000 unless they could establish that they were acting under duress or that they had neither actual nor constructive knowledge of the clandestine entrant and there was an effective system for preventing the carriage of clandestine entrants which was operated properly on the occasion in question. Once the Secretary of State had issued a penalty notice, the vehicle could be detained if it was considered that there was a serious risk that the penalty would not be paid. The penalty imposed was fixed and cumulative; no flexibility was allowed for degrees of blameworthiness or mitigating circumstances. Even if a carrier was determined not to be liable, his vehicle may have been detained and he would receive no compensation for this unless the Secretary of State acted unreasonably in issuing the penalty notice.

---

[147] *Ibid*, at [67]. See also *R (Hoverspeed Ltd) v Customs and Excise Commissioners* [2002] EWCA Civ 1804, [2003] QB 1041.

[148] *Fox v HM Customs and Excise* [2002] EWHC (Admin) 1244, [2003] 1 WLR 1331.

[149] *Customs and Excise Commissioners v Newbury* [2003] EWHC (Admin) 702, [2003] 2 All ER 964.

[150] *Ibid*, at [21].

[151] *Ibid*, at [23]. Cf. *Helman v Commissioners of Customs and Excise*, Administrative Court, 18 October 2002; *Crilly v the Commissioners of Customs and Excise*, VADT 28 July 2003; *Harding v The Commissioners of Customs and Excise*, VADT, 4 August 2003. See also *Gascoyne v HM Customs and Excise* [2004] EWCA Civ 1162, [2005] Ch 215; *Golobiewska v The Commissioners of Customs and Excise* [2005] EWCA Civ 607; See further A Lidbetter, 'Customs, Cars and Article 1 of the First Protocol' [2004] *EHRLR* 272.

[152] [2002] EWCA Civ 158, [2003] QB 728.

A majority of the Court of Appeal held that there was a wide discretion in the Secretary of State in his task of devising a suitable scheme and a high degree of deference due by the court to Parliament when it came to determining its legality.[153] However, it was also held that it was the court's role under the HRA to be the guardian of human rights.

> It cannot abdicate this responsibility. If ultimately it judges the scheme to be quite simply unfair, then the features that make it so must inevitably breach the Convention.[154]

It concluded that the scale and inflexibility of the penalty, taken in conjunction with the other features of the scheme, imposed an excessive burden on the carriers in breach of Article 1.

> Even acknowledging, as I do, the great importance of the social goal which the scheme seeks to promote, there are nevertheless limits to how far the state is entitled to go in imposing obligations of vigilance on drivers (and vicarious liability on employers and hirers) to achieve it and in penalising any breach.[155]

It was declared to be incompatible with Article 1 and Article 6.

9.3 Child Support

Whilst the payment of child support has a number of legitimate aims, it is considered in this section as it has been held that one of the aims of recovering maintenance from absent parents is to reduce the burden on the taxpayer of the single parent.[156] In *Denson*[157] the claimant argued that the Child Support Agency's attempts to make him pay maintenance in accordance with the Child Support Act 1991 were in breach of Article 1. The Administrative Court held that it was

> in the interests of the general community that the state should be able, by recovering maintenance from absent parents, to reduce the burden on the tax-payer of single parent families.[158]

It concluded that the statutory scheme, and the Child Support Agency's administration of it, struck a fair and reasonable balance between, on the one hand, the absent parent's responsibilities for his or her children and, on the other hand, the need for a system that (i) produces fair and consistent results, (ii) preserves the parents' incentive to work, (iii) reduces the dependency of parents with care on income support and (iv) provides consequent savings to taxpayers.[159]

---

[153] *Ibid*, at [26] and [139].
[154] *Ibid*, at [27] and [139].
[155] *Ibid*, at [53] and [183], [187] and [188].
[156] Above n 13.
[157] *Ibid*.
[158] *Ibid*, at [31].
[159] *Ibid*, at [32]. See also *R (on the application of Qazi) v Secretary of State for Work and Pensions* [2004] EWHC (Admin) 1331.

Index